Coriolanus on Stage
in England and America,
1609–1994

Coriolanus on Stage in England and America, 1609–1994

John Ripley

Madison • Teaneck
Fairleigh Dickinson University Press
London: Associated University Presses

Associated University Presses
440 Forsgate Drive
Cranbury, NJ 08512

Associated University Presses
16 Barter Street
London WC1A 2AH, England

Associated University Presses
P.O. Box 338, Port Credit
Mississauga, Ontario
Canada L5G 4L8

The paper used in this publication meets the requirements
of the American National Standard for Permanence of Paper
for Printed Library Materials Z39.48–1984.

Library of Congress Cataloging-in-Publication Data

Ripley, John, 1936–
    Coriolanus on stage in England and America, 1609–1994 / John
Ripley.
        p.   cm.
    Includes bibliographical references and index.
    ISBN 0-8386-3741-8 (alk. paper)
    1. Shakespeare, William, 1564–1616. Coriolanus. 2. Shakespeare,
William, 1564–1616—Stage history—England. 3. Shakespeare,
William, 1564–1616—Stage history—United States. 4. Coriolanus,
Cnaeus Marcius—In literature. 5. Heroes in literature. 6. Rome—
In literature. 7. Tragedy. I. Title.
    PR2805.R56   1998
    822.3'3—dc21
                                                                    97-36482
                                                                    CIP

For Jessica

Contents

Acknowledgments

To engage in theater history research is to find oneself in happy debt to a host of collaborators, for whose generosity no words of formal thanks seem adequate.

My most profound obligation is to the late Charles Shattuck, mentor and friend, not only to myself, but to theater researchers everywhere. His encouragement, practical assistance, and scholarly example touch almost every page of this study.

In the course of preparing his stage-sensitive edition of *Coriolanus,* Brian Parker generously shared with me many of his own critical insights and research findings.

I am particularly indebted to the formidable expertise and research assistance of the late Eileen Robinson, formerly of the Shakespeare Centre Library; and for the dedicated support of the research assistants associated with the McGill *Shakespeare in Performance* project—Iona Brindle, Marcel DeCoste, Felicity Enayat, Michael Morgan Holmes, and Jessica Slights. Staff members of the Cork City Library; the Mitchell Library, Glasgow; the Central Library, Edinburgh; the Carlisle Library; the Central Library, Liverpool; the Central Library, Bristol; the New-York Historical Society; and the New Orleans Public Library contributed information for the Handlist of Performances.

In specific and varied ways I have benefited from the kindnesses of the late Geoffrey Ashton, the late Kathleen Barker, Marilyn Berger, Michael Bristol, Adèle Brodeur, David George, Russell Jackson, Alexander Leggatt, Leanore Lieblein, the late George and Doris Nash, Niky Rathbone, Edward Pechter, Marian Pringle, Christopher Robinson, the late Sybil Rosenfeld, Denis Salter, Catherine Shaw, Carol Jackman Schuller, Gerald and Renée Sims, John Tearle, and the late Mary White.

Curators and staffs of theater collections and libraries have made me welcome, and responded knowledgeably and patiently to my importunities. I owe a special debt to the Billy Rose Theater Collection, New York Public Library; the British Library; the Print Room of the British Museum; the City of Birmingham Public Library; the Ellen Terry Memorial Museum; the Folger Shakespeare Library; the Garrick Club Library; the Harvard Theater Collection; the Henry Huntington Library; the Library of Congress; the Manchester Public Library; the Reference and Inter-Library Loans Departments of the McLennan Library, McGill University; Nottingham County

Library; Norfolk Record Office; the Shakespeare Centre Library; the Shakespeare Institute Library; the Archives of the Festival Theatre, Stratford, Ontario; the Theatre Museum; the University of Bristol Theatre Collection; the Walter Hampden Memorial Library, The Players; and the Warburg Institute.

I am deeply grateful to the Fonds pour la Formation de Chercheurs et l'Aide à la Recherche (Government of Québec), the Social Sciences and Humanities Research Council of Canada, and the Faculty of Graduate Studies and Research, McGill University, for the financial assistance which made this study possible.

Last, but far from least, my loving thanks to my daughter Jessica for being always her joyful and caring self.

NOTE

All books and periodicals cited are published in London or New York unless otherwise indicated.

Promptbooks dated before 1963 bear the numbers allotted them by Charles H. Shattuck in *The Shakespeare Promptbooks* (Urbana: 1965) which contains full descriptions of each. For later promptbooks, I have simply provided current locations.

All line numbers refer to *The Riverside Shakespeare*, ed. G. Blakemore Evans (Boston: 1974).

Coriolanus on Stage
in England and America,
1609–1994

1

Introduction

Coriolanus, stage and study agree, is not a comfortable play. Hacked as it were out of granite, its austere grandeur invites admiration rather than affection. Although one of Shakespeare's longest dramas,[1] its design suggests a rigorous economy. The action is uncompromisingly linear with no subplot to slow its forward thrust. The cast of principal characters is small, and their passions are crude and elemental. None, save perhaps Virgilia, stakes any unequivocal claim to our sympathy. Language has little more affective appeal than character. The ear is denied lyrical harmony and satisfying metrics; the eye seeks in vain for pictorial color. Fractured, harsh rhythms, dissonance, repellent imagery, and a monochromatic palette bespeak a calculated assault upon the senses. The play's conclusion brings no comforting insight, no reassuring accommodation with destiny: merely a deafening crash as irresistible force meets immovable object.

Coriolanus is a relentlessly political work, an exploration of the acquisition, use, abuse, and loss of power at both the institutional and individual level. And the low ground in the struggle is not the exclusive preserve of any one party or individual. As Eric Bentley puts it, "Shakespeare's *Coriolanus* is the struggle of wrong and wrong. That's what makes the play so hard to take."[2] The characters who engage in political activity are to some degree all lacking in spiritual integrity. "[Y]ou can't fully identify yourself with anyone in *Coriolanus,*" argues Bentley.[3] Worse still, Shakespeare's relativistic treatment of power relations offers the reader or theatergoer no secure ethical or psychological vantage point from which to view the action. Almost every line exudes ambiguity and ambivalence. Paradox is endemic. Perhaps no work of literature so mercilessly cuts the ethical ground from beneath our feet just as we feel we have found firm footing, so maddeningly shifts the balance of sympathy from one moment to the next, or so cynically presses the recognition that "our virtues / Lie in th'interpretation of the time" (4.7.49–50). The disorientated reader/theatergoer might be forgiven for feeling an unwritten contract between dramatist and audience has been violated; the playwright no longer seems to mediate reality but exposes one to the overwhelming complexity of life itself.

Despite its inhospitable character, or perhaps because of it, *Coriolanus* has challenged throughout its history the ingenuity of critics and theater artists alike. And few have emerged from the encounter indifferent. T. S. Eliot's judgment of the play as "Shakespeare's most assured success" and Henry Irving's dismissal of it as "not worth a damn" reflect the range and intensity of reaction.[4]

While it is the purpose of this study to chart *Coriolanus*'s theatrical career, the reaction of the play's critics throughout its history is by no means irrelevant. Criticism and performance are both valid modes of encountering the piece; both involve the construction of a performance text, one in the imagination, the other on the boards. Criticism and performance are parallel and complementary, yet independent, exercises: one need not be made to serve the interests of the other.[5] Since critics and artists of any given period share a common cultural environment, it is only to be expected that the findings of readers would from time to time throw light on stage practice, while stage practice might not be entirely without effect on criticism, although that is not a concern of this study. I therefore begin this account with a survey of major trends in *Coriolanus* scholarship from John Dryden to the present, not with the object of pressing a relationship between study and stage, or of using the insights of one to justify or refute the claims of the other, but rather as an intellectual backdrop to the theatrical narrative, an articulation of issues about which theater artists at a particular historical moment may be silent or only subconsciously aware of.[6]

CORIOLANUS AND THE CRITICS

Criticism from the Restoration until the early nineteenth century suggests that consideration of the play's politics was subordinated to moral and aesthetic critique; like some baroque history painting, it was judged as a moralized historical reconstruction. Dryden, the earliest commentator on the play, found "something in this very Tragedy of *Coriolanus,* as it was written by *Shakespear,* that is truly great and truly *Roman*";[7] and thus linked for the first time the play's greatness with its Romanness. Dryden's conflation seems to have been silently adopted by his contemporaries and immediate successors, but their appreciation of the play's Romanness, and presumably its greatness, was less sweeping.

Instances of Shakespeare's historic inaccuracy were not hard to come by, and were rigorously catalogued and chided. John Dennis found the character of the historical Menenius misrepresented: "Whereas *Menenius* was an eloquent Person *Shakespeare* has made him a downright Buffoon," he complained; and "whereas *Shakespeare* has made him a Hater and Contemner, and Vilifyer of the People, we are assur'd by the *Roman* Historian that *Menenius* was extremely popular."[8] Equally reprehensible was the depiction of Aufidius as "a base and a profligate Villain."[9] Lewis Theobald raised an eyebrow at the fact that Shakespeare "makes *Rome,* which at that time was a perfect Aristocrasy, a Democrasy."[10] Charles Gildon objected to the portrayal of "the Commons of *Rome,* as if they were the Rabble of an *Irish* Village, as senseless, ignorant, silly and cowardly, not remembring that the Citizens of *Rome* were the Soldiers of the Common-wealth by whom they Conquer'd the World."[11] Instances could be multiplied.

Worse than *Coriolanus*'s historical inaccuracies, in John Dennis's opinion, was its want of poetic justice, or clear-cut demonstration of Divine Providence triumphant: "The Good must never fail to prosper, and the Bad must be always punished," he insisted. "The want of this impartial Distribution of Justice makes the *Coriolanus* of Shakespear to be without Moral. . . . For Aufidius the principal Murderer of Coriolanus . . . not only survives, and survives unpunish'd, but seems to be rewarded for so detestable an Action. . . . But not only Aufidius, but the Roman Tribunes, Sicinius and Brutus, appear to me to cry aloud for Poetick Vengeance. . . . And yet these Tribunes at the end of the Play, like Aufidius, remain unpunish'd."[12] Shakespeare's untidy moral universe, however true to life, clearly diminished the play's value as art.

Coriolanus's art was as suspect as its history and morality. Shakespeare's neglect of the unities, particularly those of place and action, was endlessly censured. Thomas Sheridan found the play "purely historical, and had but little or no plot,"[13] that is to say a mere series of historic episodes without classical unity of design. Dr. Johnson found "too much bustle in the first act and too little in the last,"[14] while Francis Gentleman judged the play's theme of "heroism, and that rather of a savage kind, without any additional concerns that might engage attention or touch the heart" rather "too limited an idea for five acts."[15]

Only isolated voices acknowledged the political character of the piece, and then merely to denounce the playwright's class bias. Gildon, a Whig apologist, sniffed antipopulism. "Our Poet," he maintains, "seems fond to lay the Blame on the People, but this is contrary to Truth, for the People have never discover'd that Changeableness which Princes have done."[16] Four decades later Gildon's hints gave place to John Upton's indictment. "The patricians," he wrote in 1746, "were the few in conspiracy against the many, and the struggles of the people were an honest struggle for that share of power which was kept unjustly from them. . . . One would think our poet had been bred in the court of Nero when we see in what colours he paints the tribunes of the people: he seems to have no other idea of them than as a mob of Wat Tylers and Jack Cades."[17] In both cases, however, potential contemporary political relevance was contained by historical critique.

Most commentators, whatever their reservations on the grounds of historical inaccuracy or political partiality, doted on *Coriolanus*'s characters. Rowe, unlike Dennis, found them "as exact in the Poet as the Historian," and particularly commended "the Fierceness and Impatience of *Coriolanus,* his Courage and Disdain of the common People."[18] Gildon praised the "Manners," or in contemporary parlance the motivation, of the protagonist. "The Character of *Coriolanus* in *Shakespeare*," he noted, "prepares us to expect the Resolution he will take to disoblige the People, for Pride naturally contemns Inferiours and overvalues it self." In the early domestic scene (1.2) he found "[t]he noble Spirit of *Volumnia . . .* well express'd in her Speech," and "the Character . . . admirably distinguish'd from *Virgilia* and *Valeria*."[19] Samuel Johnson commended "the pleasing and interesting variety" of the characters: "the old man's merriment in Menenius; the lofty lady's dignity in Volumnia; the bridal modesty in Virgilia; the patrician and military haughtiness in Coriolanus; the plebeian malignity and tribunitian insolence in Brutus and Sicinius."[20] Thomas Sheridan thought the portraits of Coriolanus and Volumnia "masterly."[21]

Stronger than Johnson's approval of Shakespeare's characterization, however, was his rejection of historical accuracy as a criterion for judging them. "Dennis and Rymer think his Romans not sufficiently Roman," he remarks in a much quoted passage:

> Dennis is offended that Menenius, a senator of Rome, should play the buffoon. . . . But Shakespeare always makes nature predominate over accident; and, if he preserves the essential character, is not very careful of distinctions superinduced and adventitious. His story requires Romans or kings, but he thinks only on men.[22]

In a few brief sentences, Johnson shifted criticism from a conception of the play as an idealized dramatization of a specific moment in history to a notion of it as a mirror of human behavior in all times and places. Francis Gentleman, actor, critic, and editor of Bell's edition of Shakespeare, enthusiastically appropriating Johnson's insight, was one of the first to generalize Shakespeare's observation to contemporary society. Emptied of Roman or Elizabethan specificity, *Coriolanus*'s citizens in 1.1 seemed to him admirably to embody "the variety and quick changes of opinion which prevail among such assemblies"; and in the sequence in which Martius threatens Rome (4.6), "[t]he change of the Plebeians upon appearance of approaching danger" struck him as "very characteristic; and every man striving to throw blame off himself, laughable."[23] Martius was judged not as an historical figure but a modern, and no dinner invitation was forthcoming. "If any justification," wrote Gentleman, "can be offered for conspiracy against the life of a man, *Aufidius* seems to offer a very good one [at 5.6.28–40]; for both certain it is from the face of affairs that *Coriolanus* behaved like a traitor, abroad, intirely like a brute, and partly like a fool, at home."[24] "Courage, accompanied with an extreme degree of military ardour and activity, seems to have been the only good quality possessed by Coriolanus," asserted Wolstenholme Parr (1795). "Valour tinctured with ferocity becomes an object of terror and disgust to the very people for whose honour or protection it has been nobly and successfully exerted. It produced in Coriolanus a rude and barbarous demeanour, which we should not be extremely sorry even in real life to see chastised, much less in the shadows of a theatrical Representation."[25]

In the wake of the French Revolution, Romantic and early Victorian critics, freed, thanks to Johnson, from the eighteenth-century obsession with dramatized Roman history, discovered not only the contemporary resonance of *Coriolanus*'s characters but the play's political relevance. Hazlitt (1817) found it "a store-house of political commonplaces," and judged the "arguments for and against aristocracy, or democracy, on the privileges of the few and the claims of the many, on liberty and slavery, power and the abuse of it, peace and war" were "very ably handled."[26] Beneath Shakespeare's dialectic competence, however, he claimed to detect "a leaning to the arbitrary side of the question," attributable partly to "some feeling of contempt for his own origin" and partly to the fact that tragedy is an absolutist genre which "puts the individual for the species, the one above the infinite many, might before right."[27] Coleridge, in opposition to Gildon, Upton, and Hazlitt, discovered in Shakespeare's politics a "wonderfully philosophic impartiality": the alleged antipopulism behind his treatment of the plebeians was no more than a "good-natured laugh at mobs."[28] Nathan Drake (1817), perhaps with a patronizing glance across the Channel, commented approvingly on the naturalness of the picture of "what may be termed a Roman electioneering mob; and the insolence of newly-acquired authority on the part of the tribunes, and the ungovernable license and malignant ribaldry of the plebeians."[29]

While Coleridge, Hazlitt, and Drake recognized the play's political content, they regarded it as almost incidental to the characterization. Other commentators, however, saw the piece as primarily a political study in which the characters, however fine, are subordinated to a unifying theme. Schlegel in 1815 was the first frankly to designate the play a "political drama";[30] Hermann Ulrici argued in 1839 that its "principal object is to illustrate the struggle of democracy and aristocracy, as the conflicting *principles* of a republican polity," and lauded the very aristocratic absolutism Hazlitt had decried. Shakespeare, he remarked with some satisfaction, had "discerned the inherent rottenness and ruinous nature of popular rule."[31] Charles Knight, with less obvious partisanship, reiterated unequivocally a decade later that "[t]he leading idea of 'Coriolanus'—the pivot upon which all the action turns . . . is the contest for power between the patricians and plebeians."[32]

Whether critics took the view that politics supported character or character, politics, analysis and appreciation of the portraits of Coriolanus and Volumnia continued unabated. For Hazlitt, however, aesthetic approbation was not to be confused with moral or political approval. While he admired

Coriolanus as "a complete character," he was forced to concede that his and our response to the hero derives ultimately, not from Martius's moral or political authority, but the human instinct to side with power, the sad fact that "our vanity, or some other feeling, makes us disposed to place ourselves in the situation of the strongest party."[33] Ulrici had no such compunctions; his overt sympathies with "the right hand file" led him instinctively and unapologetically to side with Martius, "the living impersonation of the aristocratic principle." Casting textual evidence to the winds, he concludes that while Martius is "by no means free from personal pride and ambition . . . his foremost wish, on all times and occasions, is the good of his country . . . and even the very war which he wages against it has for its sole aim the emancipation of Rome from the degrading supremacy of the plebeians with which it appears to be threatened." It is, he is obliged to admit, "a sin against humanity for any individual to become a mere conventional formula of existence," and thus finds himself obliged to acquiesce to the justice of Martius's fate. "[B]ecause [Coriolanus] places the man so far below the citizen, the general principles of humanity revenge themselves upon him, and its simplest and most natural feelings ultimately work his downfal and ruin."[34]

Anna Jameson, largely untroubled by the ethical correctness of aesthetic response or the inherent right of the aristocracy to rule, directed her energies toward recognition of the strategic importance of female influence in the play's power structure. "Although Coriolanus is the hero of the play," she argued in the first extended critique of Volumnia (1832), "yet much of the interest of the action and the final catastrophe turn upon the character of his mother . . . and the power she exercised over his mind."[35]

She was not prepared to concede, however, that the matron's influence was in any way malign: indeed, she took pains to suppress her less attractive features. In Mrs. Jameson's eyes, Volumnia could be charged with little more than "aristocratic haughtiness" and "supreme contempt for the plebeians" which she neither condemns nor excuses, contenting herself with the observation that her sentiments are "very like what I have heard expressed by some high-born and high-bred women of our own day."[36]

The intense focus on character by Romantic critics yielded not only shrewd psychological insights, but acute aesthetic observations, many of which have had their full impact only in recent decades. Coleridge, for example, noted for the first time Shakespeare's construction of Martius from multiple viewpoints, "not by any one description; but by such opinions, half right half wrong, as the friends, enemies, and the man himself would give— and the reader left to draw the *whole*."[37] It is precisely this aesthetic strategy, combined with a virtual absence of soliloquies, which accounts for the enigmatic nature of Martius which has recurrently troubled critics since World War I.

A particularly rewarding aperçu was Jameson's appreciation of Volumnia's silent stage-cross in 5.5, finally recognized by Bridges-Adams in 1933 as a major performance crux. "It is an instance of Shakespeare's fine judgment," she writes,

> that after [the Intercession scene] . . . Volumnia should speak no more, for she could say nothing that would not deteriorate from the effect thus left on the imagination. She is at last dismissed from our admiring gaze amid the thunder of grateful acclamations.
> Behold our patroness,—the life of Rome![38]

Franz Horn in 1826 made the surprisingly modern observation that "[i]n *Coriolanus* almost every character taking part is in the wrong; the hero himself and his opposer, Aufidius, Menenius and the Tribunes, the Volscian as well as the Roman Senate." His confidence that despite human frailty "the Idea of State and Country stands forth predominant"[39] has not always been shared by critics, theater artists, and playgoers.

The play's incarnation as political object lesson had a relatively brief shelf life. Although as late as 1877 D. J. Snider continued to assert that "*Coriolanus* is essentially a drama of Political Parties,"[40] the Coleridge-Hazlitt-Drake notion of the play as a psychological study with political overtones had long since triumphed; and this largely through the influence of the German critic G. G. Gervinus's *Shakespeare Commentaries* (1849–50). While recognizing that "political relations are inherent in the subject," he insisted that "[t]he sort of characters which have to decide in these situations, and the prominent qualities in them, by means of which they decide in this way or that, this is everywhere the actual centre towards which the poet worked, and his leading thought here . . . is of a moral psychological nature."[41] The battle was decisively won in England and America when in 1875 the influential Edward Dowden endorsed Gervinus's position. "Although the play of Coriolanus almost inevitably suggests a digression into the consideration of the politics of Shakspere," he maintained,

> it must once again be asserted that the central and vivifying element in the play is not a political problem, but an individual character and life. The tragic struggle of the play is not that of patricians with plebeians, but of Coriolanus with his own self. It is not the Roman people who bring about his destruction; it is the patrician haughtiness and passionate self-will of Coriolanus himself.[42]

Five years later Swinburne moved to suppress the political character of the play altogether. "I cannot think," he insisted,

> that enough at least of time has been spent if not wasted . . . on examination of *Coriolanus* with regard to its political aspect or bearing on social questions. It is from first to last, for all its turmoil of battle and clamour of contentious factions, rather a private and domestic than a public or historical tragedy. . . . The subject

of the whole play is not the exile's revolt, the rebel's repentance, or the traitor's reward, but above all it is the son's tragedy. The inscription on the plinth of this tragic statue is simply to Volumnia Victrix.[43]

Throughout the second half of the nineteenth century, Coriolanus's Roman remoteness was relentlessly domesticated. The hero's relationships with himself, his troops, his family and friends, his community were exhaustively probed; formative influences were identified, and strengths and weaknesses catalogued. Gervinus set the tone with his distinction between the claims of nature and nurture. Volumnia's influence was recognized, if hardly in the benign light Mrs. Jameson would have wished, and Martius's individual responsibility highlighted: "The mother had instilled into Coriolanus his bravery and desire of glory; these had led to pride; his pride had grown to excess, to a more than human strength of will and action. But the extreme in his nature, we have said, passed everywhere over into its opposite."[44]

The crucial role played by Martius's pride was thereafter taken for granted, but its nature, as distinct from its heroic scale, remained problematic. Most critics found themselves somewhere between the extremes represented by Dowden and the American critic and editor H. N. Hudson. Dowden described Coriolanus's pride as "two-fold, a passionate self-esteem which is essentially egoistic; and secondly, a passionate prejudice of class."[45] Hudson found Coriolanus's pride more complex and epic than did Dowden, and somehow morally more acceptable. "Far from being of a mean and narrow cast" and "nobly elemented out of the various regards of rank, family, country, talents, and courage, [Coriolanus's pride] therefore partakes the general greatness of his character; is of a towering and majestic pitch . . . so it is of that high and generous scope that commonly issues in great virtues as well as great faults," he argued.[46]

In the main, criticism until the Great War tended to take the most amiable view, lauding Martius's physical courage, his sense of honour, integrity, and devotion to family and friends, while censuring and moralizing his pride and its lamentable outcome. Denton J. Snider's (1877) assessment may be taken as typical:

> In Coriolanus we behold an heroic character which, in its very heroism, bears the seeds of its tragic destiny. The poet brings before us a man who, having done a great and worthy action for his country, turns about and seeks to undo both his action and his country, but really undoes himself. . . . Apart from his valor and soldierly greatness, Coriolanus is a great moral hero. No flattery of the people or of anybody, no lying or tergiversation, no avarice, no mere desire to please, no office-hunting, no tuft-hunting, no vanity or love of adulation can be laid to his charge. . . . He has a high sense of honor, . . . he has lofty ideals, we say.[47]

Although occasional critics, like Paul Stapfer,[48] echoed Dowden's jaundiced assessment, no concerted attack upon the traditional heroic reading was made until the first decade of the present century.

The pivotal figure here, as so often in the history of Shakespeare criticism, is A. C. Bradley whose notion of the character shifted over a period of about eight years from Hudsonian deference to iconoclastic condescension. In *Shakespearean Tragedy* (1905), his voice is hardly distinguishable from Hudson's: "[T]he pride and self-will of Coriolanus," he writes, "though terrible in bulk, are scarcely so in quality; there is nothing base in them, and the huge creature whom they destroy is a noble, even a lovable being" (p. 83). Within Bradley's hulking but unterrifying hero, however, lurked Martius's twentieth-century avatar—the mother-dominated child of Aufidius's image[49]—who took unambiguous shape in 1912 at Bradley's British Academy lecture. "Often he reminds us of a huge boy," he observed in the course of analyzing the sequence in which Volumnia persuades her son to return to the plebeians; "and here he acts like a boy whose sense of honour is finer than his mother's, but who is too simple and too noble to frame the thought."[50] Bradley clearly had not meant to undermine Martius's heroic nobility, but his identification of a pervasive psychological malaise had that effect, and critics on both sides of the Atlantic flocked like crows to roadkill. Brander Matthews a year or so later declared Martius "narrow-minded and lacking in any genuine magnanimity of soul"[51] George Hookham in 1922 concluded that "Coriolanus has absolutely no good attribute except physical courage, which he shares with most men and many animals."[52] Wyndham Lewis (1927), with a degree of familiarity unimaginable a century earlier, found him

> an astonishingly close picture of a particularly cheerless and unattractive snob . . . such as the English public-school and university system has produced ever since. He is a fearless and efficient leader in war. . . . In every other respect he is a glum, vain and extremely peevish dog.[53]

And by 1945 John Palmer was well-nigh abusive, designating him a "splendid oaf who has never come to maturity."[54] Granville-Barker, however, perhaps recalling Olivier's 1938 performance, found in his immaturity an "unruly charm" which somewhat mitigated the harshness of the portrait.[55]

Castigating Martius's failings ultimately proved to be a less rewarding pursuit than trying to account for them. And around the midcentury mark psychoanalytic theory was conscripted.[56] Although Freudian studies of *Coriolanus* were published as early as 1912 by Otto Rank and in 1921 by Jackson E. Towne,[57] it was Harold Goddard who, in a groundbreaking essay in 1951, popularized the potential of psychoanalytic theory as an aid to understanding the action. "Shakespeare was naturally unacquainted with twentieth-century psychiatry," he acknowledged. "Yet, whether by instinct or wisdom, what he sets down in this play with clinical precision is a case of not wholly normal mother-son relationship. . . . Until this is analyzed, it is futile to say anything about the politics of the play in the narrower sense."[58]

Among the first fruits of Goddard's insight was Hofling's effort (1957) to identify Martius as a phallic-narcissistic character, a type first classified by Wilhelm Reich in his *Character Analysis* (1933). Gordon Ross Smith (1959) two years later labeled him, along with Volumnia, Virgilia, and Menenius, an authoritarian personality of the kind remarked by Fromm and Adorno. Robert J. Stoller (1966) hypothesized an Oedipal combat to the death between mother and son, with Martius's attraction to Aufidius motivated in part by "homosexual needs." More recent studies include Janet Adelman's (1978) influential analysis of the theme of feeding, dependency, and aggression, and James E. Calderwood's (1987) intriguing exploration of Martius's "death intoxication."[59] Similar efforts abound, and, if Stanley Cavell is right, no end may be in sight. Contemporary criticism, he argues, sees the play as lending itself to two types of readings—the psychological and the political—and the psychoanalytic perspective yields more interesting results: "A political reading is apt to become fairly predictable once you know whose side the reader is taking, that of the patricians or that of the plebeians."[60]

The forces that shaped the history of critical response to Martius's character had a similar impact on other major figures. Neoclassical historicists seemed satisfied enough with the correctness of Volumnia's portrait, or at least did not complain. Only Dennis noted that Shakespeare had incorrectly designated her Volumnia rather than "Veturia" as Livy calls her. Johnson remarked in passing "the lofty lady's dignity," but her presence was generally ignored until Mrs. Jameson called attention to her influence in the passage cited earlier. Jameson's heroic, and profoundly biased, portrait of the matron set the tone for criticism throughout the Victorian era: "Her lofty patriotism, her patrician haughtiness, her maternal pride, her eloquence, and her towering spirit are exhibited with the utmost power of effect," she wrote, "yet the truth of female nature is beautifully preserved."[61] Jameson's evaluation was very much Volumnia's own, and most criticism for two generations thereafter collaborated unquestioningly in a portrait of a severe and patriotic Roman mother who put country first and maternal feelings second. Indeed, one of Martius's more amiable features was reckoned to be his filial reverence for such a figure. Hudson (1872), too, found her "though something more admirable than lovely in her style," nevertheless "a capital representative of the old Roman matronly character, in which strength and dignity seem to have had rather the better of sweetness and delicacy, but which enshrined the very soul of rectitude and honour."[62] Furnivall, not to be outdone, saw her not merely as "the embodiment of all the virtues that made the noble Roman lady," but as the idealized hand that rocked the cradle of European Imperialism: "[F]rom mothers like Volumnia," he concluded, "came the men who conquered the known world, and have left their mark for ever on the nations of Europe."[63]

As the century neared its end, some attempt was made to domesticate Volumnia's remote severity. Grace Latham (1880) fantasized into the matron's silence at the conclusion of the Intercession scene and her mute stage cross in 5.5 a maternal warmth she could not discover elsewhere:

> Volumnia answers not a word; too well she knew that when she begged mercy for her country she devoted her only son to death; neither when the populace receive her on her return with shouts of joy and gratitude can she respond; she feels she has lost her one son, and that the voices which shout her welcome are those which hounded him to his death. She has made the greatest of all sacrifices for her country; and just as she would not show her anxiety when her Marcius was at the wars, so now she hides her pain and goes home to weep.[64]

The impulse to domesticate the Roman character once more opened the door to its devaluation. As early as 1849–50 Gervinus had recognized in Volumnia the pernicious influence Mrs. Jameson suppressed. Volumnia's manipulation was responsible, he insisted, for Martius's successive betrayals of both Rome and the Antiates: "This mother, the giver and the shaper of his life, had brought him into both situations; she, therefore, meets her punishment [the loss of her son] with him."[65] Gervinus's assessment failed to win immediate acceptance. Latham, judging Volumnia by the severest standards of Victorian motherhood, brought herself to admit that the matron had gravely erred in her son's upbringing, and mapped with frankness and sensitivity her exploitation of Martius's consequent weaknesses; but she refused to credit Volumnia with anything but the highest maternal and patriotic motives. Stopford Brooke (1905), well in advance of the psychoanalytic critics in his conviction that the mother-son relationship "is the inmost heart of the drama, where the deepest affections play," found Volumnia bereft of both maternal altruism and ethical principle. "Her honour slips away," he writes, "when she advises Coriolanus to deceive the people in order to get the consulship. . . . As to her tenderness, she has it for her son and friends, but it is tenderness modified by the hunger for fame, for glory in war. The thoughtless militarism which has in all ages infected her class has made her its victim."[66] M. W. MacCallum lays heavy emphasis on her essentially selfish "visions of glory for herself and her son," and notes that "[i]n her covetousness for the consular dignity she recommends such hypocrisy, trickery and base cringing as the self-respect of no honest man . . . could tolerate."[67] "Indeed if we would mitigate our judgment of Coriolanus it would be on the ground of his unforunate maternal parentage," added Hookham.[68] Ethically deficient and power driven, not even a vestige of maternal affection was allowed her. "[S]he has shown love for [Martius's] glory, not for him," wrote G. Wilson Knight. "She loved him as a box to be crammed with honours."[69]

As early as 1910, with a nod in the direction of Freud, MacCallum remarked that "Modern conjecture points to the mother rather than the father as the source of will-power and character in the offspring; and in the upbringing of the boy Volumnia has had it all her own way,"[70] but it was again

Goddard who directed critical attention to Volumnia's pivotal, one might say primal, importance. For him the "'education' of Coriolanus by his mother becomes of consuming interest."[71]

Goddard's searching, commonsense examination of Volumnia's psychological relationship to her son inspired, as for Coriolanus himself, a host of more overtly "scientific" analyses of her character and motives. Hofling identified her as "an extremely unfeminine, non-maternal person, one who sought to meld her son to fit a preconceived image gratifying her own masculine (actually pseudo-masculine) striving. Her method . . . was to withhold praise and the scant affection she had to give from any achievements except aggressive and exhibitionistic ones."[72] Gordon Ross Smith saw her as a caricature of "feminine authoritarianism"; Stoller hypothesized her notion of her son as "the literal embodiment of her phallus which from infancy she had wished to attain by one means or another";[73] Ralph Berry similarly noted her fixation on "Coriolanus's person and fame as a sort of sexual surrogate";[74] Janet Adelman focussed upon her attitudes toward feeding and dependence, the fact that she is "not a nourishing mother,"[75] while Phyllis Rackin blames her for giving her son an education which "taught him a morbid horror of everything associated with femininity, the virtues no less than the vices, and an exaggerated devotion to a limited ideal of manliness."[76]

While over the past two centuries criticism has viewed Shakespeare's portraits of Martius and Volumnia with an increasingly jaundiced eye, his depiction of the plebeians, once the play's politics had been suppressed, has been more favourably reviewed and the charges of antipopulist prejudice leveled by Gildon, Dennis, and Hazlitt conclusively dismissed. Coleridge initiated the trend with an invitation to his readers to "observe the good nature with which Shakespeare seems always to make sport with the passions and follies of a mob, as with an irrational animal," and "to trace a tone of almost affectionate superiority, something like that in which a father speaks of the rogueries of a child."[77] Gervinus reckoned the faults ascribed to the people hardly damning in any case. "If we observe closely," he urges, "we cannot even find that the people are here represented as so very bad. We must distinguish between the way in which they really act, and the way in which the mockers and despisers of the people represent them."[78] And, as Hudson took occasion to point out, it is only to be expected that Coriolanus, as prime mediator between reader and citizens, seizes greedily on their faults, and "winks away whatsoever there is in them of a redeeming quality."[79] To Dowden Shakespeare's representation of the people was neither harsh nor ungenial: if the playwright "does not discover in them heroic virtues," he nevertheless "recognises that the heart of the people is sound; [and] their feelings are generally right," although "their view of facts is perverted by interests, by passions, by stupidity."[80] Brander Matthews found it easier to exonerate Shakespeare of antidemocratic sentiment by reidentifying his target: "It is the mob that Shakspere seems to despise, and not the whole people, of which the mob is only a single constituent element and the least worthy. The mob is the residuum of the populace, the baser part in its aspects."[81]

Bradley attempted to solve the problem once and for all by designating the plebeians an aesthetic rather than a political feature of the drama, a move entirely consonant with the received view of the play as a character study. The maneuver freed twentieth-century critics, or at least all but Brecht and a few like-minded souls, from the necessity of confronting uncomfortable political questions. Bradley simply displaced the plebeians as representatives of a political position with a notion of them as merely "part of a dramatic design." No longer need reader or playgoer take sides.

> This design is based on the main facts of the story, and these imply a certain character in the people and the hero. . . . The necessity for dramatic sympathy with both sides demands that on both [sides] there should be some right and some wrong, both virtues and failings; and if the hero's monstrous purpose of destroying his native city is not to extinguish our sympathy, the provocation he receives must be great. This being so, the picture of the people is, surely, no darker than it had to be. . . .[82]

Bradley's strategy effectively silenced discussion of the issue in this century.

The tribunes, it should be noted, have never enjoyed the critical goodwill extended to the plebeians: when noticed at all, they have been uniformly demonized. Granville-Barker reflects the critical consensus when he designates them "the unqualified 'villains of the piece' [with] a surface of comic colouring . . . the only mitigation allowed them."[83] Denton J. Snider and John Palmer, however, have leapt to their defence; Snider, to remark that they share the popular wisdom characteristic of the plebeians, along with "a good deal of political courage";[84] Palmer, to describe them as "Shakespeare's counterfeit presentment of two labour leaders [who] use their wits to defend the interests of the popular party and to remove from power a declared enemy of the people."[85]

The treatment by character critics of the three other figures closest to Martius—Menenius, Virgilia, and Aufidius—must not be ignored, although it may be outlined more briefly.

Johnson's and Schlegel's references to "the old man's merriment" and "the original old satirist Menenius" suggest that the character was initially regarded as primarily a source of humor. Gervinus, however, dimly perceived in him a foil to Martius, "a man contented to be a man amongst men."[86] Snider found him "a mediator of patrician blood,"[87] while E. K. Chambers noted "his share in spoiling Coriolanus' character."[88] A. P. Rossiter, in a major critique in 1961, definitively identified his function in the dramatic pattern as "a humorous, ironical, experienced, sensible, critical commentator; and, simultaneously, in the Roman political world, an 'antitype' and counterpoise to everything that is Marcius."[89] Subsequent criticism has had little to add.

Virgilia throughout most of her critical history was regarded as a peripheral character, when she was noticed at all. Johnson, as we noted earlier, glancingly remarked her "bridal modesty,"[90] while Jameson was taken by the counterpoint offered to the severity of Volumnia by her "modest sweetness," "conjugal tenderness," and "fond solicitude."[91] Bradley found impressive "that kind of muteness in which Virgilia resembles Cordelia, and which is made to suggest a world of feeling in reserve."[92] E. K. Chambers felt "her sole function [was] to touch the tragedy here and there with tears."[93] Middleton Murry found her the only "truly congenial" character in the drama, although the least substantial; and in a valiant attempt to lend her materiality, he stretched the meaning of her every word to the limit and beyond, while ingeniously appropriating the speeches of others to her use and reallocating to her peers lines he considered at odds with his own notion of her.[94] Una Ellis-Fermor suggested that she might represent for Coriolanus "a longing for the balancing silences, graces, and wisdom banished from the outer world but vital to wholeness of life."[95] With the advent of psychoanalytic criticism she has received increased, but hardly less fanciful, attention. Goddard claimed Volumnia's contribution in the Intercession scene "would have amounted to nothing if the wife and the boy had not been there to translate its logic into love and imaginative power."[96] Hofling, bringing science to the support of Goddard's observation, argued that "through his marriage to the emotionally healthy and feminine Virgilia, Coriolanus has had a 'corrective emotional experience' and has undergone a partial emotional maturation. . . . [T]he healthier influences of the marriage have not been without effect and make possible the relenting which takes place in the final act."[97]

Aufidius, oddly enough, has received relatively little critical attention. Midway through the nineteenth century, Gervinus identified him as a counterpoint to Coriolanus, but little was done with the suggestion. Bradley judged him "by far the weakest spot in the drama" and "wanted merely for the plot."[98] In more recent times Robert J. Stoller and Ralph Berry postulated a homosexual attachment between Aufidius and Martius,[99] while Stanley D. McKenzie argued that Aufidius must be understood as a cynical political relativist, like Volumnia, in contrast to the absolutist Coriolanus.[100]

Although scholars from Dennis onward kept the play's characters obsessively within their sights, they were not insensitive to its structure. Dennis scolded Shakespeare's neglect of the unities; Johnson vented his dissatisfaction with the distribution of "bustle" as noted earlier; and Gentleman, while disapproving of the fourth act, concluded that "[t]he fifth act rises very considerably above the fourth . . . but what comes after [the Intercession scene] falls off, and we are not interested by the catastrophe."[101] Nineteenth-century commentators from Schlegel onward were united in a common, often ecstatic, appreciation for the play's design. Schlegel praised Shakespeare's capacity to "give unity and rounding to a series of events";[102] Hudson held the play to be "among [Shakespeare's] greatest triumphs in organization";[103] Swinburne claimed "[a] loftier or a more perfect piece of man's work was never done in all the world than this tragedy";[104] while MacCallum, with somewhat more restraint, pronounced it "[t]echnically and artistically . . . a more perfect achievement than either [*Julius Caesar* or *Antony and Cleopatra*]." The "balance and composition of the whole" he reckoned "admirable" and the construction "very perfect."[105]

The advent of literary modernism[106] in the early decades of this century, without mitigating the longstanding critical obsession with characterization and construction, focussed attention upon a new, and disquieting, issue: when *Coriolanus*'s language, imagery, and rhythms, and the reader's response to them, were subjected to New Critical scrutiny, the play's aesthetic effect declared itself to be unlike that of the other major tragedies.

The New Critical revelation was not entirely original, however; from the early eighteenth century to World War I, more than one commentator voiced an aesthetic unease. In 1730 Lewis Theobald felt moved to remark that although "Coriolanus is much my favourite . . . I had rather it sometimes wanted of the *sublime,* so it had more of the *pathos* in exchange."[107] Franz Horn, nearly a century later, observed that while the play leaves "hardly a wish . . . unfulfilled," nevertheless, "there remains in the inmost soul of the reader a longing that is unsatisfied; it is that feeling which in its tenderest depth cannot be adequately expressed."[108] It remained for Bradley to articulate precisely what the play lacked: the "*imaginative* effect or atmosphere" characteristic of the great tragedies "is hardly felt"; the supernatural element is absent; the sense of nature as "a vaster fellow-actor and fellow-sufferer" is missing; the hero offers no "exhibition of inward conflict, or of the outburst of one or another passion, terrible, heart-rending, or glorious to witness"; and, at the end, the reader experiences not transcendence but something close to disgust. "Such an emotion as mere disgust is out of place in a tragic close," he admits, "but I confess I feel nothing but disgust as Aufidius speaks the last words."[109]

Two approaches to the play's anomalous character presented themselves: the drama might be regarded as a flawed masterpiece, or its oddities might be considered features of a deliberate, but as yet unidentified, aesthetic strategy. In 1907 E. K. Chambers opted for the former, detecting in the play "the exhaustion of a mood," a "slackening of the creative energies."[110] Brander Matthews (1913) sensed "no weakening here of the poet's power or of his intelligence," but rather "a slackening of enthusiasm and a consequent diminution of emotional appeal."[111] Hookham (1922) discovered in Shakespeare at this period a "perverted moral sense," and "with this perversion of moral sense perversion of style goes here hand in hand."[112]

Most commentators, however, opted to give the dramatist the benefit of the doubt; and the attempt to endow the play with a definitive stylistic identity has constituted one of the century's perennial scholarly recreations. Bradley made no attempt to posit a style, nor did he use the word; he did however credit the play with a unifying "conception": "Shakespeare could construe the story he found only by conceiving the hero's character in a certain way; and he had to set the whole drama in tune with that conception."[113]

Middleton Murry (1922) made some attempt to identify the style, although he did not give it a name. The play's "economy, its swiftness, its solidity, its astonishing clarity and pregnancy of language," he felt, "have a peculiar and profound appropriateness to the warlike argument. . . . [T]he exact and unrelenting pattern of *Coriolanus* seems essential to the unfaltering decision and the unswerving success of the . . . Roman general."[114] Muriel St. Clare Byrne (1931), in search of a more precise definition of the play's character, recognized "a definite affinity with the classical method." Unlike romantic tragedy which "centres itself upon some tremendous personality," classical tragedy, she claimed,

> is more apt to envisage certain rights as the centre of the fable; sometimes a clash of rights or of apparently-conflicting rights. . . . We are never made to care about Coriolanus in the same way [we care about Macbeth] because Shakespeare was focussing his emotion upon an idea, the idea of Rome. We are meant to care more about the saving of Rome than about the saving of the soul of Coriolanus.[115]

For Mark Van Doren (1939) the play was a rhetorical exercise, and its style that of extended debate. "The streets of Rome are conceived as rostrums," he writes,

> where men meet for the sole purpose of discussing something—the character of the hero and its effect upon a certain political situation. . . . Coriolanus is a tragic hero whom we listen to and learn about entirely in his public aspect. His heroic fault, which is pride, is announced in the first scene as a theme for discussion; and the play is that discussion.[116]

D.J. Enright pressed the same argument some fifteen years later.[117]

O. J. Campbell, taking seriously Shaw's 1903 assertion that the play is not a tragedy at all, but "the greatest of Shakespear's comedies,"[118] advanced the notion that the play is in reality an "experiment in tragical satire." "Neither in his presentation of the central figure nor in his construction of the plot does [Shakespeare]," he argues, "follow orthodox tragic principles. Instead of enlisting our sympathy for Coriolanus, he deliberately alienates it. Indeed he makes the figure partly an object of scorn. Instead of ennobling Coriolanus through his fall and death, he mocks and ridicules him to the end."[119] A. P. Rossiter (1952) dubbed Campbell's suggestion "nonsense" and termed the drama "the last and greatest of the Histories."[120]

In recent years literary genres with which *Coriolanus* might have affinities have been canvassed with a vengeance. Reuben A. Brower (1971) finds Coriolanus an epic hero in the tradition of Achilles, and the play's conventions those of epic tragedy.[121] Richard Crowley (1974) contends that Shakespeare creates a "deliberately mixed or hybrid genre" from tragedy and epic.[122] John Holloway (1961), Kenneth Burke (1966), and Jay Halio (1972) in various ways situate the play in relation to mythic patterns, identifying Martius as a scapegoat figure ceremonially expelled from his society and ritually executed.[123] More recently Stanley D. McKenzie intriguingly suggests that *Coriolanus* invents rather than follows a literary convention. "The play," he maintains, "is singularly structured to create an overwhelming sense of unresolved paradox and uncertainty in the minds of the audience; this effect consequently conditions and impels the audience to accept an ethic of dissembling as the only means of coping with the world Shakespeare constructs."[124]

One of the most provocative initiatives is the notion advanced by Arnold Hauser in 1965 and developed by Cyrus Hoy in 1973 that the play is an exercise in the mannerist style.[125] That mannerist art was in vogue in England at the time of the play's composition is undeniable, and its analogies with mannerist aesthetics are legion. Moreover most, if not all, the aesthetic conjectures surveyed above have affinities with, and may be reconciled within, the mannerist paradigm. The fact that mannerism made its point by deliberately exploiting High Renaissance conventions accounts for the classical influences in the play perceived by St. Clare Byrne; its manneristic appeal to the head rather than to the heart, its intellectual, as opposed to emotional, character, accounts for the rhetorical, debatelike quality noted by Strachey, Van Doren, and Enright; the whimsical, even comic, distortion of space and figure characteristic of mannerist art has a certain affinity with the comedic features noted by Shaw and Campbell; and its rejection of emotive landscape, psychologically revealing likenesses, and spiritual transcendence in favor of anonymous spaces and cool coloring, ambiguous and distanced portraiture, and delicate balance and unresolved tension goes far to explain the unconventional and alienating features catalogued by Bradley and others. Mannerism's fondness for paradox, not as mere ornament but as a vital aesthetic device, convincingly accounts for Shakespeare's extensive use of it.

Widespread concentration on the play's characters and style has not precluded other research. Verbal and stage imagery, linguistic strategies, sources and contexts, all have received extensive attention. In a curious parallel with the theater phenomenon, however, scholarship has shown little interest in the play's politics. Most of the ideologically committed readings available in English are translated commentaries of European critics—Brecht, Smirnov, and Kott, for example—although a major exception is Paul

N. Siegel's *Shakespeare's Roman and History Plays: A Marxist Approach* (1986).

Cavell is perhaps not alone in his lack of enthusiasm for analyses of the play's politics in terms of "political authority or conflict, say about questions of legitimate succession or divided loyalties." *Coriolanus,* he argues, treats politics at a broader and more fundamental level: "It is about the formation of the political, the founding of the city, what it is that makes a rational animal fit for conversation, for civility. This play seems to think of this creation of the political, call it the public, as the overcoming of narcissism, incestuousness, and cannibalism."[126] In a similar vein new historicist and cultural materialist scholars have extended their definition of politics to include "those areas of human life commonly thought to be antithetical to and independent of the political realm—for example subjectivity, personal identity, gender identity, the privacy of the home, the intimacy of the family, aesthetics" which, Jonathan Dollimore argues "include, and often actively reproduce, the exploitation, repression and oppression visible in the larger public realm."[127] On the broadened critical field created by Cavell and Dollimore there is ample space for the kind of broadly based political and sociological analysis typified by Dollimore's essay "*Coriolanus* (c. 1608): The Chariot Wheel and its Dust."[128]

THE PLAY IN THE THEATER

Stephen Greenblatt initiates his *Shakespeare Negotiations* by confessing an urge, familiar enough to historians of all stripes, "to speak with the dead."[129] The theater historian, however, covets less to speak with the dead than to observe them at work. And to make the most of that experience, one craves cultural empathy: to breathe as it were the political, social, and aesthetic air that filled the lungs of theater artists, critics, and audiences at any given period. Unfortunately, we are condemned to receive a period signal with a contemporary receiver, the equivalent of attempting to play a phonograph record on a compact disk player.

To attempt to recover the theatrical past in all its factual accuracy, aesthetic complexity, and cultural resonance is, it must be admitted, a futile endeavor. Yet the "textual traces" of the dead, as Greenblatt calls them, those "fragment[s] of lost life," irresistibly call to us. And none are more full of Greenblatt's "will to be heard" than Shakespeare's texts. Throughout the history of Shakespeare representation, each age in its attempt to speak with the dead, to respond to Shakespearian traces, has reinvented Shakespeare, to use Gary Taylor's phrase, in its own image.[130] To encounter that response, however imperfectly, is not only to comprehend something new about Shakespeare, but to experience an age's aesthetic, ethical, and political value system; and so to move some distance, however fractional, toward understanding the cultural past which informs our present.

To approach Shakespeare performance in this way is not to imagine some ideal Elizabethan or Jacobean creation, and then to pursue and censure subsequent stage perversions of it; rather it is to adopt the (somewhat paraphrased) view of Alice in her interview with the Caterpillar—it is not what the text *is* that matters, but what it is *becoming,* as each generation reconstructs from the "traces" offered by the verbal score itself and theatrical tradition a new aural and visual creation which bears the stamp of its unique sensibility.

My attempt has been to trace in broad strokes the life of the play in the theater from the earliest records of production to the present. In a single volume one cannot treat all revivals: choices have to be made. I have limited my focus primarily to productions in London, New York, and the British, American, and Canadian Stratfords. I have also included, somewhat idiosyncratically, other British or North American productions of particular interest.

To cover in detail all noteworthy productions, even within my radically narrowed field, is of course impossible. I have opted, insofar as evidence allowed, simply to include the most significant features of each. If my judgment seems faulty, I have, by way of compensation, documented my sources fairly fully to enable the reader to retrace my steps for him/herself. In general, earlier productions tend to be more fully reconstructed than contemporary ones, partly because I felt it important to make available relatively inaccessible eighteenth- and nineteenth-century documentation, and also because these revivals cope for the first time with production challenges which today's director not so much discovers as inherits.

To adequately situate every revival in the context of contemporaneous theater practice, politics, and aesthetics is out of the question; nevertheless I try to keep these issues continuously in mind, and to signal, often with inordinate brevity, the relevance of one or another as appropriate. In general, however, with space considerations always to the fore, I have chosen to privilege production facts over context, leaving it to the reader to situate them as he or she chooses. I have not attempted to fit *Coriolanus*'s production history to some arbitrary theoretical construct or to make it conform to some overarching narrative. I simply hope to provide a record, albeit tentative and incomplete, which may offer a starting point for further research of various kinds.

To identify the significant moments of a performance is to select from thousands of details those which for a variety of reasons seem particularly to matter, and one's criteria are inevitably subjective. Nevertheless, with such objectivity as I could summon, I have attempted to examine the verbal "score," noting cuts, additions, and alterations; the stage environment created by set, lighting, costume, and sound designers and musicians; the

actor's interpretation of the score in speech and movement; and the omnipresent influence of the actor-manager/director.

Wherever possible I have relied upon promptbooks and other theater
documents as prime sources of information, recognizing that these are only
the most trustworthy of a fallible set of witnesses. Promptbooks, unfortunately, often cannot tell us what we most need to know—exactly how an
actor looked or sounded at any particular moment. Inevitably I have been
obliged to draw upon secondary sources—letters, diaries, reviews, and interviews—with the attendant risk of seeing not the performance itself but
what an eyewitness thought had been observed. Wherever possible I have
correlated the testimony of several observers and weighed their findings
against the "feel" of theater documents. Although one can never, it is true,
catch the stage moment fully or exactly, or fix its meaning for a playgoer at
any given performance, I hope that my reconstructions, if inadequate, are
not factually inaccurate.

Coriolanus's career in both England and America is an account of a theater establishment irresistibly drawn to its acting opportunities, particularly
the Intercession scene, but as uncomfortable as the critics with its unorthodox tragic character: the precarious balance of sympathies between the
play's political factions; a protagonist as unattractive as he is heroic, and
ultimately a traitor; not to mention a conclusion lacking in both transcendence and affirmation of societal hegemony.

The first three-quarters of a century of the play's recorded stage life
(1681–1749) saw its political potential frankly recognized and exploited. Nahum Tate and John Dennis, dissatisfied with Shakespeare's evenhandedness,
stabilized the play's politics to favor the Tories and Whigs respectively,
tamed the hero's unruliness to prevailing notions of decorum, and reworked
the ending to enforce an acceptable moral. Stagecraft was summoned to
underpin the revised text and reflect contemporary aesthetic taste. James
Thomson, recognizing that the play's political ambivalence and aesthetic
uniqueness were inseparable from its theatricality, opted to create an entirely new script which emptied the drama of political content and aestheticized and historicized its action. His strategy, adapted to Shakespeare first
by Thomas Sheridan and later by John Philip Kemble, was to shape *Coriolanus*'s production tradition for decades.

With the onset of the French Revolution, John Philip Kemble astutely
defused the play's political potential by reinventing it as a Davidian history
painting, a tactic which, conjoined with the actor-manager's unique reading
of Martius, created a box office success rarely, if ever, equalled since. Posed
grandly amid as much archaeological spectacle as could be mustered, Martius's anti-heroics amounted to little more than the mildly endearing features
of a venerable art object. The play's history from Kemble's retirement in
1817 until World War I, apart from Edmund Kean's brave challenge to the
tradition, is a chronicle of British and American attempts to replicate the

Kemble formula with some aesthetic updating to accommodate contemporary taste.

At the end of World War I, in the first flush of postwar modernism, "Elizabethan Methodism" (as Bridges-Adams termed it) scrapped the heavily cut Kemble script, the proscenium pictorial presentation, and the grand tragic acting style in favor of fuller texts, swifter, more flexible, and more intimate staging, and a more natural performance mode. The interwar exploration of the play's theatrical potential was not unlike the probing of style by the New Critics. In the end, however, *Coriolanus*'s political character, camouflaged by clever stagecraft, was hardly more evident than in the Kemble era.

Laurence Olivier's groundbreaking performance at the Old Vic in 1938 initiated two decades of romantic interpretation during which, in fullish texts and modernist settings, Martius was played for virile glamour by a series of husky leading men to audiences addicted to cinematic escapism. Politics was once more contained, this time by stagecraft and sex appeal.

The obsessive narcissism and political activism of the sixties, the political disillusion of the seventies and eighties, and the postmodern materialism and cynicism of the nineties all have informed productions of the past three decades, a period which has brought *Coriolanus* increased popularity, together with a certain empathy for Martius's defiant nonconformism and the play's user-unfriendly aesthetic. Apart from the brief appearance of Brecht's adaptation in England in the 1960s and its fleeting fallout, the play's politics have been virtually as invisible to us as to the Regency playgoer.

The general reader may find my acccount too detailed, while the specialist may feel shortchanged. I have tried to reconcile the need for a readable narrative with the awareness that much of the material is not easy to come by. The nonspecialist may wish to read selectively, while the enthusiast will find additional notes at the end of the book, full documentation of my sources, and a Chronological Handlist of Performances should there be a wish to pursue the subject further.

2

The Jacobean and Caroline Era

Coriolanus's composition date cannot be fixed with precision. Scholarship generally places it between 1605, the publication date of Camden's *Remaines,* to which Shakespeare seems to be indebted,[1] and 1610, when Ben Jonson makes what appears to be a jocular allusion to the play. Attempts to narrow the time span further on the strength of alleged topical references have been unconvincing. Martius's reference to the "coal of fire upon the ice" (1.1.173) might conceivably recall the great frost of 1607/08,[2] but images of fire and ice need not be prompted by specific events. Even less persuasive is the suggestion that Coriolanus's warning to the patricians that Sicinius may "turn your current in a ditch, / And make your channel his" (3.1.96–97) derives from a water diversion scheme propounded early in 1609.[3] No theatergoer, Jacobean or modern, who in childhood played in the gutter on a rainy day needs more than memory to seize Coriolanus's point. Efforts to discover parallels between the Roman citizens' uprising and Warwickshire peasant revolts in 1607,[4] however intriguing, also fail to yield a definitive birthdate.

The firmest clue to a date for *Coriolanus*'s theatrical premiere is Jonson's apparent parody of a line from the play in his *Epicoene,* first staged late in 1609 or early in 1610. Truewit's rueful admission to Dauphine, "[Y]ou have lurched your friends of the better half of the garland, by concealing this part of the plot" (5.4.208–10)[5] seems a pointed burlesque of Cominius's "He lurch'd all swords of the garland" (2.2.10l). The use of the lines in a parodic context assumes a thoroughgoing knowledge of *Coriolanus* on the part of the audience; and where would they acquire such familiarity save in the theater since the play was not printed until the First Folio of 1623? For such a relatively subtle allusion to have its effect, the drama would need to be fresh in the audience's memory; and since the theaters were closed due to plague from late July of 1608 until at least mid-December of 1609,[6] playgoers probably saw *Coriolanus* for the first time late in December 1609 or sometime in January 1610, shortly before the debut of *Epicoene.*

A fragment of possible corroborative evidence is offered by a reference in Robert Armin's preface to his narrative poem *The Italian Taylor, and his Boy* (1609) to "a strange time of taxation, wherein every Pen & inck-horne

34

Boy, will throw up his Cap at the hornes of the Moone in censure,"[7] a plausible echo of Martius's "they threw their caps / As they would hang them on the horns a'th'moon, / Shouting their emulation" (1.1.212–14). Armin, a longtime member of the King's Men, could well have assimilated the image while both the production and his poem were in preparation sometime in 1609.[8]

If *Coriolanus* had its premiere in December or January, it must have been staged at the Blackfriars, the new winter home of the King's company. Although the play's noise, physicality, and rhetorical fireworks might have made it an ideal choice for the Globe, its intellectual complexity and aesthetic novelty would have been no less attractive to upscale Blackfriars audiences.[9] Doubtless the piece was played at both houses at one time or another,[10] and nothing in its staging requirements would have taxed the physical resources of either. No more than an apron stage with two entry doors, a balcony above to simulate the walls of Corioli, and perhaps a set of gates (placed across the curtained recess, as suggested by Irwin Smith),[11] is required.

In civilian scenes, male patricians probably wore some form of conventional costume *à la romaine,* and in military sequences breastplates, cuirasses, and helmets arguably more authentic than the Peacham drawing suggests. To judge from the popular engravings of Johannes Stradanus's scenes from Roman history,[12] to say nothing of an abundance of material elsewhere,[13] costumiers did not lack visual reference sources, although little attempt appears to have been made in either art or theater to distinguish one period from another. Plebeians no doubt sported Jacobean working-class attire, while female characters, according to custom, wore contemporary fashions.

Textual costume cues are neither frequent nor elaborate. Usually the nature of a particular scene is assumed to make the wardrobe self-evident (for example, military gear for battle scenes); but when costume effects are crucial, dress may be specified in stage directions (witness the "gown of humility" called for at 2.3.40). Occasionally, though, costume information is embedded in dialogue. At the conclusion of the Voices scene, Menenius informs his protégé:

> Remains
> That, in th'official marks invested, you
> Anon do meet the senate
>
> (2.3.139–41).

Coriolanus might readily have been instructed in a direction to don consular robes and insignia, but how much more effective is it that the presumptuous counsel comes from the overconfident and blindly loyal Menenius. That Menenius advised the gear takes nothing away from the stunning visual irony created when Martius endures the sentence of banishment wearing the very robes which should have honoured a life of national service.

On two other occasions costume is implied in dialogue rather than called for in stage directions, thus creating simultaneously a meaningful visual statement and an acting opportunity. When Martius arrives at Aufidius's house, the latter, with galling aptness, calls attention to the stranger's shabbiness: "[T]hough thy tackle's torn, / Thou show'st a noble vessel" (4.5.61–62). Volumnia, with equal propriety, is made to note her own deterioration on her arrival in the Volscian camp (5.3.94–96).

Properties, clearly identified in stage directions and dialogue, are familiar Jacobean objects: stools, ladders, a crutch, cushions, sewing gear, leaden spoons and other paltry booty, wine, a letter, improvised weapons and tools for the plebeians, and swords and shields for the military.

Nothing is known of the original casting. Richard Burbage, the company's leading tragic actor, probably created the role of Martius. Then about forty, he would have been only four years older than the age given the historical Coriolanus by Dionysius of Halicarnassus.[14] Baldwin conjectures that Menenius was played by John Heminges, whose "line" was "the faithful father, counsellor, servant, with all the privileges of oddity or whimsicality attaching to age," not the least of which was "giving advice, and laying down the law."[15] The role of Aufidius, Baldwin allots to John Lowin, a player of rude villains, gruff counselors, and outspoken friends.

The authoritarian power demanded by the role of Volumnia has prompted speculation that the part was played by an adult. Despite Robertson Davies's conviction that the part was taken by a man,[16] there is little evidence to justify such an assumption. At this point the King's Men did not want for first-class boy performers since in 1608 they had taken over the leaders of the children at Blackfriars, including Ostler, Underwood, and Eggleston. And if some of these actors were capable of playing the complex Cleopatra, as is now generally accepted,[17] then surely the fairly straightforward Volumnia need not have been beyond their powers. Moreover, Ben Jonson's assertion that Salomon Pavy, between the ages of ten and thirteen, played "old men so duely, / As, sooth, the Parcae thought him one"[18] implies that older characters posed no greater challenge to the juvenile performers than younger ones.

Any attempt to recreate a Jacobean performance of *Coriolanus* is largely a speculative venture.[19] The unfortunate truth is that, apart from information embedded in the script itself, not a scrap of solid evidence related to the play's original staging has emerged. The text, although it cannot tell us what *was* done, nevertheless offers valuable clues to what was *meant* to be done, and the kind of audience experience such theatrical strategies imply.

The play's subject, drawn from Plutarch's *Lives,* transforms Plutarch's cautionary tale of the perils of inadequate youthful education into an objective and complex examination of a series of social, political, and psychological concerns which obsessed the whole of Europe in the second half of the sixteenth and early seventeenth centuries. Although the action is laid in the Rome of the consuls, the characters breathe the intellectual and social atmosphere of early seventeenth-century England. The alienated and explosive mood of Shakespeare's Rome was less a historical reconstruction than a reflection of contemporary reality for Jacobean audiences of all classes.[20]

At the heart of *Coriolanus* is a probing of the Machiavellian notion that politics may be defined "as an activity having its own objectives, principles, and standards, an activity . . . that can and should be conducted totally independently of non-political considerations. In politics means must be chosen to meet the ends, and the best means are those that lead most surely to those ends."[21] Most inhabitants of Martius's Rome are prepared to employ any strategy necessary to obtain a desired object: Volumnia's cynical posturing, Menenius's avuncular temporizing, the tribunes' opportunism, Aufidius's expediency, and the plebeians' mindless conformity all subordinate process to product. Ultimately Coriolanus falls victim to the new political realism because he cannot adapt to a relativist code of behavior. For him, virtue does not, and never can, in Aufidius's phrase, "Lie in th'interpretation of the time" (4.7.50). Adamantly opposed to the practice of politics divorced from principle, however wrongheaded and inhumane the principle, and determined to behave "As if a man were author of himself, / And knew no other kin" (5.3.36–37), he finds himself betrayed by his society and eventually its betrayer. A social and political anachronism, like the lonely dragon of his simile, he struggles vainly against the forces of change with the weapons of another era, and goes down, uncomprehending, to defeat. Shakespeare's focus on alienation is unrelenting throughout—of government from the people, and the hero from his society, his family, and his environment. Martius's aloneness, highlighted by Shakespeare but not to be found in Plutarch, epitomizes not only the plight of an individual but the mood of an age.

Although the play reflects with apparent accuracy social stresses in Jacobean London, its incidents discover no unequivocal ideological imperatives. Its unstable signification may be identified with a deliberate Elizabethan-Jacobean literary technique, termed by Annabel Patterson "functional ambiguity," "in which the indeterminacy inveterate to language was fully and knowingly exploited by authors and readers alike" to elude government censorship.[22] Patterson's thesis is extended by Paul Yachnin to hypothesize the existence of a "powerless theatre" during the period 1590–1625 when

the players promulgated the idea of the disinterestedness of art, extended the techniques of "functional ambiguity" practiced by early Elizabethan playwrights, and advertised that plays were separate from the operations of power. . . . The dramatic companies won from the government precisely what the government was most willing to give: a privileged, profitable, and powerless marginality.[23]

The play's ambivalent and overdetermined character has been attributed with equal conviction by Arnold Hauser and Cyrus Hoy to a mannerist aesthetic.[24] Whatever its rationale, *Coriolanus*'s political ambivalence is as insistent as it is pervasive, mediated by an artistic method, more cognitive than affective in its appeal, which privileges uncertainty, incongruity, and unresolved tension.

Much of the play's ideological and aesthetic shimmer derives from its unconventional design. Its structure evinces no one center of interest, but multiple foci—the Roman-Volscian military campaign, the domestic political struggle, the mother-son relationship. *Coriolanus*'s first half is awash in military encounters and civil broils while the latter part, until Martius's assassination, is almost devoid of physical activity.

Coriolanus is constructed in two parts, the first comprising all the material leading up to Martius's banishment, concluded by the downbeat coda in which Volumnia berates the tribunes, and the second embracing the action from his arrival in Antium to his death. The two sections, which wonderfully parallel and even parody each other, are distinctly separated by the terra incognita between Coriolanus's departure from Rome and his arrival in Antium. We know nothing of what transpired in the interim, or of the state of mind which led to his act of betrayal. Plutarch has a good deal to say on the subject, but Shakespeare suppresses his comments. The Adrian-Nicanor encounter (4.3), which occupies the spatial break between Martius's exodus from Rome and advent in Antium, acts as a linking device between the play's two sections. Apart from creating a sense of passing time, the spies' problematic identities and shifting allegiances neatly invoke the bitter past and anticipate and ironize the upcoming betrayal. A failure to appreciate the pivotal function of this small scene has resulted in its absence from productions throughout most of *Coriolanus*'s stage history.

The precariously balanced triple focus is stabilized to some degree by persistent patterned repetition of visual motifs. Three major entrances in which Martius figures, for example, are made parodically to echo one another: the triumphal return (2.1.161), the dismal procession in the Intercession scene (5.3.21), and Martius's raucous arrival with Volscian commoners at 5.6.69.[25] Similarly resonant are the three parallel embassies to Coriolanus—those of Cominius, Menenius, and the Roman matrons—all differently handled and growing cumulatively in power. Again, the episode in which Martius is goaded by Aufidius to his death reprises with devastating accuracy the scene in which he was driven into exile by the tribunes, even to the repetition of the word "traitor" which triggers in both cases a ruinous loss of self-control. Examples could be multiplied.

Whatever structural stability is achieved by patterned repetition is perennially threatened by a kaleidoscopic multiplicity of viewpoint. All sides, except, possibly, the tribunes, are given a fair hearing, but each position when juxtaposed with its opposite assumes a more complex, even contradictory, complexion. When the political tangle is scanned from one direction, the plebeians seem clearly to be in the right, but regarded from a slightly different angle, the patrician platform seems rational enough. This miraculous multifacetedness of vision offers no eternal verities, only a collection of ambiguous and contradictory insights out of which one must make, as of life itself, whatever sense one can. As Stanley Cavell has it, "[T]he politics of the play is essentially the politics of a given production, so that we should not expect its political issues to be settled by an interpretation of what you might call 'the text itself.' "[26]

Of a piece with its multiple foci and equivocal perspective is *Coriolanus*'s paradoxical and ambiguous narrative technique. At its center lies the primary paradox that "the great military hero with his unbounded sense of personal pride and absolute standards of unyielding honor proves twice to be a traitor."[27] The plot is riddled with betrayals, changes of mind, doubletalk, fickleness, and contradictions, all of which weaken the spectator's grip on reality. Reversals of expectations are routine; and the play's language fairly reeks of discontinuity, ambiguity, and contradiction. The Intercession scene, which finds its heartbeat in the implicit paradox that for both mother and son to win is to lose, is permeated with paradoxes of every sort. Volumnia begins the encounter with a catalogue of the paradoxes inherent in her situation and Coriolanus concludes it with his resigned recognition of his mother's losing victory.

Dramatic interest resides ultimately in the noisy interaction of the play's characters. The urban landscape is omnipresent, even intrusive, but references to the Capitol, the Senate, conduits, shops, and the like are indicative rather than evocative. No mention is made of nature, weather, stormy or fine, season of the year, or even time of day. Plutarch records the fact that Cominius presented Martius with the horse in the morning and that the latter arrived in Antium at twilight, but Shakespeare suppresses these facts. One has only to recall the aesthetic consequence of place, time, weather, and atmosphere in *Julius Caesar* to appreciate that the repression of such details in *Coriolanus* cannot be other than deliberate.

What matters most is the human landscape; and here the playwright seems to have taken to heart aesthetically Sicinius's rhetorical question, "What is the city but the people?" (3.1.198). Not only are references to the city's inhabitants legion—"nurses, mechanics, cobblers, tailors, apron-men, actors, orange-wives, faucet-sellers, harlots, ballad-makers, mountebanks, veiled dames, and flamens"[28]—but enormous attention is paid to the theatrical blocking of its figures. Both stage directions and dialogue spell out to an unusual degree how entrances are to be handled ("*Enter Cominius the Generall, and Titus Latius: betweene them Coriolanus, crown'd with an Oaken Garland, with Captaines and Souldiers, and a Herauld*" [2.1.161] or "My wife comes foremost, then the honour'd mould / Wherein this trunk was fram'd, and in her hand / The grandchild to her blood" [5.3.22–24]); dress is stipulated when its effect is important ("*Enter Coriolanus in meane Ap-parrell, Disguisd, and muffled*" [4.4]) and special visual, and accompanying sound, effects are composed with care ("*Flourish. Alarum. A Retreat is sounded. Enter at one Doore Cominius, with the Romanes: At another Doore Martius, with his Arme in a Scarfe*" [1.9]). Throughout the play, one is supremely aware of physical gestures: swords and hats are waved, hands are held, backs are turned, characters embrace, sit, stand, and kneel. These gestures are of the most conventional sort and often smack of attitudinizing; nevertheless, their repetition in a variety of contexts allows these banal poses to accumulate particular resonance individually and collectively. Coriolanus and Volumnia alternately kneel to each other on Martius's triumphal return as Rome's defender and again on their encounter in the Volscian camp when Martius turns traitor to his country; he takes the hand of his mother at the conclusion of the triumphal return scene (2.1.194), once more, it appears, as he goes into exile (4.1.57), and finally, and most poignantly, when he capitulates to her entreaties in the Intercession scene (5.3.182).[29] He embraces Cominius after his successful attack on the Volscians and is embraced by Aufidius when he betrays Rome to the Volscians. Each time the gesture is accompanied by nuptial imagery (1.6.29–32, 4.5.106–18). The occasional unconventional, and even bizarre, gesture is all the more effective for its rarity. An obvious example is the barbaric moment in which Aufidius stands on the corpse of Martius. This image is elaborately prepared for by a whole series of ironic foreshadowings, as Stanley D. McKenzie notes:

> Volumnia earlier predicts that Coriolanus will "beat Aufidius' head below his knee, / And tread upon his neck" (1.3.46–47), and in Act 5 Coriolanus plans to "triumphantly tread" upon Rome (5.4.116); "The ground shrinks before his tread-ing" (5.4.19–20), but Volumnia tells Coriolanus
>
> > thou shalt no sooner
> > March to assault thy country than to tread
> > (Trust to't, thou shalt not) on thy mother's womb.
> >
> > (5.3.122–24)
>
> Young Martius shouts, "'A shall not tread on me" (5.3.127), and Coriolanus finally treads on no one; he instead is trod upon until a shocked Volscian Lord tells Aufidius, "Tread not upon him" (5.6.133).[30]

The degree of substantiality given to these carefully posed figures varies considerably. Most of *Coriolanus*'s characters are sketchily drawn: Titus Lartius, Cominius, the cushion-layers, the Lieutenant, the Volscian conspirators, Adrian and Nicanor, are more functionally than personally memorable. Absent are the homely touches which made secondary, and even minor, figures distinctive in the earlier plays. One seeks in vain for the determined frailty of the kerchiefed Caius Ligarius in *Julius Caesar* or the warmhearted earthiness of the Gardener in *Richard II*. Virgilia, although the wife of the play's hero, is sketched, apart from a couple of brief outbursts, as largely a creature of tears and suggestive silences.[31] Aufidius, although a key character, is perhaps the most shadowy and problematic of all. If he is intended to represent something like Martius's alter ego, then one would expect him to have a higher profile. In the first half of the play, although he is mentioned on a number of occasions, he makes only three brief appearances. In the second half, we see more of him, but do not come to know him better. His motivation is unclear, even contradictory, and his inner life a mystery. Crudely drawn and unidimensional, Aufidius is in a sense a "man of straw," but the playwright, far from "yawning as he wrote,"[32] as Bradley suggests, was never more technically alert. To this world of equivocal values and relationships, where "virtues / Lie in th'interpretation of the time," Aufidius's discontinuous and uneasy presence, like the wraithlike figures of Tintoretto or El Greco, is totally appropriate.

Coriolanus, Volumnia, and Menenius are given more substance, which is not to say that we ever get on intimate terms with them. Despite their powerful presences and fluent talk, they remain curiously distanced and enigmatic.

Coriolanus, overwhelmingly masculine and defined throughout by physical energy, seems more natural force than man. Cominius views him as a kind of epic war machine. Always his space seems too small for him; ultimately he can only be accommodated, as Menenius suggests, by "eternity and a heaven to throne in" (5.4.24).

At times Martius's epic stature is pushed to the brink of caricature, a feature which contributed to Shaw's notion of the play as a comedy and Campbell's conclusion that it is a satire. Menenius's wry exaggeration—

> The tartness of his face sours ripe grapes. When he walks, he moves like an engine and the ground shrinks before his treading. He is able to pierce a corslet with his eye, talks like a knell, and his hum is a battery. (5.4.17–21)—

like Parmigianino's playfully-enlarged hand in *Self-Portrait from a Convex Mirror*, serves to check emotional involvement and recalls us to an intellectual stance.

Martius's inner life is ultimately hidden from us. Apart from a few lines of bemused observation in the Voices scene and on his arrival in Antium, there is nothing which could be termed soliloquy. Indeed he seems to view his life as an act of role play, and resorts with some frankness to stage imagery to clarify his position. "Would you have me / False to my nature?" he demands. "Rather say, I play / The man I am" (3.2.14–16). There is always a hint of pose in his dealings with others, an awareness of being observed. His dismissal of commendation and reward strikes one as a trifle overdone perhaps; his resort to gesture at key moments hints at calculation:

Parmigianino: *Self-Portrait from a Convex Mirror.* **[By permission of the Kunsthistor-isches Museum, Vienna]**

the hand in hand exit with his mother and wife after the triumphal entry, his insistence on standing during Cominius's Senate eulogy, the flamboyant exit from the Banishment scene with "thus I turn my back" (3.3.134), the theatrical obeisance in the Intercession scene—"Sink, my knee, i'th'earth" (5.3.50)—fall just short of spontaneity. And the latter gesture loses nothing by his preceding assertion "Like a dull actor now / I have forgot my part" (5.3.40–41).

Irresistibly he recalls the withdrawn figures of Bronzino's portraits, individuals who are supremely aware of being observed, but who disdain to look toward the observer. Most of the time we see only the public man with averted eyes; although he verbalizes freely on social, political, and military

Bronzino: *A Young Woman and Her Little Boy* (ca. 1540). [Widener Collection, Copyright 1996 Board of Trustees, National Gallery of Art, Washington]

subjects, yet he never bares his soul. Apart from a shamefaced appeal for the return of a kindness to a man who had done him a favor, a half-humorous aside to his wife on his return from the wars, and the potent moment when he holds his mother by the hand silent, he says or does little which seems unintended for public scrutiny.

Even the scanty psychological detail offered is tainted with contradiction and ambiguity. What events, one wonders, filled the space between his farewells to his family and his arrival in Antium? What mental process brought him to betray his country, a piece of behavior in direct contradiction to his departing promise, "While I remain above the ground you shall / Hear from me still, and never of me aught / But is like me formerly" (4.1.51–53)? And how does one account for his broken pledge to keep in touch? Only a few scenes later, Menenius makes a point of remarking, "Nay, I hear nothing. His mother and his wife / Hear nothing from him" (4.6.18–19). Most significant of all, perhaps, is the fact that at the action's most crucial moment, his surrender to his mother in the Intercession scene, we are left in the dark as to his real motive. Does he recognize his error, as the tragic hero must, and resolve to atone for it, or is he merely beguiled, as so often before, into pleasing his mother like the overgrown boy Aufidius claims he is? On the answer to this question rests any claim he may have to tragic stature. And each reader, each theater artist, is left to read the message in those evasive eyes as best one can.

To say that Coriolanus's inner life is hidden from us is not to suggest that the character lacks variety or interest. Shakespeare's technique is to show him, albeit from the outside, but from a variety of observation points. The sum total of observations yields a kind of composite likeness. We may not see Coriolanus in his subjective mode, but we hear his character commented upon by a variety of people, including his wife and mother, close friends such as Cominius and Menenius, outright enemies like the tribunes and Aufidius, and neutral observers represented by the cushion-layers and Aufidius's servants. This technique offers a complex impression of the character, the truthfulness and reality of which is as ambiguous, unstable, and perhaps ultimately as illusory as the reality of the life it purports to imitate.

Like Martius, Volumnia and Menenius also maintain an impenetrable privacy. In flashes, as rare as they are brief, Volumnia reveals a sneaking fondness for her grandson, gruffly attempts to badger her daughter-in-law into a more militaristic stance, and evinces a momentary weakness as her son departs the city of his birth. Elsewhere, however, she slips into one public role after another without missing a beat: proud mother, shrewd politician, outraged aristocrat, altruistic intercessor for her city. Not once do we catch her alone or solely in the company of Martius. And never are we able to assess with certainty her real feelings. At the moment of her triumphal return to Rome in 5.5, when we most long to know her heart, she crosses the stage in inscrutable silence.

The portrait of Menenius too, although ostensibly complete, reveals itself to be superficial. He readily reveals his friendship for Coriolanus and his family, admits his fondness for the good life, and betrays a merry sense of humor; apart from such casual impressions, however, he allows us only an arm's-length view of a politician, kingmaker, and strategist. Even in his most potentially pathetic scene, his rejection in the Volscian camp, he remains firmly in control of his public image. We can only guess at the state of mind behind his defiant "I say to you, as I was said to, Away!" (5.2.107–8).

The citizens, the play's counterforce, are equally enigmatic. It is tempting to see them through Martius's eyes, and indeed many productions have done so, rather than for what they themselves say and do. When judged on the strength of their own words and deeds, they do nothing as mindlessly vicious as the citizens in *Julius Caesar;* their threats may well be born of desperation ("for the gods know I speak this in hunger for bread, not in thirst for revenge" [1.1.23–25]) if we accept their charges against the patricians at face value, which may be a mistake; and they are credited with a sense of fairness and generosity ("The price is, to ask it kindly" [2.3.75]), a rough and ready sense of humor, and a willingness to meet the opposition more than halfway. At the same time, they are irrational, cowardly, potentially violent, and easily led. As much a natural force as Martius, and as difficult to judge, they can be made the unequivocal villains of the piece only by textual cutting and the introduction of stage business to validate the patrician assessment of them. And the same might be said of the tribunes.

The interaction of the play's problematic characters concludes not in a release of tension, but a continuing and unresolved balance. Coriolanus attains no insight at the moment of death, and consequently achieves no transcendence. He dies unenlightened in midbellow, mindlessly responding, like the juvenile of Aufidius's image, to the taunt of "traitor" while his mother returns to Rome in triumph and the patrician-plebeian tug-of-war presumably resumes. Aufidius will shortly justify his actions to the Volscian senate, and there is no reason to believe he will not be successful. Conditions are not much different than they were at beginning of the play except for Martius's absence. In the drama's final moments we listen in vain for a note of genuine grief, a hint of hope, some harmonic chord, however faint. Instead we hear only expressions of conventional diplomatic regret from Aufidius and the 1. Lord and the voice of hard-nosed pragmatism from the 2. Lord: "His own impatience / Takes from Aufidius a great part of blame. / Let's make the best of it." As the soldiers stoop to take up Martius's body, one is aware that the Roman-Volscian tensions are not resolved, merely suspended.

In marked contrast to the overdetermined and enigmatic nature of *Coriolanus's* politics and psychology is the specificity of stage directions and dialogic performance cues. And the bulk of such guidance is understandably directed at the actor.

Throughout the play Martius's friends and foes alike pay considerable heed to his appearance. Brutus asks Sicinius, "Mark'd you his lip and eyes?" (1.1.255); or, again, Lartius is made to remind his younger colleague that "with thy grim looks. . . . / Thou mad'st thine enemies shake" (1.4.58, 60). That these directions are retrospective in no way diminishes their value to the performer. Other dialogic cues suggest movement designed to accompany certain speeches. Martius's "I am weary, yea, my memory is tired" (1.9.91) instructs the actor to let his fatigue show physically as the scene winds down. A similar hint occurs in the Farewell scene when Martius urges Cominius to "droop not" (4.1.20).

Dominant visual effects are clearly stipulated, repeated for emphasis, and cumulative references made to them. A key exemplar is the image of Martius as "the man in blood" of the 3. Servant's phrase (4.5.211). This image, which resonates throughout the play to the terror of friends and foes alike, is indelibly stamped on the audience's memory in the course of the battlefield sequences when Martius is required to retain his bloody makeup for a lengthy period while the spectator's attention is relentlessly directed to it. The first reference to his sanguinary appearance comes in the direction at 1.4.61 "*Enter* MARTIUS, *bleeding, assaulted by the enemy.*" In the next scene Lartius remarks, "Worthy sir, thou bleed'st" (1.5.14); in the ensuing episode, Cominius demands, "Who's yonder, / That does appear as he were flea'd?" (1.6.21–22). In subsequent sequences, Martius himself calls attention to his gory complexion: he appeals to the soldiers at 1.6.67–69, "If any such be here / . . . that love this painting / Wherein you see me smear'd"; he assures Aufidius at 1.8.9–10, "'Tis not my blood / Wherein thou seest me mask'd"; and announces at 1.9.68, "I will go wash." The makeup is finally removed only at the end of 1.9 when Cominius leads him off with "The blood upon your visage dries, 'tis time / It should be look'd to. Come."

Two images may have been intended as stage recreations of contemporary art. The Folio stage direction at 1.3, "*They set them downe on two lowe stooles and sowe*" recalls Furnius's 1573 engraving of Stradanus's study of the Gracchi women who are shown in precisely the position stipulated. Again, Volumnia's lines in the Intercession scene, "This boy, that cannot tell what he would have, / But kneels and holds up hands for fellowship" (5.3.174–75), may owe something to Philip Galle's reproduction of Stradanus's version of this event, which features a miniscule young Martius in the shadow of a gigantic grandmother, doing exactly what Volumnia describes. Neither of these effects is to be found in Plutarch.

Vocal cues, explicit and implicit, are frequent. Menenius insists at 3.1.187, "I am out of breath," and has no choice but to speak appropriately. Similarly, when Volumnia instructs Virgilia to "Leave this faint puling, and lament as I do, / In anger, Juno-like," (4.2.52–53) the actors are reminded to maintain a vocal contrast. On other occasions, speeches are so constructed that the actor who gives the lines their head will automatically achieve a predeter-

Forte domi Gracchus geminos ut ceperat angues   Gracche, marem, uxori: Tuscus respondit aruspex: Quid non se debere tuis, Cornelia, tandem
Marémque, fœminámque: si dimiseris,   Sin fœminam mors ingruet prior tibi.   Maritus arbitratus est uirtutibus:
Maluit ille marem, seséque proinde, necari, Tantae superstes quam manere coniugi.

J. Stradanus: *Women of the Gracchi* (1573). [By permission of the British Museum]

Si dolor et iunctis Volscorum viribus ira   Hac mucrone petes, aciem nec viscera strages   Incidat in natum genetrix, aut illa maritum,
Offensam reddunt patria, non vbera, Marci.   In tua, nec coniux quidquam commisit, ve hostem   Formidetq; trucem proles obsessa parentem.

J. Stradanus: *The Intercession of the Roman Women* (1573). [By permission of the British Museum] mined effect. Coriolanus's mocking invocation of the citizens' voices (2.3.125–29) offers a prime example:

> Your voices? For your voices I have fought;
> Watch'd for your voices; for your voices bear
> Of wounds two dozen odd; battles thrice six
> I have seen, and heard of; for your voices have
> Done many things, some less, some more. Your voices?

The repetition of "voices" and the rhythm of the street cry neatly steer the actor into the mocking lilt which so outrages the Third Citizen. At the conclusion of 3.3, Sicinius orders the citizens, "Go see him out at gates, and follow him. . . . / Give him deserv'd vexation" (3.3.138, 140); to which the mob replies, "Come, come, let's see him out at gates, come. / The gods preserve our noble tribunes! Come." (3.3.142–43). Sicinius's injunction to "Give him deserv'd vexation" and the subsequent repeated "come"'s vocally evoke a pack of hounds harrying its prey, and recall Coriolanus's description of the citizens as a "common cry of curs" a score of lines earlier (3.3.120).

Shakespeare's dialogic cues for actorial movement and gesture are frequent and illuminating. The embedding of business in dialogue, as opposed to indicating it in stage directions, permits the activity to be both precisely timed and to take its dynamic from the energy and rhythm of the lines which surround it.

Business involving two or more actors, particularly susceptible to misfiring, is cued with particular care. Menenius's encounter with Coriolanus's guard in the Volscian camp offers a useful example. When the would-be petitioner attempts to pass, the First Watch's lines run:

> My general cares not for you. Back, I say, go: lest I let forth your half-pint of blood. Back, that's the utmost of your having, back! (5.2.55–57)

To judge from the iterated "back"'s, Menenius is intended to make three separate sallies, each of which is promptly repulsed, simultaneously suggesting the old man's determination and intensifying audience sympathy for him. Timing of the embrace seems to be a key concern in the sequence in which Aufidius welcomes Martius. The preparation for the gesture comes with Aufidius's fervid, "Let me twine / Mine arms about that body" (4.5.106–7), but the audience is obliged to wait until ll.109–10 for the act itself, cued with "Here I cleep / The anvil of my sword." "Here" seems intended as the cue for the gesture. Elsewhere Shakespeare commonly uses "thus" for the same purpose. The compliant volunteer is commanded at 1.6.74 to "wave thus to express his disposition"; the Third Citizen is cued for his imitation of Martius's hat-waving with the line "And with his hat, thus waving it in scorn"

(2.3.167). Coriolanus is similarly advised of the proper moment to swing away from the plebeians in the Banishment sequence: "Despising, / For you, the city, thus I turn my back" (3.3.133–34). In the Intercession scene, Volumnia halts Martius's exit, and seals his fate, with her "Nay, go not from us thus" (5.3.131).

Entrances and exits are treated with particular care. On one occasion, by careful blocking of a single entrance and exit, the play's class tensions are subtly and economically highlighted. At 1.1.126, the Folio direction reads *"Enter Sicinius Velutus, Annius Brutus Cominius, Titus Lartius, with other Senatours."* Editors have frequently altered the order of this entry to give the senators precedence, but business implicit in the dialogue suggests that the Folio direction is correct. As the tribunes lead the procession ("pranking themselves in authority"), Martius comments ironically, "See, our best elders." Already, in this relatively restrained response, one observes the degree to which the tribunes' presumption rankles. Lartius, it appears, is no less annoyed, for at the general exit a few lines later, he teaches the status-seekers a lesson, firmly instructing Cominius "Lead you on," and, as a special compliment to Martius, deferentially insisting, "Follow Cominius, we must follow you, / Right worthy you priority" (1.1.245–47). No mention is made of the tribunes, who remain behind to gripe at Martius's arrogance.

Exits receive as much or more attention as entrances, and what might be described as delayed exits, in which departure is referred to several times before it takes place, are a crucial ingredient of scenic rhythm. At times, for example, the playwright delays an exit of particular interest to insert information which might retard the action if included elsewhere. As Martius is about to exit with his triumphal procession, the Herald orders, "Give way there, and go on" (2.1.193). With the first cornet notes, the audience anticipates noise and movement; but its satisfaction is postponed in favor of Martius's colloquy with his mother about his visit to the plebeians and her ambitions for him. Meantime, the rest of the actors are expected to remain at the ready, as if to leave momentarily, to sustain audience tension. At last Cominius gives the direction which takes the procession off—"On, to the Capitol!" (2.1.204).

On one occasion an exit is so long delayed that it is not completed at all; while the actor engages in a series of adroitly cued false starts, the audience's interest is manipulated to permit a good deal of background information to be communicated. At 2.1.97–98, Volumnia, Virgilia, and Valeria enter in a great hurry, to judge from Menenius's "Whither do you follow your eyes so fast?". Volumnia, atwitter to join Martius, agrees to stop for just a moment; indeed, only two lines later she attempts to press forward with "for the love of Juno, let's go" (2.1.101), but absorbed almost immediately in detailing Martius's past and present exploits (essential information), she forgets her haste for some thirty lines; then, abruptly recollecting her mission, she moves off briskly with "Good ladies, let's go.—Yes, yes, yes" (2.1.133).

Once again, though, she is distracted by maternal pride and finds the procession is upon her. In the excitement of the military entry, the audience fails to notice that it has been tricked, that no exit was ever intended.

One of the shrewdest uses of the delayed exit is to be found in Volumnia's castigation of Brutus and Sicinius (4.2). This neat interweaving of word and action, keyed by the iterated use of "go" and "stay," amounts almost to a lazzo in which the tribunes repeatedly attempt to evade Volumnia's tongue-lashing only to be halted each time by a fresh verbal assault.

Although the playwright's "directorial" interventions tend to be brief in most instances, occasionally he takes the reins for sustained sequences. The tribunes' and citizens' fruitless attempt to arrest Martius (3.1.173–252) evinces not the familiar rhythmic pattern of sustained acceleration or deceleration, but rather a series of ineffective surges against an immovable object. Visually, Coriolanus, sword drawn, suggests the "great sea-mark" he so admires, while waves of plebeian anger and patrician appeal roar about him.

The first attack comes from Sicinius, who tries to apprehend Martius unaided:

> *Sic.* . . . . myself
> Attach thee as a traitorous innovator. . . .
> *Cor.*   Hence, old goat.
>
> . . . .
> *Com.*   Ag'd sir, hands off.
> *Cor.* Hence, rotten thing! or I shall shake thy bones
> Out of thy garments.

(3.1.173–79)

To judge from the dialogic cues, Sicinius is expected to make two sallies. Coriolanus must shake himself at each "hence," and it is unthinkable that Sicinius could manage to maintain his grip either time. Here the action serves to juxtapose the tribune's physical debility with Coriolanus's muscle. That the feeble tribunes eventually subdue the brawny hero with a political force he consistently disdains is one of the tragedy's most telling ironies.

The ludicrously unequal encounter between Sicinius and Coriolanus gains in credibility and seriousness as Sicinius is joined by the aediles and citizens in a second phase (3.1.211–14, 221–22, 226–27). In this scenic unit, the group proves itself as ineffectual as the aged Sicinius was earlier. The tribunes make three appeals, each of which employs the word "lay" and seems a signal for the citizens to surge forward. Coriolanus, meanwhile, remains motionless with his sword drawn. On Brutus's final command (3.1.226), the citizens finally close in and are driven off.

The final unit of this "sea-mark" sequence begins with Martius still defiant, but surrounded now by friends rather than enemies. In a series of verbal onslaughts, characterized by various forms of the verbs "come" and "go," the patricians try to persuade the obdurate Martius to quit the field. Here the tone and rhythm of the speeches suggests not the attack and repulse pattern of the previous unit, but rather the cumulative effect of a series of overlapping vocal waves, each adding its force to the preceding one. Vocal appeals, the vigor of the language implies, are supported by persuasive gestures. Gradually, under this well-intentioned assault, Martius's protests soften and he finally permits himself to be led off. This pliability under pressure, demonstrated in several earlier instances, prefigures his final and fatal capitulation.

The Jacobean forestage, on which action might be viewed from three sides, was uniquely suited to *Coriolanus*'s bleak, overdetermined vision. This large, neutral canvas allowed its calculated groupings, patterned entrances, and mannered posing to shape the narrative with uncompromising clarity, while its dizzying multiplicity of perspective, linguistic indeterminacy, and repellent imagery steadily alienated the sensibilities and challenged the interpretative powers of an audience situated above, below, and around it. Was the Blackfriars theatergoer's response to *Coriolanus,* one wonders, rather like Arnold Hauser's to Michaelangelo's *The Last Judgment* which in many ways it resembles? "In comparison with most of the works of the High Renaissance, the *Last Judgment* is unattractive, inhospitable," he writes:

> It makes a cold and rigid, severe and repellent impression, and does nothing whatever to satisfy the spectator's desire for a sense of Utopian happiness or to fulfil his dream of harmony. . . . It does not even make the concession to the spectator of presenting its theme coherently and logically. It is full, not only of unattractive details, but also of gaps and contradictions. The whole consists of loosely composed groups and more or less isolated episodes that create the impression of being the scattered fragments of a vision, the eruptive force of which provides the connecting link between the different parts of the picture.[33]

Nothing is known of the play's initial reception, but to judge from Jonson's willingness to parody it, one must assume that it met with either fame or notoriety. It is possible that its profile continued high for at least a year or two, and that the Intercession scene soon established itself as a highlight, since Beaumont and Fletcher's *A King and No King* features a mother-son vignette which owes a good deal to *Coriolanus*'s 5.3. Arane, the penitent parent of King Arbaces, kneels to him as she says:

> As low as this I bow to you, and would
> As low as to my grave, to shew a mind
> Thankful for all your mercies.
> *Arb.*   O stand up,
> And let me kneel, the light will be asham'd
> To see observance done to me by you.
> *Ara.* You are my King.
> *Arb.* You are my Mother, rise. (3.2)[34]

Since *A King and No King* premiered in 1611, the evidence suggests that
Coriolanus was either consistently popular for the intervening year or more,
or may have had a recent revival. A further hint that the play enjoyed a
continued stage success, or at least a recent performance, comes from the
Fletcher/Massinger/Field *Queen of Corinth,* which premiered sometime between 1611 and 1618. Coriolanus's lines to Virgilia in the Intercession
episode:

> Now, by the jealous queen of heaven, that kiss
> I carried from thee, dear; and my true lip
> Hath virgin'd it e'er since.

(5.3.46–48)

are recalled in Beliza's assertion:

> . . . by my life,
> The parting kiss you took before your travel
> Is yet a Virgin on my lips, preserv'd
> With as much care as I would do my fame
> To entertain your wish'd return.

(2.2)[35]

The vogue of the Coriolanus story as a theme for drama and art on the
Continent might conceivably argue some degree of interest in England. Alex-
andre Hardy's *Coriolan,* had its premiere in 1607 and was published in
1626; V. Chevreau's *Coriolan* was performed and published in 1638, as was
Chapoton's *Le Véritable Coriolan.* Treatments by painters include versions
of the intercession by Pieter Lastman (1622, Provost's House, Trinity College, Dublin), Nicolas Poussin (1635–55, Musée Poussin, Les Andelys), and
Giovanni Francesco Romanelli (1610?–62, Collection of Her Majesty the
Queen at Windsor Castle).

Pieter Lastman: *Coriolanus and the Roman Matrons* (1622). [By permission of the Board of Trinity College Dublin]

Nicolas Poussin: *Coriolan vaincu par sa femme et sa mère* (1635–55). [By permission of the Musée Nicolas Poussin, Les Andelys, France]

3

From Tate to Thomson: The Age
of Propaganda (1681–1749)

The premiere of Nahum Tate's adaptation of *Coriolanus* in 1681 inaugurates both the play's recorded theatrical career and seven of the most politically turbulent decades in England's history. The struggle for power between king and parliament, recurrent Jacobite crises, and the birth pangs of the party system created a mood of national anxiety not unlike the Jacobean-Roman apprehension which inhabits *Coriolanus,* a circumstance not lost on contemporary playwrights and theater managers. Tate's adaptation was succeeded by John Dennis's in 1719, which was followed in turn by James Thomson's entirely new drama, dating from 1745 although not staged until four years later. Each redaction, it will be noted, coincides with a period of intensified Jacobite unrest. Shakespeare's unadulterated text also seems to have received occasional stagings, but little is known of these revivals.

All three responses to Shakespeare's play, two adaptations and one rejection, frankly recognized that the drama is political, and that the playwright's treatment of class struggle is theatrically attractive but potentially subversive. Each innovator sought in his own way to exploit the stageworthiness of the Roman narrative, while redirecting its energies to legitimate a favored social order. Tate reworked the play as a Tory tract; Dennis rewrote the piece as Whig propaganda; and Thomson created a totally new text which, while unexceptionably Whig in spirit, substantially aesthetized the drama's politics and initiated the production strategy which shaped the presentation of Shakespeare's *Coriolanus* in British and American theaters for a century and a half. All three scripts differ markedly in the nature and strength of their political commitment, yet all manifest a verbal and visual impulse toward stylistic stability, clarity, and affect. Intellectual stimulation takes second place to moral and political indoctrination.

THE INGRATITUDE OF A COMMON-WEALTH:
A TORY MARTYRDOM

No performances of *Coriolanus* are recorded immediately after the Restoration. The first mention of the play comes with the division of the traditional theater repertory between the patentees in January 1668/9 when *Coriolanus* was allotted to Thomas Killigrew's King's Company then in residence at the Theatre Royal.[1] The drama apparently lay neglected for more than a decade until poet-playwright Nahum Tate, struck by "no small Resemblance" between the play's political turmoil and "the busie Faction of our own time,"[2] attempted an anti-Whig adaptation.[3] Under the title *The Ingratitude of a Common-wealth: Or, the Fall of Caius Martius Coriolanus,* the playtext was entered in the *Term Catalogues* in February 1681/2 and advertised for sale in *The Loyal Protestant* 7 March 1681/2.[4] William Van Lennep places the premiere in December 1681.[5] The only recorded performance dates from 14 January 1681/2 when *The Calendar of State Papers Domestic* notes that:

> This evening the Morocco ambassador with all his attendants will be treated at the King's playhouse with a play that has relation to that country, viz., Caius Martius with dancing and volting.[6]

The theater for which Tate redesigned *Coriolanus* was not the "powerless" institution of the late Elizabethan-Jacobean period posited by Yachnin, but effectively a tool of the state.[7] The day-to-day survival of players and playwrights depended on political patronage, and they were expected to pay their dues as often as called upon.[8]

Tate's adaptation of *Coriolanus,* unlike its original, decisively identifies itself in the *Epistle Dedicatory* with a political position: "*The Moral therefore of these Scenes,*" he writes, "*being to Recommend Submission and Adherence to Establisht Lawful Power, which in a word, is* Loyalty" (A2). *The Ingratitude of a Common-wealth* is one of a number of dramatic contributions to an anti-Whig propaganda campaign waged by the Tories between 1680 and 1683.[9] Three years before Tate's play appeared, the Popish Plot intensified anti-Catholic sentiment and strengthened the power of the Whigs. In May 1680 an Exclusion Bill was introduced in the House of Commons, denying the Roman Catholic Duke of York the right of succession to the throne, a bill which proved so divisive that Charles II dissolved Parliament in March of 1681 and over the next few months missed no opportunity to discomfit the Whigs. At this point the theaters rallied to the Tory cause with a series of productions attacking those who would threaten the peace, overthrow authority, and return the country to the miseries of civil war. Tate's *Ingratitude* was one of the first propaganda rounds fired.

The aesthetic form in which Tate recast Shakespeare's creation was precisely contrived to modulate its disorientation and alienation into fully declared meaning, to stabilize its moral and tragic focus, to enforce credibility through sensibility, and to consummate the exercise in a burst of quasi-religious transcendence.

Any consanguinity between Rome's political crisis and Jacobean exigencies was left by Shakespeare for his public to intuit: Tate's audiences were given more limited hermeneutic rein. *"Upon a close view of this Story,"* he informs his readers, *"there appear'd in some Passages, no small resemblance with the busie Faction of our own time. What offence to any good Subject,"* he argues, *"in Stygmatizing on the Stage, those* Troublers *of the* State, *that out of private Interest or Mallice, Seduce the Multitude to* Ingratitude, *against Persons that are not only plac't in Rightful Power above them; but also the Heroes and Defenders of their Country"* (A2). For Tate resemblances between consular Rome and Restoration England apparently lay in the characters of Coriolanus and James Duke of York, and the political turbulence of both periods in which the citizenry and their leaders played a key role.

Like Martius, James had a distinguished military record, but was politically naive and incompetent, and wanting in tact and moderation. Both men were banished by the country they served. In the public turmoil that attended the Bill of Exclusion (to say nothing of the Popish Plot and the threat of a French invasion), Tate found the Whigs, in much the same fashion as the tribunes, to be exploiting the tensions of the times and the gullibility of the citizenry. He seems to have had no ambition to allegorize the Jacobean narrative, but chose less ambitiously merely *"to set the Parallel nearer to Sight."* In Shakespeare's account of an aristocrat driven into exile by an ungrateful rabble, spurred on by irresponsible leadership, he found a subject which could be reworked to carry a contemporary visual and verbal warning: Whig opposition to established authority was dangerous; indeed, the fomenting of popular discontent of the sort advocated by the Earl of Shaftesbury could well return the country to the horrors of the Civil War era. The racked young Martius, the dying Virgilia, the mad Volumnia at play's end speak eloquently and emblematically to the perils of factionalism.

The impartiality (or ambivalence) of *Coriolanus*'s politics, later remarked by Coleridge, had scant attraction for a propagandist. Tate's first task, then, was to tilt the play's precariously balanced sympathies significantly to the right, which meant that Martius had to be written up and the plebeians and tribunes written down. While Tate allows Martius a want of political sensitivity, he takes particular pains to purge the character of serious anti-democratic sentiment. His outburst beginning "'Shall'?" in which he demands why the senators have "Given Hydra here to choose an officer" (3.1.90–112), and the tirade shortly afterward in which he scorns a governmental system in which "gentry, title, wisdom / Cannot conclude but by the yea and no / Of general ignorance" (3.1.125–57) are excised. His plea for the repeal of the tribunate (3.1.166–70) is abbreviated and his arrogant assertion "I do despise them! / For they do prank them in authority, / Against all noble sufferance" (3.1.22–24) disappears. His observation when required to beg plebeian voices—"It is a part / That I shall blush in acting, and might well / Be taken from the people" (2.2.144–46)—is rephrased to run rather more tactfully: "It is a Part, that I shall Blush in Acting; / Methinks the People well might spare this Method; / Better Constraind to do it" (19). The tribunes' assertion that their power will sleep if he is elected (2.1.222–23) and Sicinius's contention that Martius has "Envied against the people, seeking means / To pluck away their power" (3.3.93–99) are also blue-penciled.

However conscientiously Tate might ameliorate Martius's antipopulist views, it was impossible to purge his radical elitism entirely without doing serious injustice to the historical character or destroying the energy and tension which animate the Shakespearian original. In a strategy adopted many times since, Tate opted to denigrate the character and behavior of the plebeians, and thus render Martius's contempt for them less a political act than a civilized response to barbarity.

Tate's retouching required a delicate hand: his political parable must not defame the English underclass as a whole since Charles relied on broadly based public support. In the end, however, not even the most naive theatergoer could descry any decent citizen of his acquaintance in Tate's caricature of an ignorant, thoughtless, and violent rabble; nor could he miss the consanguinity of Tate's plebeians with the frenzied mobs, inflamed by Popish Plot hysteria and Whig manipulation, who roamed the streets staging popeburnings and other incitements to civil disorder.[10] Comic and brutish, they are deliberately shorn of any redeeming features Shakespeare allows them. The excision of Menenius's "For they have pardons, being ask'd, as free / As words to little purpose" (3.2.88–89) may be taken as representative.

The mob's callous stupidity is epitomized by the First Citizen, a role now fattened by the reallocation of other citizens' speeches and some new material. Mindlessly overconfident, he sets the tone for the rabble's senseless, yet bitterly comic, abuse of power with his line, "Let 'um feel our Swords, that take away the Use of our Knives; not that I mean any Harm Neighbours" (2). Their willingness to vote in accordance with the last suggestion they hear is highlighted in an insertion preceding the Voices episode; and in an expanded sequence following the Voices scene the 1 Cit. demonstrates a lamentable inability to weigh accurately the most obvious evidence of his eyes and ears.

Stupidity is compounded by cowardice. Not content with retaining Shakespeare's indication that the plebeians "steal away" when invited to attack the Volscians in order to obtain grain (1.1.251), Tate reduces them to terrified hysterics when Cominius returns from his Volscian embassy. Similar examples of rabble-baiting abound. On Martius's departure into banishment, he consigns them, in a rewritten execration, to human society's outer reaches:

> Poyson each other;
> Devour each other: Commerce cease amongst you;

> Rob one another: nothing you can Steal,
> But Thieves do lose it. . . .

(35)

Toward such louts, Martius's behavior would have been judged not only appropriate, but obligatory.

Hard as Tate is on the "blind Compliance" of the people, it is their "popular Misleaders," the tribunes, epitomized offstage by Shaftesbury, his minions, and organizations such as the Green Ribbon Club,[11] for whom he saves his heaviest salvos. Shakespeare treats Brutus and Sicinius with unusual harshness, but allows them at least some degree of political sagacity and psychological insight. Tate lets no mitigating feature remain. Sicinius's shrewd counsel to Coriolanus, "If you will pass / To where you are bound, you must inquire your way, /.Which you are out of, with a gentler spirit" (3.1.53–55) is a typical excision. Martius's execration of them, cast in contemporary political vernacular lest the point be missed, fairly reeks of Tory wrath at the popular threat to aristocratic exclusivity:

> *You, Faction-Mongers,*
> *That wear your formal Beards, and Plotting Heads,*
> *By the Valour of the Men you Persecute;*
> *Canting Caballers, that in Smoaky Cells,*
> *Amongst Crop-ear'd Mechanicks, wast the Night*
> *In Villanous Harrangues against the* State.
> *There may* Your Worship's *Pride be seen t'embrace*
> *A smutty Tinker, and in extasy*
> *Of Treason, shake a Cobler be th' wax't Thumb*

(27).

In the end, the tribunes receive their comeuppance at the hands of the rabble they sought to exploit. At their last appearance, the 1 Cit. is shouting, "Some comfort yet, that we have these Vipers to *Carbinado;* Come Neighbours, we'll see them smoak before us. Away, away with 'em." And without Shakespeare's humane intervention by Menenius, the company exits, "*Haling and Dragging off the Tribunes*" (46) to an unwholesome destiny.

Although in Tate's parti pris Tory universe, the subverters of public order receive their just deserts, the evil that they do lives after them. The expulsion of Martius, and the civil and domestic disorder that ensues, brings disaster upon the innocent as well as the guilty. The climax of Tate's political homily, far from being gratuitous sensationalism or defective poetic justice as his critics have contended,[12] aims at a catharsis vital to stabilizing the moral and tragic focus.

In the play's final moments, as vividly and horrifically as possible, Tate limns the outcome of civil strife. Factionalism, he implies, is an inevitable prologue to disaster in the national family, emblematically portrayed at curtain-fall by the dead Martius with his lifeless wife and child on either arm.[13] Tate's projected audience response must have been not unlike the viewer's reaction to baroque religious art envisioned by Cardinal Paleotti: "[I]f we see the martyrdom of a saint rendered in lively colours . . . we must be of marble or wood . . . if our piety is not stimulated afresh."[14] Political piety, expressed in "Submission and Adherence to Establisht Lawful Power," could hardly fail to respond to Tate's passionate theatricality. A greater contrast with the morally ambivalent finale to Shakespeare's play, in which the hero expires in a blind tantrum, can hardly be imagined.

The didactic function of Tate's project found expression in an uncomplex and profoundly unified structure based on a rigorous reorientation of perspective. His decision to set *"nearer to sight"* the parallel between Shakespeare's Rome and Restoration England, which amounted to a redrafting of Shakespeare's overdetermined design, demanded that the audience's attention be confined to a single theme—the dangers of factionalism. The multiple foci in Shakespeare's *Coriolanus,* the ongoing Roman-Volscian military struggle, the patrician-plebeian conflict, and the mother-son attachment, rendered it as ineffective a vehicle for political indoctrination as Parmigianino's *Madonna of the Long Neck,* with its anatomical distortion and perverse perspective, would have been as an aid to pious contemplation.

Tate's revision was thorough and radical.[15] In order to highlight the patrician-plebeian struggle, he downplayed considerably the Roman-Volscian conflict. His act 1 comprises four scenes, as compared with the original ten: Shakespeare's 1.1, in which Menenius and Martius meet with the plebeians, 1.3, the episode between Volumnia and Virgilia in Martius's house, and two brief battlefield sequences (part of 1.4 and a consolidation of 1.8 and 1.9). Only enough warfare remains to establish Martius's military stature and introduce Aufidius. The effect is to remove the equivalent of foreground clutter, and to place the plebeian-patrician friction at center stage with minimal distraction or delay.

From 2.1 Tate dispatched all the preliminaries to Martius's triumphal return, including Menenius's contretemps with the tribunes and his encounter with Volumnia and Virgilia, 166 lines in all. No scene is cut in its entirety, since this act is the play's political core, but the internal revision is substantial. The sequence in which the cushion-layers assess Martius's character (2.2.1–36) is eliminated, as is the tense exchange between the tribunes and Menenius prior to Cominius's eulogy (2.2.37–66). The plebeians' good-natured banter at 2.3.18–35 is replaced by a sequence after the Voices episode in which they are shown as slow-witted and lacking in judgment. Several of Martius's more defiantly ungracious exchanges are cut (2.3.94–102; 108–10), and the tribunes' inflammatory appraisal of the Voices ritual is rendered more pointed and succinct.

In act 3 the introductory update on Aufidius's status (3.1.1–20) is deleted to maintain the focus on the growing patrician-plebeian tension. The confrontation itself is considerably abbreviated and recast, partly to accelerate the narrative, but mainly to mitigate Martius's antipopulism and to magnify the tribunes' knavery. The episode in which Martius is persuaded to reconcile himself with the plebeians (3.2) becomes less an exercise in maternal blackmail than the impassioned plea of a Roman matron for compromise in the face of potential national disaster. Martius accedes, not out of conditioned reflex, but patriotic sensibility. His concession, however, proves futile, and 3.3 sees him banished with greater expedition than Shakespeare allows.

Martius's farewell (4.1), which Tate appends to act 3, is heavily rewritten to highlight the strength of the familial bond in anticipation of the Intercession scene and the act 5 denouement. Tate's Volumnia is mellower, his Virgilia more vocal, than Shakespeare's originals. And as a final touch, Young Martius is summoned to add pathos to the leavetaking. The subsequent slanging match between Volumnia and the tribunes (4.2) and the colloquy between Adrian and Nicanor (4.3) vanish.

Martius's arrival in Corioli and his abbreviated reflections on the world's slippery turns (4.4) launch Tate's act 4. The role of Aufidius's servants in 4.5 is curtailed to expedite Martius's pact with Aufidius, now shorn of its nuptial imagery. To clarify Aufidius's hitherto obscure motivation for Martius's assassination, Tate replaces the Aufidius-Lieutenant episode (4.7) with a new unit introducing the villain Nigridius, the play's *diabolus ex machina,* who for his own purposes whips Aufidius's jealousy to fever pitch and looses the forces which precipitate the ugly finale. Shakespeare's 4.6 and 5.1, in which the Roman citizens learn of Martius's approach, are abbreviated, combined, and transposed to follow the Nigridius episode. Act 4 concludes with the Intercession scene (5.3), in the course of which Menenius makes an abridged appeal as prologue to the women's embassy. The matrons' suit is not the psychological subjugation of a man-child by a manipulative parent, but a reasoned and humane petition by an individual family on behalf of the national family to one who is at once protector and aggressor; and, as on an earlier occasion, Martius is persuaded against his better judgment to place patriotic duty above personal pique. The moral mechanism is perfectly clear; Shakespeare's ambiguities are fully resolved. Martius's cynical inversion of a cliché of classical Renaissance art:

> Behold, the heavens do ope,
> The gods look down, and this unnatural scene
> They laugh at.

(5.3.183–85)

is now rehabilitated and celebrated as a moment of mystical transcendence:

O Mother-Goddess, dread *Volumnia,* turn:
What have you done? Behold the Heav'ns divide,
And *Gods* look down on this amazing Scene!
O Mother Goddess, Heav'n-born Advocate. . . .

(51)

Menenius's sour chat with Sicinius on his return to Rome (5.4) is cut, together with the news that Volumnia's suit has succeeded. The enigmatic episode in which Volumnia and Virgilia cross the stage in silence (5.5) disappears in favor of an explicit civic welcome, dominated by a loquacious Valeria, and acknowledged by its recipients.

Most of act 5 is Tate's own. Volumnia, Virgilia, and Young Martius return to Corioli to warn Martius of impending danger; Aufidius confesses to Nigridius a longstanding passion for Virgilia, and on the arrival of the Martian family has them confined. He then proceeds to accuse Martius before the Volscian council. In a much revised 5.6, Martius and Aufidius quarrel before the Volscian lords, and at a predetermined moment the Volscian general "*Stamps with his Foot, the Conspirators Enter, and help him to Wound* Martius, *who kills some, and hurts* Aufidius." (59). The Lords conveniently rush off to deal with civil unrest elsewhere, leaving the two ailing combatants to expire at leisure amid the accelerating violence of the play's final moments.

A telling apotheosis at play's end, and the ultimate success of Tate's political homily, relies heavily upon the audience's affective response to the principal characters. And Tate's dissatisfaction with Shakespeare's portraiture was as acute as his discontent with his tripartite structure. Character commentary from a variety of sources, ambivalent and contradictory speeches and actions, ambiguous silences and lacunae, not to mention the almost total absence of self-revelation, represented the very antithesis of transparent communication. Martius posed the prime challenge.

Shakespeare's churlish, alienated, and elusive hero, although an improvement on Plutarch's lout, was patently not a type to pluck the heartstrings. Not only must his political position be harmonized with the play's propaganda objective, as noted earlier, but his portrait must be redrawn more sympathetically if his death was to assume the status of martyrdom. Martius's act of national betrayal was therefore downplayed, and his attack on Rome rationalized as a legitimate reprisal against an ungrateful city for the excesses of mob rule. By astute textual cutting, highlighting, and strategic insertions, the renovated avenger, in contrast to Shakespeare's alienated, enigmatic, almost mystic, machine, stands forth as an unequivocally pious and noble warrior, dutiful son, and loving husband and father. In the play's final moments, his grief-stricken endurance of his family's pain was finely calculated to win the audience's compassion and initiate them into the horror and exaltation of the martyred family.

Psychological complexities have no place. All references to Martius's aloneness are excised; suggestions that he is a victim of reflex behavior (1.1.41–42 or 3.1.256–57) disappear. Intimations that he is susceptible either by nature or childhood conditioning to manipulation by the tribunes, Volumnia, or anyone else are rigorously pruned. The tribunes and plebeians are permitted to rail at him from time to time, but their charges are meant to be discounted. Anything like unworthy comments or actions by himself or censure by his equals are suppressed. The shifting, often contradictory, assessments of his character from a variety of observation points (the cushion-layers, Menenius, Volumnia, Aufidius, Cominius) are cut, pruned, or somehow harmonized to create a unified impression.

In a series of insertions, he is shown as pious as he is brave. At the conclusion of act 1, following his battlefield triumphs, he cries:

> Now let us Sacrifice to th'*Gods,* and Pray
> For many Rival Days, to This on *Rome;*
> Then Yield our Pious Rites, to our Slain Friends.
>
> (14–15)

Piety is complemented by warm domestic feeling: as he goes into exile, for example, the doting parent, overcome with emotion at Young Martius's request to accompany his father, is obliged to have the boy removed since "he raises in my Breast / A Tenderness that's most Unseasonable" (37). Examples could be multiplied. At play's end the figure who greets death in sentiments suggestive of artistic treatments of the flight of the redeemed soul:

> So, grasping in each Arm my Treasure, I
> Pleas'd with the Prize, to Deaths calm Region Fly.
>
> (64)

attains the status of secular saint. To his enemies, only opprobrium remains.

The pursuit of a unified vision meant for Tate not only the domestication and demystification of Martius, but the reduction of the play's subordinate characters to a strictly functional role. Volumnia, with her unhealthy hold on her son excised, emerges as an idealized mother figure selflessly committed to family and country. All idiosyncrasy is suppressed. No mention is made of wound-counting; she evinces no uncertainty over Martius's new name (2.1.174); nor is she overtly ambitious for the consulship for him (2.1.198–202). On Martius's banishment, Tate's matron discovers a "Womans Tenderness," a "Mothers Fondness," and a fund of "panting Fears" (36) unknown to her Junoesque original. The difference between the Volumnias of Shakespeare and Tate is tellingly epitomized in the handling of her final lines in the Intercession scene in which the understated, suggestive force of the Jacobean matriarch's "I am hush'd until our city be afire, /

And then I'll speak a little" (5.3.181–82) yields to the flamboyant explicitness of:

> We'll speak no more, till *Rome* be all on Fire.
> Then joyning Curses with the Crowd, expire.

(51)

In similar fashion, the wordless, maddeningly inscrutable stage-cross with which Shakespeare's Volumnia quits the play is superceded by a display of partizan-wielding madness. The averted eyes of the Jacobean matriarch have been repainted to stare back unambiguously at the Restoration spectator with maternal love, patriotic ardor, and finally terrifying irrationality when the forces of disorder have done their work.

Tate's decision to domesticate Martius meant that Virgilia would consequently assume a higher profile. Not at all taken by Shakespeare's whim to render Martius's spouse virtually mute, Tate makes her a veritable chatterbox, and a markedly more assertive soul than her Jacobean counterpart. In 2.1 she voices her abhorrence of the rabble quite as firmly as her mother-in-law. Her assessment of Valeria is more caustic than in the original ("Let me Retire from her Impertinence; / A heavier Burden than the Grief I bear" (8), and tongue-tied tearfulness on Martius's victorious return is overcome by spousal solicitude: "Ah my Dear Lord, What Means that Dismal Scarf?" she demands, "My Joy lies folded There!" (15). The Intercession scene, thanks to the appropriation of a fair number of Volumnia's lines, finds her impassioned and persuasive. Her determination to return to Corioli to rescue her husband completes the portrait of a woman of spirit, fortitude, and decisiveness. All in all, she is a fitting wife for a Roman general and an effective counterbalance to Volumnia. Her suicide, to avoid rape by Aufidius, and the noble character of her final moments identify her with a long line of female martyrs enshrined in baroque art.[16]

Young Martius, who is given several more appearances than Shakespeare provides, invariably accompanies his mother, as in so many seventeenth-century paintings where, as affective devices, children cling to, peep round, fly above, or are carried by their elders. Here the harrowing sadism of the boy's murder is crudely exploited to prompt revulsion at political upheaval and the barbarity it implies. The sensational pathos of his exchange with his dying father tints the moral in precisely the "lively colours" advocated by Paleotti:

> *Boy.* I fain wou'd clasp you too; but when I try
> To lift my Arms up to your Neck,
> There's something holds 'em.
> *Cor.* Thy Torturers my Boy have crippled 'em,
> And gash't thy pretty Cheeks.
> *Boy.* I know you Lov'd 'em;

But truly 'twas no fault of mine; they did it
Because I wou'd not cry. . . .
Cor. O Nature! A true Breed!
Boy. 'Tis grown all Dark o'th sudden, and we sink
I know not whether; good Sir hold me fast.

(63–64)

Menenius, like Volumnia, loses much of his unique individuality. To avoid diversion of interest from the nuclear Martian household, Tate purges all hint of the frail and endearing humanity with which Shakespeare graces him. His relationship with the citizens is downplayed throughout in favor of highlighting Martius's encounters with them; and only a few lines of his moving appeal in the Volscian camp survive. Little more than a judicious statesman and model Tory, he perishes in an offstage attempt to rescue Young Martius from the clutches of Nigridius.

Tate's Aufidius, unlike Shakespeare's, who exists in the most complex and ambiguous relationship to Martius, is little more than a plot device: a mean-minded foil to Martius's high-minded nobility, a convenient enemy to whom he can desert, and the instrument of his destruction. To render the audience's antipathy doubly certain, he is made the would-be ravisher of Virgilia as well. The portraits of Aufidius and Nigridius call to mind the sadistic torturer/executioners in baroque pietistic art, who by their craven viciousness heighten sympathy for the long-suffering martyr.

Hardly less attractive to the propagandist than *Coriolanus*'s evenhanded politics and capricious characterization was its want of what Bradley was later to term "*imaginative* effect or atmosphere."[17] To supply affective resonance, Tate invokes a veritable armory of florid, if somewhat hackneyed, imagery—fire, stars, Roman gods and goddesses, winds, storms, darkness and light, sunset, dying roses, owls, ravens, and vultures—and for good measure contrives several passages of portentous atmospherics, typified by Martius's premonition of catastrophe as he exits through Rome's gates:

I know not what presage has struck my Breast;
But Oh! Methinks I see Destruction teem,
And waiting for my Absence, to Discharge
The battering Storm on this perfidious Citty:
So when the murmering Wind, from out his Nest,
Jove's Royal Bird to the open Region calls;
Aloft he Mounts, and then the Tempest Falls.

(37)

Ultimately, however, the creation of persuasive ambiance was for Tate less a function of verbal imagery than of mise-en-scène. In contrast to the fluid, revolving action on the Jacobean platform, thrust into its audience and permitting a multiplicity of observation points from each of its three sides, the Theatre Royal, Drury Lane, which housed his adaptation, was a structure designed to contain, control, and frame the dramatic event in the interest of a predetermined aesthetic and emotional response. The major novelty of the Restoration stage was its painted shutters and wing flats, placed behind a proscenium arch, and offering, aided by artists' obsessive attention to sightlines, a unified pictorial effect from any point in the house.

Scenic elements were not intended to be in any way realistic, but rather a colorful background to the dramatic action which proceeded for the most part on a seventeen-foot-deep apron to which the actors gained access directly from the upstage area or through proscenium doors.[18] The play was now situated within a niche from which it spilled at intervals onto the apron to interface in a controlled manner with the world of the spectator. The visual realization of a particular dramatic moment, pictorially composed and framed by the proscenium arch, was quite as important to the cathartic climax as the text itself.

If Tate's directions represent theatrical fact rather than a playwright's wishful thinking, the visual realization of his political morality must have been fairly lavish. The 1681–82 season was a financially difficult one for the King's Company,[19] but the management may have regarded Tate's production as a last-ditch investment. The theatricality of the stage directions tends to support the claim of the text to represent the play "as performed," and the fact that the court considered the entertainment fit for the Moroccan ambassador suggests that some money had been spent on it.

Tate's adaptation reduces the twenty-nine scenes of modern editions to fourteen;[20] and immediately apparent is the concern for locale. The provision of two major backshutters, one designated "The City Rome" (act 1) and the other "The City of Corioles" (act 4), lends a physical rootedness foreign to the nonevocative geography of the Jacobean text. Everywhere mass, movement, color, and light are pressed into service to captivate the senses and touch the emotions.

The first scene of act 1 was played on the apron and backed by the "City Rome" flat in the first grooves. The citizens enter through the proscenium doors on either side of the apron and exit the same way. At the play's outset the audience is drawn into the action as bystanders who share the same fictive space as the citizens, participants, it goes without saying, in Tate's propaganda exercise.

The second scene, in Coriolanus's house, is described as "A Palace," no doubt a stock interior set in the second or third grooves and revealed when the "City Rome" flat was drawn off.[21] No exit is marked, so we must assume that a new shutter closed on the group. The shutter which masked the ladies from view is described as "*the Walls of* Corioles," and would logically have occupied the first grooves. Marcius and Decius (an officer of Tate's invention) enter through the proscenium doors, and at the sound of their "parley," "*the* Senators *Appear on the Walls,*" perhaps on balconies over the doors.[22] The battle flows back and forth across the apron and through the proscenium entrances until apparently practicable gates in the backshutter are opened and "Martius, *with a few follows them to the Gates, and is shut in.*" A moment later, as an "*Alarum continues, Re-enter* Martius *with his Party, as having Forc't their Way through the Citty; his Followers with Spoils.*" As Martius exits in search of Aufidius, the "Walls of Corioles" shutter is drawn off to reveal further upstage, probably in the second grooves, a shutter described as "a Camp or Field," no doubt another stock flat. An alarum is sounded, and "Cominius *and* Aufidius *are seen Engaging each Other, with their Parties:* Cominius *is Beaten off;* Martius *with his Souldiers Enters Hastily on the other Side.*" Another alarum is heard, and Martius and Aufidius "*Fight off; after which, a Retreat Sounded: Re-enter* Martius *and* Cominius, *at several Doors.*" Here, with impressionistic brevity and focused intensity, in contrast to the epic sprawl of Shakespeare's narrative, Martius's military prowess is impressed upon an audience, who share, as they did in scene 1, a common space with the participants.

On Martius's triumphal return to Rome, battlefield hurly-burly gives way to formal spectacle. Shakespeare appears to anticipate only modest visual display. The Folio direction at 2.1.161 reads, "*Enter Cominius the Generall, and Titus Latius: betweene them Coriolanus, crown'd with an Oaken Garland, with Captaines and Souldiers, and a Herauld.*" The people are deliberately excluded, and their reaction is later narrated by Brutus (2.1.205–21). What matters to Shakespeare at this point is the distanced, formal encounter between mother and son. Tate, however, substitutes a Roman victory parade, presumably before the "City Rome" shutter, in which Coriolanus enters "*in Triumph, met by the* Nobility and Commons *of* Rome" (15). Precisely what spectacle was offered is not indicated in the text, but it must have been considerable to prompt Volumnia's observation, "Not Thee this Pomp, but Thou Adorn'st thy Tryumph" (15). Here Tate seizes an opportunity simultaneously to celebrate the grandeur of republican Rome just before factionalism mars it, to elevate the hero by colorful display, and, as the procession crosses the forestage from one proscenium door to the other, once again to draw the audience into the action.

A different visual tactic animates the scene in which Martius is proposed for consul (2.2). Shakespeare provides for two Officers "*to lay Cushions, as it were, in the Capitoll,*" that is, on the unlocalized apron. Their conversation is followed by "*A Sennet. Enter the Patricians, and the Tribunes of the People, Lictors before them: Coriolanus, Menenius, Cominius the Consul: Sicinius and Brutus take their places by themselves: Coriolanus stands.*" Shakespeare's conservative, kinetic processional entry is restaged by Tate as a spectacular and static discovery. The direction runs "Scene *Opening, shews the* Senate *sitting in the Capitol;* Coriolanus *in a White Robe, as Candidate for the* Consulship" (17). Shakespearian attitudinizing and the byplay with sitting and standing, which allows Martius to signal his political intractability, are excised in favor of an exercise in history painting: within a post-proscenium setting, the general, dressed in white, stands in the foreground against a formal spectacular human and architectural backdrop to receive due recognition from representatives of a thriving and grateful state. This scene powerfully reinforces the impression of Roman grandeur created by the triumphal procession, the sense of a society engaged in the orderly institutional rituals of power.

The Voices scene (2.3) which succeeds it is staged on the apron, backed by a "Street" shutter which closes on the Senate setting. The political heart of the play, from the Voices episode to Martius's departure into banishment, seems to have been played as a continuous unit on the forestage before the same "Street" shutter. The Jacobean direction *"Enter seven or eight Citizens"* is replaced by *"Enter the Citizens in vast Numbers."* The throng of supers, their dynamic entry, and their proximity to the audience as they give and withdraw their voices, demand the death of Martius, and ultimately hound him into banishment underlines with devastating clarity the risks inherent in popular suffrage. By collapsing real and fictive space, Tate makes affective capital of an ugly political coup, rendered all the more disturbing by the aloof grandeur of the Senate episode which preceded it. Confronted on the one hand by the citizens' bovine stupidity and violence, and on the other by Volumnia's patriotic eloquence and Young Martius's pathetic attachment to his exiled father, playgoers were affectively beguiled into knee-jerk support for the Tory position.

On his arrival in Corioli, Martius delivers his "A goodly city" apostrophe in front of "The City of Corioles" shutter. References to Antium are deleted here and elsewhere. At the conclusion of his abbreviated soliloquy, the shutter is withdrawn to reveal *"The Inside of the Palace; Musick Plays; Servants pass hastily over the stage."* Shakespeare's encounter between Martius and Aufidius requires no background beyond the tiring-house facade; Tate shifts the action to an elegant interior, exploiting color and light to pictorialize the interview.

As a backshutter closes on the Corioli episode, Brutus and Menenius enter through the proscenium doors, and shortly the forestage is thronged with vicious Roman riffraff, who, at the news of Martius's imminent invasion hysterically rend the air "with a confus'd Cry, and Lamentation" before *"Haling and Dragging off the Tribunes"* to taste poetic justice. Tate's contempt for the mob in this his last glimpse of them is almost palpable.

The Intercession scene, in its turn, evinced an atmospheric richness reminiscent of Rembrandt or Rubens. Shakespeare sets the episode on a bare stage, furnished merely with some sort of seat. Only Aufidius and Martius are present at the top of the scene; later the matrons enter in clothing indicative of hard times, accompanied only by whatever attendants are proper to such a down-at-heel troop. The temper of the episode is more intellectual than emotional: the eye notes the bodies of the principals as they self-consciously stand, kneel, and hold hands, while the ear grapples with the paradoxical and tortured rhetoric. The playgoer is aware that beneath the alienating artificiality a dominant mother is engaged in a life-and-death struggle with her emotionally dependent son, but one is essentially an observer, not a participant in the event. In the end, the episode leaves unanswered as many questions as it resolves.

No scene in Tate's adaptation better illustrates the triumph of clarity over ambiguity and feeling over intellect. Like the earlier Senate sequence, it is staged as a discovery, with all the visual thrill revelation affords: "Scene *Opening, shews* Coriolanus *seated in State, in a rich* Pavilion, *his Guards and souldiers with lighted Torches, as ready to set Fire on* Rome; *Petitioners as from the* Citty offer him *Papers, which he scornfully throws by: At length* Menenius *comes forward, and speaks to him:* Aufidius *with* Nigridius, *making Remarks on 'em*" (46). While speech yields to mime, the audience feasts its eyes on the rich pavilion and its colorful masses of guards and soldiers over which chiaroscuro effects produced by the torches play. Here is a grand frame for a grand action—in Tate's reading, not the subjugation of an overgrown boy by a hectoring matriarch, but the conquest of a warrior's passion by the rational and patriotic appeals of a Roman wife and mother. Through interpolated gesture the audience is prepared for Coriolanus's obduracy, and the probable futility of the suit the women will press. After the summary dispatch of Menenius, Martius orders, "[N]ow plant our Fires against the Gates of Rome"; and as the soldiers "*Advance with their Lights, Enter from the other side,* Volumnia, Virgilia, *and* Young Martius, *with the rest of the* Roman *Ladies all in Mourning*" (47). The line of matrons, tastefully attired in black gowns of contemporary cut,[23] must have created a stunning effect as they passed slowly downstage, juxtaposed against the colorful, torch-lit military figures opposite. It is within this spectacular visual context that the women make their case, gaining affect all the while from the painterly ambiance. Tate's atmospherics might not have supplied what Bradley missed in Shakespeare's script, but the imagination could not fail to be seized, or the emotions stirred. So impressive was Tate's spectacular (re)vision of this scene that the procession of mourning matrons backed by flamboyant military masses, as appropriated by Thomson, remained a fixture of *Coriolanus* revivals until World War I.

Following the episodes in which Volumnia and her party return to Rome and Nigridius and Aufidius plot, both played on the apron, the shutters were drawn off to reveal "A Palace," perhaps the interior of Aufidius's palace employed earlier. Upstage the Volscian lords are discovered "*as set in Councel,*" presumably picturesquely grouped at a table. Aufidius and Coriolanus enter from opposite proscenium doors not long after. Their fight takes place downstage of the stunned assemblage of Volscian senators, who rush forward as Martius falls, only to exit a moment later. The rest of the scene makes its impact, not by visual splendor but the intense and controlled exploration of human pain, each unit of which is marked by precise blocking. Martius falls somewhere near the curtain line, facing outward toward the audience, and struggles into a semireclining position. Aufidius and Nigridius die upstage of him, perhaps near the conspirators killed earlier by Martius. Virgilia, brought in by way of a proscenium door, is placed on one of Martius's outspread arms, and proceeds to her death speech. Volumnia then enters, and apparently places Young Martius on her son's other arm, thus marking a new unit of action. Volumnia's mad soliloquy follows, concluded by her murder of Nigridius. Her exit cues the beginning of the death throes of Young Martius, terminated by his vain attempt to embrace his father. On his son's death, Coriolanus confronts his own dissolution, leaving the audience to contemplate an empty upstage council table, downstage of it the bodies of the play's villains, and nearest the audience the tableau of the martyred family. Tate's final scene, growing in disciplined intensity throughout, is not mere sensationalism for its own sake, but a theatrical exemplar of Judith Hook's observation that in baroque art "ultimate reality in the shape of some all-embracing unity was perceptible only in moments of intense passionate experience."[24] The sequence asks to be regarded as an attempt at secular transcendence:[25] even as the contemplation of the sufferings of religious figures led to spiritual insight, so, Tate might have argued, could the contemplation of political martyrdom in the theater foster wiser statecraft.

Only one other feature of Tate's adaptation remains to be accounted for—the fattening of Valeria's role and her transformation into a Restoration coquette, trading on "Allurements of Dress and Face," visiting endlessly, preening herself on her knowledge of state affairs, the real or imagined idol of throngs of lovers. Her presence seems to be a pragmatic response to the popularity and availability of a particular actress, rather than any political or aesthetic imperative. The role may have been written for Mrs. Corey who had a reputation for playing empty-headed society women.

No cast list for the production survives, but aging Charles Hart, the company's leading actor, seems the most likely candidate for the role of Martius. He played with success a series of heroic military parts including Arbaces in *A King and No King*, Amintor in *The Maid's Tragedy*, Othello, Alexander in Lee's *The Rival Queens*, and Mark Antony in *All For Love*. According to Downes, he acted Alexander "with such Grandeur and Agreeable Majesty, That one of the Court was pleas'd to Honour him with this Commendation; That *Hart* might Teach any King on Earth how to Comport himself."[26] In his hands, Martius would have been exactly the noble military figure that Tate envisioned.[27] Attempts to allocate roles to other company members can be only conjecture.

No record of the production's reception survives, but the fact that the script was published several months after its premiere suggests that it aroused some interest.

*   *   *

Nothing more is heard of *Coriolanus* until 1698 or 1699 when Shakespeare's text apparently enjoyed a successful revival. John Dennis, in a letter to Sir Richard Steele in 1719, remarks that when "the *Coriolanus* of *Shakespear* . . . was brought upon the Stage twenty Years ago, it was acted twenty Nights together."[28] Advertisements in the *Daily Courant* for the Lincoln's Inn Fields revival in December 1718 note that the play was "Not Acted these Twenty Years," which probably suggests that the earlier revival took place at that theater. If so, the leading roles must have been taken by Thomas Betterton and Mrs. Barry. In their hands, the play's formidable success would have been understandable. Some further evidence of a 1699 revival is offered by David Erskine Baker who records a quarto edition of the play printed in 1699 but which seems to be no longer extant.[29]

The only other recorded production prior to Dennis's adaptation took place at Lincoln's Inn Fields theater in December of 1718. This seems to have been an attempt to preempt the interest in Dennis's redaction, originally scheduled for production at that time, but subsequently delayed (see below). The text is advertised in the *Daily Courant* (13 December 1718) as "by Shakespear," and probably was, but Tate's spectacle was also incorporated. The play was to be presented, the advertisement promised, "With Scenes, Machines, Triumphal Arches, and other Decorations after the Custom of the Romans." Nothing is known of the casting except that a youthful James Quin probably played Martius.

The Invader of His Country: A Whig Warning

Political calm proved as elusive in the decades which followed Tate's adaptation as in those which preceded it. In 1688, James II was effectively deposed by the Whig Revolution, and died at St.-Germain in 1701. Louis XIV immediately recognized his son, James Edward Stuart (The Old Pretender), as the rightful English king, and British Jacobite sympathizers rallied to his support. The next year Anne, the Pretender's sister, succeeded William, and as a firm defender of the Protestant Succession denied her brother's claim to the throne. The Pretender consequently formed an alliance with the French and in March of 1708, at the invitation of Scottish Jacobites, made a futile attempt to land near the Firth of Forth with a French force of six thousand. Two months later, the Tories, portrayed by the Whigs as party to the Jacobite invasion, were as soundly defeated at the polls as the Old Pretender had been at sea.

John Dennis's "warm attachment . . . to the Whig Interest"[30] and keen eye to his own advancement moved him to catch the wave of anti-Jacobite sentiment, and the cautionary tale of the traitorous Martius lay conveniently to hand. "They who thro' Ambition or Revenge," his epilogue warns,

> Or impious Int'rest, join with foreign Foes,
> T'invade or to betray their Native Country,
> Shall find, like *Coriolanus,* soon or late,
> From their perfidious Foreign Friends their Fate.[31]

The adaptation, titled *The Invader of His Country: or, The Fatal Resentment,* was probably begun in 1708, about the time of the Firth of Forth fiasco, and was finished early in 1711 when Dennis sent a copy to a correspondent.[32] For some reason he seems not to have approached a theater until 1718.[33] On 28 February 1717/18, he read the tragedy to Steele, Cibber, and Booth, the Drury Lane proprietors, who agreed to stage it in the early winter of the next season (1718–19). The proposed timing of the production could not have been better. In the first months of 1718 the Old Pretender obtained the assistance of Sweden and Spain, and by the autumn an invasion of England seemed imminent; but the managers chose not to capitalize on the play's timeliness. Despite the dramatist's exasperated demand whether "any Dramatic Performance could be more seasonable in the beginning of a Winter, when we were threatened with an Invasion from *Sweden* on the North, and from *Spain* on the West"[34] Drury Lane mounted a lavish revival of *All For Love.* Meanwhile, John Rich, in anticipation of Dennis's adaptation, staged at the rival house the elaborate production of Shakespeare's script noted earlier. The Drury Lane managers fearing, with some justice, that Dennis's tragedy would suffer by comparison if it followed too closely on the heels of its original,[35] postponed the production indefinitely.

The Invader finally reached the stage only a year later (11 November 1719), when the invasion threat had subsided. To Dennis's chagrin it opened when the king was out of the country and the courtly audience sparse. Box office receipts fell short of expectations, and after the third performance the managers announced another piece for the following evening, "Insolently declaring," the enraged playwright noted, "that no Play was worth their Acting any longer than it brings a Hundred Pound."[36]

The Invader's chief interest lies in Dennis's crafty reformation of Shakespeare's text to render it as uncompromisingly Whig as Tate had made it Tory. While Shakespeare's capricious politics was subdued to the demands of partisan propaganda, the play's stylistic singularity was assimilated to the conventions of classical aesthetics.

In shaping his political moral, Dennis had to tread a treacherous path between patriotic censure of the Pretender's invasion attempt and denigration of a relative of the ruler; the result is consequently, like Tate's, less an allegory than a series of suggestive correspondences between consular

Rome and contemporary England. Dennis's Coriolanus is a thoroughly admirable figure save for the antipopulist attitudes which ultimately precipitate his exile and the betrayal of his country. Resemblances between Martius and the Old Pretender could scarcely be missed by the average theatergoer: both aspired to power; both showed little enthusiasm for popular democracy; both found themselves in exile and dependent on the support of their country's major foe; and both, with the enemy's aid, attempted to invade their homelands. From Martius's (spelled "Marcius" by Dennis) fate, the prologue insists, Jacobite traitors and their sympathizers should take a salutary warning:

> For as when Britain's Rebel Sons of late
> Combin'd with Foreign Foes t'invade the State,
> She to your Valour and your Conduct owes,
> That she subdued and crush'd her num'rous Foes:
> We shew, to Night, such Treasons to prevent,
> That their Guilt's follow'd by their Punishment.

While the play inveighs against collaboration with foreigners, it simultaneously launches a libertarian Whig attack on domestic Tory treatment of the common man and the Jacobite (and by implication Tory) legitimist denial of the people's right to a choice of ruler. Political attitudes at home constitute, Dennis argues, as great a danger to national peace as the threat of invasion from abroad.

Again, as in Tate's play, political positions are crudely simplified in order to clarify the moral. Dennis's Marcius is apostrophized by Cominius as "Brave beyond Example":

> Thy Soul's possest of ev'ry peaceful Virtue,
> Temperate, chast, observant of the Laws,
> With an Integrity like that of *Jove*,
> Above the Pow'r of Fortune or of Fate. . . .

(10)

In such a superior mortal, the fatal flaw, disdain of the common people, is all the more evident and damning.[37] To Marcius's arrogant assertion, "I hate the People," Cominius responds that it is "to this very People, whom you hate, / You more than half your matchless Conquests owe, / And more than half your Glory" (11). In the end, it is Marcius's refusal to recognize the social compact that brings about his exile, his treasonous reaction to it, and finally his death.

The plebeians, in keeping with Dennis's populist sympathies, are made to appear to be well-intentioned, unsophisticated, good-humored souls, victimized by Marcius's totalitarianism on the one hand and the power-hunger of their leaders on the other. Dennis cuts 1.1 completely, and with it disappears most of the plebeians' claim to three-dimensionality—their violence, shrewdness, hunger, and frustration, together with Marcius's assessment of them as cowardly, mutinous, and variable. In battle Dennis's citizens are heroic altruists to a man: "Lead on, brave *Marcius,* thee we follow all / To Death or Victory," shouts the lst Soldier in response to Martius's appeal, and all echo "To Death or Victory we follow all" (7). When asked for their voices, the 1 Cit. urges:

> Now let us passing one by one salute him,
> And be saluted by him, and desired
> To give our Voices.
> And now a Wager on the handsom'st Bow.
>
> (25)

Unable to respond to their rough generosity, it is Marcius who appears uncouth and ungracious. When Coriolanus returns in vengeance to Rome, and the citizens realize that the tribunes were responsible for their plight, their disposition of poetic justice is prompt and definitive:

> 2 *Cit.* Have our Tribunes done all this?
> 3 *Cit.* The Furies break their Necks for it.
> 4 *Cit.* What need we trouble the damn'd Neighbours,
> for what we can do ourselves. We are the Furies.
> *All Cit.* Ay, we are the Furies, we are the Furies.
> To the Rock, to the Rock with them.
>
> (62)

The role of the citizens is ultimately neutral: they represent an idealized version of the common man, mistreated by Marcius and misled by their own representatives. The dramatic outcome, however, turns on the contest between Marcius and the tribunes.

The latter again are made the undisputed villains of the piece. "They are guilty of two Faults," maintained Dennis:

> to get the Champion and Defender of their Country banish'd . . . could proceed from nothing but that Hatred and Malice which they had conceiv'd against him, for opposing their Institution. Their second Fault lay in procuring this Sentence . . . by exasperating and inflaming the People by Artifices and Insinuations, by taking a base Advantage of the Open-heartedness and Violence of *Coriolanus.* . . . So that this Injustice of the Tribunes was the original Cause of the Calamity which afterwards befel their Country. . . .[38]

However misguided the principles of Dennis's Marcius may be, he holds them with sincerity and integrity. The tribunes, on the other hand, are self-serving hypocrites, cynical about democracy, contemptuous of the citizens, and greedy for personal power. Dennis, as fearful of civil discord as Tate, makes their fate a potent warning to fomenters of popular discontent of all stripes.

Dennis's aesthetic debt to Dryden, his friend and mentor, is evident throughout *The Invader,* particularly in its quest for a beau ideal vision realized through a unified aesthetic effect. Unity of action, Dennis contended, was the prime concern, and the unities of time and place were expected to subserve it. Shakespeare's multiplicity of focus in *Coriolanus* was an inviting target. "The Faults of *Shakespear,*" Dennis wrote Barton Booth, who was to play Marcius in his adaptation, ". . . are his perpetual Rambles, and his apparent Duplicity in some of his Plays, or Triplicity of Action, and the frequent breaking the Continuity of the Scenes."[39] As a first step, Dennis reduced Shakespeare's twenty-nine scenes to ten, a considerable decrease on Tate's fourteen.[40]

Act 1 again receives radical revision. The scene in Marcius's house (1.2) is transposed to act 2, and 1.1, 1.4, 1.5, and 1.7 are cut altogether. The remaining material, considerably abridged and rewritten on the grounds of clarity and propriety of expression, is arranged in one long scene set on the battlefield before Corioli. Lucius Cluentius, a new character, narrates to Cominius the conquest of the city, Marcius arrives "painted . . . with Hostile Blood" to update his colleagues, and Titus Largius [sic] sings Marcius's praises. The latter seeks permission to return to the fray, rouses the troops and leaves, and a moment later is seen doing battle with Aufidius. Shortly after, Cominius rechristens Marcius and prepares to return to Rome where the consulship awaits. The action is now totally linear and unified, its spatial and temporal fluidity stabilized.

Shakespeare's act 2, already exclusively set in Rome, posed no threat to Dennis's sensitivity to unity of place; the action's "perpetual rambles," however, were another matter. The renovated act 2 opens with the Volumnia-Virgilia episode transposed from 1.3, but without Valeria's visit. In the midst of the matrons' chat, Cominius, Coriolanus, and Menenius abruptly arrive from the Volscian expedition. All the intervening matter is cut—Menenius's verbal skirmishes with the tribunes, his meeting with Volumnia en route to greet Coriolanus, the formal entry of Coriolanus with the herald and captains. In 2.2, set in the vicinity of the Capitol, Sicinius and Brutus engage in an abridged and revised discussion of the threat posed by Coriolanus's bid for the consulship (2.1.205–270). Shortly after, Coriolanus, Menenius, and Cominius enter, and the latter reports the Senate's decision to make Coriolanus consul, subject to his bespeaking the people's voice. The entire Senate scene thus disappears. Here and elsewhere, in order to avoid shifts of both place and focus, much of Shakespeare's staged action is displaced by reportage. The Voices scene, much inflated with comic material, comprises 2.3. The colloquy between the tribunes and citizens after the exit of Menenius and Marcius is heavily abridged.

Act 3, although abbreviated and frequently rewritten, retains most of

Shakespeare's content. As the plebeians leave at the end of the Banishment sequence, Volumnia and Virgilia arrive, and the act concludes with a much-revised version of the Farewell sequence (4.1).

In act 4, doubtless to his considerable chagrin, Dennis found himself compelled to set one of its two scenes in Antium and the other in Rome. By way of amends, however, his insistence on linear action is unremitting. Both Volumnia's encounter with the tribunes (4.2) and Adrian's meeting with Nicanor (4.3) vanish, and the act opens with Coriolanus's arrival in Antium (4.4). In a new episode, which follows Marcius's exchange with the servants, Aufidius confers with Volscian senators. In the course of the conclave, Coriolanus arrives, reveals himself to Aufidius, is welcomed, awarded a generalship, and sets out for Rome. In Dennis's 4.2 (Shakespeare's 4.6), the news of the Volscian invasion reaches Rome. The scene between Aufidius and his Lieutenant (4.7) is excised.

Act 5 is one long scene, set on the battlefield somewhere near Rome. Only a fraction of Shakespeare's material survives. The sequence in which Menenius is persuaded to appeal to Marcius (5.1) is blue-penciled, together with the appeal itself (5.2). The episodes in which Menenius and Sicinius hear the news of Volumnia's success (5.4) and the latter returns victorious to Rome (5.5) also disappear. The effect is to keep the audience's eye unwaveringly fixed on Marcius. The act opens with the Intercession scene, followed by a new-minted and windy dispute between Coriolanus and Aufidius which culminates in a brawl. Coriolanus kills Aufidius, is stabbed in the back by a Volscian tribune, and dies with his wife and mother at his side.

Like the lucid, intensely focused history paintings of Nicolas Poussin or Guido Reni, it is the hero's action that rivets the gaze as he moves from military success to rejection of the democratic process and banishment, from his act of national betrayal to capitulation, and finally to death. In one way or another the bare bones of the historical narrative are there, either dramatized or narrated; but the textural richness of Shakespeare's creation, to say nothing of its (equi)vocal and multivocal resonance, is sacrificed to clarity and celerity. It is also worth remark that the break between the two parts of the play is closed. Marcius departs with the promise to Virgilia, "I that depart from hence an empty Cloud, / Fraught with Destructive Thunder will return, / And break upon them with avoidless ruin" (44). Only the dimmest playgoer would be surprised to find him in Antium in the ensuing scene.

In Dennis's idealized universe, the distribution of justice is as straightforward and comprehensible as the action which precipitates it. Shakespeare's Coriolanus, Dennis notes, seems made to be "a dreadful Example to all who lead on Foreign Enemies to the Invasion of their native Country; if there were not something in the Fate of the other Characters, which gives occasion to doubt of it."[41] In a fairer world than that of Tate and Shakespeare, "in which the Guilty and the Innocent perish promiscuously," Dennis discovers "a particular Providence . . . protecting the Good, and chastizing the Bad."[42]

Virgilia, Volumnia, and Young Marcius are spared the grim fate allotted them by Tate, while the tribunes and Aufidius receive the retribution they escape in Shakespeare's Machiavellian republic.

Along with moral uplift and structural clarity, Dennis, in common with other advocates of classical aesthetics, gives a high priority to authenticity and decorum in the recreation of historical figures. For him, as for his contemporaries, psychological individuality had no charm: dramatic characters should simply be consistent with their historical portraits, with the sociopolitical type they represent, and with the moral purpose they are intended to serve.[43] The austerely chiseled Roman who dominates Dennis's *Invader* owes less to Shakespeare than to the neo-Stoicism of Poussin and Corneille; the contradictory, ambiguous, inarticulate struggle of the Jacobean lonely dragon is modulated into a rhetorical duel between passion and will in the French neoclassical manner.[44] Its climax, the Intercession scene, like Poussin's painting of the same episode, *Coriolan vaincu par sa femme et sa mère*, is heroic, graceful, and expressive, yet impersonal.[45]

Acutely vexed that Shakespeare "offended against the Equality of the Manners even in his Hero himself,"[46] Dennis takes considerable pains to reinvent Shakespeare's war machine and truculent boy as a mellow, charismatic career officer and family man. Surrounded by doting troops, the monosyllabic "thing" becomes a veritable spellbinder. "Ay, in that Shout the Volscian Army fell," he cries:

> Yes, my brave Friends, ye have already conquer'd,
> I see it in your Eyes, I hear it in your Voices.
> Come on, and I, as Time does Fate, will lead you.

(7)

In civil life his class prejudice is undeniable; but it seems more a matter of personal idiosyncrasy than the combination of political conviction and maternal brainwashing Shakespeare implies. His fears of social upheaval, his assertions of personal integrity, and his fluent defense of his views in 3.1 are all cut.

However militarily amiable Dennis's Marcius may be, it is within the family that he shines. Dennis, like Tate, goes out of his way to remove all suggestion of maternal dominance. Marcius's homecoming from the Volscian campaign becomes a domestic rather than a public occasion; and in a patent attempt to ameliorate his spousal credentials, Dennis gives the couple an immediate ecstatic reunion. Some twelve lines later Virgilia, in a marked reversal of Shakespeare's strategy, calls her husband's attention to his mother, only to hear him protest:

> I knew not till this Moment she was here,
> So much my Eyes and every busy Power
> Of my rapt Soul were taken up with thee.

(26)

Marcius's conjugal priorities are further underlined by the pair's fifty-six line leavetaking in the Farewell episode, from which Volumnia makes a point of absenting herself.

Not only are Marcius's marital ties strengthened, but Volumnia's wheedling manipulation is largely removed. In their interview (3.2) after Marcius's contretemps with the tribunes and people, her interventions, while acute, never violate the etiquette appropriate to a Roman matriarch in conversation with a national hero. Marcius's capitulation in the Intercession scene is, as in Tate's version, no longer the product of maternal exploitation of filial immaturity, but a noble sacrifice of personal ambition to national loyalty in response to an anguished appeal from a selflessly patriotic mother.

Poetic justice is abundantly justified and fully satisfied. Shakespeare fails to make it clear whether Marcius's death is retribution for his treason or merely the casual outcome of Aufidius's perfidy. Nowhere does he stand objectively guilty of having killed a single Roman. Dennis, in order to vindicate his fate, accuses him of wreaking national havoc: "Ten thousand Widows, and as many Orphans," Volumnia tells him, "Already has thy dreadful Vengeance made" (68). His death is merited, deliberately chosen, and meant to be grandly cathartic in a way Shakespeare's ugly finale is not.

In lieu of the pietistic martyrdom favored by Tate, Dennis opts for a neo-Stoic exit in which Marcius atones with dignity and resignation. There is no assassination conspiracy. When Aufidius learns that Marcius has broken his oath, he warns him that the lapse must be answered to the avenging gods and to him personally. A quarrel ensues during which Coriolanus kills Aufidius, and in the course of his valedictory—"Hail! and eternally Farewell, brave *Tullus!*"—three tribunes, bent on revenge, attack. Unlike Shakespeare's sudden and inglorious quietus, Marcius is permitted to resist his would-be assassins and dispatch all three of them. Then, to offstage warning cries from Volumnia and Virgilia ("Behind, Oh, look behind"), he is run "thro' the back" by a fourth tribune, whom he levels before he falls. The women rush to his side, and Marcius quits them with becoming nobility and warmth. Cominius and Menenius arrive with improved peace offers, and decide to return the hero's body to Rome for burial. Marcius's end, shorn of Shakespeare's Volscian citizens and senators, and staged with a few grand strokes, recalls the calm grandeur of Poussin's neo-Stoic death scenes (e.g., *The Death of Germanicus* or *The Death of Phocion*). If theatergoers failed to achieve some sense of transcendence or emotional release, it was not for want of effort on Dennis's part.

Volumnia, shorn of her unhealthy hold on Marcius and virtually any hint of common clay, is more sculpture than woman. She is not permitted to sew, to describe herself as a clucking hen, to experience a momentary memory lapse, to engage in wound-counting, to appear in destitute garb, or to make her silent cross in 5.5. Her appeals to her son are impassioned rather than calculated, and her final assessment of her role in Marcius's death—"I was the fatal, I the only Cause"—is as heroic as it is inaccurate.

Virgilia, without enjoying the primacy accorded her by Tate, is more visible and articulate than in Shakespeare's script. On Marcius's return from the wars, rather than the silent weeper of Shakespeare's devising, Dennis's Virgilia is vocal and exultant; when her husband is banished, she asserts her determination to accompany him; at the conclusion of the Intercession sequence she vainly urges him to return home; and just before curtain-fall she delivers a high Roman lament over his body. Her first and last appearances are neatly utilized by Dennis to lend that whiff of the supernatural missed from Tate to Bradley. When first introduced she tells Volumnia of a frightening dream in which she has seen Marcius "Surpriz'd, surrounded, murder'd by the *Volscians*" (13). In the final scene, as she stands by Marcius's body, she brings the action to full closure with an apostrophe to the "prophetic Vision of the Night" (78).

Particularly offensive to Dennis's fastidious historicism was Shakespeare's depiction of Aufidius, a distinguished general, as "a base and profligate Villain."[47] Not only is he now cleared of all villainy, but he is well-nigh canonized. In an addition to act 4, Aufidius is recast as the very epitome of the chivalric hero. Unlike Marcius, who places pride above patriotic duty, Aufidius insists, "Yet always shall my private Passions yield / To what's my Country's universal Good" (51). And it is on Aufidius's selfless patriotism that Dennis constructs his denouement. When Marcius sacrifices the well-being of the Volscian state to personal concerns, Aufidius is implacable in calling him to account, and the act costs him his life. Even at the moment of death, however, he nobly, but unsuccessfully, attempts to warn his enemy of the lethal approach of the Volscian tribunes. Poetic justice demanded Aufidius's death,[48] but his demise was made as impressive as circumstances permitted. In the end, however, Aufidius was for Dennis, as for Tate, little more than a dramatic device: one adaptator makes him a virtuous patriot, the other an utter villain. In both instances, superficial clarity is purchased at the expense of a devastating, if untidy, demonstration of realpolitik.

As in Tate's version, Menenius undergoes a remarkable sea change. Dennis castigated Shakespeare for making the senator "an errant Buffoon,"[49] and when the opportunity arose to correct the error, fabricated an historical shadow. The excision of 1.1 eliminates much of his interaction with the citizens; the disappearance of some two hundred lines of act 2 costs him his hard-hitting verbal skirmishes with the tribunes and his endearing portrait of himself as "a humorous patrician." He makes his first appearance on Marcius's return from the wars when he speaks nine lines of formal welcome. Gone is the whooping joy at his protégé's return and his paternal pride in his wounds. With the elimination of the Senate scene (2.2) much of his political sensitivity disappears; and most of his shrewd counsel to Coriolanus during the confrontation with the tribunes and plebeians (3.1) vanishes

as well. He is absent from Marcius's farewell, and his embassy to the Volscian camp is merely reported. His final appearance occurs after Marcius's
death, when he arrives with fresh peace offers from Rome. But Cominius
does most of the talking. His virtual absence from Dennis's redaction discovers his critical importance to Shakespeare's text—as consummate political pragmatist, the only patrician with a sense of humor, and a mellow
paternal presence which mitigates somewhat the overwhelming severity of
Volumnia.

In contrast to the verbal floridity of Tate's script, Dennis's idiom is bleakly
literal and uncompromisingly lucid. Shakespeare's already minimal imagery
is reduced almost to the vanishing point, together with all trace of ambiguity,
contradiction, paradox, and, indeed, resonance. Decorum and propriety of
expression are pressed to the point of flatness and monotony.[50]

Dennis's alterations, like Tate's, cannot all be ascribed to political or
aesthetic motives; at least one feature must be attributed to theatrical exi-
gency. Despite berating Shakespeare for introducing "a Rabble" which offended "not only against the Dignity of Tragedy, but the Truth of Fact, the
Authority of all the *Roman* Writers, the Customs of Ancient *Rome,* and
the Majesty of the *Roman* People,"[51] the adaptator finds himself confessing
somewhat shamefacedly:

> that after all I have said . . . [I] have not only retain'd in the second Act of the
> following Tragedy the Rabble which is in the Original, but deviated more from
> the *Roman* Customs than *Shakespear* had done before me.[52]

In his act 2, prior to the entrance of Marcius for the Voices scene, he
inserts a comic debate, riddled with topical reference, between the party of
Sempronius, another candidate for consul, and the party of Marcius. Later,
in the course of the Voices scene, he provides a crude "turn" for the 1 Citizen
who pretends not to know what Marcius wants or who he is, and receives
a slapstick thrashing for his pains. In act 4 he elaborates the encounter
between Marcius and Aufidius's servants when two of the lackeys, after
receiving a kicking from the anonymous visitor, lure a third into a similar
misfortune. Dennis, it is certain, did not willingly contaminate his austere
classical study: his assertion that the insertions were "a Trespass against
Conviction"[53] prompts the conjecture that under pressure from the Drury
Lane management (probably Cibber), compounded perhaps by his perennial
shortage of cash, he reluctantly supplied farcical sequences for the company's highly popular comedians.

The Invader's scenic effects are of a piece with its austere moral, structure, and characters. Like the paintings of Poussin, there is little in the way
of spectacular crowds or lavish settings. A few artfully posed individuals
before simple painted backgrounds seems to have been Dennis's aesthetic
desideratum. Advertisements make no mention of new scenery, and it is

likely that, as in *Julius Caesar* productions, only stock shutters were employed: perhaps a landscape for act 1, a "Hall" or "Chamber" for Coriolanus's house (2.1), and some sort of townscape for the Capitol and Forum sequences (Dennis's 2.2, 2.3, 3.1).[54]

The first noteworthy stage effect takes place in 4.1. Coriolanus apparently arrives by way of a proscenium door, and delivers his "A Goodly City is this *Antium*" speech standing before backshutters depicting Aufidius's house. Aufidius's servants challenge Marcius on the apron, and the 3 Servant who agrees to escort him to Aufidius leads him off by a proscenium door. On their exit, the "SCENE *draws and discovers* Aufudius *and the Senators at Table.*" Staged as a discovery, this episode, in which Marcius makes his fatal commitment to the Volscians, assumes particular importance. After Aufidius and the senators have conversed for some time, "*Enter 1 Servant and* Coriolanus *at a Distance; the other two Servants appear at the Door*" (51). While Coriolanus remains downstage on the apron, the servant moves within the proscenium to Aufidius. Simultaneously, in a commonplace of eighteenth-century caricatures, two other servants observe proceedings through the half-opened proscenium door. In response to the servant's request, Aufidius "*Comes to the front of the Stage.*" Foregrounded on the apron, as in some period history painting, Marcius reveals himself and forms his unholy alliance, while in the farther reaches of the postproscenium, the senators group themselves picturesquely as background. On Aufidius's "Let me present you to our Friendly Senators, / Who now to take their leaves of me are here," "*They go to the Table,*" thus underlining Marcius's desertion to the enemy by a physical shift from his downstage isolation to the welcoming fellowship upstage.

No indication is given of the setting for act 5. Perhaps some sort of wooded landscape was employed, as in *Julius Caesar,* for battlefield sequences. Again, with a Poussinesque preference for pictures with relatively few figures, Dennis has Coriolanus receive the women alone. The direction reads "*Enter* Virgilia, Volumnia, Valeria, Y. Marcius, *with other Ladies and Attendants.*" Just before his exit, Aufidius refers to them as "a mournful moving Train," presumably suggesting a formal procession attired in funereal black after the manner of Tate. Just how many supers were employed is not indicated, but the tone of the scene suggests less spectacle than in Tate's production, if only because the military is absent. The only other notable visual moment is a sequence in which Volumnia threatens to take her own life with a dagger. "Here, here's the Dagger," she cries, "but thou giv'st the Blow" (70). This piece of business was to have a lengthy stage history.

Coriolanus's death is staged with as much restraint as the intercession. There are no senators or Volscian citizens present as in Shakespeare and Tate. In the same space in which the intercession occurred, an effective touch, Aufidius and Marcius meet and fall alone. In the play's final moments the women enter to make their farewells, and Cominius, Menenius, and "Attendants" arrive to dress the stage. Eloquent groupings, graceful speech, and tranquil grandeur are everything. A greater contrast with the hurly-burly of Shakespeare's climactic moments can hardly be imagined.

Whatever Dennis's complaints about the timing of the production, he had no cause to blame its actors, who were the finest the age had to offer. In the leading role was Barton Booth, the premier performer of the time and, at the age of thirty-eight, at the meridian of his powers. Educated at Westminster School, he had a sound background in the classics and a cultivated taste for sculpture and painting. "These he frequently studied," Theophilus Cibber tells us, "and sometimes borrowed Attitudes from, which he so judiciously introduced, so finely executed, and fell into them with so easy a Transition that these Masterpieces of his Art seemed but the Effect of Nature."[55] Given Booth's knowledge of art, and the fact that he was a member of the theater's management team, it is likely that not only Booth's Marcius, but the production's entire visual presentation would have reflected the restrained classical spirit which permeates Dennis's text.

Already celebrated for his Brutus and Cato, Marcius was a logical addition to Booth's Roman repertory. Although only "of a middle Stature," according to Cibber, he had no cause to be intimidated by the physical demands of the role. "There was such an exalted Dignity in his Appearance," Cibber continues, "no body on the Stage looked taller."[56] Davies notes that he "walked with the ease of a gentleman and the dignity of a monarch";[57] and if, as Colley Cibber argues, he sometimes "contented himself with too grave a Dignity" and lacked "Taste of Humour,"[58] the want would scarcely be noticed in Dennis's Roman. Booth's primary strength, however, lay in his vocal musicality, his careful wedding of sound and sense, his tasteful restraint. No living actor could have given Dennis's text a better chance of success.

Equally well cast was Mrs. Porter as Volumnia. "Though plain in her person," Cooke tells us, "with not much sweetness in her voice from nature, yet . . . with an excellent understanding, and a good ear, she acquired an elevated dignity in her mien, a full tone, and a spirited propriety in all characters of heroic rage."[59] Dignified, strong, severe, and vocally resonant, her Volumnia was probably all the text allowed. John Mills, Drury Lane's leading supporting actor, doubtless proved a satisfactory Aufidius. Indeed, it is rare in the play's history to find the part played by a performer of such stature. The citizens and servants, taken by the company's comedians—Bickerstaff, Penkethman, Johnson, Miller, Norris, and Cross—lent welcome, if incongruous, relief from the overwhelming seriousness of the rest of the play.

It is clear in retrospect that *Coriolanus* did not readily lend itself to anti-Jacobite propaganda, and that Dennis's political didacticism, although the justification for the revision, is somewhat perfunctory. The play's real interest, one suspects, lay in its potential for neoclassical reinvention. But even here *The Invader* falls short: the stylistic uniqueness of the original defied transformation to a conventional classical format, as Dennis came to recognize. His tragedy in the end was not, he confessed in a letter to Sir Richard Steele, "a just and a regular one"; it was simply "as just and as regular as I could make it, upon so irregular a Plan as *Shakespear*'s."[60]

The day after the Drury Lane production closed, Lincoln's Inn Fields theater staged a revival, pointedly advertised as "*The Invader of His Country; or, The Fall of Coriolanus,*" but identified as "Written by Shakespear." Presumably the Drury Lane fiasco offered an excuse to revisit the original script. The production saw only one performance, and a further revival on 1 January 1719/20 met the same fate. In the following season (1720–21) the company revived the play three times under the title "*The Tragedy of Coriolanus.* Written by Shakespear." No cast lists survive, except for a note to the *Daily Courant* advertisement for the performance of 26 December 1720—"Comic parts by Bullock, Sr., Griffin, Spiller, and C. Bullock." It would appear that by this time the company was attempting to sell the production on the strength of its comedy. Dennis's interpolations had perhaps not been without influence. For the season's final performance, the comic parts are again listed, with no mention of principals: Rob-Sack, the Miller-Bullock Sr.; Mend-foul, the Cobbler-Spiller; Nitt, the Tailor-Griffin; Burn-crust, the Baker-Pack; Fat-Dab, the Cook-Hall; Washball, the Barber-H. Bullock. Two further performances were advertised in the 1721–22 season.

James Thomson's *Coriolanus* (1749): A Painterly Morality

For more than a quarter-century after the Lincoln's Inn Fields production of 1 January 1721/2, *Coriolanus* in any form was a stranger to the London stage until fears of an imminent war with France and renewed Gallic interest in the restoration of the Stuart dynasty intensified Jacobite feeling about 1742, and reminded James Thomson,[61] author of *The Seasons* and controversial playwright, of the pertinence of the Coriolanus theme.[62] He seems to have begun the play at this point, only to put it aside for several years.[63] By the spring of 1745 he had taken it up again, and as Bonnie Prince Charlie led his army into England in November of the same year, Thomson had advanced at least to the third scene of the third act.[64] The piece was completed in the spring or summer of 1746.

Thomson expected his old friend James Quin to take the title role, with Garrick supporting him as Attius Tullus; but the Drury Lane proprietor apparently refused to defer to his erstwhile competitor, and the production was indefinitely postponed. By the spring of 1748, Thomson's exasperation with Garrick was total: "Coriolanus has not yet appeared upon the Stage," he wrote William Paterson, "from the little dirty Jealousy of Tullus—I mean of him who was desired to act Tullus, towards him who alone can act Coriolanus."[65] A few months later, Thomson was dead, leaving behind a host of grieving friends, a quantity of debts, two indigent sisters, and an unproduced tragedy.

At the request of Lord Lyttelton and Andrew Mitchell, the poet's executors, the Covent Garden management agreed to mount *Coriolanus* as a benefit to discharge Thomson's financial obligations to his creditors and family. Quin, who owned a script, volunteered to play the titular hero and oversee rehearsals. The premiere took place on 13 January 1749.

The play's object, to sound a grave warning against treason, although hardly as apt as it would have been four years earlier, was unexceptionable at any time:

> Then be this truth the star by which we steer,
> *Above* ourselves *our* COUNTRY *should be dear.*[66]

Although framed by a Whig propagandist and intended to be played during, or in the aftermath of, the '45, Thomson's piece is less partisan than one might expect, markedly less so than his *Agamemnon* (1738) or the banned *Edward and Eleonora* (1739). Parallels between Martius and Bonnie Prince Charlie are clear enough, but Thomson's *Coriolanus,* like those of Tate and Dennis, is less an allegorical indictment of specific acts and persons than a generic caution to all Jacobite sympathizers against betrayal of the national interest. "This man," Galesus sermonizes at the play's conclusion,

> was once the glory of his age,
> . . . .
> His only blot was this; that, much provok'd,
> He rais'd his vengeful arm against his country.
> And, lo! the righteous gods have now chastis'd him,
> Even by the hands of those for whom he fought.
>
> (286)

Thomson's drama derives its interest not from its humdrum political moral, but its radical affirmation of neoclassical aesthetics and its innovative and spectacular stagecraft, both of which were to have their influence on subsequent stage realizations of Shakespeare's text.

Where Dennis had opted, like contemporary architects, merely to graft neoclassical features onto a Jacobean structure, Thomson rejected such a strategy outright. His *Coriolanus* owes next to nothing to Shakespeare; indeed, even the playwrights' sources were different. Where Shakespeare relied upon Plutarch, Thomson went to the briefer and drier Livy, and to one of Plutarch's major references, the *Roman Antiquities* of Dionysius of Halicarnassus.

For Thomson, as for Dennis, the moral effect of a work is inseparable from the unity of its design. And freed from the Shakespearian constraints under which Tate and Dennis labored, he was able to lend his homiletic narrative a fearful and wonderful symmetry. Coriolanus's act of treason, and its unhappy consequence are the drama's sole interest. The motivation for Coriolanus's decision is of no consequence: "Whatever private views and passions plead, / No cause can justify so black a deed" (286), Thomson insists. He initiates his action with Coriolanus's arrival at the Volscian camp just outside Rome where the play's five acts unfold correctly, if somewhat implausibly, within the space of twenty-four hours.

Act 1 finds the Volscians awaiting the Roman reaction to a humiliating peace offer. In the interim, Coriolanus arrives with his tale of Roman ingratitude. The serpentine intertwining of war and politics of the first half of Shakespeare's play is compressed by Thomson into an eight-line speech by Martius (spelled Marcius throughout):

> Yes. I am *Caius Marcius;*
> Known to thy smarting country by the name
> Of *Coriolanus*. That alone is left me,
> That empty name, for all my toils, my service,
> The blood which I have shed for thankless *Rome*.
> Behold me banish'd thence, a victim yielded
> By her weak nobles to the maddening rabble.
> I seek revenge.
>
> (216–17)

The entire political dimension of the Roman patrician-plebeian conflict is suppressed. Coriolanus offers his services to Attius Tullus (Tullus Attius in Dionysius of Halicarnassus, Attius Tullius in Livy), who promptly accepts, justifying his action on the grounds that Rome is ungrateful: "All should unite to punish the ungrateful / Ingratitude is treason to mankind" (217). Marcius is promptly endowed with half the Volscian command.

In act 2, Titus, the Volscian ambassador to Rome, returns with the city's rejection of the shameful Volscian terms, and narrates to Galesus, a Volscian philosopher earlier rescued by Marcius during the Roman-Volscian war, the circumstances of Coriolanus's banishment and his pathetic leavetaking. Coriolanus and Galesus are reunited a moment later, and the latter, an inveterate moralizer, warns his erstwhile benefactor to

> Be to the Volscian nation and himself
> The dread, the godlike instrument of justice!
> But let not rage and vengeance mix their rancour.
>
> (230)

Tullus presents Coriolanus to the deputies of the Volscian states (who improbably have chosen to convene in a military camp), his appointment as cogeneral is approved, and preparations are made to march immediately on Rome.

Act 3 finds Marcius successful in his first military maneuvers, and tactlessly thrusting Tullus into the background in a drive for personal vengeance. The subversion of his reason by passion, earlier feared by Galesus, vitiates his usefulness as an instrument of divine justice. Tullus accepts Marcius's ascendency with outward grace, but finds himself increasingly a prey to resentment, a circumstance exploited by the Iago-like officer Volusius. Meanwhile, a deputation of Roman senators, led by Minucius, arrive to sue for peace, only to be arbitrarily dismissed by Marcius.

In act 4, Tullus's earlier magnanimity fades as Marcius, with a fine disdain of his partner's feelings, unilaterally determines military policy, which Tullus ultimately rejects. The colleagues consequently become estranged. At this point, the deputation of Roman matrons is announced. Tullus, in a brief conversation with Volusius, concludes that whether Coriolanus resists or yields to the matrons' appeal "the Volscian honour / Will be alike betray'd":

> If Rome prevails,
> He stops our conquering arms from her destruction;
> If he rejects her suit, he reigns our tyrant.
>
> (265)

Marcius's death offers the only satisfactory resolution, and Volusius volunteers as executioner.

Act 5 sees the arrival of Veturia (as Volumnia is designated by Livy and Dionysius of Halicarnassus) and Volumnia (as Virgilia is known in the same sources), accompanied by a number of Roman ladies. Veturia makes her plea with the support of her daughter-in-law, procures her son's acquiesence, and returns to Rome. Tullus now finds ample justification for Coriolanus's death, but offers him safe-conduct home if he will quit the country. Marcius, determined to justify himself to the Volscian deputies, curtly rejects Tullus's overture. Marcius's intransigence provokes Tullus to summon Volusius and the conspirators; and in the ensuing broil, Marcius is dispatched. When Galesus and the Volscian authorities arrive, Tullus proudly confesses to the assassination, and he and his minions are led off to answer for their crime.

Thomson's didactic project demanded not only unified place, time, and action, but characters who evince unequivocal virtues and vices. Thomson's hero, like the Coriolanuses of Tate and Dennis, breathes the rarified air of Roman epic. On the battlefield, he is Rome's "wisest captain, and their bravest soldier"; in civil life he is "No less renown'd for piety, for justice, / An uncorrupted heart, and purest manners"(221). How then can the banishment of such a paragon be explained? "The charge against him was entirely groundless," Titus informs Galesus:

> His real crime was only some hot words,
> Struck from his fiery temper, in the senate,
> Against those factious ministers of discord,
> The tribunes of the people.
>
> (222)

In the Intercession scene, the only occasion on which Marcius appears with his family, no effort is spared to create a thoroughgoing man of feeling. Much is made of the stress he undergoes in the course of the women's petition. On the entrance of Volumnia and Veturia, "*after some struggle, he advances, and goes hastily to embrace them.*" In the course of the women's speeches he is wracked by emotion. At one point he "*appears in great agitation,*" and is subsequently described as "*highly agitated.*" Finally, when Volumnia (Virgilia) asks him to tell her what to say to their children, he weeps:

> Tell thee! What shall I tell thee? See these tears!
> These tears will tell thee what exceeds the power
> Of words to speak, whate'er the son, the husband,
> And father, in one complicated pang,
> Can feel . . .
>
> (276)

Once revealed, Marcius's softer side receives increasing play until the final "Thine is the triumph, Nature!" and the resigned recognition, "Ah *Veturia!* / *Rome* by thy aid is sav'd—but thy son lost."

Superior Marcius is, but he cannot be, according to the canons of classical tragic theory, perfect. "As for a perfect character of virtue," Dryden reminds us, "it never was in nature, and therefore there can be no imitation of it."[67] Thomson, like his predecessors, endows Marcius with a set of potentially dangerous character traits: he is proud, quick-tempered, and a snob. It is precisely these weaknesses which lead him to desert to the Volscians and subsequently compromise his reason and his potential as an instrument of divine retribution.[68] In the end, however, his defects are redeemed by an invincible patriotism which surfaces despite his best efforts to quell it. "He will betray himself," Tullus tells Volusius with prophetic insight,

> Whate'er his rage
> Of passion talks, a weakness for his country
> Sticks in his soul, and he is still a *Roman*.
>
> (243)

This instinctive patriotic reflex expiates his errors even as it precipitates his death. When Tullus refers to Romans as the "genuine seed of outlaws and of robbers," an enraged Coriolanus replies with consummate contempt for his safety:

> The seed of gods! . . .
> Whate'er her blots, whate'er her giddy factions,
> There is more virtue in one single year
> Of *Roman* story, than your *Volscian* annals
> Can boast thro' all your creeping dark duration!
>
> (282)

Stung by Marcius's transcendent nationalism and disdain for his benevolence, Tullus summons Volusius and the conspirators.

Marcius's demise comes more swiftly than in the readactions of Tate or Dennis. As the assassins approach "*with their swords drawn,*" Marcius, "*Laying his hand upon his sword,*" warns, "Who dares approach me, dies!" "*As* Coriolanus *draws his sword,*" the stage direction runs, "Volusius *and the Conspirators rush upon and stab him.*" Marcius, "*Endeavouring to free himself,*" shouts "Off!—Villains," and, as he falls, cries defiantly, "O murdering slaves! Assassinating cowards!" A moment later he is dead. "*Upon the noise of the tumult,*" according to a direction, "*enter hastily to them* GALESUS, *the other deputies of the* Volscian *States, Officers, friends of* Coriolanus, *and* TITUS *with a large band of soldiers*" (283–84). Civil and military masses dress the stage for Galesus's final homily. The effect is severe, masculine, and grand, a marked contrast to the flamboyantly pathetic and domestic denouements of Tate and Dennis.

Thomson's Tullus, unlike Shakespeare's insubstantial, infrequently seen, and ambiguously motivated Aufidius, is strongly, if simply, etched, present throughout, and crucial to the action from first to last. In a portrait clearly indebted to Dennis, Tullus appears as a humane, gracious, and heroic figure. Even when smarting from his defeats by his mortal enemy, he tells Volusius:

> My soul, my friend, my soul is all on fire!
> Thirst of revenge consumes me! the revenge
> Of generous emulation, not of hatred.
>
> (213)

His response to Marcius's plight is open-hearted and immediate. Within seconds, he offers him "half of my command," and in the national Volscian interest puts his personal inclinations aside.

Although sorely tempted to treachery by Marcius's insolence, he decrees his death only when he finds his Roman partner has betrayed the Volscian cause. And before he allows Volusius to strike, he offers means of escape. Tullus takes no active part in the assassination, "*standing by without having drawn his sword*"; and when it is over, he assumes full responsibility:

> This deed is mine: I claim it all!—These men,
> These valiant men, were but my instruments,
> To punish him who to our face betray'd us.
>
> (285)

Like Shakespeare's Aufidius, he closes the play with a promise to justify his actions. There is no indication that he will suffer for Marcius's murder, and perhaps in Thomson's view he does not deserve to do so.

The character of Veturia (Shakespeare's Volumnia) is much diminished. She appears only in the Intercession scene, after which she is escorted back to Rome. Throughout her brief but powerful appearance she is the embodiment of Roman grandeur, which, although mellowed at times by tears, never loses its intrinsic severity. Her mission, she insists, is not official:

> Behold me here,
> . . . .
> Commission'd by my own maternal heart,
> To try the soft, yet stronger powers of Nature.
>
> (269)

Her appeal, in contrast to that of Dennis's matron, is less to the head than to the heart, to innate patriotic feeling, to filial piety, and paternal responsibility. Without a trace of the calculation of Shakespeare's Volumnia, Thomson's Veturia guilelessly remonstrates, weeps, supplicates, and finally defies her son out of simple greatness of spirit and patriotic duty. Despairing of success, she offers her life in a final, grand gesture, destined to become a highlight of productions for a century afterwards:

> I came not hither
> To be sent back rejected, baffled, sham'd,
> A Roman matron knows, in such extremes,
> What part to take—And thus I came provided.
> 　　　　　[*Drawing from under her robe a dagger*]
> Go! barbarous son! go! double parricide!
> Rush o'er my corse to thy belov'd revenge!
> Tread on the bleeding breast of her, to whom
> Thou ow'st thy life!—Lo, thy first victim!
>
> (277)

Even with her suit granted, she allows herself no sentimental indulgence. To Marcius's premonitory recognition, "*Rome* by thy aid is sav'd—but thy son lost," she responds with more patriotic fervor than maternal anxiety, "He never can be lost, who saves his country." And on this high-minded note she quits the stage.

Volumnia (Shakespeare's Virgilia) also makes her only appearance in the Intercession episode. Here she serves merely to second her mother-in-law, and speaks about three dozen lines. Her only contribution of note is an overwrought display of baroque sentimentality which very nearly travesties Shakespeare's eloquently mute direction "*holds her by the hand silent.*"

When Veturia completes her plea, Volumnia seizes the initiative. "O permit me," she begins, "*taking his hand,*"

> To shed my gushing tears upon thy hand!
> To press it with the cordial lips of love!
> And take my last farewel!

She then proceeds to rain tears over it for some seventeen lines, and is only halted by her husband's peremptory "Leave me."

Menenius disappears from the play entirely. His monitory function is assumed by Galesus and Cominius, while Minucius, a consul, leads the deputation to Coriolanus's camp. No substitute for the blustering, humorous, sagacious father figure is anywhere to be found.

In keeping with the classical austerity of the text (Virgilia's lapse aside), Thomson's staging is tasteful and dignified, even painterly. Where Shakespeare's script delights in movement of all sorts, Thomson's mise-en-scène amounts to a series of static discoveries, picturesquely composed, with two processions offering the only dynamic spectacle. Each act, except for act 4, has a discovery as a feature.

Most of act 1 is played on the forestage against a Camp shutter showing Rome in the distance. At the end of 1.4, an officer announces the arrival of a stranger. "One of exalted port, his visage hid," he tells Tullus,

> Has plac'd himself upon your sacred hearth,
> Beneath the dread protection of your *Lares;*
> And sits majestic there in solemn silence.

> (215)

When asked why he did not ask the stranger's identity, the officer replies:

> My lord, I could not speak; I felt appall'd,
> As if the presence of some God had struck me.

With this exchange by way of prelude, "*The back-scene opens, and discovers* CORIOLANUS *as described above,*" that is, seated grandly in a classic pose, probably just above the first grooves. The discovery of the hero on his first appearance in Antium was to become one of the most durable production highlights of Shakespeare's *Coriolanus.*

In 2.5, after a series of scenes set against the Camp and Tullus's Tent shutters, an officer informs Marcius and Galesus: "My lords, th'assembled chiefs desire your presence." As the actors turn upstage, "*The back-scene opens, and discovers the deputies of the* Volscian *States, assembled in council. They rise and salute* Coriolanus; *then resume their places.*" Here the spectacular effect arises from the painterly grouping of a mass of carefully costumed supernumeraries who make a single grand gesture—rising and saluting. This effect, in germ the inspiration of Dennis, was to become a hallmark of the Shakespearian Senate scene (2.2) as staged by William Charles Macready and Henry Irving.

Although act 3 opens with a stirring entry by Coriolanus after his first victories, accompanied by Tullus, Volusius, Titus, and "*a crowd of* Volscian *officers*" to "*Acclamations behind the scenes*," the major visual treat was reserved for the last scene of the act—the petitionary embassy of Minucius. Here no expense seems to have been spared. "*The back-scene opens*," we are told,

> *and discovers* Coriolanus *sitting on his tribunal, attended by his lictors, and a crowd of* Volscian *officers. Files of troops drawn up on either hand. In the depth of the scene appear the deputies from the* Roman *senate,* M. Minucius, Posthumus Cominius, Sp. Lartius, P. Pinnarius, *and* Q. Sulpitius, *all consular senators, who had been his most zealous friends. And behind them march the priests, the sacrificers, the augurs, and the guardians of the sacred things, drest in their ceremonial habits. These advance slowly betwixt the files of soldiers, under arms. As* Tullus *enters,* Coriolanus *rising salutes him.*

Thomson's reasons for including this scene, apart from the fact that it is recorded by Dionysius of Halicarnassus, are several. Spectacular parades in Shakespeare's plays had been commonplace since the coronation procession of Anne Boleyn in a Drury Lane revival of *Henry VIII* in 1727.[69] Also, the scene lends some visual warmth to the play's austere theme, glamorizes Coriolanus who is the focus of the action, and creates a striking counterpoint to the procession of mourning Roman women which follows in act 5. This procession, adapted by Sheridan to Martius's triumphal entry in Shakespeare's 2.1, perhaps with Tate's inspiration, lingered in the theater until World War I.

Act 4 is without visual effects, presumably to maximize the audience's appreciation of two pieces of spectacle in act 5—the procession of Roman women and Marcius's death. The arrival of the Roman matrons, with which act 5 opens, is planned by Thomson with a keen eye to pictorial composition. The direction reads:

> *Trumpets sounding. The Scene discovers the camp, a croud of* Volscian *officers with files of soldiers drawn up as before. Enter* Coriolanus, Tullus, Galesus, Volusius. *The* Roman *ladies advance slowly from the depth of the stage, with* Veturia *the mother of* Coriolanus, *and* Volumnia *his wife at their head, all clad in habits of mourning.* Coriolanus *stands at the head of the* Volsci, *surrounded by his lictors; but, when he perceives his mother and wife, after some struggle, he advances, and goes hastily to embrace them.*

Two contemporary engravings of this scene survive: one from the *Universal Magazine* of 1749, the other an anonymous print in the British Museum.

Designd & Engravd for the Universal Magazine. 1749. for J. Hinton at the Kings Arms in S.t Pauls Church Yard London

Thomson's *Coriolanus* at Covent Garden, 1749. *Universal Magazine*, 1749. [Author's collection]

Both suggest that the scene was played in front of a drop or shutter depicting the Volscian camp on the outskirts of Rome, although they differ in matters of detail. Both illustrations suggest some effort to reproduce Roman architecture. To judge from the directions the backshutter was probably placed against the back wall of the stage to allow the full depth of the post-proscenium area to be used.

As the shutters open, the Volscian officers and soldiers are grouped in files on the diagonal from down right to up left. Downstage of them at stage right, presumably at something like the lst Grooves position, is a tribunal for Coriolanus, a platform with a most un-Roman chair upon it. Coriolanus enters with his party, and they station themselves near the tribunal as the trumpets sound. The procession of Roman ladies, led by Veturia and Volumnia, moves on the diagonal from up left to down right, to judge from their final stage position in both engravings. The *Universal Magazine* shows Veturia and Volumnia companioned by eight women, with the suggestion that there may be more just out of sight. This illustration less accurately reflects eighteenth-century costume practice than the Quin print. There is no record

James Quin as Coriolanus at Covent Garden, 1749. [By permission of the British Museum]

of the use of classical drapery for actresses, but plentiful references to the custom of wearing contemporary fashion in plays of all periods. The Quin print, which shows the two women tastefully outfitted in white-trimmed black dresses of contemporary cut and some form of headdress, has an air of authenticity about it. The effect, however, denotes tasteful simplicity rather than the hardship implied in the lines of Shakespeare's Volumnia at 5.3.94–96. How many military supers Rich employed is unknown, but given his fondness for pageantry, their numbers must have been as large as the budget would bear. Whatever the count, the aesthetic effect intended is clear: the long diagonal passage of a troop of fragile females in mourning dress between glittering files of colorfully garbed soldiery was designed to heighten the pathos of the scene and the glory of Veturia's ultimate triumph. The tradition of the diagonal procession of mourning women was to thrive until the era of Frank Benson.

The assassination of Coriolanus takes place in the same setting, not in the curious interior depicted in the inset to the *Universal Magazine* engraving. The engraving captures with apparent accuracy, however, the moment when, just as Marcius is stabbed, the Volscian deputies and others arrive. The direction runs:

> *Upon the noise of the tumult, enter hastily to them* GALESUS, *the other deputies of the* Volscian *States, Officers, friends of* Coriolanus, *and* TITUS *with a large band of soldiers.*

With soldiers, deputies, and officers picturesquely disposed about the stage, Galesus moralizes Coriolanus's life and death.

Nothing specific is known of the costumes for the production, save for hints offered by the engravings discussed. Both illustrations show Quin wearing a Roman "shape," consisting of a lorica or cuirass, the Roman breastplate shaped to the figure, with a matching "base" or skirt below the cuirass.[70] A Covent Garden inventory of 1744[71] abounds in such items in a plethora of colors and fabrics. To add significance to the figure, players of Roman roles wore a full-bottomed peruke surmounted by a grotesquely plumed helmet. Again the print of Quin as Coriolanus seems accurate enough. Both engravings show the hero wearing a plumed helmet. A midcalf boot completed the costume.[72]

The principals, statuesquely posed against artfully grouped supers and unobtrusive landscape vistas, were as good as the age had to offer, in the absence of Garrick himself. Quin, at the age of fifty-six, was Thomson's own choice for the title role; and Davies' assertion that "in characters of singular humour and dignified folly, of blunt and boisterous demeanor [and] contemptuous spleen . . . [he] had no equal"[73] suggests that the playwright's judgement was not far wrong. Veturia was played with skill by an artfully wrinkled Peg Woffington, at the time only thirty-one. Archly she challenged male playgoers in the epilogue:

> If with my grave discourse, and wrinkled face,
> I thus could bring a hero to disgrace,
> How absolutely may I hope to reign,
> Now I am turn'd to my own shape again!

The popular George Anne Bellamy did what she could with the teary Volumnia, while Lacy Ryan, a veteran player of tragic lovers and fine gentlemen, was a handsome, if somewhat harsh-voiced Tullus. Denis Delane, who specialized in playing well-bred men, was astutely cast as the wise and rational Galesus. Isaac Sparks played the sinister Volusius. The play ran for ten performances, a more than respectable showing for the time, but its audiences were motivated more by respect for Thomson than enthusiasm for his play. As one theatergoer informed a correspondent:

[W]e have had a Play of Thompson's [sic] called Coriolanus which by the power of good friends ran nine nights, but was however generally disliked and was in my opinion a very unentertaining dull piece.[74]

The play was never again staged in London in its original form.

4

From Sheridan to Kemble: The Making of a Production Tradition (1752–1817)

Thomson's *Coriolanus,* albeit ideologically a halfhearted effort, marked the last overt attempt until the present century to constrain the play's political ambivalence in the interests of party propaganda. From the mid–eighteenth century to the end of the nineteenth, actor-managers opted to contain its potential political subversiveness by staging it as antiquarian reconstruction within a privileged and aestheticized space.

Although no longer a partisan instrument, *Coriolanus*'s Roman narrative, in the hands of Thomas Sheridan and John Philip Kemble, the two figures most responsible for its production style, could not escape a contemporary political and social coloration. From Sheridan's first production in 1752 through Kemble's final performance in 1817, England was almost constantly at war, and military figures, whether Wolfe, Nelson, Napoleon, or Martius, were icons of popular culture. Government in the England of the Georges, like that in consular Rome, was in the hands of an aristocratic oligarchy; and the lower orders, despite the efforts of reformers, were kept firmly in their place. Notwithstanding the social stresses contingent on the Industrial Revolution, English workers, unlike their French counterparts, seldom sought to transcend their station or interfere in the affairs of their betters.[1] Meanwhile the rising middle classes prospered through manufacturing and trade at home and abroad, and succeeded in considerably extending their commercial and political influence. Although major domestic upheavals were rare, consciousness of the French Revolution, and the possibility of its spread to England, was never far from the minds of all classes, sympathizers and opponents alike. Apprehension was omnipresent, if not always voiced, and educated members of society sought some measure of reassurance in the arts. At a moment when the classical baroque movement was running to seed, the excavations at Herculaneum (1737) and Pompeii (1749) gave fresh impetus to classical studies; and in the rediscovery of Greek and Roman culture, an anxious age found aesthetic and moral orientation and inspiration, a grandeur, simplicity, elegance, and idealism which steadied its nerves in revolutionary times.[2] The only way to become great, the influential art theorist Johann Winckelmann told them, "is to imitate antiquity."[3] The neoclassical movement, although not so described until later, was fueled by a feverish traffic between England and Greece and Italy. Tourists, scholars, and artists found a ready market for lectures, books, periodical pieces, and artistic creation among the prosperous bourgeois who had now become significant patrons of the arts, and particularly the theater. Throughout the period, playhouses increased enormously in size to service the new clientele, and rapidly adjusted their repertoire to accommodate demand for examples of high classical culture.

Over some six decades the *Coriolanus* revivals of Sheridan and Kemble, to the immense satisfaction of their middle- and upper-class audiences, celebrated the individualistic struggle of an antique Roman military figure, while largely suppressing the class conflict which animates Shakespeare's narrative. The package was wrapped in fetching archaeological trimmings, and marketed as the last word in contemporary art. Sheridan established the structural production pattern, which Kemble later refined and improved. The capacity of the Sheridan version to seize the taste of the age is attested to by the fact that although Garrick staged a competitive revival of *Coriolanus* in Shakespeare's authentic, if abbreviated, text, it did not last beyond one season, while the Sheridan redaction, as modified by Kemble, endured for a century and a half.

THOMAS SHERIDAN'S ADAPTATION (1752–1768)

Some two months after the conclusion of its Covent Garden premiere, Thomas Sheridan, the entrepreneurial actor-manager of Dublin's Smock Alley theater, had Thomson's *Coriolanus* in rehearsal, and informed his public that they would shortly see this "new Tragedy . . . as it was lately performed at the Theatre-Royal in London" (*Dublin Journal,* 8–11 April 1749).[4] On closer examination of the script, he concluded that the play "was defective in some essential points, and must always appear tedious in the acting";[5] and about six weeks later postponed the venture to the following autumn. When the promised treat reached the stage after a three-year delay, Thomson's defects had been ameliorated by liberal applications of Shakespeare. The advertisement for the production, in the *Dublin Journal* of 18–22 February 1751/2, ran:

> Never acted before. On Saturday next will be presented a Tragedy called Coriolanus, Taken partly from Shakespear and partly from Thompson . . . With new Scenes, Dresses, and Decorations.

Featuring Sheridan as Coriolanus and Peg Woffington once more as Veturia, the piece opened on 29 February and was repeated a further three times before the end of the season, a noteworthy achievement given the small size of Dublin's potential theater audience. The play was revived at Smock Alley in the seasons of 1752–53, 1753–54, 1756–57, and 1757–58.

The adaptation's most influential revival, however, took place in London in 1754 when, driven out of management at Smock Alley by a riotous public, Sheridan took refuge at Covent Garden. Here he restaged his Dublin success with appropriate visual splendor, and again cast himself and Woffington as the Roman son and mother. The revival was pronounced a hit, playing no fewer than eight times in the 1754–55 season, and was restaged at intervals thereafter in London until 1768. From 1757 until Kemble's revival of 1789, it was the only version of the play mounted. Sheridan's "Advertisement" to the Covent Garden acting edition, published in 1755,[6] gives us some indication of the principles which guided his revision.[7]

TEXT

Sheridan found himself, he tells us, dissatisfied with both the Shakespeare and Thomson texts. Although Shakespeare's Coriolanus and Volumnia were "drawn in as masterly a manner as any that came from the pen of the inimitable *Shakespear*," the play in general, he thought, "was purely historical, and had little or no plot"; by which he means that the drama is too much a straightforward dramatization of Plutarch, with too little regard for the claims of the ideal and their embodiment in classical dramatic form. "*Thomson*'s plot," on the other hand, "was regular, but too much of the epic kind, and wanted business"; which is to say that Thomson's drama had classical structure but little dramatic interest. By blending the two scripts, he argued, "a piece might be produced, which, tho' not perfect, might furnish great entertainment to, and keep up the attention of an audience." In his desire to have the best of both worlds, the authenticity and richness of Shakespeare's characterization and action and the regularity and formal dignity of Thomson's composition, he authentically reflects the aesthetic taste characteristic of the third quarter of the eighteenth century described by Hauser as "rococo classicism," a carefree mixture of styles "in which there is not even an attempt to reduce the different stylistic elements to a common denominator."[8]

Most immediately apparent, although significantly he fails to mention it, is Sheridan's concern to depoliticize the action. Gone is the whole of 1.1, with its conflict between patricians and plebeians, the citizens' view of Martius and his reaction, and Menenius's belly fable. The Voices scene is carved up to render Martius less provocative and disdainful of the popular will, little more indeed than a rough spoken victim of military modesty. The "corn" debate between Martius and the tribunes virtually disappears with the excision of 3.1.41–155, and with it a rational statement of Martius's political position. The citizens are allowed to drive Martius out since the dramatic action requires it, but Sheridan makes it clear that the hero's treatment is unjustified.

Undoubtedly the strongest influence on the adaptation is the neoclassical concern for unity of action. Sheridan excises the battle scenes, but is obviously not prepared, like Thomson, to subordinate all emotional and physical turbulence to the pursuit of Poussinesque tranquillity and intensity of focus. He restores to the play a series of incidents merely narrated by Thomson— the Voices scene, various encounters between Menenius and the tribunes, the Banishment sequence, and the reception by the tribunes of the news of Martius's march on Rome. In these bursts of nonmediated Shakespearian passion he found the dramatic interest Thomson's play lacked.

Unity of place is not rigorously observed; the first three acts are set in Rome and the latter two take place primarily, though not exclusively, in Corioli. Time is left indeterminate.

The play begins with the entrance of Veturia and Volumnia (1.3), who retain the names with which Thomson christened them. The gentlewoman who in Shakespeare enters to announce Valeria informs Veturia in a speech tailored by Sheridan:

> Madam, here's a messenger arrived, who says the army is on its march back to Rome, having obtain'd a great victory over the Volsci—the honour of which is chiefly given to your son. He brings letters from him. (3)

The women rush off to greet the returning hero, thus eliminating Valeria's visit. In Sheridan's 1.2, Menenius encounters the tribunes (Shakespeare's 2.1), and as he prepares to leave them, Veturia and Volumnia arrive to announce Martius's return. Sheridan begins a new scene (1.3) with the Herald's speech (2.1.162), and it is played virtually uncut. The exit of the procession marks the end of the episode. The colloquy between Brutus and Sicinius (2.1.205–70) is treated as a separate scene (1.4). The Senate sequence (2.2) becomes Sheridan's 1.5, and begins with the entry of the patricians and tribunes at 2.2.37. Martius does not appear until he is summoned at 2.2.131. Thirty-three lines of preliminary skirmishing (2.2.48–81) between Menenius and the tribunes and instances of Coriolanus's intractable and boorish behavior are blue-penciled.

The Voices scene (2.3), substantially cut, becomes Sheridan's 1.6. All the citizens' jocular exchanges (2.3.14–39) vanish in the interest of tragic decorum and speed. Fully one-half of Martius's interview with the citizens disappears with the removal of 2.3.85–124—his encounter with "*two other Citizens*," his muttered moment of self-communion beginning "Most sweet voices!" and his meditation on custom. The tribunes' advice to the citizens after their encounter with Coriolanus is curtailed by some fifty-seven lines (2.3.176–99, 220–252): detailed portrayal of their political machinations constituted a distraction in what was designed purely as a grand recreation of a classical historical event. Act 1, then, with admirable succinctness, introduces the major Roman figures, establishes the conflict, and concludes with the pivotal moment at which Martius offends the citizenry.

Sheridan's act 2 begins with Shakespeare's 3.1 and features the hostilities leading to Martius's banishment. Most of the preliminaries are removed; and Shakespeare's "Gentry" are absent, although the super senators he calls for are on hand. After a contretemps of only about thirty lines, the tribunes demand Martius's arrest on a charge of treason. One of Thomson's characters, Marcus Minutius, takes Titus Lartius's lines. The plebeians' attempt to have Coriolanus arrested (3.1.180–228) is reduced to a dozen or so staccato exclamations; and after one brief skirmish, "the Tribunes, the Aediles, and the People, are beaten in." Speed and directness are everything; intellectual complexity and rhythmic subtlety count for nothing. Martius's interview with Volumnia (3.2) and the Banishment episode (3.3) are played virtually uncut save for the odd alteration on the grounds of propriety or clarity. The only major change in the latter sequence is Sheridan's use of Coriolanus's "There is a world elsewhere" (3.3.135) as a curtain-line. Shakespeare's finale, which has the citizens swarm around Sicinius with their reiterated "Ho! Hoo!" and "Come"'s, reminiscent of the baying curs Marcius claims they are, vanished in favor of a strong, clean exit for the star. The practice was to become enshrined for a century and a half thereafter.

With Sheridan's act 3, Thomson's text, albeit heavily cut, comes to the fore. Tullus and Volusius await the return of Galesus, and the stranger arrives. The reconciliation between the enemy generals is momentarily vitalized by the incorporation of Shakespeare's 4.5.101–3 and 4.5.106–13, but the bulk of the encounter employs the frigid phrasing of Thomson. Galesus and Coriolanus are reunited as in Thomson's text, but with greater moral terseness. Tullus informs Martius near the end of the act that the senators "With eager joy agreed to my request, / And give thee rule o'er half the Volscian powers" (51). As the curtain falls the pair anticipate the dawn and their departure for Rome. Thomson's scene in which Martius meets the Senate (2.6) is cut.

Act 4 opens with Coriolanus victorious in his first military encounters while Volusius whets Tullus's jealousy of his partner. Thomson's episode in which Roman senators and priests arrive in full state is cut. Instead, with a fine disregard for unity of place, Sheridan, like Dennis, returns to Rome for a sequence which merges parts of Shakespeare's 4.6, 5.1, and 5.4 to limn a terror stricken populace, desperately awaiting the outcome of the matrons' appeal. Sheridan has little appreciation for Shakespeare's cinematic intercutting, and opts for a single, animated sequence to lend dramatic contrast to the lengthy static episodes which precede and follow it.

In the next scene, set in the Volscian camp, Tullus ponders, as in Thomson, the folly of having given Martius half of his command. Immediately after Tullus's soliloquy Volusius announces the approach of the Roman matrons, and Tullus decides that whatever the outcome of the matrons' embassy, Martius must be removed, and by nonviolent means if possible.

The Intercession scene is entirely Thomson's.[9] After the exit of the Roman women Tullus makes his offer of safety to Martius, and the quarrel ensues. The first sixty-nine lines of the altercation are Thomson's, and are subsequently supplemented by Shakespeare's 5.6.90–103 (slightly modified):

> perfidiously
> He has betray'd your business . . .
>
> . . . .
> *Cor.* Measureless liar, thou hast made my heart
> Too great for what contains it. "Boy"? O slave!

The wrangle continues with 5.6.113–116:

> *Cor.* If you have writ your . . .
> . . . Alone I did it. "Boy"!

The assassination sequence follows Thomson. When Coriolanus falls, Galesus arrives with soldiers and friends for a didactic finale. Tullus initiates his response to Galesus's reproach with Shakespeare's "My rage is gone, / And I am struck with sorrow," and continues with the following valediction, penned by Sheridan:

> Tho' he has been our foe,
> Yet as a soldier, brave, unmatch'd in arms,
> With martial pomp, let these his sacred reliques
> Be consecrate to the dread god of war,
> Whose favourite he liv'd. His noble memory,
> His deathless fame remain; but be his faults,
> Be our resentments bury'd with his dust.
>
> (78)

Galesus then moralizes the play in Thomson's fashion, although at somewhat less length, concluding with the unexceptionable:

> Then be this truth the star by which we steer,
> Above our selves our country should be dear.

In all, Sheridan retained 1080 of Shakespeare's 3409 lines, to which he added 784 from Thomson and a further 71 of his own devising.

Although Sheridan claimed his acting edition was designed to preserve the characters of Martius and Volumnia, he found nothing sacrosanct about Shakespeare's portraiture. Like his predecessors, he appreciated the dramatist's ability to vivify a character through a deft touch here and there, but placed a higher value on character consistency and decorum. No more than Dennis and Thomson could he stomach a hero less than ideally heroic. His Martius is in the end as innocent of serious wrongdoing as Thomson's, even if he evinces rather more human frailty than did his antecedents.

Sheridan's Martius enjoys a full measure of patrician pride, reckless independence, and gritty integrity. He asserts as in Shakespeare that he had rather be the patricians' "servant in my way, / Than sway with them in theirs"; he frankly objects to the practice of soliciting the people's voices and remarks that the custom "might well / Be taken from the people." In the Voices scene, he is less cynically contemptuous than in Shakespeare's text, but hardly complaisant either. He opposes popular government in some half-dozen lines in his subsequent confrontation with the tribunes and citizens (3.1.38–41, 155–57), but without the lengthy rationale Shakespeare permits him. His function in the production is, after all, historic and heroic rather than political. In general, we are invited to take him at Menenius's assessment—"His nature is too noble for the world . . . ." (3.1.254–59).

It is his outspoken, inflexible integrity which provokes his opposition to the tribunes, and earns him banishment; and it is his sense of outrage at his country's ingratitude which leads him to the enemy and treason. Ultimately, however, his innate spiritual nobility triumphs. Or as Tullus puts it,

> What'er his rage
> Of passion talks, a weakness for his country
> Sticks in his soul, and he is still a Roman.

And this instinctive patriotism finally costs him his life. Sheridan's Martius is less elegant than Thomson's, more vital and authentic, but entirely bereft of the traits which cost Shakespeare's hero audience sympathy. With 1.1 and the battlefield episodes excised, his vituperative hatred of the citizens and his abusive treatment of the military rank and file disappear. The elimination of his ill-mannered display in the senate (2.2) has been noted earlier. There is no suggestion of his obsessive love-hate relationship with Aufidius, and as a result his desertion to the Volscians loses much of its resonance. Once Coriolanus's actions and reactions have been laundered, clarified, and simplified, the audience is expected to make a straightforward, and favorable, judgment. The multiplicity of viewpoint provided by Shakespeare's cushion-layers (2.2.1–36), tribunes (2.3.176–99), and Aufidius (4.7.19–53) is excised.

In private life Martius is shown to be a good husband, father, and son, although less stress is laid on his domestic persona than by Tate and Dennis. Since 1.1 is omitted, the 1st Citizen does not suggest that his heroic acts were done "to please his mother," but Volumnia's influence is more apparent than in previous versions. On his triumphal return, Veturia (Volumnia) brings forward Volumnia (Virgilia) as in Shakespeare's text. Elsewhere, as indicated below, Martius is subjected to more maternal pressure than in previous adaptations. Again, since the Intercession scene is Thomson's, Martius displays a degree of overt emotion denied him by Shakespeare.

Sheridan retains enough of Thomson's death scene to allow Martius's exit a measure of transcendence. Again he is permitted to redeem his traitorous impulse by the speech:

> The seed of Gods!—'Tis not for thee, vain boaster!
> 'Tis not for such as thou, so often spar'd
> By her victorious sword, to talk of Rome . . .

And once more, as in Thomson, he dies resisting his assassins.

Sheridan's subtitle "OR, THE ROMAN MATRON" says more about Veturia's pivotal importance in the dramatic action than the size of her role; for, although she has more lines than Thomson allows her, and many of them Shakespeare's, she is denied some of her finest Jacobean moments. Few of her lines are cut prior to the Farewell scene (4.1), but several crucial touches disappear. The excised lines in which she expresses her pride in her grandson's preference for swords and a drum rather than his schoolmaster (1.3.55–56) and her grim delight in the butterfly-mammocking (1.3.66) offer essential insights into her upbringing of the elder Martius. Sheridan is also at pains to downplay her antidemocratic views to some degree, even as he ameliorates those of her son.

She regains, however, a good deal of her edge with the restoration of her ghoulish wound-counting (2.1), and her outspoken political advice in 3.2, the fullest recorded version of the episode played to date. Since the Intercession scene is Thomson's, she is obliged to share the honors with Volumnia (Virgilia). Once more she produces a dagger at the strategic moment, offers her life as a national sacrifice, and leaves the stage on Thomson's exit line "He never can be lost, who saves his country." Her poignantly subdued appearance in the Farewell scene (4.1) and the release of her pent-up grief and rage in her subsequent encounter with the tribunes (4.2) remain unplayed.

Virgilia, so delicately etched by Shakespeare in small outbursts, tears, and silence, is now more crudely drawn. With the disappearance of the Valeria episode, she loses the opportunity to defy her mother-in-law. Equally unfortunate was Sheridan's decision to transpose the appearance of Young Martius from the Intercession scene to the Triumphal Return episode, and to have his mother put him forward for the paternal blessing. The integrity of Shakespeare's portraiture is irrevocably compromised, however, in the Intercession scene, when in Thomson's account, she forgoes all claim to silence, and joins Veturia in impassioned rhetoric, highlighted by hand-holding and hysterical weeping.

Sheridan's Tullus, like his Virgilia, is more Thomson's creature than

Shakespeare's. Although he is referred to several times in the first part of the play, he does not appear until Coriolanus arrives in Antium. Thereafter he is a constant presence. As in Thomson's version, despite the retention of some Shakespearian lines, Tullus shows himself a noble soul inflexibly dedicated to the national interest, which Martius, at his family's insistence, betrays. He is not faultless; jealousy is an ever present companion; yet he manages to maintain a firmer hold on disinterested principle, despite his moments of unworthy impulse, than does his vengeance-seeking partner. Once more, as in Thomson's drama, he *"stands, without drawing"* as Volusius and the rest attack, and speaks the curious eulogy cited earlier. Galesus promises vengeance for Martius's death, but there is no indication that Tullus will individually be called to account. Sheridan's transformation of Aufidius into a less ambiguous figure, and a more aesthetically satisfying foil to Martius, was but another in a perennial series of attempts to stabilize the role and thus the audience's reaction to it.

Menenius receives somewhat more importance than Dennis gave him, but his political function is largely nullified with the excision of the belly fable. Nevertheless he is allowed his fine banter with the tribunes in 2.1 and his admitted fondness for the good life; his ecstatic welcome of Martius from the wars is also restored, together with his futile efforts to teach his protégé diplomacy. His exchanges with the tribunes and plebeians in the Banishment scene and afterwards make a welcome return, if in abbreviated form. Unfortunately his embassy to Martius with its understated nobility and pathos is cut.

Sheridan's subordination of the play's politics to a celebration of heroic individualism demanded a radical lowering of the plebeians' profile. With the disappearance of 1.1, in which the citizens critique the power structure and advance their own alternatives, they become merely the passive and inarticulate tools of the tribunes. Thanks to the cuts in the Voices scene noted earlier, they dwindle into little more than the good-natured targets of Martius's disdain. In the clashes between the tribunes and patricians in act 3, they merely mill about and offer the odd exclamation. On Martius's "There is a world elsewhere," they promptly *"shout, throw up their caps, and exeunt."* In the wake of recent popular protests against calendar reform (1751), the Gin Act (1752), and the Jew Naturalisation Bill (1753), Sheridan may have judged it unwise to further highlight the disruptive potential of the lower orders. On their final appearance, in Sheridan's conflation of 4.6, 5.1, and 5.4, the citizens are more flatteringly portrayed than in Shakespeare. They do not obsequiously laud the tribunes, and although they are understandably fearful of Martius's approach, they decisively opt to expiate their past errors by throwing the tribunes from the Tarpeian rock. Milder souls than the citizens of Tate and Dennis, however, they agree to suspend their anger until the results of the matrons' suit is known. All in all, the underclass is neutrally treated: they are allowed no political status, but neither are they held up to ridicule in the manner of Dennis. They are purely functional devices, nothing more. Since their presence is no longer political, token numbers suffice: a mere half-dozen seem to have been employed to judge from the cast lists.

As in previous adaptations, the blame for Martius's defection belongs exclusively to Sicinius and Brutus, depicted as unredeemed knaves rather than the seasoned wardheelers of Shakespeare's contriving. The cutting of 1.1 eliminates their bumbling attempts to understand the patrician mind. Their strategic intervention in the Senate scene beginning "We are convented / Upon a pleasing treaty" (2.2.54–60) also disappears, to say nothing of their perceptive rehearsal of tactics after the Voices scene. Sicinius's canny advice to Martius—"If you will pass / To where you are bound, you must inquire your way, / Which you are out of, with a gentler spirit" (3.1.53–55)—is removed, as are a number of their equally apt assessments of Martius's fitness for consul. Their role in the Banishment sequence requires them only to provoke Martius, allow him to fulminate briefly, and then accuse him of treason. With the excision of 4.2, they miss Volumnia's tongue-lashing, and appear only once more—to receive their comeuppance from the citizens on Martius's approach to Rome.

Sheridan's text, then, is an example of Shakespeare methodized, not so much in the interests of overt propaganda as inspirational art. Psychological and political texture is ruthlessly sacrificed to create an epic figure of superlative heroism, integrity, and frankness who, unjustly exiled by tribunitian ambition, commits treason through wounded pride and atones for his error when instinctive patriotic sentiment is awakened by the pleas of his family. The action is clean, severe, and unified, although more animated than in previous versions. Poetic justice is finally meted out to the hero, if not to Tullus or the tribunes. The audience makes its way homeward in a mood of spiritual transcendence, social reassurance, and moral elevation.

STAGECRAFT

As an active member of the London and Dublin artistic and intellectual communities, Sheridan was alert to the public taste for historic spectacle; and as a classical scholar, he was thoroughly familiar with Roman culture and the latest archeological research. His staging, an amalgam of Thomson's innovations and his own, was no doubt executed with the careful attention to antiquarian and artistic detail for which he was famous,[10] but its quality and accuracy were inevitably limited by the scholarship available and the resources of the theater.

Since Sheridan's drama is not nearly as sensitive to unity of place as Thomson's, the audience was treated to more frequent scene changes. Shutter indications include "Coriolanus's House," "Senate-House," "The Forum," and "The Volscian Camp." Martius makes his treasonous pact, as in Thomson's version, not in Shakespeare's Antium, but in the Volscian camp.

Sheridan shares Thomson's fondness for the discovery, and appropriates several of his pictures. On Martius's first appearance in the Volscian camp, he is once again revealed, sitting "majestic . . . in solemn silence" beneath Tullus's lares. The action takes place, appropriately enough, in a military tent: a stage direction in Sheridan's 1757 acting edition calls for "Tent, Table, Stool, Lares, &c." (34).

The by now traditional procession of Roman women is once more a feature. The direction reads "SCENE *a Camp with* Volscian *Soldiers, as before. Enter* CORIOLANUS, TULLUS, GALESUS, VOLUSIUS. *The* Roman *Ladies advance slowly, with* VETURIA *and* VOLUMNIA, *all clad in mourning.*" Presumably the women pass between diagonal files of military as in the Thomson/Quin staging. "CORIOLANUS," we are told, "*sits on his tribunal; but seeing them, advances, and goes hastily to embrace his mother,*" ordering as he does so, "Lower your fasces, Lictors" (65).

Again, as in Thomson's version, the final scene is staged as a formal tableau. After Coriolanus falls, "*Enter* GALESUS, *the Volscian states, officers and friends of* CORIOLANUS, *and* TITUS, *with a large band of soldiers, &c.*" (77). With friends and foes picturesquely grouped around the body, Tullus speaks his eulogy.

The visual novelty of Sheridan's production was a lavish procession to mark Coriolanus's triumphal return. This "*Roman* Ovation" Sheridan described to his archaeologically curious audience as "a lesser sort of triumph":

It had its name from *ovis,* a sheep, which was sacrificed on this occasion, instead of a bull, used in the great triumph. The ovation was granted upon any extraordinary success against the enemy. . . . But a triumph was never obtained, unless a kingdom was entirely subdued, and added to the *Roman* territories.[11]

He went on to explain that in an ovation "all marched on foot, but in the triumph the victor was carried in a chariot drawn by horses, and followed by horsemen." Even had a triumph been appropriate to Martius's achievement, the "representation of the latter" would have been "impracticable" on the Covent Garden stage.

As it was, no antiquarian or spectacle lover had cause for complaint. Veturia's "These are the ushers of Martius: before him he carries noise, and behind him he leaves tears" (2.1.158–59), instead of heralding Coriolanus's arrival, served merely as an exit cue for herself and her party. Not long afterwards they were back, as part of a civil procession, to begin a fresh scene. The civil parade, which clearly owed something to Thomson's senatorial procession, featured "Priests, Flamens, Choiristers, Senators, Tribunes, Virgins, Matrons, and the Mother, Wife, and Child of *Coriolanus.* These walked to the sound of flutes and soft instruments, and lined the way to behold the military entry, and congratulate the victor."[12] For Volumnia and her companions to enter formally in procession, it goes without saying, is not at all the same thing as to be overtaken naturalistically by Coriolanus while *en route* to meet him. With the religious and civil elements artistically disposed about the stage, the military entered to the sound of drums, fifes, and trumpets. Highlights of the procession were "Four [Soldiers] carrying a Bier with Gold and Silver Vases, Part of the Spoil," "Four [Soldiers] carrying another Bier with a large Urn and Four Vases," "Four [Soldiers] carrying a Bier loaden with Trophies, Armour, Ensigns, &c. taken from the Enemy," "Five Souldiers with mural and civick Crowns," and "Four Captive Generals in Chains." Also included were lictors, incense-bearers, standard-bearers, musicians, and miscellaneous groups of troops. "In the military Procession alone, independent of the Civil," Sheridan tells us, "there were an hundred and eighteen persons." Unlike Shakespeare's plan, in which Coriolanus enters almost immediately and takes up a position between his fellow generals, Sheridan has the hero arrive almost at the end of the parade, following two consuls and followed in turn by standard-bearers and soldiers. Coriolanus's "No more of this," must have rung somewhat hollowly after his willing participation in pageantry on such a scale. Sheridan's ovation, which at once glamorized Martius, mitigated the play's visual chill, and titillated antiquarians and spectacle-lovers, was destined to become a production fixture.

Performance time was one hour and forty-one minutes, excluding about a half hour of entr'acte music.[13]

THE ACTORS

Sheridan was not an ideal Coriolanus, but less criticized in this role than in many others. Although not of heroic bulk, he surprised at least one spectator by his skill "in making his Person appear of that athletick Proportion, and giving that Ferocity to his Countenance which so remarkably distinguishes that Character."[14] His costume struck the same theatergoer as "one of the most finish'd Things I ever saw, and gave me a much stronger Idea of an old Roman Warrior, than ever I had got from Books, Pictures, or Statues."[15] A contemporary recalls him in the role of Cato, in which he wore "bright armour under a fine laced scarlet cloak, and surmounted by a huge, white, bushy, well-powdered wig (like Dr. Johnson's), over which was stuck his helmet";[16] and he probably looked not much different as Martius. Most critics, if they could not judge his interpretation brilliant, praised his conscientious craftsmanship and sensible reading. Tate Wilkinson felt he "conveyed a masterly knowledge of the character";[17] and if his action tended to be somewhat "solemn, stiff, and confined," or his voice "unequal, harsh,

Thomas Sheridan as Coriolanus, ca. 1755. [Author's collection]

and discordant,"[18] these deficiencies were less marked in the unpolished
Martius than in some less rugged soul.

Peg Woffington, at thirty-five, was again a satisfactory Veturia, one gath-
ers, but no record of her performance has come to light. Lacy Ryan, who
had played Tullus in the premiere of Thomson's drama, returned to the

part. Volumnia was again played by the beautiful George Ann Bellamy and Menenius by Ned Shuter.

Critical reaction to the production was mixed. Paul Hiffernan derided the venture as "*Shakespear,* put into his Night-Gown by *Messire* Thomson; and humm'd to Sleep by *Don Torpedo* [Sheridan] infamous for the *Mezentian Art* of joining the *Dead* to the *Living.*"[19] The *Monthly Review* (January, 1755) critic was harsher still. Sheridan, the writer contended, "has joined *Shakespear* and *Thomson* as awkwardly together, as if a man should tack, to the body of one picture, the limbs of another, without considering what an uncouth figure they might make together." A correspondent of the *Public Advertiser* (13 December 1754), on the other hand, thought the alteration had been made "with great Art":

> The gross Absurdities of Shakespear in Point of Time and Place, have in a great Measure been amended; those Scenes, which in their own Nature are improper for Representation, have been judiciously omitted: At the same Time, all the fine Passages and Incidents, have been preserv'd, which serve to mark strongly the two Characters of Coriolanus and Veturia . . . [W]hether it was owing to the Skill of the Performers or whether Thompson [sic] having Shakespear in View, was inspired with an unusual Warmth of Imagination, the Characters appeared supported throughout with the same Fire, and seem'd to be of a Piece.

Playgoers apparently seconded the opinion of the *Public Advertiser* contributor. Apart from Garrick's production (see below), all London revivals until Kemble's time (1757–58, 1758–59, 1759–60, 1764–65, 1767–68) employed Sheridan's adaptation.

The only other actor besides Sheridan to play the role in Covent Garden revivals prior to Kemble's performances (see Chronological Handlist) was William "Gentleman" Smith, an actor best known for his performance of men of fashion. According to one witness, he cut a very martial figure on his triumphal entry "to the tune of violins and hautboys." With his complexion darkened by the aid of burnt cork and wearing "a real coat of mail,"[20] he was a far more convincing warrior than Sheridan. Thomas Wilkes found his figure "very pleasing" and his performance "very tolerable."[21] His speaking, however, was somewhat monotonous, and further marred by "keeping too much at the top of his voice."[22] He was partnered by the Veturias of Esther Hamilton and George Ann Bellamy. Mrs. Hamilton was particularly well received. Her speaking of the line "He never can be lost who saves his country" was the highlight of her performance, according to the *London Chronicle* (7–9 November 1758).

GARRICK'S REVIVAL AT DRURY LANE (1754)

When Thomson first approached Garrick with the script of his *Coriolanus,* the actor-manager was keen to mount a revival, but rapidly lost his enthusiasm when asked to yield the title role to Quin. The premiere of Thomson's piece at the rival house, with Quin in the "lead," apparently tempted Garrick to revive Shakespeare's text with himself as the doughty hero. On 17 August 1751 he wrote Somerset Draper from Londesbrough, "I am working and studying here like a horse.—I intend playing *Coriolanus* and the *Rehearsal,* alternately."[23] The idea came to nothing, however, perhaps because, as Thomas Davies suggests, "he would never willingly put on the Roman habit."[24] The announcement in the autumn of 1754 of Rich's intention to stage Sheridan's adaptation at Covent Garden "with infinite pomp and splendour . . . struck terror to the whole host of Drury," according to Wilkinson. "Eager to get the start of the rival theatre,"[25] Garrick announced a revival of *Coriolanus* as written by Shakespeare for 11 November 1754, a month before Sheridan's piece was scheduled. Garrick's experiment marks the first time in more than thirty years that *Coriolanus*'s unadulterated text had been mounted. Bell's edition of 1774, with notes by Francis Gentleman, is clearly taken from the Drury Lane promptbook for this production. The script is very carefully prepared and, although lines and words are cut and altered in the interests of propriety, clarity, and simplicity of syntax, a sensitive hand is at work throughout. In all about a thousand lines are cut, not many more than in most twentieth-century productions; and a surprising number of the passages edited are those which trouble modern directors.

In act 1, the battlefield action is cut (1.4, 5, 6, 7, and 8) to accelerate and clarify the narrative. Aufidius is not permitted to appear with the Volscian senators (1.2), to fight with Martius (1.8), or to soliloquize (1.10). Act 1 consists only of the plebeians' encounter with Menenius and Martius (1.1) and the episode in Martius's house (1.3). The action of act 1, then, is confined to Rome, preserving unity of place and substantially reducing the need for scene shifts.

Act 2 opens with the only battlefield sequence Garrick preserves, the episode in which Martius receives his title (1.9). The only significant excision is the sequence in which the officers lay cushions in the Capitol (2.2.1–36), removed to accelerate the action. A number of speeches are curtailed, particularly the tribunes' reproaches to the plebeians in 2.3, but the sense is preserved throughout.

Act 3 follows Shakespeare's design in the main, with several noteworthy adjustments.The brawl between the patricians and aediles disappears, together with the exchanges of Brutus and Menenius (3.1.213–21, 224–28). Martius simply draws his sword, threatens to "die here," and the citizens exit. The ensuing patrician discussion is made a separate scene, as is the negotiation between the patricians and tribunes after Martius's departure, but there is no indication of a change of locale. The episode in which Volumnia persuades her recalcitrant son to return to the plebeians is lightly cut and amended on the grounds of clarity and propriety. Volumnia and Martius enter together at the start of the scene, in contradistinction to Shakespeare who has them enter separately, and the scene ends with Volumnia's "Do your will" (3.2.137). The "mildly" dialogue between Martius and Menenius vanishes. The Banishment episode (3.3) omits most of the tribunes' strategy session prior to Martius's arrival and begins with Brutus's "Put him to choler straight" (3.3.25). A number of speeches are subjected to internal cuts, but on the whole the scene substantially resembles its original. Interestingly enough, however, it concludes in the Sheridan manner on Martius's "There is a world elsewhere," at which the "people shout, and throw up their caps." In act 4 the Farewell scene (4.1) and Volumnia's slanging match with the tribunes (4.2) are played virtually in their entirety; but the Adrian-Nicanor episode (4.3) is once more cut. Martius's oblique and suggestive soliloquy on his arrival in Antium (4.4) is pellucidly rewritten:

> O world, thy slippery turns!
> My birthplace have I and my lovers left;
> This enemy's house I'll enter; if he slay me
> He does fair justice; if he give me way,
> I'll do his country service.

His encounter with Aufidius's servants (4.5) is abbreviated, and the comic episode in which the three servingmen compare the generals (4.5.148–235) is dispatched. In 4.6, where the tribunes and citizens fearfully await the Volscian invasion, the citizens' entry is made to mark the beginning of a new scene, a change doubtless editorial rather than theatrical since no alteration of setting is indicated or required. Significantly Aufidius's observation that "our virtues / Lie in th'interpretation of the time . . ." (4.7.49–55) is removed: ethical certainties were demanded of residents of the antique world.

Cominius's report of his petitionary visit (5.1) is played virtually uncut and Menenius's embassy (5.2) is tastefully abbreviated by some fifty lines. To allow him to exit with a flourish on "I say to you, as I was said to, Away!", the last lines of the scene are cut. The Intercession sequence (5.3) is shortened by about thirty lines, mostly to secure simplicity and directness of speech. Young Martius is present but not permitted to interject. Curiously enough, the scene's concluding lines, "Ladies, you deserve to have a temple built you . . ." (5.3.206–9), meant to be spoken by Martius, are reallocated to Aufidius. In order to secure the exit line for the star, Coriolanus's "Come enter with us" (5.3.206) is transposed to the end of the scene. The arrival in Rome of the news of Volumnia's success (5.4) is played uncut, but her provocative stage cross (5.5) is excised. The assassination sequence is somewhat altered. Coriolanus enters not to the beat of a drum and accompanied by commoners, but alone and in silence. Since the Volscian people are absent, their lines are removed. Martius dies as Shakespeare designed, but Aufidius's disrespectful treatment of Martius's body and the Lord's reproach are cut. The Second Lord's jaded observation, "His own impatience / Takes from Aufidius a great part of the blame. / Let's make the best of it" (5.6.144–46) also disappears.

Very few of Garrick's cuts may be attributed to the eighteenth-century obsession with character consistency. In the main, Shakespeare's figures disport themselves in their pristine ambiguity, inconsistency, and even ugliness. Martius, as one might expect, is subjected to more pruning than others. Somewhat inexplicably he is robbed of two of the rare moments of self-communion Shakespeare gives him: his aside in the Voices scene beginning "Why in this wolfish toge should I stand here . . ." (2.3.115–24) and his brief exclamation in the Intercession scene, "Like a dull actor now / I have forgot my part . . ." (5.3.40–42). More understandably, several of his excessively uncouth moments vanish, including his cynically mocking "For your voices I have fought . . ." (2.3.126–30). His well-deserved rebuke from Sicinius, "You show too much of that / For which the people stir" (3.1.52–57), is also cut; and Aufidius's unsubstantiated allegation that Martius flattered and seduced his friends (5.6.20–30) is removed. A more crucial cut, and one made before and since Garrick, is Martius's fluent and rational, if impassioned, attack on plebeian suffrage (3.1.90–112, 119–161). Here he reveals himself as more than an inarticulate military man and victim of maternal prejudice: he is clearly capable of staking out an intellectual position and sustaining it with grace and conviction when his precarious self-image is not threatened. But, these deletions aside, Martius remains the brash bully, the antidemocrat, the mother-dominated boy of Shakespeare's creation. Volumnia is allowed all of her warlike mania, her driving ambition, and her manipulative wiles; she is not, however, permitted to kneel to her son at the beginning of the Intercession scene (5.3.52–62), perhaps because it might preempt her "Down, ladies; let us shame him with our knees" (5.3.169) which marks the climax of the episode. Virgilia and Menenius are left virtually untouched. Aufidius, denied three of the appearances Shakespeare gives him, is a much diminished figure, hardly more than a plot device.

Stage directions call for "*a Street in* Rome," "*the* Forum," "*the house of* Coriolanus," "*the Gates of* Rome," "*a hall in* Aufidius's *house,*" "*a camp, at a small distance from* Rome," and "*a wood*" (in which the battlefield scene in 2.1 was staged), but no evidence of the nature or quality of the settings survives. Advertisements for the production make no claim to new, or archaeologically accurate, shutters.

Wilkinson claims that the revival was mounted at considerable expense; and if he is correct, one must assume that most of the expenditure was directed to costumes and supers. Some sort of procession seems to have marked Coriolanus's return to Rome after the defeat of the Volscians: newspaper advertisements promise, with a fine disdain for Sheridan's historical research, that "In Act II. will be introduced the Representation of a ROMAN

TRIUMPH" (*Public Advertiser,* 13 November 1754). No mention is made
of the spectacular procession of matrons which traditionally introduced the
Intercession scene. The stage direction suggests a simpler entry, but in the
usual black weeds—"*Enter* Virgilia, Volumnia, Valeria, *young* Martius *with
attendants, all in mourning.*" Eye-catching wardrobe was to be a primary
attraction elsewhere in the production; advertisements stressed daily that
"the Characters [were] new dress'd" (*Public Advertiser,* 15 November 1754).
Music was introduced at every opportunity. A march accompanies the exit
from the battlefield at the conclusion of 1.9, and "A grand march" concludes
the Roman Triumph (2.1); another march marks the entry of Coriolanus and
Aufidius in 5.3, and Aufidius's arrival in 5.6. Supers appear to have been
used liberally, and kept in action as a kind of living scenery. In contrast
to the nightgowned *Coriolanus* of Sheridan, Hiffernan thought Garrick's
production "the most mobbing, huzzaing, shewy, boasting, drumming,
fighting, trumpeting Tragedy I ever saw."[26]

Garrick's visual effects, unlike those of Sheridan and Rich, attracted little
attention. The acting, however, since Garrick's company was stronger than
that of the rival house, elicited almost universal praise. In the end, Garrick
did not appear as Martius, a wise decision since he was physically too small
for the role. Instead, the part was taken by the Irish actor Henry Mossop,
who achieved an instant success. Mossop's figure, "rising above the middle
size," we are told, "was in just symmetry and proportion";[27] and to judge
from a surviving engraving of him in the role, he seems to have been an
impressive figure, even without the traditional peruke affected by Sheridan.
Although he was, in Davies's opinion, "utterly void of grace in deportment,
and dignity in action,"[28] he disguised this defect by specializing in parts
calling for rough militarism, vehemence, and rage. His voice was described
as "manly, strong, and of great compass . . . harmonious from the lowest
note to the highest elevation."[29] As Coriolanus, John O'Keeffe recalls, "his
port was majestic and commanding; his voice strong and articulate, and
audible in a whisper . . . his excellencies were the expression of anger and
disdain; in the former terrific."[30] Robert Hitchcock felt that "all the stern
fierceness of the proud, haughty, unrelenting Roman was admirably adapted
to his powers," and rated his performance in the last act "uncommonly
fine."[31] When the Coriolanuses of Sheridan and Mossop were compared,
Hiffernan reports, "the Generality of Spectators [declare] in Behalf of the
young Warrior."[32]

Mossop was companioned by Hannah Pritchard, whose merit, according
to Hester Thrale, "overbore the want of Figure." Her "Intelligence pervaded
every Sense," Mrs. Thrale continues, and her Volumnia was the "loftiest
Roman matron that Shakespear could conceive."[33] Wilkinson nevertheless
thought her "tiresomely blubbering" in the Intercession scene.[34] Edward
Berry, who specialized in playing old men, seems to have been a satisfactory
Menenius, and the Virgilia of Susannah Davies and the Aufidius of William

Henry Mossop as Coriolanus, ca. 1754. [By permission of the Theatre Museum, Victoria and Albert Museum]

Havard, whose line was "remorseless tyrants, savage conquerors, and state villains,"[35] evoked no adverse comment. According to one critic, "the characters were finely cast, and the whole action performed with the greatest applause" (*The Entertainer*, 12 November 1754).

The production ran for eight nights on its initial appearance, and was revived on 22 April 1755 for the benefit of the Ballet-Master. Thereafter Garrick's script was performed no more. Perhaps once the Covent Garden revival had been satisfactorily upstaged, Garrick saw no reason to star Mossop in a role likely to add to his reputation as the country's third leading actor. Or, more probably, Shakespeare's maneristic artistry, no matter how well interpreted, was unsympathetic to neoclassical tastes. In any event,

Sheridan's spectacular adaptation reigned supreme thereafter; and audiences were to wait for close to three-quarters of a century before they again witnessed Shakespeare's unadulterated text.

JOHN PHILIP KEMBLE (1789–1817)

John Philip Kemble, London's premier actor-manager for some three decades, is the most influential figure in *Coriolanus*'s stage history. He singlehandedly canonized the text played in the theater for a century after his death on both sides of the Atlantic; he created the visual tradition which, with minor variations, accompanied the play until World War I; and in the title role he gave birth to a conception which became the stuff of theatrical legend.[36]

While acting manager at Drury Lane under Richard Brinsley Sheridan's proprietorship, Kemble staged his first *Coriolanus* on 7 February 1789 and repeated it six times in the first season. He played it twice in the 1791–92 and 1792–93 seasons, once in the 1795–96 season, and twice in the 1796–97 season. The production was then withdrawn for nine years, Elizabeth Inchbald tells us, "for some reasons of state."[37] With General Bonaparte momentarily threatening an invasion of England, ruthless impressment of workingmen into military service until twenty percent of the adult male population was under arms, the Irish Rebellion (1798), a succession of bad harvests leading to food riots in 1800, to say nothing of intensifying punitive taxation, the English theater audience, particularly the working class portion of it, needed no reminder of the parallels between their own plight and that of Martian Rome or of the historic solution adopted.[38] "When the lower order of people are in good plight," placidly observes Mrs. Inchbald, "they will bear contempt with cheerfulness, and even with mirth; but poverty puts them out of humour at the slightest disrespect. Certain sentences in this play are, therefore, of dangerous tendency at certain times."[39] Nelson's victory at Trafalgar in 1805 dissipated the longstanding threat of a French invasion of England, and fostered a somewhat greater sense of social stability. With Grenville's "Ministry of all the Talents" in control at Westminster and himself in sole charge at Covent Garden, Kemble ventured a grand revival of *Coriolanus* in the 1806–7 season and played it to enraptured audiences some fifteen times, and a further three times the next season. Less than a year later, settings, costumes, and promptbooks were destroyed in the Covent Garden conflagration. In 1811 he launched a splendid revival in his newly built playhouse to mark Mrs. Siddons's valedictory performances, during which the play was offered on nine occasions; and from 1814 onwards he revived the piece annually until his retirement in 1817, when he chose it as the vehicle for his farewell appearance. In all performances until her retirement in 1811, he was partnered by the enormously popular Volumnia of

Siddons. After 1811, he was companioned by a series of inadequate matrons, and his Coriolanus became largely a solo recital.

Educated at Douay, Kemble was thoroughly conversant with the classics, knowledgeable about art, and a friend of scholars and artists. Like many of his contemporaries, he was profoundly convinced that England's international supremacy derived not from her military and economic achievements, but from her moral qualities; and that moral standards might best be maintained and strengthened through the civilizing power of the arts. For him Winckelmann's conviction that "[t]he only way for us [moderns] to become great or, if this be possible, inimitable, is to imitate the ancients"[40] was nothing less than an article of faith. As the son of a provincial actor-manager, however, Kemble's aesthetic idealism was tempered by a hardheaded approach to business and a thoroughgoing familiarity with the nuts and bolts of stage tradition and contemporary practice. While acting manager at Drury Lane (1788–1802) under R. B. Sheridan, son of Thomas, he sought to convince his financially inept employer that "it was a waste of time and money" to lavish the theater's resources on ephemeral pieces when "a grand and permanent attraction might be given to Drury Lane by encreasing the power of Shakespeare."[41] But it was only with his assumption of the Covent Garden management and a one-sixth share of the patent that he found himself completely free to stage Shakespeare as he saw fit. From 1804 to his retirement in 1817, one glittering, influential, and profitable revival followed another. And *Coriolanus* was one of his greatest successes.

Kemble, like the elder Sheridan, had little interest in making the play serve the interests of any specific political party, but shared the Dublin manager's reactionary stance together with his predilection for neoclassical aesthetics; and, thanks to three decades of advances in archeology and art theory and criticism, complemented by the example of a host of painters and sculptors engaged in ever stricter application of neoclassical principles, he was able to realize his artistic conceptions more fully than his pioneering predecessor.[42]

Kemble's conception of Shakespeare production, and of *Coriolanus* in particular, owed much to contemporary art theory and its emphasis on the classical ideal.[43] For him, however, imitation of the antique did not mean copying: rather it implied a rigorous distillation of the quintessence of the antique experience. It is not the task of the artist, Kemble's close friend Sir Joshua Reynolds argued in his discourses to the Royal Academy, "to amuse mankind with the minute neatness of his imitations" of nature as she is, but "to improve them by the grandeur of his ideas." The true artist must carefully "distinguish the accidental deficiencies, and deformities of things, from their general figures" and so depict an "abstract idea of their forms more perfect than any one original."[44] Likewise, the recreator of the classic world, whether painter, sculptor, or actor-manager, must aspire to a synthesis of timeless perfection by combining the best of inspiration from a wealth of classic art and archaeological artifacts. Works of real genius, as distinct from the products of mere artistic competence and good taste, might be expected to evoke the aesthetic experience described by Edmund Burke as "the sublime": a response to objects whose properties seemed repellent, "such as excessive size, darkness or infinite extension,"[45] characterized by transcendence, mystery, and exultation. Giovanni Battista Piranesi's engraved views of Roman monuments, in which proportions were exaggerated to provide an overpowering and cathartic sense of grandeur, were judged prototypical.

As early as the 1760s Gavin Hamilton and Anton Raphael Mengs popularized vast, solemn, static treatments of classical subjects animated by "high-minded and instructive themes of an austere and stoic morality."[46] In the later years of the century, however, the neoclassical ideal was realized most fully by Jean-Louis David's grand and rigorously controlled treatment of neo-Stoic subjects such as *The Oath of the Horatii* (1784–85) or *Brutus* (1789), or *The Intervention of the Sabine Women* (1799).[47]

Kemble's revivals of *Coriolanus* are virtual stage equivalents of the paintings of David. He saw in Coriolanus the kind of severe, antique hero of ancient times who would provide, like David's classic subjects, a moral example in an era of political and social upheaval. Shakespeare's narrative had, however, to be given a beau ideal shape, to have what Reynolds called its "excrescences" pared away to reveal a purer, simpler, and more elevated design than either Plutarch's original or Shakespeare's recreation. Idealized action, grandly and severely heightened through art and craft, was intended to awaken in the theatergoer a sense of the sublime, a kind of cathartic awe at the exploits of the heroes of old. Art must, in the words of David, "make the soul of the spectator vibrate."[48]

A sine qua non of Kemble's art, as for the antiquarian painters and sculptors of the period, was research; and his starting point was the text. It was not Kemble's "notion of the business," Boaden tells us, to order the prompter "to write out the parts from some old mutilated copy lingering on his shelves," but "to consider it attentively in the author's genuine book."[49] That Kemble consulted Shakespearian quartos or folios is highly unlikely; he did, however, familiarize himself with readily available editions, and supplemented his findings with advice from the textual critics Steevens, Malone, and Reed, which he as often as not ignored. Having established what he considered to be a sound text, he then proceeded to carve it into a beau ideal shape.

His enthusiasm for historical research matched his concern for textual investigation. All too often, he argued, traditional Shakespearian stagecraft had made "too many and too considerable demands . . . upon the imagination of the spectator, 'to piece out with their thoughts' the imperfections of the stage. He saw no reason why the representation in the seeming magnificence of the action could yield to the reality; and that it should be *true* as well as splendid."[50] To the achievement of correctness and artistic excellence in decor, he felt that "the prevailing studies of the times" had much to contribute. He utilized the innovations of the pantomime designers and avidly followed the work of contemporary artists and antiquaries, but treated their insights as cavalierly as he did editors' counsel. For the implementation of his scenographic vision, Kemble employed the best craftspeople available and supervised them meticulously.

Kemble's painted backgrounds owed much of their effect to his living scenery—massive processions and statuesque groupings of supernumeraries roughly comparable in function to drapery in beau ideal paintings. Costumes, based on antiquarian scholarship, were relatively accurate, colors were simple and subdued, movement was kept to a minimum, and groupings were arranged according to the sculptural principles enunciated by Reynolds. Where Sheridan employed supernumeraries purely as spectacle, Kemble made them a compositional feature.

If the performer was not to be overwhelmed by the mise-en-scène, acting style must be comparably heightened. Scenic grandeur demanded a histrionic grandeur in which "everything should be raised and enlarged beyond its natural state; that the full effect may come home to the spectator, which otherwise would be lost in the comparatively extensive space of the theatre."[51] The expansion in the capacity of playhouses from about two thousand in Garrick's Drury Lane to some four thousand in Kemble's new Covent Garden (1809) rendered a heightened performance style not only aesthetically desirable but pragmatically essential. With the best models of classic art before them, Kemble and Mrs. Siddons cultivated what became known as "the grand style," characterized by a deliberate and majestic step, a statuesque grace of action, and formal, stately declamation.

TEXT

The results of Kemble's textual research were made available to the public in the form of acting texts, usually, but not exclusively, issued just prior to a revival. Jaggard lists *Coriolanus* editions in 1789, 1800, 1801, 1806, 1812, and 1814.[52] Subsequent acting versions conform closely to the 1789 script, with minor changes in the 1812 and 1814 editions.[53] Three promptbooks are extant: the official promptbook, now in the Folger Shakespeare Library (*Cor* 2), a similar book in the Garrick Club Library (*Cor* 3), and the Wister copy, also in the Folger Shakespeare Library.[54] All three represent the production as it stood in the 1811 season, probably the revival which best represented Kemble's intentions. Earlier books were destroyed in the disastrous fires at Covent Garden and Drury Lane in 1808 and 1809 respectively. My reconstruction is based on the official promptbook, although all three manuscripts have been consulted.

Kemble's acting text, far from being "the author's genuine book," is a modified version of Sheridan's acting editions of 1755 and 1757 with further Shakespearian lines restored, some Thomsonian material deleted, and a few managerial lines added. Unchanged, however, is Sheridan's depoliticized action. Shakespeare's complex exploration of alienated individual and collective experience becomes simply a high-minded chronicle of a national idol who suffers banishment for his principles, commits treason out of wounded pride, and is redeemed by the radiant grandeur of his mother's patriotism.

Kemble's act 1 restores 1.1, cut by Sheridan, but excludes the crucial belly fable (1.1.50–162). Kemble had no more enthusiasm for politics than his predecessor, but he could not forgo the opportunity for Martius to strut at the earliest possible moment. The citizens consequently engage in abbreviated conversation until Martius and Menenius enter together on Martius's "What's the matter, you dissentious rogues?" (1.1.164). The antagonism between Martius and the plebeians is apparent, but Kemble's cuts make the antipathy seem more personal than political. Kemble follows Sheridan in removing 1.2, the colloquy between Aufidius and the Volscian senators, and five of the seven battlefield episodes (1.4, 1.5, 1.7, 1.8, 1.10). Act 1 consists of the contretemps with the citizens, the scene featuring Volumnia and Virgilia, who enjoy the names with which Shakespeare christened them, and two battlefield scenes—Shakespeare's 1.6, in which Martius rallies Cominius's troops, and 1.9, in which his military achievements are honored. In this first act, rigorously pruned, Martius's relationship to the plebeians, his family, and his military confreres is highlighted.

Kemble's act 2 opens, as does Shakespeare's, with the exchange between Menenius and the tribunes (Sheridan's 1.3), followed by the entrance of Volumnia and Virgilia with the news of Martius's approach. As in Sheridan's text, Volumnia and her party exit at the sound of trumpets announcing Martius's revival, to return a few moments later marching in the procession. Just prior to the trumpet cue, Volumnia launches into a verbal fanfare comprising lines from Cominius's senate eulogy and several of Kemble's own devising:

> Where'er he went, before him fortune flew,
> While victory upon his dreaded brow
> Sat thron'd, and joyful clapp'd her silver wings:—
> Three times mine eagle singled out Aufidius,
> And thrice the Volscian sunk beneath his thunder,
> Bending the knee, as 't were in adoration.

Kemble follows Sheridan in making separate scenes of the Ovation episode and the ensuing, but more heavily cut, sequence in which the tribunes voice their concern about Martius's future influence (2.1.204–70).

The Senate scene, Kemble's 2.4, is played much as in Sheridan's version, except that Coriolanus is onstage from the beginning, and is permitted his ungracious Shakespearian departure. Cominius's panegyric is somewhat abridged, and the scene ends, unlike Sheridan's version, with a flourish of trumpets as Cominius proclaims "To Coriolanus come all joy and honour!" The cynical observations of Brutus and Sicinius are removed to permit Martius a stylish exit.

The Voices scene, Kemble's 2.5, apart from the addition or subtraction of the odd line or two, and some curtailment of the citizens' comic exchanges at the beginning of the sequence, is played in the text of Sheridan's 1757 acting edition. In order to obtain a stronger curtain, however, Kemble departs from Sheridan by ending the scene with Brutus's order, "Repair to the capitol" and the citizens' enthusiastic "We will; we will." The tribunes' subsequent strategizing disappears.

Kemble's act 3 (Sheridan's act 2) again follows Sheridan's 1757 text, but with even heavier abridgement of Shakespeare. Some two hundred lines, approximately seventy-five more than Sheridan excised, are removed to accelerate the action and to render it grander and less restless. Like neoclassic painters, Kemble and, to a lesser degree, Sheridan, favored single, strong movements without fussy detail. Again, as in Sheridan's adaptation, Coriolanus's justification of his political position is cut, leaving his attitude toward the plebeians largely one of instinctive class consciousness, although Kemble restores some forty-seven lines of mutual patrician-tribune recrimination. Shakespeare's physical encounters between the tribunes and plebeians (3.1.176–206, 213–21, 223–24, 225–28) are all eliminated, including the one skirmish permitted by Sheridan. In keeping with the neoclassical preference for moments of statuesque crisis, Coriolanus is required merely to pose grandly with sword in hand on "No; I'll die here." The plebeians are not driven off; Coriolanus exits at the urging of Cominius, while the tribunes and citizens remain on stage for an abbreviated exchange with Menenius. The effect of Kemble's cuts is seriously to weaken the credibility of the tribunes' allegations of Martius's violence. The episode in Martius's house (3.2), reduced by about one-third from Sheridan's virtually full text, is played initially as a private interview. Menenius enters alone later, and Cominius later still; and at no time are others present. Cuts are designed to lend momentum to the action and eliminate what struck Kemble as extraneous detail.

The strategy conference between Sicinius and Brutus which launches 3.3 is reduced from about thirty lines to six, a much heavier cut than Sheridan's. Only a few lines are removed from the confrontation between Martius and the tribunes, mostly on the grounds of repetitiveness, and Cominius's protest on Martius's behalf (3.3.109–16) is blue-penciled. The scene, as in Sheridan's version, concludes with "There is a world elsewhere" (3.3.135). Kemble follows Sheridan in cutting the Farewell scene (4.1), the encounter between Volumnia and the tribunes (4.2), and the meeting of Adrian and

Nicanor (4.3), all because they keep the star off the stage. Martius's arrival in Antium (4.4) and his skirmish with Aufidius's servants (4.5.1–49) are removed to allow him to be discovered in a spectacular pose.[55]

Kemble's act 4 (Sheridan's act 3) opens with a shortened conversation between Aufidius (his Shakespearian cognomen now restored) and Volusius. Aufidius's account of Galesus's embassy to Rome is cut along with a number of Thomson's more rhetorical flourishes. By way of compensation, however, Kemble gives Aufidius a few lines from Thomson not included by Sheridan:

> This happy Roman, this proud Marcius, haunts me.
> Each troubled night, when slaves and captives sleep
> Forgetful of their chains, I in my dreams
> Anew am vanquish'd; and, beneath his sword
> With horror sinking, feel a ten-fold death,
> The death of honour.

The scene concludes with the Thomson-Sheridan announcement of the mysterious stranger's arrival. The officer reports, however, that the visitor has placed himself not beneath Aufidius's lares, as Thomson and Sheridan stipulate, but "beneath the statue of / The mighty Mars." Moreover, he "majestick stands / In solemn silence" rather than sits. Aufidius goes to meet him.

Act 4, scene 2 opens with Coriolanus discovered in the pose described by the officer. The reconciliation takes place predominantly in Shakespeare's rather than Thomson's idiom. Aufidius's more ecstatic transports (4.5.114–36) are cut. The scene concludes as Martius and Aufidius go off to meet the senators, and the servingmen's chatter (4.5.149–241) is excised. Galesus disappears from the play, and with him the sequence in which he and Martius are reunited. Kemble partially restores Shakespeare's 4.6 (cut by Sheridan) in which the tribunes taunt Menenius and news arrives of the Volscian advance on Rome, designating it 4.3. The citizens do not appear, nor do Menenius and Cominius mock the tribunes' folly. Kemble then introduces the Sheridan-Thomson scene in which a victorious Martius peremptorily imposes strategy on Aufidius, and Volusius arouses Tullus to retaliate. The scene is generally faithful to Sheridan's adaptation, although about sixty-five lines of Thomsonian rhetoric are struck, and a couple of new Thomsonian lines added. This episode replaces Shakespeare's conversation between Aufidius and his Lieutenant (4.7). Kemble retains as 4.5 Sheridan's amalgam of 4.6, 5.1, and 5.4 in which Cominius reports his failure to move Martius, Menenius refuses to intervene, and the terror-stricken citizenry suspend the tribunes' execution while they await the outcome of the matrons' embassy.

Act 5 opens with the Intercession scene, drawn largely from Sheridan's 1757 text with some minor alterations.[56] He eliminates the Thomsonian lines retained by Sheridan in which Volumnia arrests Martius's welcome with the demand "Whom am I to embrace, a son, or foe?" He also excises Volumnia's Shakespearian lines "Should we be silent and not speak, our raiment / And state of bodies would bewray what life / We have led since thy exile" (5.3.94– 96), since presumably the ladies wear the traditional mourning outfits. The sequence in which Young Martius is put forward to receive his father's blessing is restored. Volumnia's appeal, albeit abridged, is drawn from Shakespeare; but midway in her harangue Kemble self-indulgently inserts a Thomsonian aside by Tullus to Volusius, directing the audience's gaze to the star for a virtuoso "reaction shot":

> See, see, Volusius, how the strong emotions
> Of powerful nature shake his inmost soul!
> See how they tear him!—If he long resist them,
> He is a god, or something worse than man.

At the conclusion of Volumnia's truncated Shakespearian petition, Kemble resorts to the Sheridan-Thomson narrative in which Virgilia weeps, Martius offers his family refuge in Antium, and Volumnia produces the dagger and departs victorious.

Aufidius, as in the Thomson-Sheridan versions, offers Martius safe passage back to Rome, and the two quarrel in the Sheridan manner, in the course of which Martius again enjoys his redemptive outburst beginning "The seed of gods." Just before Volscian officers arrive to carry out the assassination, he is allowed his (slightly emended) Shakespearian death-speech, "O, that I had thee in the field, / With six Aufidiuses, or more, thy tribe, / To use my lawful sword" in lieu of Sheridan's "Oh murdering slaves! Assassinating cowards." Once Martius falls, Kemble loses no time in reaching the final curtain. Aufidius's last two speeches, with a few words from the l. Lord, are run together as a eulogy. Everything else is cut.

For Kemble, as for Sheridan, the creation of a unified and uncomplex line of action was only half the task. Characters, too, must be pruned to a simple, grand, and decorous form. Kemble's treatment of the character of Coriolanus, as one reviewer (*News,* 29 June 1817) put it, was

> distinguished by the unity of design, the severe grandeur, and the majestic simplicity which characterized the fine arts in the classic ages. . . . [I]t was massive, grand, severe and lofty.

Less concerned than either Dennis or Sheridan with keeping Martius's conduct within the bounds of conventional propriety, Kemble allowed him to retain even his most vicious moments, including the barbaric threat to "make a quarry of these quartered slaves as high as I could pick my lance." In Kemble's view, the sheer scale of both Martius's integrity and his aristocratic arrogance was what mattered; and even though the portrait is no more conventionally attractive than the ruins of Piranesi, its monumental grandeur might constitute a comparable source of the sublime. For Kemble Martius's only aesthetic offense would be a descent into everyday realism. He was not permitted to refer to itching scabs at 1.1.165–66, or jokingly to ask Menenius, "And live you yet?" (2.1.180), or to address one of the tribunes as "old goat" and "rotten thing" (3.1.176, 178). Battle scenes, which might fracture the heroic illusion, were to be avoided at all costs.

Complexities, ambiguities, and contradictions, enemies to clarity of outline, were not to be tolerated: the assessments of the cushion-layers, Aufidius, Menenius, and the tribunes disappear. Most of what we learn about Martius, we observe first hand, and it is as uncomplex as can be. His aristocratic integrity and fatal arrogance blaze in ever-growing splendor from his first appearance with the citizens to his final defiance of Aufidius. At the moment of his death, fueled by national pride as he lauds his country and shares its glory, his patriotic arrogance is incandescent and his transcendence complete.

In keeping with Kemble's painterly bent, Martius was furnished with at least one great visual moment in each act: in act 1, his first entrance in scarlet dashing in among the plebeians; in act 2, his statuesque pose under the arch during the ovation; in act 3, his defiance of the plebeians and tribunes, sword in hand; in act 4, his discovery beneath the statue of Mars; and in act 5, a series of living pictures worthy of David—his reception of the matrons, his hand-holding capitulation, his epic demise, and the funeral cortege.

The role of Volumnia, the quintessence of maternal pride and severe Roman patriotism, the source of both Martius's arrogance and its undoing, was chiseled with similar simplicity and severity. Kemble allowed her a full measure of bloodthirsty imagery and delight in her savage grandson in 1.3. Her interview with Martius, now largely private, finds her alternatively coaxing and berating her offspring as Shakespeare intended, including the devastating allegation, "Thy valiantness was mine, thou suck'st it from me; / But owe thy pride thyself" (3.2.129–30).

Like her son, Volumnia may be as grandly barbaric as she pleases, but must not be caught in an act or expression of mundane humanity. She is not permitted to sew in her first scene, to speak of her womb (1.3.6), "the embracements of his bed" (1.3.4–5), or the "good lady that lies in" (1.3.76–77), to cite a few typical examples. Talk of spurting blood and mammocked butterflies was quite acceptable. Particularly unapt was any betrayal of personal weakness. Her almost wordless, yet pathetically eloquent, presence in the Farewell scene (4.1) and her impotent rage as she encounters the tribunes in the subsequent episode (4.2) disappear. Her great moment, of course, came in the Intercession scene where with the aid of solemn procession, mourning costume, and dagger she turns aside her son's treasonous fury. And with her final observation, "He never can be lost, who saves his country," she quits the stage without a scintilla of self-pity or sentiment.

Aufidius, here as in Sheridan's version, is the character most abused. Again he is not permitted to make an appearance until after Martius's arrival in Antium. When he does appear, he is the worthy general, the noble humanitarian of Thomson and Sheridan, not Shakespeare's violent, fiery, testy, and ultimately unprincipled villain. His speeches are considerably shortened; and he is much less tediously introspective. His moral superiority to Coriolanus is now no longer as emphatic as it was in Thomson's, or even Sheridan's, treatment. He dwindles into little more than a high-principled deus ex machina.

Menenius continues to be the good-natured, apolitical nonentity of Sheridan's creation. In the Banishment scene, his participation is limited to a few lines of ineffectual protest and sage advice. Like Aufidius, he lacks ideological and psychological texture, and functions merely as a dramatic device.

Virgilia remains much as Sheridan left her, although with the return of Valeria to the play, she gains an additional opportunity for self-assertion. Like the grieving background figures in neoclassical scenes of stoic triumph,[57] she serves mainly to heighten by contrast the epic sternness of Martius and Volumnia and to lend a sentimental touch to the narrative's otherwise unrelieved grimness.

Kemble's radical depoliticization and aestheticization of Shakespeare's drama reduces the citizens to little more than theatrical furniture—mindless, capricious lumps on whom Martius might vent his spleen and an apolitical mass ripe for exploitation by self-interested demagogues. Despite the partial restoration of their initial conversation (1.1.1–50), they are made, by astute cutting, to focus their antagonism on Martius personally. Suggestions of a wider patrician-plebeian class struggle (1.1.15–25) disappear. In the patrician-plebeian contention (3.1) and the Banishment scene (3.3), their interventions are fewer and their behavior even more restrained than in Sheridan's version.

In the now traditional manner, the tribunes are allotted the role of villains. As usual they are permitted no hint of political altruism: their opposition to Martius is driven by purely private motives—the threat his integrity poses to their personal ambitions. And with two further cuts, their astute reading of the future political scenario (2.1.224–31, 243–59) and their detailed planning of the final confrontation with Martius (3.3.1–24), Kemble vitiates much of the already limited claim to strategic insight Sheridan allows them.

STAGECRAFT

Kemble's 1811 revival, which opened on 14 December, was the first *Coriolanus* production in the rebuilt Covent Garden theater, and while it did not differ substantively from the revivals which preceded it, the manager spared

"A Street in Rome" (1.1.). John Philip Kemble Production, Covent Garden, 1811. [By permission of the British Museum]

no expense to make it the most spectacular to date.[58] The settings, attributed to Phillips, Pugh, and Whitmore, with a street scene contributed by John Hodgins,[59] were better painted and more authentic than anything yet seen. Copies of most of the settings, reproduced in 1815 by William West in his Juvenile Drama series, survive.[60] Costumes, to judge from reviews, were unprecedentedly elegant and historically correct. Supers were deployed with a lavish hand; and Sheridan's ovation was increased to some two hundred and forty persons, according to Charles Mayne Young. "The military part of the spectacle," Thomas Goodwin recalls, "was composed of a portion of the famous organization known as the Life Guards. They were a magnificent set of men, every one of whom was over six feet in height. . . . In a stage procession a hundred or more such men with their natural military bearing, clad in the costumes and bearing the arms and armor of Roman soldiers and the insignia of the Roman senate and people, could hardly fail to make a grand and imposing feature."[61]

ACT I

With the proscenium doors locked and the stage cloth (a green carpet indicating tragedy) down, the curtain rose on "A Street in Rome," a setting upstage of the second grooves since the citizens are instructed to enter RUE (Right Upper Entrance).[62] Despite Kemble's claims to historic accuracy, he chose to set *Coriolanus* in the Rome of the Caesars rather than the Rome of the consuls partly because the Imperial city offered more picturesque visual opportunities and partly because archaeological scholarship did not yet permit fine distinctions to be made between the architecture and costume of adjacent historical periods. "Three Shouts by Citizens" are heard RUE and "a Company of Mutinous Citizens" enter. After their conversation, as the citizens rush to exit left, Menenius enters R and Martius abruptly emerges L to confront the mettlesome troop. "When he came on in the first scene," recalls a contemporary, "the crowd of mob-Romans fell back as though they had run against a wild bull, and he dashed in amongst them in scarlet pride, and looked, even in the eyes of the audience, sufficient 'to beat forty of them.'"[63] Menenius remains on the R of the stage for quite some time to allow Martius to defy the plebeians without distraction. When Martius threatens to "make a quarry / Of these quartered slaves," the "Citizens retire R" in alarm; and only then does Menenius "advance" to Martius to discuss the crowd on the other side of the city.

On Menenius's "This is strange," a Roman Officer enters from R, and asks "Where's Caius Marcius?" His message delivered, he "retires to 1st Wing L." A moment later, Cominius enters R with 12 Lictors and Sicinius and Brutus. The lictors bear "Fasces without axes," and "X behind and stand behind the officer L.[eft] H.[and]," that is, downstage left. The tribunes "join the Citizens R.[ight] H.[and]." Already an inviolable Kemble production principle declares itself: the star occupies center stage at all times, and the action in which he is engaged is the exclusive focus of interest. Other characters move to the center momentarily for their contacts with him, but when not directly involved in the action, they group themselves, like drapery in beau ideal paintings, to add mass to the back and sides. Kemble's blocking, here as elsewhere, is not only pictorial but narrative. To clarify visually the story line in a vast auditorium where seeing and hearing are both problematic, he blocks with care the play's opposing forces—the tribunes and plebeians at stage right and the patrician element at stage left. The scene concludes uneventfully with Cominius and the officers and lictors exiting L, followed moments later by Menenius and Martius. The citizens go off R. The tribunes converse alone and then exit L.

The mise-en-scène for 1.2, described as "An Apartment in Caius Marcius's House in Rome," is an elegant reconstruction of a Augustan Roman interior, with Ionic columns and curtains adorned with laurel wreaths and key pattern, with a tessellated floor and elegantly decorated ceiling. It seems to have been set well forward, since all entrances take place downstage. Only entrances and stage crosses are indicated.

The first of the two battlefield scenes (1.3) is set in "A Wood, near the Camp of Cominius," a shutter apparently run on in the third grooves to allow the functional tent setting for the next scene to be put in place upstage. This "Wood" was doubtless a stock piece, which may account for West's

"An Apartment in Caius Marcius' House in Rome." John Philip Kemble Production,
Covent Garden, 1811. [By permission of the British Museum]

failure to reproduce it. From R there are "Shouts & Charge. Then Trumpets
sound a Retreat." From RUE enter "Cominius, 1st Roman Officer, 2 Standards *S.P.Q.R.,* 2 Standards *Eagles,* 12 Lictors, 6 Spears & Shields, 8 Swords
& Shields."[64] "[A]ll range R" to dress the stage for Martius's entrance. The
2nd Officer arrives L2E to announce that Martius has been driven to the
trenches by the Volscians. Offstage Martius is heard shouting, "Come I too
late?", and a moment later he enters LUE. Once he is down center, "the 12
Lictors spread into the Centre at the back of the Stage." Throughout the
play, Kemble uses splendidly costumed military figures bearing banners,
spears and shields, or symbolic civic objects as a kind of living scenery.
These groups take little or no part in the action, but merely lend pictorial
effect. Cominius demands "Where is that slave, / Which told me they had
beat you to your trenches?", "The 2nd Roman Officer advances, and two
Soldiers prepare to seize him" before Martius intervenes. Towards the end
of the scene, when Martius rallies the troops, trumpets sound, and "Soldiers
shout thrice, and wave their swords." Martius and Cominius exit R together,
with the soldiers in pairs following smartly.

The decor for the second battlefield sequence (1.4) is described in the
Garrick Club book as "Open Country" and in the Wister book as "Cut
Wood." The setting as represented by West depicts a series of tents on a
plain, with "tree" wing flats at the sides. The accuracy of West's setting is
confirmed by a note in Kemble's partbook[65] reminding him to "Exit with

Com. into the Tent." At least one of the tents must have been functional. The scene opens on an empty stage to a suggestive series of offstage sounds—"A loud Flourish.—A Battle.—A Retreat sounded." Comininius, Martius, and military supers from the previous scene now reenter in the same order in which they exited earlier. The only noteworthy feature of the scene is the fact that rhetorical high points are highlighted with flourishes of trumpets and other wind instruments.[66] All exit LUE to a march as the act curtain falls.

"A Street in Rome" (2.1). John Philip Kemble Production, Covent Garden, 1811. [By permission of the British Museum]

ACT 2

The "Street in Rome" setting for 2.1 by John Hodgins, the original design for which survives,[67] is painted in careful perspective and with a close eye to historically accurate detail. The vast spaces in the foreground and the enormous architectural masses at the sides and in the distance lend the scene a grandeur and simplicity which precisely match the character of Kemble's text and the acting style which realized it. The shutter was probably run on in the first or second grooves to allow the upstage tent scene to be struck and the ovation setting to be erected. The conversation between Menenius and the tribunes is played quite straightforwardly as is the subsequent conversation between Menenius and the women. On "True? I'll be

"A Street in Rome" (2.1). Original design by John Hodgins for John Philip Kemble Production, Covent Garden, 1811. [By permission of the British Museum]

sworn they are true," Menenius crosses to the tribunes to fling in their faces, "Marcius is coming home: he has more cause to be proud." At the conclusion of the scene, a "Flourish of Trumpets—Shouts &c." signal Martius's arrival, and all exeunt L.

The Street shutter is now drawn off to reveal the setting for 2.2, titled "A triumphal Arch in Rome," a three-dimensional cityscape featuring a gigantic functional arch flanked on the sides and downstage by examples of familiar Roman architecture. Upstage, viewed through the arch, is a perspective backcloth. The procession enters RUE, passes through the arch, curves down left onto the apron, crosses it, and proceeds up right to allow the audience a theatrical close-up of Roman culture resurrected. The parade comprises four divisions as compared with Sheridan's two. First, heralded by "Three Loud Shouts with Drums &c.," came some forty soldiers and officers bearing banners with representations of Corioli, followed by "Civic crowns," "Silver Eagles," "Golden Eagles," trophies, and other objects of visual interest. After a further three shouts came the second division, a civil display, featuring "4 Boys—2 & 2 with Censers," "2 Priests—Fires & Staves," two others with sacrificial knives, "6 Girls—bearing the Lamb,"[68] "2 Priests—axes," "2 Priests—Fires,"[69] "6 Ladies—2 & 2," and "6 Senators—2 & 2." Another three shouts introduced a third division, largely military, comprising soldiers flourishing banners and trophies, trumpeters,

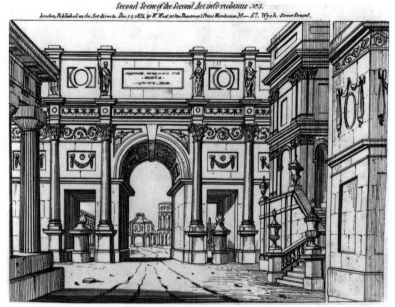

Second Scene of the Second Act in Coriolanus No 5.
London, Published as the Act directs, Dec. 24, 1824, by W. West, at his Theatrical Print Warehouse No — 57, Wych Street Strand.

"A Triumphal Arch in Rome" (Ovation setting). John Philip Kemble Production, Covent Garden, 1811. [By permission of the British Museum]

officers in chains, and soldiers bearing biers loaded with spoils. A further three shouts announced a fourth division comprised of musicians and choristers rendering "See the conquering hero comes!" from Handel's *Julius Caesar.* The musicians line up at the back of the stage, and divisions which had exited earlier reenter to group themselves picturesquely as living decor for the interview between Martius and his family. At the very end of the cavalcade come 28 Senators, 27 Ladies, 4 Roman Matrons, Valeria and Servilia (a name given by Kemble to Volumnia's female servant), Virgilia, Volumnia, Menenius and Cominius, and finally Coriolanus followed by the "Chief Eagle." As the hero appears in the arch, he stops, and is greeted by a "Flourish of Trumpets—Three Shouts—&c." That moment lingered in the minds of theatergoers for decades. "The spoils, the captives, the soldiers, the citizens had passed over," recalls one such,

> and there, *alone,* beneath the triumphal arch, stood the hero, in his simple, graceful, crimson robe, with his black head uncovered, and his attitude dictated by the very spirit of classic taste! . . . The exquisite beauty of the statue struck even the most uncultivated mind, and . . . the spectators were in an absolute ecstasy of delight. . . .[70]

After a suitable period of admiration, Martius protests a trifle belatedly, "No more of this, it does offend my heart," and kneels to his mother who

Second Scene of the Fourth Act in Coriolanus. N° 6.
London, Published as the Act directs, Dec.14,1824, by W.West, at his Theatrical Print Warehouse, 57, Wych Street, Strand.

"The Capitol in Rome" (Senate setting). John Philip Kemble Production, Covent Garden, 1811. [By permission of the British Museum]

"X to Corio. & raises him." A moment later, she "puts Virgilia next him." No other business for the scene is recorded. On Martius's "On, to the Capitol," the procession moves off R to "A grand March." The "Street in Rome" shutters close on the ovation, and the tribunes engage in mean-spirited speculation on the forestage.

Meanwhile the ovation setting is struck and replaced by "The Capitol in Rome," the mise-en-scène for 2.4,[71] a grand columned court featuring a "Consul's Chair" well upstage and occupied by Cominius, with twelve lictors arranged upstage of it. In front of them, immediately behind and to the right and left of the chair, stand two soldiers bearing Golden Eagles, with the Chief Eagle between them. Two benches are arranged at oblique angles to the consul's chair with three senators occupying each. Down right stand Coriolanus and the 1st Roman Officer and opposite them down left are Menenius and the 2nd Roman officer. Sicinius and Brutus are located L, slightly upstage of Menenius. Only one piece of business is worth remark: as Coriolanus reenters R after being summoned and crosses toward C, "Comin[ius] comes down R. [and the] Senators rise" as the consul informs Martius of the senate's decision. The scene concludes with a "Flourish of Trumpets" on "To Coriolanus come all joy and honour!", and all exeunt R.

The shutter for the Voices scene, probably the "Street" flat employed in 2.3, is run on downstage to permit the deep "Street" scene for 3.1 to be set behind. The forward position allows the Voices encounter to take place as near the audience as possible. The directions for this scene relate almost exclusively to entrances and exits.

1st Scene of 3d Act in Coriolanus. No 7.
London Published as the Act directs Dec. 4, 1814 by W. West, at his Theatrical Print Warehouse No. 57. Wych Street, Strand.

"A Street in Rome" (3.1). John Philip Kemble Production, Covent Garden, 1811. [By permission of the British Museum]

ACT 3

The shutter for the Voices episode is now withdrawn to reveal a deep "Street in Rome" setting for 3.1, featuring a colonnade from up left to down left, terminating upstage in a double-arched wall with a backcloth behind. In keeping with the notion that the dramatic action represents a purely personal conflict between the noble Martius and the ignoble tribunes and their plebeian-dupes, the supers called for by Shakespeare to represent *"all the* GENTRY . . . *and other* SENATORS" are absent. Only Cominius, Coriolanus, Menenius, and the tribunes grace the early part of the sequence, apart from twelve lictors who dress the stage. As Sicinius orders "Go, call the people," Brutus, according to the Wister book, "beckons to the Citizens, who rush on immediately—R." Sicinius, "Laying hold on CORIOLA-NUS,"[72] in the scene's only violent act, insists, "Obey, I charge thee, / And follow to thine answer" (3.1.175–76). When Sicinius orders the citizens to seize Martius, the latter simply draws his sword in a monumental gesture of defiance. A moment later, Cominius and Coriolanus exit L. When Brutus orders, "Pursue him to his house," "All [the citizens] rush tumultuously towards L," but are halted by Menenius's "One word more, one word." At

1.ᵗ Scene of 4.ᵗ Act in Coriolanus. N.º8.
London,Published as the Act directs Dec,4,1813, by W.West,at his Theatrical Print Warehouse,Exeter House,Exeter St.ᵗ Strand.

**"The Forum in Rome" (3.3). John Philip Kemble Production, Covent Garden, 1811.
[By permission of the British Museum]**

the end of the scene they exit with the tribunes R, and Menenius goes off
L in search of Martius.

The promptbook notes for Martius's interview with Volumnia (3.2) indicate only entrances, exits, and crosses.

The setting for 3.3, described as "The Forum in Rome,"[73] consists of a
facade, pierced with three severe arches and flanked by downstage columns.
The scene is very sparsely marked, save once more for entrances, exits,
and crosses. At its conclusion, on "There is a world elsewhere," "The People
shout & follow Coriolanus" as he strides off R.

ACT 4

West provides no setting for "A Room in Aufidius' House in Antium"
(4.1). Aufidius and Volusius enter R. A little later, the "1st Volscian Officer,
very pale" interrupts their conversation to announce the stranger's arrival.
All exit R.

The opening of 4.2, according to West's reproduction, discovered a heavily columned court with a statue of Mars at stage center beneath and to the
left of which Coriolanus stands grimly as indicated in the promptbook and
by Bourgeois in his splendid painting of the moment. The promptbook records only that Aufidius enters R at the beginning of the scene and the cogen-
erals leave by the same exit at its close.

"A Hall, in which stands a Statue of Mars." John Philip Kemble Production, Covent Garden, 1811. [By permission of the British Museum]

The much abbreviated sequence in which the news of Martius's approach reaches Menenius and the tribunes (4.3) takes place against a "Street in Rome" shutter, probably placed in the first grooves to allow the forthcoming deep scene to be arranged upstage. The promptbook again records only entrances and exits.

To underscore Martius's military success, Kemble inaugurates 4.4 with an eyecatching pageant on "A Plain, near Rome," probably a stock shutter placed well upstage. To a flourish of drums and trumpets, some forty soldiers enter RUE bearing spears, shields, and banners, and mass themselves above and to the left of Volusius, Aufidius, and Coriolanus, leaving them in spendid isolation down right. The Second Officer announces the approach of the deputation from the Roman senate, and Coriolanus exits L with his entourage. Aufidius and Volusius, now alone, ponder the former's humiliation to which the audience has been witness. As an offstage "Trumpet sounds" to mark Martius's reception of the senatorial deputation, Aufidius and Volusius exeunt L.

The "Street in Rome" shutter, probably in the first grooves, closes on the "Plain, near Rome." Menenius baits the citizens and tribunes; Cominius, companioned by six senators, confesses the failure of his mission; and Brutus futilely begs Menenius to intervene. At the end of the scene, the tribunes, Cominius, and the senators exeunt L, and the citizens R.

Sir Francis Bourgeois: *John Philip Kemble as Coriolanus beneath the statue of Mars.*
[By permission of the Trustees of Sir John Soane's Museum]

First Scene of the Fifth Act in Coriolanus. № 10.
London, Published as the Act directs Dec 14, 1811. by W. West at his Theatrical Print Warehouse, No—57, Wych Street, Strand.

"The Volscian Camp" (act 5). John Philip Kemble Production, Covent Garden, 1811.
[By permission of the British Museum]

ACT 5

While the scene with Menenius, Cominius, tribunes, and citizens proceeds on the forestage, the entire postproscenium area is transformed to a
"Volscian Camp." A line of tents stretches more or less diagonally from up
right to down left; and those nearest the audience appear to be functional.
Down right two chairs stand side by side on a "pedestal" beneath a canopy.
To a "Flourish of Drums and Trumpets," Coriolanus, Aufidius, and Volusius
enter L, accompanied by "Senators, Officers, Soldiers, & Standards." A
promptbook direction reads "Every body to the last Act," so presumably
the two hundred-odd supers who participated in the ovation now animate the
play's final moments. The Volscian officers, soldiers, and standard-bearers
arrange themselves in two diagonal files the full depth of the stage. Coriolanus sits and asks Tullus to join him, and as he does so "Soft Musick" is
heard from off R, "at first distant. Louder by degrees." Now from RUE
"Enter VIRGILIA, VOLUMNIA, *young* MARCIUS, VALERIA, and Roman Ladies, in mourning habits." The procession slowly advances down L,
the black gowns and flowing veils a melancholy contrast to the colorful
metallic display of the militia. As Virgilia nears Martius she bows, as does
Volumnia a moment later, and the music ceases. On Virgilia's "My lord and
husband!" she tentatively "Advances a step"; Coriolanus, in lines transposed from slightly earlier in the scene, replies, "I melt, and am not / Of

stronger earth than others," and "Runs down to her" and kisses her. He then kneels to his mother, who "X to him, & raises him." Young Martius in turn kneels, afterwards positioning himself between his mother and grand-mother. Martius sits to hear the ladies' suit. When all hope seems lost, and the women prepare to exit, Virgilia, on "O, permit me, / To shed my gushing tears upon thy hand," "advances fearfully." At Martius's "Leave me," "Virgilia starts, like one who never heard such a word before." And as she replies, "I obey" and moves left, she "looks back" to observe "How bitter thus to part." When an outraged Volumnia rejects her son's invitation to live in Antium, Coriolanus rises to protest, "By the immortal gods." Virgilia, terrified, exclaims "O, vow not our destruction!", falling to her knees as she speaks. Volumnia "Raises her sternly," and a few lines later produces the dagger. Coriolanus seizes her hand and ultimately yields as in Sheridan's script. On "Volscians, we raise the seige," "CORIOLANUS turns to the Roman Ladies, who retire in the order they entered. RUE." As the procession exits, Aufidius "Rushes forward" to Volusius to exult, "'Tis as we wish'd, Volusius." The latter "Retires a little R" as Coriolanus remarks, "I plainly, Tullus, by your looks perceive, / You disapprove my conduct." The promptbooks contain no instructions for the management of the quarrel. On Volusius's "Insolent villain," "VOLUSIUS and other Volscian Officers draw, and kill CORIOLANUS," and "The Senators start up" in astonishment. The serried ranks of soldiery apparently adorn the stage in frigid immobility throughout. When Aufidius orders, "Beat, beat the drum," "Trumpts. & Muffled Drums" are heard; the soldiers "Lower Ensigns & arms"; and, bearing the body, the military procession moves off to "A dead March" from the orchestra. Running time for the production was three hours and ten minutes, including "waits."

THE ACTORS

The production was built from first to last around Kemble and Mrs. Siddons, and their acting was a living realization of the principles governing beau ideal painting and sculpture. Like David or Reynolds, their goal was a transcendent, spiritually elevating portrait of their subjects. The *Bell's Weekly Messenger* critic (29 June 1817) judged Kemble's performance "an art" which

> consisted in selecting beauties wherever he found them, and then uniting them, according to nature, in a whole, of which every part was natural but the composition artificial. . . . He . . . gave us a Roman such as Virgil would have drawn him. It is impossible to conceive any thing of more majesty. It was an epic painting— not of what Rome was, and still less of what *Coriolanus* was; but of that *beau ideal* of Rome and *Coriolanus*, which existed in the imagination of Virgil, of Shakespear, and of Mr. Kemble.

Kemble's performance owed much to his heroic build, Roman features, flattering costumes, and picturesque poses drawn from painting and statuary. "His figure," recalls a contemporary,

> was tall and majestic . . . elegance of form and strength of muscle being combined. . . . His face was rigid; and the general expression of his countenance was that of hauteur; as though he always bore in mind the consciousness of superiority. His brow was scowling and supercilious, and his eye penetrating: while his lips seemed, almost naturally, to take an expression of scorn. His nose was large and of the true Roman arch; and his chin was very prominent (*Minerva*, New York, 4 October 1823).

"The dresses which Mr. KEMBLE wears," one theatergoer noted, "fall about his form with peculiar richness and beauty in broad wavy folds. . . . The cloak in *Coriolanus* . . . hangs in exquisite curves, never losing the true line of beauty. . . . He is the only man on the stage that could boast before the people that 'on fair ground he could beat forty of them,'—and not be laughed at" (*Champion*, 25 May 1817). To augment his natural advantages, he wore special sandals from which, according to John Howard Payne, he "derived an additional elevation of perhaps two inches."[74]

His Coriolanus, as text and stagecraft suggest, was conceived in straight-line terms: the complexity of Shakespeare's Roman was simplistically metamorphosed into "the haughtiness of the man, the valour and wildness of the soldier, the proud affection of the Roman Son" (*Champion*, 25 May 1817). And "the same haughty dignity of demeanour, the same energy of will, and unbending sternness of temper" was preserved throughout. "He was swayed by a single impulse," we learn. "His tenaciousness of purpose was only irritated by opposition; he turned neither to the right nor the left; the vehemence with which he moved forward increasing every instant, till it hurried him on to the catastrophe" (*The Times*, 25 June 1817).

Kemble's performance was largely rhetorical, complemented by a series of carefully contrived poses, each held for just the right length of time. "[W]e never saw any thing," reported an eyewitness, "that resulted from the chisel of the Greek sculptors, or from the artists of the intermediate ages, that was more consonant with the enforcement of awful dignity, than what this excelling gentleman displayed."[75]

His first entrance, when the scarlet-cloaked Coriolanus (which he pronounced "Cor-eye-olanus") confronted the startled rabble, is described by an audience member more as sculpture than life. "It is impossible not to admire," he writes,

> the noble proportions and majestic *contour* of his figure; the expression of his face, naturally of the Roman character; his right arm erected in conscious authority; his chest thrown forward, and his head slightly back; his right leg fearlessly advanced,

and firmness in all his attitude, together with the exact adjustment and tasteful folds of the classical drapery with which his person is invested.[76]

Shortly after, however, when informed that the Volscians are in arms, the sculpture was wonderfully quickened: "a glow of exaltation and anticipated triumph plays upon his features," we are told, "while he quickly exclaims—'I'm glad on't.'"[77] In the battlefield episodes, he was apparently adequate, but few critics provide details.

In the Ovation scene, despite the presence of some two hundred supers, he was never for a moment overshadowed. "No stage effect," wrote William Robson, ". . . was equal to that produced by his appearance in the Ovation" as he posed beneath the arch.[78] His picturesque act of homage to his wife and mother, following a slow move downstage to a trumpet flourish,[79] was also much praised.

His treatment of the Voices sequence was rather more controversial. He played the scene brutally and inflexibly, a disgusting exhibition of "patrician pride compelled to prefer a request, unable to condescend to the slightest courtesy, but with a haughtiness which could brook no dissimulation, claiming his boon as a right, and spurning the low-born granters" (*Morning Post,* 29 October 1816). His "snatching away his hand from their friendly familiarity—and bidding them adieu with a withering *sangfroid*" (*News,* 24 November 1816) were frequently cited with approbation; but more than one critic thought his highhandedness somewhat overdone, particularly his reading of "Kindly, sir, I pray let me ha't. . . . Your good voice, sir, what say you?" (2.3.76–78). John Ambrose Williams judged it a mistake to deliver the lines "with the same inflexible mien, and tone of defiance, which characterise the other parts of his performance" rather than "with an affected cringing air of supplication, an assumed mask of humility, in defiance of the peoples' wishes."[80] Another observer queried his response to the citizens' observation that the price of their voices is "to ask it kindly." Here, he remarked, Kemble "bawls out 'Kindly?' as if he wondered they could ask him so to demean himself, and then blusters out in defiance, 'Give me your voices.'"[81] A third commentator thought his entire conception of the scene was mistaken, and a blot on the beau ideal scutcheon: "*Coriolanus* treats the Roman people with contempt," he concedes, "but not with disgust and abhorrence, which sentiments appearing in the action of Mr. Kemble, take away from that nobility of mind possessed by *Coriolanus,* and make us rather think that he deserves his exile, than incline us to despise the ingratitude of his persecutors."[82]

In 3.1, Martius's first meeting with the tribunes after the Voices scene, his response to Brutus's suggestion that his anti-populism was known "Not to them all," was widely admired. "[T]he tone and manner in which he rejoined 'Have *you* informed them *since?*' was inconceivably fine," reported the *Morning Post* critic (16 December 1811). "The suddenness of the retort

. . . together with the look which accompanied it, confounded the envious cunning, and abashed the petty souls of the tribunes," another spectator recalls.[83] Later in the scene, when Menenius urges Martius toward calm, Kemble won "repeated thunders of applause for his reply "with half-smothered wrath, in a rapid utterance and under-tone":

> It is a purpos'd thing, and grows by plot,
> To curb the will of the nobility.[84]

Equally popular was his delivery of

> How? no more?
> As for my country I have shed my blood,
> Not fearing outward force, so shall my lungs
> Coin words till their decay against these measles.

"The whole of the force of this passage," we are told, "was concentrated in the word *measles*. Mr. Kemble collected all his energy, pride, scorn, and indignation, which he threw into the expression of that single dissyllable."[85] He also won accolades for the "uncontrollable bursts of passion in the very teeth of the tribunes, when they brand him with the name of Traitor" (*Champion*, 25 May 1817). In the episode in which Volumnia persuades him to temporize with the plebeians (3.2), "the conquest of filial duty . . . and its conflict with patrician arrogance"[86] powerfully foreshadowed the Intercession sequence. And his incandescent exit on "There is a world elsewhere" (3.3.135) was one of the legendary masterstrokes of the nineteenth-century stage.

After the sound and fury which attended his Roman adieu, the serene grandeur of his first appearance at Antium left theatergoers awestruck. As the shutters withdrew, "he stood at the foot of the statue of Mars, himself another Mars!" (*The Times*, 25 June 1817). Isolated in alien space and wrapped in unwonted silence, "his visage was so communicative, and his attitude was in such harmony with the fact, that the tenor and direction of his perturbed and wounded spirit could be seen and known, although his tongue was not obedient to the offices of sound."[87] In the ensuing interview, "his high deportment towards Aufidius" indicated no attenuation of his "lofty and commanding" spirit. "Aufidius," wrote one witness, "shrinks into insignificance in the presence of his exiled conqueror."[88]

His performance in the Intercession episode, however, was the highlight of the production. Here "the conflict between pride and natural affection was depicted with such force and truth, that the effect was sublime," wrote the *Morning Post* critic (29 October 1816). Nor was he less impressive "when Nature finally overcomes, and, bending on the neck of his mother, he exclaims, 'Rome is saved, but thy son is lost.'"[89]

Equally memorable were the production's final moments when, with statuesque pose and Thomsonian eloquence, he redeemed his venal past in patriotic reaffirmation. "Never shall we forget," writes an observer, "how that great actor himself, in answer to his rival's [taunt] that his countrymen were 'the seed of outlaws and of robbers,' exclaimed 'the seed of Gods!'— how he dashed his own disgraces in the teeth of him who dared 'to speak of Rome but with respect and awful veneration,'—how, above all, in the midst of his glorious passion, the memory of his own wrongs just fell on his soul like a summer cloud, and his lip for an instant quivered, as he gave utterance to the line *'whate'er her faults, whate'er her giddy factions,'* and was borne triumphantly onward by his noble ardour" (*Champion,* 29 January 1820). Just before his assassination, according to Ludwig Tieck, "When Coriolanus exclaims, 'Hear'st thou, Mars?' and Aufidius says 'Name not the God, thou boy of tears!' the exclamation 'Ha!' to which Coriolanus gives vent in the height of his rage was terrible."[90] In the "Alone I did it. 'Boy'!" passage, the mingled rage and astonishment with which he repeated "Boy" were particularly praised. "It is apparently with difficulty," a theatergoer noted, "that the word finds a passage from the throat; but when at last it rushes forth, its emphasis is terrible. His whole soul seems convulsed, and rent asunder by the effort."[91] When the Volscian assassins approached him "from behind in the very midst of the triumphant vaunt of his repeated victories over their countrymen [and] seemed to pass their swords through the body of Coriolanus," Walter Scott recalls, "[t]here was no precaution, no support; in the midst of the exclamation against Tullus Aufidius, he dropped as dead and as flat on the stage as if the swords had really met in his body." This scene, Scott thought, "had the most striking resemblance to actual and instant death we ever witnessed."[92]

Kemble's interpretation was perfectly attuned to the taste of the time, the love of things Roman, the *goût de grandeur,* and was greeted with the same hysteria which accompanied exhibitions of David's Roman paintings in France. Somehow by miracles of scale and severity, Kemble managed to befuddle the audience's intellect, to make irrelevant questions of right and wrong, to put beyond question Martius's humanity and integrity or lack of it. Through theatrical alchemy, as a contemporary put it, "This man, who being justly banished for his attempt against the Roman constitution, joins the enemies of his country for the satisfaction of a childish revenge, whose duty stoops to that family affection before which his pride would not bend, who, after his accumulated treachery and weakness, dies by too noble a death, becomes . . . almost amiable, and is pitied by those who abhor him" (*Morning Chronicle,* 29 October 1816). Which was precisely the object of Kemble's exertions.

Never, perhaps, have both major roles been so well filled in any one production; and despite the relative brevity of the part, Mrs. Siddons's Volumnia ranks among her greatest achievements. Public demand for paintings of heroic women of antiquity was already enormous, and no actress was better able to offer a stage equivalent.[93] The effect she created was, quite simply, overwhelming, so devastating in fact that critics, to the dismay of the stage historian, sought relief in etherial superlatives to the neglect of earthbound detail. A handsome woman of majestic proportions, she looked the part to perfection whether at thirty-four when she first played it or at fifty-six when she quit it.

While she was "as firm and as eloquent in her expression of dignity as her elevated son," she was careful to make a clear distinction between their basic characters: "her loftiness of soul was sweetened by morality, while that of *Coriolanus* was upheld by fierceness and inflexibility."[94] On her initial appearance with Virgilia, her "tones of familiar elegance" (*World,* 9 February 1789) were approvingly noted, but her first great coup came with the ovation procession, in the special entrance invented by Sheridan for Woffington. Here, "the proud mother of a proud son, and conquering hero," "with flashing eye, and proudest smile, and head erect, and hands pressed firmly on her bosom, as if to repress by manual force its triumphant swellings . . . towered above all around her, and rolled, and, almost, reeled across the stage; her very soul as it were, dilating, and rioting in its exultation; until her action lost all grace, and, yet, became so true to nature, so picturesque, and so descriptive, that, pit and gallery sprang to their feet, electrified by the transcendent execution of the conception."[95] In the course of the episode in which she instructs Martius in diplomacy, "her rebuke to her son for his overweening arrogance was duly and feelingly administered"[96] by the only contemporary performer who could match his hauteur. Her "artful persuasions" (*World,* 9 February 1789) were also favorably noticed. In the Intercession scene she scored her greatest triumph. Here, we are told, "in her maternal solicitude, at the head of the matrons of Rome . . . she never forgot her station or her greatness—she was ardent in her solicitude to rescue her country from impending desolation, yet she would not even do so much by means which were incompatible with her honor."[97] An "irresistible tenderness, maternal dignity, and female patriotism" (*Star,* 4 October 1796) characterized her plea throughout, and the "pathetic and chilling accents" of "This fellow had a Volscian to his mother" (*World,* 9 February 1789) echoed in the mind's ear long afterwards. The uniqueness of her achievement became apparent only after her retirement when contemporary actresses of the caliber of Eliza O'Neill and Mrs. Faucit attempted the role, and failed dismally.

The production designed as a showcase for Kemble and Mrs. Siddons served its function so admirably that supporting actors were largely ignored. The citizens, about twenty in the 1789 production and some thirty in the 1811 revival, were little more than a group voice. In 1811, their similarity to a herd was underlined by dressing them all identically in the toga alba. One critic thought them "more like a parcel of mad millers running about Brentford to hoot their employer, than the chequered *comitia* of the world's capital" (*News,* 22 December 1811). Most of the plum speeches were allotted to the 1st Citizen, played by the company's leading comedian, first Suett and later Simmons, who enjoyed some degree of license. In the Voices scene, Simmons "used to peer about for Kemble's wounds like a flimsy connoisseur examining a statue of some mighty Roman,"[98] and when he later recounted Martius's solicitation of the citizens' voices,

> The manner in which he caught the peculiarities of the great tragedian, and trans-ferred them to his own small person, was irresistibly comic—the original scarcely excited more applause than did Simmons, when he waved his hand in imitation of the would-be consul, and exclaimed, "Your voices! your most sweet voices!"[99]

The tribunes, although the villains of the piece, received next to no critical attention. Their role, like that of the citizens, was merely to serve as a foil for Kemble; in 1806, for example, Messrs. Chapman and Murray "appeared so contemptible," according to Henry Crabb Robinson, "that [Coriolanus] drew down hisses on them."[100] Aufidius and Menenius, played by a variety of actors, were rarely noticed unless they proved incompetent. Egerton's Aufidius was censured for being "rather too coarse and blustering" by the *Times* critic (29 October 1816) and Baddeley as Menenius was chided for mistaking "the eccentric Roman for *Polonius*" (*Star,* 11 February 1789).

5

The Kemble Tradition Challenged:
Elliston-Kean (1820)

John Kemble had been retired three years; yet his *Coriolanus* lingered in memory "as clear and distinct as though even yet it were palpable to the senses"[1] when Robert Elliston and Edmund Kean challenged its near mythic status at Drury Lane on 25 January 1820.[2] Young William Charles Macready, a disciple of Kemble, had played the role, it is true, a month or so earlier at Covent Garden, but he trod so closely on the heels of his mentor that his performance was less a threat than a tribute to the tradition. The Elliston-Kean revival, by way of contrast, was a calculated act of iconoclasm.

Elliston, a successful provincial theater manager, popular actor, and proprietor of London's Surrey playhouse, became lessee of the troubled Drury Lane in the summer of 1819 and promptly redecorated the interior and recruited a strong company. Old Drury's leading, but profoundly unhappy, light was Edmund Kean who had successfully starred there for several seasons only to see his bid for the lesseeship rejected in favor of Elliston's. In a fit of pique he booked a tour of America, but was sharply reminded by the new proprietor that his contract for the upcoming season had been bought with the lease. Threatened with legal action, Kean had little choice but to capitulate.[3] His bruised ego was salved to some degree, however, by the promise of a new Shakespearian role.

Elliston's decision to stage *Coriolanus* and Kean's agreement to star were dictated less by fondness for the play or each other than pure self-interest. Elliston's program badly needed a novelty, since two of his best prospects had recently evaporated with Mrs. Siddons's refusal to come out of retirement and Sir Walter Scott's reluctance to write him a tragedy. A production designed to challenge *Coriolanus*'s success at the rival house offered piquant box-office bait; and Kean, whose vanity had been wounded by Macready's well-received Martius, welcomed an occasion to settle accounts.

Elliston's *Coriolanus* was as distinctively Romantic a product as Kemble's was neoclassic. His rejection of textual impurity and insistence on scholarly scenography, together with Kean's commitment to psychological process, not only marked a decisive break with Kemble but foreshadowed Charles

Kean and Henry Irving. Elliston's innovative artistry, however, proved to be his undoing. As a longtime manager of minor theaters, where novelty was the lifeblood of the box office, he made the false assumption that theater-goers at patent houses prized change above all else, and consequently under-valued the charm of the familiar. Elliston, like the ultra-conservative Kemble, had little sympathy with the play's political features—an apt exam-ple of that "growing gulf between the realities of the early industrial age and the escapist tendencies in the arts" remarked by William Fleming.[4] At the time of the production's premiere, some five months after the "massacre of Peterloo," the alienation of the British working class from its legislators mirrored with uncanny accuracy the social and political tensions of Shake-speare's Rome. "Seldom in English history," writes Anthony Wood, "has a government been so hated by the people. . . ."

> If, for example, the taxes on food had been remitted, the situation of the poor might have been relieved a little; instead, the income tax, which weighed most heavily on the upper and middle classes, was dropped. Yet the removal of the taxes on food would barely have scraped the surface of the problem. Only a nation-wide system of economic control could have eased the birth-pangs of a new industrial society, and such measures of interference were beyond the power and knowledge of any government of this time.[5]

Precisely, perhaps, because of the perils inherent in *Coriolanus*'s political aptness, Elliston, like Kemble during the French Revolution, opted to stage the play as a celebration of bourgeois individualism. But where Kemble invited awe for a neoclassical demigod by the epic scale of his drives and the grandeur of his surroundings, Elliston and Kean begged sympathy for a Romantic noble savage, a creature of primordial integrity victimized by corruption at both ends of the social scale.

Elliston's revival, for the first time in the play's history, staked its claim to singularity on the grounds of authenticity—textual, scenic, and histri-onic—and thus declared its consanguinity with a major contemporary move-ment in the arts. In the latter decades of the eighteenth century, the unprecedented scholarly research undertaken by John Singleton Copley for his *Charles I Demanding the Surrender of the Five Impeached MPs* (1785)[6] had made authenticity a vital feature of history painting, while Edmond Malone's 1790 attempt to establish the authenticity of Shakespeare's biog-raphy and texts brought a comparable thrust to literature.[7] As aware as the next manager of the direction of the aesthetic winds, Kemble had laid claim to textual and antiquarian scholarship; but, as we have seen, his editorial research went not much beyond a survey of traditional acting editions. And historical correctness in decor as often as not ran a poor second to visual effect.

Elliston enjoyed no reputation for scholarship, but he was not without education or contacts in the world of art and letters: he had attended St.

Paul's school, boasted two uncles who were Cambridge professors, and was on social terms throughout his theatrical career with most of London's leading artistic, intellectual, and political lights.[8] The range of entertainment he offered at the Surrey, the Olympic, the Theatre Royal, Birmingham, and elsewhere, puts beyond doubt his familiarity with contemporary developments in both high and popular culture. And all of his experience, for good and ill, was brought to bear on his *Coriolanus.*

His quest for authenticity, that rising lodestar of high art, began, understandably enough, with the text. In an "Advertisement" to his published acting edition, roughly parallel in function to the "Prolegomenon" to Malone's Shakespeare, he invokes the principle of authenticity and claims uniqueness for his own script on this ground.[9] The Sheridan-Kemble hybrid is summarily discredited at the outset, and indeed the practice of adulteration altogether. "To represent SHAKESPEARE's CORIOLANUS in its original form would, from the length of the Play, be impossible," he conceded.

> But though we cannot bring upon the stage all that the great poet has written, there yet appears no just cause for interpolating his text with the works of others. Any alteration, but that of omission, seems a sin against the majesty of our poet. . . . It is, perhaps, scarcely requisite to observe, that the Coriolanus of the modern stage is very freely interpolated with extracts from Thomson. (v)

Elliston's text lived up to its billing. Not a word of Thomson or any other adaptor contaminated the Shakespearian landscape, or what was left of it; for almost half the play, some 1780 lines, vanished. The manager was not, however, quite as innocent of Kemble's influence as he implied; indeed, a Covent Garden acting edition lay at hand as he worked to judge from the numerous cuts common to both texts, to say nothing of his appropriation of Kemble's names for Shakespeare's anonymous messengers, servants, and senators (Appius, Lucius, Navius, Arnus, Servilia).

Elliston's textual cutting was dictated by three major concerns: the sublimination of political and military content to character revelation; a marked distaste for having the star absent from the stage for any lengthy period; and a preference for action and spectacle over speech.

The citizens' political profile is reduced to near invisibility: they function largely as an object of Martius's scorn and an animated and colorful backdrop to patrician grandstanding. As usual, the tribunes are the motors of the action, and their motives are again personal rather than political. The Volscian-Roman conflict with its disillusioned view of militarism shrinks to several animated vignettes in which the hero demonstrates his physical prowess and receives martial honors. Scenes in which Martius does not appear are cut wherever possible, and heavily abridged when they cannot be eliminated. When the star is onstage, his speeches are curtailed to minimize rhetoric in favor of movement, and scenes are rushed to a conclusion once he exits.

Elliston's script, despite a certain affinity with Kemble's, marches to a different aesthetic drummer: in lieu of the Covent Garden manager's succession of static tableaux with a highly finished characterization forever in the foreground, Elliston offers a series of impressionistic action sequences each of which reveals the star in a moment of crudely emotional crisis against a spectacular setting. The eye consistently preempts the ear; speech unsupported by action, particularly if not delivered by Kean, receives short shrift. Elliston's predilection for visual over auditory communication owes its origin to decades spent in the minor theaters where dialogue was largely illegal. "The emphatic gesture," he informed audiences in an "Occasional Address" to his 326-line *Macbeth* burletta at the Royal Circus a decade earlier:

> eloquence of eye,
> Scenes, music, every energy we try,
>
>   . . . .
>
> To prove we keep our duties full in view,
> And what we must not *say,* resolve to *do;*
> Convinc'd that you will deem our zeal sincere
> Since more by *deeds* than *words* it will appear.[10]

In fairness to Elliston, it must be admitted that had he chosen to use more dialogue, there was no guarantee that it would be heard. The need for narrative clarity in an acoustically problematic three thousand-seat playhouse inevitably forced literary art to play second fiddle to visual splendor.

However swingeing the cuts elsewhere, audiences were treated to a fuller version of 1.1 than was characteristic of Kemble. Menenius, enjoying a rare instance of managerial largesse, is allowed to speak the belly fable despite the production's apolitical character. The scene is shortened by some eighty lines altogether, with most cuts designed to clarify syntax, eliminate rhetoric, and hasten the action. In an effort to diminish the play's political dimension, the citizens' subversive potential is markedly underplayed. Significantly, Menenius's challenge, "But make you ready your stiff bats and clubs. . . . The one side must have bale" (1.1.161–63) is cut. Aufidius's encounter with the Volscian senators (1.2), thirty-seven lines in all, is again eliminated. The scene between Volumnia, Virgilia, and Valeria (1.3) is curtailed by about one-third, mostly by reduction in the length of speeches. There is no talk of visiting "the good lady that lies in"; Valeria merely invites the women to "play the idle huswife with me this afternoon." Most of Virgilia's resistance to leaving home (1.3.78–88, 102–110) disappears. It is worth noting, perhaps, that the women are permitted to sit and sew for the first time since the Commonwealth.

The battle before the walls of Corioli (1.4) is restored, but the ensuing scene, with its cynical glance at military heroics, is absent, as is the impres-

sionistic sequence in which Titus Lartius moves toward the camp of Cominius (1.7). The fight between Martius and Aufidius (1.8) is also removed
together with the episode in which Tullus vows revenge (1.10).

Act 1, then, comprises five scenes: the encounter between Martius, Menenius and the plebeians (1.1), the Volumnia-Virgilia domestic sequence (1.2),
and three battlefield episodes—1.4, 1.6, and 1.9. Elliston's version, although
radically shortened, offers more of the play's martial dimension than had
been seen since the seventeenth century.

To open act 2 with the ovation, which he had no inclination to omit,
Elliston slashed the preliminary 161 lines in which Menenius harangues the
tribunes and anticipates, with Volumnia and Virgilia, Martius's triumphal
return. At the exit of the procession at 2.1.204 Elliston, like Kemble, makes
a separate "carpenter's scene" of the strategy discussion between Sicinius
and Brutus. The Senate episode (2.2) opens with the entry of the senators;
and as usual, the cushion-layers vanish. In 2.3, the Voices scene, Martius
encounters only two groups of citizens, as in Kemble's time. In the subsequent citizen-tribune caucus, the instructions of the latter are substantially
shortened, particularly by the removal of 2.3.222–51. The scene ends, as in
Kemble's script, with the exit of the plebeians. The tribunes' final observations (2.3.255–63) disappear.

In 3.1, deferring to Kemble's practice, physical aggression (3.1.180–206)
is excised along with Menenius's interjections and appeals. Martius, in the
approved Kemble manner, simply draws his sword and defies his opponents
on "I'll die here." Once the star quits the stage, Menenius's pleas are
abruptly stifled. The scene in which Volumnia persuades Martius to temporize with the electors (3.2) is reduced by about one-third. The Banishment
episode (3.3), shortened by a similar amount, loses most of the initial strategy conference between Sicinius and Brutus (3.3.1–24) and concludes in
traditional fashion with "There is a world elsewhere."

Act 4 opens with the Farewell scene, now happily restored, although some
thirty-odd lines briefer than its original, and is followed by Volumnia's contretemps with the tribunes (4.2). Adrian and Nicanor (4.3) are blue-penciled
as is Martius's arrival in Antium (4.4), cuts favored by Kemble. Elliston's 4.3
begins with a much abbreviated encounter between Martius and Aufidius's
servants. The Volscian general arrives more speedily than in Shakespeare's
text, and the pact between the deadly enemies is struck with minimal debate.
The scene ends on Aufidius's strong exit line, "Your hand: most welcome!";
the servants' colloquy (4.5.148–235) is cut as in Kemble's text. The Roman
reception of the news of Martius's approach (4.6) is lopped less severely
than by Kemble. Aufidius and his lieutenant are again denied their interview
in 4.7.

Shakespeare's 5.1, in which Menenius agrees to approach Martius, and
5.2, in which his appeal meets failure, disappear. Elliston's act 5 opens, as
did Kemble's, with Menenius's grim assessment of Volumnia's prospects

(5.4), transposed to precede rather than follow the Intercession episode (5.3), and thus crudely to hike dramatic tension. The announcement of the matrons' success is, of course, removed, since the event has not yet taken place. The intercession is purged of Sheridan-Thomson-Kemble corruptions, but less than three-quarters of the Shakespearian text survives. In keeping with tradition, Volumnia's victorious return to Rome (5.5) is omitted to allow Martius's assassination to follow without change of locale. The women and Martius withdraw at the conclusion of the intercession sequence, and Aufidius exchanges with Volusius (who retains his Thomsonian designation but takes the speeches of the 1st Conspirator) nineteen lines of his sixty-line colloquy with the conspirators from 5.6. The lords then enter, and Martius returns with the Roman women and Young Martius. The quarrel is played in Shakespeare's text, save for the absence of the Volscian citizens; but in a curious reversion to Dennis's practice, Martius is struck down in full view of his family. Aufidius is permitted to stand on the body for the first time since the Restoration, and the Third Lord fails to remonstrate.

The Elliston-Kean revival fully convinced the *Examiner* critic that "Mr. KEMBLE made a fine picturesque mistake of this character." Coriolanus, he informed his readers, "is not a Roman of the elegant fashion of after times":

> He is one of the rougher soldiers of the early republic; and SHAKESPEARE himself evidently intended him for such. An apology is made to the people by his friends on the very score of his rough reading and want of address (31 January 1820).

It was precisely toward this historically and textually authentic conception of the hero's character that much of Elliston's pruning was directed. What he seems to have envisioned was a series of rapid-fire confrontations between a primitive creature of absolute *virtus* and a temporizing and corrupt society. At breakneck speed, a roughcast Martius defies the plebeians, scales the walls of Corioli, receives military honors, returns home in triumph, solicits the citizens' voices, confronts the plebeians and is banished, bids farewell to his family, joins the enemy, approaches Rome, is turned aside by his family, and dies. Kemble's Roman was a figure of antique splendor; Kean's, of exploited integrity. Significantly, the "lonely dragon" simile, long cut, is restored, and serves throughout to animate a kind of Byronic hero, described by Hauser as "the eternal stranger among men. . . . lonely, silent, and unapproachable with his inner loneliness, his secret which is never revealed . . . his childish and animal-like 'self-sufficiency and unapproachability.'"[11] Where Kemble's portrait was distanced and generalized, the Elliston-Kean study was immediate and personal. As a creature of a prehistoric time, rudeness and brutality are essential to his authenticity: little attempt is made to mitigate his anti- or predemocratic convictions, his disdain of plebeian aspirations, or his lack of social ease. Although the "flower of warriors," he remains in touch with his feelings. Unlike Kemble's Roman, he is allowed to confess to weariness, to forget his Volscian host's name, to betray a vein of domestic tenderness. What is missing, however, is some evidence of intellectual capacity; for example, although more of his crucial defence of his political position (3.1.90–161) is spoken than in Kemble's script, the audience still hears less than half the original. But of course ratiocination sorted ill with instinctive goodness.

The Martius of Elliston's text, although nearer Shakespeare's than any yet encountered, exists in outline only. Detail and texture are almost non-existent. Elliston is no more ready than his predecessors to engage in analysis of Martius's character from multiple points of view, some of them contradictory; consequently, the observations of the tribunes, Menenius, Volumnia, and Aufidius, not to mention the views of the cushion-layers, disappear or are radically curtailed.

Volumnia loses some of the histrionic opportunities provided by Kemble, including her separate entry in the ovation and the dagger sequence in the Intercession scene; but by way of compensation she is granted the histrionic challenges of the Farewell episode (4.1) and her subsequent altercation with the tribunes (4.2). To speed the reentry of the star, she forgoes her scene of high excitement prior to Martius's triumphal return, for which her gratuitous appearance as a mute in the play's final moments is scant redress. The primitive period in which the action is set offered sufficient warrant for her Amazonian flights and little attempt was made to ameliorate them.

Menenius enjoys a slightly greater prominence than in previous versions. In 1.1 he is permitted to converse with the plebeians prior to Martius's arrival. With the restoration of the Farewell scene and Volumnia's contretemps with the tribunes, he regains a few finely dramatic moments denied him by Kemble. The excision of his confrontation with the tribunes in 2.1 is a considerable loss; and it is a pity, too, to miss his good-natured assessment of himself as a "humorous patrician" (2.1.46ff.) and his exhibition of boyish high spirits as he awaits Martius's return. Since the patrician-plebeian fisticuffs in 3.2 disappear, as in Kemble, he loses much of his diplomatic dimension; and most of his defense of Martius after the latter's departure also disappears. While he continues to taunt the plebeians and tribunes when news arrives of Martius's impending invasion, he takes no active role in averting the impending disaster. The scenes in which he agrees to approach Martius and the encounter itself (5.1 and 5.2) are cut. While he is a more obvious presence than in Kemble's production, the wholesale and haphazard butchery of his lines denies him any coherent function.

Aufidius continues to fare badly. Although freed from Thomsonian humanitarianism and allowed some degree of Shakespearian opportunism, his appearances are too few and brief to have much impact. The importance attached by Shakespeare to the interaction of Martius and his alter ego throughout the play's early scenes is ignored. He does not appear with the Volscian senators in 2.1, nor does he battle Martius in 1.8, or renounce chivalry in favor of opportunism in 1.10. As in Kemble's text, he is not seen until Martius deserts to the Volscians. Even then his ecstatic nuptial imagery (4.5.103–26) is cut, as well as the entire scene in which he assesses Martius's character for the Lieutenant (4.7). His justification of, and strategy for, Martius's assassination (5.6) are much reduced, and the thrust altered. When Volusius offers to "deliver you / Of your great danger," Aufidius replies "We must proceed as we do find the people." The lords arrive before he can make a decision. Later, the conspirators kill Martius, apparently without the aid of Aufidius, although he later stands on the body. As usual he speaks the perfunctory, "My rage is gone, / And I am struck with sorrow" and orders the cortege. Shakespeare's integral, if ambiguous, Volscian, shrinks in Elliston's text to a mere cipher—a convenient foe to whom Martius deserts and the contriver of his death.

However emphatically Elliston might reject certain aspects of the Kemble tradition, he was wholly in sympathy with its spectacular character: on the grounds of authenticity, however, Kemble's mise-en-scène, like his text, was open to challenge. Coriolanus is an early Republican historical figure; the visual milieu should therefore, Elliston argued, suggest that period rather than the Imperial grandeur long familiar at Covent Garden. But research into the era was not easy, and imagination had frequently to be summoned to assist fact. "Not even a fragment remains to us of the Roman buildings or dresses in the time of Coriolanus," he confessed in the "Advertisement" to his acting edition. "Whatever therefore has been done, in the way of decoration, must be received with indulgence." Nevertheless, he did what he could. "The nearest approach to the time, is to be found in a basso relievo from Herculaneum, which represents Coriolanus receiving his wife and mother, as the advocates of Rome," he informed his audiences, anticipating by some decades the erudite program notes of Charles Kean. For "Roman dresses" and "head dresses" he drew on vase paintings.

Although he freely acknowledged that much of his reconstruction was open to question since "[e]ven the manners of the period are but imperfectly known," he was concerned lest archeologically correct costume features fail to be appreciated due to a casual resemblance to "the costume of the French peasants" or "prototypes in the fashions of our modern world." Audiences were duly reminded "that the more remote fashions of antiquity are the nearest allied to the present period" (vi).

His decision to enrich Kemble's Davidian palette with gilding and vibrant color also demanded advance explanation lest cynics invoke the ghost of his pantomimic past. "Much has been said of the severe taste of ancient times," he conceded, and it is probable therefore, that the gilded splendor of the scenery may be objected to;—it would, perhaps, be a sufficient answer to such cavils to state, that truth must be sometimes sacrificed to stage effect; but I may go farther; we know that the Greeks, with all their supposed purity of taste, painted and gilded their finest statues. . . . Let me hope, therefore, on this head to escape censure, where I may not have deserved praise" (vi).

No visual record of the production has come to light; the only concrete reference is the playbill's list of new scenes with the names of the artists responsible: "A View in Rome . . . Marinari," "View near the Camp of Cominius . . . Andrews," "The Camp of Cominius . . . Ditto," "The Capitol of Rome . . . Hollagan," "Another View in Rome . . . Marinari," "The Walls of Rome . . . Dixon."[12] Despite Elliston's archaeological dedication, few critics noticed the mise-en-scène. The *Morning Post* reviewer (26 January 1820) found the settings "beautiful and effective," while *The News* (30 January 1820) judged them "very beautiful and correct." And no one felt moved to say more. On the positive side, the censure he had anticipated on the grounds of historical inaccuracy did not materialize. The *Morning Advertiser* reviewer identified two "violations of historical truth": that he "could not distinguish [the citizens'] trades" by their costumes and that "all were provided with sticks" (26 January 1820). There was also criticism of the fact that "in the camp of TULLUS, the *Roman* banners are waving" (*British Monitor,* 30 January 1820). But these complaints were virtually unique.

Living scenery remained as popular as in Kemble's time. The ovation, "which combined the fasces, eagles, and other various insignia of Roman dominion, with the costume in classical precision" (*British Press,* 26 January 1820), but without the reeling matron evoked by Mrs. Siddons, found general approval. "See the Conquering Hero Comes," which accompanied Kemble's procession, was replaced by "An Ode of Triumph Written by Mr. G. SOANE, and Composed by Mr. T. COOKE" and sung by a sizeable male and female chorus of Flamens, Vestals, and Soldiers. The first two stanzas offer a fair sample of its quality:

> Strew the way with all that blushes,
>   Sweetest in the bowers of Spring,
> 'Till each footfall odour crushes
>   From the flowers blossoming.

> Io Paean! swell his glory
>   'Till it beat the star-lit sky;
> Io Paean! write his story
>   In thy book, Eternity.

There was also the procession of Roman matrons, and interpolated spectacle whenever occasion offered. "One would think there were processions enough in this play, as it was acted in John Kemble's time," complained

Hazlitt; "but besides these, there were introduced others of the same sort, some of which were lengthened out as if they would reach all the way to the Circus" (*London Magazine,* February 1820). Precisely where the new pageantry was inserted cannot be determined.

The restored battle of Corioli was not well-received. Hazlitt described it as "a sham-fight, of melodramatic effect . . . in which Mr. Kean was like to have lost his voice" (*London Magazine,* February 1820). Another theatergoer wryly recalled that "when the city of *Corioli* is attacked by the Roman army, four men are defending it from the ramparts, cutting away with as much *non chalance* as if they were carving a buttock of beef at a cook's shop" (*British Monitor,* 30 January 1820). A third simply advised Elliston "to get rid of the rambling fight . . . as quickly as possible" (*Morning Advertiser,* 26 January 1820).

It was, however, primarily for Kean's Martius that audiences crowded the theater on the first night, and it was here that the Kemble tradition was most decisively challenged. At his first entrance audiences witnessed not the towering grandeur of John Kemble, but a Martius of five feet six and three-quarter inches.[13] Kean had "rather a compact and not disproportioned nor ill-formed figure," recalls Hackett. "His face"

> beamed with intelligence, and its muscles were plastic and suggestive of the passions; his eyes were black, large, brilliant, and penetrating, and remarkable for the shortness of their upper lid. . . . [H]is action and gesticulation, though ever easy and natural, were generally quick and energetic, and very earnest-like.
> . . . His voice, when raised or strained, was harsh and dissonant, but in level speaking, and especially in poetic measure, its undertones were charming, musical, and undulating. . . .[14]

His acting style, characterized by Hazlitt as "radical," was more natural than Kemble's; it relied for its effect on a series of flamboyant, discrete moments, rather than on the gradual accretion of detail. Where Kemble's performance was statuesque, controlled, even chilly, Kean's was energetic, spontaneous, and vehement.

Whatever the virtues of Kean's Martius, and there were some, audiences refused to overlook his want of size. Here as in no other Shakespearian play the hero's epic physicality confronts the theatergoer at every turn; and if the actor does not measure up to reasonable expectation, credibility is compromised. As one reviewer put it:

> To say that a hero should be of a certain height, or that it is indispensable that he should possess a particular cast of features, would be to court ridicule; but yet we think that those who have seen Mr. KEMBLE in *Coriolanus* . . . will be ready to adopt our opinion that the figure, face, voice, and deportment of Mr. KEAN, are but little calculated to satisfy the admirers of SHAKSPEARE's *Caius Marcius* (*Morning Post,* 26 January 1820).

Edmund Kean as Coriolanus (1820). [By permission of the Folger Shakespeare Library]

"We must be pardoned," wrote another, "if, in fancying the *beau ideal* of a Roman warrior, we imagined his stature *somewhat* to exceed 5 feet. . . . [I]t is this which makes the threat to the Tribune:

> 'Hence, or I will shake thy bones
> Out of thy garments!'

with other passages of the same kind, to which Mr. KEMBLE's form, eye, and action, gave so terrible an emphasis, utterly ridiculous from the lips of Mr. KEAN" (*News*, 30 January 1820).

Even with greater physical advantages, however, Kean's romantic Martius would have seemed aesthetically sacrilegious to a generation weaned on the Kemble Roman. John Philip's marmoreal figure may have been "a fine picturesque mistake," as Leigh Hunt maintained, but "the town judge[d] of a *Coriolanus* by his, and not by Shakespeare's [character]" (*Examiner,* 31 January 1820). However faithful to Shakespeare's text a reading might be, and Kean's was not exceptionally so, contemporary taste preferred Kemble's misreading.

The chief virtue of Kean's characterization, and the source of its undoing, lay in its originality. "Our modern Roscius," wrote the *Mirror of the Times* reviewer, had the wisdom to abandon all former models, and to strike out a path for himself."

> He reflected, probably, that *Coriolanus,* with all the dignity of a Roman, is vulnerable to the feelings of a man: that dignity, like a state dress, cannot be consistently worn on every occasion, and that its representation is subordinate in effect on the stage, to the delineation of human agony and suffering that comes home to the bosom of every spectator (22–29 January 1820).

Where Kemble incarnated physical dignity and spiritual grandeur, Kean, making a virtue of necessity, eschewed both. Kean's Coriolanus was "a barbarian soldier of primitive Rome, graced only with a barbarian's virtues—courage, generosity, and filial obedience."[15] In keeping with his determination to humanize the character, "[t]he style of the lofty Roman," one critic remarked, "was frequently abandoned in favour of colloquial, but popular touches," "fire and energy," and a "vehement picture of the passions" of a barbaric spirit (*Morning Chronicle,* 26 January 1820).

Even as Elliston's scenery invoked the picturesque authenticity of early Republican Rome, Kean's Martius probed the unrefined, but uncorrupted, sensibility of a primitive military man, the diametric opposite of Kemble's Imperial icon. Nowhere was the difference between the two characterizations more marked than in the portrayal of Martius's pride. The pride of Kemble's Roman was not personal, but, as one critic observed, "it rather relate[d] to his order than to his person and repose[d] on times which then were old" (*New Monthly Magazine,* April 1820). The pride of Kean's Martius, by way of contrast, was entirely personal, based on individual accomplishment, and betraying when affronted a psyche "o'er-informed with feeling, which is just elicited and cannot last" (*New Monthly Magazine,* April 1820). Kemble's demigod, remote and unimpassioned, now yielded pride of place to a rugged individualist "with all the infirmities of man about him," as one reviewer put it:

> Passionate and headstrong, obstinate and fierce. He despises the Plebeans, not because he is a Patrician, but because he is brave, and esteems them as cowards. His contempt is that of a soldier towards a recreant. . . . The *Coriolanus* of Mr. Kemble bore no resemblance to this. His was merely Patrician pride (*Imperial Weekly Gazette,* 29 January 1820).

This conception of Coriolanus as a primitive military man, champion and victim of a code which gave no quarter to human weakness, licensed Kean to posture at will in a series of almost discrete situations in which uncompromising honesty confronts expediency. Indeed, to one theatergoer, the performance seemed "to comprise a certain number of intense expressions of rage—a certain number of hysteric laughs—and a certain number of rapid transitions—all separately striking—but harmonized by no universal feeling, nor producing in the whole any impression of a great individual character" (*Champion*, 29 January 1820). The conception was, as we have seen, fostered by Elliston's text.

What audiences missed most was the sheer scale and monumentality of the character. Hazlitt, unconsciously in thrall to the Kemble icon, found Kean's Martius altogether too frenetic, self-conscious, even déclassé. "[I]nstead of remaining fixed and immovable (for the most part) on his pedestal of pride,"

> [Martius] seemed impatient of this mock dignity, this *still-life* assumption of superiority; burst too often from the trammels of precedent, and the routine of etiquette, which should have confined him; and descended into the common arena of man, to make good his pretensions by the energy with which he contended for them, and to prove the hollowness of his supposed indifference to the opinion of others by the excessive significance and studied variations of the scorn and disgust he expressed for it (*London Magazine*, February 1820).

Heroic authority of the Kemble variety was in short supply throughout, but particularly in act 1 where Martius's epic mystique must be established. In the recuperated Battle of Corioli episode, Kean's "comparative smallness of stature and weakness of voice were unquestionably adverse to his exertions" (*British Press*, 26 January 1820); nevertheless, "his energy made him appropriately conspicuous" (*Morning Post*, 26 January 1820), if not awesome, and fighting "with a lighted torch in his hand" (*Courier*, 26 January 1820) lent the character a swashbuckling air. His awareness of his physical deficiencies, however, was pervasive, distracting, and ultimately destructive. Theatergoers were disconcerted to find him "contract[ing] his person and gesture as if to collect his passions and his force for more powerful expression" (*English Chronicle*, 25–27 January 1820), or, as part of the same attempt at compensation, "literally rant[ing] in those scenes which required a dignified energy of expression, and bustl[ing] *à la Richard*, through those which demanded calm fortitude, or lofty contempt" (*Courier*, 26 January 1820).

He was at his best, of course, when he could give emotion full rein. The "bitter contempt" with which he spoke "They said they were an-hungry" (1.1.205) and the "beautiful and engaging simplicity" with which he begged the freedom of his Volscian host were much praised. The effect of the latter was somewhat vitiated, however, when "the name of his host being de-

manded, [he] made a long pause—tapped his forehead two or three times—
but finding *nothing there,* said, in a low and hurried voice—'By Jupiter,
forgotten!'" (*News,* 30 January 1820). The Voices scene was judged a triumph. "Only a great actor," maintained John Doran, "could have played the
scene . . . as Kean did,"[16] although he received some criticism for the long
pauses at every repetition of the word "voices." His playing in 3.1 was a
popular rather than a critical success. His "first amazement at the presumption of the tribunes" promised much, but reviewers rapidly lost enthusiasm
as Kean strayed from high Roman solemnity. His "dialogues with the Tribunes were mere farce and low buffoonery," complained *The Champion.*
The lines

> Shall remain?
> Hear you this Triton of the minnows? Mark you
> His absolute "shall"?
>
> (3.1.88–90)

were delivered "in the most flippant and affected manner, and terminated
like the other speeches, in stammering farce" (29 January 1820). "The ridicule thrown on the pompous Tribune . . . was laughable, and it obtained
great applause," admitted the *Morning Post,* "but it was downright farce,
and therefore out of its place in *Coriolanus*" (26 January 1820). Behind these
cavils lurks the intriguing possibility that Kean found humor in the character,
a possibility overlooked until Olivier tackled the role more than a century
later. Whatever their reservations, however, reviewers found the scene not
entirely meritless: Martius's "terrific bursts of passion where he is accused
as a traitor to the people" (*Champion,* 29 January 1820), and the "sublimely
awful" visual effect of his "No, I'll die here" (*Imperial Weekly Gazette,* 29
January 1820) won golden opinions. It was precisely the devastating intensity
of his rage that lent credibility to Martius's desertion to the Volscians, always a weak spot in Kemble's cold-blooded reading. The subsequent episode (3.2) in which Volumnia persuades her near hysterical offspring to
temporize with the citizens was described as one of several "masterly pieces
of acting" (*British Press,* 26 January 1820).

To assess fairly Kean's Banishment scene is next to impossible: the ghost
of Kemble shadowed his every move and inflection, and eyewitnesses were
incapable of critiquing the performance save as a desecration of the Kemble
rite. Hazlitt, from whom one expects better, faulted Kean's reading, not
because it was unjustifiable, but because it was not the Covent Garden
revelation. His "I banish you," he wrote, in a typical reaction:

> was given with all the virulence of execration, and rage of impotent despair, as if
> he had to strain every nerve and faculty of soul to shake off the contamination
> of [the plebeians'] hated power over him, instead of being delivered with calm,
> majestic self-possession, as if he remained rooted to the spot and his least motion,

word, or look, must scatter them like chaff or scum from his presence! (*London Magazine*, February 1820).

Despite the fact that Kean's Roman was an emotionally overwrought tribesman driven to near hysteria by assaults on his integrity, only John Philip's imperial iciness would do. The lines, insisted one such devotee, "convey a solemn, dignified, and bitter rebuke, and require not a burst of hysteric laughter to strengthen them. The lofty-minded *Coriolanus* would be better portrayed . . . if he left the stage breathing his indignation in the calm tone of collected scorn, instead of running off in a paroxysm of frantic or rather silly rage" (*Morning Post*, 26 January 1820).

Critics who blamed Kean for excessive emotion in the Banishment scene faulted him for want of it in the Farewell and Intercession episodes. "The parting scene of Coriolanus and his friends at the gate of Rome does not draw forth a single tear," reported *The Champion* (29 January 1820), and the Intercession sequence "passed over the house without the slightest expression of applause," according to the *English Chronicle* (25–27 January 1820). Indeed, if one is to credit Hazlitt's account of the intercession, "this decisive and affecting interview passed off as if nothing had happened, and was conducted with diplomatic gravity and skill" (*London Magazine*, February 1820). Is one to conclude that without the florid Thomsonian rhetoric, drawn dagger, and tear-drenched hand the text seemed tame? Or were the actors somehow defective? Of one fact there can be no doubt: Kemble Romans absent were somehow more potent than Kean-Elliston Romans present.

Martius's death, in its turn, was less censured, although not uniformly praised. The "fiery impetuosity with which [Martius] repelled the taunts of *Tullus*" (*Morning Post*, 26 January 1820) was just the sort of emotional gymnastics at which Kean excelled; but even as he soared, the Kemble shade stalked. Some critics disparaged the stammering bluster of "Alone -I -I -I -I -did it," eulogizing John Philip's bleak stoicism at the expense of Kean's flamboyant sensibility: "the one was a mighty mind betrayed unwillingly into the expression of an exulting consciousness of his great deeds, the other the egotism of an enraged bully" (*Theatrical Inquisitor*, January 1820). Even the timing of his death fall was unfavorably compared with Kemble's abrupt crash: to at least one observer, Martius seemed "to remain standing too long after receiving the fatal stabs from the Volscians" (*British Press*, 26 January 1820).

While Kean was dispraised, his supporting performers were ignored or received only general and perfunctory mention.

The Elliston-Kean challenge to the Kemble tradition, premised on authenticity and originality when audiences and critics wanted neither, ultimately proved as misjudged as it was brave. The restored scenes awakened no enthusiasm, and theatergoers missed Kemble's interpolations. "Some of the

noblest pieces of scenic effect, in KEMBLE's composition are not in Shakespeare," argued the *Champion* (29 January 1820) reviewer:

> but we do not think this any reason why they should be omitted. The discovery
> of the hero beneath the Statue of Mars was not the less impressive because
> Shakespeare had not devised it. In the last scene between Coriolanus and Tullus
> Aufidius, the speeches taken from Thomson produced almost an equal effect with
> those of Shakespeare, and, on the Stage, the difference between their poetical
> merit never disturbed the impression produced by the sweeping Majesty of the
> sentiment and of the action.

The *New Monthly Magazine* (April 1820), equally committed to the status
quo, reported "that the restored scenes were past [sic] over without notice,
the battles appeared childish, and the interest in the last act was divided
and feeble." "The truth is," their critic concluded, ". . . that the fact of a
certain scene being Shakspeare's is no presumption that it must tell on the
stage when common sense and experience are against it."

Kean's attempt at interpretative originality was as unappreciated as Elliston's uncorrupted text. "An affected departure from the best models is
not originality, but only alteration," the *News* critic insisted:

> and an actor may take a bad model, and reject a good one, and yet be as little
> original as ever. It is this contempt of those who have gone before him, and a
> paltry ambition of originality . . . which lie at the bottom of all Mr. KEAN's
> faults of style. . . . (30 January 1820).

The box office quickly ratified the verdict of the critics. After a satisfying
first-night gate of £561, receipts fell off precipitously, and the production
was withdrawn after the fourth performance.

Disparaged in its own time and neglected by theater historians since, the
Elliston-Kean *Coriolanus* ranks high among the play's pivotal productions,
not so much for its realization as for its vision. Decades before it was fash-
ionable to do so, Elliston placed his faith in the play's uncorrupted, if curtailed, text—a circumstance not to be duplicated until the time of Frank
Benson. For better or worse, his early-Republican scenography was clearly
the (unacknowledged) inspiration for Macready's antiquarian spectacle in
1838 and Irving's 1901 mise-en-scène, shaped in its turn by the Macready
precedent. Kean's much maligned Martius was in its way as radically pro-
gressive as Elliston's text and stagecraft. Although far from perfectly realized, something of the character's original roughness and inconsistency, long
smoothed by beau ideal cosmeticians, stood revealed. In contrast to the awe-
inspiring icon incarnated by Kemble, Martius at last assumed a dynamic,
passionate individuality. The romantic recognition of his pride as the product
of his unique psyche, rather than the trademark of an aristocratic society,
underpinned the more sophisticated psychological reading pioneered by Ma-

cready almost two decades later. The characterization was, of course, incoherent and unpolished, but its originality was striking, its potential profound, and its influence far-reaching.

For the moment, however, the challenge to the Kemble tradition had been met and vanquished. If actors and managers learned anything from the Kean-Elliston experiment, it was that the Kemble *Coriolanus* was less a cultural artifact than a theatrical rite, and seriously to tamper with it was to invite aesthetic and financial disaster.

6

The Kemble Tradition in England (1819–1915)

From Macready's first appearances as Martius in 1819 until World War I, Kemble's production served as the benchmark for *Coriolanus* interpretation on the English stage. On the strength of the popularity won for it by Kemble, *Coriolanus,* during the half-century after his retirement, enjoyed an unprecedented number of revivals. Twenty or more touring provincial stars (see *Chronological Handlist*)—among them William Augustus Conway, Charles Mayne Young, J. W. Wallack, Samuel Butler, Charles Dillon, and G. V. Brooke—scorned the plebeians in the Voices scene, repelled them heroically with sword in hand in the Forum, posed loftily beneath the statue of Mars, capitulated magnanimously to Volumnia, and dropped like felled trees in the play's final moments. The degree of historical authenticity and decorative splendor varied from theater to theater, but some attempt was invariably made to provide impressive ovations and sizable processions of mourning matrons. Few of these provincial Martiuses reached the theaters of the capitol, and if they did so, seldom found success. The sole exception was John Vandenhoff who offered Macready his only credible competition.

While itinerant stars aped John Kemble to the best of their limited talents and resources, actor-managers—William Charles Macready, Samuel Phelps, Henry Irving, and Frank Benson—attempted to lend novelty to the play by bending the Kemble production style without quite breaking it. Tricks were played with the Kemble text: Thomsonian interpolations were gradually removed, Shakespearian passages were restored and cut afresh; yet the Kemble script remained the reference point. Mise-en-scène became ever more historically accurate and realistic, but its aesthetic function was unaltered. The character of Martius, as played by Macready, Phelps, Irving, and Benson, proclaimed its beau ideal origins throughout the Victorian era, although the portrait steadily became softer focused until, in Benson's revivals, its remote and elevated character threatened to disappear altogether.

John Vandenhoff (1820–1848)

Between November of 1819 and December of 1820, a period of just over a year, no less than three youthful actors attempted Coriolanus in London theaters. Macready played the role at Covent Garden in November 1819 with considerable acclaim, and Kean ineffectually challenged him, as we have seen, in January 1820. In the autumn of 1820, when Kean was finally permitted to undertake his postponed tour of America, he recommended to the Drury Lane Committee as his replacement John Vandenhoff, a promising provincial stroller. The Covent Garden management, alert as always to competition from the rival house, rushed to hire Vandenhoff themselves. His Coriolanus debuted in December of 1820 to a lukewarm reception, and he returned, chagrined, to the hinterland. Over the next decade, however, he established an enviable reputation in Liverpool, Manchester, Edinburgh, and elsewhere, with Coriolanus as a feature of his repertory; and in the spring of 1834, some fourteen years after his first London appearance, he returned to star at the Haymarket where his Martius won instant acclaim. The following season (1834–35), as a member of the Covent Garden company, he repeated his performance with renewed success. Four years later, and just a few months after a lavish but financially disastrous production, Macready ameliorated his losses somewhat with a well-received *Coriolanus* revival featuring the previous season's sets and Vandenhoff in the title role. Thereafter, although Vandenhoff played Martius in the provinces for another decade and made the part a highlight of his American touring repertory (1837–41), London saw his Coriolanus no more.

Where other performers earn a place in *Coriolanus*'s stage history by their originality, Vandenhoff gains a niche through his dedicated perpetuation of the Kemble tradition. No actor played the part as often, throughout so extended a period (twenty-eight years), and over such a wide geographical area. And each appearance was a compulsively painstaking invocation of the Kemble ghost.

His best performances were doubtless those at the Haymarket and Covent Garden in 1834, and at Covent Garden under Macready's management in 1838. In these revivals, he seems to have been adequately, if not brilliantly, supported; stage effects were at least passable, and, under Macready's aegis, outstanding.

Vandenhoff, at his London appearance in 1834, was forty-four years of age, and the most physically impressive Roman then on the stage. Tall, heroically built, and rich-voiced, he represented for James Murdoch "the true ideal of the Roman character more thoroughly than any actor I had ever seen."[1] Kemble devotees, it is true, found Vandenhoff's interpretation rather "deficient in the colouring, spreading too dull a tone over the character," but they were simultaneously obliged to acknowledge him as "the only actor now upon the stage who can embody the prominent attributes—the dignity, the power, and the stern-heartedness" with which their idol had stamped the role on the popular imagination (*Atlas*, 29 September 1838). If he lacked something of Kemble's patrician sublimity, Vandenhoff lent the "rough, manly vigour" of the soldier a welcome "infusion of feeling and tenderness" by way of compensation (*Spectator,* 29 September 1838).

His performance in the first two acts received little critical notice, although in the Voices scene, "the proud reluctance with which he stooped to solicit, and the shuddering with which he shrunk from the touch of one of the people" (*Morning Chronicle,* 17 June 1834), a Kemble trick, was much applauded. He came into his own, however, in the act 3 confrontations. His challenges to the tribunes, "Have you not set them on?" and "Have you informed them since?" were delivered "with a force and point as if he looked them through." The "tone and smile of contempt" (*Albion and the Star,* 19 June 1834) with which he exclaimed, "Hear you this Triton of the minnows? Mark you / His absolute 'shall'?" invariably drew a round of applause. His delivery of the lines "pent to linger / But with a grain a day. . . . / To have't with saying, 'Good morrow'" (3.3.89–93), "growing on fuller and firmer as each succeeding word brought out the stern framing of his purpose," was a much admired piece of vocal pyrotechnics, as was his defiance of the mob as he went into exile. "His appearance at the statue of Mars" was regarded, like Kemble's, as "really a study for a painter" (*Morning News and Public Ledger,* 17 June 1834), while "the struggle with his feelings on the approach of the Roman matrons . . . the struggle between pride for Rome, and desire of faith with the Volscians were depicted with feeling force, and truth." In the final scene, "his heart truly seemed, as he said, to have become too big for what it contained; so that the scorn with which he denounced the Volscians, and *Tullus Aufidius* as a 'measureless liar,' had the most appalling and withering effect" (*Morning Advertiser,* 3 October 1834).

Vandenhoff's major defect, apart from his failure to attain his model's overall perfection, was a tendency to overplay Kemble's subtle gestural touches. During the Voices sequence, in an outburst of disgust with the plebeians, he appeared "to blow along the stage, as if oppressed with heat, or offended by the intrusion of some bad odour" (*Sun,* 25 September 1838). In the episode in which his mother and Menenius persuade him to be reconciled with the tribunes and people, as he spoke the lines "A beggar's tongue / Make motion through my lips" (3.2.117–18) "he rather degraded the lofty scorn he ought to feel by slightly (and it was but slightly) mimicking 'a beggar's tongue' and supplicating deportment" (*Morning Chronicle,* 17 June 1834). On "Sink my knee, i'th' earth," as he knelt to his mother in the Volscian camp, one critic recalls, "he literally clutches hold of his knee, forces it down as if it recalcitrated at volition, and apostrophises it" (*John Bull,* 30 September 1838). When Volumnia drew the dagger at the conclusion of the Intercession episode, instead of merely arresting her gesture, as Kemble had done, Vandenhoff on at least one occasion "wrested the weapon from her grasp and flung it away" (*Albion and the Star,* 19 June 1834). Almost universally execrated was his attempt to reproduce Kemble's legendary mime which accompanied his reference to fluttering the Volscians (5.6.114–

15). Vandenhoff never managed to get the movement right, but persisted in it nonetheless. "His arms, we think," wrote the *Morning Chronicle* reviewer (17 June 1834), "are at all times a trifle too long; but they seemed remarkably so, when, at the words 'fluttered your Volsces in Corioli,' he swung his right [arm] round, as if it were the fly of a windmill." Vandenhoff's failure to control his flamboyant taste even in his death throes led a critic to remind him that "a noble Roman rather covered his face in dying with his mantle than became in his mortal agony 'a driveller and a show,' with his teeth grinding like a slave beneath the lash" (*Satirist,* 30 September 1838). The Kemble inspiration for this bizarre effect is not immediately apparent.

Whatever its faults, it is no small tribute to Vandenhoff's Coriolanus that it commanded the respect of audiences who had witnessed Kemble, and constituted for theatergoers for whom Kemble was only a legend a living and poignant relic of vanished neoclassical grandeur for close to three decades on both sides of the Atlantic.

WILLIAM CHARLES MACREADY (1838)

William Charles Macready in 1819, at the age of twenty-six, played Martius for the first time, at Kemble's theater and only three years after the retirement of its proprietor. With a sensitivity to popular taste considerably greater than Kean's, he played the Kemble text more or less in the Kemble manner, and enjoyed a warm reception.[2] Over the next eighteen years he repeated the part occasionally in London and the provinces, but it was never a staple of his repertory. After his London debut as Coriolanus, he played the role in the capital only four times prior to undertaking management— at Drury Lane in 1821, 1824, 1831, and 1833. "I am very anxious to make a part of [it]," he confided to his diary in 1833, "but fear the uninteresting nature of the story and the recollection of Kemble are objections too strong to overcome."[3]

During his management of Covent Garden in the 1837–38 season, however, he screwed his courage to the sticking place and, despite physical disqualifications for the role, launched a major revival on 12 March which proclaimed its loyalty to the Kemble tradition but asserted a marked degree of aesthetic autonomy.[4]

Macready was no more taken than Kemble with *Coriolanus*'s political character, and was equally disinclined to exploit its contemporary relevance. "[A]rt and literature," he told an audience shortly before *Coriolanus* opened, "have no politics."[5] While depression, bad harvests, trade union unrest, Chartist riots, and outrage at the fate of the Tolpuddle Martyrs obsessed the public mind, Macready's production remained wonderfully innocent of sociopolitical reference.[6] Like Kemble, he deliberately suppressed the play's politics whenever possible, and when the patrician-plebeian conflict could not be ignored he aestheticized it. Located in the remote past and swamped with exotic spectacle, the drive of the underclass for a place in the sun became little more for both managers than an incidental dash of period color in theatrical celebrations of bourgeois individualism.

Coriolanus's idiosyncratic structure and characterization had no more charm for Macready than for his distinguished predecessor, and the beau ideal reinvention of Caius Martius was again the key challenge. Their sources of aesthetic inspiration differed radically, however: Kemble's superman owed his appeal to the stern grandeur of neoclassicism; Macready's sought charisma in the rugged authenticity of Romantic primitivism.

Macready's text for the 1838 production does not survive, but it is fairly clear from playbills and reviews that he played something close to the Kemble script. He restored, it should be noted, Menenius's belly fable (1.1), Coriolanus's Farewell scene (4.1), his arrival in Antium, with its "O world, thy slippery turns!" soliloquy (4.4), and Menenius's mission (5.2) to the Volscian camp. Aufidius's anonymous servants, now christened Nautius, Servius, and Cotus, appear in the playbill; presumably some of their lines were reinstated.[7] In order to secure a crudely theatrical finale to Volumnia's appeal, he transposed her "thou shalt no sooner / March to assault thy country than to tread / . . . on thy mother's womb" (5.3.122–24) to follow her brilliantly understated "I am hush'd until our city be afire" lines (5.3.181–82).[8] Throughout the play he seems to have deleted a fair number of Thomsonian interpolations, but retained in act 5 the episode in which Aufidius offers Coriolanus the opportunity to return to Rome in safety. Act 5 was played as one long scene in the Kemble manner, so Menenius's deputation must have been inserted at the conclusion of act 4.

Macready's Romantic conception of the play drew its visual, and undeclared, inspiration from the Elliston-Kean revival of almost two decades earlier. Exploiting the contemporary fad for historicism, which made Sir Walter Scott a cultural icon, Macready set the action in the Etruscan period, now susceptible of something like credible reproduction thanks to the growing archive of antiquarian research.[9] Within a primitive Roman society just beginning to taste the bittersweet fruit of democracy, Macready situated a Rousseauesque Noble Savage, a creature of an earlier, more heroic ethos, unable to temporize with ignoble power seekers and consequently destroyed by them.

The curtain rose on "Rome, seen from the south-west side of the Tyber, which forms part of the foreground;"

> beyond the river rises the steep height of the southern summit of the Capitoline hill, crowned with its *Arx* and temples; underneath, to the right, are seen the *Cloaca Maxima* and the Temple of VESTA; whilst the remainder of the picture is occupied by the Palatine, crested with a few larger mansions, but its shelving

side, up which a rude street winds its way, densely crowded with . . . thatch covered huts (*John Bull,* 18 March 1838).

Offstage was heard "the roar of the many-headed monster, like the surging murmurs of the sea . . . till the multitude burst on the stage, rivalling in numbers and violence probably the actual Roman mob that thronged to the Capitol" (*Spectator,* 17 March 1838). "Their varied and sordid garbs, their excited looks and gestures, the miscellaneous weapons of their insurrection, and the truth of their movements" struck more than one critic as "a rare contrast to the rows of human clothes-pegs usually stuck up for this sort of stage duty" (*Morning Chronicle,* 13 March 1838). "They fluctuated to and fro," recalled another reviewer, "as their violent assent or dissent impelled them, with a loud and overwhelming suddenness, and one-minded ponderosity, truly fearful to think of encountering" (*Examiner,* 18 March 1838). Unlike Kemble's token, and comic, stage rabble, Macready's citizens were a numerically convincing and credibly dangerous opponent.

The next scene, Coriolanus's House, was a primitive Roman atrium, "lighted through its *compluvium,* and adorned by the tesselated floor, and shining brickwork of the period" (*John Bull,* 18 March 1838). Furnished with earthen vases and a bronze candelabra, it struck one reviewer as having an "almost pathetic simplicity" (*Examiner,* 18 March 1838). The battlefield sequences, abbreviated as in Kemble's version, offered a splendid opportunity for the reconstruction of an early Roman square camp, complete with vallum and fosse, "a field of battle covered with dead," and Corioli in the distance (*Examiner,* 18 March 1838).

A highlight of the play, as usual, was the ovation, staged in the Forum, "with, above, a glimpse of the still proud Capitol" and on the right the rostrum. In an innovative coup, the citizens, some two hundred in all, were brought on stage, despite Shakespeare's deliberate exclusion of them.[10] Volumnia, to Macready's credit, ceased to be a feature of the procession as in Mrs. Siddons's time, and assumed her original position among the spectators.

The procession, preceded by a crowd waving laurel and cheered on by citizens at second-story windows, passed through a rude brick arch rather than the monumental Republican structure of the Kemble era. "The emotion of the vast crowds as the passage of the procession through the gate brings nearer and nearer its renowned hero—," enthused one theatregoer,

the forest of laurel boughs rustling through the air as each hand seeks to contribute something to the glory of the scene. . . . the triumph, surpassing all this, of the mother and wife of the great soldier, as . . . they see him enter at last covered with the light purple and crowned with the oaken garland—these were the elements of a picture of life and excitement . . . the noblest . . . we ever witnessed (*Examiner,* 18 March 1838).

The Ovation. William Charles Macready Production, Covent Garden, 1838. [By permission of the British Library]

Quite as impressive was Macready's Senate scene, an episode to which Kemble paid little attention. Here, in a patent appropriation of a visual effect from Thomson's 2.5, the audience viewed the interior of the temple of Capitoline Jove, with between a hundred and two hundred white-robed senators seated on three sides of the stage on triple rows of stone benches, "the lighted altar in the midst, the Consul on his curule chair, backed by the bronze wolf . . . with no other ornament than its simple columns, and the vaulted heavens seen through its open roof" (*John Bull,* 18 March 1838). When the carefully grouped assembly rose as one man and with uplifted arms saluted their consul, critics were left vainly groping for adequate superlatives.

The Forum scenes in which Martius sought the citizens' voices and later incurred their disfavour and sentence of banishment were characterized by scenic beauty, archaeological accuracy, and finely managed and realistic crowds. Two settings were provided: "one displaying the tribunal and the warning statue of *Marsyas* in front, whilst high above tower the *Arx,* the Tarpeian rock, and the fane of JUPITER CAPITOLINUS . . . stretches with its hundred pillars and massy porticos, half across the scene; the other showing the Forum lengthwise, looking towards the Temple of VESTA,

The Senate Scene. William Charles Macready Production, Covent Garden, 1838. [By permission of the British Library]

which is seen through a centre arch" (*John Bull,* 18 March 1838). The specific setting used for each episode cannot now be determined.

To the archaeological interest and spectacular thrills characteristic of Kemble's decor, Macready added the emotional evocativeness of Romantic painting. Throughout the first half of the play, Charles Marshall, the scenic artist, utilized the architecture of early republican Rome, as Turner and Friedrich did landscape, not as an interest in itself, but to lend spiritual resonance to the figures placed against it.[11] The rude authenticity of Marshall's brick and stone cityscape constituted a visual equivalent of Martius's rugged value system which the self-interest of the rabble, tribunes, patricians, and even Volumnia conspire to corrupt.

The first two settings for the second half of the play romanticized and spiritualized Martius as an abused outcast; physical environment was subtly manipulated to endow the character with the affect Shakespeare denies him. He arrived at the house of Aufidius by starlight. "[I]n the centre of the stage," we are told,

Macready stood alone, the muffled, disguised, banished Coriolanus. . . . Behind him were the moles running out into the sea, and at the back of the scene the horison drawn beyond the sea in one long level line, interrupted only by a tall solitary tower, the pharos, or watch-tower of Antium (*Examiner,* 18 March 1838).

Marshall's exploitation of natural imagery to resonate human action and emotion was not lost on reviewers. "[The scene's] wide and barren aspect presents the simplicity and large-minded poverty of those old times, and the tower looks like *Coriolanus* himself in a less mortal shape, rising in lonely grandeur, but with still unextinguished light, above the melancholy of his exile and the level sternness of his contemporaries," noted the *Morning Chronicle* (13 March 1838). To add pathos to Martius's "O world, thy slipp'ry turns" soliloquy, music drifted through the open door of a brightly lighted house at stage right, where Aufidius feasted his nobles.

In the interior scene in which Martius revealed himself to Aufidius, Macready rejected Kemble's grand pose under the statue of Mars in favor of a more romantic (and Plutarchan) discovery in the aula of Aufidius's house, where, "lit by the glimmering brazier on the hearth," he sat shrouded in his mantle, flanked by statues of the household gods (*John Bull*, 18 March 1838).

The staging of the remainder of act 4, with its scenes in the Volscian camp and in Rome, was largely ignored by reviewers overwhelmed by the splendor of the final act, where Macready, like Kemble, marshaled all his scenographic resources to create a series of splendid and pathetic pictorial diversions as partial compensation for the text's want of transcendence and release.

The drop ascended on the final act to reveal the Volscian camp. "The city frowns in the distance," we learn, "begirt with the walls of *Servius,* and encircled . . . by his wide moat" (*John Bull*, 18 March 1838). "Various moving towers and battering rams" indicated preparations for a seige. "The number of brilliantly equipped soldiers on the stage," recalled one reporter, "was truly startling." According to the *Theatrical Observer* (13 March 1838), some "200 soldiers of the Guards," painstakingly grouped, suggested the Volscian army. The appearance of Volumnia and her train of matrons (23 are listed in the playbill), "stretching obliquely across the stage, in the midst of these brilliant warrior-files, one long, dreary, sable line of monotonous misery" (*Examiner,* 18 March 1838), seemed to divide as with a black thread the red masses of the enemy. Against this massive military backdrop, the confrontation between mother and son assumed something like cosmic dimensions.

Having attained their object, the women left the stage as in Kemble's version, while the military remained in place. Martius and Aufidius quarrel in the Thomsonian manner, and Martius is given his quietus by Volscian officers. John Coleman vividly recreates the play's concluding moments:

When Caius Marcius had fallen beneath the assassin's steel, horror and shame struck the Volscians dumb. Each man looked upon the other. . . . Then came silence—silence, awful and profound. Presently was heard the sound of a distant trumpet, followed by another and yet another. Men passed rapidly forth in answer to the signal, doubtless to relate how Caius Marcius fell. Again silence. . . . From afar arose the cry of women and children; then there came hurrying through the camp a host of fair maidens and stately matrons, piercing the air with lamentations, as they waved their arms aloft, and tossed their dishevelled hair. Before them strode a majestic figure, like one of the Eumenides. It was the Roman mother, Volumnia, who confronted, with pale face and flashing eyes, the men who had done to death her lion-hearted son. Next came his fair young wife, Virgilia, and his boy . . . followed by Valeria. . . . While with tears and piteous cries they bewailed their warrior dead, the murderers stood aghast, conscience-stricken, and appalled, until at a signal from their leader, the muffled drums and the shrill trump of the clarion made mournful music.[12]

As Aufidius speaks the eulogy, "the warriors around lift up the dead body of the conqueror on their shields, hang around it the splendidest trophies of war, and trailing their steel pikes in sorrow, move with it slowly up the stage to the sound of mournful music" (*Examiner,* 18 March 1838) as the curtain falls.

Macready's mise-en-scène was designed not as a discrete production feature, although it was viewed as such, but rather as an affective resonator for his groundbreaking Coriolanus, an interpretation which must have seemed less revolutionary to those who had seen Kean. Described as early as 1820 as "the most romantic of actors" (*New Monthly Magazine,* March 1820), Macready long since realized that any serious challenge he might make to the memory of Kemble's Martius must derive, not from physical grandeur and Davidian severity, but impassioned sensibility. The Macready Coriolanus, when it came to fruition, proved to be no Kemble demigod, but rather a noble and passionate, if rough-hewn, military man, the product of a time when physical valor and moral integrity, rather than political wardheeling, were the qualifications for state office. Macready's reading, no less beau ideal in its way than Kemble's, took its inspiration, not from the classical baroque tradition of Poussin, Dennis, and Thomson, but from the Romantic wellsprings which nourished the art of Rousseau, Chateaubriand, and Goethe.[13] And the ghost of Kean's fiery outsider forever hovered in the wings.

For Fox, Macready's reading was designed to reveal the struggle of "an individual nature with the spirit of an age." Rome, in the birth-pangs of democracy, demanded new sorts of leadership for a changing political system. Martius, product of a ruder aristocratic era, cannot accommodate his principles to the times: "The vices of a state of semi-civilisation, where pride and baseness, ferocity and hypocrisy, blend together, perpetually jar with his nature. They excite his contempt, mar his course of life, falsify his position, and co-operate with his own best feelings to work his destruction" (*Morning Chronicle,* 22 March 1838). Patrician pride, the key to Kemble's characterization, was a minor feature of Macready's reading: Martius merely "assume[d] pride as a means of subduing the violent passions by which his breast is torn" (*Courier,* 13 March 1838). The "scorn which *he*

The Funeral Procession. William Charles Macready Production, Covent Garden, 1838.
[By permission of the British Library]

gives vent to, wrong and misplaced as it often is, has its unfailing source in
what his own heart believes to be noble in thought and just in action" (*Exam-*
iner, 18 March 1838). In the end, as Macready saw it, he became a victim,
not of his own folly, but of a "filial veneration" which allowed his mother to
sacrifice his best interests to the exigencies of the Roman state. Fox summa-
rizes the tragedy of Macready's Martius thus:

> The heart of *Brutus* could joy that in all his life he found no man but he was true
> to him. Nobody is true to *Coriolanus*. His dearest friends, and the mother whom
> he reverences with an instinctive homage so profound, all conspire to persuade
> him into inconsistencies with himself. When seeking most to serve him they con-
> sult, not his nature and tendencies, but their own. . . . The web is woven around
> him more fatally by the patriotism of *Volumnia* than by the jealousy of *Aufidius*
> (*Morning Chronicle,* 22 March 1838).

In the early scenes of the play, although now forty-five, Macready admirably suggested "a young soldier overflowing with enthusiasm, love of country and of arms, and flushed with victory" (*Morning Advertiser,* 13 March
1838). His contempt for the citizens, unlike that of Kemble, was not an
inborn class reflex, but the reaction of crude integrity to moral corruption.
"He scorns the multitude," writes Fox, "because they are base-minded,
not because they are plebeian born," a view abundantly justified by the

demonization of the citizens throughout the production. His "irritability and unrestrained emotion" in the Voices scene and his subsequent confrontations with tribunes and citizens were symptomatic of an inner chafing at a society whose values pained him (*Morning Chronicle*, 13 March 1838). Where Kemble repulsed the tribunes and plebeians with cold disdain, Macready's reading was marked by "passion, almost wrought up to madness." He darted at the tribunes, we are told, "like a tiger at his prey" (*Sunday Times*, 18 March 1838). His pent-up disgust found satisfying release in the Banishment scene when with "an outbursting of hitherto smouldered, crushed-within fire, on the words, 'How! traitor!' . . . with all the mighty gush of its bound-up strength, the lava of indignation, scorn, and rage poured forth as he said 'The fires i'the lowest hell fold in the people.' Mother, honours, friends, Rome, all creatures, and all things, were whelmed and forgotten in the destructive sweep of that massive burst!," recalls Charles Pemberton, "—It was truly sublime!"[14] The cold scorn of "I banish you" and his exit on "There is a world elsewhere!" with "a look of unutterable contempt at the monster multitude" (*Sunday Times*, 18 March 1838) constituted a definitive repudiation of both his countrymen and his political ambitions.

His moral dilemma—the conflict between personal integrity and filial duty—was brutally highlighted in the episode in which Volumnia persuades him to placate the people. It was one thing to find himself at personal variance with a morally reprehensible society, but quite another to find his mother urging coexistence with it. Pemberton recalls Martius's "surprise, grief, and regret that his conduct is not appproved by [Volumnia]" at the beginning of the scene, the "look of pain and doubt" with which he listens to her appeal to temporize, "as if wishing *she* would not give such counsel, yet showing that he hears it, for that it is his duty to hear her." For his speech beginning, "Well I must do it," he compelled his voice into calm; "each syllable was distinctly pronounced: the thoughts gradually swelling with disgust at the picture which they drew, the face increasing its flush of shame, at the prospect of so degrading his habit and his nature." Finally his indignation burst out on "I will not do it," not loudly, but "in a dense, hard, iron tone, which told the full mastery with which the passion had grappled him."[15] "The look towards her which precedes his consent to humble himself before the people" (*Morning Chronicle*, 13 March 1838) was apparently devastating.

The lonely integrity of the outcast, symbolized by the solitary lighthouse and described by Fox as "most beautiful and touching," was underscored during pauses in the "O world, thy slippery turns" speech by "the faint but lively notes of the 'music within'" (*Morning Chronicle*, 22 March 1838). The wretchedness of exile gained fresh force with the revelation of a muffled, seated figure, illuminated by the firelight of Aufidius's hearth. "In the dialogue which follows," we are told, "there was no point-making, but the whole was one strong poetical and dramatic action" (*Morning Chronicle*, 13 March 1838).

The Intercession scene's visual splendor preempted the reviewers' attention to the neglect of the performers. It is clear, however, that Macready milked Martius's conflict between personal integrity and filial devotion for every ounce of sentiment it could yield. He "suffers as much as he sways," we are told, "and, conflicting with opposite emotions in his soul, sinks at last beneath the struggle" (*Examiner*, 18 March 1838). Macready's technique was as crude as it was effective. In a virtuoso display of brilliantly counterpointed emotional outbursts following closely one on the other, Martius unpacked his heart; lovers of impassioned sensibility thrilled to "the settled defiance of entreaty, the gushing fondness towards his wife and child, the horror at the idea of his mother's kneeling to him [a sequence now restored], the consciousness of ebbing resolve, and the entirely vanquished spirit at the final suggestion of *Volumnia*" (*Morning Chronicle*, 13 March 1838).

Still finer effects were held in reserve for the death sequence. Throughout the early part of the episode, in which Aufidius offers him safe passage to Rome, Martius was "most equable in his grandeur, and dignified in his contempt . . . until *Aufidius* would strip him of his quality of manhood" (*Guide*, 18 March 1838). The "noble indignation" of his reproach to Aufidius, "'Tis not for such as thee . . ." and "the grandeur of voice and action" which characterized the Volsces-fluttering speech were warmly praised (*Sun*, 13 March 1838). As he flung back on Aufidius the epithet "Boy," he delivered "the triumphant taunt with the fury and bitterness of one frantic with rage and indignation, the tempest of whose wrath has swept away the extremest bounds of discretion" (*Spectator*, 17 March 1838). A moment later, under "the onslaught of a dozen Volscians, who transfix him at once with their swords" (*Morning Post*, 13 March 1838), he fell in the Kemble manner, "as though that excess of vitality was only capable of instantaneous extinction" (*Morning Chronicle*, 13 March 1838). Round the corpse, the impression of those last moments of transcendent passion lingered. "The body lay dead," reported a witness, "but the passion of sublime wrath still glowed all livingly about it" (*Magnet*, 19 March 1838).

Macready's interpretation, although it had sterling virtues, fell short of success. Kemble-worshippers, and the audience was riddled with them, claimed that "he vulgarised *Coriolanus*" (*News and Sunday Globe*, 25 March 1838). Martius's passionate, almost frantic, intolerance of his society struck others as untrue to the character and ultimately monotonous. "Mr. Macready denudes *Caius Marcius* of the dignity of his nature," maintained the *Sunday Times* critic, "and represents a tetchy waspish caviller; he alternately frets and fumes and ever and anon falls into fits of fury which border on the ridiculous" (18 March 1838). Still others missed the character's epic dimension. "We feel," remarked the *Morning Post* (13 March 1838), "that the . . . actor's performance does not fully satisfy our notions of the man whose presence could turn the tide of battles and of empires, and whose mere name in arms against his ungrateful country could change its all-conquering valour into a pitiful universal panic." Most production notices treated the acting almost as a postscript to a detailed catalogue of visual effects. "A prettier pageant than the scenic representation . . . can hardly be conceived," wrote the *News and Sunday Globe* (25 March 1838) critic. "It is so good, in fact, as to render the absence of the chief character ex-cuseable. The way in which this fine drama is presented reminds us of a landscape where all is good save the figures in the foreground."

Macready's supporting players were probably the most competent avail-able, but in an era of mediocre talent the assertion means little. The crowd was for most reviewers the star of the show. No longer identically dressed as in Kemble's time, their outfits varied "in every degree from the complete toga to the savage strip, [and] were in the highest degree accurate" (*Exam-iner*, 18 March 1838). Divided into sections, each of which was under the direction of a speaking citizen, Macready's crowd was a revelation to the-atergoers long accustomed to incompetence, comic irrelevance, or mere static presence. The citizens were now a crucial component of the action, ignoble representatives of the public corruption Martius so despised. "The populace of old Rome, in their numbers, their varieties of half-clothed and famished wretchedness, their cowardly ferocity, their wild impulses and fickle waywardness, their insolence, and their baseness," asserted the *Morn-ing Chronicle* (22 March 1838), "are realised with a vividness perfectly new to the stage." Although shorn of political significance and reduced to little more than a villainous foil against which Martius's pristine virtues might show to advantage, they were at least a credible force.[16] The tribunes, re-duced to little more than the leaders of a disreputable mob, largely escaped the notice of reviewers.

Mrs. Warner, at only thirty-four, proved an impressive Spartan parent to Macready's hypersensitive son. Gifted with "a beautiful person" and "more physical power than any lady on the stage," she created for the first time since the Restoration a "real Roman virago matron," we are told, "prompt to assert, insist, command, harangue, exhort, entreat, and denounce, without allowing any etiquette, or delicacy, false or real to thwart her purpose in the slightest degree" (*Morning Post*, 13 March 1838). On her first appearance, in domestic surroundings, she "seemed an Amazonian leader, wiping from her brow the bloody stains of battle," while later her anticipation of Martius's return from the wars was marked by "restless and over-flowing excitement." In the Intercession scene "her flushed face, bending knee, and tremulous hands" betrayed "a fearful intensity" (*Morning Chronicle*, 22 March 1838); and even without the benefit of dagger, her appeal was overwhelming. The "apprehensive thrill that passe[d] over her look of exultation in success at the ominous words in which Coriolanus grants her prayer" (*Observer*, 30 September 1838) was an unusually subtle touch.

Bartley's Menenius, "a sturdy, aye, and active, middle-aged gentleman, with amplitude of calf, and a voice that made the welkin ring" (*Sunday Times*, 18 March 1838) was "a rollicking, yet at the same time aristocratic" figure.[17] J. R. Anderson's Aufidius, despite pounds of padding, "sandals raised an inch in the soles, a fine helmet and magnificent crest, hair cropped to 'the short warrior cut,' together with a full crisp beard," was largely ignored by the critical fraternity.[18]

Although the production gleaned a good deal of critical praise, audiences were less than charmed; and once the novelty of the scenery and spectacle palled, the box office went into an abrupt decline. On 20 April, not quite six weeks after *Coriolanus*'s premiere, Macready ruefully noted in his diary: "Account from the theatre most wretched, £55. So that this at least tells us the value of 'Coriolanus.'"[19]

The historical importance of Macready's revival was considerable, if, unfortunately, not bankable. His modest attempt to purify the text of Thomsonian interpolations and his restoration of a fair amount of Shakespeare is altogether laudable. His attempt to make the citizens a serious dramatic, if not political, force rather than mere stage dressing was a singular innovation. Perhaps his major achievement, however, was the revelation of the vulnerable humanity of Coriolanus, a feature overlooked since Tate's time. Finally, he sensed, as no post-Restoration artist had done, the play's alienated mood. He erred, however, in identifying it exclusively with Martius's character which he sought to mellow into a comfortable humanity. He failed to recognize, and who can blame him, that the source of the play's estranged character is a social and political vision which lacks a fixed observation point, and of which Coriolanus is both agent and victim.

SAMUEL PHELPS (1848–1860)

When Macready withdrew from the management of Drury Lane after the 1843 season, recalls Phelps, "many ladies and gentlemen who had been members of his company, were left without a stage on which their talents could be employed." "Having been given to understand," he continues, "that the then managers of . . . [Sadler's Wells] were about to abandon it, an arrangement was made, and myself and Mrs. Warner assumed its directorship."[20] Located in the unfashionable suburb of Islington, the theater was not nearly as attractive to audiences as those in the city center, yet Phelps managed between 1844 and 1862 to attract profitable houses to revivals of all but half a dozen of Shakespeare's plays.[21] Although his texts were not as pristinely Shakespearian as is sometimes claimed, they were nearer their originals than anything available elsewhere. "Shakespeare's plays," maintained Henry Morley, "are always poems as performed at Sadler's Wells." The scenery, although constrained by a limited budget, was "always beautiful," but "not allowed to draw attention from the poet, with whose whole conception it is made to blend with most perfect harmony." The actors, Morley tells us, were "content also to be subordinate to the play," taking care "to subdue excesses of expression that by giving undue force to one part would destroy the balance of the whole." Even more remarkable, if Morley is right, the actor-manager "never . . . drag[ged] [the starring role] out of its place in the drama."[22] As a result, Phelps's productions more closely approximated an ensemble than anything the stage had seen since the Restoration.

In the 1848–49 season, four years after he assumed the Sadler's Wells management, Phelps staged his first revival of *Coriolanus,* and others followed in the seasons of 1850–51, 1856–57, 1859–60, and 1860–61. His *Coriolanus* productions, unlike those of certain other Shakespearian plays, were in no way revolutionary. He was content to honor the Kemble tradition, indeed to a greater degree than Macready had done, while incorporating a number of Macready's more eye-catching innovations.

The promptbook (*Cor* 12), with notations in the hands of Phelps himself and his prompter, Pepper Williams, provides solid evidence of the text spoken and a fair indication of the visual effects.[23]

The fact that Phelps chose to use as his script a copy drawn from a *Works* rather than a Kemble acting edition suggests that he initially intended a radical restoration of the text. In the end, however, apart from removing all the Thomson interpolations except for a few lines in act 4, he found himself with a virtual clone of the Kemble script. Certain departures from Kemble's text clearly betray a debt to Macready, for whom Phelps played Aufidius to Vandenhoff's Martius, albeit with little success, during the latter's Covent Garden visit in the autumn of 1838.[24] In the absence of the Macready promptbook, the precise extent of Phelps's debt cannot be determined.

In act 1, he follows Kemble and Macready in cutting the exchange between Aufidius and the senators (1.2), two of the Battle of Corioli scenes (1.4, 5), and the brief colloquy between Lartius and the Lieutenant (1.7). On his own initiative, or following Macready's example, he restores the fight with Aufidius (1.7); and at its conclusion he appends most of Shakespeare's 1.10, in which Aufidius vows vengeance on Martius by fair means or foul, an episode cut by Kemble. Act 2 closely follows Kemble's text. At the conclusion to 2.1 he rehabilitates Volumnia's long-absent finale: "Death, that dark spirit, in's nervy arm doth lie, / Which, being advanc'd, declines, and then men die" (2.1.160–61) and permits the Herald to proclaim Martius's fame at his homecoming (2.1.162–66). Martius's exchange with the second group of citizens in the Voices scene (2.3.85–111) also makes a welcome comeback. Act 3 is virtually unadulterated Kemble. Phelps allows rather more shouting and bustle in the patrician-plebeian confrontation, but continues to have Martius grandly defy his opponents ("I'll die here") in the Kemble manner. Martius's farewell (4.1), Volumnia's encounter with the tribunes (4.2), and the meeting of Adrian and Nicanor (4.3) are once more cut.

Macready's influence makes itself indisputably felt in Phelps's act 4, which opens, unlike Kemble's, with Martius's arrival in Antium (4.4), to which he adds some of Martius's conversation with the servants (4.5.7–15) and a scattering of lines in which the latter discuss the Roman visitor. The fact that the servants bear the names given them by Macready—Nautius, Servius, Cotus—suggests that this revision may not have originated with Phelps. Martius is again discovered at Aufidius's hearth, but in the Macready, not the Kemble, pose. The ensuing discussion among the servants (4.5.148–235) is as usual excised.

Phelps restores the first 35 lines of Aufidius's conversation with the Lieutenant in 4.7, then transposes from 1.10 Aufidius's "Mine emulation . . . Or wrath or craft may get him" (ll.12–16), and concludes the sequence with the curtain lines: "Come, let's away . . . then shortly thou art mine" (4.7.56–57). The act ends with Kemble's abbreviated version of Shakespeare's 4.6 in which the plebeians learn of Martius's impending invasion. Menenius's expedition to the Volscian camp (5.1,2), restored by Macready, again vanishes. As in Kemble's text, Menenius responds to Brutus's plea, "Stand our friend!" with "[N]ot I; they may hang, drown, burn, or break your worthless necks from the rock; 't is all one to me," and exits.

Phelps's act 5 is played as the now traditional single scene. The act opens, not with Thomson's "Here, noble Tullus, sit, and judge my conduct . . ." but with Shakespeare's "My partner in this action, / You must report to th'Volscian lords, how plainly / I have borne this business" (5.3.2–4) and continues as in Kemble's version with the arrival of the matrons. Phelps returns Coriolanus's "I melt, and am not / Of stronger earth than others" (5.3.28–29) to its proper place, and reinstates substantial amounts of Volumnia's plea, particularly her "Thou know'st, great son . . . / Still to remember wrongs?" (5.3.140–55). Less admirable is his Macreadyesque reconstruction of the climax of her speech. Happily, there was no need for dagger-drawing: Coriolanus capitulates promptly with Shakespeare's "O mother, mother!", and quits the stage on his appeal to Aufidius, "Stand to me in this cause" (5.3.199). After Martius's exit with the women, an abbreviated version of the conversation between Aufidius and the conspirators (5.6) concludes the scene. The latter's lines, however, are now appropriated by Volusius.

Martius's speech to the Volscian lords incorporates lines from the Intercession scene, "Aufidius, though I cannot make true wars, / I'll frame convenient peace" (5.3.190–91), and is also shortened and slightly emended. Phelps restores Aufidius's appeal to the senators (5.6.116–19) and the conspirators' cries of "Kill, kill, kill, kill, kill him!" (5.6.130) and the Second Lord's reproach "Thou hast done a deed whereat valour will weep" (5.6.132). Aufidius's final speech is more like Shakespeare than Kemble, although the 1. Lord's "Let him be regarded / As the most noble corse that ever herald / Did follow to his urn" (5.6.142–44) is transposed to become part of the eulogy, and Aufidius's offer to act as a pallbearer is cut.

Phelps's notion of the play is encapsulated in the introduction to his edition of it. "In *Coriolanus*," he writes:

> we have the proud, unbending Roman, whose conduct must command respect, if it does not extort unmingled approbation. We are presented with a succession of grand and animated tableaux, in which the imagination realises, by sculpturesque draperies and picturesque groupings, the scenes which were enacted in the streets of old Rome with patricians and plebeians for performers. The excited populace, whirled to and fro by the breath of eloquence . . .—the insurrectionary atoms now raised to a rampant height, and presently scattered abroad passive and harmless—form a spectacle of popular vacillation at once ludicrous and melancholy.[25]

Phelps, like Kemble and Macready, found in the drama scant political interest; and his production once more featured an idealized character study, embellished with historical tableaux and counterpointed by a "ludicrous and melancholy" display of popular caprice.

Phelps's staging, like his text, owed much to Kemble and Macready, particularly its commitment to visual grandeur. Following the Kemble example, he set the Roman sequences in the Imperial rather than the early republican era, but borrowed Macready's Etruscan mise-en-scène for the Volscian episodes, the first recorded attempt to distinguish visually between Roman and Volscian cultures. While formal groupings of lictors and soldiers recalled Kemble's practice, Phelps's realistic crowds and Martius's Romantic arrival in Antium and discovery at Aufidius's hearth evinced Macready's influence.

Act 1 opens with a "Rome. A Street" setting in the third grooves, described as "very beautiful and very appropriate" (*Douglas Jerrold's Weekly Newspaper,* 30 September 1848). Twenty citizens are heard shouting at LUE who shortly enter at RUE, talking, realistically enough, as they appear. Phelps's supers, although fewer than Macready's, were equally well-trained and effective:[26] "the crowds of tumultuous citizens rushing in headed by Mr. Scharf . . . were life itself," reported the *Daily News* (28 September 1848). From the outset the plebeians are the violent and cowardly rabble of Kemble and Macready. After Menenius's belly speech they are about to leave R "until Menenius says aloud "hail Noble Marcius" [.] Citizens then turn saying "Where. Where is he." meaningly [presumably threateningly]— until Coriolanus on—when they cower."

After the exit of Sicinius and Brutus at the end of the scene, the "Apartment in Marcius' house" flat is run on in the second grooves. In a neat tribute to Victorian domesticity and Shakespearian authenticity, the long-time ban on sewing is lifted with the direction, "2 Stools with Embroidery lying thereon brought on by Servants." At the end of the scene Virgilia exits R1E and Volumnia and Valeria exeunt L, while "2 Servants clear stage R & L." The "Apartment in Marcius' house" flat withdraws to reveal a "Cut

Wood" shutter in the third grooves suggesting a locale "Near the camp of Cominius." From LUE "Distant Shouts" are heard and "Trumpet sounding a Retreat." At this point "Enter Cominius in armour and Forces, retreating LUE." With a degree of realism not previously evident, "18 Roman Troops Enter PS [L] 2 & 3rd E looking back and walking as if fatigued. not in marching order." The rest of the scene has no effects worthy of record. In 1.4, before a shutter described only as "The Field of Battle," Phelps inserts an impressionistic, almost cinematic, mimed sequence. To the accompaniment of "Drum. Trumpets. Shouts," "[t]he whole of the Roman Troops of Scene 3rd are now driven across by Volscian Soldiery. [F]rom P.S. 2nd & 3rd Entrances—Alarums—Trumpets—Clashing of Swords &c. and they all Exeunt O.P. [R] 2. 3rd 4th Entrance." Next "Enter Aufidius L.U.E. & Coriolanus meeting U.E.L.H." To continued "Shouts—Drums—Trumpets," Martius and Aufidius "fight off." Volusius and four officers "rush across stage and off R and return with Aufidius." The latter, after vowing revenge on Martius, exits L1E. This gesture toward realistic action as opposed to static pictorialism owes more to Macready than Kemble. The sequence in which Martius is rechristened takes place against the same setting with some two to three dozen troops decoratively disposed about the stage to lend visual interest.

The Ovation scene (2.1) seems to have featured the usual procession in 1848, but was staged as a discovery in subsequent revivals. In 1848, the set was designated "Rome. The Forum." At the end of the acrimonious conversation between Menenius and the tribunes, the latter "retire to the back of the scene" as Volumnia, Virgilia, and Valeria enter R1E. On Volumnia's "These are the ushers of Martius," the procession enters to a trumpet fanfare, replete with troops, lictors, chariots, and spoils, although in smaller quantities than in Kemble's or Macready's revivals.

From 1850 onwards, it appears, Menenius and the matrons exit prior to Martius's arrival. The flats then withdraw to reveal a setting described as "City of Rome" with Coriolanus "disc[overe]d standing in in War Chariot" at stage center. According to a direction in the Plowman transcript (*Cor* 14), the tableau was arranged as follows:

    4 Boys in front with incense
    4 Volscian Prisoners R & L of chariot
    Trophies &c. each side of d[itt]o
    11 Roman Lictors ranged across at back
    20   "   Troops   "   R & L
    4   "   Officers

The prompt copy also mentions the presence of citizens, but their blocking is not indicated. Once the discovery is complete, Volumnia, Virgilia, and Valeria enter with six Ladies from L1E with Menenius following. It is their entry which prompts Cominius to call Martius's attention to his mother. As Volumnia says, "But O, thy wife," "Virgilia rushes to Coriolanus and throws herself on his neck." Directions for the remainder of the scene are unremarkable. The conversation between Brutus and Sicinius, treated as a carpenter's scene, was placed well downstage in front of the "Forum" shutter to allow the deep Capitol setting to be erected behind. To cover the construction noise, "March of Last Scene [is] played Piano throughout."

The Senate episode, located in "the interior of the Capitol, with the august white-robed assembly and the old wolf in the background" (*The Times,* 29 September 1848), was as nearly a copy of Macready's spectacle as Phelps could afford. In contrast to Macready's one hundred to two hundred supers, Phelps provides only thirty, but so artistic was their arrangement that critics found no cause for complaint. Once more, as in Macready's production, the scene concludes with the senators "all rising" to salute Martius with "To Coriolanus come all joy and honour!". The Voices scene was straightforwardly staged against the Forum shutter.

Martius confronted the plebeians and tribunes in 3.1 within a "street" setting located in the fourth grooves. Twelve lictors, "who range across stage" at the back, and six senators, grouped downstage of R2E, lend static pictorial interest. When the people rush on in response to Sicinius's summons, the lictors abruptly abandon their passivity and "wheel from center to RH Wing up stage and place themselves in a posture of defence. Fasces lowered waiting for orders." The tense moment amounts to no more than that, however; as in Kemble's production, Phelps's Martius simply defies the citizens on "I'll die here," and the physical conflict goes no further. Coriolanus's house is set in the first grooves to allow a deep setting for the Banishment scene to be readied, but directions are otherwise sparse. The Banishment episode occupied the full stage, with a platform approached by steps well up center, and was played in the Kemble style. The citizens, numbering thirty-four in at least one revival according to the Plowman copy (*Cor* 14), were particularly vociferous. They enter murmuring, and on seeing Coriolanus, they "express their disapprobation by a yell." On "It shall be so," "All the Citizens rush towards Coriolanus brandishing their staves and yelling 'It shall be so' till Coriolanus is on top of platform, and he raises his arm to speak." He exits on "There is a world elsewhere" to a "Loud demonstration of joy by the Mob—throwing up caps and dancing &c."

Martius arrives in Antium in 4.1 "by the light of the rising moon"[27] rather than Macready's starlight. Again lights glow in the windows of Aufidius's house (in the second grooves) and "Festive music" is heard off R. There is no mention of the Macready seascape in either the prompt copy or notices, but it is clear that physical environment is again exploited to romanticize the exile. Coriolanus engages in brief exchanges with the servants, then exits to be discovered a moment later in another Macready pose. In the fourth grooves, audiences now witnessed the interior of Aufidius's house with "A Fire in Antique Fireplace on Platform. . . . 2 Tripods . . . with Lighted Lamps. Small Grotesque Pedestals [the household gods] at the foot of Fireplace." On a "Stool L of Platform" Coriolanus is discovered seated LC in the firelight. Aufidius enters R. After much gallant embracing and hand-clasping the pact is concluded, and the generals exeunt R1E to "Festive Music as before." The remaining three scenes of the act—the episode in which Rome learns of Martius's impending invasion, the dialogue between Aufidius and Volusius [Shakespeare's Lieutenant], and the sequence in which Menenius taunts the citizens—seem to have been simply and swiftly played.

The curtain rose on act 5 to reveal "The Volscian Camp," with the stage, as usual, "filled with Volscian Troops & Officers with Trophies Pikes etc." Coriolanus and Aufidius are positioned in the Kemble manner down right on "2 Seats covered with Splendid Drapery." Phelps's desire to emulate the Kemble-Macready spectacle is obvious, but where his predecessors counted their supers in hundreds, the Sadler's Wells manager could muster only fifty-two, all of whom dressed the stage. On Martius's assertion "Fresh embassies and suits, / Nor from the state nor private friends, hereafter / Will I lend ear to" (5.3.17–19), "Shouts & Music" are heard "off R.U.E.," and in the century-old manner "The Troops on the OP [R] side of stage open R & L facing about & forming an Avenue for the Ladies to advance," fitted out yet again in neat mourning outfits. Weeping, they pass diagonally downstage, Virgilia foremost, trailed by Volumnia leading Young Martius, with Valeria and "6 Ladies in Single File" bringing up the rear. Phelps makes a particular attempt to emphasize Martius's familial attachment, since it is as much through domestic pressure as force of argument that he is finally brought to heel. On "I have sat too long" (5.3.131), he rises. As he is "going up RC," "Volumnia LC catches his Robe"; and on "Speak thou, boy," she calculatingly places Young Martius "in a posture of entreaty." On her mother-in-law's "Thou art not honest" (5.3.166), Virgilia "passes at back to RC" to block Martius's exit. When ordered to kneel by Volumnia, she "has got to Coriolanus R.H. with the child, [and] kneels R, in front of him. Volumnia L. all the Ladies around him." To leave the stage at this point, Martius would be obliged to walk over the suppliants, a visual realization of his mother's earlier assertion that to refuse her request is to tread on her "grave." Moments later, Martius surrenders and leaves the stage with the matrons, while Volusius and Aufidius talk briefly. During their conversation "Drums, Trumpets & Shouts" are heard. Troops enter and "form a lane or avenue." Coriolanus re-enters, and "Volscian Officers form a Semi-circle in front so as to prevent Coriolanus's return," much as the women had earlier blocked his exit—a telling visual touch. After Martius is stabbed by the conspirators, the "Lords gather around forming a 1/2 circle and hiding the body of Coriolanus" while the "Soldiers with shields form bier and place Coriolanus thereon" in the Macready manner. "As Dead March Begins All the Troops lower their Weapons & Standards and throw the Stage open forming on either side." The body is raised aloft. "Aufidius goes up C. Volscian Officers & Troops follow up Centre in order as the Curtain descends."

Although forty-four when he first played Coriolanus in 1848, Phelps looked a good deal younger. "[A] little over middle height" and "slender rather than sturdy," according to John Coleman,[28] Phelps was no rival to Kemble, although a somewhat more physically convincing Roman than Macready; but his notion of Coriolanus as the blunt military man and devoted paterfamilias idealized by Victorian imperialist culture depended less on physique than moral muscle. "The pride of Coriolanus," writes Morley,

> is heroic, and is a man's pride, from which vanity is altogether absent. That which he is, he is. . . . Upon comparisons between himself and the base multitude he never wastes a thought. It matters not at what level other men are content to dwell; his mind abides on its own heights (*Examiner,* 22 September 1860).

This pride in his military capability and his role in Rome's (and by implication, Britain's) imperial destiny was complemented by "the utmost purity and tenderness of home affections." "Next to his love of honour," maintained Morley, "is his love of home." This conception of a heroic military officer and devoted family man invalidated comparisons with the grandeur of Kemble or the exoticism of Macready, and allowed Phelps to tap the vein of domestic tragedy in which he excelled.

Phelps's conception of the character was clear from the outset, but in his initial performances he failed to suggest a commanding military presence. "Mr. Phelps, who has a world of pathos but a limited stock of dignity," wrote the *Spectator* critic (30 September 1848), "probably could not have selected in the whole Shaksperian range a character less adapted to display his histrionic merits, than that of the Roman patrician." Too often instead of cold, unbending pride, he gave the impression of "testiness and ill-humour." "When railing at the weak, vacillating, low-bred Roman rabble," the *Morning Chronicle* reviewer (2 October 1848) thought "he showed that he was subject to the same infirmities of temperament as themselves." The same brusque impatience, however, made his reading of the Voices scene a success from the first. "The struggle between compliance and unwillingness when with ill-grace he supplicates the votes of the citizens" gratified the *Times* critic (29 September 1848), while the bitter energy of "Your voices! For your voices I have fought" (2.3.126–31) delighted the *Observer* (1 October 1848). By his last appearances in the role in 1860, he had the heroic side under better control. In the scene in which Martius is renamed and exhorted to "Bear the addition nobly ever," Morley tells us, Phelps played him as "stirred by the warning into a large sense of what is in his soul, and lifted upon tiptoe by his soaring thought." At his banishment, he confronted the

MR PHELPS as CORIOLANUS

Samuel Phelps as Coriolanus. [Author's collection]

mob "with all the signs of suppressed passion, and impatient, yet in itself
almost heroic endurance of what is really intense torture." When called
"traitor" by the tribune, "he recoils as from a blow," writes Morley, "and
lets his wrath have way"; yet a moment later, when the citizens expel him,
he was again in complete control. "He mounts proudly the steps," Morley
continues, "from which as from his mental height he looks down on them,

and he is lord of himself, lord as he feels of Rome. With a sublimity of disdain he retorts on them . . . 'I banish you'" (*Examiner,* 22 September 1860). His death scene, which passed in early years almost without comment, by 1860 was a hit. Moments before he was struck down, roused by "the taunt of an enemy basely triumphant," we are told,

His whole frame enlarges, and his hands press on the expanding breast, as he cries,

> "Measureless liar, thou hast made my heart
> Too great for what contains it!"

And so at last the loftiness of his disdain carries all sympathies with it when he whets the swords of the conspirators by telling them . . . "Alone I did it.—Boy!" (*Examiner,* 22 September 1860).

From his first performances Phelps's interpretation of the domestic and pathetic side of the character left little to be wished. Virgilia set the tone of familial warmth when in the interpolated business in the Ovation sequence she "rushes to Coriolanus and throws herself on his neck," a gesture pathetically echoed in the Intercession scene when Martius "comes quickly from tribunal towards Virgilia who rushes to meet him." To the indications of filial love and respect given the character by Shakespeare, Phelps added a couple of additional touches. In the scene in which he is persuaded to mollify the citizens, immediately after Volumnia urges him to "perform a part / Thou hast not done before," the direction runs "Volumnia looks at Coriolanus," and he instantly exclaims, "Well, I will [sic] do't." In the Intercession scene when his mother insists, "Say my request's unjust" the promptbook direction reads "Coriolanus turns away"; Morley notes that he was distinctly seen to flinch at his mother's disapproval, and at that moment his fate was sealed. Phelps took pains not only to establish Martius as loving husband and dutiful son, but made him an affectionate and demonstrative father as well. In the Intercession scene, as Volumnia says to Young Martius, "Your knee, sirrah" (5.3.75), "Young Marcius [is] about to kneel" when his doting father "catches him up [and] Kisses him." Throughout the interview "the struggle of conflicting emotions going on within his breast" (*Morning Chronicle,* 2 October 1848), the contending forces of wounded pride and family affection, was powerfully depicted.

In the revivals of 1848 and 1850, Phelps was supported by the Volumnia of Isabella Glyn, a young performer and pupil of the aging Charles Kemble, described as "tall—her figure rather slight, though well proportioned" with a face "capable of great expression" (*Theatrical Journal,* 5 October 1848). To play at the age of twenty-three a convincing mother to the middle-aged Phelps was an impossible task, and the challenge was hardly ameliorated by her affectation of Mrs. Siddons. In later revivals, the role was played by

Rosalind Atkinson, with not much greater success. Atkinson, although a more natural actress, lacked dignity and emotional range. "When she desires with face and gesture to express scorn," remarked Morley, "it not seldom happens that she fails to suggest more than intensity of spite" (*Examiner,* 22 September 1860).

The Meneniuses of A. Younge (1848, 1850), Henry Marston (1857, March, 1860), and George Bennett (September, 1860) were praised in general terms, as were the Aufidiuses of Marston (1848) and Hermann Vezin (1860). But details of specific performances yield in most cases to general praise for the excellence of the ensemble.

Phelps's productions were not in themselves landmark events in *Coriolanus*'s stage history. They were workmanlike, rather than inspired, straying only slightly from the example of his immediate predecessors, and modified, one suspects, more out of economic necessity than artistic conviction. His conservative, yet generous, attitude to mise-en-scène, his attention to ensemble performance, and his own thoughtful, if simplistic, interpretation of the role nevertheless kept the play before the public longer than did the more spectacular revivals of Macready. Phelps's promptbook and memories treasured by aging actors and theatergoers allowed Henry Irving and Frank Benson, for better or worse, to carry something of the Kemble tradition into the twentieth century.

Throughout his years at Sadler's Wells, Phelps had few rivals as Coriolanus. The aging Vandenhoff continued to play the part in the provinces, but his palmier days were over. The only other serious contender was J. R. Anderson who starred in the provinces and on American tours between 1844 and 1853 and staged a moderately successful revival in 1851 during his brief management of Drury Lane. After Phelps's withdrawal from management in 1862, the play was kept alive chiefly by provincial performers including Charles Dillon, William Creswick, Henry Loraine, G. V. Brooke, and Osmond Tearle. None achieved much success.

HENRY IRVING (1901)

Henry Irving's revival, which premiered at the Lyceum 15 April 1901, was distinguished by the most spectacular scenography and the weakest performance by a major actor in the play's entire stage history.[29] Although undeniably in the Kemble-Macready-Phelps bloodline, the production owed its most striking features to the spectacular-realist convention popularized by Charles Kean's midcentury Shakespeare productions at the Princess's.[30] Like the baroque and neoclassical styles which preceded it, spectacular realism reflected the tastes of its age: the Victorian love of architectural grandeur, microscopic detail, and lush color. Forever lurking in the wings is the simultaneous threat and stimulus offered the stage by the nascent art of photography.

Irving's promptbook[31] makes it clear that, as always, his primary concern in Shakespeare production was popular accessibility; clarity, brevity, and picturesqueness were cardinal virtues. His skeletal text with its "heroic cutting, a massacre of whole legions of iambics" thoroughly delighted William Archer: "I never saw a play of Shakespeare's so uncompromisingly curtailed, and I never found curtailments less regrettable." A particular target of Irving's and Archer's disapproval was Shakespeare's diction, "so condensed, so mannered, so full of inherent obscurities, that when the sense of a passage fails to get over the footlights, the fault may just as well be with the poet as with the actors" (*World*, 24 April 1901). By the time Irving's blue pencil ceased its work, the script was a triumph of Victorian plainspokenness.

While the ears of the Lyceum's middle-class patrons imbibed a transparent text, their eyes luxuriated in picturesque antiquarianism. "A visit to *Coriolanus*," claimed the *Era* critic, "is a liberal education in the attire, the furniture, the weapons, and the architecture of Rome five hundred years before Christ" (20 April 1901), and, of course, a celebration of Imperial Britain's capacity to rediscover, comprehend, and recreate through its omnicompetent science, arts, and crafts the best of all civilizations which preceded it.

The epitome of Victorian cultural achievement, although now, like the age, fast approaching dissolution, was Sir Henry himself. And the production was designed, as always, as a showcase for his talents. "There was," as Frances Donaldson puts it, "an absolute integrity about his egotism. He saw the picture as a whole and in the middle of the picture he saw himself. His loyalty was entirely to the picture and it would have been quite impossible for him to compose it in any way except to enhance and set off himself as the central figure."[32] To highlight the hero's already ubiquitous presence, Irving carved the play into three acts, each of which focused relentlessly on a colorful chapter in Martius's career. Act 1 comprised the action from his first appearance among the citizens to his acclamation by the senate in a splendid final curtain; act 2 embraced the narrative from the Voices scene to the Banishment, and concluded with another powerful curtain on "There is a world elsewhere"; act 3 opened with Martius's arrival in Antium and terminated with his death and funeral cortege.

Although his act arrangement was original, Irving's text evinces throughout the lingering, if diminished, strength of the Kemble tradition; indeed, he seems to have edited the script with a Kemble acting edition and a copy of Phelps's promptbook at his elbow.[33] He did not, however, adopt his predecessors' emendations uncritically: the text is riddled with minor alterations indicative of his careful adaptation of traditional practice to his own taste and needs.

In the time honored manner, he cuts from Shakespeare's act 1 the scene between Tullus and the Volscian senators (1.2), the Corioli battle scenes (1.4,5), the scene between Titus Lartius and the Lieutenant (1.7), the fight with Aufidius (1.8), cut by Kemble and restored by Phelps, and the sequence featuring Aufidius and his soldiers (1.10). The Farewell scene (4.1), Volumnia's encounter with the tribunes (4.2), and the Adrian and Nicanor sequence (4.3) are excised as usual.

Heavy internal cuts and adjustments are made in the material retained, many of them traditional. In act 1, in an original stroke, he combines 1.6, in which Martius arrives breathless, and his victorious return from the fight with Aufidius (1.9). Martius exits in 1.6 with the volunteer soldiers, and returns moments later to the same setting. Cominius's "Therefore be it known . . . Caius Martius Coriolanus" (1.9.58–65) is transposed to the end of the scene to heighten the finale.

Like Kemble and Phelps he makes the ovation a separate scene, but retains the Herald's proclamation as did Phelps. The conversation between the tribunes after the ovation is made a discrete unit in the Kemble manner to allow the Capitol setting to be mounted behind. In the Senate scene (2.2), the officers laying cushions vanish as usual. The text spoken closely resembles Kemble's and the episode once more concludes with the senators' acclamation "To Coriolanus come all joy and honour!" (2.2.154).

Act 2 opens with the Voices scene (2.3). Irving abbreviates the preliminaries even more harshly than did Kemble, and, like the Covent Garden manager, cuts Martius's encounter with the second group of citizens (2.3.85–111), a sequence restored by Phelps. Like Phelps, however, he retains Shakespeare's scene ending. In 2.2 (Shakespeare's 3.1), he savages, like his predecessors, Coriolanus's reactionary political analysis, and again robs him of any ciaim to an articulate intellectual position. In the patrician-plebeian confrontation (3.1) the latter are "beaten in" as stipulated by Shakespeare, a feature Irving may have borrowed from Frank Benson, who had been routing the citizens since 1893. And in the Kemble manner, the scene is rushed to a swift conclusion once the star exits. In 2.4 (Shakespeare's 3.3), although Irving restores a fair amount of the strategy session between the tribunes and the aedile, the format is Kemble's, including the inevitable curtain on "There is a world elsewhere."

Act 3 begins with Coriolanus's arrival in Antium (4.5), an episode cut by Kemble, but restored by Macready and Phelps. In the subsequent episode in Aufidius's house, he retains more of the exchanges with the serving men than did Kemble or Phelps, although Martius's aggressiveness is downplayed. Aufidius's reconciliation speech is more harshly abridged than by earlier actor-managers; and after the exit of the generals, the conversation among the serving men is again cut. In Irving's 3.3 (4.6) interest is tightly focussed on the news of Martius's impending invasion, the patricians' taunts, and the citizens' panic. Irving removes from the early part of the scene the discussion of Martius's character by the tribunes and Menenius (4.6.29–37) and the aedile's account of the slave's story (4.6.37–57). Toward the end of the scene, an abbreviated version of the baiting of the citizens by Menenius and Cominius is restored, and the episode concludes with a curtailed plea to Menenius to intercede. Cominius's account of his failed mission is excised. In a lengthy 3.4 Irving provides an abridgement of Menenius's embassy, cut entirely by Kemble and Phelps, followed by a change of lighting from "Night to morning," and a fragment of the conversation between Aufidius and his Lieutenant transposed from 4.7. Volusius at last disappears. The intercession, barbarously slashed, concludes the scene. Irving's 3.5 comprises an extract from the sequence in which Menenius and the tribunes learn of Volumnia's success (5.4) and the long-unplayed episode in which the matron crosses the stage to the acclamation of the lords (5.5). The recuperation of this material precluded the customary staging of events from the intercession to Martius's death as a continuous dramatic unit.

The scene of Martius's death (Irving's 3.6), although shortened, is truer to Shakespeare's text than either Phelps's or Kemble's. The most serious excisions are some twenty-five lines of Aufidius's conversation with the conspirators, the Third Lord's admonition "Tread not upon him," and Aufidius's offer to be a pallbearer. Aufidius's concluding speeches are combined and transposed to offer a more overtly theatrical finale with "Let him be regarded . . . Did follow to his urn" as the curtain lines. In all Irving reduced Shakespeare's five acts and twenty-nine scenes to three acts and seventeen scenes.

Irving's production amounted to little more than a series of animated historical tableaux, assiduously researched and designed by the eminent academic artist Sir Lawrence Alma-Tadema,[34] painted by Frederick Harker, Walter Hann, and Hawes Craven, and animated by throngs of well-trained and splendidly costumed supers who lent period realism to the background and compositional significance to the central figure. So technically intriguing, aesthetically irreproachable, and archaeologically accurate was Alma-Tadema's reconstruction that the *Architectural Review* devoted to it a substantial illustrated essay.[35]

Alma-Tadema's historicism was not, however, as thoroughgoing as reviewers initially claimed. He inaccurately employed distinctive Etruscan structures, in the manner of Phelps, to distinguish Corioli from Rome, and for the Roman scenes allowed himself "a little latitude in bringing the date of the play in architecture a little nearer to a period which can be recognised as definitely Roman."[36] His sources, primarily Etruscan and Lycian tombs, Vitruvius's description of a Tuscan temple, and excavated architectural fragments in museums, are catalogued in some detail in the *Architectural Review*.

The curtain went up on 1.1 to reveal the Roman Forum, an intricately detailed backcloth. The "Temple of Jupiter Capitolinus crowns the summit of the Capitol," we are told, "being enclosed on three sides by a *stoa* or *porticus* with projecting balconies on an upper story."[37]

> An arch and flight of steps led down from the Temple to a wall, and below the wall was an open arcade. On each side was a temple, that on the stage right with a double row of columns in front but with plain sides represented a stone building with a red tiled roof. In contrast on the left was an Etruscan temple with characteristic wooden projecting eaves and with two columns and piers squared at the angles.[38]

Bathed in the brilliant Italian sunlight characteristic of Alma-Tadema's paintings, flower girls wove garlands, others, "carrying great water-jars flit across the stage," while from stage left a group of patrician ladies enter "wearing robes of silk of every soft shade of green, brown, and purple, carrying great bunches of yellow lilies" (*Westminster Gazette,* 16 April 1901). The mood of picturesque peace is abruptly broken by a "Drum Roll" and the abrupt and noisy arrival of a crowd of citizens, "unkempt and unwashed . . . with dull-coloured tunics" (*Westminster Gazette,* 16 April 1901) and "hard angry faces," and "armed with clubs and axes" (*Daily Express,* 16 April 1901). As the mob rushes on, the "Ladies exit in alarm" and a "citizen is knocked down by the first group entering." The mood of the crowd is distinctly ugly. Once more the plebeians are represented as the dirty and dangerous force the patricians claim them to be, their depravity heightened by the surrounding magnificence. When Menenius enters LUE[39] they "growl" and raise their weapons, and he pacifies them only with difficulty. By contrast, as Martius enters RUE, attired in "the scarlet tunica palmata worn by Roman generals in times of peace, with an embroidered border and fringe of gold" and over it "the toga praetexta in a deeper shade" (*Daily Express,* 16 April 1901), they again growl, but timidly "fall back L & R." Further cowed by the appearance of "12 Lictors [who] enter LUE ranging at back," they "steal away R" at the end of the scene.

The episode in Martius's house (1.2) was staged in "a lofty room leading to the courtyard through a portico of fluted columns. At stage left was an enclosed bed chamber decorated with frescoes, and on the back wall was painted a sundial as described by Vitruvius."[40] Directions call for "One chair 2 Stools Settee & footrest. Basket of wool. Sewing frame." In an atmosphere of antiquarian elegance, Volumnia and Virgilia are discovered at their housewifery. There are few indications of business. The major attraction seems to have been their costumes, recreated by journalists in excruciating detail.

The military scene for 1.3, described as "Near the Camp of Cominius," indicated "a landscape viewed amid the gathering shadows of night" (*Daily Chronicle,* 16 April 1901). In a production style trembling on the brink of cinematic realism, the episode opens on a darkened stage with three parties of soldiers in retreat. The 2d Party is seen "carrying wounded & dead. all are battle worn with hard fighting." Shortly after, they prepare to make camp: "one group [goes] off LUE for Tent poles, canvas etc. one group off RUE for water for wounded one group off R.3E. for wood for fire which is built near tent. Some soldiers lie down others take off armour others give up spears & pile their shields LC at back." On this exhausted and dispirited bivouac, Martius bursts in charismatic splendour from R2E; and with "Those are they that are most willing," the men take "one step eagerly forward." A moment later as he urges "And follow Marcius," a trumpet sounds and "Ten soldiers rush C swords in air & *shout* 'Marcius.'" All exit L3E in renewed high spirits. There is no scene change: lights are lowered to indicate a time lapse, and silhouetted military figures cross the stage in the course of routine duties. Eventually trumpet calls are heard in the distance, the soldiers and officers manning the camp "point off L. in excitement," and the "sound of returning victorious soldiers singing" is heard. Shortly after "*Enter* Soldiers full of joy all excited some wiping foreheads. etc. etc.," led by Martius and Cominius. "Two stools with Leopard skins are brought out of tent & placed L.C.," and near them sits a "Lantern" for picturesque effect. The proclamation of Martius's new name is reserved for the end of the scene. As Cominius is going "up with Cor" toward his tent, he turns to address the soldiers who come to attention. After his announcement, "Two soldiers raise Cor on shield, then all shout 'Caius Martius Coriolanus.'" To trumpet blasts "Soldiers L & R. close in & all shout 'Marcius' till curtain is down." Here Irving neatly captures Coriolanus at the height of his success in a visual masterstroke ironically echoed at the final curtain when he is again lifted high on a shield—now in death and by the enemy.

The next major pictorial effect, the ovation, was staged, in the style of Phelps, as a discovery. The Forum setting of 1.1, now modified by the introduction of a triumphal arch, was "crowded with girls carrying palms, men with branches of green trees, children scattering flowers, senators in white and purple, and lictors in brown tunics" (*Westminster Gazette,* 16 April 1901). The usual collection of patricians, senators, and named characters was grouped in front. With a fine disdain for Sheridan's antiquarian accuracy, Irving horsed the ovation into a triumph. At center stage Martius stood in a chariot drawn by four cream-colored horses, "gay with trappings of buff and red" and "followed by a crowd of soldiers in their gay uniforms, carrying the eagle and other emblems of Rome." At the end of the scene, a tableau curtain fell on the picture.

Irving's Senate scene, its debt to Macready unmistakable, was probably the visual highlight of the production. "Against grey stone walls, with little ornamentation," Frederick Harker recalls, "tier upon tier of seats filled the whole back of the scene, on which were seated the white-robed, grey-bearded senators, whose interest in the proceedings was intense."[41] Irving used only sixty senators, a third, perhaps, of the number featured by Macready, but the effect seems to have been quite as powerful. As the curtain rose, all the senators were seated except for Cominius. Cominius then enters and "walks C to altar puts powder on altar," and as "smoke rises All bow slowly. Cominius get[s] to his place C turns & Bows L[.] All L Bow slowly. Cor Bows R. All R. bow. slowly." In an atmosphere of studied formality, Martius's feats of valor are catalogued and his achievements hymned, although he absents himself throughout Cominius's recital, returning only when summoned. At the close of the scene, the senators rise and salute in the Macready-Phelps fashion. For Harker, when the senators "exclaimed with one voice: 'To Coriolanus come all joy and honour,' one felt it was no ordinary crowd just speaking in unison, but there was individuality in it, as if each senator was speaking for himself."[42] The actors were directed to "Hold picture" as a medium slow curtain descended to a trumpet flourish and "plaudits again and again renewed" from an appreciative audience (*Stage*, 18 April 1901). A stronger ending to the act could hardly be wished.

Act 2 opened with the Voices scene, set in the Forum of act 1. Traditional comic byplay seems to have been minimized, but the citizens were no more flatteringly represented than in earlier revivals. "All who know what a political mob is like know that it is under the sway of men whom people out of the fanatic throng deem 'cranks,'" wrote one spectator. "The cranks are here and the 'First Citizen,' Mr. C. Dodsworth, and the others—especially he, with his keen, conceited, unquestioning positiveness—are cranky in their stupidity and stupid in their crankiness" (*Liverpool Daily Post*, 17 April 1901). After the exit of the citizens, followed shortly after by Martius and Menenius, the tribunes remain on stage, and the citizens reenter. In a sequence reminiscent of Herbert Beerbohm Tree's Forum scene in *Julius Caesar* (1898),[43] the tribunes gradually work up the citizens to a mutinous pitch. "As each Tribune speaks Citizens turn from one another in perplexity" until on the Third Citizen's "He's not confirmed; we may deny him yet," all shout "Yes." Eager to be gone, they make for the exits, only to be detained several times by the tribunes, with a consequent rise in tension. Finally they are released on a flood of hysterical energy, and as Brutus and Sicinius exeunt LUE, they "exchange looks of triumph."

The patrician-plebeian clash was staged against Harker's "Street" drop, placed well upstage and featuring "a narrow alley of shops through which were seen a distant temple and part of a house with a pergola. The shop for pots, seen at right angles on the stage right, was protected by an awning; the frontal vegetable stall on the left was garlanded and behung with dried fish. . . . In the foreground was a raised street."[44] As the lights come up, Martius and Menenius enter R with lictors and a substantial group of senators and patricians. Sicinius and Brutus enter LUE and stop Martius's party. The quarrel intensifies, and Sicinius summons the people. At this point,

> Lictors see citizens coming & march down double file from R back to C up & down stage ranging in front of Senators & Patricians. Citizens are armed as in

Act I Sc. 1 & brandish their weapons at each cue with deep murmurs of rage &
hate. *Citizens* when they enter rush down round Cor. brandishing weapons & are
beaten back by Men. Lar. Com. & 1st Senator.

In due course the citizens are driven off LUE, after which, realistically
enough, the senators and patricians "return in exitement rearranging their
robes." Once Martius is safely out of the way, the "Citizens re-enter L4E
in groups all excited" for the debate between Menenius and the tribunes.
At the end of the scene as Menenius and the First Senator exeunt, "Two
groups of citizens go off LUE [and] 3 groups advance toward R2E shaking
weapons after Coriolanus [in the direction of his exit] & uttering low growl
as scene closes in," clearly establishing the threat which motivates Volumnia's lecture on political diplomacy, which was cleanly staged.

The Banishment scene finds the action back in the Forum. After the brief
conversation between the tribunes and the aedile, Coriolanus, Menenius,
and Cominius arrive from RUE with "3 Senators and 2 Patricians." The
citizens then enter LUE in groups, and "as soon as [they] see Cor. *low
growl*." In the scene's early moments the citizens are "silent but [in] movement." As the exchange becomes more heated, movement intensifies and is
accompanied by murmurs. On Sicinius's "He's sentenced. No more hearing," "Citizens all shouting waving weapons croud round Cor. Those *down*
R (25) rush across L stage [.] those *up* stage (rest) rush *round* Cor at back
& down L [.] when Cor turns round *all fall back*." On "There is a world
elsewhere," Martius sweeps off with the patricians while "All Citizens stand
looking at [him] as he exits R.U.E. bending forward perfectly still." After a
prolonged pause, the curtain falls on act 2.

Act 3 got underway with Martius's arrival at Aufidius's house, which took
place in Phelps's moonlight rather than Macready's twilight. "The central
feature was a great olive tree" by the side of which was a reproduction of
the Chimaera from the Florence Museum. "The tree partly hid a temple in
the center background with steps leading down to the street. On the stage
left was part of another temple portico. . . . On the stage right was depicted
the three storey house behind a wall."[45] "Its outlines," we are told, "are
clearly shown by the glow of the light from within, and this also reaches the
gloom and reveals the forms of trees and stone terraces. Overhead is a sky
packed thick with clouds, from behind which the moon's clearness is
dimmed" (*Vanity Fair,* 18 April 1901). The continued influence of Macready's Romantic aesthetic is patent. Martius enters L, and at the conclusion of his soliloquy, after a "dark change," the lights come up for 3.2 on
"A hall in Aufidius's house," a drop painted in perspective and inspired by
an Etruscan tomb at Corneto. Furnishings included a "chair, Lamp [and]
Stone Tripod." A fire burning in the tripod casts a red glow on the face of
the exile seated RC in the Macready pose. Aufidius's servants pass back
and forth bearing wineskins; and when they notice the strange guest, they

The Banishment Scene (Coriolanus-Henry Irving). Henry Irving Production, Lyceum, 1901. [By permission of the British Library]

halfheartedly (since most of their lines are cut) urge him to depart. Aufidius is summoned and arrives promptly, but no business for the interview is indicated. Irving's 3.3, in which Rome learns of Martius's approach, was swiftly staged in the Forum.

After another "dark change" the Volscian Camp setting stood revealed. No design survives, but a sketch of the scene in the *Lady's Pictorial* (27 April 1901) features a drop showing the distant battlemented walls of Rome with tents and woodland in the foreground. It is night and two sentinels are on duty when Menenius arrives. His plea is uneventfully made and swiftly dismissed. A time lapse is suggested by a pause, a change of lighting from "Night to Morning," and a fresh pair of sentinels. The Intercession scene is dressed by far fewer military figures than in the Kemble or Macready productions, perhaps fifty in all. At the appropriate moment, music is heard. Martius looks L1E, exclaims, "Ha! what sight is this?", and somewhat abruptly, he and Aufidius sit.[46] Then, in a tradition at least a century and a half old, "Enter, in mourning habits, VIRGILIA, VOLUMNIA leading young MARCIUS, VALERIA, and 20 attendants." As usual, the women wear identical outfits, this time "white girdled chitons of crepe de Chine, with their heads bowed and draped in large togas of black crepe de Chine" (*Daily Express,* 16 April 1901). Nowhere is there any sign of war-weariness or deprivation. The picturesque moment when "the black and white clad ladies occupy one side of the stage and the Volscians, in superb armour and tunics of gloriously rich colour, the other" (*Daily Telegraph,* 16 April 1901) was nevertheless judged beyond praise.

Apart from cues for bowing and kneeling, the scene is very lightly marked. Volumnia, it should be noted, on "And then I'll speak a little," "Holds [her] hand out," inviting Martius's subsequent gesture. As the curtain falls, the ladies kneel beneath the fixed gaze of the barbarically splendid Volscian soldiery.

Irving's 3.5 returns to the Forum where Menenius receives the news of Volumnia's success. As he enunciates a somewhat revised version of the 1. Senator's speech beginning "[P]raise the gods, / And make triumphant fires" (5.5.2–3), from LUE a procession enters comprising "Group of citizens and citizens ladies with Palms etc.," "Group of Senators who walk from LUE to R1E," and Volumnia's entourage "with Black & white dresses but hoods off heads on shoulders," followed by "Volumnia & Virgilia (wreathed)." Volumnia, her purpose gained and her black veil thrown back, triumphantly sports a "beautiful flame-coloured chiton, almost hiding the white tunic, which is embroidered with gold" (*Westminster Gazette,* 16 April 1901). The Senator's cry "Welcome, ladies, welcome!" is "taken up by soldiers off L." And to "A flourish with drums and trumpets," the scene concludes on a tableau.

Coriolanus's quietus was administered in "Antium. A Public Place," a simplified version of the Roman Forum, with at its center an elevated temple from which steps descended. "In front was a high bronze altar with bulls' heads and horns. On each side were portions of temples on plinths joined, as in the Roman Forum, to the central one by arcades."[47] The lights came up to discover a group of Volscian lords near a stone seat at RC, and a group of conspirators and the Lieutenant placed at LC. Aufidius enters with officers RUE, and dispatches the paper to the lords of the city. As he speaks with the conspirators, drums, trumpets, and the shouts of a crowd are heard. A moment later Coriolanus enters in procession with standard bearers, Volscian soldiers, spoils, and officers. A throng of citizens, present for the first time on record, "fill up wings L2 and L3." There are few directions for the conduct of the quarrel, save that on Martius's "To use my lawful sword" (5.6.129), "Lieutenant has crept round Cor & at cue stabs him." On "Bear from hence his body," "Two soldiers come forward from L. up stage & lay their shields alongside Cor L. Six Soldiers (bearers) range 3 each side of body." On "Take him up," "Body is lifted on to the two shields (still on ground)." At "Yet he shall have a noble memory," the "Body is lifted up till it rests (on shields) on *straight* arms of 6 Bearers." Soldiers with round shields form up three on each side "hiding heads of Bearers with shields." Standard-bearers place themselves at the head and feet, and with the conclu-

The Intercession Scene (Coriolanus-Henry Irving; Volumnia-Ellen Terry). Henry Irving Production, Lyceum, 1901. [By permission of the British Library]

sion of Aufidius's eulogy, the "Cortege moves slowly up C." While the actors "Hold picture," a slow curtain falls.

At over six feet in height Irving was taller than many earlier Martiuses, but he was unheroically built and his movement was ungraceful. Despite the splendid trappings, his Martius was militarily unconvincing: "Sir Henry Irving in armour," sighed the *Daily Telegraph* (16 April 1901), "is never Sir Henry Irving at his happiest." Worse still, at the age of sixty-three and weakened by illness, he lacked energy and vital spirits. But even with a different physique, fewer years, and better health, Martius's crude splendor would probably have been beyond him. Irving's forte lay in the subtle realization of complex personalities, the delicate baring of inner conflict, the lyrical delineation of loneliness, guilt, and despair. The uncommunicative Martius had little need of Irving's legendary talent for playing introspection, but received the dubious benefit of it just the same.

Well aware of his defects as a military figure, he followed Kemble, Macready, and Phelps in cutting the Corioli scenes; but where earlier players had physical and vocal grandeur sufficient to persuade audiences to take the word for the deed, Irving's patrons could not readily grant his Martius Homeric stature or overlook his disdain for weaker souls. Instead they discovered in the character merely a neurotic and alienated outsider, "a man haughty and intolerant, struggling not with the people, but with himself, and whose passionate self-will brings his doom on his own head" (*News of the World,* 21 April 1901). Martius's hatred of the plebeians seemed to have little to do with politics or principle. "[T]hough stiff enough in opinion," wrote one reviewer, "he has no impregnable strength of purpose. In the hands of his mother . . . he is as putty" (*Pall Mall Gazette,* 16 April 1901). Irving's Martius took its inspiration not from the etherial splendor of high tragedy but the banalities of melodrama.

Martius's first entrance, unlike Kemble's dash in scarlet pride into the midst of the plebeians, was almost unobtrusive. Sporting "a close-cropped brown wig, moustache, and incipient beard" (*Daily Express,* 16 April 1901), he suggested not so much an epic hero as a more or less commonplace "lean, thoughtful soldier" (*Star,* 16 April 1901). His first encounter with the plebeians was noticeably underplayed. "His glance at the assembled revolutionists" was "replete with bitterest contempt" (*Standard,* 16 April 1901). "Restrained in scorn, he kept throughout an attitude of disdainful pride, the face, the eyes, set, while only the mouth twitched, seeming to chew his words with the disgust of one swallowing a painful morsel" (*Star,* 16 April 1901). Here was no blunt warrior, but "a thinker, exclusive, proud, subtle, courageous . . . a mind at work—a proud, resolute spirit far beyond the claims of friendship, of patriotism, or even of domestic ties." His tragedy, as one critic put it, "is the fall of the man who refuses to enter into relations with his fellow-men, or to find out what is in their thoughts" (*Daily News,* 16 April 1901).

In the battle sequences, Irving resorted to melodramatic artifice, befuddling audiences with "Machiavellian chuckles between lines of quite ingenuous intent and such inappropriate decorations as not only hindered the understanding of what one heard, but made the character yet more mystified." When honored by his military confreres, he "changed his mind continually as to whether he would receive the applause of his fellow countrymen with disgust or gratification" (*Morning Leader,* 16 April 1901).

His performance in the Ovation and Senate scenes was apparently upstaged by the scenery: scarcely a critic mentions it. In the Voices episode, however, he discovered a touch of humor rare in earlier performances.[48] Ellen Terry recorded in one of her studybooks the "Grim humour" in his protests to Menenius before he confronts the citizens; and nearer the scene's conclusion she found Coriolanus's enquiry "Is this done?" "Funny," and his "May I change these garments?" "Very funny."[49]

Throughout his clash with the citizenry after the withdrawal of their voices, we are told, "until the tribunes proceed to deeds of active hostility, laying upon him violent hands, he scorns to recognize his antagonists, speaking of them to the aristocrats and not to themselves" (*Athenaeum,* 20 April 1901). As he braved the mob, "he stabbed at it again and again with his quiet contempt and scorn, but he never condescended to sneer."[50] The scene in his house in which his mother advises him to temporize was "enacted with playful, if at times grim humour,"[51] a strategy later rediscovered by Olivier. His treatment of the Banishment scene was highly praised for its understated power. "Apparently unmoved and unconcerned, he stands in the middle of the stage, while the crowd swirl round him pressing the decree which seems to matter so little to him," reported the *Daily News* (16 April 1901). "Where other actors would have ranted," Arthur Symons recalls, "he spoke with bitter humor, a humor that seemed to hurt the speaker, the concise, active humor of the soldier, putting his words rapidly into deeds" (*Star,* 16 April 1901). His climactic "I banish you," instead of being shouted, was "hissed with an intensity that caused the crowd to involuntarily fall back a few paces" (*Daily Chronicle,* 16 April 1901); and "saying this, he with consummate art, gathering the folds of his toga in both hands, and, sweeping it hither and thither, seemed, as though with the wind it caused, to clear away the mob like dust in the swirl" (*News of the World,* 21 April 1901).

On his arrival in Antium, "[e]nveloped in a toga which looks like part of the blue of the moonlight" (*Daily Telegraph,* 16 April 1901), "the solitary exile waiting outside the house, uncertain of his reception,"[52] staked a forceful claim to the audience's sympathies, a claim pressed even harder in the subsequent scene, "when the hero, concealing his face, bends over the burning logs whilst questioned by the servants in the dimly-lighted, lofty hall" (*Daily Chronicle,* 16 April 1901). At no time, however, was there any hint of self-pity. As Aufidius questioned him, "It was the soldier who answered. . . .

Irving never lost his dignity nor became a suppliant; it seemed as if he conferred a favour."[53]

In his meeting with Menenius he revealed a gentleness little evident elsewhere: "He was firm in his refusal to discuss matters with him, but tempered his refusal with kindly remembrance of their former friendship."[54] In the Intercession scene he sought, like Phelps, to exploit domestic sensibility. His study book[55] records a variety of shameless stratagems designed to compel theater patrons to reach for their handkerchiefs: on "But, out, affection," "Strikes breast"; on "and my young boy," "breaking down at young boy"; on "These eyes are not the same," "Trying to be hard"; on "Like a dull actor," "Turning to her—then striking breast before speaking." But his efforts were largely wasted: his earlier arrogance and meanmindedness had put him beyond compassion. At the moment of death, however, he to some degree redeemed himself. "There was resignation in Irving's Coriolanus," Harker recalls,

> as, facing the conspirators, after calmly stating his case, he realized that he had sealed his doom. With every inducement for ranting . . . he answered the taunts and insults of Aufidius with quiet disdain. . . . Then, with flashing eyes, and defiance in his voice and whole bearing, he reminded them of their former humiliation.[56]

His fall nevertheless evoked no cosmic vibration. To watch the disintegration of this "very picturesque, strange creature" (*Sketch,* 24 April 1901) was intriguing, sometimes pathetic, and even painful, but nobody made the mistake of confusing psychological interest with tragic catharsis.

After viewing Irving's revival, one reviewer came away convinced that *Coriolanus* is "a play made up principally of one character and a crowd, the crowd being a sort of moving background" (*Star,* 16 April 1901). Since *Coriolanus,* as usual, was permitted no political dimension, the crowd served merely as his antagonist and foil, a vicious rabble which would to some degree justify his antipopulist sentiment and render his personality almost amiable by comparison. And Irving's mob, although but a score or two as compared with Macready's hundreds, succeeded splendidly. "It was of vital importance that this crowd should be truly life-like," wrote the *Stage* (18 April 1901) reviewer, "truly human in motion, gesture, and ejaculation; and happily this result has been triumphantly achieved." Beneficiary of the innovations in crowd management effected by Macready, Phelps, and the Meiningen Court Company, Irving's mob was individualized yet capable of functioning credibly as a mass. "One of the characteristics of this crowd is that no two members are exactly alike," Harker remarks."[57]

The interest provided by the stage crowds was particularly welcome since the theatrical impact of Ellen Terry's Volumnia was so weak as to be almost nonexistent. Famed for her delicate femininity, warmth, and sex appeal, a more unlikely representative of the Spartan Volumnia could hardly be imagined. By bleaching her hair white she managed physically to suggest the Roman matron, but the psychology of the character eluded her. Her study books are scrawled with reminders to herself of what to think and feel. Beside "Then his good report should have been my son," she reminds herself "Not 'taken down' by a *girl.*" Next to Volumnia's "Think with thyself" speech in the Intercession scene, she notes "Keep it *old.*"

She and Irving seem to have concluded that Volumnia's more Amazonian flights would be beyond her, and a number of these were cut. With what was left she fashioned a character "poetical and radiant rather than heroic" (*Globe,* 16 April 1901). "Her Volumnia," wrote the *Sketch* (24 April 1901) reviewer, "instead of being a noisy, fierce, scolding patrician dame, is a proud but charming creature who wisely places more reliance on persuasion than coercion." In sum, her portrait was hardly more than that of a contemporary society matron in fancy dress: "of the appalling and imposing woman in whom the patriotic feeling was more developed than the motherly there was hardly a trace" (*Westminster Gazette,* 16 April 1901). To her credit it must be said, however, that her unorthodox reading discovered in Volumnia a fund of "humorous common sense" which eluded her grander predecessors and lightened the performances of her successors. Her "Pow waw," Sir Edward Russell rightly observed, had "never . . . been said with such sardonic playfulness"(*Liverpool Daily Post,* 17 April 1901).

Having admired Alma-Tadema's art and archeology, lamented Irving's Martius, praised the crowd, and indulgently chided Terry's Volumnia, critics considered their job done. The Polonius-like Menenius of J. H. Barnes, the "subtly malevolent Brutus of Laurence Irving, and the "robust and choleric" Sicinius of James Hearn seldom excited comment.[58] W. E. Ashcroft, shorn of most of his lines as Aufidius, was little more than a sword for Coriolanus to run upon, as Alan Hughes puts it.

Out of respect for Irving's status as a cultural institution, reviewers were kind when they could not be enthusiastic. But the box office spoke with implacable directness. After an initial thirty-six performances and a final one at the close of the season, the play was withdrawn. In September the production was included in the repertory for a provincial tour, but it enjoyed as little success away as it had done at home.

SIR FRANK BENSON (1893–1919)

Although Irving's *Coriolanus* could claim consanguinity with Kemble's original, the legitimate heir to the Kemble tradition was the young provincial actor-manager Frank Benson, who paraded *Coriolanus* in beau ideal splendor up and down the English countryside for close to three decades. His production premiered at the Shakespeare Memorial Theatre in Stratford-upon-Avon in 1893, and he repeated it there in 1898, 1907, 1909, 1910, 1912, 1915, and 1919 (in a shortened version). London audiences viewed the production at the Comedy Theatre in 1901, the Coronet Theatre in 1907, and at Herbert Beerbohm Tree's Shakespeare Festival in 1910.

Benson, unlike previous actor-managers, did not learn his craft through apprenticeship in the stock system. As a student at Oxford, he mounted a successful amateur production of the *Agamemnon,* and on the strength of it determined to pursue a theatrical career. His only professional education was a year in London beginning in the autumn of 1881 where he haunted the Lyceum and studied privately with the veteran actors William Creswick (1813–88), Walter Lacy (1809–98), and Hermann Vezin (1829–1910). Their encyclopaedic knowledge of Shakespeare performance tradition offered him in months a lifetime of information about texts, business, deportment, and verse-speaking; thereafter he was an unremitting defender of the classical style against all comers. Sensitive to the threat posed to traditional Shakespeare performance technique by realistic interpretation, epitomized in the informalities of Robertsonian comedy, Benson found a shield and buckler in the remote splendour of beau ideal aesthetics. "I conceived it my job," he tells us, "to preserve what was best in the old and blend it with the constructive forces of the new."[59]

In 1883, at the age of twenty-five and with only a year of undistinguished professional engagements behind him, he took over the bankrupt Walter Bentley Company, made Shakespeare the staple of his repertory, and assumed the leading roles. Throughout the next fifty years he recruited young actors, trained them in classical practice as he understood it, and toured them indefatigably throughout the provincial hinterland.

Convinced that the built-up settings of the spectacular realists were smothering Shakespeare and distracting attention from the actor, he returned to the simple and flexible scenery employed by Phelps—painted drops, a few flats, and matching wings; but, like the Sadler's Wells proprietor, he found simplicity no excuse for visual shoddiness. Graphic business and eye-catching tableaux were also advantageous, although not at the expense of narrative flow.

No promptbook survives for any of Benson's *Coriolanus* revivals, but to judge from the synopsis of scenes contained in his programs and remarks by reviewers, he seems to have played something close to the Phelps text.[60] Indeed, nothing is more likely than that the aging provincial troupers, Creswick, Lacy, and Vezin, would have introduced their protégé to the Kemble text, long a staple in the provinces, and supplemented it with their recollections of the alterations effected by Phelps, with whom all three had worked.[61]

Programs indicate that act 1, as in Kemble's version, consisted of only three scenes: "A Street in Rome" (1.1), "Room in Coriolanus's House" (1.3), and "Near the Roman Camp" (probably Kemble's amalgam of 1.6 and 1.9). Everything else in the act was removed.

Act 2 follows Phelps's 1848 arrangement of four scenes rather than Kemble's five: the ovation is not staged as a separate unit as in Mrs. Siddons's heyday. Benson's 2.1 opens in "The Forum" with the discussion between Menenius and the tribunes, continues with the arrival of Volumnia and Virgilia, and concludes with the ovation. The cranky colloquy of the tribunes is set in "A Street in Rome" and treated as a discrete episode as by Kemble. The Senate scene becomes Benson's 2.3, and 2.4, set again in "A Street in Rome," is the Voices sequence. The three scenes of act 3 follow Kemble's division; and as in Kemble's format, the first clash between Coriolanus and the people takes place on a "Street in Rome," while the Banishment episode is located in the Forum.

In act 4 Benson reinstates Coriolanus's Farewell scene, cut by Phelps, and merges it with Volumnia's rating of the tribunes. Yet again the Adrian and Nicanor episode vanishes, together with Martius's arrival in Antium, rehabilitated by Macready but excised by Phelps. Martius's pact with Aufidius constitutes Benson's 4.2, and the act ends with Rome's apprehension of Martius's approach. Aufidius's conversation with his lieutenant (4.7) once more vanishes.

Act 5 in Benson's early performances was played in three scenes rather than the one long episode sanctified by tradition. Benson's 5.1, designated "The Volscian Camp," deals with Menenius's embassy and its unhappy outcome (5.2). His agreement to undertake the mission (5.1) is blue-penciled. The Intercession episode, set in "Coriolanus's Tent," occupies 5.2. The final scene, located in "Antium—A Public Place," features Coriolanus's death. After the turn of the century, to judge from his programs, Benson usually played the act in two scenes (merging Menenius's and Volumnia's appeals) and on at least one occasion (1905) as a single continuous scene. Playing time was under three hours according to the *Daily Telegraph* (14 February 1901).

Settings and costumes for the revivals of 1893 and 1898 were designed by Alma-Tadema, and no doubt benefited from the research he had done in 1879 or thereabouts for Irving's projected revival. In keeping with the needs of an itinerant company, settings were of necessity lighter and simpler than those fabricated later for the Lyceum, but were reckoned by fin de siècle audiences to be the last word in historical accuracy and pictorial realism. Reviewers revelled in "the narrow streets and stately public buildings of . . . [Rome] in the time of the Republic."

> Before us were the haughty patricians, or patrons, in their stately togas and gowns, the free citizen soldiers with their picturesque varieties of arms and armour, and in their sandals and homespun tunics . . . the mere workers and traders. . . . And here, too, were the powerful, wealthy Plebeians, or land-owners,

the men whose political factions and blind partisanship had brought their Republic to the verge of destruction. . . . (*Stratford-upon-Avon Herald,* 25 August 1893).

If the five Street scenes employed the same flat, and both "Coriolanus's House" sequences and the two Forum episodes required only one unit each, the production would have needed only ten flats or drops. After the Newcastle fire of 1899, in which Benson lost his entire stock of scenery, he seems to have further curtailed his decor. The Forum episodes are staged in Street settings, and the whole of act 5, divided into two scenes as noted above, is staged against a flat designated "The Volscian Camp before Rome."

For Benson, as for all of Kemble's progeny, supernumeraries, or living scenery, were as crucial as the painted variety. In 1893, the *Birmingham Daily Gazette* (18 August 1893) reported "upwards of 80 persons" involved in the performance, of whom approximately seventy must have been supers. Like Phelps, Benson employed as many as he could afford, dressed them as well as his budget permitted, and drilled them to whatever degree of competence time allowed. Since supers were frequently recruited off the street on the day of the performance, the air of professional expertise they exuded a few hours later was little short of miraculous. The picturesqueness of Benson's groupings covered a multitude of sins in static scenes, while episodes demanding realistic group movement found leading company members, who routinely played in crowd scenes, leading and animating subgroups of amateurs.

As tradition demanded, historical spectacle was a sine qua non of performance; and the ovation, as for the past century and a half, retained its wonted popularity. "The triumphant return of the army into Rome," reported the *Stratford-upon-Avon Herald* (25 August 1893), "with prisoners and spoils and the lamb for sacrifice, the flower strewing, dancing, shouting, standards, banners &c., awakened enthusiastic approbation." Nor, of course, could the procession of mourning matrons in act 5 be forgone. Additional excitement was generated by Benson's restoration to act 3 of the fisticuffs between patricians and plebeians. Instead of Martius's traditional grand defiance of the people with sword drawn, "the Senators, suddenly banding themselves together, somewhat after the fashion of a Rugger scrum" drove the rabble from the stage (*Sketch,* 18 March 1908). To lend further excitement, Benson reverted to the practice of Tate and Dennis, and had the tribunes meted out poetic justice. As the curtain fell on act 4, the pair were "most realistically strangled and battered to pieces by the ungrateful mob" (*Globe,* 20 April 1910). As in Phelps's productions, however, scenery and spectacle seldom drew attention from the actors; it was invariably performances, rather than decor, that caught the critic's eye.

Like Macready and Phelps, Benson lacked the physical impressiveness that made Kemble's Coriolanus such an awesome figure; and his interpretation of the character reflected a realistic assessment of his strengths and weaknesses. His slim build and medium height ruled out much suggestion of the warrior-dragon, but his "fine Dantesque features," "steel-knit frame," and "transparent honest nature" ideally suited him to portray a noble, athletic, young aristocrat with some pretensions to intellect. A thoroughgoing patrician and patriot, "a hard shell Reactionist" in his politics, Benson's Martius manifested throughout "a superb independence [and] a lofty disdain of consequence" (*The Theatre*, 1 October 1893).

In the first scene, he was much praised for "the unconscious dignity, the utter fearlessness, the quiet scornfulness, the firm sure tread and soldierly carriage . . . as he came into the midst of those who were, as howling wolves, gnashing their fangs and thirsting for his blood." Interestingly enough, "neither the sharp unsparing rudeness of his retorts, the mocking jests with which he taunted their cowardice, nor the scathing severity of his sarcasm were weakened" (*Stratford-upon-Avon Herald*, 25 August 1893) by his understated style. His pride, like Kemble's, was a pride of class, but it revealed itself less in Jovian grandeur than "patrician austerity" (*Birmingham Daily Mail*, 1 May 1915) with "an almost ascetic flavour" (*Era*, 23 April 1910). In the battlefield sequences, curtailed as usual to become less action than rhetoric, his voice rang out "more clearly and more valiantly than . . . in any other play," according to the *Morning Post* (28 February 1908). In the fight with Aufidius, however, his only physical combat, he recklessly sacrificed dignity "to the joy of getting his man to the ground." In the Voices scene, attired in a white smock, "a natural note of aristocratic exclusiveness" (*The Theatre*, 1 October 1893) stood him in good stead, but he weakened his effect to some degree by incorporating business for which Kemble had been censured by his critics a century earlier: when demanding the citizens' voices, "his contempt for them [was] shown by mimicking their antics and treating them to ironical curtsies" (*Morning Post*, 28 February 1908). He was much more successful in the scenes leading to his banishment. Here "there was something in his presence, his voice, and his fine reserve" that "seemed to place him in the right and his enemies in the wrong" (*Stratford-upon-Avon Herald*, 22 April 1898). One playgoer noted, however, perhaps with some justice, that he failed to suggest that "those violent upbraidings of the plebeians were not deliberately said by Coriolanus, they came out of the man of themselves, and made themselves heard, sometimes in spite of him, he could not check or restrain them, not even when policy, his own safety, and his promise to his mother and friends bound him to do so" (*Sunday Times*, 17 February 1901). Unlike Phelps, he did not mount a flight of steps to deliver his "You common cry of curs" speech. He spoke it from floor level, and with a "scathing bitterness and power" (*Stratford-upon-Avon Herald*, 22 April 1898) which left audiences loudly appreciative at the fall of the act-curtain. The *Sunday Times* (17 February 1901) lauded "his extremely dignified delivery of the fine scene in the hall of Tullus Aufidius," although the *Era* (16 February 1901) reviewer missed the "muffled figure of

Coriolanus seated by the glowing embers of the brazier" popularized by Macready and Phelps.

The high point of Benson's performance, however, was the Intercession scene. At his best "where anger and pride struggle with the softer emotions" (*Daily Telegraph,* 14 February 1901), he made his audiences feel "by the simplest means, the tragedy of [his] surrender" (*Pall Mall Gazette,* 29 February 1908). In his dealings with his family throughout the play he revealed "a soft side to his character—the domestic." "Struck there," in the Intercession scene, "he perishes, but not until he has revealed . . . a world of tenderness for mother, wife, and child" (*Stratford-upon-Avon Herald,* 7 May 1915). At the moment of his death, he trembled on the brink of tragic splendor, thought one playgoer, as "he throws aside the cold severity of his attitude, and his voice vibrates with the triumph of these words, 'False hound, if you have writ your annals true. . . . Alone I did it.'" (*Leamington Spa Courier,* 19 August 1893).

The Benson Coriolanus, although carefully wrought and beautifully spoken, ultimately fell short of tragic sublimity. As the *Star* (14 February 1901) critic put it, "Mr. Benson gives us a rather self-conscious young man, who ought hardly to come to so much harm because he is so young, and so little aware of what he is doing. That is not tragic; it is only pathetic. . . . We find ourselves vexed that he comes to grief, rather than vexed that he is such as must come to grief." The overpowering majesty which surrounded the Kemble Coriolanus, although to some degree imposed on the text rather than intrinsic to it, carried tragic conviction. Benson's athletic young aristocrat, despite its creator's *goût de grandeur,* rose little above the level of melodrama. Concluded the *Illustrated Sporting and Dramatic News* (23 February 1901), succinctly if a trifle inelegantly, "You cannot do justice to the Hallelujah Chorus with a tin whistle, even though that whistle be very skilfully played." Benson's reading richened somewhat with the years, but never quite attained tragic stature.

His Coriolanus most nearly approached beau ideal stature in scenes with Genevieve Ward, who partnered him in all Stratford and London revivals save three;[62] and if contemporary critics are to be believed, her Volumnia merited comparison only with Mrs. Siddons's legendary creation. A pupil of Regnier and disciple of Ristori, Ward appeared early in her career with Phelps and later starred with major English, French, and American performers. Like Benson she was devoted to the beau ideal tradition, but her commitment derived from a lifetime of experience, while Benson's was the product of study.

At the age of sixty-three, when Ward first appeared with Benson as Volumnia, she struck Richard Dickins as "the ideal embodiment of the Roman mother who loved her son beyond everything in the world, except only her country."[63] She dominated the role for two decades thereafter, and rendered all competitors intolerable. Although a small woman, "her vitality was dynamic," Harcourt Williams remembers. Dressed in a gold circlet and blue robe in the early scenes, she was "a good, easy-going, well-conditioned English lady, who had doubtless a will of her own upon occasion, but who was loth to let it be seen" (*Birmingham Post,* 23 April 1907). With the ovation, however, the characterization took on grandeur and power. "The sweep of her entrance to greet her victorious son on his return from the Volscian war," we learn,

> was ecstatic and triumphant. As she first entered telling the great news her eyes flashed excitement, and her gaiety as she told of the letters that had come was infectious. And who that heard it can forget the scornful retort to Virgilia's weak "The gods grant them true!" or the curl of her lip on the final syllables: "True? Pow waw!"[64]

Her "O welcome home!" speech was delivered "with uplifted arms and eyes, as a thank-offering to the gods" (*Pall Mall Gazette,* 20 April 1910), a piece of business as old as Macready's revival. In the episode in which she persuades Martius to return to the tribunes and people, "her passion," notes one reviewer, "flashed very like a sword itself about the head of her son, whose immovable obstinacy alternately frightens and angers her" (*Stratford-upon-Avon Herald,* 26 April 1907). Her "contemptuous yet burning anger mitigated by appeal" (*Stratford-upon-Avon Herald,* 26 April 1907) and the bitterness of her "You have done a brave deed!" were particularly noted. Her entrance for the confrontation with the tribunes after Martius's banishment was unforgettable. "How she strode on to the stage to pour the vials of her wrath on the two Tribunes," recalled Harcourt Williams. "[S]he had a way of holding her head and whole body so as to dominate the scene. She could well exclaim: ' . . . lament as I do, in anger, Juno-like,' as with blazing eyes she swept from the stage".[65]

Her finest effects though were reserved for her intercession. Here "[h]er voice in potency and emotion might have moved stones, so strong and yet so tender was it, so broken and tremulous, and yet so direct and searching" (*Stratford-upon-Avon Herald,* 26 April 1907). "The reasoned appeal, the poignant, bitter warning, the broken supplication and the scorn," recorded an eyewitness,

> are spoken with a very touching dignity of realism. The long speech utterly convinces; and one looks on at the picture, the watching Volscian chiefs and Coriolanus, with his back turned, grasping, motionless, the arm of the stool, as if at a scene of real life in which great destinies were in the balance. She prevails, but wins no show of affection, and there is much pathos in her stumbling, quiet exit. (*Pall Mall Gazette,* 29 February 1908).

Apart from Ward as Volumnia, Benson rarely enjoyed first-class acting support. Many of his players were young and inexperienced, mere appren-

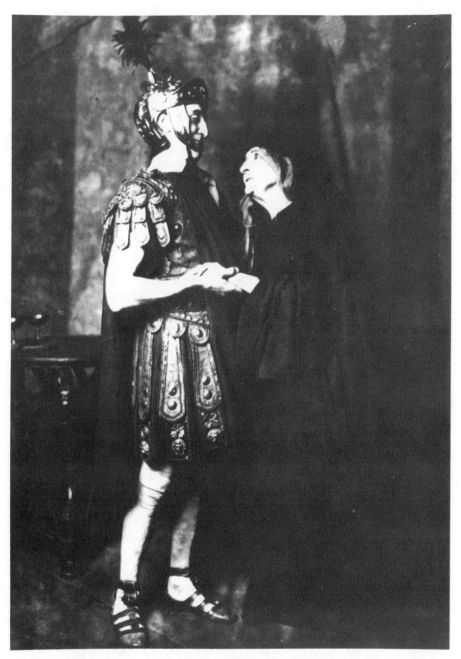

**Frank Benson as Coriolanus; Genevieve Ward as Volumnia. Frank Benson Production
ca. 1910. [By permission of the Shakespeare Centre Library, Stratford-upon-Avon]**

tices in the classic tradition; and all too frequently, as soon as they achieved something more than competence, they defected to more glamorous London managements. Even had Benson's auxiliaries been better, however, his severely curtailed script would have prevented them from doing their parts much justice. Menenius was probably best played by Lyall Swete (1893, 1898, 1901) as one who "although his sympathies are with the people, out of love for Coriolanus becomes his parasite" (*Stratford-upon-Avon Herald,* 22 April 1898), and by H. O. Nicholson (1905, 1907, 1909, 1910) who limned a sympathetic portrait of "the kindly, persuasive, and pacific" old counselor (*Stage,* 21 April 1910); but neither did him much credit as a political strategist.

That Aufidius, variously played by Otho Stuart (1893, 1915), Frank Rodney (1898), Alfred Brydone (1901), George Buchanan (1907), Arthur Goodsall (1909), and Baliol Holloway (1912), aroused little attention is hardly surprising. Rather than the complex, indeterminate Jacobean creation, Benson's pared-down Volscian was a shopworn dramatic convenience. As long as the actor was stalwart and picturesque, little more was required.

The real antagonist of Coriolanus in Bensonian productions was the crowd, "not to be regarded as a mere congregation of atoms," as one critic has it, but as "a consistent and coherent character" (*Stratford-upon-Avon Herald,* 23 April 1909). And as the citizens' leaders, the tribunes came in for unwonted attention. Rarely indeed have reviewers been so conscious of their presence. In 1893, Ashcroft and Grenville "were party politicians to the life—crafty, cruel, unscrupulous, vehement, and skilful with tricks of oratory" (*Stratford-upon-Avon-Herald,* 25 August 1893); in 1907, E. A. Warburton and Clarence Derwent, more longshoremen than politicians, were censured for their too frequent resort to farce; in 1910 Murray Carrington and J. Moffat Johnston provided contrasting portraits, "the former as the lean, cadaverous agitator, the latter as the hail-fellow-well-met popular leader" (*Birmingham Gazette,* 3 May 1910). Probably the most memorable realization was the Sicinius of Oscar Asche (1901). "You thought," wrote Gordon Crosse, "you had never seen anything so undignified as this coarse, shambling demagogue with his low cunning and his envious temper."[66] "The surly insolence of the man, his contempt for the patrician, and his sublime belief in the power and rights of the proletariat," left the *Era* reviewer fairly agape (16 February 1901). His best moment came at the conclusion of act 4 when "after the expulsion of Coriolanus [he was] seated on a stone in the Roman street, contentedly peeling and eating an orange,"[67] only to find, moments later, that the "gloating enjoyment of his popularity was followed by his violent and realistic death at the hands of the fickle mob."[68]

Benson's last full-length *Coriolanus* performances at Stratford during World War I effectively marked the end of the Kemble tradition.[69] Thanks largely to the dedication of one who had not shared the beau ideal tradition, something of its legendary nineteenth-century glory, however imperfectly realized, was passed on to the twentieth. It was destined, however, to be an heirloom without an heir.

7

The Kemble Tradition in America (1796–1885)

Coriolanus, unlike *Julius Caesar,* found little critical favor in late eighteenth- and nineteenth-century America, primarily because its subject failed to pluck postcolonial heartstrings. Although Plutarch's *Lives* was widely read as a moral and political guide to fledgling nation builders, his life of *Coriolanus* offered less uplift than his biographies of *Caesar, Cato, Cicero,* or *Solon.*[1] The antidemocratic turn Shakespeare was alleged to have given Plutarch's narrative rendered the dramatization even less congenial than its original. "What a vast and godlike influence [Shakespeare] might have exerted in moulding the public mind and guiding the upward progress of nations," lamented William Leggett, "if his great genius had not been dazzled by the false glitter of aristocratic institutions, and blinded to the equal rights of the great family of man."[2] "His humanity," concluded a fellow journalist in the same vein,

> was not as comprehensive as his genius. His genius encircled, with its radiant girdle, all mankind. His humanity buckled with so intense a clasp around the individual as to shut out that great collective individuality, the people (*New-York Daily Tribune,* 24 April 1855).

As late as the fourth quarter of the century, with the iconization of Shakespeare in full flood, *Coriolanus* remained under a critical cloud. The "main purpose" of the play, George Wilkes felt obliged to warn his countrymen in 1877, "is to deride the principle of popular suffrage; nay, to deny and scoff at popular rights of all sorts, and especially to make the working classes look mean, meritless, and cowardly."[3] Attendance at *Coriolanus* performances from Cooper to McCullough was a potentially unsettling experience; as one theatergoer put it, "[T]hough [Shakespeare's] mastermind so shaped [the play] as to disguise its evident aims from the first glance of the people, yet the entire tendencies of it are not of a nature ever to create a favorable or a lasting impression in a republican audience" (*New-York Dispatch,* 29 April 1855).

Actors, not surprisingly, failed to share the widespread critical distaste for the play: indeed, the temptation to grandstand on "There is a world elsewhere" or yield meltingly to familial woe was irresistible to leading men of heroic bulk. Pit, boxes, and galleries could only be filled, however, by the adoption of a performance convention which would vitiate political discomfort. In the early years of the republic, revivals exploited the widespread passion for Roman art, history, and literature, to say nothing of the vogue for oratory. As an exemplar of Roman *virtus,* of masculine energy directed against epic odds, Martius offered an admirable role model to post-Revolutionary youth, provided his antipopulist stance could be mitigated: and here the adoption of John Philip's aesthetic strategies, the packaging of the play as antiquarian reconstruction rather than political preachment, subverted contemporary relevance as effectively on one side of the Atlantic as on the other. Liberal applications of neoclassical spectacle, epic characterization, and rhetorical pyrotechnic by Thomas Abthorpe Cooper and a bevy of itinerant English stars soothed Jeffersonian anxieties sufficiently to secure the play a fair stage popularity throughout the first three decades of the nineteenth century. On Cooper's retirement in 1838, Thomas Hamblin, with more tenacity than talent, managed to wring an additional decade or so of service from the now-enfeebled tactic. Towards the midcentury point, Edwin Forrest appropriated and refurbished the Kemble formula as a tonic for antebellum and Civil War angst: in the stern *virtus* of a Roman frontiersman, in which roughhewn integrity companioned familial devotion, audiences found a welcome antidote to a perceived contemporary moral enervation. Forrest's disciple and successor John McCullough in his turn briefly tamed Martius's bellicose manners to the parlor etiquette of the Brown Decades, and with his efforts the Kemble influence in America ended.

The first version of *Coriolanus* staged in the New World was Thomson's, mounted 8 June 1767 by the American Company at Philadelphia's Southwark Theater "For the Benefit of Mr. TOMLINSON." No account of its reception survives, but the fact that it was not repeated may be significant. Shakespeare's text received its first recorded airing, albeit by amateurs, when soldiers based in Portsmouth, New Hampshire mounted a production in 1778 to protest their new country's lack of appreciation for their services. In an epilogue one Jonathan Sewall drew a parallel between his military confreres and Coriolanus, both of whom were obliged to endure their "country's base ingratitude."[4] *Coriolanus* reached the professional stage on 3 June 1796 in Philadelphia when Kemble's version was performed by the Wignell-Reinagle company, with John Moreton as Martius and Elizabeth Whitlock (a younger sister of John Philip Kemble)[5] as Volumnia. The audience was promised, in the Sheridan-Kemble tradition, "AN OVATION, in honor of the victory of Caius Marcius Coriolanus, over the Volscians at Corioli" and "A PROCESSION OF MATRONS for the purpose of entreating Terms of Peace for Rome, after the revolt of Coriolanus to the Volscians." For good measure the play would conclude "With a DEAD MARCH, after his Death" (*Gazette of the United States,* Philadelphia, 3 June 1796). Moreton was rather too lightweight an actor for Martius, and Mrs. Whitlock, "short and undignified" with a "heavy, thick voice," was not a prepossessing Volumnia, although John Bernard tells us her "genuine passion . . . could kindle the sympathies and blind the spectator to every deficiency."[6] Apart from advertisements, no details of the performance have come to light. Whatever the immediate outcome of the venture, its long-term impact was profound: with Elizabeth Whitlock's performance, the Kemble convention gained a foothold in America where it shaped production style for more than three-quarters of a century. For the first thirty-odd years, Thomas Abthorpe Cooper guarded the sacred flame.

Thomas Abthorpe Cooper (1799–1831)

Thomas Abthorpe Cooper first appeared as Martius at New York's Park Theater 3 June 1799 at the age of twenty-three and dominated the role until he was past fifty. Still a novice when recruited from the English provincial circuit, Cooper's grasp of stage technique was precarious; nevertheless, his heroic dimensions, handsome face, and golden voice captivated American audiences. Over the next few years he established himself as the country's first star, and a specialist in Roman roles: Damon in Banim's *Damon and Pythias,* Brutus in Payne's play of the same name, the title character in Knowles's *Virginius,* and Shakespeare's Mark Antony (in *Julius Caesar*) all received his stamp in turn. After his 1799 debut as Coriolanus, the role became a feature of his starring tours; and during his management of the Park from 1806 to 1815 he revived the play almost annually. Before coming to America, Cooper appeared briefly at Covent Garden while Kemble was playing Martius with the Drury Lane company, and studied his legendary performance with care. When he assumed the role himself, the Kemble influence was palpable: even the hero's name was pronounced in the Kemble manner.[7]

Cooper's promptbook does not survive, but an acting edition, published by Thomas H. Palmer in Philadelphia in 1823 and purporting to represent the text "As performed at the Philadelphia Theater," probably offers something close to it. The script is virtually a reprint of Oxberry's version which in turn trod on the heels of Kemble. All stock companies of the period, it should be remembered, played uniform scripts with standardized business to allow visiting stars to be incorporated into productions with a minimum of rehearsal. The persistence and stability of the Kemble adaptation is confirmed by the fact that Noah Ludlow's promptbook (*Cor* 11), used as late as 1845,[8] was made on a 1823 Palmer edition, as was Edwin Forrest's for his 1855 revival.[9]

Conditions on the touring circuit forbade detailed reproduction of Kemble's labored archaeology and picturesque composition, but some degree of imperial splendor was imperative. No revival worthy of the name lacked an ovation and a procession of grieving matrons. Cooper's assumption of the role at the Park Theater was accompanied by an unusual degree of display. According to an advertisement in the *Daily Advertiser* (New York, 3 June 1799), the "Grand TRIUMPHAL ENTRY" included:

> Two Boys bearing Incense,
> An Officer with a Roman Eagle,
> Eight Senators, Four Trumpets,
> Two Boys bearing Incense,
> Four Priests with Torches,
> Two Officers,
> Six Lictors with Fasces,
> Two Officers with Standards,
> Six Soldiers bearing a Bier laden with Spoils.
> A CHOIR *consisting of*
> Four Boys,   Six Virgins,
> Four Priests with Torches,   Six Lictors with Fasces.
> Senators-Soldiers-Standard Bearers-Fifes-
>   Drums-Trumpets-Priests, &c. &c.
>   A CAPTIVE GENERAL IN CHAINS
>   *Volumnia, Virgilia, Valeria*
> Six Virgins strewing Flowers, before a Triumphal
> Car, bearing CORIOLANUS, drawn by
>   TWO WHITE HORSES,
> Accompanied with a full band of Instrumental
> Music and a Grand Chorus,
>   "*See the Conquering Hero comes*".

Cooper's white horses, it is worth noting, preempted Henry Irving's equine exhibition by more than a century. Horses were a rarity in processions,[10] but sheep were common. The first *Coriolanus* performance in Boston on 30 December 1805 boasted "2 Priests, leading a Ram adorned for sacrifice" (*Boston Gazette,* 30 December 1805), while "Priests with a LAMB adorned for sacrifice" were a feature of a revival in Philadelphia on 15 March 1813.[11]

The rarity of references in advertisements to new shutters suggests that scenery was judged less vital to visual effect than supers and livestock, a conclusion strengthened by frequent indictments of managerial disdain for, or ignorance of, history.[12] As late as 1845, during James Anderson's appearances at the Park Theater, an exasperated observer found the scenery "so perfectly out of keeping as to destroy the necessary illusion requisite to the perfect success of the Dramatic art." "Gothic Cathedrals in ancient Rome, and streets of the Elizabethan period, to represent the Imperial City, when she was mistress of the world! Can any thing be more preposterous?", he demanded (*Albion,* New York, 19 April 1845). Even Cooper's costume did not escape criticism. In the Voices scene he was censured on one occasion for appearing "in a *black* gown, whereas, according to Roman custom, it should have been *white*" (*Columbian Centinel,* Boston, 1 January 1806).

Ensemble performance was almost unknown: supporting players were often incompetent, and supers were worse, while the stress of staging a fresh play almost nightly forced even the most conscientious actors into textual inaccuracy and improvisation. But audiences bore such defects with tolerance; when stars topped the bill, only their performance mattered. Indeed *Coriolanus* was deemed less vulnerable to weak company work than other Shakespearian plays since, reviewers argued, it was "written peculiarly to evince the powers of the principal personage concerned" (*Columbian,* Boston, 20 April 1811).

In the early days of the republic, if stage Romans were massive, graceful, and full-throatedly declamatory, the role was already half-played; and Cooper, ideally qualified for these parts, could hardly fail. According to William Wood, he was "not quite six feet high,"[13] an above average height for the period. Another contemporary found him in 1807 "extremely graceful, slender, and inclining to tall" with a face "peculiarly handsome, and his features uncommonly expressive." His voice was "strong, clear, and capable of infinite modulation" (*Port Folio,* Philadelphia, 31 January 1807).

Cooper's acting style John Howard Payne identified as "of the Kemble school," with "less tricks of the stage than Kemble," and greater naturalness.[14] "[T]he deep, the terrible, the strong and overwhelming passions of the soul" were considered his forte;[15] and Coriolanus was precisely the role to challenge his powers. On his first entrance, his "classical costume, the graceful dignity of his carriage, the expressiveness and flowing ease of his action" invariably disposed the audience in Martius's favor. In his encounters with the squalid and underplayed plebeians, his "unconquerable, sneering haughtiness, which even mingles itself with the sweetness of his smile," his "unyielding stubbornness and stern intrepidity" suggested not contemporary antipopulism but historic individualism on an epic scale (*Boston Weekly Magazine,* 21 February 1818). The Voices sequence saw him "beg, as if he would demand"[16] in all the "towering grandeur of Roman majesty" (*New-England Galaxy & Masonic Magazine,* Boston, 31 December 1819), while the Banishment episode, in which his gift for "the silent and gradual approaches of the storm of passion" had full play, left audiences, if Noah Ludlow is to be believed, "transfixed with the grandeur of the scene."[17] In the early part of the Intercession sequence, the "workings of his countenance" and his portrayal of "the restraint which pride and false honour lay upon nature and humanity" were warmly praised; as he approached the moment of capitulation, his depiction of "those workings of the soul, when anguish shakes her" and finally the manner of "testifying his broken pride and returning tenderness"[18] left critics bereft of superlatives. In the final scene, when Aufidius "casts the opprobrious epithet of *boy* upon him," one reviewer reported him "fierce as ten furies, and terrible as hell"

(*New-England Galaxy & Masonic Magazine,* Boston, 31 December 1819). Isaac Harby, educator and editor of the *Southern Patriot,* found himself, "in spite of the cold dictates of judgment . . . hurrie[d] along in the rapidity and glow of [the actor's] conceptions." As the hero fell beneath the assassin's swords, Cooper, ever conscious of picturesque detail, "judiciously covered his face with his garment."[19]

Although often ill-rehearsed, careless, and frequently underplayed,[20] Cooper's Martius, at its best, had moments of grandeur and sublimity to be found only in Kemble's reading. And for these moments, audiences forgave him much. Period journalism indicates that audiences and reviewers rarely troubled their heads about Shakespeare's politics. Like Kemble's public, they were drawn into a recreation of Roman history so aesthetically distanced as to make contemporary relevance next to unthinkable.

Cooper's monopoly of the role, if complete, did not go unchallenged. Occasionally American stock actors like William Wood and John Duff displayed their wares, but lasted only a night or two. Touring English provincial stars fared somewhat better. J. W. Wallack, the first actor to commute regularly between England and the United States, played a Kemblesque Martius a number of times between 1818 and 1824. A typical reviewer found "the eye . . . gratified by the novelty of attitude and the graces of gesture and motion; but the ear and the understanding . . . unsatisfied and disappointed" (*New-England Galaxy & Masonic Magazine,* Boston, 11 December 1818) when compared with Cooper's reading. Indeed, the same critic judged Wallack's patrician superior to Cooper's "only in the sumptuousness of the consul's wardrobe." Wallack's handsome person and masculine magnetism allowed him occasionally to attract good houses for the play, but it was never a highlight of his repertory. His brother Henry also attempted the part from time to time (see *Chronological Handlist*). Macready tried his luck at the Park Theater once during his 1826 visit, but after a lukewarm reception did not brave Cooper loyalists again.

William Augustus Conway, an English provincial star and protégé of Hester Thrale Piozzi, offered Cooper his only serious competition. Worn out with cabals and theatrical quarrels in England, he arrived in America in 1823, and appeared as Coriolanus for the first time at the Park Theater 14 January 1824. Over the next three years his reading caught the wave of enthusiasm for classical studies then sweeping the country,[21] and was wildly acclaimed for its historic grandeur and picturesque elegance in the course of several tours of the south and northeast. His dethronement of the middle-aged Cooper was a virtual certainty when he impulsively leapt to his death from a steamer near Charleston four years after his arrival.

Conway, like Cooper and Kemble, was an impressive physical specimen. "He is rising six feet in height," a New York critic reported,

and his form is so exquisite that it might serve as a model for an Apollo . . his countenance is expressive and his eye penetrating. He carries his person erect, and his step is firm and majestic. He possesses, likewise, the control of every muscle of his body, which, when necessary, he brings into action with the greatest ease, and in strict conformity to nature (*Minerva,* New York, 21 January 1824).

His acting style, like Cooper's, was indebted to Kemble; indeed, he aped the master sufficiently well to replace him as Coriolanus at Covent Garden in 1813 when the star was incapacitated for a time. A decade later the Kemble influence remained potent. One critic, who had seen the Coriolanuses of both Kemble and Conway, found "so striking a resemblance to [Kemble] in many of the scenes, and in the voice of Conway, that we imagined, at times, it was Kemble himself who stood before us" (*Minerva,* New York, 21 January 1824). One of his promptbooks, presented to Thomas Hamblin when they were working together at the Theatre Royal, Dublin in 1823 (*Cor* 8), suggests that he scrupulously followed the Kemble script.

His eye-catching physique, like Kemble's, gave his interpretation particular fascination. His "gigantic form," impressive at any time, seemed, when warmed by passion, "to dilate and become yet more grand," we are told, "as if the very god Mars walked in our presence" (*New-York Mirror,* 31 January 1824). Quite as fetching in a different way was the moment when "his martial form kneeled down with the utmost grace to receive the blessing of his mother, and rose again with perfect elegance and ease" (*New-York Mirror,* 31 January 1824).

Superb physical control was complemented by emotional versatility. In the Voices scene "the indignation breaking through the constraint imposed upon [Martius], and finding relief in a most bitter irony" (*New-York Mirror,* 31 January 1824) was warmly praised. In the subsequent scene, when the tribunes forbid him to pass, "the astonishment of his manner at first—the anger which followed—the unconcealed fury that glances like lightning against the tribunes, drew down the applause of a crowded audience" (*New-York Mirror,* 31 January 1824). In the exchange with the tribunes which runs:

> *Cor.* Why this was known before.
> *Bru.* Not to them all.
> *Cor.* Have you informed them since?

he unashamedly appropriated Kemble's *coup de maître:* "'Why, this was known before,' was spoken in a tone of expostulation; but when he receives answer, 'Not to them all,' quick as lightning he turns to the guilty tribune, and catching him in his own toils, he asks, 'Have you informed them since?'". The Kemble business on "I'll die here" during the citizen-patrician confrontation in 3.1 was also poignantly evoked. "In the heat of the debate," we are told,

the indignant soldier walked to the farthermost part of the stage, and the rabble, rash and impetuous, and infuriated by the hypocritical tribunes, prepared to seize him, and throng around him with fierce looks and uplifted clubs; but the Roman hero draws up his lofty figure to its full height, silent and majestic he stood among them, like some god, whose glance could awe down their inferior spirits, and look them from his presence. The crowd are appalled at the sight, and retreat in terror (*New-York Mirror,* 31 January 1824).

In the Intercession scene, according to the *Boston Patriot* (2 March 1824), "the struggles of nature with his idol honor, of relenting affection with the passion of revenge, were expressed by the most powerful and emphatic combinations of word, look and gesture." With Conway's suicide, the Cooper Roman lost its only serious competition and its only credible heir.[22]

THOMAS HAMBLIN AND THE BRITISH PROVINCIAL STARS (1825–1855)

A youthful Thomas Hamblin shared English provincial stages with Conway for a year or two before following him to America in 1825 with his own fascimile of the Kemble Martius, painstakingly fashioned on the British touring circuit. His New York welcome was less delirious than his predecessor's, but a measure of fame came eventually, if slowly. His conscientious starring tours and well-mounted revivals during his management of the Bowery and Park theaters kept the Kemble Roman alive, if hardly thriving, from Cooper's retirement until the midcentury mark. The only other significant residents to undertake the role were the juvenile Edwin Forrest, whose early attempts at the patrician were ill-received, and the lightweight J. W. Wallack Jr., who was largely ignored. The extensive and lengthy junkets of the British stars John Vandenhoff and James Anderson account for most other noteworthy *Coriolanus* performances in the second quarter of the century.

Hamblin's 1825 debut as Martius at the Park offered no threat to Cooper or Conway; and over the next few years he seldom undertook the part. In 1831, a year or so after he assumed the management of the Bowery, he mounted the play with himself in the title role, and almost a year later revived it with the English provincial star Samuel Butler as Martius. He then seems to have left the field to Cooper until the latter's retirement. He returned to the role in 1837 while on a brief starring visit at Covent Garden, and critical reaction ranged from lukewarm to downright damning. Back in the United States in 1838, his Martius found an enthusiastic reception at New York's National Theater, and he played the part fairly regularly thereafter in a variety of venues until 1852.

Like most American stage Romans, Hamblin was heroically proportioned. According to his one-time partner, James Hackett, he "was in height above the ordinary stature of men, and his frame was more bony than fleshy." "His head," he recalls, "was remarkable for its covering by a shock

Thomas Hamblin as Coriolanus. [By permission of the Folger Shakespeare Library]

of thick and curly dark-brown hair; his nose was high and thick, and long like his visage." With his tall figure costumed to advantage and skilled in "such artificial bearing as has become consonant with our modern ideas of the manner of ancient Romans," Hackett allowed that he made "a respectable stand."[23] A reviewer who saw his London performances found his action "easy and natural" and his declamation "sonorous and distinct" (*Sunday Times,* 19 February 1837), but rated his interpretation rather "a correct than a powerful delineation of character" (*Sunday Times,* 26 February 1837). American audiences did not share his reservations. At his 1843 Bowery performances the house, we are told, "was crowded in every part, and it was utterly impossible for all who applied to obtain seats, such was the rush" (*Morning Courier and New York Enquirer*, 10 October 1843). The 1848 revival, probably his best, was described as "a splendid performance of the true, old stamp." "He looked, moved, and acted the haughty patrician," an observer noted, "with a classic dignity and finished style of delivery that stamped him as being 'the last of the Romans' now left of the Kemble school" (*Albion*, New York, 16 September 1848). His final appearances in 1852 were greeted with undiminished enthusiasm. "His Coriolanus, last evening," reported the *Evening Mirror*, "was witnessed by a full and appreciative house, who repeatedly applauded his powerful acting" (New York, 8 June 1852). That he managed to play to packed theaters in an age which routinely witnessed Vandenhoff's touring copy of the Kemble Martius is a remarkable tribute to either Hamblin's talents or his audience's loyalty, or perhaps both.

Although American patriotic sympathies were with the Hamblin Coriolanus, Vandenhoff (1837–38, 1839–40, 1841) and James Anderson (1844–45, 1846) received warmer welcomes than London offered. Even Vandenhoff's maligned dovecote-fluttering gesture was hailed as "true to the passion" and enthusiastically applauded (*Evening Signal*, New York, 13 January 1840). When Anderson entered in the play's first scene, the Park Theater audience rose and "continued standing, for some minutes" (*New York Morning Express*, 16 April 1845), and the slanging match with Tullus Aufidius at the play's climax "brought down thunders of applause" (*New York Herald*, 15 April 1845).

Nowhere does one come upon a Volumnia of much power, or a Menenius or Aufidius who receives more than casual mention. The citizens, few in numbers, ill-rehearsed, and shorn of all political significance, were totally overlooked by critics bewitched by spectacular processions and virtuoso oratory.

Edwin Forrest (1838–1864)

Although Edwin Forrest[24] played the Kemble text and offered a beau ideal Roman of Kemble-Macready-Phelps ancestry, his Martius was no mere copy, nor was his scenography exclusively indebted to any single London or New York antecedent. He owed as much to Kemble as to anyone, but tempered Kemble's production practice with effects borrowed from Macready and Phelps which he augmented in turn with his own eccentric invention. The result was not a tasteless muddle, as might be expected, but an identifiable style which overlaid English high culture with the swashbuckling brashness, gushing sentiment, and vivid palette of native melodrama. In *Coriolanus* the stern grandeur of Kemble, the tremulous spirituality of Macready, and the decorous domesticity of Phelps were not rejected outright; rather, individual elements were heightened and the whole reshaped to catch the contemporary market for unconfined sentiment and flamboyant spectacle.[25]

Forrest, tempted perhaps by the success of Vandenhoff's touring performances in the autumn of 1837, added Coriolanus to his repertory early in 1838, but enjoyed little success. He arrayed his talents against Vandenhoff again during the latter's 1841 tour with no better result, and did not attempt the part again until after Hamblin's retirement. His most successful *Coriolanus* revivals took place at New York's Broadway Theater in 1855 and Niblo's Garden in 1863. In 1855 his production suffered from inadequate technical support; but the 1863 revival, supervised by the brilliant manager William Wheatley, did all possible justice to Forrest's conception.[26]

For Forrest, champion of the common man, rabid democrat, and proud and outspoken patriot, Martius's antipopulism and treason were unequivocally distasteful. Unlike Cooper, he disdained simply to obscure *Coriolanus*'s antidemocratic bias beneath heroic physique, rhetorical flash, and visual historicity. If the play was to be performed, its political character must be erased, not disguised; and the craft of melodrama, in which Forrest had few equals, offered a tempting strategy. Through imaginative characterization and ingenious stagecraft, Shakespeare's class struggle was metamorphosed into the moral and social crusade of a Roman frontiersman against a rabble of degenerate ruffians who had violated the historic social contract. Forrest's reading shrewdly targeted a variety of anxieties related to uncontrolled antebellum economic expansion and urbanization: a perceived decline in moral integrity born of unprecedented prosperity, a loss of rootedness and family values attendant on increased mobility, and a sense of physical danger associated with the proliferation of urban slumdwellers, described as early as 1817 by Reverend Ward Stafford as "a great mass of people beyond the restraints of religion," among whom "thousands . . . are grossly vicious."[27] Against a stirring evocation of antiquarian splendor, Forrest offered jittery antebellum and Civil War audiences an inspirational parable of a youthful republic threatened by moral outlaws and bravely defied by a muscular family man "with every virtue of civil life adorned." Shakespeare's aesthetic complexity has probably never been more rigorously simplified.

The promptbook for the 1863 production (*Cor* 20) is made on a Spencer's Boston Theater edition, another derivative of Oxberry and thus of Kemble's script. Forrest, ignoring the textual restorations of Macready and Phelps, retained Kemble's Thomsonian interpolations. He treated act 5 as one continuous scene, as did Kemble, but added two tableaux numbered 5.2 and 5.3 to which we shall return. Kemble's 2.1, the sequence in which Menenius verbally jousts with the tribunes and later awaits the ovation procession with Volumnia and Virgilia, and Kemble's 2.2, the ovation itself, Forrest appends to act 1 as 1.5 and 1.6. He also divides the Voices scene (Kemble's 2.5) into two parts: the first comprises the citizens' conversation prior to

Martius's entry, after which they exit; the second begins with Martius's entrance.

Forrest situates the action within Kemble's Imperial rather than Macready's Republican decor, a tactic calculated simultaneously to satisfy the contemporary appetite for classical grandeur and to glorify American expansionistic aspirations of which he was a champion. At the same time, he did not hesitate on occasion to enlist elements of Macready's Romantic scenography in the service of picturesque sentimentalism.

Forrest's Eternal City, designed by J. H. Selwyn and H. Hillyard, was visually fetching and historically derived, although wanting something of the artistic finish which distinguished the Romes of Kemble and Macready. The setting for 1.1, in the "3 or 4 G[rooves]," was an elaborate reconstruction of a Roman street with authentic Imperial architecture. The flat before which Menenius berated the tribunes in 1.5, described as "A Street in Rome," was a particular source of pride. Located at the 1st Grooves and presumably a drop,[28] it featured, according to the playbill, "THE ROMAN WOLF Placed in the Comitium, near Fig Tree 'Ruminalis,' under which tree Romulus and Remus were suckled, and which was preserved with great veneration by Romans for nearly four hundred years from the building of the city."[29]

The ovation was, as usual, the play's visual highlight. Occupying the "whole extent of stage, including paint Room," "the Capitol of Rome on paint frame" against the back wall lent the picture distanced splendor and perspective; the foreground was "divided by two Streets" up which "thro' arches" could be seen the "distant backing view of Rome." In the middle distance were "steps ascending to the Capitol" in front of which was a platform designed to accommodate the chorus. An altar was located C.

The Senate hailed Martius in a three-tiered amphitheater located just below the 4th grooves, while the Voices episode took place before "The Temple of Jupiter." Martius outfaced his plebeian opposition in 3.1 downstage of a representation of the "Tarpeian Rock, ascended by the hundred steps," located in the 2d grooves. Its foreground, in emulation of the antiquarian pedantry beloved of Charles Kean, depicted "one of the branches of the Cloaca Maxima draining the Marshes of the Velabrum." The Banishment episode (3.3) was assigned the same locale as the ovation, a clever thought.

Martius arrived in Antium before a carpenter's scene (1st grooves) described as "A Room in AUFIDIUS' House," while the upcoming setting was readied behind. His meeting with Aufidius, staged in the Kemble rather than the Macready manner, took place in a "Grecian Hall" with a "Marble Platform in 3 G [rooves] Centre" graced with a gigantic statue of Mars. On the right of steps leading to the platform stood an altar fitted with a gas flame which, filtered through red glass, cast a ruddy glow on the immobile figure, sentimentally mellowing it with Macready's firelight effect.

The Intercession scene employed the traditional background flat or drop

Promptbook sketch of the Ovation setting. Edwin Forrest Production, 1863. [By permission of the Folger Shakespeare Library]

depicting "The Volscian Camp and Distant View of Rome"; at downstage right was located a platform with two seats beneath a canopy. The only novelty was the provision of eight seats for Volscian senators at upstage right.

Again, as the Kemble tradition dictated, supers were an integral feature of the decor. Forrest's "auxiliaries" for the 1863 revival numbered more than a hundred,[30] and he paraded them on the slightest excuse. Only stock shutters seem to have been used for the two battlefield sequences (1.3 and 1.4), and colorfully garbed troops were the exclusive source of eye-appeal. In 1.3, after "noise of battle, clashing of swords [and] 4 shouts" succeeded by "Drums and trumpet charges then Trumpet Retreat," "Enter R.H.3.G. 24 Roman soldiers with Fulvius, Navius, Lucius, Aruns, Decius, armed with spears and shields, & range on R.H." to dress the stage for Martius's arrival. In 1.3, in which Martius is new-christened, the same twenty-four military bodies "Enter Marching R.H.3.E." Once down center they are instructed to "divide R & L upstage Counter march and range on R & L" once more to act as a breathing backdrop to the heroic moment.

Living scenery, if useful on the battlefield, was crucial to the ovation. Forrest arranged his procession in Kemble's five divisions, retaining most of his content; the numbers in each unit were reduced, however, to reflect the fact that the production had at its disposal less than half the supers

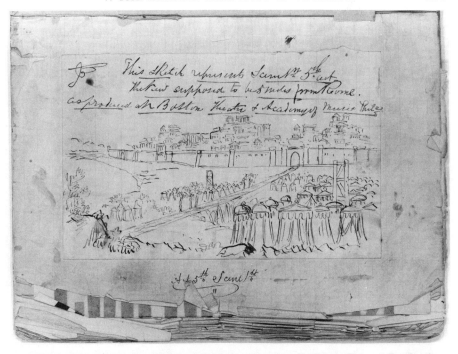

Promptbook sketch of the "Volscian Camp" setting (act 5). Edwin Forrest Production, 1863. [By permission of the Folger Shakespeare Library]

available at Covent Garden. In blatant disregard of the Shakespearian design he followed Macready in making the plebeians an obtrusive stage presence at Martius's homecoming. As the curtain rises, "Citizens of Rome" are positioned "at Windows and Balconys [sic] of Houses." Others in high excitement "run across, shouting from the arch R.H.U.E. and ascend the steps to Capitol" and exit. The procession now enters, passing "down the Street R [and] X'es in front and up Street L." In a piece of gratuitous showmanship that would have appalled Macready and Kemble, Forrest posed grandly in a triumphal car drawn by plebeians, while their compatriots watching above showered the victor with wreaths. The effect, although undeniably picturesque, was utterly at odds with both Martius's modesty and his contempt for the riffraff throughout. "Imagine," fulminated the *Albion* (New York, 5 May 1855) critic, "the fiery patrician submitting to this kind of exhibition, when even in the Senate he will not hear his merits discussed." Even less acceptable was the notion "of *Coriolanus* permitting the greasy plebeians to make an exhibition of him" (*New-York Daily Times,* 24 April 1855).

If the ovation's introduction of plebeian spectators betrayed a debt to Macready, the Senate staging proved to be an outright appropriation.[31] Although he mustered only sixty senators, as compared with his archenemy's one to two hundred, Forrest achieved a passable facsimile by arranging thirty on each side of the stage in three amphitheatrical tiers while upstage center on a marble platform stood Cominius's consular chair with "The statue of the wolf" behind. At the scene's conclusion, the senators rose as one man to salute Martius in the approved Macready fashion on "To Coriolanus come all joy and honor." As "Cominius le[d] Coriolanus up stage centre," bowing to the Senate as he passed, "Street" shutters closed on the scene.

The curtain rose on the last act to discover the traditional throngs of military supers, colorfully uniformed and bearing handsome banners. Two groups of soldiers at extreme upstage right and left lent background mass to the picture; and at stage right, from upstage to downstage, symmetrically arranged scarlet-clad troops offered color contrast to the mourning women shortly to pass in the obligatory procession. The extreme downstage right was occupied by Volscian officers and more banners; opposite, well downstage left, sat Martius and Tullus, with eight senators slightly upstage of them. From U.L., and to music, "Virgilia—Volumnia & Young Marcius, Valeria, Servilia, & Rom. Ladies 2 & 2" progressed downstage, squired by "4 Roman Ambassadors with Gold staffs." The improbable presence of elegantly-attired diplomats on a pathetic domestic mission troubled Forrest not a whit. Pictorial effect was all.

With the intercession over and Martius and the women offstage, Forrest regrouped his troops across the upstage area at right angles to the military already arranged from upstage to downstage left. Opposite them sat the senators, with Tullus and Volusius standing just below them. The blocking design both framed the action and constructed visually the trap Aufidius is about to spring. Where in previous productions the military supers apparently stood by impassively, contrary to all probability, they now actively participate. On Volusius's "Insolent villain," Aufidius, Volusius, and the officers shout "Kill! Kill! Kill! Kill him!" According to the promptbook "Aufidius—Volusius and all the officers surround Coriolanus, draw their swords, & stab him same time they are speaking." As the officers advance the soldiers come down on R and L "and close in double lines with backs to audience." The effect is to hide the assassination behind three rows of military. "The crowd [of soldiers]," Forrest's friend William B. Maclay reported, "rush upon him, cover him from the view of the audience, and in the *melée* he is slain—but the manner of his death is left to the imagination" (*Evening Post,* New York, 25 April 1855). A treacherous murder by mean-minded conspirators and a ritual execution by a vengeful militia are not at all the same thing. Forrest may have been motivated by a desire to ennoble Martius's departure, or perhaps to vitiate Shakespeare's brutality by hiding it; in any event, the moment of death, so essential to some sense of tragic closure, was missed.

Once Martius falls, "Officers and soldiers separate R & L and his body is discovered lying on stage. The Senators on R.H. rise in astonishment."

On this picture, a "Dead March" begins, and "4 Soldiers bring on Bier" from up right and place it at center stage. Officers and soldiers "close in front" while the body is readied. As the bier is raised shoulder high, senators, soldiers, and officers assume a processional formation and exit up left.

In two ensuing gratuitous mimed scenes, Forrest strained ingenuity, not to mention the limits of good taste, to endow the death of nature's nobleman with an aura of spirituality not conspicuous in his lifetime. In a new unit numbered 5.2 the cortege which just exited crosses backstage from left to right while a "Black Drapery Drop" is flown in in the 1st grooves to allow the upstage area to be reset. With wing lights, border lights, and footlights out, the procession reenters L.H.1 E., attended by priests and lighted by torches, and slowly crosses the stage to "Dead March Continued."

As the cortege disappears, the black drop rises on Forrest's 5.3 to reveal "A closely shaded Grove" by night in the 6th grooves. A pyre is discovered C at the 4th grooves "with the body of Coriolanus (Dummy) on raised trap platform behind Pyre." A "Calcium [Lime] Light to strike on Body from flies R.H." creates an ambiance of moonlit tranquillity. Two Priests are positioned at either end of the Pyre, bearing lighted torches, and at R a chorus of male and female citizens await their cue. Officers, senators, virgins, and soldiers with banners are picturesquely disposed about the stage. Well down left stand Volumnia, Virgilia, Valeria, Young Martius, and a contingent of Roman ladies. On cue, the chorus launches into a dirge:

> The Funeral pyre we rear
> The Funeral dirge we sing
> For you we shed a tear
> For you the trophies bring.
>
> Farewell, farewell, farewell
> Son of the mighty Mars
> Thy body to the flames we give
> Thy soul unto the stars.

In the course of the requiem, the priests ignite the pyre, and the trap bearing the body slowly sinks as the fire takes hold. In a climactic affirmation of immortality and spiritual renewal, "A phoenix rises from the flames" and "all on stage kneel" as the curtain falls. Here the entire melodramatic kitbag was emptied to canonize the martyr to moral integrity and filial piety and to reinforce socially the values he was made to represent. If after such a surfeit of picture, atmosphere, pyrotechnic display, and elevating sentiment there was an earthbound soul or a dry eye in the house, Forrest could hardly be blamed.

Forrest's evocative mise-en-scène was designed from first to last to flatter his idealized Martius. Physically the part was tailored to measure for him. At five feet ten inches he was about the same height as Cooper, while grueling daily conditioning gave him arms, legs, and chest of epic proportions. When he stepped upon the stage, writes his biographer Alger,

> quivering with vital power, his skin polished by exercise and friction to a smooth and marbly hardness, conscious of his enormous potency, fearless of anything on the earth . . . he used to stand and receive the long, tulmultuous cheering that greeted him as immovable as a planted statue of Hercules.[32]

His strapping physique, admirable as it was, nevertheless lacked the classic proportions of Kemble and Cooper, nor was he master of the statuesque movement which was their trademark.

His temperament was, if possible, more suited to the character than his frame. "He was constitutionally a savage and always in rebellion," writes William Winter.

> Forrest was always the slave of his ignorance, his passion, and his prejudice, and was always in a fume over his own limitations. . . . He believed himself to be a man of genius, but to his mind this meant that he was unlike other men and superior to them, and therefore ordained and privileged to dominate everything. . . . He liked to feel his royal authority and to make the weak tremble. He could, indeed, be magnanimous, loving and kind—for he was human and had warmth as well of the affections as of the passions. . . . But nothing like self-government . . . appeared in any important moment of his life.[33]

If anyone could understand and sympathetically recreate Shakespeare's Martius, it was Forrest; yet the hero's politics cut him off from the actor's sympathies. For years, however, he struggled to interpret the character as theatrical tradition construed him. In his early performances at the Park in 1838, his imitation of Kemble's reading as derived from Cooper[34] was ill-received on political grounds.[35] When he revived the part at the Broadway in 1855, it was not his politics which displeased, but his faulty evocation of the beau ideal style: the stoic grandeur of Kemble and Cooper had dwindled into self-conscious posing. Martius was uncharitably characterized by one critic as "a large phlegmatic man with a strong predilection for standing in one place, and a tedious habit of pausing between his sentences" (*New-York Daily Times*, 24 April 1855). Another, remarking Forrest's natural inability to suggest "lofty dignity and arrogant hauteur," alleged that "in the solemnity of the attempt [to assume them], the principal elements in the character of Coriolanus—its naturalness and impulsiveness—are lost" (*New-York Daily Tribune*, 24 April 1855).

When he tackled the role in 1863, Forrest finally put the Kemble-Cooper example firmly behind him, and shaped Martius to his own artistic strengths and ideological sympathies. The Martius theatergoers saw at Niblo's Garden was a Roman pioneer, brawny of body, honest of heart, physically fearless but socially inept, gallant to women, and tender to the weak; in fact, the protagonist of heroic melodrama and close kin to Forrest's iconic Spartacus and Metamora, what the *Sunday Mirror* (New York, 8 November 1863) called "not so much a patrician by status as by mind."

"Shattering virtue's temple was the job of the villain," as David Grimsted puts it,[36] and rarely have tribunes and plebeians, as joint malefactors, been more unflatteringly represented. Brutus and Sicinius, as played by Frank Mordaunt and John Nunan, were a pair of unredeemed demagogues. The rabble, in no way to be confused with honest workingmen, were the lazy, greedy, senselessly violent dregs of an otherwise wholesome republic. The *Sunday Mercury* (New York, 8 November 1863) aptly labeled them "the scum of a great city." The dramatic conflict consequently identified itself as a struggle between Martius's roughhewn integrity and the street gang's moral corruption with the future of legitimate government at stake. On his exile, Martius was reinvented not as a traitor but a "bandit for the sake of virtue," a type of melodramatic hero Grimsted identifies as:

> separated from society by banishment or withdrawal for some wrongdoing, real or alleged . . . [I]f he had been guilty of some breach of social bonds, there were extenuating circumstances to lessen the trespass; if he were wholly a victim of social injustice, he scorned society in terms that showed he possessed its virtues in abundance and reentered it when occasions for protecting the pure and innocent demanded.[37]

In the end Martius's transgression was redeemed by the greatest of melodramatic virtues next to sexual purity, filial piety. The triumph of domestic and patriotic feeling over private pique cost him his life but earned him spiritual immortality.

Forrest's reinvention of *Coriolanus* as heroic melodrama struck precisely the right note. "As the physical Roman he presented a magnificent appearance," reported the *Sunday Mercury* (New York, 8 November 1863); "as mental as well as accidental patrician he did not fail in one instance." Forrest's Roman "thrills sensibility, it kindles the imagination, it stirs the heart by high ideals of valiant manliness," gushed *Wilkes' Spirit of the Times* (New York, 14 November 1863), and few reviewers disagreed. "On his first appearance," noted one observer,

> he seemed to shrink, with all the acute sensibility of a superior mind, from too familiar a contact with natures that are vulgar. His abhorrence of the mob of Rome is not because it is composed of a ragged crew; not even because it is dirty . . . not because it is what is commonly called ignorant: but because it is brutal as well—fickle and insolent all the while . . . arrantly coward, too—with stones and knives, ready to work vengeance on the patrician (*Sunday Mercury,* New York, 8 November 1863).

The thirty citizens provided did their best to justify Martius's repugnance. Armed and threatening on their entry in 1.1, they loudly and abrasively

Edwin Forrest as Coriolanus beneath the Statue of Mars. [By permission of the Folger Shakespeare Library]

made their presence felt until Martius's arrival when "All retreat in fear towards R.H.1.E. step by step." When invited by Martius to "follow," "all the citizens sneak off 1 E.R. & 2.E." Clean, stalwart, and fearless, Martius declared himself their natural superior in every way.

In the military scenes, Forrest was at his swashbuckling best, awash in waving spears and heralded at every turn by trumpet flourishes. As one reviewer put it, "Case him in armor, put a falchion in his hand and a helmet on his head, place him on the boards strung up to the good old Roman pitch, and he is one of the greatest actors the world ever saw" (*New York News*, 3 November 1863). In the post-battle episode which sees Martius renamed, his modesty was urged without stint. Flanked by twenty-four soldiers and half a dozen officers, artfully marshalled, his gruff "I do refuse it" was highlighted by "Flourish R.H. Soldiers and officers raise spears & shields and shout 3 times." Similar business on "false faced soothing," the investiture itself, and "bear the addition nobly ever," carried him inexorably on a cresting wave, toward a fame he merits, but does not seek.

To a society apprehensive at the disappearance of the patriarchal family, Forrest offered a comforting paterfamilias. Taking a hint from Macready and Phelps, he amplified the domestic moments throughout, beginning with Martius's homecoming. One reviewer noted the particular "delicacy with which he threw in the tender touches, the almost childish delight with which he lingered over every opportunity for private and domestic feeling" (*Express*, New York, 3 November 1863). The warmth and strength of the familial bond established by Forrest early in the play was to serve him well later.

Forrest's interpretation, he well knew, would stand or fall by his handling of the Voices episode, and it was crucial that here the rabble appear at their grossest. As Martius awaited their arrival before the Temple of Jupiter, "Enter First and Second Citizens L.H.1 E. Arm in Arm. Pompous," strutting about the stage in complacent self-satisfaction at their newfound influence. "The Citizens on first seeing Coriolanus," according to the promptbook, "are somewhat abashed." Their confidence grows apace, however, and on Martius's "I've wounds to show you," "1st Citizen advance[s] to examine the wounds"; Martius, affronted at his presumption, abruptly "closes his Mantle" on "Which shall be yours in private," leaving "1st Citizen abashed." On "A match, sir," the "2nd Cit rubs his hand to clean it," and advances eagerly to take the hand of Coriolanus, who, copying Kemble's time-honored business, "proudly withdraws it." On "An't were to give again," the 2nd Citizen menacingly "advances on Coriolanus, who motions him away." It is clear from the promptbook that Forrest played this sequence with considerable restraint, allowing the mob's insolence full rein, and his own precariously controlled outrage to mount in direct response. His sense of physical and moral violation found satisfying release in the patrician-plebeian donnybrook in 3.1. Here, with less squeamishness than shown by Kemble, Forrest calls Sicinius a "rotten thing" and throws him to R.H. on "I shall shake thy bones out of thy garments." Confronted with imminent arrest, he draws his sword and makes the most of the Kemble tour de force on "No, I'll die here." Just before Martius reacts, in the mistaken assumption that he will compliantly exit, "all the citizens advance towards Coriolanus," but with customary cowardice "they [retreat] back again to R corner as he draws sword upon them." Throughout Forrest kept Martius on the defensive: the national hero was not the initiator of violence; he simply reacted, as his code of honor demanded, to social anarchy. As Cominius urges "Come, sir, along with us" (3.1.236), "All the Citizens advance again on Coriolanus—and shrink back with fear" at his glance as he quits the stage.

Martius's interview with his mother (3.2), in which she persuades him to trim his sails to the prevailing wind, although more lightly handled than in earlier productions, subtly and richly revealed the strength of the mother-son relationship and Martius's recognition of his filial obligation. "This scene," wrote one reviewer, "was conceived in the grand spirit of that serious comedy which old Kean was so marvellous in—comedy that translates the tragic nature without stilts" (*New York Dispatch,* 8 November 1863). In a delicate interaction, by turns gently amusing, tender, and finally ominous, Mme. Ponisi's Volumnia pellucidly revealed her strategy from moment to moment to everyone but Martius.

Forrest's promptbook allows the encounter to be reconstructed with fair precision. "[C]oaxing and persuading Coriolanus" on "I pr'ythee now, my son," she enjoys some initial success; but with "He must, and will," however, she betrays her determination rather too much, and "Coriolanus looks at Volumnia indignantly." She cunningly resumes her former tactic, and once more "proceeds coaxingly." Gradually, as she warms to her appeal, her inexorable will inadvertently asserts itself. To Martius's demand, "Must I / With my base tongue give to my noble heart / A lie that it must bear?", "Volumnia in action [indicates] 'Yes!'". The intensification of his mother's suasion, which leads her wheedlingly to "pat him upon the cheek" at one point, serves only to aggravate Martius's impatience. On her defiant boast, "I mock at death / With as big heart as thou," he "motions Volumnia to be calm," and she sensibly assumes a more moderate tone. Shortly after, however, her will to win overtly resurfaces: she "manifests impatience," and even becomes downright "angry" at her son's recalcitrance. Martius's filial devotion shortly after prompts his submission to the maternal will; and on "I'll return consul," in a fine prefiguration of his intercession capitulation, he "takes her hand." Forrest's "mingling of playful tenderness . . . with the haughtier nature of the patrician" in this scene one theatergoer found "indescribably beautiful" (*Frank Leslie's Illustrated Newspaper,* New York, 14 November 1863).

The Banishment episode offered Forrest, like his predecessors, an unrivaled opportunity for physical, vocal, and emotional gymnastics, and he made the most of it. Again, he relied strongly on the provocative behavior of tribunes and plebeians to mitigate his subsequent behaviour: the "representatives of the *vox populi,*" we learn, "were as patronizing and insolent as they well could be; and the crowd in the back ground . . . in their turn, assumed the part of masters." Throughout the early part of the scene, as in the Voices sequence, Martius "seemed to be mentally writhing under the infliction of the popular address; and when it came his turn to talk, his words, though conciliatory in sense, were leavened with a satire of tone" (*Sunday Mercury,* New York, 8 November 1863). Baited beyond endurance by the epithet "traitor," Martius's controlled scorn gave way to untrammeled fury. On "It shall be so!" the mob, feeling they now enjoyed the upper hand, were seen "advancing with their staves on Coriolanus"; but when the object of their attentions moved towards them from C, "they retreat[ed] from him step by step as he advance[d] on them into R Corner with great fear." His "You common cry of curs" diatribe was a deeply satisfying moment for long-suffering urbanites all too familiar with contemporary gang-violence.[38] "In the position where Forrest stood," recalled William B. Maclay, "he seemed to have acquired additional height, as with flashing eyes and dilated form he rushed toward the retreating rabble and thundered out his concentrated scorn in the exclamation, 'I banish *you.*'"[39] Not content with multiplied examples of Martius's intrepidity and the mob's cowardice, Forrest offered one final demonstration at the act's end. His "There is a world elsewhere" (which he gave with a stress on *is,* despite vociferous protests from reviewers) was followed by a pause. Coriolanus then "turns his back goes up stage R.H. followed by Cominius and Menenius." The plebeians, eager as always to defy authority from a safe distance, "follow Coriolanus up R." To their surprise, however, the wounded lion once more "turns upon them, [and] they retreat back again into L corner shouting 'Whoo'! 'Whoo'!" Martius immediately leaves the stage without a backward glance, while his tormentors "all follow [him] up shouting till Drop Down." This curiously delayed exit, so unlike the swift Kemble departure, was calculated to stamp on the collective emotional canvas an indelible recollection of mob viciousness and heroic resistance. Martius was to need all the sympathy thus generated in the scenes to follow.

Critics were apparently so overcome with the Banishment episode that they failed to remark upon Martius's discovery in Aufidius's house. It is difficult to understand how a scene so integral to the Kemble production tradition should have passed unnoticed when played by an actor renowned for his statuesque glamour.

In the Intercession scene, as in earlier domestic contacts, Forrest's Martius relentlessly idealized the patriarchal family, its relationships mellowed throughout by masculine tenderness. Phelps's innovations had clearly not gone unheeded. The emotional temperature of the scene's climax was raised considerably by Forrest's restoration of Martius's lines beginning "O, my mother, mother!" (5.3.185–89).

As the procession halts, and its participants dispose themselves about the stage, the promptbook reminds Martius to look at his son who "holds out his hands beseechingly" and at his supplicating spouse and parent. On "I melt, and am not / Of stronger earth than others," he "throws away his truncheon and rushes to his wife."[40] After embracing Virgilia and doing obeisance to his mother, he "Raises and kisses Boy," as did Phelps. The claims of familial affection established, Forrest proceeded to underscore the demands of personal honor. Prior to Volumnia's speech the "grand self-confidence in his impregnability to all entreaty, the apparent immobility with which he seat[ed] himself to listen" (*Frank Leslie's Illustrated Newspaper,* New York, 14 November 1863), indicated that the struggle would be of epic dimensions. "The suppressed passion with which he listens to his mother pleading for their common country, the veiled anguish with which he hears her indignant taunts, and the final breaking down of his revenge under the attempt at self-immolation, were indescribably and sublimely touching," reported the *New York Dispatch* (8 November 1863).

Some of his finest effects, however, were reserved for his final confrontation with Aufidius in which, we are told, "he rose to the very sublimity of heroic passion" and his response to the "Boy" taunts was "simply magnificent" (*Frank Leslie's Illustrated Newspaper,* New York, 14 November 1863). Forrest's idiosyncratic blocking of the assassination denied him the Kemble back-fall.

In most of his revivals, Forrest was poorly partnered, but Wheatley went out of his way in 1863 to ensure that support was at least adequate if not ideal. The citizens, so crucial to Forrest's conception, were superbly drilled; Mme. Ponisi's Volumnia was stately and powerful; and Burnett's ascerbic Menenius and Shewell's fiery Aufidius received general but undetailed praise.

Forrest's *Coriolanus,* although it lacked the artistic homogeneity and high finish of the Kemble and Macready revivals, nevertheless attests with equal eloquence to the aesthetic imperatives of its time and place. Forrest's appreciation of structural integrity, character consistency, and visual subtlety was tenuous at best; but his ear for the heartbeat of his audience was infallible. His muscular, great-hearted, and tender hero staring down the forces of disorder amid scenes of imperial magnificence, pathetically capitulating to familial grief, and dying heroically in a military coup offered an insecure nation a two-hour retreat into patriarchal security, moral integrity, and familial sensibility, what McConachie calls "a utopian vision of an Arcadian past."[41]

JOHN McCULLOUGH (1878)

The Forrest style was perpetuated by his protégé John McCullough (1832–85)[42] for a decade or more after the master's demise, but its expression was refined, mellowed, and sentimentalized even as the robust manners of the fifties were chastened by the Brown Decades.[43] McCullough, a handsome Irishman as heroically built as Forrest himself, joined Forrest's company in 1861 at the age of twenty-nine, and in short order became a leading member. His Cominius in the 1863 revival was favorably noticed. When in 1866 he left Forrest to make a bid for stardom in California, his mentor's blood and thunder heroics were cheered to the rafters by audiences who thrived on muscular theater. After eight successful years in the West, he returned east in 1874 to find Forrest's Herculean grandeur had been displaced by Edwin Booth's poetic soulfulness. Under the tutelage of Steele MacKaye, who favored a Delsartean approach to acting, McCullough sought repose, disciplined focus, and graceful and expressive gesture dictated by character rather than potential applause points. On 7 February 1878 he premiered his *Coriolanus* in Boston with great success, and the following December brought the production to New York's Grand Opera House where it enjoyed a lucrative two-week run. Curiously enough, he played the role only occasionally during the five years before madness overtook him in 1883.

The text used by McCullough was basically Forrest's, with a few restorations, including the belly fable. The two scenes associated with Martius's cremation he counted as one act, thus making the play six acts rather than five. Like Forrest, and indeed all producers in the Kemble tradition, he doted on historical authenticity, pictorial composition, and the corporeal splendor of massed ranks of supers in motion and at rest. For good measure, he added a chariot drawn by horses to the Ovation scene, only to find his realistic gesture rebuffed: "We need not enter a theatre to behold a horse," the *New-York Daily Tribune* (19 December 1878) reminded him.

Audiences witnessing McCullough's New York revival in 1878 found little to distinguish this production visually or textually from Forrest's. What was different, however, was McCullough's Roman. Neither the class-conscious patrician of Kemble, nor the noble savage of Macready, nor the pure-spirited frontiersman of Forrest, this Martius was a spit-and-polish military man, whose life and actions are dictated by disinterested principle, and whose fatal flaw lies in his intellectual pride. "He is of an icy purity, physical as well as mental," noted William Winter,

and his nerves tingle with an absolute disgust of the personal uncleanliness of the mob. His is not the aristocracy which sits in a corner, deedless and meritless . . . but the aristocracy of achievement and of nature—the solid superiority of having done the brightest and best deeds that could be done in his time, and of being the greatest man of his generation (*New-York Daily Tribune,* 19 December 1878).

Reviewers were swift to give Shakespeare's Roman narrative American cultural reference, and to draw inspiration from it. "It is as if a Washington, having made and saved a nation, were to spurn it from him in lusty, and by no means groundless, contempt for the ignorance, pettiness, meanness and filth of mankind," wrote Winter, and went on to instance modern parallels in the blighted careers of Benedict Arnold and Aaron Burr. An object lesson to the Gilded Age's self-made aristocrats, the production was read as a plea for humane tolerance, sympathy for misery, recognition of one's own fallibility, and for oneness with the world.

Throughout the early scenes of the play, McCullough was "an imperial figure that move[d] with a mountainous grace through the fleeting rabble of Roman Plebeians and Volscians, dreadful in war, loftily calm in peace, irradiating rather than expressing the conscious superiority of power, dignity,

John McCullough as Coriolanus (1878). [By permission of the Folger Shakespeare Library]

worth and honorable renown." Here his action had "the splendid repose, not merely of great strength, but of intellectual poise and native mental supremacy" (*New-York Daily Tribune*, 19 December 1878). Unlike the essentially disjointed series of virtuoso moments offered by Forrest, McCullough managed to create a closely woven characterization in which a series of previously isolated strands came together. While audiences admired the inherent grandeur of his patrician, they revelled in the "tenderness, reverence, . . . proud humility and the softer graces which harmonize the character of one 'born to command'" (*Daily Graphic*, New York, 17 December 1878).

The early scenes were marked by a "simple dignity" (*Spirit of the Times*, New York, 21 December 1878) which, in his encounters with the plebeians, betrayed beneath it a "fierce haughtiness and scarcely restrained fury of disgust" (*Spirit of the Times*, New York, 21 December 1878). In the battle scenes, his fine military presence in armor, "the most massive, and the handsomest ever seen on our stage" (*Spirit of the Times*, New York, 31 December 1878), could hardly have been bettered. He made more of the Senate scene than most of his predecessors in the role. Here, according to Winter, "the delicacy of vocalism, movement, tone of sentiment and manliness of condition—the true royal fibre of a great mind—in the act of withdrawal from the Senate, was right and beautiful" (*New-York Daily Tribune*, 19 December 1878). In the Voices sequence, he apparently reined in the open disgust which characterized Forrest's reading in favor of "contemptuous irony" (*Spirit of the Times*, New York, 14 December 1878),[44] while in the Banishment episode he attained a "lofty repose, the ineffable disdain of the innate superiority of the patrician, too proud to show how strongly he was moved" (*Daily Graphic*, New York, 17 December 1878).

McCullough's splendid display of intellectual pride would have gone for nothing had he not shown to climactic effect its ultimate conquest by humane feeling. To have full effect in the play's final moments, as William Winter put it, "The deep heart as well as the imperial intellect must speak" (*New-York Daily Tribune*, 19 December 1878). His basically affectionate nature emerged in the Ovation sequence when military severity gave way to a touching "sweetness and tenderness"; in his conversation with his mother, we are told, "there was added to these a grave, deep-reaching reverence, through which breathed the peculiar virtue of the ancient republic" (*Spirit of the Times*, New York, 14 December 1878). Essential preparation for his disintegration in the Intercession scene was the Admonition episode. Here, Winter thought, "the stormy utterance of revolted pride and furious disgust, in the denial of Volumnia's request—the tempestuous outburst, 'I will not do it'—made as wild, fiery, and fine a moment in tragic acting as could be imagined" (*New-York Daily Tribune*, 19 December 1878). The groundwork was thus well and truly laid for the subsequent and decisive battle between heart and head, and audiences were not disappointed. The *Daily Graphic* critic (17 December 1878) found himself at a loss for words, save to observe that McCullough throughout the intercession "vibrate[d] the chords of feeling until they can scarcely bear the tension" and left the audience at its close seized with "a prophetic sadness." Even in the Assassination scene, McCullough's artistic restraint did not desert him: the explosive "measureless liar" and "boy," so dear to the hearts of earlier Martiuses, "were treated with abundant power and yet with the nicest shades of meaning" (*Daily Graphic,* New York, 17 December 1878). And as the McCullough Martius received his quietus, so too did the last vestiges of the Kemble *Coriolanus* tradition in America.

The supporting company, from the Walnut Street Theater in Philadelphia, was competent if apparently overwhelmed throughout by McCullough. An awed *Advertiser* (Boston, 12 February 1878) reviewer concluded that "the mighty personality of *Caius Marcius* so fills each act and scene that there is little need and indeed little room for aught else." The plebeians, apparently not the villains painted by Forrest, were seldom, if ever, mentioned.

A European Footnote: Visits by Barnay (1883) and Salvini (1885)

Even as John McCullough commenced his horrifying descent into insanity, hints of twentieth-century modernism were in the air. In 1883 Ludwig Barnay, at the Old Bowery, scene of so many of Forrest's triumphs and now rechristened the Thalia, brought to Shakespeare's intractable Roman the latest in Meiningen Company practice. In 1885, two days after John McCullough was buried with pomp and circumstance, Tomasso Salvini played the role in New York, offering an interpretation based on character analysis rather than the conventions of history painting. Neither production made any attempt to temper the play's antidemocratic sentiments to American sensibilities, nor was the rugged Martius rendered any more alluring than Shakespeare makes him. Reviewers significantly make no mention of an ovation, a discovery beneath the statue of Mars, a train of mourning matrons, or a cremation. Critics of both productions had eyes only for Martius, his relationships with his peers, his family, and the plebeians.

The precise text played in the Thalia revival cannot be determined with accuracy. It seems likely that the Schlegel-Tieck translation was used, and that it was cut to some extent. The only specific comment on excisions, however, is the *Evening Post* critic's remark that omissions included "portions of the first act, which require frequent change of scene" (New York, 4 January 1883).

The Thalia, a German-language house, was well-known for the high quality of its sets and its careful drilling of supers, both specialities of its exemplar, the Meiningen Company, which until recently had counted Barnay among its leading members. The *New York World* (4 January 1883) reviewer judged the supporting company "excellent" and reported that "in matters relating to the corps of supernumeraries, the scenic setting and costumes the traditions of the Meiningen stage were followed as closely as possible."

The prime attraction, however, was not settings or supers, but the Martius of Barnay himself. And critics were unanimous in lauding his physical fitness for the role. The *Evening Post* (New York, 4 January 1883) noted that he possessed "a remarkably handsome, imposing, muscular and heroic *Siegfried* figure, with dark eyes, finely-chiselled features, and an expressive mouth." His acting style was praised for its freedom from artifice, and its combination of "mental subtlety with abundant physical powers of expression" (*New-York Daily Tribune,* 4 January 1883).

In singular contrast to the spiritually-superior creations of Forrest and McCullough, the Barnay Roman was an unmitigated and unrepentant patrician, "the incarnation of superb, defiant egotism; a man so proud of his birth, so filled with the inherent glory of the Roman aristocracy, that he recognizes none but its members as worthy of his notice. To him the reforms tending towards popular government are dangerous innovations, and in spurning them he spurns the rabble who are to profit by them" (*New-York Daily Tribune,* 4 January 1883). In his first clash with the citizens and in the battle sequences, "the whole man spoke," we are told, "features and limbs and carriage of the body and attitudes" (*New York Times,* 4 January 1883). In the Voices scene, in contrast to the Kemble tradition, he made an effort to dissemble his true feelings. The Banishment scene, in which he expressed his determination "to brave all and suffer all rather than yield," was played in a manner, one critic thought, "that would have made Edwin Forrest glow with delight" (*Daily Graphic,* New York, 4 January 1883). This scene marked the conclusion of the unsympathetic part of the portrait.

Beginning with the farewell at the city gates, Barnay attempted to make the figure more attractive. Although he saved most of his pathos for the Intercession scene, he here displayed a filial warmth which was profoundly affecting. In the sequence in Aufidius's house, where the Kemble tradition commanded awe, Barnay invited empathy, and in his "manner and bearing," according to one critic, "seemed to give new justification, beyond what the spoken lines afford, for the traitorous course he was about to pursue" (*Daily Graphic,* New York, 4 January 1883). In the Intercession scene, "the tender emotions [were] suppressed to the last moment" (*Evening Post,* New York, 4 January 1883) in order to make the most of "the struggle of an affectionate heart against an imperious, arrogant and vengeful will" (*New-York Daily Tribune,* 4 January 1883), and at his death "the actor gave a nobility to the character which brought to it more of sympathetic appreciation than was its due" (*New-York Times,* 4 January 1883). Stripped of its Forrest-McCullough disguise, the play again revealed its unacceptability to American palates.

Through firmly clenched teeth the *Spirit of the Times* critic urged audiences to "go to see the actor, if not the play" (New York, 6 January 1883).

Two years later the maligned script served as a star vehicle for the Italian actor Tomasso Salvini,[45] who considered Coriolanus uniquely suited to his temperament: "I felt I could divine that character, which resembled my own in some ways—not, certainly, in his warlike exploits, but in his susceptibility, in his spurning of the arrogance and insolent pretensions of the ignorant masses, and, above all, in his filial submissiveness and affection."[46] "My conception of the individuality of Coriolanus," he insisted with delightful irreverence in an interview with the *World*, "accords so exactly with that of Shakespeare that I cannot but think that in its delineation the poet had prescience of my being" (New York, 12 November 1885).

Salvini began his study of the character in 1883, but finding the costs of mounting the play in Italy excessive, postponed production until his tour of the United States in 1885 when he could take advantage of relatively cheap American scenic artists and supers. His revival premiered at New York's Metropolitan Opera House 11 October 1885, with the title role spoken in Italian and the other parts in English, and over the next four months traveled to Boston, Philadelphia, Washington, Chicago, and San Francisco. Critics found the supporting players less than adequate, and the supers execrable, but their praise for Salvini's unique interpretation was unanimous; he must, they insisted, give Coriolanus a permanent place in his repertory. But after the 1885 American tour he played it no more.

Salvini's acting text, sold at performances,[47] suggests that he followed generally Kemble's arrangement, without, of course, the Thomsonian inter-polations. There were also several restorations. Aufidius now enjoys rather more prominence than Kemble gave him.[48] The scene in which Tullus con-fesses, "Mine emulation hath not that honor in't it had" (1.10) is restored, although transposed to come before 1.9, which now ends the act. The fiery Volscian is also at last permitted his fight with Martius (1.8) and his tête-à-tête with his Lieutenant (4.7). Less squeamish about stage battles than the Covent Garden manager, Salvini reinstates the brawl in which the citizens are driven in at 3.1.228, and also rehabilitates, albeit in abbreviated form, the farewell at the city gate (4.1) and Volumnia's encounter with the tribunes (4.2). Again no mention is made of ovations or processions of mourning matrons: if spectacle there was, Salvini seems to have upstaged it by the sheer size and uniqueness of his reading.

Massive and muscular, Salvini was quite as well equipped physically for heroic roles as were Forrest and McCullough. Not content with his native qualifications, however, he added a certain picturesque charm through makeup. On his first appearance, his "rather neglected blond beard, the thick, obstinate growth of crisply curling light-brown hair, indicative of a super abundance of animal vigor, the bluff burliness of his bearing" (*Boston Evening Transcript*, 4 December 1885), all suggested a freer, more natural, less deliberate figure than audiences were accustomed to. And this was precisely Salvini's point: Martius was not an Anglo-Saxon but a Roman. "The *Coriolanus* of Salvini glows with the warmth of the southern blood which flows in his veins," wrote John Ranken Towse, and was palpably more warrior than patrician. His disdain for the commons sprang from "his scorn for their cowardice and pride in his own physical rather than intellectual superiority. His unwillingness to beg favors at their hands does not originate in the pride of his order, but in an honest disgust at the idea of boasting of the courage which to him seems to be no virtue at all, but the physical inheritance of every proper man" (*Evening Post,* New York, 12 November 1885). Or as another critic put it, "Salvini's Coriolanus is as proud as Lucifer, but his pride seems a . . . personal matter":

> the fact that he is Caius Marcius is in his eyes quite as important . . . as that he is of noble birth. He is not much inclined to stand upon his dignity, but is content to believe that every one takes his dignity for granted; with his friends his manner is outwardly rough, yet with a very sensible undercurrent of patrician courtliness, even of gentleness, as befits a burly giant; at moments he is even expansive, with a trifle of *bonhomie* (*Boston Evening Transcript,* 4 December 1885).

Unlike the disciples of Kemble, Salvini aimed at a gradual intensification of dramatic tension throughout rather than a series of isolated histrionic effects. Until almost the moment of his banishment, the tribunes and plebeians were no more than a casual nuisance, never a serious threat to his well-being. On his first entrance, he seemed to view them "in the light of a bad joke which Providence has played on the upper classes; the humorous side of a plebeian attempting to be or do anything is what strikes him first." In the Voices scene, "his general air," we are told, "is that of sheer weariness at having to go through with an unpleasant duty; he is even almost civil. . . . His manner is cold, but not quite offensive." On his first encounter with the plebeians after the Voices scene, he became momentarily aware that they have "carried the joke of their existence so far as to interfere with his personal comfort," and resorted to scornful sarcasm; he directed it, however, "to the bystanders of his own order, as something too precious to be wasted on an unappreciative rabble." "Before the people," recalled one critic, "he felt himself as strong as Jove," but in the privacy of his own house and forced by his mentors and his mother to come to terms with realpolitik, "a suspicion of his own impotence dawns upon him." As he confronts the necessity of swallowing his pride, "he pours forth the vials of his wrath in open sneers and biting sarcasms." Later, in the Banishment scene, "the revulsion of feeling from the first outburst of wrath at the word 'traitor' to shame and horror as he begins to appreciate that these vile plebeians have really the power to dishonor him," provided a mighty climax to the growing awareness of his vulnerability. The actor seized the moment, however, to demonstrate Martius's self-control rather than his flamboyant eloquence. Regaining "sufficient self-command to repress all exhibition of shame," he delivered "There is a world elsewhere" "with a very bravado of grim, scornful humor." Where "Forrest used to thunder like *Jupiter tonans,* like an outraged divinity," Salvini ended "by finding the whole affair too utterly despicable even for cursing" (*Boston Evening Transcript,* 4 December 1885).

Although Salvini kept Martius's relationship with the plebeians in the foreground throughout the first half of the play, he delineated with care the military ideals and family loyalties which both define and undo him. "Salvini's *Coriolanus* is predominantly martial," noted the *Sun.* "In every passage he is, he breathes, the very soldier and highbred Roman" (New York, 12 November 1885). In the battle scenes, "that great voice becomes as a trumpet of prodigious depth and power, and its tones resound with effect so stirring that few auditors can control their feelings." Although his portrait was of epic dimensions (Towse wondered "whether the Old Roman patrician has ever found before so magnificent a representative, so far as the mere grandeur of physical proportion is concerned," (*Evening Post,* New York, 12 November 1885), his grandeur was totally natural. The apostrophe to the martial feats of Aufidius (1.1.228–36) was "not made the burden of a shout," as in so many previous interpretations, but was "an honest and thoughtful expression of admiration for a brave foe whose arms may prove victorious" (*New-York Times,* 12 November 1885). His forgetfulness of the name of his Coriolian host, in which he demonstrated an engaging frailty (1.9.79–92), was also a much admired feature: "He asks the favor in a tender, compassionate tone," recorded the *New York Times,* "but when the name is demanded, he staggers, grasps the arm of Cominius, and smiles as he presses his hand to his brow and shakes his head [on "By Jupiter, forgot!"]. The hero needs rest for the day has been a hard one. 'Have we no wine here?' he feebly asks" (12 November 1885). "Forrest's Coriolanus would have died before he would have shown a sign of physical weakness," wryly observed another theatergoer; and the same might be said of a host of Forrest's predecessors. Again on his arrival in Antium, unlike Forrest who stood revealed "like some great god visiting a mortal," Salvini came "quite humanly, with manly dignity and courtesy, but still as one who is not quite sure of what his reception will be" (*Boston Evening Transcript,* 4 December 1885).

His most moving moments, predictably enough, were those with his family. At his homecoming, he was "the simple, courteous gentleman"; "the scene of hesitation and remonstrance with Volumnia" was described as "one of wonderful beauty" (*New-York Times,* 12 November 1885); and his farewell at the city gates struck one critic as "inexpressibly pathetic" (*Evening Post,* New York, 12 November 1885). The Intercession scene elicited unalloyed approval. "His silence during [Volumnia's] long plea," recalled a playgoer, was eloquence itself, for though his back was turned on her one could see in his face and in the heaving of his chest that a mighty struggle was going on within between pride and outraged honor and filial love. And what a world of meaning there was in his heart-broken cry, "O Madre!" and in his outstretched arms, as Volumnia turns to go! All of his resolution "never to be such a gosling as to obey instinct" melts away in an instant (*Boston Evening Transcript*, 18 November 1885).

Where Coriolanuses from Kemble onwards had relied for their effects on virtuoso displays of physical and vocal heroics, Salvini won the sympathy and admiration of audiences by deliberate underplaying. The *World* reviewer (New York, 12 November 1885) remarked throughout "a sense of subdued emotion that becomes actually appalling. The spectator comes to hope in vain for the breaking of the storm. There is an uncanny sensation of thunder—of thunder without noise." Nowhere was this technique more finely utilized than in the "speechless horror" of the final scene when, charged by Aufidius with perfidy (*Boston Evening Transcript*, 4 December 1885), he coolly recognized the approach of the retribution he had invited, withdrew with dignity into the fastnesses of the self, and with contained contempt accepted the inevitable.

Despite inadequate supporting players, incompetent supers, and scenery which Towse termed only "a collection of odds and ends,"[49] Salvini's triumph in city after city throughout his American tour can only be attributed to his discovery in Shakespeare's text of a human being rather than an orating statue. The insight was, unfortunately, wasted both on the American theater which staged no *Coriolanus* productions for another half century, and on the British theater establishment where the Kemble tradition, as modulated by Benson and Irving, held sway for another thirty years.

8

Modernism and Elizabethan Methodism
(1920–1938)

In 1913 Charles Péguy could claim with fair accuracy that "the world has changed less since the time of Jesus Christ than it has in the last thirty years."[1] And the next three decades proved hardly more stable. Revolutionary advances in the physical and social sciences, to say nothing of a World War, an international depression, and the threat of a second call to arms, evoked an intellectual and emotional anxiety throughout Europe unparalleled since the sixteenth century.

Realism, judged an inadequate idiom for the alienated mood, suffered eclipse in all the arts, but painting led the way: history painting lost its privileged status, and the moral mission of art was repudiated. In England, in the aftermath of the revolutionary Post-Impressionist exhibitions of 1910 and 1912, Clive Bell and Roger Fry concluded that art existed only to reflect the imagination of the creator, to permit the contemplation of subjective experience. "Paradoxical as it may seem," wrote Bell in his enormously influential *Art,* which went through nine impressions between 1913 and 1930, "the only relevant qualities in a work of art, judged as art, are artistic qualities."[2] The form in which the art was cast, as the key to aesthetic response, became all-important: "We all agree, now", Bell insisted, "that any form in which an artist can express himself is legitimate. . . . We have ceased to ask, 'What does this picture represent?' and ask instead, 'What does it make us feel?'"[3]

Theatrical Shakespeare[4] was as vulnerable to the influence of modernist aesthetics as any other cultural product: and William Poel's laboratory productions bore much the same relation to Irving's gaslit extravaganzas as the iconoclasm of Cezanne, Gauguin, and Van Gogh did to the obsessive historical realism of Alma-Tadema. For the first time Shakespeare's plays were credited with an intrinsic aesthetic which merited study within an approximation of its original creative context. Poel's pursuit of Shakespearian design through vocal realization of the text in Elizabethan-style acting spaces differed little from the quest by modernist artists for "Significant Form."[5] The Shakespeare performance was for Poel neither an excuse for what Van

Gogh termed "stereoscopic realism," nor a vehicle for moral or political preachment, but an end in itself; or as Bell put it in relation to painting, "not a means to anything except emotion."[6] And emotion must arise, as in all modernist art, through a direct interactive encounter between the art object and the viewer. The starting point was textual authenticity, from which all else flowed. "It is indeed to be regretted," Poel wrote in 1913, "that no scholar nor actor has thought it necessary to study the art of Shakespeare's dramatic construction from the original copies."

> Some of our University men have written intelligently about Shakespeare's characters and his philosophy. . . . But it is doubtful if any serious attention has been given yet to the way Shakespeare conducts his story and brings his characters on and off the stage, a matter of the highest moment, since the very life of the play depends upon the skill with which this is done. And how many realize that the art of Shakespeare's dramatic construction differs fundamentally from that of the modern dramatist?[7]

Almost four decades of theatrical experimentation, beginning with his groundbreaking production of the First Quarto *Hamlet* in 1881, were dedicated not to a pedantic reconstruction of the Elizabethan theater for its own sake, as was sometimes alleged, but to a rediscovery of its aesthetic as a mode of contemporary experience: "Some people have called me an archaeologist," he informed an interviewer, "but I am not. I am really a modernist."[8] His championship of the Elizabethan apron effectively repudiated the representational theater from the baroque era onward, with the scenic extravagance, the extrinsic grandeur, the primacy of the star, and the indifference to text the aesthetic implied.

Poel's audiences, like viewers of Post-Impressionist art, were expected not simply to admire, but to interact with the work. No longer in thrall to "correct perspective," Poel's Shakespeare, in common with modernist paintings, offered theatergoers multiple visual and intellectual viewpoints.

The restored Shakespearian text revealed its complex structure and rhythm (a new notion), Poel contended, when allotted a ludic space designed as a site for speech rather than a scenic showcase; on a bare apron backed by traverse curtains and some rudimentary provision for discoveries, poetry, spoken swiftly and musically, enabled playgoers to create in the mind's eye appropriate visual effects without loss of dramatic momentum or obstruction of the rhythmic flow. Poel's *Twelfth Night* (1903) made the distinguished painter Byam Shaw an instant convert to verbal scenography:

> I told several of my artist friends [he wrote Poel] to go and see it and they were all simply delighted. I only wish that others would follow your noble example and allow us to listen to Shakespeare instead of looking at what Mr. So-and-So thinks is like a sunset or a cherry tree.[9]

Poel's early experiments, although acted by amateurs in recalcitrant proscenium houses where Elizabethan conditions were suggested rather than recreated, nevertheless sensitized audiences and actors to the advantages of what Bridges-Adams was later to christen "Elizabethan Methodism." More importantly, the principles he championed, sometimes more effectively in theory than practice, profoundly impressed a succession of young men who worked with him. It was the twentieth-century theater's good fortune that a number of them became managers, and used their positions and influence to bring Poel's revolutionary vision into the professional mainstream.

Coriolanus, if not so radically Elizabethanized as some other plays, did not escape Poel's influence. Although Poel himself failed to tackle *Coriolanus* until 1931, and then in an avant garde stylization, a group of his protégés—Robert Atkins at the Old Vic in 1924, William Bridges-Adams at the Shakespeare Memorial Theatre in 1926 and 1933, and Nugent Mock at the Maddermarket Theatre in 1928—all brought his modernist stagecraft to bear. Hugh Hunt, too, although never a Poel associate, appropriated his innovations for a production at Dublin's Abbey Theatre in 1936; and about the same time, Elizabethan Methodism crossed the Atlantic to shape an American revival of *Coriolanus* by the Federal Theater Project.

While all modernist directors shared a distaste for nineteenth-century realism, Poel's radical Elizabethanism was not universally seen as the sole alternative. "We shall not save our souls by being Elizabethan," insisted Harley Granville-Barker, Poel's most influential collaborator.[10] What mattered was to reproduce "those conditions of the Elizabethan theatre which had a spiritual significance in the shaping of the plays themselves."[11] His three Shakespeare productions at the Savoy—*The Winter's Tale* (1912), *Twelfth Night* (1912), and *A Midsummer Night's Dream* (1914)—were swiftly spoken in largely uncut texts on a modified apron with dress-circle lighting.[12] But at the same time they sported an eye-catching stylized decor which owed much to Cubism and Futurism, not to mention the Craigian atmospherics of Max Reinhardt's London productions of *Sumurun* (Coliseum and Savoy, 1911) and *Oedipus Rex* (Covent Garden, 1912). Granville-Barker's mise-en-scène was neither an illusionistic environment at one extreme, nor a functional space for speech at another, but rather a visual and emotional correlative to a play's dramatic character. His strategy served at once to subvert the audience's traditional perceptual patterns and elicit, through its reliance on contemporary idiom, a radically fresh aesthetic response.

Granville-Barker's stylizations were widely influential, but cast their spell most potently on Nigel Playfair at the Lyric, Hammersmith, Barry Jackson at the Birmingham Repertory Theatre, and Terence Gray at the Cambridge Festival Theatre. Playfair, for a controversial production of *As You Like It* (1919), frequently perceived as Futuristic, drew upon the visual conventions of late medieval French tapestries and illuminated manuscripts. Jackson, in a series of revivals beginning with *Cymbeline* in 1923, explored the modern dress convention. Both Playfair and Jackson, however different their stylistic strategies, shared Granville-Barker's respect for the Shakespearian text and his conviction that visual effects must subserve it. Gray, on the other hand, viewed the text as an excuse for scenographic exhibitionism. Throughout a succession of drastically cut and expressionistically lit turntable productions beginning with *Richard III* in 1928, he baited lovers of "nineteenth-century hocus pocus and bamboozle" and Elizabethan purists alike with mischievous delight: Shylock fished in a Venetian canal; Toby Belch and Andrew Aguecheek made their entrance on roller skates; Rosalind and Celia cavorted as Boy Scout and Girl Guide; and the court of Henry VIII appeared as playing cards.[13]

Stylization came late to *Coriolanus;* and when it arrived, in the shape of William Poel's eccentric Directoire revival in 1931, it owed more to Gray than to Granville-Barker or Playfair. The modern dress convention manifested itself in a Manchester Repertory Theatre revival in 1935, a dozen years after Jackson's groundbreaking *Cymbeline,* too late and too obscurely to have much impact on mainstream *Coriolanus* production, shortly to succumb to the epic romanticism of Olivier.

Coriolanus's stage history from the first postwar performance in 1920 to Olivier's conquest of the title role in 1938 is less an account of great productions greatly acted than of a series of modest modernist explorations based for the most part on the Poelian thesis that if a play's original scenograpic environment was functionally reproduced, its unique aesthetic would declare itself. And to some degree the assumption was justified. Within slightly less than two decades, the play burst its Kemble cerements, and text unheard for centuries was spoken fluidly, naturally, and swiftly in ludic spaces which fostered scenic continuity and hence some degree of structural and rhythmic integrity. Interwar productions, with one or two noteworthy exceptions, revealed more about the play's shape than its characters; directorial fascination with the interrelationship of dramatic form and stagecraft was partly responsible, but a lack of interest in the play by first-rate actors was a major contributing factor, to say nothing of totally inadequate rehearsal conditions.

OLD VIC (1920, 1924)

Two years after the Great War ground to a halt, Russell Thorndike and Charles Warburton in a coproduction at the Old Vic brought *Coriolanus* to its modernist avatar, albeit with debris from its Kemble incarnation still affixed. In a run of six performances, audiences encountered a new Martius, not so much a Poussinesque icon as a relic of prewar class prejudice, "a nobleman of extravagant arrogance and not very nice feeling" (*Westminster Gazette,* 15 April 1920). No mention is made in programs or reviews of the ovation or the procession of mourning matrons, and one must assume that they had finally been retired.[14] Volusius and Kemble's other named minor characters are happily absent from the cast-list. The play nevertheless remained heavily cut, and in the traditional manner, while Genevieve Ward's Volumnia, grandly oblivious to the unheroic modernist turn taken by her filial offspring, splendidly if somewhat incongruously dominated the revival as the selfless mother of her country in unabashed imperial grandeur.

The textual arrangement, to judge from the program, seems to have been Benson's. Act 5 comprised two scenes, the intercession and the assassination, both set in "The Volscian Camp Before Rome," an occasional Bensonian practice; and the tribunes were lynched by the incensed populace in the Benson manner.

Critics were tactfully silent on the subject of settings: no doubt the decaying and unapt Victorian flats and drops which served Old Vic Shakespeare in season and out did duty yet again. But, in a first modernist gesture toward scenic flexibility, Thorndike had the ancient fixed grooves removed from the Old Vic stage.[15]

With only a week's rehearsal, Lilian Baylis's time limit, nothing resembling a polished production was possible; that there was a coherent presentation at all was little short of miraculous. "Played throughout in [a] full-blooded, highly-coloured, and slightly melodramatic style" (*Daily Telegraph,* 13 April 1920), the production disdained Kemblesque formality and hinted at bold new initiatives. Harcourt Williams was later to describe the revival as "the high peak of the season."[16]

The political character of the play, if not highlighted, was allowed to surface to the degree the curtailed text permitted; and seldom since Kemble's heyday had social conditions offered apter parallels. Trade was depressed; prices were high; unemployment was rising, and strikes were endemic. F. W. Brockway's speech to the 1922 conference of the Labour Party is, for all practical purposes, a modern paraphrase of the 1 Citizen's plaint (1.1.15–22, 79–86). "[W]e pay," he maintained,

> a terrible tribute to Rent, Interest and Profit . . . [which] enrich mainly the class which has already more to spend than it can usefully spend.
>   It is this class which gives us the spectacles of senseless and wasteful display at race meetings, royal levees and royal weddings, hunting and shooting parties and gatherings of the swell mob at continental pleasure resorts.
>   For the Royal homecoming it is "roses all the way". For the miner's wife, trudging to the guardians for relief, it is tears all the way. . . .[17]

It was, perhaps, because the Old Vic was a working-class theater that Martius's class prejudice was allowed full play, and no apparent attempt was made to justify his contempt by rendering the citizens unduly comic, stupid, or vicious—save for the Bensonian execution of the tribunes which came too late to matter. Once his target was no longer demonized, the beau ideal veneer which hitherto camouflaged Martius's offensiveness showed signs of cracking, and this less than a decade after Bradley precipitated a similar deconstructive process within the scholarly community. The abrasive treatment of the lower orders by an unredeemed elitist, familiar enough to the Old Vic's postwar playgoers, moved an uncomfortable American journalist to wish Warburton had "not reserved so much of his soldier-like bluntness for the plebeians only" (*Christian Science Monitor,* Boston, 1 June 1920).

Charles Warburton was physically slighter than tradition demanded, but his reading required no demigod: aristocratic boors come in all sizes. Martius nevertheless displayed the requisite "robust force and picturesqueness" (*Daily News,* 13 April 1920), and, when called for, authority was not lacking: "In facing the mob in the market-place," noted the *Era* reviewer, "he really gave the impression of a superman among pygmies" (*Era,* 14 April 1920). For a change Martius was granted some measure of intellect; indeed, the *Christian Science Monitor* (Boston, 1 June 1920) thought he might "have hinted rather less at the thinker."

Although descriptive detail is sparse, the modernist thrust of Warburton's performance is patent. To limn Martius's "pig headed splendour" against the cumulative force of the Kemble tradition, and to allow the citizens' complaints some legitimacy, was no small achievement, especially given the time constraints under which the play was rehearsed.

The laurels of the evening, however, were reserved for Genevieve Ward who, in an age when the classical tragic tradition was *in extremis,* incarnated its best features. "When coaxing her son," we are told,

the mother's voice has all its familiar tender, maternal note. When confronting his enemies the woman was erect upon her feet, eyes flashing, arm extended, her tones ringing with anger; and when, in the last act, she pleads with Coriolanus for Rome, there was in her voice a strength and touching earnestness of appeal that greatly moved the house (*Christian Science Monitor,* Boston, 1 June 1920).

"The audience shed tears with sheer joy," reported the *Globe* (13 April 1920), a response noted by a number of critics. "Hardened theatre-goers," wrote another, "moved to tears by her magnetic force, rose from their seats in a body at the end of the performance, and the little woman, with her triumphs behind her, was recalled again and again before the curtain" (*Daily Mail,* 13 April 1920). To assert that audiences witnessed the finest performance of the role since the age of Siddons is probably no exaggeration. Ward's legacy to her successors was the conviction that there need be "no trace of severity or gloom about [Volumnia]: only the radiant pride which was one of Siddons's secrets" (*Daily Chronicle,* 13 April 1920). That insight was to stand Sybil Thorndike in good stead some eighteen years later.

In 1924, after a four-year interval, the Old Vic again tackled the play, this time under the direction of Poel's protégé Robert Atkins,[18] who energetically took up the modernist cudgels precisely where Warburton and Thorndike had dropped them. For *Coriolanus,* as for his other Shakespeare productions, Atkins determined to play close to a full text[19] for the first time since the Commonwealth in a space sufficiently Elizabethan/Jacobean to do justice to its structure and rhythm. Like his mentor, however, Atkins's ambitions were thwarted by the reality of a proscenium arch and an auditorium with fixed seating oriented to baroque sightlines. In the end, he was forced to accept the Poelian compromise: the stage was modified enough to allow a script to be staged without sacrifice of continuity, and the Elizabethan experience of sitting and standing around an open platform was postponed to another day. According to a contemporary journalist, the Old Vic stage was

> slightly advanced (but not into the full apron), and scenes in street or open country, were played on the fore-stage in front of plain black curtains. These can be raised to form an arch revealing similar curtains. In this second stage room-scenes are played. . . . Behind this a third stage is available whereon scenery of the old type is used in a modest way (*Manchester Guardian,* 4 October 1921).[20]

Atkins's abbreviated apron, flanked by proscenium doors, was cause for rejoicing, but it evinced precisely the limitation that dogged Poel's miniature platform: the actor escaped the picture frame, but failed to achieve audience intimacy. "The shape of the theatre made it impossible to be truly Elizabethan," Atkins freely admitted, "but the forestage helped rapidity of speech and with staging obeying the author's construction of the plays, it was possible to catch the spirit of the Elizabethan presentation."[21] Whatever their shortcomings, Atkins's innovations marked a vital advance on traditional stagecraft: Poel's discoveries at last entered the professional mainstream, and in consequence Shakespeare's formal artistry could be popularly demonstrated if not fully experienced.

Coriolanus's mise-en-scène, comprising "curtains and back cloths slung behind . . . three semi-permanent arches" (*Queen,* 2 April 1924) with only two upstage set scenes—one for the Capitol and the other "the interior of the city of Corioli" (*Stage,* 27 March 1924)—allowed Atkins "to get the play through without cuts before 11 o'clock" (*Queen,* 2 April 1924). An impressionistic, some might say Spartan, simplicity evident in the decor owed something to Atkins's dedication to Poelian fluidity, but more to Lilian Baylis's notorious parsimony: "A Gothic hanging used in Henry VIII," noted the *Queen* reviewer, "had been made Roman by the simple device of hanging it with the golden fleurs-de-lys backward . . . in a room in Volumnia's house" and a couple of cypress trees "now hoary and almost bent with age, appeared as part of Corioli" (2 April 1924). Costumes were "properly 'Roman' with the men in long robes and togas, bare arms and legs, and the ladies in the graceful clinging robes of the same period."[22]

Once a virtually full text was spoken under a semblance of Jacobean

stage conditions, the political nature of the drama was recognized and its
contemporary relevance acknowledged: indeed, Herbert Farjeon found "its
application . . . so enduring that it would, to-day, quite comfortably carry
the title of *Strife* or *Loyalties*."[23] Since the last Old Vic production, the
country had acquired its first Labour government and with it widespread
public concern, fueled by Conservative Diehards and power-hungry Lib-
erals, of an immediate Bolshevist takeover. Atkins, notwithstanding the
sympathies of his audience, cast in his lot with the forces of reaction and
chose to stabilize the play's ambivalent politics by "underlin[ing] the nobility
of the nobility." Justifying his artistic choice as conformity to Shakespeare's
intention, he went so far as to depict the tribunes as "a couple of outrageous
Hebraic scarecrows, fit for bonfires."[24] A bemused Farjeon, himself a man
of conservative sympathies, was appreciative if somewhat bemused.
"Whether Mr. Robert Atkins is a Bolshevik I do not know," he wrote,

> but it is pretty safe to conjecture that, as director of a People's Theatre, he does
> not find the lower classes all foul breath and grease: and he is therefore to be
> congratulated on underlining the spirit of the play so emphatically . . . by shrewd
> touches of Elizabethan realism.[25]

To stress the nobility of the nobility, however, was not to romanticize
Martius; compared with Menenius, Cominius, and Volumnia, he came off
badly. "To our modern ideas," wrote the *Daily News* critic, "he stands as a
pig-headed soldier not fit to govern, for he has so little of sympathy in him
or of common humanity." "The character is really," he concluded, "a fine
and subtle study in the limited man of action as ruler or leader of men" (25
March 1924).

A major achievement of the revival was the reassessment of features long
obscured by textual mutilation. The military skirmishes, when staged uncut,
struck Farjeon as "unconvincing":[26] but the play's final scenes, played fully
and continuously, revealed a rhythmic complexity and power totally foreign
to the isolated static tableaux of the Kemble tradition. The intensifying pulse
of the action can be felt beneath even the prompter's [Doris Westwood's]
diary entry:

> Now comes the news, in Rome, that Coriolanus has joined with the enemy and
> is approaching against them. The failure of his former friends to prevail with him
> for his mercy. The appeal of his wife and mother as a last hope. His cold reception
> of them. . . . the old love stirring within him as he kisses his wife. . . . The soldier
> fighting with the man in him all through Volumnia's long speech. The last subduing
> of her pride into the dust as she kneels before him. . . . Her final words that
> break, at last, his will—and then his bitter cry as he turns to her. . . . It is the
> beginning of the end.[27]

The end, when it came, at last smacked of Shakespeare rather than Kemble, and in its stark minimalism fittingly complemented Martius's unheroic

demise and the script's visual severity. At the conclusion of Aufidius's eulogy, the curtain "came down on the murderers of Coriolanus kneeling beside his body ready to 'bear him away.'" A moment later it rose again as
the soldiers lifted the corpse to shoulder height; "Coriolanus let his head
fall back as a dead man's head would fall, and the four bearers turned slowly,
with the body between them, and faced the wings" as the curtain dropped
for the last time.[28]

Characters long mere adjuncts to the starring role, once their lines and
scenic continuity reappeared, assumed a new importance. With the demise
of Martius's godlike manifestation in Antium, Aufidius attained a status
hitherto denied him. In Atkins's production, his "sudden compassion on the
fallen soldier" in the speech beginning "O Martius Martius! / Each word thou
hast spoke" (4.5.101–2) now became a highlight. "At rehearsals," Westwood
recalls, "that speech of Aufidius would break upon us in a flood. He always
knew it well and put into it such emotion that we would hush ourselves to
listen. It was like a quiet pool in a roaring sea, and every word, spoken
slowly and distinctly, was full of meaning."[29]

With the demise of Kemble's vast military processions, the citizens also
gained a new political and visual significance. And Old Vic crowds, comprising all performers available regardless of rank, were a force to be reckoned
with. "I saw men," wrote Westwood, "who had played long speaking parts
now put their best into the delivery of one line; I saw girls who yearned to
be leading ladies shouting enthusiastically as units in the mob." At the center
of the crowd at one point, "disguised in a rough serge tunic and hood," was
Atkins himself.[30]

Unfortunately Atkins's achievement must be measured more in terms of
his conception than its realization, which was irrevocably compromised by
lack of rehearsal. "It is impossible to produce so great a play as Coriolanus
in so short a time," lamented the prompter, "a little over a week. . . . To
see Mr. Atkins grappling with it is like watching a wrestler, already tired,
clinching with a fresh opponent, gritting his teeth, determined to get him
down. But Coriolanus cannot be the production it might have been if we
had had more time."[31]

Whatever Atkins's progress toward recognition of *Coriolanus*'s formal
strengths, and it was considerable, the leading performers, miscast and
underrehearsed, largely vitiated his efforts. Ion Swinley looked Martius to
perfection, but his failure to memorize the lines in time for opening night
gravely marred the production.[32] Westwood's admiration of "the intonation
of Coriolanus' voice . . . so boyishly boasting sometimes, sometimes so
wisely gentle"[33] in the Farewell scene, hints at the success it might have
been under different circumstances.

The Volumnia of Hutin Britton, though word perfect and "wonderfully
beautiful . . . in face and raiment" (*Queen*, 2 April 1924), belonged in an
Edwardian drawing room rather than a Roman camp: Farjeon found her "a

burlesque of an old lady on a flag-day rather than the Olympus to which she is compared."[34] She did, however, have some effective moments: in the Admonition scene, when she "lean[ed] over [Martius] as he sat silent in his chair, pleading with him until at last his answer comes," she subtly and deliberately foreshadowed the graver battle of wills in the Intercession scene.[35]

Whether due to the weakness of the leads or the dynamics of a full text, more of the secondary parts than usual caught the eye of reviewers. Wilfrid Walter's Menenius, Rayner Barton's Cominius, George Hayes's Aufidius ("exactly like a Norwegian viking blown into Corioli by mistake," Westwood thought), even Hay Petrie's 1st Citizen, received favorable mention.

WILLIAM BRIDGES-ADAMS AT STRATFORD (1926, 1933)

It is matter for regret that the two major centers of Shakespeare production in England between the wars, the Old Vic and the Shakespeare Memorial Theatre at Stratford-upon-Avon, were both strongholds of administrative conservatism: Lilian Baylis ruled the Old Vic with a prayerbook in one hand and a cash book in the other while Sir Archibald Flower and the Board of Governors at Stratford deified tradition and elevated parsimony to high art. Shakespeare directors with a modernist bent were condemned at both institutions to perpetual compromise and artistic frustration, as Atkins discovered in his tempestuous five years with Baylis.[36] That Bridges-Adams completed a fifteen-year stint at Stratford, during which he dramatically cleansed the Bensonian stables, owed more to his gift for institutional politics than the artistic vision of his employers.

"Futurism has no beauties for me," announced Lady Benson after seeing a Stratford performance of Nigel Playfair's As You Like It[37] shortly before Bridges-Adams assumed the management of the SMT in 1919. And the one-time colleague of Poel and Granville-Barker knew better than to force a showdown between traditional and modernist aesthetics on hallowed Bensonian ground. Gradually, however, the mutilated Benson texts were replaced with something closer to their Shakespearian originals, if only to be curtailed once more on the basis of unsatisfactory theatrical experience; ancient flats and footlights in turn yielded to atmospherically lit semi-permanent settings (which sold themselves to the Governors on the grounds of economy) with sufficient pictorial realism to keep traditionalists in their seats; and a swift and uncluttered production style was complemented by natural movement and verse speaking.

Bridges-Adams was not eager, however, to follow Barry Jackson or Terence Gray down the road to contemporaneity. His Shakespeare revivals, like Post-Impressionist art as viewed by Fry and Bell, were autonomous aesthetic enterprises exempt from the contemporary sociopolitical dynamic.

Admonition Scene (Coriolanus-Ion Swinley; Volumnia-Hutin Britton). Robert Atkins Production, Old Vic, 1924. [By permission of the British Library]

Although his 1926 *Coriolanus* opened less than two weeks before the General Strike, the major and arguably the most influential political event of the decade, he insisted, with admirable commitment to the play's shiftiness, that the production remain nonpartisan. "When I proposed including this play in the year's repertoire it was felt, vaguely perhaps, that if there were Bolsheviks about this play, if any, would 'learn' them," he told the Shakespeare Club.

> Well, it does, and I am glad of it. But I would submit that it 'learns' the Diehards too. Coriolanus is a very noble Roman, but we cannot justly deny that he is a little bit of an ass—a noble ass, and dies nobly for his asininity and for something bigger than that, but, in point of tact at least, an ass. . . . The two Tribunes who fire the people against him are asses too—prodigious, unworthy, place-hunting asses. . . .[38]

Although politics offers dramatic context, "the theme of 'Coriolanus' is not politics, but pride. . . . Manners may change, coded morality may change, but human nature is unchanging. Our poet-playwright wrote primarily not of politics, not of morals, not of philosophy, not of religion, but of men."[39] Bridges-Adams's *Coriolanus* revivals, whatever twentieth-century political and social cataclysms shook the world beyond Stratford, remained aesthetic essays in timeless human behavior set in a functionally Jacobean stage space. Of course, as Dennis Kennedy observes, Bridges-Adams's "very resistance to the partisan content of *Coriolanus* can be read as a conservative political act."[40]

For both his revivals, one in 1926 and another in 1933, Adams used basically the same text. His promptbook,[41] the first extant for a postwar production, shows him quicker with the blue pencil than Atkins. Apparently the full-text experiment at the Old Vic merited no repetition. Gone from act 1 are the scenes in which the Roman soldiers examine their spoils (1.5), Martius appears at Cominius's camp (1.6), and Aufidius vows revenge by fair means or foul (1.10). The Adrian and Nicanor encounter (4.3) also vanishes, together with Menenius's reluctant decision to petition Martius for mercy (5.1). In a curious transposition, reminiscent of nineteenth-century fiddling, the return of the suppliant women (5.5) is made to follow the Messenger's "Sir, if you'd save your life, fly to your house" (5.4.35). At this point, to secure a strong curtain, the women enter and exit amid a singing crowd with hands uplifted.

Internal cuts are numerous, and include most of the exchange before the walls of Corioli prior to Martius's invasion (1.4), the cushion-layers' speeches (2.2.1–34), and much of Martius's argument against giving the plebeians corn in 3.1. The Banishment scene in the bad old tradition ended with "There is a world elsewhere." The servingmen's banter, restored by Atkins, again disappears from 4.5; and the news of Volumnia's success (ll.

36–62) is displaced in 5.4 by her processional entrance. In the play's final moments Bridges-Adams proved surprisingly squeamish when confronted with Martius's ugly quietus: Aufidius does not tread on the body, nor does he attempt to justify his deed; nor does the 2. Lord urge his colleagues to "make the best of it." Once Martius falls, Aufidius launches into his eulogy almost at once. In all an astonishing thirteen hundred lines vanish.

While hardly an advertisement for textual integrity, Bridges-Adams's *Coriolanus,* like Atkins's, broke fresh scenographic ground. Confined for the 1926 revival to the Greenhill Street cinema while his new theater was being built, the director-designer found visual inventiveness challenged to its limit by the shallow proscenium box. Ultimately flights of steps from the stage to the orchestra pit, a staple of German stagecraft, yielded something of the flexibility of the Poelian apron; the strategic use of curtains and lighting "dissolves" facilitated scene changes; and intriguingly illuminated scenic units, such as the gates of Rome and Corioli, lent visual interest without loss of space, pace, or continuity. In the 1926 revival, as in Atkins's two years earlier, structure and rhythm were better served than characterization. Rehearsal time was absurdly short, and the actors, none of them of the first rank, proved inadequate to the challenges that confronted them. The citizens, drawn from local townspeople, were barely passable; and a shortage of military types may well explain Bridges-Adams's radical cutting of the battlefield sequences, a conjecture supported by a reviewer's observation that "the mimic battles by the gate of Corioli, with hardly any battlers" was "too thin for words" (*Stratford-upon-Avon Herald,* 27 August 1926).

George Skillan, physically impressive and suitably resonant, was an adequate but unmemorable Coriolanus. Somehow he managed to make "the Roman soldier's unbending pride the comprehensible effect of a noble character" (*Daily Telegraph,* 24 April 1926), altogether, one theatergoer thought, "a much more amiable man than we had expected" (*Stratford-upon-Avon Herald,* 30 April 1926). An agreeable Martius and a clutch of innocuous citizens were not the stuff of which cosmic conflict could be fabricated. And Ethel Carrington's lightweight and inoffensive Volumnia did little to raise the temperature. Once again, it is worth noting, the scene in Aufidius's house claimed attention, and the secondary roles enjoyed some prominence. Menenius, played by Randle Ayrton with "dignity and a sly humour" (*Daily Telegraph,* 24 April 1926) received frequent praise, as did the Sicinius of Fred Morgan and the Brutus of Roy Byford, now given more "light and shade" than heretofore.

In 1933, with a new state-of-the-art plant at his disposal, Bridges-Adams mounted a better *Coriolanus,* but it still remained a triumph of mise-en-scène rather than interpretation. While fascism gained strength daily in Europe (Hitler had become Chancellor of Germany only three months earlier) and Britain's ineffective National Government ignored the threat in favor of parochial concerns, Bridges-Adams continued to downplay *Coriolanus's* political character. His script remained unrevised, save for the restoration of the episode in the camp of Cominius (1.6).

Playgoers were invited to revisit the Greenhill Street cinema design, now better realized thanks to a more spacious stage and access to new technology. The director's plea for a highly flexible performing space had failed to impress the Governors, and he was compelled to coexist with an obtrusive proscenium arch: once more, then, as in the productions of Poel, Granville-Barker, and Atkins, audiences were offered an impression of Elizabethan scenography rather than the experience itself. In a modulation of the 1926 design, steep flights of steps rose from the stage towards the skyline and descended into the orchestra pit; a feature which not only brought the action nearer the audience, but facilitated vertical blocking, a directorial technique which allowed dramatic rhythm to be visually mapped, and eloquent and picturesque groupings. The steps were supplemented with rudimentary arches, gates, stone blocks, and columns placed, at times on a rolling stage, against the new cyclorama. Bridges-Adams's mastery of chiaroscuro lighting lent the most minimal arrangements stunning pictorial effect. Costumes, as in the 1926 revival, were conventionally Roman.

Making a virtue of economic necessity, Bridges-Adams convincingly demonstrated that pictorial quality need be neither ruinously expensive nor inimical to continuity and rhythmic integrity. Particularly noteworthy were "the scene where the gates of Corioli crashed under the Roman battering-rams" (*Stage,* 27 April 1933), Martius's "There is a world elsewhere," spoken at the top of a flight of steps, with the lone figure "a silhouette, against the sky" (*Birmingham Post,* 25 April 1933), and Volumnia's return from the Volscian camp when "the Roman crowd, women and men, came, chanting slowly, up the steps to meet the women coming slowly down" (*Manchester Guardian,* 26 April 1933).

Bridges-Adams's conviction that the theme of the play was pride did not preclude effective representation of the political context to Martius's tragic narrative once production conditions permitted. The crowd, again composed of townspeople but larger, better drilled, and less confined than in 1926, proved an altogether worthy counterbalance to the epic hero. Exploiting the verticality of the setting, the mob "surged up and down the steps, toppled its enemies down them, crouched on them, and generally managed to give an impression of being only the fringes of a greater mob elsewhere" (*Manchester Guardian,* 26 April 1933). Nowhere was it seen to greater effect than in its Bensonian dispatch of the tribunes when, according to the prompt-book, "Sicinius & Brutus see crowd coming from orch: They rush up C & meet crowd coming down. Brutus is seized & dragged down orch: steps. Sicinius is carried down C. and laid head downwards on slab L.C. Brutus is carried to upper steps & hanged." Here, wrote the *Birmingham Mail* reviewer, "heights of frenzied excitement were scaled" (25 April 1933).

In 1933, as in 1926, Bridges-Adams's artistic vision was vitiated by a

The Seige of Corioli. Bridges-Adams Production, Shakespeare Memorial Theatre, 1933. [By permission of the Shakespeare Centre Library, Stratford-upon-Avon]

rehearsal period of less than a week[42] and a want of first-class actors. Anew McMaster, a young Irishman "who might have walked from a Florentine canvas of the high Renaissance,"[43] captured "the swollen pride of [Martius], and suggested also the nobility of spirit which alone could make us sympathise with him" (*Manchester Guardian Weekly*, 28 April 1933), but in no more than outline; and his inclination to mouth the text and "grimace at moments of emotional distress" (*Daily Telegraph*, 25 April 1933) did little to ameliorate the reading. Fiery and full voiced, he nevertheless matched the crowd roar for roar throughout, and in a unique finale fell beneath the Volscian swords in a burst of savage laughter. The Volumnia of Alice O'Day, an actress of the old school, evinced "plenty of vigour but no great distinction" (*Birmingham Post*, 25 April 1933). The tribunes (Sicinius-Eric Maxon and Brutus-Reginald Jarman), "windy demagogues" in earlier scenes transformed to "terror-striken cringers as the mob rose against them" (*Birmingham Mail*, 25 April 1933), were little more than caricatures. The compelling humanity of Stanley Lathbury's Menenius, "a shrewd and gently caustic old observer and commentator . . . with an accession of forlornness in the moment of his rejection" (*Stage*, 27 April 1933), was all the more noteworthy by comparison.

Bridges-Adams's revivals, if models neither of textual integrity nor interpretative subtlety, were nevertheless scenographically groundbreaking: as respect for the interplay of scenic continuity and dramatic rhythm gained currency among directors over the next few years, his pioneering efforts to

make the poetry of representation serve the poetry of the text, to use Co-
peau's phrase, became a kind of grammar of practice.

NUGENT MONCK AT THE MADDERMARKET (1928)

Early in February 1928, four years after Atkins staged *Coriolanus* at the
Old Vic and two years after Bridges-Adams's first Stratford revival, their
onetime colleague Nugent Monck mounted the play at his Maddermarket
Theatre in Norwich.[44] After a long apprenticeship with Poel (1902–10),
Monck had in 1911 founded in the cathedral city an amateur troupe known
as the Norwich Players, and directed them in one Shakespeare production
before the war intervened. On his return from military service in 1919 he
reorganized the company and installed it in a Georgian structure remodeled
at considerable expense along Elizabethan lines. Here, over the next thirty
years, he devoted his time, energy, and whatever cash he could muster to
the implementation of Poel's production theories.

Monck's 220-seat playhouse, advertised as the first non-proscenium theater built since the Commonwealth and an approximation of an Elizabethan
ludic space inspired by the Fortune contract, featured "a gallery round three
sides of the hall, connected with the balcony over the stage" beneath which
was located a discovery area. The forestage, thirty-two feet wide and twenty
feet deep,[45] was divided into downstage, center, and upstage areas by traverse curtains frequently drawn by the actors themselves. Set pieces could
thus be placed and removed at will without impeding dramatic momentum.
Doors surmounted by windows gave ready access to the foremost section,
where the bulk of the action took place.

Flexible stagecraft and the swift speech which identified Monck's productions obviated the need to cut the play to fit theatergoing hours; his excisions, some six hundred lines in all, seem primarily designed to clarify
meaning and accelerate action. His promptbook[46] indicates that he removed
only four scenes entirely: Aufidius's conference with the Coriolian senators
(1.2), Martius's arrival at the camp of Cominius (1.6), Lartius's instructions
to the Lieutenant (1.7), and the Adrian and Nicanor episode (4.3). He also
made heavy internal cuts to the battle scenes in act 1, the cushion-layers'
speeches (2.2), the exchange between Menenius and the tribunes in 3.1, and
Menenius's encounter with the Watch (5.2). The performance seems to have
occupied about three hours, including two intervals: one after 2.1, Coriolanus's triumphal return, and the other after Volumnia's slanging match with
the tribunes (4.2).

Monck's promptbook is very sparsely marked, but makes his staging technique clear enough: and a glance at a scene or two is adequate to demonstrate its effectiveness. A traverse curtain, presumably just behind the
forestage doors, opened at the beginning of the play to allow the entire stage

Owen P. Smyth Design. Nugent Monck Production, Maddermarket Theatre, 1928. [By permission of the Maddermarket Theatre and The Norfolk Record Office]

area to be used for the citizens' confrontation with Menenius and Martius in 1.1. At the conclusion of the scene the curtain closed to permit Volumnia and Virgilia to play 1.3 in the extreme downstage area, which they enter by the forestage doors. Meanwhile gates were placed upstage of the traverse. As the women exit, the curtains open for the battle sequence (1.4) on a full stage, complete with city gates. Throughout the play only one traverse curtain seems to have been used; unless large numbers of performers were involved, or set pieces were called for, action was located as close to the audience as possible. Perhaps inspired by Bridges-Adams's 1926 revival, Monck introduced "a broad flight of steps" (*Eastern Evening News,* Norwich, 7 February 1928) upstage of the traverse curtain for some scenes.

Speed and intimacy were achieved without sacrifice of visual interest. From Poel Monck acquired a taste for dressing productions in what was judged to be the Elizabethan/Jacobean theatrical mode—for the Roman plays, a combination of contemporary and conventional gear. He found his immediate inspiration in Veronese's *The Family of Darius before Alexander:* the men accordingly sported period tunics and tights complemented by Roman boots and armor, while the women wore contemporary Jacobean fashions.[47] Theatergoers accustomed to the traditional "Saturday night at the Turkish baths" wardrobe found the warm Renaissance coloring a distinct and welcome change. *Coriolanus*'s Renaissance fashions owed much of their effect, however, to modern lighting technology. Painterly stage groupings, masterfully illuminated, made the play, in one critic's opinion, "much more spectacular than it could possibly have been with conventional scenery." "Could there have been," he demanded, "anything finer, for instance, than the stormy scene at the gates of Corioli, the austere beauty of some of the later groupings on the steps, or the warm colouring, like an Italian fresco, of the banquet of Aufidius?" (*Eastern Evening News,* Norwich, 7 February 1928). Another playgoer lauded "the delightful blend of colours in the scene before Coriolanus' tent" (*Eastern Daily Press,* Norwich, 7 February 1928), while a third was struck by the way "figures grouped [on the steps] were thrown up against a background, often illuminated" (*Christian Science Monitor,* Boston, n.d.).

Although Monck's company was entirely composed of amateurs, it was widely conceded, at its best, to be of professional caliber; and *Coriolanus* was judged one its finest achievements.[48] Monck's production notebook[49] lists only eight supers, yet Norman Marshall, a professional director, thought the production offered "the best crowd scenes I have seen in any theatre";[50] and the battle scenes for once received favorable notice. "They really 'fight' on the Maddermarket stage," noted a local reviewer, "and the clash of sword on breastplate, the wild cries of the combatants, made the taking of Corioli, for instance, as exciting as any screen battle with a thousand times as many people taking part" (*Eastern Daily Press,* Norwich, 7 February 1928).

Maddermarket Shakespeare was routinely ignored by the London critics, and the local press sketched individual performances with the broadest of strokes. The Martius of C. Miller[51] was described as "finely conceived, dignified," and played "with power without exaggeration," but detail is in short supply. Miss Diver's Volumnia was characterized by "dignity, distinction and womanly tenderness, with great charm of voice"; Sicinius's (T. Stevens) "malevolence" was approved, and the Brutus of O. P. Smyth was deemed "forcible and virile" (*Eastern Daily Press,* Norwich, 7 February 1928). With such vague intimations, one must rest content.

Monck's production, lamentably ill-documented, remains a key modern revival. Mounted on a thrust stage in a relatively full text, swiftly spoken, and picturesquely realized, it doubtless revealed much about the play's theatrical character, but the critical community was not on hand to observe and record. One provocative insight hints at what must have been a host of theatrical aperçus. When played as Monck staged it, according to the *Christian Science Monitor, Coriolanus* declared itself unequivocally a political drama. It became clear that the play "deals with opposing and exterior forces"

> rather than the inner tragedies which belong to the individual. After all Coriolanus comes and Coriolanus goes; but you know no more about him, or rather you know as much, at the beginning as you do at the end. You have, in fact, a curious contrast throughout—the contrast between the swift and ever increasing movement of the story and the stationary pose of Coriolanus. . . . The profoundest, the most enduring experiences of mankind are deserted for an Elizabethan view of the great political problems (Boston, n.d.).

About a month later (3 March 1928) the Marlowe Society at Cambridge University staged an unremarkable revival save that the women's roles were played by men. And at least one reviewer found the masculine dimension of Volumnia's character "more convincingly played than we have seen it hitherto" (*Cambridge Daily News*, 6 March 1928).

Hugh Hunt at the Abbey (1936)

In January of 1936 Hugh Hunt, the newly appointed manager of Dublin's Abbey Theatre, drawing upon the experience of Atkins, Bridges-Adams, and Monck, designed and directed a production visually indebted, like Monck's revival, to the paintings of Veronese. A curtain, painted by a youthful Tanya Moiseiwitsch "after a picture of Coriolanus by Genga," was also a feature. The Atkins-Monck system of alternating shallow and deep scenes separated by traverse curtains enabled Hunt to offer a fairly full text in two hours and fifty minutes, including two intervals totaling twenty minutes. The wardrobe, as in Monck's revival, was Renaissance Roman. Hunt's modernist scenography was warmly approved, but it was the Martius of a rising young Stratford actor, Reginald Jarman,[52] which captivated reviewers. For the first time modernist characterization complemented modernist stagecraft.

As early as 1912 Bradley had called attention to the fact that "often [Martius] reminds us of a huge boy,"[53] a perception Jarman now realized in theatrical practice. And the reading was a revelation to the *Irish Independent* reviewer. "Properly understood," he wrote, "[Martius] . . . has the mind of a child."

> His virtues and his vices are those of a small boy. He loves fighting, he is full of the most sentimental kind of patriotism, the kind that wants to fight and die for his country without knowing or caring what the quarrel is about, but has no interest in his country's welfare and no love for its citizens.
> He has at once the selfishness and the generosity of childhood. The stupid intolerance of his aristocratic snobbery brings about his own banishment and

almost the ruin of his class, but he is not ignoble and will not stoop to plead his wounds or service to the State in extenuation. . . .

When banished he rushes away in a huff, like any small boy determined to have revenge at all costs, but it is only the furious, short-lived hatred of a child that would unthinkingly destroy the world, but is easily turned from its purpose. . . . [T]he final small boy touch is the fact that it is his mother who has real influence over him (Dublin, 14 January 1936).

Physically massive, Jarman "towered properly over everyone about him on the stage. "He tore through them," we learn, "embarrassing his senatorial friends as much as he made his enemies not merely fear him, but hate him."[54] "As a fighting man," remarked one playgoer, "he showed us Coriolanus the joyous swashbuckler" (*Irish Independent,* Dublin, 14 January 1936); but at the same time his predilection for confrontation revealed "the violent man who, had he come to power might have been a tyrannical dictator." In his "uncontrolled fury," the observer continues, "he annotated as much the dangers of privileges as the weakness of the 'many-headed' and timorous mob."[55] Throughout he was a creature of moods, the whole harmonized by a pervasive immaturity. "Even when his folly was most crass," the *Irish Independent* critic found his behavior "perfectly understandable, and so we never lost our sympathy—why preach worldly wisdom to a child, for childhood despises commonsense above all things" (Dublin, 14 January 1936). Among the high points of his performance was the banishment, where the indomitable pride which had sustained him throughout deserted him; "his body," we are told, "quivers with anger" and, in spite of himself, "he descends to the level of those whom he so despises" (*Christian Science Monitor,* Boston, 10 February 1936). In the scene in Aufidius's house, Martius was "every inch the aristocrat" (*Christian Science Monitor,* Boston, 10 February 1936); his chilly superiority, however, dissolved under Volumnia's intercessional onslaught into "a bewildered pathos" (*Irish Independent,* Dublin, 14 January 1936). Neither Hunt nor Jarman sought sympathy for the character in his final moments, during which, according to the *Christian Science Monitor,* Martius became "a snarling, tearing tiger-cat in his attitude toward Aufidius, and his cutting-off appear[ed] a just fate." He died as he lived, "a man of impossible outlook, who was unquestionably a hero to himself" (Boston, 10 February, 1936).

Throughout Jarman was ably, if unremarkably, supported by May Carey's aristocratic and canny Volumnia, and Barry Fitzgerald's Menenius, a "shrewd old man who despised the people, as Coriolanus did, but knew that in politics one must stoop to conquer" (*Christian Science Monitor,* Boston, 10 February 1936). Michael J. Dolan and Fred Johnson were conventionally sinister tribunes.

Jarman's was unquestionably one of the most original readings in the first half of this century, and in many ways the precursor of Olivier's. Hunt's dozen or so citizens, however, unable to compete with the power and originality of the new-minted Martius, were reduced to mere instruments upon which the star played, and the play's political complexity was hardly noticed.

Politics was in fact more evident off the stage than on it. Outraged nationalists, who saw the production of Shakespeare as a subversion of the Abbey's mission, mobilized public opinion against Hunt's experiment: "Since there is only one national theatre in the whole of Ireland," one writer reminded the company, "Mr. Hunt and his co-workers must not think too badly of us for preferring that it should remain national, and for preferring that the particularly Irish qualities of its company should be devoted to Irish plays" (*Sunday Dispatch*, Dublin, 19 January 1936). Nationalism triumphed. At first, feigning injured incomprehension, Hunt pronounced himself "anxious to discover the reason for the complete lack of support the public have so far afforded to the play" (*Irish Times*, Dublin, 16 January 1936), but soon bowed to the inevitable and closed the production after only a week of performances.

FEDERAL THEATER PROJECT (1938)

Two years later New Yorkers were treated to a dual theatrical novelty: the first production of *Coriolanus* in almost four decades[56] and, as an added fillip, outfitted in Elizabethan Methodist gear. Prompted no doubt by the success of Orson Welles's anti-fascist *Julius Caesar*, still enjoying a triumphant run at the Mercury, Charles Hopkins' Repertory Branch of the Federal Theater Project launched its *Coriolanus* at the Maxine Elliott Theater on 1 February 1938.[57] Although bent on competition with Welles, Hopkins eschewed both politics and contemporaneity, the key ingredients of *Caesar*'s box office appeal; and even as Mussolini bombed Barcelona and Hitler readied his invasion of Austria, Hopkins plumped for the isolationist aestheticism championed by Bridges-Adams and Monck a decade, and Macready a century, earlier.

Like his counterparts in British professional houses, Hopkins was obliged to coexist with the intractable proscenium arch; but quick to tap the British experience, he found partial escape from constriction, some degree of intimacy, and the impression of Jacobean scenic continuity in curtains and flights of steps. Opting for a permanent setting, he constructed a massive stairway from the center aisle position on the auditorium floor to the rear of the stage. Part way up, square pylons supported grey traverse curtains which were opened à la Nugent Monck when spaciousness was demanded and drawn whenever possible to bring the action forward. Costumes, like those of Atkins and Bridges-Adams, were conventionally Roman. Light, in keeping with modernist practice, was an indispensable adjunct to form— marking locale changes, creating atmosphere, defining groupings, modulating rhythm, and lending color and picturesqueness. The lighting design, by Abraham Feder, one of America's leading innovators, was widely praised.

Hopkins's key objective was to play, with Jacobean proximity and rhythmic integrity, as full a text as possible; and in this he succeeded. In a more intimate ambiance than that of Atkins or Bridges-Adams, exits and entrances were frequently made from the aisles, Roman supers flung themselves down the steps at the very feet of playgoers, and trumpet blasts assailed the ear from deafening arm's length. Critics lauded the production's vigor and immediacy: "the swift pace of the present production maintains a steady sweep of action," wrote one, "and as it culminates before the doomed gates of Rome with a mother's plea to her son to spare his native city, it finds an impact that vouches for its magnificence as sheer theater" (*New York Journal and American,* 4 February 1938). But, as so often in British modernist revivals, sensitive staging was compromised by inadequate acting. In this case, all the performers were too youthful for the roles. Erford Gage was a picturesque and boyish Martius because he was little more than a boy, but when heroic stature was called for, he was unable to summon it. Lenore Sorsby was an elegant and dignified, if also too youthful, Volumnia.

However conscientiously directed and designed, the FTP *Coriolanus* proved poor competition to the Welles *Caesar.* "You will find the 'Coriolanus' the better Shakespeare," Burns Mantle reluctantly informed his readers, "but the 'Julius Caesar' the more exciting production" (*Daily News,* New York, 3 February 1938). Audiences apparently chose excitement, and the revival closed a week later.

After prolonged exposure to scholarly, conscientious essays in Elizabethan Methodism, one turns with somewhat guilty relief to the two lone modernist attempts at stylization.

STYLIZATION AND MODERN DRESS

When William Poel mounted *Coriolanus* for a single 11 a.m. performance at the Chelsea Palace Theatre in 1931, he was approaching eighty, and no more the servant of convention than he had ever been—even of conventions he had himself popularized. Having managed after half a century to convince his theatrical colleagues that Shakespeare's texts deserved respect, he now proceeded to flout his most cherished principles, all the while using supposititious scholarship to justify pure whimsy.

Ignoring the fact that the play had demonstrated its theatrical viability in several recent, and relatively full-text, revivals, Poel declared the play unactable as written. Its defects, he argued in a "Producer's Note" to the program, were attributable to the fact that by 1610, the composition date he favored, Shakespeare was an invalid and only "outlining the action" of his scripts. The dialogue was supplied by Fletcher, Massinger, or, in the case of *Coriolanus,* Chapman. "There seems to be in the composition of "Coriolanus," he maintained, "the product of two different minds; Chapman, that is, adheres to Plutarch's story, while Shakespeare wishes to regard it with more freedom than the text of Plutarch allows."[58] The conjectural intervention of Chapman allowed Poel to tamper with a license he denied himself in texts wholly attributable to Shakespeare.

For Poel *Coriolanus's* subject was not politics, but "the ageless spirit of militarism," epitomized in the destruction of an heroic son by a saber-rattling mother. The key to the play, he claimed, lay in Martius's stunned and disbelieving "O, mother, mother! What have you done?" (5.3.182–83). "Well may he ask this question," he says,

> for it is his mother who has taught him to look upon war as the sole aim and end of his existence, and now he finds that to save her life he must sacrifice his own! . . . Volumnia is not the tragic queen of the play; she has educated her "boy" to his ruin, and is responsible for his death.[59]

While stoutly denying *Coriolanus's* political character, he silently removed several hundred lines of political comment, and argued with vigor that the plebeians were no more than a mere dramatic device. "[T]he crowd is not used as political opponents to the patricians or to exploit political animosities," he insisted. "It is no question of the Labour Party versus the House of Lords. Before Coriolanus can be killed he must be banished from Rome and the plebeian crowd in the play is used for this purpose."[60]

The nature of Poel's script was further dictated by his newfound conviction that "no modern audience would sit through the full length of a Shakespeare play,"[61] although audiences at the Old Vic, the Shakespeare Memorial, and the Maddermarket were by now doing so almost routinely. As a result, when Poel laid down his blue pencil, playing time occupied about one and one-half hours thanks to the excision of some 2000 of the text's 3409 lines.

Three annotated scripts associated with the production[62] indicate that although Poel hacked with abandon, his modernist concern for Shakespeare's overall design led him to preserve at least a part of every scene in the first four acts. His respect for scenic integrity, however, was another matter; and few escaped curtailment, internal mutilation, transposition, or rewriting. The surviving text was rearranged without scene divisions as a continuous narrative, with intervals at the end of the Senate episode (2.2) and the conclusion of the pact between Martius and Aufidius (4.5.147). The action thus fell into three movements: Martius's military career, culminating in his nomination for the consulship; his confrontation with the Roman tribunes and citizens leading to a Volscian generalship; and his struggle with his mother terminating in his defeat and death.

The initial confrontation between Menenius and Martius and the plebeians (1.1) is reduced from 277 lines to 82. Most of the political comment is excised, including, of course, the belly fable. The citizens and Martius vent their mutual antipathy in a dozen or so lines, just enough to set the plot in motion. The rarely played sequence in which Aufidius confers with the Coriolian senators (1.2), abridged by about two-thirds, becomes a conversation between Aufidius and his Lieutenant. The domestic scene with Volumnia, Virgilia, and Valeria (1.3) is less heavily curtailed. The Battle of Corioli episode (1.4), on the other hand, retains just sufficient lines to motivate Martius's entry into the city. Menenius receives a gratuitous appearance at the top of the scene, inciting the citizens to come to Martius's aid. The episode in which soldiers enter with spoils (1.5) sees Martius make his bloody reentry from the city, an event placed by Shakespeare in the previous scene. The eighty-odd lines of the sequence in Cominius's camp (1.6) shrink to half-a-dozen, hardly more than Martius's request to be set against Aufidius. By way of compensation, the short transitional scene between Lartius and the Lieutenant (1.7), traditionally cut, was restored. The fight between Martius and Aufidius (1.8) loses only four of its lines, but 1.9, in which Martius is renamed, chronicles only the bare event; Martius makes no request for mercy for his host, nor does he suffer a memory lapse. In 1.10 Aufidius's decision to square accounts is reached without a spare word.

The near ninety-line verbal brawl between Menenius and the tribunes in 2.1 shrinks to an eighteen-line skirmish. Martius's triumphal return is heavily cut, and the conversation between Brutus and Sicinius after the exit of the procession is savaged. The Senate scene (2.2) is also radically pruned: the officers who lay cushions speak only some half-dozen lines, and the commendatory speeches of Menenius and Cominius are whittled to token dimensions. An interval follows.

The Voices episode (2.3) is not heavily cut, but after Coriolanus leaves the stage, the tribunes' manipulation of the plebeians is trimmed almost to the vanishing point. Martius's altercation with the tribunes and plebeians in 3.1 contains next to no indication of the general's political consciousness. The action hurtles forward to Martius's denunciation as a traitor; his outraged defiance and the diplomatic protests of his friends amount to only a line or two before he is led off. The exchange between Menenius and the tribunes after Martius's departure is completed in a dozen or so lines. In the Admonition scene (3.2) Volumnia's dialectic is heavily curtailed, as are her son's diverting antics when he imagines himself the people's wooer. Prior to Martius's reentry in 3.3, the tribunes are allowed only five lines in which to strategize as compared with Shakespeare's forty. The remainder of the scene is a headlong rush toward Coriolanus's banishment.

The family farewell at the city gates (4.1) is perfunctory: only twenty-five out of sixty lines are left standing. And Volumnia's indictment of the tribunes (4.2) fares no better. Although Poel retained the Adrian and Nicanor episode (4.3), a rare event indeed, he inexplicably made it follow rather than precede Coriolanus's arrival in Antium. Martius's conversation with the Volscian citizen in 4.4 is reduced by about one-half. The first seventy-odd lines of 4.5 are summarily dispatched, and with them Martius's scuffle with Aufidius's servants and the revelation of his identity to Aufidius. The scene opens as the generals enter on Martius's "The cruelty and envy of the people . . ." (4.5.74). Their subsequent conversation is heavily truncated, with the nuptial imagery a particular target. The exit of the pair through the city gates, "both talking with animation," is the cue for a second interval.

The play's final movement begins with the entry of Aufidius's servants on the lines "Why, he is so made on here within as if he were son and heir to Mars" (4.5.191–92). Their exchange is succeeded by the colloquy between the tribunes, Menenius, and the citizens, played relatively uncut until the arrival of the messenger at 4.6.57 after which all but a few lines, including the stategy conference and the citizens' panic, are excised. In 4.7 only eleven lines of the fifty-seven-line conversation between Aufidius and his lieutenant survive, and these are transposed elsewhere.

Prior to act 5 Poel's textual alterations consist mainly of cuts, the rewriting of an occasional line or two, and the frequent reallocation of speeches. With act 5, however, all pretense to a modernist respect for form is abandoned. After the exit of Menenius on his embassy in 5.1, word arrives of the departure of Volumnia's mission, a sequence cobbled together from the account of her victorious homecoming at 5.4.30–55. The servants' response to Martius's reception (4.5.191ff.) follows, followed in turn by an abbreviated version of the conversation between Aufidius and his Lieutenant (4.7) and a quick chat with the conspirators, borrowed from 5.6. With Volscian treachery established, Menenius arrives, converses with Aufidius who appropriates the Watch's lines from 5.2, and is dismissed by Martius before he can make his case. The Intercession scene ensues.

Most of Martius's introspective musing as the women approach disappears; and his salute to Valeria launches her into into a peroration appropriated from Plutarch:

> We address ourselves to you without any decree of the senate or order of the consuls. But our god, we believe, lending a merciful ear to our prayers, put in our minds to apply to you and to entreat you to do a thing that will not only be salutary to us and to the other citizens, but glorious for you if you hearken to us.

The poetic grandeur of Volumnia's appeal, perhaps in Poel's opinion too sublime for a battlefield vulture, is reworked into stilted prose, the quality of which may be indicated by a brief sample:

> You see, my son, by our attire to what condition your banishment has reduced us. Think with yourself whether we are not the most unhappy of women whom

fortune has changed the spectacle that should have been the most pleasing in the world, into the most dreadful; camped in a hostile manner before the walls of his native city. . . .

After his capitulation, Martius bids his family farewell with a reassuring flourish, the conclusion of which owes more to the baroque than the modernist spirit:

> —and you shall bear
> A better witness back than words, which we
> On like conditions, will have counter-sealed.
> Go enter the gates. Farewell! Weep no more, all
>   will yet be well.

Martius now watches his family "pass through the gates where they are received by the villagers with much cheering."

> [The Mother turns and makes signs to her son to come who replies—]
> Ay, by and by;
>   [The curtains of the gate close.]
> (Alone) O, mother, my mother!
> What have you done? Behold, the heavens do ope,
> The gods look down, and smile in dismal wonder
> As at one forsworn. O my mother, mother! O!
> You have won a happy victory to Rome;
> But for your son—believe it, O, believe it,
> Most dangerously you have with him prevail'd,
> If not most mortal to him, But, let it come. O
>   Mother! Wife!
> [He buries his face in his hands then he walks closely towards the Corioli door, and gives two loud knocks with his fist. The door opens, he enters and it closes. Singing and dancing heard in the Roman City followed by tumult and killing of CORIOLANUS in the city of Corioli.]

And, incredibly enough, there the play ended. With the departure of Volumnia, in Poel's opinion, the action reached its climax. "For a satisfactory ending," he wrote, "Coriolanus must be shown as a sympathetic figure. . . . Coriolanus's last speech is harsh and leaves a bad impression."[63] Martius need only reap with minimal delay the harvest of his mother's heartlessness. There was no Martius-Aufidius showdown, no attack by the conspirators, no standing on the body, and no eulogy. The audience contemplated instead a tableau of rejoicing Gypsy girls.

The production was staged on a large open platform built out over the first rows of the Chelsea Palace stalls with steps at the sides to permit entrances and exits to be made by way of the auditorium. The proscenium opening was closed, probably by curtains, immediately behind which seem to have been a set of gates used for the Corioli battle, Martius's farewell to his family, and Volumnia's departure after the intercession. At either side of the platform stood flats with functional doors, one designated as leading to Rome, the other to Corioli.

Poel's fluid and rhythmic scenography was by now no novelty, but his costumes must have come as a distinct shock to theatergoers habituated to his Elizabethan antiquarianism. To highlight "the ageless spirit of militarism" which he found at the heart of the play, Poel situated the action more or less in the Directoire era: I say "more or less" since he undermined his own conception with a series of visual caprices. Martius, played by Robert Speaight, was obliged to make his first appearance in a leopard skin and toting an enormous two-handed sword. On the battlefield he wore a semblance of Roman military gear; and for his victorious return he sported "the full-dress uniform of a Colonel of the Hussars." Volumnia, in her turn, "was dressed as an imperious Gainsborough in hat and plumes and Virgilia was a pure Pre-Raphaelite" whose dress Poel copied from the photograph in a society journal of a contemporary beauty at a fancy-dress ball.[64] The tribunes "were in the black gowns and white wigs of barristers" while the plebeians "were attired in costumes which made them look like a cross between decayed members of the French Foreign Legion and English engine-drivers," a bemused observer reported (*Manchester Guardian,* 12 May 1931). The Roman military wore relatively authentic Napoleonic uniforms, and the Volscians rang the changes on oriental gear. Aufidius himself was garbed "in the gorgeous robes of an Oriental potentate" (*Manchester Guardian,* 12 May 1931).

Actors in Poel's productions were little more than puppets, and critics and audiences were accordingly disinclined to censure them. As Speaight put it, "They might commiserate, but they would not criticise; they might be bewildered, but they would not blame. They would assume, quite rightly, that you were simply doing what you had been told."[65] Speaight's Coriolanus, if physically lightweight, was judged appropriately passionate and bravely declaimed; but Poel's determination to stress the mother-son relationship to the exclusion of everything else robbed the role of epic dimension. In the opinion of the *Everyman* reviewer, "There was no tragedy, only a weak man who blamed his mother for bringing him up badly!" (21 May 1931). Sara Allgood's Volumnia, disdaining the Poussinesque splendor of Genevieve Ward, turned out to be "a blatant and bragging Lady Britomartish sort of person" (*Everyman,* 21 May 1931) with "a hearty Irish bloodthirstiness" (*Daily Telegraph,* 12 May 1931) curiously at variance with her feathered hats and powdered hair. The plebeians, recruited from the ranks of the Shaftesbury Boys of Fortescue House, were hardly a menacing political force, nor were they meant to be. Theatergoers found the costumes of the rest of the dramatis personae more remarkable than their characters.

Even the crankiest work of a theatrical genius may have value and influence, and Poel's *Coriolanus* is no exception. His apron setting, perhaps inspired by the Swan drawing, provided a more effective escape from the proscenium arch than any director had achieved to date; its size and position gave the play greater spatial freedom than Bridges-Adams's steps or even Monck's smallish forestage; and his use of front-of-house entrances and exits realized something closer to Jacobean intimacy than anything yet experienced at the Old Vic or the Shakespeare Memorial. The pity is that, having created an expressive ludic space, he denied the play the opportunity to assert itself there in its fullness.

Poel's scenographic relocation of the action to the Napoleonic period was, like the Roman decor of Bridges-Adams or the Renaissance Roman mise-en-scène of Monck, an acknowledgment of the play's political and social unpalatability for contemporary audiences. His relocation of the action to a period associated with neither the play's subject nor its original performance was, however, unique; and the tactic was to become a commonplace of twentieth-century production. The Directoire stylization itself, rather more consistently realized by Michael Langham and Tyrone Guthrie, went on to influential, if controversial, airings at Stratford, Ontario (1961) and Nottingham (1963). As recently as 1994 it was reinvented by the RSC.

Although Poel's suppression of *Coriolanus*'s political character was unfortunate, his stress on the mother-son relationship, particularly Volumnia's less than wholesome mind-set, offered a welcome antidote to the traditional Poussinesque reading of the Intercession scene as an exhibition of patriotic duty by one party and filial piety by the other. Poel's unflattering portrait, reflecting criticism by Gervinus, Brooke, MacCallum, and Hookham, pointed the theater toward a reinterpretation of the characters in the light of contemporary psychoanalytic theory, an approach which for good and ill has shaped most productions since the mid-thirties.

Even more importantly, perhaps, the Chelsea Palace *Coriolanus* may be seen as the harbinger of contemporary "director's theater" approaches to the play. Three years earlier Wilson Knight concluded that each Shakespearian drama contained a "particular and peculiar vision of human existence," a vision which "determines not alone the choice of the main plot, but the selection or invention of subsidiary scenes and characters, the matters brought up for discussion within the scenes, and the very fibre of the language."[66] This vision would not declare itself simply by the fastidious speaking of full texts on functional replicas of Elizabethan stages: indeed, in contemporary productions, Knight was later to complain, "[t]he play's surface has been merely translated from book to stage, it has not been recreated from within."[67] To avoid what he described as "inorganic" productions, directors must identify each play's inner uniqueness, and intervene actively to communicate it to an audience using whatever strategies suggest themselves: the director enjoys "full powers to cut, adapt, even, on rare occasions, transpose, according to circumstances. . . . The producer's business is not translation, but recreation."[68] Whether Poel was familiar with Knight's ideas or not, he instinctively practiced what Knight preached, and, along with Terence Gray, pioneered in Britain the notion of directorial creation which, pursued more sensationally by Peter Brook and others, was to become theatrical orthodoxy a couple of decades later.

While Britain's major directors denied to their last breath Coriolanus's relevance to contemporary politics, a 1934 Paris revival at the Comédie Française, employed by royalists and fascists alike as a weapon against the left-wing Daladier government, decisively proved them wrong. In the wake of serious riots the production was suspended, the theater was closed for several weeks, and the police prefect and the director of the Comédie Française were dismissed. Perhaps it was the widespread media coverage of the event which inspired Dominic Roche in 1935 to defy conventional British theatrical wisdom and mount the century's first patently political production at the Manchester Repertory Theatre, and in modern dress at that.

Roche presented the play in three acts and eleven scenes.[69] Only four sets were used—"A Cafe in Rome," "A Lobby in the Capitol," "Outside Aufidius' House," and "A Hall in Aufidius' House." The "Lobby in the Capitol" was described as "a spacious and pleasant setting with a long balcony from which the unseen mob [was] harangued, and a council table at which Coriolanus [was] honoured, indicted, and banished" (*Manchester Guardian*, 12 November 1935). Roche removed the milling crowd from the stage, although they could be heard off from time to time. The curtain rose for the first scene, not on a mob of mutinous citizens, but on "half a dozen cafe loungers discussing the topics of the day" (*Daily Dispatch*, 12 November 1935) at a sidewalk bistro. Later an insolent Martius hurled defiance at an unseen opposition from a balcony, while infuriated offstage hordes alternately raged and sang the Internationale. The battle scenes were cut, and the Corioli victory celebrations were heard on radio by Volumnia, Virgilia, and the theater audience. Menenius was informed by telephone of Martius's impending invasion, and the hero in the play's final moments was shot in the back by a revolver.

Martius appeared in his moment of triumph "resplendent in white uniform, topee and glistening revolver-holster" and went into exile "in a tired blue double-breasted suit and a black slouch hat" (*Manchester Evening News*, 12 November 1935). The tribunes, one of whom bore a marked resemblance to Lenin, were "tweed-suited with red ties" (*Manchester Evening News*, 12 November 1935). Menenius sported a morning coat; Cominius appeared as "an elderly officer in khaki and monocle" (*Stage*, 14 November 1935); and Volumnia, for the Intercession scene, wore "a rich and heavy gown of white satin in which Queen Victoria might have held a garden party" (*Stage*, 14 November 1935). Aufidius was conceived in the Poel manner as "a slightly Oriental potentate with be-fezzed servants" (*Stage*, 14 November 1935).

Like previous interwar productions, the revival boasted adequate rather than brilliant performers, and once again acting proved less imaginative than the production style. John Citroen looked Martius to perfection, played with "both passion and dignity" and, in the Intercession scene, achieved "a moving tenderness" (*Manchester Guardian*, 12 November 1935). Eileen Draycott as Volumnia admirably realized the "unbending pride . . . and ultimate humility" (*Manchester Guardian*, 12 November 1935) the role demands, but failed to put any original stamp on it. Brutus (Charles Lamb) and Sicinius (Fred A. Essex) "looking like American party bosses" (*Daily Dispatch*, 12 November 1935), were routinely demagogic, while the Aufidius of D. W. King was little more than "properly crafty and malevolent" (*Manchester Guardian*, 12 November 1935).

Whatever the production's shortcomings, however, it obliged audiences and critics to confront, however briefly, the play's contemporaneity. "The politics of Rome, as Shakespeare conceived them," conceded the *Manchester Guardian* reviewer,

> bear a singular likeness to the politics of to-day, and can almost as cogently be argued on the contemporary stage as on that of Elizabeth. He is a confident politician who will deny that Governments in our time still suffer the masses to go hungry while the storehouses are filled with grain; he is a brazen one who dare assert that "that most grave belly," on whose function of distributing life to the body Menenius dwelled, is to-day doing its work. We have not passed the stage when many in authority believe with Caius Marcius that the best way to distract discontent at home is to plunge into war. Nor . . . is the sort of publicity now forced upon the prominent widely different from the compulsion to boast his exploits and show his scars to the mob which so violently offended the sensibilities of Coriolanus (12 November 1935).

Unfortunately Manchester was off the beaten theatrical track, Roche was not a member of the professional establishment, and the modern dress convention had long since lost its power to shock. Despite the fact that the little-known director preempted many of Welles's innovations by two years, his production disappeared without a ripple after a handful of performances.

9

From Olivier to Olivier:
A Romantic Interlude (1938–1959)

By the time Lewis Casson staged *Coriolanus* at the Old Vic in 1938, Elizabethan Methodism was theatrical orthodoxy. Robert Atkins, Nugent Monck, and others had demonstrated that a full text could be played in about three hours, and there no longer seemed any good reason for not doing so. Unfortunately, to stage the play in something like its entirety, with scenic continuity and rhythmic integrity, was not to render it more audience friendly. As a theatergoer put it after Bridges-Adams's 1926 production, "[*Coriolanus*] will never achieve popularity purely as a stage production. For a stage production must always make strong calls upon the emotionalism of the audience, whereas here the appeal is almost entirely to the intellect. . . . Coriolanus commands neither our love nor our pity. . . . We do not feel passionately about the vicissitudes of his life. His victories do not lead us to invest him with the glamour of a romantic hero" (*Stratford-upon-Avon Herald,* 30 April 1926).

From the thirties to the fifties the play's want of affect was a particular drawback. Audiences battered by a depression, the rise of fascism, World War II, and its aftermath demanded from their entertainment media not hard-nosed reality, but romantic escape. And the cinema, with its stalwart, swashbuckling young heroes in quest of love and glory, offered precisely what the age demanded.[1] To retain a place in the theatrical repertory, it was apparent, *Coriolanus* needed romantic cachet.

Competition with cinematic spectacle was out of the question. Biblical and Roman epics featuring lavishly costumed casts of thousands in actual and reconstructed locations of stunning authenticity had set visual standards the theater could not match. It was nevertheless possible to compete in a small way by creating significant pictorial moments, as it were in close-up, and, with the aid of skilled costume and lighting design, to color them effectively in a way film technology did not permit until the fifties.

Ultimately, however, the theater's trump card was not its decor, but the three-dimensional performer. The public's appetite for charismatic film stars in romantic stage roles was insatiable, and a generation of young leading actors, skilled in the techniques of both stage and screen, stood ready to meet the demand. Their presence gave new life to the shopworn classical repertory, brief fame to a number of bad original scripts, and a highly marketable romantic ambiance to a number of Shakespeare's dramas. The recalcitrant *Coriolanus* over a period of two decades was a periodic object of their attentions.

Only a year or so before the outbreak of war, Lewis Casson, firmly rejecting any hint of contemporary relevance, mounted *Coriolanus* with spectacular success at the Old Vic in a romantic style destined to shape revivals for two decades. Politics were yet again displaced, this time in favor of a fervid account of a virile war hero's quest for a political career, its frustration by self-seeking wardheelers and a malignant street mob, his disillusioned desertion to the enemy, surrender to the heartbroken entreaties of his mother, and subsequent assassination. The titular hero, as played by the rising stage and screen star Laurence Olivier,[2] was handsome, athletic, and abundantly charismatic, if hardly brawny. Settings, pioneered by Casson and elaborated by his successors, were not so much indications of place as spaces designed for the exhibition of the actor: arches and pillars against which to pose picturesquely, flights of steps up and down which to measure swords, and projections from which to hurl oneself. An elegantly colored wardrobe and carefully lighted groupings were de rigueur.

If the Casson-Olivier revival did not win the play permanent popularity, it at least inspired a bevy of fetching experiments as Alec Clunes (1939), John Clements (1948), Antony Quayle (1952), Robert Ryan (1954), and Richard Burton (1954), with varying degrees of success, tried to coax admiration and sympathy from audiences which denied the hero love. Olivier's return to the role at the Shakespeare Memorial Theatre in 1959, in a reading alternately scorching and glacial, definitively put the romantic interpretation beyond all competition and marked the end of an era.

OLD VIC (1938)

The *Coriolanus* which opened at the Old Vic 19 April 1938, with fascism rampant in Europe and the onset of war only a year away, was, like its immediate predecessors, miraculously uncontaminated by contemporary reference: a Jacobean text, it was made clear in preproduction interviews, was to be staged with respect for the theater conventions of its period. In keeping with his Elizabethan Methodist roots, Casson, a onetime associate and admirer of Poel and Granville-Barker, cut only "passages that by their obscurity or awkwardness would necessitate slowing up the pace of speaking in order to obtain clarity" (*Stage*, 7 April 1938). None of Shakespeare's named characters was absent: even Adrian and Nicanor made an overdue appearance.[3] In a bid for romantic allure, however, some of Martius's less

Sketch of Permanent Setting. Lewis Casson Production, Old Vic, 1938. (*The Sphere*, 7 May 1938). [By permission of the *Illustrated London News* Picture Library]

winning remarks were apparently suppressed: "All that mock modesty. . . . All that stuff about 'Don't praise me,' a sort of inverted Henry V. . . . I cut it all," Olivier told Peter Hall in 1959.[4]

In front of the proscenium Casson constructed a modest forestage backed by a permanent set, textured to suggest weathered stone (some said Stonehenge), in which a large curtained central arch framed action within itself or revealed vistas upstage. Lower arches to right and left functioned as entrances, and a flight of steps connected the architectural components with the apron. The somber decor admirably highlighted Bruce Winston's vivid Renaissance Classical costumes, while Casson's dress-circle lighting, rich in chiaroscuro effects, defined groupings, harmonized sets and wardrobe, and lent emotional tonality. Conspicuous among a series of brilliantly photographic compositions, was the "arresting picture . . . when Coriolanus, in amethyst, white and scarlet, stood with his gentle wife, Virgilia, in shimmering white satin, and Volumnia magnificent in floating draperies of purple" (*Birmingham Post*, 22 April 1938). Equally impressive were moments of "fine darkness . . . in which the red cloak of Coriolanus glow[ed] like a sullen fire" (*Sunday Times*, 24 April 1938). Without color technology, film at such moments found itself *hors de combat*.

For Casson, *Coriolanus*'s politics, which he limited to Shakespeare's allegedly unsympathetic portrait of the plebeians, was treated as an aesthetic issue, and summarily dismissed. "[M]ost people seem to feel that Shakespeare is unduly hard on the tribunes and the common people. . . . But, as Professor Bradley says, this is better for the play, and that probably is the main point the dramatist considered" (*Stage*, 7 April 1938). The citizens' profile was hardly ameliorated in Casson's production by reducing their numbers to eight, dressing them in rags, and using them as mere obstacles to Martius's success, ill-mannered butts of aristocratic abuse, and a source of low comedy—when they were allowed any visibility at all. The tribunes fared no better.

Without credible political tension, the play became, as in the Kean-Elliston revival, an extended exhibition of the protagonist in a variety of sensational situations. And whatever drawbacks attend upon that strategy, the role of Martius benefits markedly. Now with all the dramatis personae present and endowed with most of their lines, Casson was able to demonstrate that it was "the smaller parts . . . that render the motives of the main characters clearer" (*Stage*, 7 April 1938). When viewed from a multiplicity of perspectives, Martius's multifaceted, paradoxical identity emerged in sudden splendor. Desmond MacCarthy for one was bowled over by it: "As a character-drama, and that is what *Coriolanus* is," he concluded, "it is a magnificent play. Coriolanus himself is a masterpiece. He is not a sympathetic character, and hence the play's comparative unpopularity. We watch him with moments of exhilarating wonder, but without acute sympathy, stumbling blindly to his end" (*New Statesman and Nation*, 14 May 1938).

Olivier at thirty, fresh from the film romance *Fire Over England*, was a considerable box office "draw," even without the publicity attendant on his affair with Vivian Leigh. Despite a physique less stalwart than some of his contemporaries, punishing physical workouts, judicious use of padding, and painstaking makeup (Agate found his face "not so much made-up as buried beneath loam and plaster," *Sunday Times*, 24 April 1938) allowed him to communicate a powerful physicality.

On his first entrance, Martius's "mien was austere and Roman, having the right youth and wilfulness, and being rather more impetuous than imperious." "His gait," we are told, "had in it nothing but the highest sort of pride and dignity, so that the wading walk . . . assumed in retrospect . . . the motion of a man knee deep in blood" (*Manchester Guardian*, 20 April 1938). His patrician nobility, in both deportment and spirit, was total and disarmingly natural: his pride was consummate, his courage complete, his spontaneous affection for family and friends endearing. And from the outset, his "Horatian aversion to the profane rabble was a thing of ice" (*Manchester Guardian*, 20 April 1938). The epic Roman presence was animated, not by Kemble's stoic principle, but the whims of a "superb, overgrown child." In Bradley's notion of the boy/man, advanced a quarter-century earlier, Casson and Olivier managed to reconcile the role's contradictory facets and simultaneously tap a hitherto unsuspected vein of humor.

In an article written about this time, Casson described Martius as a victim of "arrested development," instancing "his reliance on and subservience to his mother, his almost schoolboy hatred of Aufidius, and the special fury at the taunt of 'boy of tears' which cost him his life."[5] Throughout the play, and at considerable risk, "the humour of his tantrums was brilliantly revealed, but without losing a jot of natural nobility and warlike courage."[6] In the Voices episode, for example, the note of "contemptuous amazement that *he,* Coriolanus, should be asked to demean himself or beg for votes ('Here come *more* voices')" (*New Statesman and Nation,* 14 May 1938) elicited a half-complicit audience laughter unknown to earlier revivals. One critic found, to his surprise, that he could "almost sympathise with this superb, overgrown child in his embarrassment at having to sire to men instead of blackguarding them" (*Evening Standard,* 20 April 1938).

Whatever his infantile weaknesses, Martius's heroic splendor was never for a moment in doubt. On the battlefield Olivier's love of breathtaking swordplay and athletic exhibitionism found full vent, and Martius's anger and physicality when confronting the people in 3.1 were of epic scale. In the Banishment scene (3.3), however, innate nobility and granite pride forbade any expression beyond a devastating quiet contempt, underscored, at the words "For you, the city," by "an inspired pause and a backward-gazing gesture which suddenly conjured a vista of the whole of attendant Rome."[7] His subsequent self-revelation in the house of Aufidius was described as "strangely powerful" (*Evening News,* 20 April 1938). In a verse-speaking performance unrivaled in living memory for its musicality, volume, rhythm, and lucidity, his final indictment of Aufidius exceeded all expectation: "Measureless liar, thou hast made my heart / Too great for what contains it," one spectator thought, evinced "a sheer superbity probably never surpassed in this theatre."[8] The assassination itself, no less romantically fraught, concluded with a crashing death-fall in which Martius "somersault[ed] down the staircase and roll[ed] over three times to end within a foot of the footlights."[9] "The whole theatre seemed to reel at it," recalled Audrey Williamson, "and the curtain fell amid the hush that precedes the most violent thunder of applause."[10]

Martius was, in Casson's revival, precisely what Volumnia made him; and at last, with two first-rate actors playing a relatively full text, the twisted mother-son relationship, pioneered by Poel, was given full value. Dame Sybil Thorndike's Volumnia, to the astonishment of playgoers, was neither an icy grande dame nor a warmongering harridan,[11] but a very human, even humorous, matron, whose very agreeableness made the exploitation of her son all the more terrifying. In the conversation with Virgilia and Valeria, Thorndike established "a cheerful relationship" (*Sunday Times,* 24 April 1938) with the audience, animating the character with "her own warmth of

Homecoming Scene. Lewis Casson Production, Old Vic, 1938. [Photograph by J. W. Debenham. By permission of the Theatre Museum, Victoria and Albert Museum]

heart and abundant vitality" (*Observer,* 24 April 1938). Rejecting the chilly regality of high Victorian Volumnias, Thorndike's matriarch was "a kind of war-time county lady bursting with maternal pride at her son's fighting prowess, and revealing all those somewhat ridiculous, fussy, conceited forms of delight in reflected glory that make the type so tiresome" (*Jewish Chronicle,* 29 April 1938). Nowhere was innovation so evident as in the traditional gloomy enumeration of Martius's wounds prior to his triumphal entry, where the wrangle with Menenius became "as merry a war as ever shook the Old Vic rafters."[12] With the return of the victorious Martius, however, maternal ambition lent her geniality a darker coloring. Agate bade his readers "mark this actress's face" as she welcomed her son (*Sunday Times,* 24 April 1938), and the character's subsequent assumption of full tragic dimension. Theatergoers watched with mixed horror and amusement as her marmoreal determination to have Martius temporize with the plebeians crushed his infantile resistance like the ripe mulberries of her image. The suppressed outrage of the recalcitrant man/child and the "flint-flashed snap of 'The word is *mildly*'" were to haunt J. C. Trewin for decades.[13] Her "agony of solicitude for her hero-son" in the Farewell episode Desmond MacCarthy found even more moving than her intercession (*New Statesman and Nation,* 14 May 1938).

Few playgoers, however, would have shared MacCarthy's preference. For in the Intercession sequence the remarkably sensitive subtext written during

earlier familial encounters proclaimed disaster with an almost Greek inevitability as the "tortured soul of the soldier" was excruciatingly racked by the
mother's "bowed and compassionate spirit" (*New Statesman,* 14 May 1938).
"The dignity and pathos and human sweetness of this black-robed Volumnia's last appeal to her son struck a symphonic key which hushed the
house," we are told (*Stage,* 21 April 1938); and in the silence, Martius's
"choking cry, 'O mother, mother! what have you done?'"[14] and the four blunt
words "But let it come," little noticed heretofore, "magnificently caught the
note of destiny."[15]

Seldom in the history of the play have its stars been better supported.
The Menenius of Cecil Trouncer, one of the finest character actors of the
period, was "a beautiful piece of oddity, warm and shrewd, testy and true
to life" (*Sunday Times,* 24 April 1938), while the "corroding sense of inferior-
ity"[16] with which William Devlin endowed his Aufidius gave that character
unusual credibility. The Sicinius of Stephen Murray and the Brutus of
George Skillan, if rather "too much alike in their lean malignity,"[17] were the
unredeemed villains the romantic reading demanded.

However purists might censure Casson's reductive approach, there was
no denying that he had accurately taken the pulse of his times. A witness
to the second night's performance records that at its conclusion "a very
large audience remained on its feet cheering for a good three minutes" (*John
O'London's Weekly,* 29 April 1938), and the play enjoyed more than thirty
further performances before the end of the season.

Shakespeare Memorial Theatre (1939)

Just a year later, in May of 1939, as Mussolini invaded Albania, Hitler
threatened Poland, the two fascist leaders signed their Pact of Steel, and
Britain introduced conscription, Ben Iden Payne, Bridges-Adams's successor as director of the Shakespeare Memorial Theatre, with a fine disdain
for real and present danger, mounted a serenely nostalgic Jacobean-dress
Coriolanus evocative of little more than "old unhappy far-off things and
battles long ago." In the title role was twenty-seven-year-old Alec Clunes,
a rising young stage star, destined for his first cinema experience (*Convoy*)
a year later. Handsome, well-built, talented, and, to the delight of the Governors, happy to work for the Stratford pittance, Clunes rehearsed in a brief
five weeks Petruchio, Richmond in *Richard III,* Iago, and Benedick, as well
as Coriolanus.

In a gesture uncharacteristic of a director respected for his Elizabethan
scholarship, Payne reduced the text by some eight hundred lines in all.[18]
Many of the cuts were internal, and designed, like Casson's, to remove
obscurities and syntax inimical to swift speech. Political reference was frequently abbreviated or removed. Much of the tribunes' insightful comment,

particularly Sicinius's prophetic assessment of Martius's future behavior—
"He cannot temp'rately transport. . . . / Lose those he hath won" (2.1.224–
26)—was cut in an apparent attempt to render their depravity complete.
Much of the reflection on Martius's character was also deemed expendable.
Payne's blue pencil fell most heavily, however, on the battle scenes: the
Roman-Volscian military clash (1.4) was substantially shortened; the conquest of Corioli (1.5) was entirely excised; the episode in which Martius is
renamed (1.6) was curtailed by sixty-seven lines; and Titus Lartius's instructions to the Lieutenant (1.7) disappeared altogether. In a curious return to
nineteenth-century practice, Payne concluded the Senate scene (2.2) with
"To Coriolanus come all joy and honour," as Macready and Irving had done,
and ended the Banishment episode on the traditional "There is a world
elsewhere." After a brief appearance in the Casson revival, Adrian and Nicanor again vanish. Quite inexplicably, twenty-six lines of Volumnia's intercession were removed; and the 2. Lord's cynically telling "His own impatience /
Takes from Aufidius a great part of blame. / Let's make the best of it"
(5.6.144–46) was cut. Two intervals were provided for, each preceded by a
strong curtain: one after the Senate scene and the other after the
banishment.

Not only was the text attenuated, but the plebeians were denied their
proper function. Surging up and down the steps at every opportunity, they
were more numerous and visible than in Casson's revival, but their raison
d'être remained spectacular rather than ideological. The tribunes were as
usual mere comically scurrilous foils to the romantic hero.

J. Gower Parks's Rome was identified by hefty columns in front of which
stairs descended to the orchestra pit, while behind the proscenium line a
second flight of steps climbed skyward in the Bridges-Adams manner. Corioli was defined by arches and a gate which, when opened, revealed distant
architectural pieces looming against the sky. An artfully lighted cyclorama,
visible throughout the play, lent atmosphere and spaciousness. The setting
for the intercession, "a tent of brightest blue and gold standing out brilliantly
against a sky of storm" (*Punch*, 12 July 1939), was a visual highlight. A
traverse curtain at roughly center stage facilitated the manipulation of scenic
units upstage of it, thus permitting virtually pauseless action.

Payne's most controversial tactic was his introduction of Elizabethan/
Jacobean dress with casual Roman touches: "conventional Roman costumes," he explained, "would be inaccurate, since the historical period of
'Coriolanus' was in the fifth century B.C."; moreover, "Shakespeare, like
all Elizabethans, regarded a play as a contemporary happening, with the
result that the feeling and tone of "Coriolanus" are essentially of the Renaissance and should be so expressed" (*The Times*, 8 May 1939). Payne's Roman
effects, limited to military gear, served only to confuse audiences by their
failure to differentiate Romans from Volscians. Quaintly pictorial rather than
dramatically telling, pancake velvet hats, ruffs, jerkins, and farthingales, it

was generally agreed, "blurr[ed] the hard pagan spirit of old Rome, and soften[ed] a play which, of all things, should be brassy" (*Birmingham Gazette*, 10 May 1939).

Alec Clunes, as Martius, glamourously virile and dashingly athletic, "rode the play as a Cossack might ride a horse" (*Birmingham Gazette*, 10 May 1939), "carr[ying] most of the show on a pair of very strong shoulders" (*Birmingham Evening Dispatch*, 10 May 1939). With only a week's rehearsal, subtlety was out of the question; nevertheless, he established satisfyingly "the pig-headed splendour" of Martius's military idealism and "put an exciting edge upon his love of glory and contempt for popular favour" (*The Times*, 10 May 1939), even if patrician grandeur of the Olivier stamp was in short supply. In the end, he discovered "sufficient dignity in adversity to support that 'noble memory' which the triumphant Aufidius conventionally stipulates for him" (*The Times*, 10 May 1939). Reviewers applauded the robust physicality of the character as he swept "through fight and forum without sparing limb or lung" (*Observer*, 14 May 1939), the "torrential surges of scornful declamation" (*Stage*, 11 May 1939), and his "handsome dashing impatience" (*Punch*, 12 July 1939); but overall he appeared "too much . . . a romantic juvenile lead" (*Birmingham Mail*, 10 May 1939), a warlord without iron in his soul. And the humor Olivier exploited so effectively was sorely missed.

Reviewers failed to remark the boyishness so crucial to Olivier's reading; and for this want Dorothy Green's lacklustre Volumnia must bear some responsibility. "[L]ess effective in a farthingale than she usually [was] in classical draperies" (*Daily Telegraph*, 10 May 1939), Green compounded the handicap by a grand and sonorous acting style. Her efforts to feminize the character in the Thorndike manner were "soft and honeyed" rather than "nobly tender" (*Stratford-upon-Avon Herald*, 12 May 1939), and the disconcerting gaiety of the Old Vic matron seems to have eluded her entirely.

Andrew Leigh's Menenius, "a dapper little man of the world" (*Daily Telegraph*, 10 May 1939) and "a jovial, pursy digger into the ribs of other men's follies and foibles" (*Birmingham Mail*, 10 May 1939), lacked paternal and political authority. John Laurie's Sicinius, "a gaunt, forbidding figure with frightening fingers and a positively terrifying reserve of private and professional hatred" (*Birmingham Mail*, 10 May 1939), was just what the romantic reading demanded, and Stanley Howlett's fawning Brutus proved an ideal second. Aufidius (James Dale), "a bluff, breezy soldier with sardonic undertones to his heartiness" (*Birmingham Mail*, 10 May 1939), received more notice than usual.

OLD VIC (1948)

Coriolanus did not again see the stage for almost a decade. In the intervening years, as the protagonist in an international struggle between fascism and democracy, the soldier-hero became an icon of contemporary culture; and in war's aftermath, the reintegration of the veteran into peacetime society proved a major preoccupation. The reabsorption of wartime leaders posed particular challenges, and Churchill, de Gaulle, Eisenhower, and MacArthur at one time or another all tested the public patience.

Against this background the Old Vic, at the New Theatre while wartime damage to the Waterloo Road house was repaired, revived the play in the spring of 1948 under the direction of Martin Browne, with John Clements and Rosalind Atkinson in the key roles.

Coriolanus's contemporary aptness could hardly have been more striking. "It is impossible," wrote one critic, ". . . to avoid the suggestion of certain parallels with these times. A postwar mob is short of food, oblivious of the plight of its late defeated enemies and easily roused by a few agitators into active hostility to the one man who has saved the nation from foreign servitude" (*Truth,* 9 April 1948). Beverly Baxter, in a review in the *Evening Standard* (2 April 1948), drew an implicit parallel between Coriolanus and Churchill, only to be roundly chastised by indignant readers.

Whatever contemporaneity the production itself evinced was largely in the eye of the beholder: Browne, like his immediate predecessors, was bent on a romantic romp. And that implied a judiciously pruned text.[19] The battlefield scenes were shortened to maximize swordplay and minimize the hero's uncongeniality; much of the political material was excised; and a good deal of the character analysis of Martius by friend and foe disappeared. Volumnia's exchange with the tribunes was also eliminated, together with the Adrian-Nicanor sequence.

For the first time in decades, the action took place entirely within the proscenium where, in Stella Mary Pearce's design, two massive pillars suggested a close-up shot from a cinema epic. Costumes, created by Kathleen Ankers, were safely Renaissance Classical in cut. In keeping with Browne's apolitical interpretation, crowds were small, dwarfed by the pillars round which they were compelled to maneuver, and played merely for comedy. This "circle of gaping village idiots, [a] bedraggled band of Zanies. . . . could have broken no one," complained T. C. Worsley. "The crowd in *Coriolanus,* like any other crowd, contains its fools," he reminded the director, "but they are human people, with starving women and children in their homes, and a collective strength sufficient to unseat a potential tyrant" (*New Statesman and Nation,* 10 April 1948). But for Browne, as for Casson and Iden Payne, politics were an unwelcome distraction in a romantic character study.

John Clements, at thirty-seven an established stage star with a clutch of romantic film roles to his credit, possessed a better natural physique than Olivier's, and Browne posed it becomingly against the stage architecture in season and out. On his first entrance, Harold Hobson reported, "[h]e slid unobtrusively from behind one of the tall pillars . . . and greeted us all with a happy smile. He stood for a moment, curled and handsome, undeniably a most agreeable sight" (*Sunday Times,* 4 April 1948).

Extensive experience as a romantic leading man ill prepared him to suggest patrician grandeur and roughhewn integrity. "[G]ood stage presence, poise, dignity, and clear enunciation" were simply not enough; he was, in the words of one reviewer, "far too 'gentlemanly'" (*Christian Science Monitor,* Boston, 24 April 1948) when titanic abandon was demanded. His "rueful assumption of the 'garment of humility,'" Philip Hope-Wallace felt, was handled "with ease and charm" (*Manchester Guardian,* 2 April 1948), as was the almost silent meeting with Virgilia on his triumphal return; and his speaking of "I banish you" at "a slow, level, and measured pace as though it soiled his tongue" (*Sunday Times,* 4 April 1948) was a triumph. But Martius's epic surrender in the Intercession scene and cosmic defiance in the assassination episode lay well beyond the actor's reach, and the play's tragic dimension was irrevocably compromised as a result. "One is sorry to see [Martius] come to grief," concluded W. A. Darlington, "but one's deeper feelings are hardly engaged" (*Daily Telegraph,* 1 April 1948).

Rosalind Atkinson's fragile Volumnia, more gracious than grand, caught something of Thorndike's geniality but missed her tragic power; and without that, the rich complexity of the mother-son relationship and its profoundly moving denouement went for very little. Perplexed by what he regarded as excessive good nature on the part of the matron, Harold Hobson confessed himself unable to "believe the ancient Romans to have been so gay a people" (*Sunday Times,* 4 April 1948).

The undisputed star of the production was Alec Guinness's Menenius, a figure "rich in wisdom, heart and dignity" (*News Chronicle,* 1 April 1948) in which "the physical appearance of old age, the devotion of a hero worshipper and the cleverness of a compromising . . . politician" were intricately blended. This Menenius, as much a product of subtext as text, clearly had "a full life before, and outside, the events of the play, a mind rich and stocked but cynical and opportunist, a man who has learnt from a wide experience only not to expect too much from life and people" (*Manchester Guardian,* 2 April 1948). For Philip Hope-Wallace Menenius's rejection offered "the one really moving moment of the evening" (*Manchester Guardian,* 2 April 1948). Guinness's performance was to remain the benchmark interpretation of the role for decades thereafter.

The tribunes of Mark Dignam (Sicinius) and Peter Copley (Brutus), described as "hovering over the Senate House like a pair of baleful crows" (*Birmingham Post,* 1 April 1948), were the usual malignant caricatures. Gordon Crosse found Brutus's "giving the time to the crowd for their shouts of 'It-shall-be-so'" a neat touch, as was "his clinging in terror to Sicinius while bearing the marks of his rough handling by the mob."[20] The Aufidius of Harry Andrews proved a potent "mixture of chivalry and baseness."[21]

SHAKESPEARE MEMORIAL THEATRE (1952)

Four years later, on 13 March 1952, Glen Byam Shaw directed the Shake-speare Memorial Theatre's hefty artistic director Anthony Quayle in a hand-some production which owed more to the current vogue for military romance than to the tragic muse. Text, mise-en-scène, and the treatment of the citi-zens and tribunes all were neatly manipulated to focus attention on a vet-eran's frustrated aspirations, his act of national betrayal, and his destruction at the hands of an overpowering parent. Quayle's wartime experience as a major in the Royal Artillery lent the role a unique authenticity.

Byam Shaw slashed the play by approximately a thousand lines, mostly through internal cuts. The battle scenes, in keeping with his production thrust, were reduced less than in Payne's revival, although the sequence in which the soldiers enter bearing spoils (1.5) was excised in its entirety, together with Titus Lartius's injunction to the Lieutenant to guard the ports (1.7). Martius's pep rally at Cominius's camp (1.6) was curtailed by some thirty-seven lines. Other major cuts included the entire Senate scene (2.2), an episode played at least in part by the most wanton actor-managers, Mar-tius's political polemic in 3.1, and the Adrian and Nicanor episode (4.3).

The decor by Motley, combining visual variety with flexibility, featured a newly created forestage which brought the action closer to the audience than usual, while an ingenious complex of steps and arches facilitated innovative blocking. The basic Roman setting became Corioli when "a gate [rose] in the background and sharp spikes [were] thrust out from the scene."[22] Strate-gically placed fabrics and screens suggested interiors, and tents flown in front of the Roman locale established the Volscian camp. During the inter-cession, which took place at night, "stars twinkled from behind the tents giving the impression of tremendous depth" (*Western Daily Press*, Bristol, 17 March 1952). Colorful costumes, of no particular period but indicative of barbaric splendor, lent pictorial interest without preempting attention.

Byam Shaw's battles carried more conviction than usual thanks to Quayle's military expertise and intensive drilling of the soldiery as the care-fully marked promptbook attests.[23] Sequences featuring the citizens, as in previous romantic productions, fared less well: a handful in all, the plebeians were little more than "semi-comic malcontents" bent on frustrating the am-bitions of their erstwhile savior. The impotence of Martius's opponents was hardly mitigated by tribunes described as "creatures of straw": one "a fat Egyptian-looking fellow with an impediment in his speech: the other an old thin greybeard who squeak[ed] like a castrate." "How two such incompe-tents succeeded in rousing and directing a mob to the pitch of throwing out and banishing the great general-hero, it is impossible to imagine," asserted one reviewer. "It happens, but somehow in spite of them. A noble, brave, soldierly, virile Coriolanus seems to be winning easy round after easy round

over these two impotents when suddenly you find he's got himself banished"
(*New Statesman,* 22 March 1952).

Quayle at thirty-eight, like Olivier, Clunes, and Clements a virile and
athletic romantic lead, specialized in characters with roughcast charm. His
Martius had as little patrician ice about him as those of Clunes and Clements; instead, audiences were confronted by the "tough soldier" of postwar
stage and cinema "with a parade ground rasp in his voice, wearing his
wounds aggressively as badges of rank." Behind the toughness, in the Olivier
manner, he allowed "something attractively boyish to peep through at times"
(*The Times,* 14 March 1952). His scorn of the mob, it was evident, owed
less to patrician temperament than military prejudice; and without Martius's
splendid if wrong-headed commitment to the patrician ideal, "the greatness
of the man," and hence his tragedy, "[was] never very compelling" (*The
Times,* 14 March 1952).

What Quayle did, however, he did superbly; the "obstinate aristocrat who
recognised only one obligation to his country, and that to place his efficient
sword at her service" (*Birmingham Post* 14 March 1952), a signal feature of
the character, has seldom been better realized. His brawny physicality rendered his demonstrations of soldiership, although wonderfully effective, almost redundant. Nor in verbal confrontations did he carry less conviction:
exasperated by civilian insurgency in 3.1, for example, "[h]is body tremble[d] with suppressed disdain: his voice thicken[ed] with provoked gorge"
(*Manchester Daily Dispatch,* 14 March 1952). His "vilification of the mob
that had banished him, and his seeking out and meeting with his old enemy
in Antium" were described as "gripping in their power" (*Birmingham Mail,*
14 March 1952). But while he caught with rare skill "the tenacity of the
idealist," "the honesty of the fanatic" (*Birmingham Post,* 14 March 1952),
whatever power he evinced was born "of sheer force rather than of natural
nobility" (*Birmingham Mail,* 14 March 1952). Without patrician grandeur,
Quayle's Roman bespoke sordid realism rather than high tragedy and consequently alienated audience sympathy. "We have suffered too deeply from
egomaniacs to regard them with admiration," observed W. A. Darlington
(*Daily Telegraph,* 14 March 1952).

Mary Ellis, the revival's Volumnia,[24] an American actor best known as a
star in Ivor Novello's musicals, was unable to summon the indomitable
authority and emotional sweep the role demands. Too young for the part,
and unconvincingly made-up, Ellis's matron revealed only "beautiful dignity
and a warm-hearted maternity" (*Stage,* 20 March 1952). As a result, the
mother-son relationship evinced neither texture nor conviction. The intercession, was, in Philip Hope-Wallace's view, "never tragic, at the best only
touching" (*Manchester Guardian,* 5 March 1952).

The "fine donnish humour" (*The Times,* 14 March 1952) of Michael
Hordern's Menenius came close to rivaling Guinness's reading. In a nicely
balanced portrait, "he wore the tolerance as well as the impatience of the

ageing patrician" (*Birmingham Mail,* 14 March 1952); for Alex Guinness's ascerbic wit, he substituted "a satirical suavity and a philosophic sweetness of a most engaging kind" (*Observer,* 16 March 1952).

Laurence Harvey's red-haired Aufidius, in appearance "like one of the subtler and crueller emperors" (*News Chronicle,* 14 March 1952), carried "an exotic and feline menace" (*Spectator,* 21 March 1952) that satisfyingly counterpointed Martius's earthy bluntness. On one of the few occasions when a first-rate performer has played Virgilia, the brilliant Siobhan McKenna found little more in the role than fragile sweetness.

The relative failure of the Byam Shaw/Quayle revival did nothing to deter further romantic essays, however: for John Houseman and Robert Ryan and Michael Benthall and Richard Burton, the Olivier/Casson torch continued to burn bright.

PHOENIX THEATER, NEW YORK (1954)

Houseman, partner of Orson Welles in the Mercury Theater venture in the late thirties and more recently a Hollywood producer, when invited to direct at New York's Phoenix theater a major production of a new or classic play unlikely for one reason or another to get an airing on Broadway, chose *Coriolanus* on the grounds of its timeliness: "DeGaulle and Churchill (and to a lesser degree Eisenhower) had raised the question of the wartime hero as political leader," he wrote; "elsewhere in the world men were testing the perennial alternatives of government by the people or by the elite."[25] As he prepared *Coriolanus*'s production text, he found himself, unlike Stratford and Old Vic directors, "emphasizing its political aspects and minimizing the military manoeuvers."[26]

For virtually the first time in the play's stage history, a director was not only prepared to do justice to the play's political character, but to be as ideologically evenhanded as Shakespeare himself. "I was determined," Houseman recalls, "(and it was the principal virtue of my production) that I would not take sides—that I would give both parties equal time and the same opportunity to state their case." With considerable astuteness, he saw that an unslanted representation of the play's politics is inseparable from the treatment of the tribunes. "In the way in which those two were interpreted," he argued, "lay the key to the play."

In most productions they are treated mainly as trouble-makers—inciters and manipulators of an unthinking, greasy, dangerous mob. . . . I wanted the Tribunes to be credible as duly elected representatives, speaking with the eloquence of union organizers or Labor Party M.P.'s.

To ensure as sympathetic a reading as possible, he opted "to cast [the] Tribunes from the ranks of the Left—with actors who held radical convictions of their own."[27]

It went without saying that the citizens must also be presented "in a convincing and exciting manner"; not only were they cast and costumed with care, but their visibility was higher than in recent British productions. Throughout much of the first half of the play they were stationed on "a long, wide ledge three feet below the level of the stage [i.e., in the orchestra pit]," a tactic which allowed Houseman "to keep the crowd in view, in dim silhouette" as a compelling presence "without interfering with the visibility of the principal characters." When required to participate more actively, they were neatly positioned to "surge forward in a menacing wave onto the stage." Houseman's blocking also permitted "the Tribunes to make their speeches directly to the crowd in the pit at the same time as they were addressing the theatre audience."[28]

Reversing Byam Shaw's strategy, Houseman removed most of the military scenes, save for the fight between Martius and Aufidius, but left the political matter largely untouched. Other passages excised included Martius's plea for the release of his Volscian host (1.9.79–90), the assessment of Martius by the cushion-layers (2.2.1–36), the Farewell episode (4.1), Volumnia's indictment of the tribunes (4.2), and the Adrian and Nicanor colloquy (4.3).[29]

The setting, designed by Donald Oenslager, was "a handsome but simple two-story structure [at stage level] with wide symmetrical steps rising on both sides to a large platform some ten feet high, over an archway or tunnel running the full depth of the stage."[30]

The principal challenge was to find a satisfactory Coriolanus, and Houseman finally settled on Robert Ryan, veteran of some thirty romantic film roles. A physically more impressive Roman than Ryan, an ex-Marine and onetime truckdriver, six feet four inches in height "with a heavyweight boxer's body,"[31] could hardly be imagined. Unfortunately, however, his voice was weak and his verse speaking technique nonexistent. As Volumnia Houseman cast the film comedienne Mildred Natwick, another performer with little classical experience. The want of technical expertise in the leading roles fatally compromised one of the most interesting production concepts of the century.

Houseman's high-profile crowd and sympathetic tribunes counterbalanced by a Herculean Martius allowed at least a simplistic version of the play's politics, the conflict between the will of the people and a would-be overlord, to declare itself. The more fundamental Shakespearian struggle between patrician paternalism and proletarian aspiration was largely vitiated by the inability of Ryan and Natwick to simulate nobility, to say nothing of spiritual grandeur. As a result tragedy dwindled into political romance.

In the play's first scene, Ryan's failure to suggest patrician elitism led to a fatal misrepresentation of Martius as "an attractive, well-bred son of the upper classes who despises the people . . . out of intellectual sluggishness" (*New York Times,* 24 January 1954), an error which scuttled the entire project. The Voices scene, in which Houseman maintained the focus as much on the plebeians as their petitioner, worked better: "A row of heads rises silently over the footlights to listen to Coriolanus' grudging appeal for the people's votes," noted Kerr, "and there is steady menace in the image" (*New York Herald Tribune,* 20 January 1954). Martius's contretemps with the citizens in 3.1, although played with fiery intensity, proved more noisy than caustic.

Despite the production's political thrust, it was Ryan's more romantic moments which caught reviewers' attention. His fight with Aufidius, choreographed by a Judo expert and featuring "hair-raising acrobatics,"[32] was a predictable hit. Martius's arrival in Antium, usually not much noticed, also proved to be a performance highlight, a happy consequence of Ryan's bulk, the passive and subdued nature of the speeches, and the eloquent ambience. Staged as "a chill night sequence," "[t]he aristocrat's grotesque reception at the hands of some bumptious servants ha[d] an aching edge of mockery to it," Kerr reported; "the lighting, movement, and hollow offstage gaiety combine[d] to foreshadow this hero's grim ending" (*New York Herald Tribune,* 20 January 1954). His juvenile gaucheness with his mother, his "gangling, inarticulate, and . . . boyish charm with his wife. . . . not wholly unlike that of a cowboy hero in the moving pictures" (*New Yorker,* 30 January 1954) touched but failed to shake the emotions. The assassination was virtually ignored by reviewers.

Natwick, a seasoned character actor, was effective enough in the quieter domestic passages: "As she suggest[ed] to Coriolanus that 'honor and policy' may somehow be joined, [and] as she chat[ted] hopefully with his wife about the great man he is to become," Walter Kerr discovered in her reading "a luminous lyrical quality" (*New York Herald Tribune,* 20 January 1954), although the *Cue* reviewer thought her aristocracy smacked more of Victorian England than "the barbaric nobility of the earthy Volumnia" (30 January 1954). Even the most sympathetic critics were compelled to admit that the intercession was a disaster, an assessment in which Houseman frankly concurred: "No matter how hard we tried to make the scene work in human, dramatic terms, mother and son ended up in a formal debate—not a scene of personal emotion."[33]

The play's supporting roles were in many cases better played than the "leads." The tribunes (Brutus-John Randolph; Sicinius-Will Geer) offered a welcome relief from their clownish British counterparts, particularly Geer's Sicinius, "rugged and unyielding and with a sort of dignity which it was surprising to find the part admitted."[34] It was a particular irony that on the well-nigh unique occasion that tribunes of quality appeared, they lacked a Martius worthy of their opposition. John Emery's Aufidius, "a dark, menacing, and formidable antagonist whose growing jealousy of his unexpected ally [was] readily understandable" (*Christian Science Monitor,* Boston, 23 January 1954), lent rare clarity to the often murky relationship. His servants also received unwonted attention. Menenius, played by Alan Napier with "benevolent distinction and with some of the comic quality of the part" (*Christian Science Monitor,* Boston, 23 January 1954), fell short of the creations of Guinness and Hordern.

Whatever the faults of Houseman's revival, want of interest was not one of them. While critics agreed that the actors failed to scale the technical and spiritual heights of tragedy, they nevertheless applauded the production as swashbuckling political romance, what Brooks Atkinson called "a merchantable piece of drama that deals in the vendable goods of tensions, crises and disasters" (*New York Times,* 24 January 1954). It enjoyed a respectable run of fifty performances, but ultimately failed to convince either critics or audiences that America had suffered any serious artistic loss by its absence (except for the 1937 FTP production) from the country's stages since the late nineteenth century.

OLD VIC (1954)

On 23 February 1954, as Ryan's Martius received his quietus for the last time in New York, the Old Vic, back home in Waterloo Road, launched its third romantic *Coriolanus,* now directed by Michael Benthall and starring yet another screen idol, Richard Burton, still aglow with his cinematic triumph in *The Robe* (1953). Benthall's production, clearly indebted to the revived cinema epic, subordinated politics to personality, sacrificed verbal subtlety to picturesque action, and showcased the charismatic Burton in all his sulky sexuality at every opportunity.

Like most directors in the romantic tradition, Benthall made considerable adjustments to the battlefield sequences, removing about one-third of the scene before the walls of Corioli (1.4), half of the scene in which the Roman soldiers enter with spoils (1.5), all of the inspirational militarism of the episode in Cominius's camp (1.6), and Titus Lartius's instructions regarding the security of the ports (1.7). What remained was played as a fast-moving action sequence in which Martius, in a series of mimed military encounters, fended off all comers. The Senate scene (2.2), curtailed by some 140 lines, opened with Menenius's "The Senate, Coriolanus, are well pleas'd / To make thee consul" (2.2.132–33) and concluded twenty-two lines later with the senators' "To Coriolanus come all joy and honor!" (2.2.154). The Adrian-Nicanor sequence (4.3) was once more excised, as was the entire conversation between Tullus and the conspirators (5.6.1–69), presumably to restore Martius to center stage with minimum delay, even though subsequent events were as a result ill-prepared for. The Coriolian lords were eliminated from the Assassination scene, and the script modified accordingly. In perhaps the most striking cut of all, Benthall concluded the play with Martius's execution, a feature to which we shall return. In all Benthall shortened the text by more than 700 lines.[35]

Since the play's political character was again suppressed, the citizens' role was predictably attenuated and their image besmirched. Mitigatory lines such as the 1 Cit.'s "the gods know I speak this in hunger for bread, not in thirst for revenge" (1.1.24–25) and Menenius's "For they have pardons, being ask'd, as free / As words to little purpose" (3.2.88–89) were removed, along with their self-deprecatory jocularity in 2.2. In the now conventional manner, the crowd was made a grubby, even comic, foil to the hero. "The Roman mob is presented through Coriolanus's eyes," complained Richard Findlater, "as stinking curs or filthy rabble, fit only for his revengeful sword; its spokesman . . . as a sinister murderer" (*Tribune,* 19 March 1954). To add insult to injury, in a gratuitous appearance in the Farewell scene, according to the promptbook, the citizens "yelling [,] throwing abuse[,] follow [Martius] off" as he goes into exile.

The tribunes were once more shorn of much of their leadership potential. A particular loss was their prescient analysis of Martius's character (2.1.224–31) and the thirty-line strategy session at the opening of 3.3. The fact that they were played as "a pair of nervous teetering old gentlemen" (*Birmingham Post,* 24 February 1954) did little to heighten their impact.

With his corn speech heavily curtailed (3.1.141–61), and some of his more vicious pronouncements on the underclass excised, Martius emerged as a proud young veteran who, when his political ambitions are frustrated by an ungrateful public, defects to the enemy, then capitulates altruistically to his mother's petition, and finally suffers martyrdom at the hands of an outraged military.

The action unfolded on a permanent set intended to accommodate, with variations by individual designers, the entire season's repertory. Three Palladian arches two feet behind the proscenium backed a seventeen-foot multilevel apron over part of the orchestra pit from which stairs led downward. Proscenium doors to right and left kept the action well forward. Audrey Cruddas's *Coriolanus* decor identified Rome by a great golden eagle on a plinth upstage of the central opening; and for scenes in Corioli or Antium, a green Volscian standard was dropped in front. Huge doors placed within the central arch indicated the gates of Corioli and Antium, while interiors were evoked by a painted drop curtain and a heavy chair. Roman costumes, of Renaissance Classical cut, created a rich palette of hot reds, gold, and purple, dominated throughout by a great red cloak worn by Martius. The Volscians appeared in smoky blue-green uniforms.[36] Drawing upon his consummate command of lighting technique, Benthall contrived one visual coup after another, "fading and even dissolving scenes as if in a film."[37]

Although a wonderfully handsome and magnetic figure, Burton, like so many of his predecessors, found patrician grandeur beyond him; and it was only by comparison with the ill-dressed and unmitigatedly vulgar citizenry that he achieved measurable superiority. In the play's opening scene a want of aristocratic authority led him to "rail at the mob like a thoroughly embittered corporal whose chances of promotion were nil" (*Manchester Guardian,* 25 February 1954), but lack of "effortless, genial superiority of manner" (*Manchester Guardian,* 25 February 1954) was to some degree redeemed by mesmeric physicality as he strode in splendor throughout the early episodes, "all sinews tightened, the insolence burning like a hot iron through leather" (*Financial Times,* 24 February 1954). At the seige of Corioli, "with a sword in his hand, the scowl of battle on his face" (*Stage,* 25 February 1954), his performance could hardly be bettered.

In the postwar passages, however, he made the mistake of romanticizing Shakespeare's chilling war machine into a "lonely, neurotic soldier" (*Tribune,* 19 March 1954), "a doomed man, isolated in his own conceit, who carried his tragedy with him" (*Theatre World,* April 1954); and Martius's epic stature was in consequence diminished. Even his withering "There is a world elsewhere" seemed to Philip Hope-Wallace "far too Byronic, far too little an arrow of disdain" (*Manchester Guardian,* 25 February 1954). He was altogether too much the boy of tears, too little the man of ice.

Burton's strengths stood transparently revealed in the play's quieter moments: his "quick and gentle recognition of Valeria as the 'moon of Rome'" (*Illustrated London News,* 6 March 1954), his "I banish you," "murmur[ed] with quiet power" (*Liverpool Daily Post,* 24 February 1954), and the unmuffling before Aufidius at Antium.

The intercession was by all accounts masterly. Here he evinced "a brooding, sulky, Celtic magnetism which was highly effective" (*Manchester Guardian,* 25 February 1954). At the outset of the encounter when Virgilia (Claire Bloom) addressed him as "My lord and husband," reported Beverly Baxter, "he moved us all to emotion with his whispered answer: 'These eyes are not the same I wore in Rome.'" A moment later as familial tenderness threatened to gain the upper hand, "there was an infinite weariness in his voice as he muttered: 'Like a dull actor now, I have forgot my part'" (*Sunday Express,* 28 February 1954). Throughout Volumnia's harangue, he stood, immovable and implacable, with his back to the audience, creating an almost intolerable tension. Just as Volumnia, and the audience, were prepared to accept her failure, he "put out a gentle hand to find his mother's," we are told. "Then he [spoke], his powerful, resonant voice cracking, like an ice-floe breaking up: 'O, mother, mother! What have you done?'" (*Truth,* 5 March 1954). This, and similar scenes of suppressed emotion, successful as they were as discrete units, might have had greater cumulative effect had Burton been able in earlier scenes to capture Martius's epic pride and super-human will.

The highlight of the Old Vic revival, unlike Houseman's production, was the Assassination episode which tipped the scales as definitively in Martius's favor as Benthall's depreciation of the citizens and tribunes. The final quarrel took place before the great gates of Corioli. When Martius roared "O that I had him / . . . To use my lawful sword!", he flung Aufidius from him and, clad in his massive scarlet cloak, stood "with arms outstretched in front of the dark city doors . . . and, in the attitude of a priest celebrating some tremendous ritual, [was] stabbed to death by his envious enemies. After the collapse of Coriolanus," Harold Hobson recalled,

> not a word is spoken. . . . Instead the murderers, appalled, not at the wickedness but at the temerity of their crime, peer at the prostrate body, and then, seized with terror of their old conqueror, slink and run and flee into the darkness, tripping over each other in panic fear, vanishing in abject alarm into the bowels of the Old Vic stage (*Sunday Times*, 28 February 1954).

Their departure was accompanied by "drum-taps whose decreasing intensity," W. A. Darlington thought, "symbolised the fading triumph of the murderers—their knowledge that the man they have killed is, for all his besetting pride, a better man than any of themselves" (*Daily Telegraph*, 24 February 1954). The play's final image was "the stiff figure of Coriolanus . . . spread-eagled on the stage, a single shaft of light catching his scarlet cloak."[38]

Fay Compton's Volumnia was better than some of her recent predecessors, but she, like her son, wanted patrician conviction. She nevertheless looked superb "with her hair greyed in ringlets, her nose like a bridge, her eyes like sleeping adders and her mouth a crooked gape of defiance" (*Daily Herald*, 24 February 1954), and spoke the verse well, if somewhat too emphatically. Her matron, flamboyant and intense, was "no sombre thoughtful figure of tragedy and pride," reported W. Macqueen Pope, but "a woman who knows no half measures. . . . so wrapped in her ideals that she spares nobody." "One sees her very fingers clutching at the mere thought of her opponents" (*Morning Telegraph*, New York, 9 March 1954). On her first entrance, in a chilling directorial invention, she was engaged in fashioning a laurel wreath which she indulgently tried on Young Martius who came downstage "fighting" to meet her. Her finest moment, however, came with the intercession where, according to Beverly Baxter, "She showed a mother's pride in having a son who was a mighty conqueror, and she showed a mother's contempt for a son whose outraged vanity could only be appeased with the blood of his fellow-countrymen." Her reading, virtually free of maternal manipulation, relied on the creation of a portrait so merciless and accurate "that at last Coriolanus sees himself as the figure of contempt which he has become" (*Sunday Express*, 28 February 1954). She quitted the stage morally victorious; but just before her exit, in an inspired actorial gesture, maternal anxiety led her to cast a "doubting glance back at Aufidius and his lieutenant" (*John O'London's Weekly*, 12 March 1954). Her final

Assassination Scene (Coriolanus-Richard Burton). Michael Benthall Production, Old Vic, 1954. Angus McBean Photograph. [By permission of the University of Bristol Theatre Collection]

appearance, the civic welcome to Rome so often cut, saw the three women and the boy "heavily and darkly cloaked, walk past the clamant crowds, silent, sad-faced, casting a mauve shadow on optimism" (*Truth,* 5 March 1954).

Little need be said of the other roles. William Squires's Menenius, dignified enough but wanting wit, was unfavorably compared with the portrayals of Guinness and Hordern. Aufidius (Paul Daneman), described by one critic as "a stubborn and shrilling general of the Volsces" (*Birmingham Post,* 24 February 1954), was no more than adequate.

The fact that the play proclaimed itself romantic melodrama rather than tragedy was hardly noticed at the box office. Thanks to picturesque staging and Burton's charisma, Benthall's revival enjoyed a well-attended run of twenty-four performances.

SHAKESPEARE MEMORIAL THEATRE (1959)

Apart from an unremarkable production at the Birmingham Repertory Theatre in 1956, the play languished until 1959 when, to celebrate its one-hundredth season, the Shakespeare Memorial Theatre featured a galaxy of stage and screen luminaries in a series of gala revivals. Laurence Olivier was invited to revisit *Coriolanus* after an absence of two decades, directed by twenty-eight-year-old Peter Hall and partnered by Edith Evans.[39] The romantic production mode, with its suppressed politics, swashbuckling action, cinematic images, and muscular protagonist, pioneered in 1938, was again, and for the last time, regnant.

Hall's text was shortened by some eight hundred lines, mostly through internal cuts.[40] The only scenes eliminated in their entirety were the Adrian and Nicanor sequence (4.3) and the Senate scene (2.2), excisions made by Byam Shaw in 1952. Martius's "sort of inverted Henry V" speeches, omitted by Olivier in 1938, were now restored at Hall's insistence.[41] An interval was placed after Volumnia's encounter with the tribunes. Total playing time was two and a half hours.

Boris Aronson's set, a permanent multileveled complex of steps, platforms, upstage doors, and primitive columns, featured a central, twelve-foot stage-level projection, likened to the Tarpeian rock by some critics, which opened to reveal interiors. Textured in bronze and red, thrust against the proscenium line, and lapped in shifting shadows, the massive structure evoked an archaic, vaguely pre-Incan, savagery.[42] Although horizontally cramped, the set's vertical potential permitted issues of status to be visually stressed, and Martius to enjoy myriad coigns of vantage from which to see and be seen. The expansive crowd movement characteristic of earlier productions was, for better or worse, impracticable. Riette Sturge Moore's Renaissance Classical gear for Romans and barbarian furs for Volscians were uninspired.

The play's political content, as usual, counted for very little. The crowd, a dozen semi-comic provincial toilers led by an outrageously opinionated Albert Finney, lacked political credibility. Making good in noise what they lacked in movement, they served sometimes as an intensifier of excitement, sometimes as comic relief, and invariably as "straight men" for Martius's grandstanding. Shakespeare's tribunes were parodied by Peter Woodthorpe (Brutus) and Robert Hardy (Sicinius) as "a couple of shifty, thrifty local aldermen who run the local Tammany Hall for the swift advantage and short-term profit" (*Spectator,* 17 July 1959). Neither the people nor their leaders posed any real threat to Martius, whose patrician scorn, military glamour, disarming childishness, and grotesque demise left them as short of sympathy as corn.

What captivated audiences, as in the 1938 revival and its romantic successors, was the three-dimensional presence of a star; and here Olivier, hotfoot from the role of Marcus Crassus in the cinema epic *Spartacus,* did not disappoint. Now fifty-two, he was brawnier than twenty years earlier; his good looks and athletic flair remained unimpaired; and his art and craft had matured. Nothing fundamental to the 1938 reading was altered: the portrait was simply better focused, more richly textured, and more subtly colored. "We found what we thought were a few more secrets about the part," Olivier told an interviewer, "and it was chiefly these that we worked on—the business of his not being able to accept praise although his great fault was pride."[43] On the whole, however, Olivier did not consider Martius a first-rate challenge. "Coriolanus doesn't require very great cerebral heights in the artist performing him," he maintained.

> He's a very straightforward, reactionary son of a so-and-so, and it's quite easy to get on to him as his thoughts are not deep. You've just got to appreciate what he is and make quite sure that he is a patrician first and foremost. . . .[44]

It was precisely in the recognition and incarnation of Martius's heroic patricianism that the greatness of both Olivier's initial and latest performance lay. Like Kemble, he understood that the driving force behind the character is class pride, that Martius's sensibility must be epic in scale, and the action it motivates of a magnitude sufficient to defy the standards applied to the products of mundane realism.

Olivier's Martius, physically magnificent and vocally splendid, was as implacably "absolute" as his mother alleged; his pride, his obstinacy, his courage, were all of Homeric dimension. Again, as in the 1938 revival, the actor discovered comedy in the role, and used it to vitiate what might otherwise seem repulsive boorishness. Here "a hothead who cannot suffer fools gladly," and there "a colossally conceited young devil who is aware of his impudence all the time" (*Plays and Players,* September, 1959), he effortlessly seduced playergoers into a half-guilty admiration of one they could not love. And once in possession of some degree of audience sympathy, he held them captive through the devastating narrative of "a man whose pride and wilful judgment slowly obscures from him the truth that his narrow conception of honour has brought him to think of his country's good only as the ladder of his own reputation" (*The Times,* 8 July 1959), in short, the tragedy of an egoist.

His first appearance, atop the rocky promontory at stage center, the first of three key scenes played in this locale, revealed him as nothing short of physically magnificent. He made no entrance; "There like the apparition of an eagle, he suddenly was,"[45] "with a sardonic smile constantly playing round his lips" (*Evening Standard,* 8 July 1959). "His preliminary scorn of the plebeians," recalls Laurence Kitchin, he "flicked casually, like a man so much in the habit of it that no effort is required. 'Go, get you home,' it ended, 'you . . .', and Olivier paused, searching for a fresh term of abuse, before he came out with 'fragments'"[46] At the mention of Aufidius, impatience with his inferiors abruptly gave way to another kind of impatience, a chivalric eagerness to confront a worthy rival. "He seemed to expand with spontaneous joy at the very mention of this man,"[47] simultaneously adding a flattering brush stroke to the portrait and highlighting his relationship with Aufidius, so often no more than a perfunctory gesture.

In the battle scenes he was splendidly acrobatic, predictably cocky, alternately bullying and jovial, and totally, ludicrously, unable to accept praise. "When this Coriolanus refuses money for his victories," wrote Harold Hobson, "he is not magnificently indignant, but impatient like a man ill at ease with a compliment he does not know how to answer" (*Sunday Times,* 12 July 1959). But Martius's modesty, Olivier made it clear, is false, "the result of the man of action's narcissism held back by the necessity to belittle success in the presence of social equals": he "writhed in discomfort at the praises heaped on him by his fellow generals," Kitchen noted, "only to release a cold smile, unabashed, at the sound of his new title."[48]

His triumphant return to Rome, graced by some thirty participants and observers, and including the citizens as Macready had done, betrayed the same embarrassed impatience, but modulated now by an awareness of his mother's pride at his achievement and his own delight in her approval. Although he greeted Virgilia "with a tender break in his voice," his concentration remained on the jubilant Volumnia whom he favored with "a long smile with the spoilt son's immodest complacency."[49]

In the Voices scene (2.3), another dissection of inverted modesty, he definitively evoked "the awkward adult boy sickened equally by flattery and the need to flatter,"[50] artfully exploiting the unconscious humor which had earlier bewitched Old Vic audiences. Martius's entrance in a floppy hat (a textually warranted accessory), and Menenius's fussy positioning of him, like some wayward child, teetered dangerously on the brink of farce. At the scene's conclusion the relieved petitioner doffed his gown and hat, and with supreme nonchalance tossed them at the tribunes.

The confrontation sequence (3.1) was played with greater subtlety and less bluster than usual. Martius's historical-political diatribe on the popular franchise, left textually intact, was delivered with full-throated conviction and consummate insensitivity. Toward the end of the scene, however, the citizens' infuriated reaction suddenly gave him pause: his face "registered a few seconds of bewilderment . . . a marked surprise that arrogant statements habitual in the family circle and among patricians could have such an inflammatory effect." Just before drawing his sword, in a revealing innovation, the enraged fire-eater seemed "disorientated for a time . . . briefly in need of reassurance, presumably from his mother."[51]

As the Admonition sequence opened, Olivier's delivery of "I muse my mother / Does not approve me further" (3.2.7ff) caught the querulous defiance of a small boy about to have his conduct questioned, and determined to brazen it out. "He listened to his mother's reproofs," Laurence Kitchin remembers,

> with infantile sullenness and the tone adopted reduced the whole issue to the scale of some breach of etiquette. . . . Having made the most of lines which will

bear a petulant interpretation, Olivier next gave the entire scene a turn on a single one, where Coriolanus is told he must go back to the tribunes and replies: "Well, what then? what then?" He lent the first "What then?" his celebrated full brass on a rising inflection, caught Volumnia's eye, paused, deflated and repeated "what then?" quietly and deferentially.[52]

As Volumnia pressed the case for diplomacy, "the response of his sagging mouth, shuffling feet and faraway eyes" irresistibly recalled "a schoolboy reluctantly agreeing to apologise for kicking teacher on the shins" (*Daily Mail*, 8 July 1959). The encounter terminated differently, but quite as memorably as in 1938. Where at the Old Vic "the flint-flashed snap of 'The word is *mildly*'" (3.2.142)[53] marked the scene's apogee, it was now the second "mildly" of the final line. Olivier neither spoke the word nor cut it: "[i]nstead, at the moment of shaping it with lips and facial muscles, he convulsively retched."[54]

The banishment (3.3), a miracle of sustained energy and subtle craftsmanship, culminated with Martius aloft. Just before the "common cry of curs" speech, he "leaned against the masonry high up on Aronson's set, head rolling from side to side, eyes mad . . . while he listened to the tribunes." Then, advancing to the projection on which he first appeared, "he made the speech with less volume than in Casson's production, but with a terrifying concentration of contempt."[55] "You common cry of curs," Alan Brien noted, "drops from his lips in bloody icicles, each phrase a jagged spear of frozen fury" (*Spectator*, 17 July 1959). "There is a world elsewhere," flung "across his shoulder in a great and overwhelming silence" (*Lady*, 13 August 1959), "crumble[d] and melt[ed] in his mouth" (*Spectator*, 17 July 1959).

From this point onward, Martius "wore the look of a man doomed by his own conscience," his face transformed "into the mask of fatality" (*Tablet* 8 August 1959). The momentum of the scene in which he made common cause with the Volscians, from "the diffident way in which he approached Aufidius" (*Scotsman*, 14 July 1959) at the outset to the final sealing of the pact, suggested an almost Greek inevitability. "He had been very quiet during the scene," writes Kitchin. "There was a deathly, premonitory misgiving in the way he eventually shook hands; and his eyes were glazed. Whatever integration the character of Marcius had possessed fell apart at that moment. The rest was crumble, detonation and collapse, with part of him fatalistically detached."[56]

The desolation of the lonely dragon was neatly underscored in the following scene (4.6) when, during Rome's celebration of Martius's departure, the First Citizen "pass[ed] over the stage carrying his youngest child on his shoulders and followed by the rest of his family, as if he were bound for a day at the seaside" (*Scotsman*, 14 July 1959). Martius's jubilant homecoming in 2.1 was poignantly invoked, and the fatal intimacy of 5.3 foreshadowed. When at the outset of the Intercession episode, Volumnia bore down on him, with wife and child on either side, Martius seemed physically to dwindle; and as the scene progressed, his moral resolve could be seen to ebb with almost the same visual clarity. The collapse, when he sidled toward Volumnia to grasp her hand, murmuring "Oh, my mother," was as epic as it was abject; and in that moment the comic capitulation in 3.2 was poignantly recollected and brilliantly vindicated.

When the moment of death arrived, Martius, as in 1938, declined to go gently. Out of Shakespeare's abrupt, undignified, and unenlightened exit, long a histrionic embarrassment, Olivier created an event of cinematic splendor. The moment was carefully prepared for, and inimitably executed. When he returned to the Volscians in the play's final scene, he seemed "compact, dignified, alert." But at Aufidius's taunt, "his whole frame seem[ed] to inflate, he move[d] violently as though under an unbearable pressure" (*New Statesman,* 18 July 1959). No one has memorialized the scene's climax better than Kenneth Tynan: "'*Boy!*' shrieks the overmothered general, in an outburst of strangled fury, and leaps up a flight of precipitous steps to vent his rage." At the top of the Tarpian structure, where he first appeared in arrogant splendour and later defied the Roman populace, "he relents and throws his sword away."

After letting his voice fly high in the great, swingeing line about how he "flutter'd your Volscians in *Cor-i-o-li,*" he allows a dozen spears to impale him. He is poised, now, on a promontory some twelve feet above the stage, from which he topples forward, to be caught by the ankles so that he dangles, inverted, like the slaughtered Mussolini.[57]

The image remains one of the most resonant visual statements in twentieth-century theater. The funeral procession on a darkened stage, its somber solemnity bringing an ironically decorous closure to a career of absolutist excess, was a trimphant vindication of Shakespeare's dramatic judgement over Benthall's.

Olivier's characterization owed much of its texture to the seventy-year-old Volumnia of Edith Evans, who renounced the Poussinesque grandeur of Ward and the Grecian majesty of Thorndike in favor of an almost cosmic maternalism, fueled by an irresistible, and ultimately deadly, femininity. "[Volumnia] was a pagan, a Roman, and a patrician," Evans observed in a talk given not long after the opening.

But all that meant nothing unless she was also a woman. Where was the woman to be found?

In her love for Coriolanus. She did not love war for its own sake but for his. . . . Politics, again, means nothing to her in itself. All she wants is for her boy not to antagonize the City Councillors while it is in their power to spoil his chances of the consulship. . . . His banishment is not only a crying injustice done to him but

Assassination Scene (Coriolanus-Laurence Olivier; Aufidius-Anthony Nicholls). Peter Hall Production, Shakespeare Memorial Theatre, 1959. Angus McBean Photograph. [By permission of the Shakespeare Centre Library, Stratford-upon-Avon]

also means that he will be completely cut off from her (*The Times*, 22 August 1959).

Her first appearances, attired in gold, disconcertingly suggested to Bernard Levin "a priestess of some ancient, bloody religion" (*Daily Express*, 8 July 1959) even as she carried out the housewifely task of sewing.[58] The domestic and homecoming sequences, characterized by dignity, courage, and a fierce joy in military prowess, mellowed throughout by a devastating femininity, revealed the Evans Volumnia as "the almost perfect complement to Olivier's Coriolanus." "[O]ne could feel and see the blood-tie between them," insisted one reviewer (*Stratford-upon-Avon Herald*, 10 July 1959). The strength of that tie, manifest less in what was said than what was left unsaid, was omnipresent. In the Admonition sequence, after scolding Martius for his pride, she remained calculatingly rocklike until the chastened man/child crossed to her, touched her tentatively, and after a brief wait for a return to favor pleaded, "Chide me no more" (3.2.132). Moments later, when the wily matron swept from the stage in a strategic gesture of rejection, Martius followed a few steps and anxiously watched her departure. Cominius's "Away, the tribunes do attend you" (3.2.138) was designed to break his hypnotic focus on the vanished parent.

The "piercing grief and indignation" (*News Chronicle*, 8 July 1959) which marked her farewell and subsequent rating of the tribunes were prompted as much by the spectre of loneliness as outrage at injustice. Her black-clad entrance, wasted but resolute, in the Intercession scene, and the spinning of her fatal psychological web were nothing short of mesmerizing.

The supporting cast was almost as good as could be wished. The Menenius of Harry Andrews, "faintly busybody, faintly pleased with his gift of the gab, but pre-eminently sane and responsible" (*New Statesman*, 18 July 1959), was an admirable counterpoise to the emotional extravagance of the protagonists. The rejection of his petition discovered a memorable dignity and pathos. Anthony Nicholls's Aufidius, a barbarian warrior, clad in furs and half-hidden by a ragged beard and tangled shoulder-length locks, offered not only a visual contrast to Martius, but a psychological, moral, and political counterpoint as well.

The play itself was not ideally served by Hall's production, nor was it in any romantic revival; but insofar as Coriolanus is the play's nucleus, that nucleus had seldom been so convincingly, richly, and consistently imagined. One critic found Olivier's technique somewhat self-conscious; another questioned whether a character as ironically self-aware as his Martius would be capable of such stupidities; but gripes were few. Trewin's judgement that SMT audiences had witnessed "one of the most exciting Shakespearean performances of our time" (*Illustrated London News*, 15 August 1959) went virtually unchallenged.

Even as the first Olivier revival inaugurated the romantic production convention, the second ended it. After the Hall production, there was simply nowhere for the style to go. Amid the critical adulation that accompanied the revival, A. Alvarez recognized the romantic convention for what it was, and denounced its failure to serve the script. The Hall production, he argued, was "wrong because it [was], in the most stultifying way, conventional."

> The convention is that the Roman plays are boring: too much talk, manoeuvring, dull rhetoric and heroics; neither enough humanity nor quotes. Hence the conventional solution is to play them as melodrama, as horse operas with togas and short swords. The Tribunes, for instance, are evil—wealthy *petits bourgeois* who exploit the plebs against the patricians—therefore they must be for ever sneering and cowering; all they needed were moustaches to twist. The Roman generals are noble; therefore they must puff out their chests and talk with pebbles in their mouths (*New Statesman*, 18 July 1959).

If change was what Alvarez had in mind, he was about to get it. Within a year or two of Martius's last spectacular plunge, theatrical romance was displaced by calculated ugliness, escape by confrontation, the hero by the antihero, and emotional intoxication by politics, psychoanalysis, and post-modernity. Novelty was to be the alpha and omega of the new aesthetic.

10

Psychoanalysis, Politics, and Postmodernity (1961–1994)

Over the thirty-three-year period from 1961 to 1994 *Coriolanus* enjoyed some two dozen major revivals in England and North America as compared to eight in the previous twenty. The newfound popularity owed a good deal to the British and North American Shakespeare boom in the postwar decades, the result of increased access to higher education[1] and the privileging of Shakespeare in the curriculum.[2] A marked increase in production activity followed. The Royal Shakespeare Company, the erstwhile Shakespeare Memorial Theatre, extended its reach with satellite locations in Newcastle and London; provincial repertory companies, now enjoying a renaissance, found Shakespeare consumer friendly; and in North America the Shakespeare festival phenomenon proved as popular as it was ubiquitous.

Much of *Coriolanus*'s good fortune, however, must be attributed to its unique contemporary appeal.[3] Its political character, caught, however briefly, the attention of an educated elite obsessed with societal ideology; its psychological complexity captured the imagination of what Lasch labeled "the culture of narcissism,"[4] a generation preoccupied with theories of the self, most of them Freud-inspired; and the fact that the play was by a dead white European male, and capable of being read as a celebration of retrograde imperialist values, kindled the deconstructive enthusiasms of cultural revisionists.

To identify definitively the forces operative on any given *Coriolanus* production is impossible: each broadly reflected contemporary cultural concerns, but usually in no very specific or coherent way, certainly not with the aesthetic uniformity which marked the neoromantic era. During the sixties the play profited from Marxist and antiwar sentiment, epitomized by the vogue for Brecht, although Brecht-influenced revivals of *Coriolanus* in England and North America were triumphs of style rather than ideology. Psychoanalytic investigation of the characters of Martius and Volumnia was pursued with rigor throughout the entire period; but where Olivier and his imitators exploited Martius's infantile behavior as primarily a romantic acting opportunity, a chance to glamorize, soften, and lend comic appeal to an otherwise harsh portrait, the new Freudian readings rubbed audiences' noses in the psychology of alienation—military destructiveness, psychic pain, problematic sexuality—all attributable to malign maternal influence. Cultural ideology found expression in the rejection of the romantic production tradition, particularly pictorial mise-en-scène and actorial glamor, in favor of a cult of visual drabness, monochronism, and an insistent anti-heroism. Within the past decade, postmodern design has tended to prioritize the visual image, often as an independent and interpolated mediator of the text, in an effort to, in Dennis Kennedy's phrase, enforce "a disjunction between the pastness of Shakespeare's plays and the ways we now receive them."[5] Mainstream productions, however, apart from a postmodern "look" and touches of trendy revisionism, remain untouched by contemporary European developments in Shakespearian acting style. The commitment of the Shakespeare theater establishment to modernism and psychoanalysis remains fixed and pervasive.

Romanticism and Psychoanalysis (1961–1963)

The reaction against romanticism was not immediate or abrupt. Two productions, one staged by Michael Langham in 1961 at Stratford, Ontario's Festival Theatre and the other by Tyrone Guthrie two years later at the Nottingham Playhouse, each firmly clasped the romantic convention with one hand while stroking the social sciences with the other.

Michael Langham's revival, starring Paul Scofield in the title role, was, apart from its unique interpretation, a landmark in *Coriolanus*'s stage history: for the first time since the Jacobean era a professional company led by a major actor played a relatively full text on a stage functionally, not merely pictorially, approximating the one for which it was written. It is a curious coincidence that the realization of Poel's dream of an Elizabethan acting space should be companioned by the Directoire production style he advocated three decades earlier.

Langham's text, one of the fullest to date, omitted only about five hundred lines, primarily through internal cuts to minimize rhetoric and clarify syntax.[6] The sole scene completely excised was Volumnia's victorious return to Rome (5.5). The unusual presence of Adrian and Nicanor, played as a "pair of merry, mincing spies" (*Telegram*, Toronto, 20 June 1961), contributed little beyond comic diversion.

Out of deference to the neoromantic style, politics was yet again subordinated to character revelation. "It is our belief," Langham announced in his program notes, "that the political aspect of the play, intriguing though it may be, is quite secondary." The citizens, few in number and picturesquely outfitted, served mainly as a source of local color and a target for Martius's abuse. The tribunes, if as usual, the villains of the piece, were at least depicted as "chilling and unnerving schemers . . . instead of the pair of comical shop stewards"[7] endemic to British productions.

In violation of romantic precedent Langham resorted to Napoleonic dress rather than the customary Renaissance Classical trappings.[8] Civilian patricians were garbed by Tanya Moiseiwitsch in earth-toned frock coats and waistcoats, while the military donned full-dress regimentals. Plebeians, in highly individualized rags, chewed on clay pipes. Roman soldiers bore muskets while citizens were equipped with crowbars. The innovation, intended to lend the action greater relevance for contemporary audiences, misfired. "The text never stops saying 'Rome' for a moment," insisted the *New York Herald Tribune*.

> We are frequently confronted with one or another character removing his top hat to say "I am a Roman," and the final effect is not to freshen the landscape but to forcibly remind us that we have got off at the wrong stop (21 June 1961).

Whatever the drawbacks of the style, however, it lent romantic color to the play and facilitated picturesque groupings, a number of which were indebted to Goya's war paintings.

Since muskets could not be fired without deafening the audience, battles were fought with bayonets in a kind of balletic mime choreographed by Alan Lund, an innovation about to become a convention. Want of realistic cut and thrust, fatal to a romantic reading, hardly mattered in a production bent on exploiting the vagaries of Martius's psyche.

The focus of the performance, as Langham intended, was Martius, but a radically different creature than the fetching boy-hero of Olivier's imagining. Where the Olivier Roman compelled admiration for his epic drives, the Scofield Roman begged sympathy for his psychic disability.

From the outset Langham made Volumnia the mainspring of the action, directing Eleanor Stuart, who played the role, "toward a mother-son relationship which was very nearly Freudian."[9] Scofield's Martius, at thirty-nine, was a tall, gaunt, ruggedly handsome figure for whom maternal love had since childhood been made conditional on adherence to a rigid military code which demanded a physical and psychological self-sufficiency as total as it was frigid. An eloquent elaboration of Benthall's 1954 invention introduced Young Martius at Volumnia's first entrance, engaged in mock battle. Waving a wooden sword, he shouted "Charge, charge. Cowards." In a powerful evocation of his father's childhood, and to Volumnia's indulgent delight, he added, "Let me alone." Martius's epic feats were not discounted by Langham, but in no production before or since was the personal price paid, the glacial "inner isolation" of the boy-general, so insisted upon: "in the Senate," wrote one theatergoer, ". . . in the market-place; at the moment of his banishment; he stood, every inch a hero, separated by half the stage from friend and foe alike, 'alone, like to a lonely dragon.'"[10] What in other productions passed for arrogance might not have been rendered more palatable, but was at least understandable.

After a first-act demonstration of the military results of Volumnia's nurture, Martius found himself in act 2 pressed to perform a series of acts his upbringing leads him to regard as reprehensible, even outrageous. In the Senate, he turned his back on the entire debate, "listing his strained head to the vast amphitheater around him as though to ask the audience whether all political processes aren't as preposterous as this one and whether his impatience and his anger aren't wholly justified" (*New York Herald Tribune*, 21 June 1961). His suit for the citizens' voices, an outrage to his compulsively independent spirit, could be tolerated only as a perverse test of endurance. When he invited the citizens to offer him a consular appointment as a favor to themselves, his eye was "somewhat wickedly confiding,"

> suggesting that they are no more taken in by this absurd mockery than he is. The curl of his lip [was] almost joyous in its interior triumph, as though there were a deep masochistic satisfaction to be taken from acting out the farce so well (*New York Herald Tribune*, 21 June 1961).

His defiance of the tribunes and people in 3.1 and 3.3 was played, according to one critic, with "the hard brilliance of a midwinter noon," the whole building with implacable rhythm to the "hoarse, bitter, and quite moving agony [of] his abrupt headlong exit on the cry 'There is a world elsewhere'" (*New York Herald Tribune*, 21 June 1961).

Exiled from Volumnia and Rome, he finds in Aufidius and Antium a surrogate parent prepared to value him for what he does rather than for what he is. In Aufidius's house, the rediscovery of what the lonely dragon counted as love and belonging found expression "in the warmth of an embrace that seem[ed] to sweep the very past away."[11] On his first entrance after his desertion, he wore a replica of Aufidius's black uniform, at once a pathetic indication of his urge to relate in the only way he understands and an "inescapable proof of the degradation he had given himself."[12]

The era of harmony was short-lived; and with the onset of Aufidius's jealousy, the emotional temperature went into abrupt free fall, symbolized by a seasonal change from autumn to winter. Menenius wheezed his way through a countryside as chilly as his reception at Martius's camp; and the women made their appeal in a subzero ambience which immobilized human interaction. At the outset of Volumnia's petition, Martius was "a brooding figure clenching his hands and relaxing them again, as if almost unaware that his family knelt before him"; at its end he remained a "stiff" and "unyielding" presence on the edge of the platform "staring at the rear of the stage." Only "after Volumnia, the last to leave, had passed by" did he summon mobility enough to fling a "long arm behind him to stay her."[13]

It is significant that Volumnia, seizing the initiative as always, grasped his outstretched hand rather than he hers. But the choice was his: he signed his death warrant in full consciousness, accepting his fate "with a kind of serenity, as though aware finally that his mother's domination has made him the kind of man that he is, and has led him to the end that is inevitable for him" (*Stratford [Ontario] Beacon-Herald,* 20 June 1961). That end, met with becoming defiance, was brief, brutal, and degrading. Cut down by a volley of pistol shots, he lurched to the center pillar where Aufidius met him, appropriated his sword, ran him through, and stepped back. Only half-conscious, Martius instinctively staggered toward his murderer, but went "suddenly rigid, half turning, and slamm[ed] down full length on the floor" as death overtook him.[14] In a final bid for sympathy for the epic outsider, Langham insisted that the ugly moment in which Aufidius stands on the corpse be played with absolute clarity.[15]

Reviewers praised the quality of Scofield's support, but seldom added descriptive detail. The Volumnia of Eleanor Stuart, a formidable Jocasta in Stratford's earlier *Oedipus Rex,* was majestic, rich-voiced, and tastefully underplayed. Robertson Davies found it rare that "family relationship in a play [was] so easy to accept"; for him Stuart's matron was "wholly credible as the mother of such a man."[16] Which is perhaps as much as can be said of a human Juno shrunk to a figure in a Freudian case study. Douglas Campbell's Menenius, "rather like Mr. Pickwick without the specs" (*Brantford Expositor,* 20 June 1961), was a fine blend of sense and sensibility. Feisty and life-affirming before Martius's banishment, he subsequently "decline[d] into a faded dignity, his way of life wounded beyond return" (*Globe and Mail,* Toronto, 21 June 1961). His earlier vigor briefly reasserted itself when, "attired . . . in a long flowing cloak and fur hat . . . a perfect Cossack field-marshal" (*London [Ontario] Evening Free Press,* 20 June 1961), he approached the Volscian camp. The collapse of his overtaxed resources at Martius's repulse was thus doubly pathetic.

With greater attention to the subtleties of Martius's psyche, Aufidius gained a heightened profile; and, as played by John Colicos, renewed interest as a passionate, barbarian foil to Martius's icy patricianism. An inveterate hero-worshipper, habitually given to emotional excess, his alternating envy and admiration throughout the early scenes suggested neurosis; in Antium, enmity exploded with frightening whimsicality into love. When the object of his worship lived up to his military reputation, love was tainted by jealousy; and when he failed to do so, veered to murderous violence.

Langham's *Coriolanus,* although evincing certain romantic features, looked forward rather than backward. Its sustained study of male narcissism and aggression as a result of infantile deprivation was to become an interpretative commonplace over the next three decades. Martius's maternal dependence, long a source of amusement, even charm, came to be regarded, in the age of Dr. Spock, as symptomatic of a serious character disorder, from which at times, the entire society feared it might be suffering—the alienated self.[17]

Two years later, Tyrone Guthrie, the Stratford Festival's godfather and Langham's mentor, inaugurated the new Nottingham Playhouse with a production which probed Martius's enigmatic psyche with a sharper eye to box office sensation than textual fidelity. Despite widespread censure of Langham's Napoleonic mise-en-scène, Guthrie opted to repeat the experiment.

His text, although only two hundred lines shorter than Langham's, was more rashly curtailed.[18] Internal cuts were fewer, but several scenes disappeared entirely. The episode in which Martius is rechristened (1.9) was cut, as was, for the only time in the play's stage history, the Voices scene (2.3). The Adrian-Nicanor meeting (4.3) was also excised. In keeping with the play's psychological thrust, the tribune's speeches were severely curtailed, together with Menenius's extended mockery of them at 2.1.1–96. The cushion-layers vanished from 2.2; and although Volumnia's silent stage cross in 5.5 was retained, only one line—"Behold our patroness, the life of Rome!"—was spoken. The scene in which Aufidius vows vengeance on Martius (1.10) was transposed to come between Martius's triumphal entry (2.1) and the Senate episode (2.2). The latter sequence concluded with the strong curtain line "To Coriolanus come all joy and honour!" (2.2.154).

For Guthrie, as for Langham, *Coriolanus* was not a political drama, but a character study with compelling contemporary relevance. The fascination with social and psychological conditioning which led him a quarter century earlier to consult Ernest Jones before staging his Old Vic *Hamlet* and *Othello* remained undiminished. "We do well to remember," he counseled in his program notes,

> how prevalent still are notions about "honour", sportsmanship, loyalty to country, to family and class, which . . . do not stand up to one moment's serious and detached examination; how very prevalent too, and almost universally admired, are dominant Mammas who ruthlessly inculcate into the minds of sensitive male children, especially if, like Coriolanus, they have no father, the conventional morality of their own class and environment.[19]

Guthrie's stage exploration of Britain's inherited class values was perfunctory at best; the real interest in the production, for him and for reviewers, lay in his dissection of the "love-hate between Coriolanus and Aufidius; the hysterical and homosexual element which seems so useful and powerful an ingredient in the composition of intensely vigorous men of action."[20] Once again, although the precise psychological mechanism was never revealed, Volumnia was held responsible.

The first half of the drama, in keeping with his apolitical approach, Guthrie treated as largely an opportunity for byplay. In the first scene, like contemporary anti-bomb demonstrators, the citizens "storm[ed] over the stage with banners inscribed 'Corn not Scorn.'" Battles, as in Langham's revival, were suggested "with balletic strokes, in slow motion, across the stage once and back again" (*Guardian Journal,* 13 December 1963). The homecoming of John Neville's Martius was treated as an challenge to comic invention: Volumnia and Menenius discussed the hero's achievements "while skipping over ceremonial ropes and obstructing the laying of the red carpet" (*Plays and Players,* February, 1964); at one point an incompetent carpet-layer whacked his partner with a rolled-up rug; and later the pair managed to "catch a dignitary under the crutch with a barrier rope" (*Guardian Journal,* 13 December 1963).

Most of the production, sadly maimed without the Voices scene, was devoted to a demonstration of "the witless paradox of martial pride" with Volumnia "the original Imperial mother-figure pull[ing] the strings that move the honourable puppet" (*Guardian,* 13 December 1963). Arrayed in "the golden breastplate, thighboots and plumes of the Life Guards" (*Stage,* 19 December 1963), Neville's Martius cut a fine figure as he curled a disdainful lip at plebeians and tribunes, struggled vainly, "like . . . an eagle trying to chain itself down" (*Stage,* 19 December 1963), to acquire diplomacy, and finally, in an ecstasy of rage and frustration, quit the city. For a victim of social maladjustment, maternal exploitation, and aristocratic self-delusion, an audience could summon a measure of sympathy, but no reaction grander or more intense. Harold Hobson found "nothing frightening in his hatred of democracy, nothing to tremble at in his taunts" (*Christian Science Monitor,* Boston, 17 December 1963). This was no doubt precisely the response Guthrie's antiheroic strategy anticipated. But did he foresee that the play's mechanism in consequence would lack a mainspring?

The production's final movement writ large what had earlier only been hinted at—that Volumnia's dominance of her fatherless son was responsible for a homosexual orientation. As early as the hand-to-hand combat in act 1, a powerful sexual attraction led the antagonists to circle each other "uttering threats like sensual caresses" (*The Times,* 14 December 1963); and sexual motivation later explained both Martius's desertion and Aufidius's ecstatic reception. The nuptial imagery in the reconciliation scene, so often cut, was given full value: J. C. Trewin found the moment at which Martius "breaks down in the arms of Aufidius" quite "beautifully done" (*Birmingham Post,* 23 December 1963). The scene's climax, which saw the "exhausted, muffled figure rejected by Rome . . . carried into the Volscian General's house like a bride into the bridal chamber" (*Plays and Players,* February 1964), was as bizarre as it was unique. Ultimately Aufidius's jealousy, suspicion, and sense of national and personal betrayal at Martius's rejection of him in favor of Volumnia sealed his lover's fate.[21] The defiantly heroic "Alone I did it. 'Boy'!", which enraptured audiences from Kemble to Olivier, was nothing more than the hysterical cry of a "mama's boy" exploited by his country, his parent, and his lover. The murder itself, "a sudden rush of killing" (*Guardian Journal,* 13 December 1963), was brief and the death fall unremarkable. Less commonplace was the moment when Aufidius stamped viciously on the dead Martius's groin and "flung his body, with strange groans, on the prostrate form" (*Sunday Times,* 15 December 1963).[22]

Other characters were little more than caricatures. The citizens, dressed in rags, offered low comedy; the Dickensian tribunes struck one reviewer more as "jeer-leaders" than serious activists (*Evening Post,* 13 December 1963); and Leo McKern's Menenius recalled "a W. C. Fields portrayal of Mr. Micawber" (*Evening Post,* 13 December 1963).

No character in the play suffered more from Guthrie's antiheroic assault than Volumnia, played by Dorothy Reynolds. Robbed of grandeur, political conviction, and moral purpose, she dwindled into little more than an authoritarian mama with social pretensions. In the Intercession scene, now merely a display of psychological blackmail, it was "her hysterical pathos rather than any transcendent passion that . . . turn[ed] Coriolanus from the gates of Rome" (*Guardian,* 13 December 1963).

The only character to come off with credit was Ian McKellen's Aufidius. "[A] Mongol in a hussar's uniform," his performance suggested at the outset "a dark strength" (*Stage,* 19 December 1963). Later, however, he discovered "a man whose will is piteously betrayed by his nerves"; "his enormous efforts at self-mastery" Harold Hobson found "magnificent to watch" (*Sunday Times,* 15 December 1963). In the play's final moments, in the grip of sexually driven frenzy, he stabbed Martius four times before falling precipitately upon the body in abject remorse. As the lights faded, he knelt keening "a long wailing threnody" (*The Times,* 14 December 1963) of hysterical passion.

Two American productions in 1965, one directed by Allen Fletcher at the American Shakespeare Festival at Stratford, Connecticut, and the other mounted by Gladys Vaughan for the New York Shakespeare Festival in New York's Central Park, both Freud-inspired and uninventive, did nothing to ameliorate the perennial republican distaste for the play. The latter revival, the first example of multiracial casting for *Coriolanus,* featured the African-American actors Jane White as Volumnia and James Earl Jones as Brutus, with Alan Ansara as a Puerto Rican Sicinius. White received an Obie award as Best Actress of the Year for her Nefertitian matron.

Psychoanalytic exploration was briefly, and as it turned out, ineffectually, sidelined when Brecht's adaptation, titled *Coriolan,* was staged at the Old Vic by the Berliner Ensemble during the 1965 World Theatre Season. *Coriolanus*'s politics were no novelty on the continent: Piachaud's version at the Comédie Française provoked street riots in the 1933–34 season; the Allies, on the strength of the play's alleged fascist bias, banned German productions in the immediate postwar years; and, more recently, Georgio Strehler's Brecht-inspired production at the Milan's Piccolo Theater in 1957 had raised a critical storm. The British theater, long indifferent to *Coriolanus*'s political character, was now forced to confront it on its doorstep.

PLAYING POLITICS (1965–1981)

Coriolan was roughed out in Berlin in 1951 and 1952, but revision of the battlefield scenes (1.4–10), which Brecht intended to evolve in the course of rehearsal, remained unfinished at his death in 1956.

Brecht's redaction, which he termed a "tragedy of a people that has a hero against it,"[23] was born of the conviction that the plebeians and tribunes must transparently be endowed with the means to control their own destiny. His underclass are consequently neither local color, comic butts, or Forrestian thugs, but honest workmen, capable of forging their future without the aid of an aristocratic superman. After the war, they discover the joys of political solidarity under the leadership of the tribunes, no longer self-seeking demagogues but altruistic political activists; and when Martius, on the strength of his military indispensablity, assumes the right to govern, the tribunes encourage the citizens to resist. They do so; the would-be dictator is exiled; and the citizens in consequence find the city under threat of invasion. In the end Martius is turned back, not by maternal manipulation, but an awareness of his own dispensability in the face of an armed and determined citizenry.

Brecht based his adaptation on Dorothea Tieck's translation, freely rephrasing and adding as he went; but shrewd cutting and eloquent business accounted for some of his strongest effects. To render the plebeians more sympathetic, he excised all lines indicative of irresponsiblity or inconsistency. Menenius and Martius, to their discredit, were permitted to verbally assault them at length, while their targets remained stoically silent. No mention was made of their cowardice; they behaved with consummate dignity in the Voices scene (all comic lines were cut), and firmly and responsibly showed their teeth in the Banishment episode. At the approach of the invader, Brecht's common man, unlike Shakespeare's, determined to defend his freedom. To Brutus's observation that "The city fathers are leaving Rome to its fate," a citizen responded, "The majority [of workingmen] have reported for military duty" (137).[24]

To further tip the scales in the plebeians' favor, Brecht introduced The Man with the Child in 1.1 to highlight the miseries of the exploited poor, and rewrote the Adrian-Nicanor sequence to feature a Roman Rope-maker and a Volscian Tanner who agree that the lot of the workingman in all times and places is to "eat, sleep and pay taxes" (119).

The tribunes, not surprisingly, were thoroughly laundered. Menenius was not permitted his devastatingly humorous indictment of them prior to Martius's return (2.1.34–93), nor did they betray the cynical motivation Shakespeare has them voice after the patricians exit (2.1.205–61). They appeared more conciliatory in the Senate scene, and indulged in no chicanery at the conclusion of the Voices episode. In the patrician-plebeian exchange, they limited themselves to a polite request "to / Question the candidate concerning / His program and his general opinions" (99), a democratic exercise for which Martius proved ill-adapted. In the Banishment sequence they behaved with dignified restraint, and under the threat of invasion were models of strategic competence and inspirational leadership.

The patricians, in contrast, received short shrift throughout. Menenius lost his earthy shrewdness, mellow humor, paternal fondness for Martius, and altruistic mission to the Volscian camp. Volumnia, shorn of both maternal and humanitarian concern, was limned as a callous nationalist who would "rather see us plebeians trampled on by Romans than by Volscians" (138). Her mission to the Volscian camp, accompanied by a plebian woman to keep her honest, found her less a grieving mother than a diplomatic envoy. When the news of Martius's disengagement reached Rome, the people, not Volumnia, received the credit: as Brutus put it, "The stone has moved. The people take / Up weapons, and the old earth shakes" (143).

Martius, never the most congenial of creatures, emerged as an unmitigated thug. On his first entrance, during Menenius's belly fable, he was backed by a menacing company of armed men. All instances of provocation by citizens and plebeians were cut, along with many of his gentler lines to family and friends. Through a merger of the Voices episode (2.3) with the plebeian-patrician confrontation (3.1) Brecht obliged him to move with sustained irascibility from arrogant begging, to singing a taunting song, to flaunting his refusal of grain, to outright defiance of the citizens' authority. Well might an audience conclude that the Roman people had more right than wrong on their side. Little attention was paid to the mother-son relationship: the victorious return was perfunctory; the Farewell scene suggested an exercise in aristocratic chin-upmanship; and the intercession lacked intimacy and affect. At the conclusion of Volumnia's appeal, Martius neither yielded nor took her hand. Only after her exit did he speak the single line Brecht left standing—"O mother, mother! What have you done?" (142). The assassination by Aufidius's officers was swift and businesslike. In a gratuitous twist of Brecht's anti-patrician blade, an appeal by Menenius to the Senate to have Martius's name inscribed in the Capitol was summarily rejected along with the family's request to wear public mourning. Aufidius in his turn became a virtual nonentity—simply a convenient warmonger to whom Martius can desert, and a device to rid the world of an inconvenient hero.

Coriolan premiered obscurely in a production by Heinrich Koch at Frankfurt's City Theatre in 1962,[25] and came to international attention two years later when Brecht's onetime assistants, Manfred Wekwerth and Joachim Tenschert, staged it, with further revisions, at the Berliner Ensemble in 1964. The battlefield sequences, now recast, were placed "at the centre of [the] production."[26] "We show them," the directors wrote,

> as the work of great specialists of war (Coriolanus, Aufidius). Even their behavior in peacetime derives from their battle skill; even in peacetime they fight against everything that opposes the wish to fight.[27]

Only three military episodes were played—the Corioli assault (1.4), the fight between Martius and Aufidius (1.8), and the sequence in which Martius is surnamed (1.9)—and these were heavily edited and intercut with civil sequences. The Corioli battle followed the first part of the scene in Martius's house (1.3), and was followed in turn by the segment featuring Valeria's visit. The fight between Martius and Aufidius was succeeded by the abbreviated colloquy between Menenius and the tribunes (2.1), after which Martius received his battlefield honors. The civil scenes were designed to estrange the battle scenes and vice versa.[28]

Martius's dependence on his mother, downplayed by Brecht, was given somewhat greater emphasis; and to make the point more forcibly, Volumnia armed her son for battle in a sequence which owed something to *Antony and Cleopatra* (4.4). Brecht's fundamental point, that Martius's change of heart was motivated not by maternal pressure, but the recognition in the face of populist resistance that he is not indispensable, remained unaltered.

The Coriolanus-Aufidius rivalry also gained more prominence than Brecht allowed. Persuaded that "the armed games of two ambitious warriors . . . are the driving force that sets the story in motion,"[29] the directors restored the conversation between Aufidius and the Senators of Corioli (1.2), Martius's inquiries about Aufidius's progress at the opening of 3.1, and the sequence in which the conspirators (now christened Spurius and Calvus) whip up Aufidius's hostility (5.6).

The Berliner Ensemble production opened in Berlin in October 1964 after nine months of rehearsals, and arrived in England less than a year later. The show's Marxist polemic left reviewers bemused and ultimately unpersuaded, but its mise-en-scène and acting were an aesthetic revelation.

The scenic elements, mounted on a turntable, featured a towering white stone archway for Roman scenes which revolved to reveal a brown wooden stockade representative of Corioli. Staged under glaring white light against a clinically white cyclorama, the production achieved stunning visual effects by the radical exploitation of monochromism: at the conclusion of the Banishment scene, for example, after long exposure to the massive white arch and the "pale chalky greys" of the costumes, the visual relief offered by the "stupendous red leather cloak that is dropped and left" (*Observer,* 15 August 1965) proved almost painful.

Equally potent spectacle derived from actors in motion: the battle scenes in particular, brilliantly choreographed by Ruth Berghaus, have never been more epically realized. Corioli was conquered, Kenneth Tynan reported, "in three great flourishes of action, wordless except for deafening rhythmical chants of "*Cai-us Mar-cius!*" and "*Au-fi-di-us!*" yelled by the black-clad armies into the resonant concavity of their shields."

> First the gates are stormed, with attack by siege-ladders, counter-attack by vast nets of heavy rope, renewed attack by shield-plated phalanx. Next: battle in the open, with waves of soldiers clashing in the stylised manner of Chinese opera, knees akimbo and swords maniacally brandished. As they part, the mortally wounded slowly spin and fall.[30]

In the Martius-Aufidius contest, which constituted the third movement, the combatants "first stalk each other like two vizored soldiers from ancient statuary . . . and as the stage revolves, their combat becomes a ritualized dance, performed to the sound of castanets. Helmets, armor, and swords fall from each warrior in turn; hand-to-hand combat follows: Audidius's eye and nose are horribly bloodied; Coriolanus conquers and is borne aloft by his troops, down rows of dead soldiers and mangled helmets on pikes, his hands raised casually to acknowledge the general cries."[31] Brecht's lifelong detestation of war, incarnate in sound and image, was as devastating as it was complete.

The Martius of Ekkehard Schall, Brecht's son-in-law, was splendidly Teutonic, a blond, violent, war machine created by and dedicated to the service of the bourgeois elite. In peacetime he was a brute; in war, "a plump narcissist who smiles as he kills" (*Observer*, 15 August 1965). As he made his cynical bid for votes, defiantly wearing a red toga over his gown of humility, "the [revolving] stage [brought] him from plebe to plebe as if he disdained to make the conciliatory gestures himself."[32] Even his relationship with Virgilia was perfunctory and chilly: on his return from the wars, he embraced her "with his wrists turned fastidiously back." His death, as unsentimental as his life, saw him "hacked down in mid-chuckle by a ring of soldiers with their arms round each other like a rugger scrum" (*Observer*, 15 August 1965), after which the Volscian army stomped on his body, then carried Aufidius over it in triumph. "[L]eft alone on stage, his corpse composed in a hideous and grotesque death,"[33] the hero who thought himself indispensable was a potently ironic object of contemplation.

Helena Weigel's Volumnia, political signifier rather than flesh-and-blood woman, made little impression apart from the moment in the Intercession scene when she knocked her head three times on the ground. Wolf Kaiser's Menenius, merely a tough-minded defender of aristocratic privilege, found little sympathy. Aufidius (Hilmar Thate), diminished as always in political readings, was "a seething cauldron of suppressed rage" in the opening scenes, and at the end "a grey and tortured little man . . . eaten away with envy of Coriolanus as by an acid."[34]

The Berliner production, whatever its visual charms, failed to upstage Shakespeare's creation. The redaction's simplistic Marxism was no substitute for the mature, if maddening, political complexity of the original. Worse still, its elevation of the citizens to stardom drained the action of dramatic tension: their role was complete with Martius's banishment, and the play's second half amounted simply to a prolonged wait for the unlovely hero to receive his comeuppance. Finally, the mechanism which accounted for Martius's destruction was itself suspect. That Coriolanus would abandon the attack on Rome because its citizens decide to resist him was entirely inconsistent with his character. There was nothing in his earlier behavior, as Harold Hobson put it, to "suggest he had so much common sense" (*Sunday Times,* 15 August 1965).

Five years after their debut at the World Theatre Season, Wekworth and Tenschert were again invited to Britain, this time to apply Brechtian production techniques to the unadulterated *Coriolanus* text in a National Theatre revival. Through a misunderstanding they arrived prepared to stage *Coriolan,* and were abruptly obliged to shift direction. Early rehearsals were in consequence rife with conflict, and Christopher Plummer, cast in the title role, precipitately quit and was replaced by Anthony Hopkins.[35]

The production which opened 6 May 1971 suggested that the German directors had simply restaged the Berliner Ensemble concept without the Brechtian text. Barred from rewriting the play, they opted to retain most of Brecht's cuts, to implement a series of novel transpositions, and to insert material from other Shakespearian dramas. The script, a hodge-podge identifiable as neither Brechtian polemic nor Shakespearian tragedy, does not warrant detailed analysis.[36] The mise-en-scène for the production, which opened 6 May 1971, was a virtual duplicate of von Appen's Berliner Ensemble design.

This time a problematic text was not redeemed by its staging. English actors and technicians, without the Ensemble's nine months of rehearsal, could only approximate its unique choreography and stagecraft. The citizens, deprived of the earthy humanity lent them by Brecht's interpolations, seemed merely a silent and sullen mass, and the patricians, a Brechtian caricature. As a result the play evinced "no ethical centre of gravity" (*The Times,* 7 May 1971). There was no individual or group with whom any rightminded theatergoer would want to side.

Amid a monumental display of incompetence and incoherence, the Martius of Anthony Hopkins, his first Shakespearian role, shone like the proverbial jewel in the dust. Required to create a totally repellent hero, he responded with a display of imagination and technique which left critics astonished. Speeches susceptible to favorable or unfavorable interpretation were uniformly given the most vicious coloration. The lines "He used me kindly," spoken during Martius's plea for the release of his Volscian host, were articulated as "the merest hypocrisy, an attempt to impress others with his supposed moral, as well as his proven physical, calibre"; later he admitted to forgetfulness "shrugging, smiling slightly and generally indicating that he couldn't care less."[37]

Shorn of the ambivalence, charm, and disarming tenderness of Shakespeare's contriving, Hopkins's Roman emerged as a bullet headed, thick necked fascist brute. His encounters with the plebeians were characterized by "clenching of fists and complacent, oddly sly smirks, all slouch, swagger and wary, hopeful rocking from foot to foot."[38] His fight with Aufidius was an ecstatic surrender to violence which ended "in a satisfied exhaustion that ha[d] post-coital undertones" (*Sunday Telegraph,* 9 May 1971). In the Voices scene "he pace[d] between the groups like an impatient cat, his vacillations and sudden solicitings emphasized by the revolving stage until he [could] take no more humiliation and roar[ed] out with angry pride" (*International Herald Tribune,* 15–16 May 1971). The narrative of boorishness as high art could be extended indefinitely.

Constance Cummings's Volumnia, a Nordic beauty with Wagnerian ambitions, incarnated to perfection maternal influence without maternal feeling. Like her son, she was merely the representative and instrument of imperial ambition; and in the Brechtian manner, was not on stage to witness the success of her strategy.

In 1975 Geoffrey Reeves mounted a *Coriolan*-inspired production at Liverpool's Everyman Theatre. The audience was seated in the dress circle, while the orchestra was occupied by a specially built platform overlooked by an enormous gate. The production's only noteworthy moment came in the Banishment scene when Peter Postlethwaite's raw and athletic Martius "leap[t] indignantly up into the circle, pour[ed] his patrician scorn [on the astonished clientele]. . . . then jump[ed] down again with a show of martial art more akin to Kung Fu than to Shakespeare" (*Daily Telegraph,* 30 April 1975). With this unexpected flourish, Brecht's *Coriolan* made its exit from the British stage,[39] although echoes of the Berliner Ensemble stagecraft lingered.

In a startling inversion of Brecht's Marxist reading, Brian Bedford's 1981 production at the Canadian Stratford cogently indicted the debasement of contemporary democratic politics, and highlighted the ruinous consequences for the individual who defies the system. At no time, it should be noted, did Bedford suggest fascism as an alternative to corrupt democracy, nor did he recommend Martian isolation. The moral of the production, if it had one, was that "the whole world is politics; the cut and thrust of deal-making is everywhere, and the man who disdains politics, and its part in human relationships, disdains life" (*Toronto Star,* 17 June 1981).

Although Shakespeare's text accommodates itself more readily to an anti-democratic than a Brechtian reading, Bedford nevertheless excised something like one-third of the play and biased performances unconscionably to render his contemporary parable pellucid.[40]

The plebeians, who gave fresh resonance to the term "political animal," were less individuals than an animate embodiment of abstract political force. Placed at the center of the action, their conduct rendered Martius's evaluation of them blatant understatement, and his refusal to temporize with them, like that of Forrest, an act not so much of class arrogance as moral integrity. Before the lights came up, the crowd, some twenty-four in all, was heard "panting and slavering in the darkness like one single horrifying monster" (*London [Ontario] Free Press,* 17 June 1981). With their cries and silences inflected by Gabriel Charpentier's electronic soundscape, they never appeared "more than semi-savage, a faceless crowd creeping in from the aisles of the theatre and stage entrances, ready to shift its ground with each new development" (*Kitchener-Waterloo Record,* 17 June 1981). Needless to say, their good-natured banter, like other mitigating Shakespearian features, was excised.

Martius on his first entrance seemed an entirely worthy match. Len Cariou, although less stalwart than some romantic performers, walked on "with a directness that seem[ed] to clear a path as if by magnetic force." His hair close-cropped and his face "almost a skull mask," he spoke "with the natural authority of those who never stop to think about consequences, only about what is right" (*Hamilton Spectator,* 17 June 1981). His conduct throughout, thanks to textual pruning and skilled acting, seemed, if not downright admirable, at least explicable. "His crime," concluded Gina Mallet, "if it is a crime, is that he has no patience for the meaningless rituals of inferior minds. That may qualify him as an élitist of sorts, but he is neither small-minded nor vindictive about it. He simply insists on the privilege of his convictions" (*Toronto Star,* 17 June 1981).

When Martius's reactionary stance precipitates his banishment, he insists, "There is a world elsewhere." But for one who eschews the rituals of power, there is not. Volscian politics differs little from Roman politics; and moral absolutism undoes him once more. Martius's refusal to concede so much as a glance over his shoulder, when belligerently ensconced on an Antium balcony, allowed Aufidius to climb up behind him and plant a knife in his back. As the erstwhile popular favorite pitched forward and down into the enraged mob, Ralph Berry recalls, "they turned in upon him and rent him. And then the Volscian people turned out toward the theatre audience with looks of candid, open-eyed complicity. They had devoured the hero, and we became part of the eating."[41]

Like most political readings, Bedford's devalued the play's psychological content. Never, save by Brecht, had Volumnia's speeches been so savaged. Fifteen vital, carnivorous lines (1.3.19–43) disappeared from her first scene, and about the same number from the episode in which she brings her son to heel (3.2). Her acerbic exchange with the tribunes (4.2) was entirely excised, to say nothing of some fifty lines of her intercession. Due to lack of text and Barbara Chilcott's inability to summon matriarchal strength, Volumnia's attempts to make and unmake her son seemed mere grandstanding.

To focus attention on Martius's conflict with the people, Menenius's contacts with them were limited, as were the tribunes' relations with both Martius and the electorate. The Aufidius of Scott Hyland, however, "a primitive force that respects only hardness and courage" (*Toronto Star,* 17 June 1981), commanded, despite considerable loss of text, more attention than in most political readings.

ANTIHERO AND SUPERHERO (1967–1978)

Constructive societal ideologies, particularly the Marxist idealism which fueled Brechtian and other forms of committed theater in the sixties and early seventies, had a relatively brief shelf life, and by the mid-seventies were swamped by a wave of deconstructive assaults on traditional values, institutions, even authority itself. The antihero, from Woody Allen to Dustin Hoffman, was the new protagonist. Yet, even as western society demythologized its collective persona, it pressed a narcissistic quest for individual liberation and relationship as an antidote to the spiritual desolation of modern life. The dilemma of the alienated self, classically probed in *A Clockwork Orange, E. T.,* and *Who's Afraid of Virginia Woolf?,* at once fascinating and repellent, offered cinema and theatrical box offices a bonanza. And Martius was a prime candidate for exploitation.

Three Royal Shakespeare productions—John Barton's in 1967, Trevor Nunn's in 1972, and Terry Hands's in 1977—all to some degree reflect the concerns of the era. All three ignore the play's political resonance in favor of a revisionist critique of Roman history and the exploitation of the phenomenon of alienation. All place Martius at the center of the action, but unlike romantic interpretations, invite not identification but estrangement: audiences at Barton's and Nunn's productions were repelled by an antihero; at Hands's, awed by an alien superhero.

John Barton's revival, which opened only two years after the visit of the Berliner Ensemble, owed a clear debt to its Brechtian predecessor, an obligation more stylistic than ideological however.[42] The repellent features of the play, and of Martius in particular, long glossed over in British and American productions and highlighted for political ends by the Ensemble, were now ruthlessly exploited by Barton as a revisionist gesture. From a Rome just emerging from prehistory, Barton culled the bleak aperçu that humankind's triumph over nature freed it only for the pursuit of power. In a production without heroes, Irving Wardle discovered "no ideological division between the masses and the nobility; all in one sense or another are equally engaged in the fight for territory" (*The Times,* 13 April 1967).

Barton's point was made, cleverly enough, not by textual manipulation, but by stagecraft and actorial ingenuity. No scenes were removed in their entirety, and the six hundred scattered lines excised through internal cuts seem defensible attempts to clarify syntax, minimize rhetoric, and shorten playing time, which occupied, even with the abridged text, three and a half hours including intervals.[43]

In thrall to the Ensemble's monochromism, John Bury clothed Barton's nihilistic vision, predictably enough, in unrelieved black. The bulk of the action took place inside a primitive wooden compound where totems towered above the palisade. Against a permanent black backcloth, figures in black leather armor and black furs bore black shields in black-gloved hands; not surprisingly, Martius went to his death sporting a black laurel wreath. Sharp-edged metal was a pervasive presence: branched iron and copper standards, forests of spears, and gigantic, spiked, oblong shields announced a violent, even sadistic, society, dominated by a ruthless warrior class. The citizens, in straw hats and dark woolens, betrayed, by way of contrast, a visual vulnerability, if no less ferocity and cupidity than their betters. Theatergoers' depression was modulated into despair by relentless chiaroscuro lighting, mitigated only by the occasional flare of torches.

The acting style, if not designed to alienate the audience outright, deliberately constrained emotion in favor of a Brechtian rationality, coolness, even dryness. The battle scenes were staged in slow motion along Ensemble lines, and sound effects were provided by stamping feet and clanging shields in the approved Brechtian mode.

The primitive powermonger found consummate representation in Ian Richardson's Martius. Blonde-haired and bronze-bodied, godlike and glacial, blindly egotistic and aggressively self-sufficient, he seemed "the embodiment of a tragic flaw in the body—and mind—politic of Rome . . . the personification of spiritual disease." His face was "dusky, waxen, almost immobile, his eye flashe[d] icily upon his fellow human beings, his laugh crackle[d] briefly and mirthlessly." He spoke "in a voice strangulated by his distaste for the need to communicate, even vocally, with anybody" (*Stratford-upon-Avon Herald,* 21 April 1967).

More slightly built than many Martiuses, Richardson offered athleticism in lieu of brawn. The battlefield sequences, in keeping with Martius's sporting proclivities, were played as a projection of the way he sees warfare, "an extension of the gymnasium, a place where young men may flex their muscles and indulge in a ritualistic game" (*Plays and Players,* June, 1967). On one occasion, with the horrifying nonchalance of a professional sportsman, he routinely took the life of one of his own men whom he considered laggard. Barton's indictment not only of Martius's, but society's, romanticization of war was devastating.

Although a chillingly effective fighting man, Richardson's Roman betrayed an elusive weakness. "Whereas most actors play Coriolanus as if his hauteur were built on the rock of a real and not a delusory inner assurance," noted Bryan Magee, "Ian Richardson gives him that special kind of enclosed shut-off quality that is a defence against vulnerability" (*Listener,* 25 May 1967). When threatened in civil situations, Martius retreated into a fastidious narcissism: ordered into exile, he spoke "I banish you" almost in a whisper, self-consciously disdainful of wasting vocal energy on inferiors. In the Intercession scene he not so much capitulated as disintegrated; "torn between conflicting maternal commands, he [came] apart like an over-strained child" (*Observer,* 16 April 1967). "All the pride and valour and contempt [were] shaken out of him in appalling sobs" (*Daily Mail,* 13 April 1967). But the emotional collapse of an otherwise frigidly malevolent savage left audiences unmoved, and his gruesome finale, crushed between four huge spiked shields, seemed somehow no more than fitting.

Barton's *Coriolanus* amounted to little more than a star turn since the plebeians, few and ineffective, failed to discharge their function in his societal critique. Indeed, the *Spectator* reviewer found "the loutish Roman crowd . . . barely there at all" (21 April 1967). Catherine Lacey's Volumnia, "like an ancient mistress of foxhounds, glorying in her son's wounds like a huntress blooding her young" (*Daily Mail,* 13 April 1967), pleased in the play's early scenes, but lacked matriarchal authority when it was called for. Aufidius (Edward Cicciarelli), Coriolanus's blond twin and alter ego, registered little more than a visual impact. Brewster Mason's Menenius, "a conservative politician, ripe-voiced but downy, a pseudo man-of-the-people with genuine powers of opinionation and abuse" (*Listener,* 25 May 1967), more than held his own amongst fellow frauds; while the tribunes (B-Nicholas Selby and S-Clive Swift), more repulsive products of a repellent society, were hardly noticed.

The lesson of Barton's production was that unrelieved repulsiveness itself repels. "[I]nordinately protracted and ferociously boring" was Harold Hobson's verdict (*Sunday Times,* 16 April 1967), and his sentiment, more tactfully voiced, was widely shared.

Five years on, Trevor Nunn, no more dazzled than Barton by the time-honored idealization of Shakespeare's Rome, mounted (with Buzz Goodbody) the Roman plays as a chronological cycle in a renewed attempt to deromanticize critical and theatrical tradition. Although Nunn disclaimed any intention to emulate the *Wars of the Roses* experiment, he clearly hoped *The Romans,* as he titled the venture, might reveal a similar collective resonance.[44]

Unfortunately, the Roman dramas, unlike the histories, betrayed no overarching theme, unifying insight, or cumulative momentum, and Nunn's projected epic of "the birth, achievement, and collapse of a civilisation" miscarried: *Titus Andronicus,* as finale to *The Romans,* proved less an illuminating capstone than an embarrassing anticlimax. *Coriolanus,* flagship of the enterprise, premiered in the 1972 Stratford season, and, after a critical thrashing, transferred, in what amounted to a new production, to the Aldwych in the autumn of 1973.

Prior to mounting the cycle, the capacity of the Stratford auditorium was increased by seventy-six seats, and the proscenium replaced by a bare fiberboard chamber, the floor of which, comprising a series of stone-textured blocks, hydraulically rose, fell, and tilted to create with cinematic ease walls, flights of steps, or tiers of Senate seats.

Coriolanus, in keeping with its historical primacy in the cycle, incarnated the birthpangs of Roman democracy, while the remaining plays traced its maturity and decline. Although Nunn shared Barton's disinterest in the play's more obvious political issues, he, like his predecessor, was intrigued by the process of power-acquisition as a sociological phenomenon; and his revival, despite being staged on a white set in blinding white light, offered as little cause for optimism as did Barton's Stygian venture. In Rome, a power-mad patrician oligarchy was bent on creating a myth of omnipotence on the backs of a group of long-suffering craftsmen. The Volscians, whose costumes and rituals owed something to Aztec or early Amerindian inspiration, came off as aggressive barbarians, at a developmental level from which Rome had only recently emerged. Martius, like Kean's Roman, a creature of an earlier ethos, refuses to subscribe to homegrown power rituals, and betakes himself to primitive Antium, where he is welcomed, even godded. In the end, however, a vulnerability engendered by civilization undoes him in Volscian eyes, and he dies twice a victim of nationalist arrogance.

The text played was relatively full.[45] Only about four hundred lines were cut, most of them to clarify syntax and reduce performance time. The only scene wholly removed was Titus's instruction to his lieutenant to guard the ports (1.7).

Spectacle was of the essence; its function, however, was not, as in Kemble's revivals, to lend Martius reflected glory, but, through dehumanized authoritarian rituals, to estrange the audience from both Roman and Volscian positions. Huge crowds, both Roman and Volscian, filled the heaving stage. In an introductory tableau, the great bronze she-wolf was borne aloft on poles by bronze-masked automata while Romulus and Remus were held up to the vulpine teats. This image of a Rome implacably in pursuit of a national destiny, a commitment to which individual ambition must bow or be broken, set the tone for the cycle. In the wake of the procession, a ragged plebeian lay dead—a negligible sacrifice to nationalistic ambition. Martius's own destruction, another minor blip on the historical screen, could hardly have been more effectively foreshadowed. The repulsive final scene in which, in a similar chauvinistic rite, he was ceremonially lifted high by Volscian warriors, disemboweled over a fire, and left on stage under a fading spotlight, was its inevitable realization.

Nunn's sociological obsession proved to be the production's undoing. His absorption in the clash of civilizations, and the peripheral spectacle that implied, finally submerged the play's focal conflict, the clash between patricians and plebeians, against which Martius's tragedy unfolds. The casting of the diminutive Ian Hogg as an Errol Flynn-like antihero was the final nail in the production's coffin. Physically unimpressive and vocally feeble, he virtually disappeared amid undulating settings, creeping smoke and flame, seething crowds, and strobe lighting. Margaret Tyzack's Volumnia, without a Coriolanus worthy of her mettle, was a musician without an instrument.

For its Aldwych premiere in November 1973 the production was remounted and substantially recast. Stratford's surging stage was succeeded by a stable black box adorned only with scaffolding to which scenic items were attached as needed. Spectacle was downplayed, and the Roman wolf tableau dispatched. The text, abbreviated by some eight hundred lines, lost the Adrian-Nicanor sequence as well as the Titus Lartius scene.

While the production still stressed Rome's preoccupation with her manifest destiny, its focus, by accident or design, was now Nicol Williamson's highly original antihero—a stunning portrayal of a man of straw whose life was one long act of overcompensation for a gaping hollowness at his center. In a prefatory tableau, Williamson stood "in a blaze of light on a darkened stage. On his defenseless body his attendants drape[d] the trappings of war, added to disguise the weakness of the flesh, whilst his arms [were] stretched out in the attitude of a man crucified" (*Sunday Times,* 28 October 1973). This Martius was to be more victim than victor.

For the first time in the play's history, the general's aristocratic origins were put in question: he seemed to Harold Hobson "less a man nurtured on generations of wealth and social dominance than a product of the underprivileged and deprived blowing himself pathetically up into the semblance of an arrogant patrician" (*Sunday Times,* 28 October 1973). It was equally evident that a frightened child was attempting to impersonate a man. Continuous military action informed by rage was Martius's sole defense against recognition of his own vulnerability. "Throughout the play," wrote Hobson, "he drives himself to thunder out defiances and insults which his thin voice is inadequate to sustain" (*Sunday Times,* 28 October 1973). Even his modesty struck Irving Wardle as "an incapacity for any close human contact outside warfare" (*The Times,* 23 October 1973). Domestic emotions were quite beyond him: he displayed little affection for his wife, and his relationship with his mother was animated by something close to hatred. Unable to share communal pain in the Farewell scene, "he [ran] out of the gate while his friends' backs [were] turned" (*Observer,* 28 October 1973).

His desertion to the Volscians was as much an act of psychological self-preservation as of revenge: without war, no matter against whom, he has no self. Here was no misled patrician patriot, but a "professional *déraciné,* classless, mercenary, dedicated to victory, anybody's dictator but only for, and by, the power of the army" (*Observer,* 28 October 1973). Aufidius could no more elicit an emotional response from him than anyone else: when

welcomed into the Volsican ranks Martius stood impassive, "rigidly suffering the fraternal embrace" (*The Times,* 23 October 1973).

To accede to his mother's demand, Martius understood, meant not merely
the sacrifice of his military ambitions, but his precarious hold on selfhood.
"The pause after Volumnia's plea "seem[ed] to stretch out into minutes
while Williamson's face visibly turn[ed] to pulp" (*The Times,* 23 October
1973). Now as naked psychologically as he had been physically at the play's
outset, the would-be dragon was utterly without defence: "all the pretences
are stripped from him in the unbearable crisis of self-discovery" (*Sunday
Times,* 28 October 1973). After this calculated act of psychological suicide,
his physical destruction seemed little more than a perfunctory gesture. It
was entirely appropriate that he expired in a crouched fetal position.

Margaret Tyzack, better partnered than at Stratford, revealed a Volumnia
of memorable power, if scarcely of classic cut. An apt parent for Williamson's patrician *manqué*, she might have been "the widow of some Roman
property speculator who had come into money late in life" (*Sunday Times,*
28 October 1973). The son without a sense of self was the hapless issue of
a woman with infinite social aspirations but no maternal instincts. Consum-
mately manipulative at home and in the Volscian camp, she was the "lady
beast-trainer showing in the midst of a circus disaster that she can control
. . . the animal she has conditioned from birth" (*Plays and Players,* December, 1973).

In the end Williamson's brilliantly executed, and ultimately sympathetic,
antihero annihilated such vestiges as remained of Nunn's sociohistoric pre-
occupations, totally upstaging in the process Mark Dignam's unctuous and
unprincipled Menenius, Oscar James's sonorous (and black) Aufidius, and
the epicene tribunes of Philip Locke and John Nettleton, "a couple of silly
old queens, flapping their arms, widening their eyes and hissing."[46] The
citizens, fewer than at Stratford and less spectacularly deployed, almost
escaped notice, while the Volscians, now an African tribe sporting pigtails
and black jockstraps, were aggressively obtrusive.

Without a major star or press fanfare and the final offering of the 1977
RSC season, Terry Hands's *Coriolanus,* starring the forty-year-old Alan
Howard, was critically hailed as the most satisfying revival since the Hall-
Olivier partnership. After a successful Stratford run, it traveled to the RSC's
Newcastle base in March of 1978, arrived at the Aldwych in June, and in
1979 toured Europe.[47]

The text, one of the fullest on record, was abbreviated by only about
three hundred lines, some five hundred fewer than the Hall script.[48] Hands
removed no scenes in their entirety, contenting himself with minor internal
cuts. His only textual innovation was the attribution of the Officers'
speeches in 2.2 to seven citizens, who place benches as they talk, a tactic
which not only denies Martius a character reference from relatively neutral

parties, but credits the citizens with more perspicacity than Shakespeare allows. Playing time was an even three hours, excluding two intervals.

Hands's revival, innocent of political or sociological critique, simply depicted, as Irving Wardle saw it, "the conflict between those who bend to circumstances and the one character who cannot do such violence to his own nature" (*The Times,* 22 October 1977). That struggle between collective relativism and individual absolutism was played out in the context of patrician-plebeian contestation, toward which the production maintained, in Andrew Gurr's opinion, a position "as carefully neutral as litmus paper."[49]

The setting, designed by Farrah, was simply a ludic space, an arrangement of anonymous, starkly lit slabs which closed and parted in a manner suggestive of gates or walls as required. Benches were added for the Senate scene, and a table and chairs for the banishment sequence. Living scenery was not much in evidence: the numbers of citizens never exceeded seven at any time. Battles were likewise minimalistic, and staged in slow motion.

Coriolanus dominated the action from beginning to end, a looming epic figure, like the great seamark of his own image. Better, perhaps, than any actor before or since, Howard captured the alien otherness of the man: a robot designed by his mother for patrician conquest, his motivation seemed largely a matter of conditioned reflex. "His personal rivalry for Aufidius . . . his innate dislike of the lower orders, and his respect for his mother amount to the total of his opinions," wrote B. A. Young. "To turn traitor against the Romans, to shop the Volscians in their turn, these are not matters to worry his conscience; they are just instinctive reactions to his situation" (*Financial Times,* 21 October 1977).

The isolation of the epic outsider was driven home by the sociality with which he was surrounded. The tribunes, validating Menenius's observation "You do very little alone," continually "look[ed] to each other for support and often [spoke] in unison" (*The Times,* 22 October 1977). The patricians and plebeians compulsively sought solace in groups, and the Volscians, in the end, found the courage to assassinate him only in the collective hysteria of a lynch mob.

At crucial moments throughout the play, the character's heroic individualism was sculpted in rivetting images. On his first entrance, clad in skintight black leather pierced with metal studs, and lighted directionally, Howard seemed abnormally tall and long-legged, an alien giant casting huge shadows over the puny clusters of citizens and patricians around him. During the seige of Corioli he reappeared from his one-man assault spread-eagled on the city gates, like some great avenging angel, streaming with blood and thirsting for more. Later, on the battlefield, as he urged, "O me alone, make you a sword of me," the soldiers raised him on crossed spears high in the air, blood-spattered and incandescent, like some all-conquering god. When his banishment was pronounced, he snatched the trestle table at which the tribunes were seated, raised it picturesquely above his head, and dashed it

"O me alone! make you a sword of me!" (Coriolanus-Alan Howard). Terry Hands Production, Royal Shakespeare Theatre, 1977. [By permission of the Shakespeare Centre Library, Stratford-upon-Avon]

to the floor. At his homecoming and the intercession, the women were
blocked "to look like statuesque figures paying [divine] homage in a Christian tableau" (*Evening News,* 1 November 1977). After decades of reductive
portraits, Howard's epic conception prompted a response little short of awe.

While Volumnia (Maxine Audley) was clearly the creator of the dragon,
her control was less sure than usual. His agreement to temporize with the
plebeians was unconvincingly won, and his failure in the Banishment scene
to implement the new agenda did not surprise. In the Intercession scene it
was apparent that Volumnia had fashioned an instrument of war she was
afraid to use. Quite as diffident as everyone else, she made her plea with
respectful rationality, and he responded in kind. "There is no great emotional
crack-up to Volumnia's supplications," noted Wardle. "He simply chooses
to spare Rome and is never more thoroughly in command of the situation
than when he embraces his family under the baleful eye of Julian Glover's
Aufidius. He knows it means death" (*The Times,* 22 October 1977). The
motivation for Martius's surrender remained a mystery, but it was clearly
not the outcome of Volumnia's manipulation. Was he simply tired of being
the tool of others' ambition? Some such impulse might account for his
equally enigmatic gesture in the Assassination scene when, confronted by
Volscian cutthroats, he abruptly impaled himself on Aufidius's dagger before
the pikes could touch him. The overpowering black-clad superhero took his
secret to the grave with him.[50] Unfortunately, it was precisely a lack of
motivational clarity here and elsewhere that denied tragic resonance to Howard's performance and the production as a whole. To sympathize, one must
understand. The inner mechanism of Shakespeare's Martius is indeed often
mysterious, but the playwright endows him with sufficient fallible humanity
to build a bridge from his alienated world to ours. It was this connection
that Hands and Howard severed. The fate of an absolutist automaton might,
and did, inspire awe, even terror, but tragic pity reserves itself for creatures
of our own kind.

Despite Martius's epic pervasiveness, the supporting characters were
rarely upstaged. Audley's Volumnia, tiny but frigidly authoritative, was precisely the sort of mother to fabricate a military robot. Her uncompromising
drive for power through her offspring expressed itself in a frighteningly
seductive possessiveness toward him which masked her fragile sense of
control. On her final appearance, in the silent stage cross of 5.5, "she flung
off Young Martius' cloak to show him, hands crossed over a sword, black
leather armour and defiant chin, the young image of his father."[51] Matriarchal
power-madness was about to give birth to another superman.

The citizens, clad in donkey jackets and brilliantly led by the 1st Citizen
of Barrie Rutter, were honest tradesmen rather than comic foils, their
individual characters and opinions paramount rather than massed noise
and motion. The mackintoshed tribunes (Brutus-Oliver Ford-Davies and
Sicinius-Tim Wylton), if played as contemporary trades union leaders, en-

joyed a welcome measure of sincerity and humanity. The patricians, too, received their due as men born to rule rather than imperialistic caricatures. Graham Crowden's Menenius, waggishly dispensing wisdom from a shooting stick, "larding his insults with smiles when dealing with the people, embarrassingly subservient to the patricians, but notably firm in serious debate" (*Financial Times*, 21 October 1977), was a memorable creation. Julian Glover's Aufidius, garbed as Martius's alter ego and aping his mannerisms like envy personified, was picturesque, cool, and dignified, even as he held the dagger on which his erstwhile partner fell.

POSTMODERN EXPERIMENT (1979–1994)

Revivals of the past decade disclose no major common production trend, but rather a set of more or less postmodern features.[52] The modernist notion of an organic unity or totalizing narrative within a Shakespeare text to be revealed through an illusionistic production style to an emotionally involved audience has given way to a notion of the text as a series of exploitable theatrical opportunities, wherein nonhomogenous, discontinuous images unfold for a detached spectator, who thinks and evaluates as much as feels. Plays are frequently slanted to highlight contemporary concerns—racism, gender politics, sexuality, or media influence—and as often as not, the point is made through image rather than text. Frequently the images, eclectic, shocking, historically dislocated, and often spectacular, are ironically loaded, employing quotation, frequently from pop culture, to make a revisionist point for an intellectually alert audience. Between director and theatergoer is assumed to exist a playful and self-reflexive complicity based on shared values or lack of them. Most postmodern revivals are more interesting for flashes of ingenious technique than for extended, disciplined reinterpretation.

In an admirable postmodern attempt to "shatter the 'white' image of Shakespeare"[53] and make the play more accessible to New York's marginalized cultural communities, Michael Langham mounted at the 1979 New York Shakespeare Festival a *Coriolanus* with a cast of black and Hispanic actors. The experiment, more a political statement than an artistic one due to the company's want of acting and verse-speaking expertise, served only to prove to Michael Goldman "that twenty black actors can play Shakespeare just as routinely as twenty white ones."[54]

Postmodernism was more competently and imaginatively in evidence in Peter Hall's second *Coriolanus*—on the Olivier stage at the National Theatre in December of 1984, precisely a quarter century after his first. Despite the dispraise of conservative critics, the play enjoyed 102 London performances and a further two nights at the Herod Atticus amphitheatre in Athens.

The production's uniqueness, apart from the readings of Ian McKellen and Irene Worth, derived from Hall's decision to impose no unifying directorial conception, but rather to foster an environment within which the play's potential might reveal itself. Apart from an insistence on "classically correct" technique, Hall allowed performers an unusual degree of freedom to explore relationships in rehearsals, and even encouraged improvisation during performances, a tactic which lent freshness and edge from show to show.[55]

Profoundly concerned by the political and social issues which divided Thatcherite Britain, Hall challenged his company to explore the use and abuse of power, not as practiced by parties but as experienced by individuals. No attempt was made to made to demonize any character or point of view: the company's goal was simply to investigate the power process.

John Bury's setting, a circular sandpit, was backed by gargantuan reversible gates; one gold-studded side represented Rome, the other, stark black, stood for Antium and Corioli. In contrast to the recurrent monochromism of RSC productions, Hall's version, in the postmodern European manner, was a visual feast. For the triumphal return scene, for example, the stage was covered with a huge red carpet, while red banners floated everywhere.

Costumes ranging from mauve silk togas to double-breasted suits to First World War battle fatigues, to jeans, sweatshirts, and sweaters, sometimes even in combination, lent a timeless, if at times disconcerting, quality to the piece. In an amusing 1970s RSC quotation, the Volscians appeared in black leather.

To underscore the production's self-conscious theatricalism, some ninety audience members were seated nightly on risers located on either side of the stage and co-opted from time to time into the performance. Umbrellas and purses in hand, they were a forcible reminder to the audience in the auditorium proper of the nonillusionistic character of the event; but when they blocked sightlines, swamped the action, and occasionally confused the actors, some playgoers justifiably felt postmodern sensibility could carry too high a price tag. Eventually Hall reluctantly reduced their numbers.

The text was shortened by some five hundred lines, primarily through internal cutting.[56] The only scene removed in its entirety was the Adrian-Nicanor episode. The heaviest single cut was the colloquy among the servingmen (4.5.148–235) after Martius and Aufidius conclude their pact. Most excisions were pragmatic attempts to simplify syntax, abbreviate prolix speeches, or remove obscure references.

Confined spatially to the sandpit, in the manner of Hall's 1960 *Troilus and Cressida* at the RSC, the play's intricate interplay of individual and collective power hunger was tightly focused visually and aurally. Despite Hall's determination to give equal time to all points of view, Hazlitt's observation that "The insolence of power is stronger than the plea of necessity" was amply confirmed. The sheer charisma of McKellen's Coriolanus (pronounced Cor-*eye*-olanus in the Kemble manner), like that of Olivier, drew all eyes toward him, and upstaged, despite the best intentions of all concerned, not least McKellen himself, the production's thematic objective.

A "valour-drunk anachronism in a world of political calculation that has no place for heroes" (*The Times*, 17 December 1984), Martius on his first entrance, in sunglasses and an immaculate white suit with matching overcoat and shoes, was a calculated insult to hard up plebeians in sloppy sweaters and jeans. Cockily balancing a golden sheathed sword on his shoulder as an Edwardian dandy might have sported a cane, he spat his contempt at the placard-waving ("Corn for the People") populace. Hazlitt's insolence of power was incarnate in a single stroke of visual bravura.

On the battlefield, half-naked and soaked in gore, Martius found fresh opportunity for exhibitionism. For the fight with Aufidius he stripped to a bloodstained jockstrap; later as he pleaded, "Make you a sword of me," he stood, arm outstretched and streaming with blood, on a soldier's shoulders like an avenging fury. Small wonder that in the homecoming sequence his protest, "No more of this, it does offend my heart," was greeted by a burst of audience-laughter.

Like Olivier, he mined the role for humor, particularly in the Voices scene where he stood "on a stool in a floppy-hat like royalty self-consciously slumming," an antiromantic quotation from the first Hall production for stage connoisseurs with good memories (*Guardian*, 17 December 1984). When permitted to doff his gown of humility, Martius "wriggle[d] out of [it] like someone getting out of a bathing-suit at high speed" (*Guardian*, 17 December 1984). Under his mother's scolding in 3.2, in a droll evocation of childish guilt, he "alternately shift[ed] his feet in the sand and sw[ung] his sword like a pendulum."[57]

At his final confrontation with the plebeians, staged more as a people's court than a lynching party, Martius's narcissistic fury contrasted sharply with the fussy formality of the tribunes and people. Towards the end of the scene, however, the roles were reversed: as the people regressed into hysteria, Coriolanus, with consummate control, walked among them, addressing each phrase of his "You common cry of curs" speech "to individuals in the crowd, causing them to look away."[58] In a departure which must have had nineteenth-century stars spinning in their sepulchres, Martius's disembodied voice defiantly proclaimed from *offstage*, "There is a world elsewhere."

In the house of Aufidius, at the moment of reconciliation, he briefly dropped his guard. "Part of him had hoped Aufidius would say no and run him through, then and there." Now "grief and despair drain[ed] his face as Aufidius accept[ed] his offer" (*Observer*, 23 December 1984). Both McKellen and Greg Hicks (who played Aufidius) recognized in this scene a sexual dimension (as in the fight in act 1), and it was given varied emphasis in each performance, but never allowed to constitute an interest in itself.

His struggle in the Intercession scene was titanic, and clearly intensified by the familial tenderness he allowed himself at the outset. The silent hand-holding seemed to last for an eternity before he said, "You have won a happy victory to Rome." As he spoke, Bedford records, "he squeezes [Volumnia's] hand in rhythm to the lines to drive the point home. Suddenly he breaks away and crosses right, uttering an active acceptance of his fate: 'But let it come.' His movement away from his mother comes as a step towards death."[59]

To lend the play's finale a flash of postmodern theatricality, Martius entered down the central aisle of the theater to the whistles and cheers of an adoring populace, and ran a lap round the sandpit in a cloud of gold confetti. Moments later, with Aufidius's indictment, the celebratory mood turned ugly. On the lines "Measureless liar, thou has made my heart / Too great for what contains it," he suffered an apparent heart attack, and contended throughout the rest of the scene with physical pain as well as wounded pride. At last, with the conclusion of his taunt beginning "O that I had him," he drew his sword and lunged at Aufidius in blind fury, only to find himself gunned down by two volleys of rifle fire from the ramparts. Immediately afterwards, Aufidius posed triumphantly with both feet on the corpse. The funeral cortege offered cold comfort to lovers of heroic finales: as the body was carried upstage, "[p]iercing music and a high pitched whine buil[t] to ear-shattering intensity, to be cut off only with the climactic crash of the gates slamming shut."[60]

Irene Worth, like Edith Evans, found the key to Volumnia's character in a fatally attractive femininity which camouflaged a fearsome ambition. Sewing at home with Virgilia, she seemed "disconcertingly cosy" (*Sunday Telegraph*, 23 December 1984), seductively "cooing 'O, she shall' over her needlework when Virgilia decline[d] to accommodate her wishes" (*The Times*, 17 December 1984). At Martius's victorious return, her "sudden emergence as a public hero in the processional pomp of red carpet and trumpets" evoked a disarming "mixture of rapture and bewilderment" (*Financial Times*, 17 December 1984). At home after Martius offended the people, she made "a point of greeting each of the senators in turn in the gracious manner of Mrs. Reagan at a White House reception" (*Financial Times*, 17 December 1984); and when Martius briefly flouted her authority she did not deign to raise her voice: "all she does," reported one reviewer, "is to turn her back on him, and slowly restore her approval once she has reduced him to a gauche, guilty adolescent with a mouth stupidly agape" (*The Times*, 17 December 1984). Here the "superficial cosiness" she demonstrated earlier, like that of Edith Evans, rendered "her maternal hold on Coriolanus even more sinister" (*Sunday Telegraph*, 23 December 1984). Her rage at the tribunes after Martius's leave-taking owed as much to her loss of power in Roman society as maternal loneliness. "With the exile of her son," observes Bedford, "she has been robbed of the medium through which she vicariously won the wars and ruled the state."[61] And that loss of power she cold-bloodedly aimed to redress in the Intercession scene. Through "perfectly timed false exits, and low-register vocal resources," even prostrating herself in the sand at one point, she subjected Martius to what the *Times* reviewer found "as spellbinding a demonstration of emotional blackmail as I have ever seen" (17 December 1984). Approaching the climax of the petition, Bedford noticed, Volumnia "look[ed] him in the eye, then deliberately turn[ed] away" as in the Admonition scene, at which point Martius convulsively reached for her hand.[62] On her final, silent, appearance, she progressed down the central aisle of the auditorium while the stage audience stood and applauded rhythmically. Eventually she arrived at the sandpit. "Fighting back the tears," her wordless presence witnessed with consummate eloquence "to the public triumph and personal grief at war within her."[63] "[S]mall, twitching smiles acknowledge the plaudits," observed a spectator, "but the eyes express a terrible desolation, since she already realises that [Martius] must die" (*Sunday Telegraph,* 23 December 1984). And to continued rhythmical applause, her procession passed through the gates.

Seldom has Aufidius evinced greater intrinsic interest. Thanks to a full text and careful attention to stage imagery, Greg Hicks's Volscian emerged as a high-principled military man finally "gone wrong, just beaten one too many times."[64] The often neglected episode with the Volscian senators (1.2), when staged formally with appropriate numbers of supers, fully justified the Roman anxiety, and identified Aufidius, attired in a long black coat in contrast to the white outfit affected by Martius, as a force to be reckoned with, an impression confirmed by the character's compelling physical and psychological stillness. In the course of the play, his spiritual degeneration was mapped as much in images as words. A milestone was his exit after the hand-to-hand encounter with Coriolanus: virtually naked, he trudged off in utter humiliation, clutching his shield and helmet and dragging his sword behind him. At the opening of 1.10, he reappeared still naked beneath a black coat draped over his shoulders, his body streaming with blood, still trailing his sword. "The despair and anger of his opening line 'The town is ta'en!'", Bedford recollects,

> mingle with the quiet solemnity of the stage picture, as the ravages of war find visual expression in the wounded bodies lying strewn about their leader. Aufidius surveys the devastation, and makes the internal shift from humiliation at this powerlessness to regain the city . . . to a personal sense of outraged pride: "Mine emulation / Hath not that honour in't it had" . . . .[65]

In a unique innovation he delivered most of his conversation with the lieutenant in 4.7 as a soliloquy, thus obviating a concern of editors and critics from Coleridge onward that the conversation seems inappropriate between a military leader and a subordinate. In the closing moments of the play, his abrupt change of heart, often wanting in credibility, carried more than usual conviction: the unnatural callousness which had hitherto sustained him suddenly collapsed, and the full awareness of his crime flooded in upon him. "His hatred for Coriolanus," writes Bedford, "has always been personal, one individual's envy for another, and the removal of that object means that the greatest part of his own life is dead with him. . . . Thus 'My rage is gone' . . . conveys a profound sense of emptiness and desolation."[66] Frederick Treeves's Menenius provided a headily satisfying mixture of political sagacity, high spirits, and endearing fallibility with no hint of caricature. The tribunes (Brutus-James Hayes and Sicinius-David Ryall) were played more seriously than in most productions; indeed Hall discouraged the actors from lapses into slapstick, and the characters' political stance, in consequence, gained credibility. The citizens, too, viewed not through Martius's eyes but as a neutral observer might see them, commanded an unusual degree of sympathy.

In retrospect Hall's postmodernism seems less radical than it appears at first blush. "Rarely do any of the major Anglophone companies hazard the transgressive Shakespearean acting [of European companies]," writes Dennis Kennedy. "What looks postmodern in Britain or North America is nothing more than . . . an innovative visual frame for rather traditional performances."[67] His observation applies with particular force to Hall's venture. However open-endedly postmodern the rehearsal and performance process, however ingeniously metatheatrical the stagecraft and mise-enscène, the acting style would not have been incompatible with any production of the past half century.

Deborah Warner's 1986 Kick Theatre production at the Almeida was as self-awarely theatrical as was the National revival: now, however, the absence of visual diversion rather than its presence served to remind the audience of its postmodern spectatorship. In what the director described as "minimalism taken to its absolute" (*Hampstead & Highgate Express,* 12 September 1986), the play was staged by a company of twelve barefoot actors, dressed in timeless costumes, in and around a ring of a dozen wooden crates. Played in an uncut text in three and three-quarter hours, the production proclaimed itself theater of the word and the ear, but the young actors lacked the maturity and technique to meet the challenge. Starved for visual excitement, the audience perhaps gave undue weight to the candlelit fight between Martius and Aufidius, in which they cast gigantic shadows on the back wall as they circled each other, and the moment in which Martius stripped naked in the Voices scene in transparent defiance of the text.

Closer to the iconoclastic privileging of image over text typical of European postmodernist Shakespeare were Steven Berkoff's production at the New York Shakespeare Festival in 1988 and the *Coriolan* of Robert Lepage's Théâtre Repère de Québec, which gained international attention in June

1994 at the Festival de Théâtre des Amériques in Montreal and later toured to the Nottingham Playhouse and elsewhere.

Berkoff's production, more an improvisation on Shakespeare's text than an interpretation of it,[68] was a cynical montage of images presenting Shakespeare's Rome as a contemporary American cityscape. Costumes, quotations from Hollywood cinema clichés, at once underlined the action's theatricality and subjected the playgoer to an ironic juxtaposition of historic word and contemporary image. The citizens, sporting "black leather pants, black buttoned-up shirts, and pointed leather shoes," conjured up an Italian-American street gang, while the tribunes in pinstripes recalled small-time mobsters. The patricians declined into hard-eyed bureaucrats, and Volumnia (Irene Worth) into a ruthless political "fixer." Christopher Walken's Martius, attired in a long, black leather overcoat, black silk shirt, and black trousers, evoking "simultaneously Hollywood 'Nazi' and contemporary urban chic,"[69] strutted to a percussive score played by a solitary musician who accompanied the entire production. Walken's Coriolanus in the end gained the audience's sympathy, not because he was an intrinsically admirable person, but because he was the only individual with any claim to integrity in a nest of metropolitan vipers.

With a mise-en-scène consisting only of a row of slender classical columns and a dozen straight-backed chairs, the heavily cut text, thanks to stylized movement and imaginative lighting, took on something approximating the mythic dimension of oriental theater. The battle scenes were mimed without swords, but with overwhelming conviction, as was Martius's assassination. One of the play's most eloquently ironic images was a gray diplomatic envelope containing the Roman-Volscian peace treaty which Martius finally signed. At one point Aufidius held it contemptuously between thumb and forefinger; at another, Volumnia waved it aloft in her victory procession; and after Martius's death it was passed to an anonymous bureaucrat who casually popped it into his briefcase and snapped the lid shut. The act that broke Martius's proud spirit and cost him his life, far from being a cataclysmic event, was merely a minor incident in a larger scenario written elsewhere by faceless power brokers.

Lepage's *Coriolan,* like Berkoff's project, was played in a drastically cut text employed largely as scaffolding to support images, again of cinematic, and specifically of Felliniesque, origin. Set within a rectangular frame five feet by fifteen feet, cut into a black screen furnished with surtitles and scene identifications, the action featured three-dimensional performers in what amounted to a scaled-down evocation of cinemascope. In a period of just over two hours, a postmodern Martius (Jules Philip) attempted with disastrous results to come to terms with a contemporary Rome in which "what counts is PR and effective self-presentation; an inside world of spoilt celebrities, narcissistic luminaries, and fixers with agendas" (*The Times,* 26 November 1993). Theatergoers were distanced from events not only by the

Intercession Scene. Robert LePage Production. Théâtre Repère de Québec, 1993. [Copyright Emmanuel Valette 1992. Droits résérves]

voyeuristic slot through which action was viewed, but also by mediation of most of the play's action by a variety of media. Menenius (Jacques Languirand) narrated the belly fable on television to citizens who were never more than noises off; the battles were fought by military puppets; the erotic nude wrestling match between Martius and Aufidius (Gerald Gagnon) was reflected in an angled mirror; the tribunes watched Martius's triumphant return on television, and later plotted his downfall by telephone; Martius was banished in the course of a television talk show, and his act of filial submission was reduced to a filmic frame or two in which "a hand descend[ed] from a long black dress contemptuously to rumple his hair" as he knelt (*The Times*, 26 November 1993).

Recent mainstream productions, however, have tended to espouse a modernistic respect for the integrity of the text, favor a psychoanalytic as distinct from a political thrust, and timidly insinuate postmodern visual touches by way of novelty.

Terry Hands's second *Coriolanus* for the RSC, staged in 1988 with the assistance of John Barton, although an otherwise lackluster affair, demands attention for its postmodern deference to feminist politics. Women, who had almost invisibly swelled stage crowds for centuries, were not only present, but militantly active. "In 2.3 it was the women plebeians,"

who provided the switch of mood against Coriolanus with the Third Citizen's speech (2.3.166–73) divided between a group of women. In 5.1 there was a strong emphasis on the men arming for the threat of war and, by the end of the scene, a powerful image of the women left behind, the city unmanned. . . . Even more emphatically the voices of the Volscian people in 5.6 shouting against Coriolanus were all women, a female recognition of the costs of Coriolanus' actions by the people who are "widowed and unchilded" . . . The Volscian women urged their men to attack Coriolanus who was knifed by Aufidius and then mobbed and beaten to death by the crowd.[70]

The definitive feminist statement came with Volumnia's stage cross in 5.5. Where in 1978 the matron simply displayed the boy dressed as a miniature version of his parent, implicitly declaring her individual intention to create another military monster, she now engaged in a matriarchal power rite in which Valeria spoke the senator's eulogy and presented the boy with his father's sword, after which the people knelt to acknowledge their latest savior, led in triumph around the stage by his grandmother.

Postmodern features in other recent productions seem adventitious stylistic flourishes rather than key components of an animating aesthetic. Michael Bogdanov's 1990 English Shakespeare Company production, set in contemporary Eastern Europe, attempted not simply to highlight the political relevance of Shakespeare's text in the manner of the modern dress revivals of Barry Jackson's *Hamlet* or Orson Welles's *Caesar,* but to force audiences to read the Jacobean words against a set of contemporary images for whatever ironic insights might emerge. In an ambiance suggestive of Poland in the dying days of the Communist regime, corrupt patricians/Communists were confronted by plebeians/Solidarity activists. Playgoers, constrained witnesses to the birth of a democracy, were obliged to reexamine their own jaded political responses as they joined the Roman/Eastern European crowd in creating a social revolution. "The crowd's discussions," according to Peter Holland, "(for example in 2.3 and 3.3) became intense and complex political debates, conducted with the house lights up and with the people spread through the auditorium as well as on stage, debating through a microphone, prompted where necessary by the tribunes."[71] The theatricality of the postmodern aesthetic was highlighted by the abrupt violation of the illusionistic conventions which normally separate the viewer from the viewed—light and space. The play's interpersonal, as distinct from political, relationships were conventionally played.

The Renaissance Theatre Company revival in 1992 at the Chichester Festival Theatre, with Kenneth Branagh in the title role, sought postmodern theatricality through an evocation of clichés of modernist design: the Chichester apron was painted the red of drying blood and the upstage area was stripped to its structural walls and equipped with red scaffolding in a neat Wellesian quotation; a blue traverse curtain of the sort beloved by the Elizabethan Methodists and Brecht was an obtrusive presence; and more than

fifty locally recruited amateurs swarmed over the stage in the best tradition
of Benson and Bridges-Adams.

Apart from its battles, almost surrealistic in their disconcerting configu-
rations of huge oblong shields, the show's most suggestive visual device was
a recurrent ladder image: in the first scene, two ladders fixed to the upstage
scaffolding were used by citizens as rostrums from which to rouse their
compatriots; at Corioli Martius mounted a ladder, held aloft by military
admirers, from which he surveyed the battlefield and harangued the troops;
in the assassination sequence, he was raised aloft on another ladder, this
time by Volscian enthusiasts, to defy Aufidius, who leapt on it in pursuit of
his quarry. The ladder was then lowered. The citizens closed round it as
Martius received the coup de grâce, and then they half-raised it to display
the corpse as Aufidius spoke the eulogy. In a final, ironic exclamation point,
it was pressed into service as a bier.[72]

Costumes were "postmodern eclectic" in style—trousers, breastplates,
helmets, jackets, aprons, waistcoats, and rudimentary togas and gowns. In
an apparent parody of the nineteenth-century processions of Roman matrons in black mourning gear, Volumnia and her entourage arrived at the
Volscian camp in matching off white outfits of impeccable cut.

Unfortunately, the acting, rather than an intellectually destabilizing counterpoint to the modernist stagecraft, proved to be, in its tired psychoanalytic
orthodoxy, of a piece with it.

An impulse to exploit historic design conventions also animated Fran
Thompson's mise-en-scène for David Thacker's 1994 RSC production at the
Swan, where the Napoleonic decor of Poel, Langham, and Guthrie was
redeployed; not now, as Dennis Kennedy puts it, to "assist interpreted meaning or to reinforce character and fable" in modernist fashion, but "to encourage active self-consciousness."[73] The audience was cued to Thompson's
postmodern use of the convention by the stage setting which showed,
through a gap in a broken upstage brick wall a reproduction of Delacroix's
painting *Liberty Leading the People* as a work in progress, with only the
main figure complete and the others merely outlined in black. The incomplete artwork thus became a metaphor for the play's transhistorical meaning: the democratic struggle is itself a work in progress. Bloodstained
banners hanging in the auditorium, citizens present in balconies, and battles
staged in the aisles, all served to subvert the conventional audience-actor,
stage-auditorium rupture. The twentieth-century audience, willingly or unwillingly, became a participant in a Napoleonic reading of a Jacobean artistic
treatment of a Roman event.

Visual strategies were used, not only to engage the audience in an intellectual exploration of the connection between the original text and its historical
relocation, but to bias the play's political sympathies. Where traditionally
the corn shortage has been downplayed or ignored altogether, and the justice
of the plebeian complaints left for the audience to weigh for itself, Thacker's

revival unambiguously declared itself from the start: as the lights went down, a shower of golden grain poured from the flies into substage bunkers and the covers were slammed shut. After Martius's banishment, the plebeians "came in to fill their bowls from the opened grain silo and [went] thence with the tribunes' blessings."[74] The reality of the grain shortage was not in doubt, nor who was responsible for it.

Thompson's iconographically powerful decor left critics unimpressed: they saved their kudos for twenty-four-year-old Toby Stephens's Martius, who upstaged Volumnia (Barbara Blakiston) and Menenius (Philip Voss) with ease. Yet another psychoanalytic creation, Stephens's Martius was a tour de force for a man of his age, but hardly a hermeneutic landmark. He was handsome, appropriately athletic if not heroically proportioned, a convincing embodiment of "a kind of naked power lust inside a god-like casing" (*Plays & Players,* June 1994), and an object of homoerotic attraction for Menenius and Aufidius; but the middle-aged national hero was beyond him. This Martius was in reality little more than a boy; his was the pardonable arrogance of youth, which he might still outgrow, along with his mother's influence. To be called "boy" by Aufidius was less an insult than a statement of fact. Martius's response, and violent end, seemed more the product of youthful misjudgement than tragic frailty. When in the play's final moments, Aufidius cried "Assist," "the Volscian lords conspicuously demur[red], leaving it to their leader to struggle with the traitor's corpse" (*Guardian,* 26 May 1994), a cynical visual revision of Shakespeare's call to solidarity and renewal.

Afterword

Coriolanus's stage history is driven by the theater's conviction that the play is flawed, that its idiosyncratic character is the product not of aesthetic strategy but defective craft. To render the piece agreeable to actors and marketable to audiences, its wayward indeterminacy must be stabilized, its multiple perspective focused, its grim and overdetermined personalities glamorized and rendered psychologically transparent, its bleak ambiance warmed and colored, and its conclusion endowed with a measure of transcendence or emotional release. To this end, the text has been cut, transposed, and rewritten; the characters have reinvented themselves as anything from ambulatory Roman statues to contemporary urban hipsters, with psyches redolent at times of Poussinesque spirituality, and at others of Freudian nightmare. The chromatic richness of baroque scenography, the severe splendor of neoclassical painting and statuary, the awesome scale of spectacular realism, the swift fluidity of modernistic functionalism, and the cynical novelty of postmodern image-making have all been summoned to convince the playgoer that a sated eye equals a full heart. But never, it is safe to say, has the play been staged without apology by a first-class company as a fully realized masterpiece. The modernist era, with its interest in full texts and functional Jacobean staging, offered, perhaps, the best hope of rehabilitation. But the hope was frustrated by its suppression of the play's politics, its reduction of the text by as much as a quarter, and its perennial failure to attract leading actors to the major roles. It is a particular irony that William Poel, who was tutelary genius to so much Shakespearian drama, should have been one of *Coriolanus*'s greatest mutilators.

Perhaps the theater has been right all along; maybe *Coriolanus* is defective, the product of the playwright's failing powers or an miscalculated attempt to stretch the resources of theater and audience too far. But would it not be an experiment worth the making to assume, for once, that the play has a calculated aesthetic, however unconventional, and to devote the resources of a major company to its exploration? What might that exploration imply?

As a starting point, it must be accepted that playgoers will not go home happy at curtain fall; if the experience shapes itself as seems intended, they may be disorientated and unfulfilled, but this is not to say they will be dissatisfied. Perhaps the theater's error has been to underestimate its audience, to give them what it thinks they want, rather than what the play-wright offers.

To acknowledge *Coriolanus*'s aesthetic is to recognize that it privileges overdeterminacy and indeterminacy. Theater artists need to distinguish with care occasions when the action and characters demand clarification, and when their eloquent and suggestive reticence must be respected. Much of the play's indeterminacy results from the characters' failure to explain their motivation or their state of mind. We do not know why Martius does not make concessions to the plebeians, whether it is out of egotism, pride of class, or conditioned reflex. We are similarly unenlightened about his decision to desert to Aufidius, or the psychological impulse which leads him to hold his mother by the hand silent. Nor do we know precisely what motivates Volumnia to visit the Volscian camp, what principle or more personal consideration shapes her intercession, or what emotion pulses beneath her wordless stage cross afterwards. While actions are left unexplained, people talk about each other compulsively. And for the purposes of this play, talk is action. The psychological dissection of Martius by the plebeians, Menenius, the tribunes, the cushion-layers, Volumnia, Aufidius, and others approximates the enigmatic and complex character of our mundane evaluations of each other. *Coriolanus* invites the theatergoer to a demanding intellectual engagement: one is asked to observe and compare, in much the same way as mannerist art challenges the viewer to weigh its distortions and instabilities against the classical perfections of High Renaissance creations. The urge to stabilize the play's shiftiness by energetic blue-penciling is omnipresent; but what appears to be expendable character commentary is in reality the warp and woof of the play's design.

Our modernist legacy, the impulse to see in, or to force upon, the script a tight-knit organic unity should also be guarded against. The plaitlike structural coherence espoused by Doran and Parker is not self-evident;[1] rather the construction suggests the multiple centers of interest typical of mannerist painting, say in Pontormo's *Joseph in Egypt* (London, National Gallery) or Rosso's *Moses and the Daughters of Jethro* (Florence, Uffizi), each of which is to some degree discrete. Although each unit when focused upon separately may be seen to comment on other units, the effect of the whole is to create a sense of disorientation. *Coriolanus*'s centers of interest are three: the patrician-plebeian conflict, the Roman-Volscian military struggle, and the mother-son relationship. Each of the first three scenes highlights one theme: the political contest in 1.1; the war in 1.2; and the domestic issue in 1.3. The plot then proceeds for seven scenes to concentrate on the Roman-Volscian war to the neglect of political and domestic concerns. Once the Roman-Volscian enmity and Martius's military prowess are established, interest shifts, with the hero's homecoming, for two whole acts to the ideological struggle. The dramaturgical spotlight is trained three times on the mother-son motif, each at a crucial point in Martius's political project: the victory celebration during which Volumnia hints at her plans for him (2.1), the sequence in which she attempts to teach the veteran warrior political chicanery (3.2), and her farewell to him when her advice is ignored (4.1).

With 4.4 (leaving 4.3 aside for the moment) the center of interest again shifts to the Roman-Volscian conflict, with Martius now on the side of the enemy, and there it remains throughout acts 4 and 5, the play's second and final movement. The patrician-plebeian contention is suspended out of a common fear of invasion, and the mother-son relationship calls attention to itself only once, albeit powerfully, in the Intercession scene. The intercut Roman episodes are little more than extended, intensifying reaction shots. With the return of the women to Rome, after their successful petition, the Volscian-Roman conflict, now personified in Martius and Aufidius, resumes and absorbs all interest until the titular hero's death. That death, when it comes, brings no insight, transcendence, or resolution. The temptation to enforce it by domesticating, exoticizing, or otherwise softening the brutality of the play's final moments must be resisted. The dialogue and directions are clear: Aufidius must stand on the body; the 2. Lord's jaded "His own impatience / Takes from Aufidius a great part of blame. / Let's make the best of it." (5.6.144–46) demands to be spoken, and Aufidius's unconvincing volte-face allowed to remain just that.

The play's first movement, then, which amounts to its first half, comprises an introduction (1.1–3) followed by the military (1.4–10) and political (acts 2 and 3) sections to which Volumnia's encounter with the tribunes after Martius's banishment forms a coda. The ideal opportunity for an intermission comes after the exit of the matron and her party. If a second interval is to be provided, it should not be allowed to shatter the rhythmic integrity of either the military or political sections: it can only be placed after the former, and that at the risk of attenuating the complex ironic counterpoint between the two segments which demands continuity for its full appreciation.

The second movement begins with Martius's arrival in Antium. But before that, and preferably after the intermission, comes the pivotal and much neglected Adrian-Nicanor scene (4.3), which, appropriately set somewhere between Rome and Antium, looks backward at the political movement and forward to the renewed Roman-Volscian hostilities of the play's second half. This workaday exchange of information between a Roman traitor and a Volscian patriot, reminiscent of the linking devices employed in two-part mannerist paintings where gestures, oddly angled bodies, and strategically placed objects lead the eye from the lower to the upper halves, brilliantly foreshadows the epic betrayal about to be enacted and offers an unsettling preface to it. Frequently cut because it has no immediate relevance to the narrative, any more than the pointing gestures of two bystanders in Raphael's *Transfiguration,* it deserves respect as a key aesthetic device.The drama's second half, unlike the first, treats a single continuous action, the

Volscian invasion of Rome, from the time Martius allies himself with the enemy until his death.

While the centers of interest are to a considerable degree discrete, they are inextricably linked by Martius's pervasive presence as warrior, aspiring politician, and son. If the title role is to receive the importance it warrants, each center, while it is under the eye, must be given appropriate weight.

Traditionally the military unit has been scanted, primarily because battles are difficult to stage convincingly. Nevertheless the battlefield episodes bear crucial witness to Martius's martial skills, against which his inability to manage political and maternal stress must be ironically measured; and, it goes without saying, they lend much needed physical distinction to one who lacks spiritual charisma. These scenes have a rhythmic integrity, growing in intensity in a series of surges to a climax with Martius's rechristening, then slackening as his fatigue and forgetfulness surface and he allows himself to be led off for medical treatment. Conventional cuts leave the character of the titular hero and the strength of the Roman-Volscian antipathy attenuated, and the act rhythm maimed. Somehow means must be found to stage these scenes so that they make their point. The Kemblian resort to sheer numbers of military figures is not the answer; the tactic merely retards the action, and attracts the eye to itself rather than Coriolanus. Only token numbers seem envisioned by the playwright, but their deployment remains problematic. Can battle scenes be cogently staged for a contemporary audience? The static pictorialism of the Kemble tradition, the spectacular realism of Irving, the slow-motion stylization of the Berliner Ensemble, all theatrical coups of a sort, served themselves rather than the text. Nugent Monck and Glen Byam Shaw apparently achieved some degree of authenticity and speed by playing the scenes fairly fully and straightforwardly. One would give much to know how Monck, with only eight supers, managed to make the seige of Corioli "as exciting as any screen battle with a thousand times as many people taking part" (*Eastern Daily Press,* Norwich, 7 February 1928).

The challenge posed by the play's indeterminate politics is quite as daunting. Actor-managers and directors, perennially convinced that uncommitted ideological debate is potentially subversive or untheatrical or both, have either stabilized *Coriolanus*'s politics in favor of the right or left, or displaced it as much as possible by character analysis. The fact remains that the play is profoundly political, but apparently uncommitted; and perhaps the time has come to allow ideological relativism and indeterminacy their head. This means that a full text must be played, and conscious scenographic bias avoided. The citizens require respectful treatment. They need not appear overthreatening in either numbers, dress, weaponry, or actions; nor, alternatively, should their violent potential be entirely suppressed. There is justification for their behavior in their hunger and sense of injustice, if we are to believe them. And their portraits are not without rough-hewn goodwill and good humor if the relevant lines are spoken. Curiously enough, there seems little danger of playing the citizens too sympathetically; Shakespeare has inextricably interwoven sufficient negative material to ensure that they never escape censure. To create a totally positive portrait, as Brecht discovered, the director must resort to wholesale rewriting.

The tribunes must also be treated with care. They are not paragons, but neither are they unmitigated villains or a bad political joke. Gross incompetents of the sort sometimes represented cannot credibly be charged with Martius's overthrow. Brutus and Sicinius are, on the contrary, successful practitioners of the craft of realpolitik, to which are added their own particular virtues and defects. The audience may be permitted to draw its own conclusions about them as it does about any public figure.

The patricians pose different interpretative challenges. All too often, they have been flattered as unjustifiably as their opponents have been dispraised. When placed in the Tate or Kemble manner against massive architectural display and surrounded by throngs of military and civil supers, the politics of grandeur takes over, and oligarchic might implies right. Biased stagecraft is an ever present threat to ideological balance.

A politically sensitive reading of Menenius and Martius is also vital to a textured account of the aristocratic position. If Menenius is played purely as an avuncular, sybaritic paternalist, the right hand file appears more benign than if his calculated expediency, cynicism, and hypocrisy are given vent. In a world of relativistic statecraft, he is the supreme temporizer, the survivor, the fixer, everything his protégé is not and cannot become; and that needs to be made evident. Martius, too, requires careful attention: he is no naive victim of a sordid power play, as is often suggested, but a political activist. He subscribes to a classical reactionary ideology, and defends it articulately when he is permitted the "corn" speech (3.1.113ff) and similar outbursts. His antipopulist sentiments are not music to democratic ears, and may even smack of repetition and excess; but directors do the play no favor by downplaying his radical elitism. It must be given full value if the rationale for his banishment is to be fully appreciated and the authorship of his ruin identified.

Politics in *Coriolanus* is pervasive, crucial to the plot, and eternally relevant. But, as in life itself, the rights and wrongs are precisely balanced. When the text is played in its entirety, one's sympathies sway now to this side, now that. It takes only slight cuts, or fairly unobtrusive bits of business, to impair the delicate equilibrium; and on such occasions, the dramatic construction is such that the play is more apt to assume a patrician coloration than the reverse.

Throughout most of *Coriolanus*'s stage history the mother-son theme has been stressed at the expense of the play's military and political thrusts; yet it is the involvement of the protagonists in these areas which lends their characters significance. Without the crucial resonance of battlefield and Forum, their tortured attachment is at best the stuff of Tennessee Williams melodrama or at worst, Freudian analysis.

The stabilization of Volumnia as a heroic mother of the nation or a maternal vampire has repeatedly proved disastrous, especially for the Intercession scene: human warmth is compromised in the first instance, and tragic nobility in the second. It goes without saying that the text must be played uncut, and the action not unduly biased in one direction or another. Both her virtues and vices must be fairly represented, and the balance between them allowed to fluctuate. At play's end, we will not know to what degree her appearance in the Volscian camp was altruistic, nor will we have firm answers to a dozen other questions. The aesthetics of the play privilege uncertainty: Volumnia is no more addicted to self-revelation than the subjects of Bronzino's portraits.

Martius, despite Olivier's offhand dismissal of him as "a very straightforward, reactionary son of a so-and-so,"[2] cannot be played on automatic pilot if the domestic dimension is to have its effect. *Coriolanus*'s stage history indicates that to do justice to the battle sequences the actor must be physically impressive and athletic. There is no record of a slightly-built performer making a success in the role: David Garrick, Edwin Booth, and John Gielgud all avoided it, and Edmund Kean and Ian Hogg probably wished they had. The role is clearly written for an actor in his thirties or older: when youthful actors undertake it, as evinced by Toby Stephens's 1994 attempt, the point of Martius's "arrested development" is lost. In addition to physicality and seniority, Martius's intellectual capacity warrants consideration. He is not a purely physical creature, as so often depicted, but a man of fierce convictions which he defends with eloquence and passion. The dramatic point of the Martius-Volumnia relationship is that a brawny, middle-aged man, able to contend physically on the battlefield or intellectually in the marketplace, suddenly becomes a quaking, tongue-tied youngster in the maternal presence. At the moment of his ultimate surrender, he can make his feelings known only by "hold[ing] her by the hand silent." To cut his rhetorical flights, and so to deny freedom to his mind and voice, is as serious an error as to miscast him with regard to physique or age.

His character, like that of Volumnia, cannot, and should not, be stabilized. We cannot identify with any precision the emotional underpinnings to a number of his actions; but there is little justification for imposing either an arbitrarily vicious or a self-consciously noble humor. As Granville-Barker points out, "action and words are expressively keyed together"[3] to an unusual degree in this play; and the words must be permitted to take their color from the actions which accompany them. The act of judgement is the responsibility of the playgoer.

That *Coriolanus* is an exemplary tragedy, or can be made to function as one, is dubious. Nevertheless, its subject, language, and characters suggest some measure of tragic quality. Without resort to the beau ideal grandeur of Kemble and the nineteenth-century Romans, Martius, to achieve any degree of success, must seem to matter; there must be some element of greatness about him. A major challenge to the contemporary director is to discover a balance between the boyishness and maternal dependence implicit in the role and the heroic distinction which lends his fate significance. The destruction of a mere mother-dependent soldier through some replication of ingrained psychological patterns is hardly tragic; but, at the same time, the selfless submission of a demigod to maternal solicitation wants warmth and credibility. Both the heroic and human dimensions must be present and balanced; in some combination of the epic authority of Alan Howard and the psychological subtlety of Nicol Williamson may lie the answer.

Although it is conventional to focus on the mother-son relationship, the psychological forces at play are really triangular: in ways, Martius is as obsessed with Aufidius as with his parent; and his encounters with his military nemesis, as with his mother, are few and deadly.

The precise nature of the Martius-Aufidius relationship is elusive. In a purely functional sense, Aufidius provides an enemy against whom Martius can whet his sword, a rival power to whom he can desert, and the source of his quietus at curtain fall. But the Volscian general is more than a mere mechanism: he it is who enunciates and incarnates the play's philosophic and aesthetic relativism: "So our virtues / lie in th'interpretation of the time" (4.7.49–50). He begins the play as a subscriber to Martius's chivalric code only to allow his valor to become poisoned by one too many defeats. When Martius turns traitor, treacherous enmity abruptly erupts into love, which is once more tainted, this time by jealousy. And Martius's death is the immediate consequence. It is uniquely fitting that the representative of ethical relativism should be at one moment the violator of Martius's corpse and the next, marshal of his funeral procession. When compared with Aufidius's cynical shiftiness, Martius's absolutist inflexibility seems almost attractive.

That there is a powerful attraction between the two men, with possible homoerotic overtones, cannot be denied. But to make too much of the homosexual dimension, as did Guthrie, is again to diminish whatever claim to tragic stature the play may have. The notion that the nuptial imagery employed by Aufidius in the reconciliation sequence (4.5.113ff) indicates homosexual attraction is dubious: the outburst may be no more than a conventional Jacobean literary flight, since Martius addresses Cominius in similar terms when they meet on the battlefield at 1.6.29ff. Aufidius is no more Martius's alter ego than his homosexual obsession. To make him such, like the blond twin of John Barton's 1967 revival, is seriously to limit his relativistic, discontinuous contribution to the play's overdetermined ideology, psychology, and aesthetics.

The actor who plays Aufidius needs to be as physically impressive as Martius, and a suitable object of his admiration. The dramatist writes him into only eight of the twenty-nine scenes, in some to speak only a line or two. As a result, the role is frequently allocated to an inferior actor, and goes largely unnoticed. No character in the play merits more careful reconsideration.

Virgilia's dramatic function deserves brief notice—all she got from the playwright, or has since received from the study or stage. If Aufidius's character is overdetermined and contradictory, Virgilia's is almost perversely simplified. A creature of small gestures, tears, and silences, she has been little more throughout the history of the play than a live prop for the principals. And Shakespeare's bizarre restriction of her contacts and dialogue with, and response to, her husband and mother-in-law prevent her from being much more. To imagine the play without Virgilia, however, is to appreciate her function: a potent example of the disorienting clash of expectation and actuality which bedevils the theatergoer throughout; and a vexing exemplar at some of the action's most charged moments of the playwright's adamant refusal to allow emotion free rein. No actor to date, including the brilliant Siobhan McKenna, has made her more than that. And perhaps one is not meant to.

While *Coriolanus* relies for its effect on its relativistic and overdetermined vision, that vision is cogently structured and controlled as indicated in chapter 2. Few directors and designers, however, have seen fit to honor the text's stage directions and dialogic performance cues. The playwright's decisive rejection of bright color and sensuous atmosphere, the visual hardness and sharpness implied in his imagery, and the unevocative nature of his physical spaces have been largely ignored. Scenographic severity has been seen as a defect to be overcome rather than an aesthetic feature to be respected; and supers, sets, and costumes have all been misemployed in the effort. To respect the play's visual style as implied in its language is not to neglect pictorial interest; it is rather to create a decor consonant with the character of the play rather than to impose upon it an arbitrary "look."

Quite as important to *Coriolanus*'s aesthetic effect as its mise-en-scène is the movement score discussed in chapter 2: severe but eloquent blocking, patterned entrances and exits, identical gestures in multiple contexts, all of which accentuate, comment upon, and modulate particular themes, and so structure the narrative without compromising its indeterminacy.[4] The performance score has been perennially disregarded since at least the Restoration: insensitive cuts have removed crucial elements of replicated motifs; strategic entrances and exits have been whimsically shuffled; simple but eloquent gestural statements have been swamped by serried ranks of supers. Key stage images have been obliterated altogether. The "man in blood" image, for example, has been vitiated by having Martius appear with only a tasteful smear or, in some romantic productions, no sign of gore at all.

Finally, the almost symphonic rhythmic structure, cued in word and action as suggested in chapter 2, must be observed; and that implies an uncut script. Although in recent decades more of the text has been played than formerly, even the most restrained trimming can wreak havoc with the intricate pulse beat. Atkins and Monck adequately demonstrated that a full text can be played in about three hours if the speaking is swift and the staging flexible. Surely contemporary full-text revivals are not beyond the ingenuity of designers and performers and the endurance of audiences.

The theater, I suspect, will never adopt an indeterminate production mode for the play as orthodoxy. Rather it will continue to stabilize it in one way or another; and that, perhaps, is not entirely to be deplored. Each attempt to fix *Coriolanus*'s characters and action creates a new coign of vantage from which to contemplate its mysteries, and therein lies the secret of its theatrical attraction and perennial renewal.

Chronological Handlist of Performances, 1609–1994

The following calendar of performances in London, the Stratfords, and New York is, I hope, as complete as documentation permits. Productions elsewhere in Great Britain and North America are included when these are of special interest. The players of the four major roles are identified whenever possible. Actors are listed by surname only, except when one performer might be confused with a contemporary of the same name, in which case they are distinguished by initials. Productions take place in London unless otherwise indicated, and repeat performances in any Autumn-Spring season are grouped with the first. For long-run and repertory revivals in the late-nineteenth and twentieth centuries, only the date of the premiere is noted.

? December-January 1609/10	*Coriolanus* (Shakespeare). ? Blackfriars. C-?Burbage; V-?; M-?; A-?.
? December 1681	*The Ingratitude of a Common-wealth* (alteration by Nahum Tate). King's Company. Drury Lane. No cast-list.
14 January 1681/2	*The Ingratitude of a Common-wealth* (alteration by Nahum Tate). King's Company. Drury Lane. No cast-list.
? ca. 1699	*Coriolanus* (?Shakespeare). ?Lincoln's Inn Fields. C-?Betterton; V-?Barry; M-?; A-?.
13 December 1718	*Coriolanus* (Shakespeare). Lincoln's Inn Fields. No cast-list. Repeated 15, 16 December.
11 November 1719	*The Invader of His Country; or The Fatal Resentment* (alteration by John Dennis). Drury Lane. C-Booth; V-Porter; M-Corey; A-Mills. Repeated 12, 13 November.
14 November 1719	*The Invader of His Country; or, The Fall of Coriolanus.* "Written by Shakespear." Lincoln's Inn Fields. No cast-list.

1 January 1719/20	*The Invader of His Country.* Lincoln's Inn Fields. No cast-list.
24 November 1720	*The Tragedy of Coriolanus.* "Written by Shakespear." Lincoln's Inn Fields. No cast-list.
26 December 1720	*The Tragedy of Coriolanus.* "Written by Shakespear." Lincoln's Inn Fields. No cast-list for principals. Comic parts by Bullock Sr., Griffin, Spiller, and C. Bullock.
10 April 1721	*Coriolanus.* "Written by Shakespear." Lincoln's Inn Fields. No cast-list for principals. Comic parts by Bullock Sr., Griffin, Spiller, C. Bullock, Pack, and Hall.
31 October 1721	*Coriolanus.* "Written by Shakespear." Lincoln's Inn Fields. No cast-list for principals. Comic parts by Bullock Sr., Spiller, C. Bullock, Hall, and H. Bullock.
1 January 1721/2	*Coriolanus.* "Written by Shakespear." Lincoln's Inn Fields. No cast-list.
13 January 1749	*Coriolanus* by James Thomson. Covent Garden. C-Quin; Veturia-Woffington; Minucius-Bridgwater; Tullus-Ryan; Repeated 14, 16, 17, 18, 19, 20, 21, 23, 24 January.
29 February 1752	*Coriolanus; or the Roman Matron* (alteration by Thomas Sheridan). Smock Alley Theatre, Dublin. C-Sheridan; V-Woffington; M-Sparks; T-Digges. Repeated 4, 21 March; 7 May.
7 May 1753	*Coriolanus; or the Roman Matron* (alteration by Thomas Sheridan). Smock Alley, Dublin. C-Sheridan; V-Woffington; M-?; T-Digges.
22 February 1754	*Coriolanus; or the Roman Matron* (alteration by Thomas Sheridan). Smock Alley, Dublin. C-Sheridan; V-Woffington; M-Sparks; T-Digges.
11 November 1754	*Coriolanus* (Shakespeare). Drury Lane. C-Mossop; V-Pritchard; M-Berry; A-Havard. Repeated 13, 15, 18, 20, 23, 27, 29 November; 22 April 1755.
10 December 1754	*Coriolanus; or the Roman Matron* (alteration by Thomas Sheridan). Covent Garden. C-Sheridan; V-Woffington; M-Shuter; T-Ryan. Repeated 11, 12, 14, 18, 21 December; 27 January 1754/5; 31 March 1754/5.

5 February 1757	*Coriolanus; or the Roman Matron* (alteration by Thomas Sheridan). Smock Alley, Dublin. C-Sheridan; V-Kennedy; M-Sparks; T-Dexter. Repeated 17, 24 February.
14 November 1757	*Coriolanus; or the Roman Matron* (alteration by Thomas Sheridan). Smock Alley, Dublin. C-Sheridan; V-Fitzhenry; M-Sparks; T-Dexter. Repeated 6 March 1757/8.
14 March 1757/8	*Coriolanus; or the Roman Matron* (alteration by Thomas Sheridan). Covent Garden. C-Smith; V-Hamilton; M-Shuter; T-Ryan. Repeated 20 April.
11 September 1758	*Coriolanus; or the Roman Matron* (alteration by Thomas Sheridan). Theatre Royal, Cork. C-Heaphy; V-Kennedy; M-Sparks; T-Dexter.
2 November 1758	*Coriolanus; or the Roman Matron* (alteration by Thomas Sheridan). Covent Garden. C-Smith; V-Hamilton; M-Shuter; T-Ryan. Repeated 3 November; 3 February 1758/9.
18 April 1760	*Coriolanus; or the Roman Matron* (alteration by Thomas Sheridan). Covent Garden. C-Smith; V-Hamilton; M-Shuter; T-Clarke.
18 February 1765	*Coriolanus; or the Roman Matron* (alteration by Thomas Sheridan). Covent Garden. C-Smith; V-Bellamy; M-Shuter; T-Clarke.
13 April 1765	Version unknown. New Concert Hall, Edinburgh. C-Wilkinson; V-?; M-?; A-?.
8 June 1767	*Coriolanus* by James Thomson. American Company of Comedians. Southwark Theatre, Philadelphia. C-David Douglass; V-?; M-?; T-?.
20 April 1768	*Coriolanus; or the Roman Matron* (alteration by Thomas Sheridan). Covent Garden. C-Smith; V-Bellamy; M-Shuter; T-Younger.
10 February 1777	*Coriolanus; or the Roman Matron* (alteration by Thomas Sheridan). Theatre Royal, Manchester. C-Powell; V-Siddons; M-Inchbald; T-Casey.
7 February 1789	*Coriolanus; or the Roman Matron* (alteration by Kemble). [All texts played hereafter are substantially

by Shakespeare]. Drury Lane. C-Kemble; V-Siddons; M-Baddeley; A-Wroughton. Repeated 10, 14, 21 February; 3, 7, 14 March.

31 March 1792   Drury Lane Company at King's Theatre, Haymarket. C-Kemble; V-Siddons; M-Baddeley; A-Wroughton. Repeated 21 April.

11 July 1792   Theatre Royal, Edinburgh. C-Kemble; V-?; M-?; A-?.

23 February 1793   Drury Lane Company at King's Theatre, Haymarket. C-Kemble; V-Siddons; M-Baddeley; A-Wroughton. Repeated 21 May.

31 March 1794   Theatre Royal, Manchester. C-Cooke; V-Taylor; M-?; A-?.

18 April 1796   Drury Lane. C-Kemble; V-Siddons; M-Benson; A-Wroughton.

3 June 1796   New Theater, Philadelphia. C-Moreton; V-Whitlock; M-Bates; A-Green.

3 October 1796   Drury Lane. C-Kemble; V-Siddons; M-Palmer; A-Wroughton. Repeated 27 February 1797.

3 June 1799   Park Theater, New York. C-Cooper; V-Barrett; M-Bates; A-Martin.

29 May 1804   Drury Lane. C-Cooke; V-Powell; M-Dowton; A-Raymond.

30 December 1805   Boston Theater. C-Cooper; V-Powell; M-Twaits; A-Fox. Repeated 31 December; 1, 3, 4, 30, 31 January 1806.

29 March 1806   Chestnut Street Theater, Philadelphia. C-Cooper; V-Melmoth; M-Warren; A-Cain.

3 November 1806   Covent Garden. C-Kemble; V-Siddons; M-Munden; A-Pope. Repeated 5, 7, 10, 12, 14, 18, 22, 27, 29 November; 1, 3, 5 December; 18, 25 May 1807.

16 November 1806   Park Theater, New York. C-Cooper; V–Villiers; M-Harwood; A-Green. Repeated 23 November.

2 February 1807   Boston Theater. C-Cooper; V-Powell; M-Dickenson; A-Fox.

22 April 1807   Charleston (Alabama) Theater. C-Cooper; V-?; M-?;
                         A-?.

26 October 1807   Covent Garden. C-Kemble; V-Siddons; M-Munden; A-
                         Pope. Repeated 2, 9 November.

28 January 1808   New Theater Royal, Manchester. C-Barrymore; V-
                         Galindo; M-Swendall; A-Meggett.

28 November 1808   Park Theater, New York. C-Cooper; V-Twaits; M-
                         Twaits; A-Rutherford.

5 April 1810   New Theatre Royal, Edinburgh. C-Siddons; V-Siddons;
                         M-Terry; A-Putnam.

25 May 1810   Park Theater, New York. C-Cooper; V-Twaits; M-
                         Twaits; A-Simpson.

19 September 1810   Theatre Royal, Liverpool. C-Cooper; V-Beaumont; M-
                         Andrews; A-Grant.

17 October 1810   Theatre Royal, Liverpool. C-Rae; V-Stratton; M-
                         Andrews; A-Grant.

6 March 1811   Chestnut Street Theater, Philadelphia. C-Wood; V-
                         Twaits; M-Warren; A-Cone.

19 April 1811   Park Theater, New York. C-Cooper; V-Mason; M-?; A-
                         Simpson.

8 July 1811   Theatre Royal, Bristol. C-Bengough; V-Johnson; M-
                         Charlton; A-Abbott.

18 November 1811   Theatre Royal, Liverpool. C-Rae; V-Dobbs; M-
                         Andrews; A-Grant.

14 December 1811   Covent Garden. C-Kemble; V-Siddons; M-Blanchard;
                         A-Egerton. Repeated 17, 19, 21, 23 December; 14
                         April, 1812; 5, 23 May; 22 June.

10 July 1812   Theatre Royal, Liverpool. C-Kemble; V-Campbell; M-
                         Andrews; A-Bartley. Repeated 17 July.

6 November 1812   Theater, Lincoln. C-Musgrave; V-Birchall; M-
                         Robertson; A-Elston.

16 December 1812   Park Theater, New York. C-Cooper; V-Stanley; M-
                         Yates; A-Simpson.

26 December 1812	Theatre Royal, Bath. C-Kemble; V-Weston; M-?; A-?.
28 December 1812	Theatre Royal, Bristol. C-Kemble; V-Weston; M-Charlton; A-Stanley.
26 February 1813	Boston Theater. C-Cooper; V-Powell; M-Drake; A-Waring.
15 March 1813	Chestnut Street Theater, Philadelphia. C-Duff; V-Mason; M-Bray; A-Barrett.
19 March 1813	Park Theater, New York. C-Cooper; V-Stanley; M-Yates; A-Simpson.
22 March 1813	Theatre Royal, Edinburgh. C-Kemble; V-M'Namara; M-Terry; A-Jones.
2 June 1813	Covent Garden. C-Young; V-Powell; M-Blanchard; A-Egerton. Repeated 7, 21 June; 13 July.
4 October 1813	Theatre Royal, Bristol. C-Young; V-Weston; M-Charlton; A-Stanley.
11 November 1813	Theatre Royal, Dublin. C-Kemble; V-O'Neill; M-Williams; A-Neville.
3 December 1813	Covent Garden. C-Conway; V-Powell; M-Blanchard; A-Egerton. Repeated 13 December.
15 January 1814	Covent Garden. C-Kemble; V-Powell; M-Blanchard; A-Egerton. Repeated 22, 25 January; 2, 14, 16 February; 18 May.
26 February 1814	Boston Theater. C-Cooper; V-Powell; M-?; A-?. Repeated 28 February.
14 March 1814	Theatre Royal, Edinburgh. C-Kemble; V-Macauley; M-Moore; A-Jones.
18 April 1814	Theatre Royal, Bristol. C-Kemble; V-Weston; M-Charlton; A-Stanley.
20 June 1814	Theatre Royal, Liverpool. C-Kemble; V-Campbell; M-Andrews; A-Cooper. Repeated 11 July.
22 October 1814	Covent Garden. C-Kemble; V-Renaud; M-Blanchard; A-Egerton. Repeated 22 November; 15 December; 1, 15 [C-Conway] May 1815.

2 November 1814	Theatre Royal, Liverpool. C-Vandenhoff; V-Campbell; M-Andrews; A-Cooper.
13 March 1815	Theatre Royal, Edinburgh. C-Kemble; V-Douglas; M-Eyre; A-Trueman. Repeated 18 March.
9 May 1815	Theatre Royal, Manchester. C-Young; V-Ward; M-Andrews; A-Cooper.
30 October 1815	Covent Garden. C-Kemble; V-Renaud; M-Blanchard; A-Egerton. Repeated 23, 29 April 1816.
23 March 1816	Theatre Royal, Edinburgh. C-Kemble; V-Douglas; M-?; A-?. Repeated 27 March; 3 April.
27 March 1816	Charleston (Alabama) Theater. C-Cooper; V-Barrett; M-Horton; A-Tyler.
24 June 1816	Theatre Royal, Liverpool. C-Kemble; V-M'Gibbon; M-Andrews; A-Cooper. Repeated 12 July.
28 October 1816	Covent Garden. C-Kemble; V-O'Neill; M-Blanchard; A-Egerton. Repeated 31 October; 4, 9, 19, 28 November; 19 December [V-Faucit in rest of season's performances]; 26 April 1817; 10, 23 May; 23 June.
6 January 1817	Theatre Royal, Bristol. C-Kemble; V-Clifford; M-?; A-Stanley.
14 January 1817	Theatre Royal, Bath. C-Kemble; V-Clifford; M-Charlton; A-Stanley.
29 January 1817	Chestnut Street Theater, Philadelphia. C-Cooper; V-Entwistle; M-Warren; A-Wood.
26 February 1817	Theatre Royal, Glasgow. C-Kemble; V-Dalton; M-MacKay; A-Grant.
17 October 1817	Theatre Royal, Liverpool. C-Conway; V-M'Gibbon; M-Andrews; A-Cooper.
16 February 1818	Boston Theater. C-Cooper; V-Powell; M-Dykes; A-Green.
4 May 1818	Charleston (Alabama) Theater. C-Mude; V-Barrett; M-Faulkner; A-Tyler.

9 September 1818   Park Theater, New York. C-J. W. Wallack; V-Entwistle; M-Robertson; A-Simpson.

18 November 1818   Theatre Royal, Chester. C-Musgrave; V-Pitt; M-Flemmington; A-Ormond.

4 December 1818   Boston Theater. C-J. W. Wallack; V-Powell; M-Green; A-Price.

15 January 1819   Theatre Royal, Bath. C-Conway; V-Penley; M-Charlton; A-Elton. Repeated 18 January.

23 February 1819   Park Theater, New York. C-J. W. Wallack; V-Leesugg; M-Robertson; A-Simpson.

29 November 1819   Covent Garden. C-Macready; V-Faucit; M-Blanchard; A-Egerton. Repeated 1, 6 December.

10 December 1819   Federal Street Theater, Boston. C-Cooper; V-Powell; M-Dykes; A-Duff.

13 December 1819   Theatre Royal, Bath. C-Conway; V-Pope; M-Charlton; A-Williams.

28 December 1819   Theatre Royal, Bristol. C-Macready; V-Desmond; M-Telbin; A-Stuart.

12 January 1820   Chestnut Street Theater, Philadelphia. C-J. W. Wallack; V-Entwistle; M-Warren; A-H. Wallack.

25 January 1820   Drury Lane. C-Kean; V-Glover; M-Gattie; A-Penley. Repeated 26, 28 January; 22 February 1821.

8 March 1820   Charleston (Alabama) Theater. C-J. W. Wallack; V-? ; M-?; A-?.

3 April 1820   Theatre Royal, Bristol. C-Macready; V-Desmond; M-Telbin; A-Stuart.

7 April 1820   Theatre Royal, Bath. C-Young; V-Pope; M-Charlton; A-Williams.

6 June 1820   Theatre Royal, Liverpool. C-Young; V-M'Gibbon; M-Andrews; A-Bass.

13 July 1820   Theatre Royal, Edinburgh. C-Young; V-Renaud; M-Loveday; A-Calcraft.

13 November 1820	Theatre Royal, Liverpool. C-Vandenhoff; V-M'Gibbon; M-Andrews; A-Bass.
18 December 1820	Covent Garden. C-Vandenhoff; V-Bunn; M-Blanchard; A-Egerton. Repeated 21, 31 December.
1 January 1821	Drury Lane. C-J. W. Wallack; V-Egerton; M-Gattie; A-Cooper.
13 January 1821	Theatre Royal, Bath. C-Conway; V-Weston; M-Charlton; A-Younger.
30 January 1821	Theatre Royal, Newcastle. C-Hamblin; V-Leonard; M-Butler; A-Carter.
21 May 1821	Park Theater, New York. C-H. Wallack; V-Battersby; M-Kilner; A-Simpson.
27 August 1821	Theatre Royal, Birmingham. C-Macready; V-Bunn; M-Butler; A-Mathews.
2 January 1823	Park Theater, New York. C-J. W. Wallack; V-Battersby; M-Foot; A-Simpson.
6 January 1823	Theatre Royal, Edinburgh. C-Vandenhoff; V-Renaud; M-Mason; A-Butler. Repeated 8, 10, 15 January; 3 March.
18 January 1823	Chestnut Street Theater, Philadelphia. C-J. W. Wallack; V-Entwistle; M-Warren; A-H. Wallack.
21 April 1823	Theatre Royal, Newcastle. C-Mude; V-Clifford; M-Butler; A-Carr.
30 May 1823	Theatre Royal, Liverpool. C-Vandenhoff; V-M'Gibbon; M-Andrews; A-Bass.
5 August 1823	Theatre, Leeds. C-Calvert; V-Weston; M-Downe; A-Crook.
20 October 1823	Park Theater, New York. C-Cooper; V-Tatnall; M-Foot; A-Simpson. Repeated 24 October.
7 November 1823	Boston Theater. C-Cooper; V-Powell; M-Kilner; A-Barrett.
17 December 1823	Theatre Royal, Dublin. C-Hamblin; V–Vaughan; M-Williams; A-Hamerton Jr.

5 January 1824	Theatre Royal, Edinburgh. C-Vandenhoff; V-Renaud; M-Mason; A-Pritchard. Repeated 10 January.
10 January 1824	Chestnut Street Theater, Philadelphia. C-Cooper; V-Battersby; M-Warren; A-Duff.
14 January 1824	Park Theater, New York. C-Conway; V-Stone; M-Foot; A-Simpson. Repeated 26 January.
27 February 1824	Boston Theater. C-Conway; V-Powell; M-Kilner; A-Barrett.
4 March 1824	Theatre Royal, Edinburgh. C-Vandenhoff; V-Renaud; M-Mason; A-Pritchard. Repeated 5 March.
20 March 1824	Charleston (South Carolina) Theater. C-J. W. Wallack; V-Hughes; M-Horton; A-Hughes.
26 April 1824	Chestnut Street Theater, Philadelphia. C-Conway; V-Battersby; M-Warren; A-H. Wallack.
14 June 1824	Drury Lane. C-Macready; V-Bunn; M-Terry; A-Archer. Repeated 21 June.
14 June 1824	Theatre Royal, Bristol. C-Butler; V-M'Cready; M-Williams; A-Montague.
12 July 1824	Theatre Royal, Birmingham. C-Young; V-Bunn; M-Shuter; A-Mude.
9 November 1824	Theatre Royal, Liverpool. C-Vandenhoff; V-M'Gibbon; M-Andrews; A-Bass.
17 December 1824	Charleston (South Carolina) Theater. C-Conway; V-Barrett; M-Faulkner; A-Barrett. Repeated 23 December.
16 February 1825	Theatre Royal, Edinburgh. C-Vandenhoff; V-Renaud; M-Mason; A-Pritchard.
2 May 1825	Theatre Royal, Bristol. C-Barton; V-M'Cready; M-Grierson; A-Flinn.
16 September 1825	Park Theater, New York. C-Conway; V-Battersby; M-Foot; A-Simpson.
9 December 1825	Park Theater, New York. C-Hamblin; V-Battersby; M-Foot; A-Simpson. Repeated 12 December.

16 December 1825   Park Theater, New York. C-Cooper; V-Battersby; M-Foot; A-Simpson.

10 January 1826   Theatre Royal, Edinburgh. C-Vandenhoff; V-Renaud; M-Mason; A-Pritchard.

2 February 1826   Chatham Garden, New York. C-H. Wallack; V-Entwistle; M-Roberts; A-Scott.

3 April 1826   Theatre Royal, Manchester. C-Vandenhoff; V-M'Gibbon; M-Andrews; A-Bass.

11 September 1826   Park Theater, New York. C-Cooper; V-Stickney; M-Foot; A-Simpson.

23 October 1826   Park Theater, New York. C-Macready; V-Stickney; M-?; A-Simpson.

26 December 1826   Bowery Theater, New York. C-Hamblin; V-Duff; M-?; A-Duff.

24 January 1827   Theatre Royal, Edinburgh. C-Vandenhoff; V-Renaud; M-Mason; A-Pritchard. Repeated 17 March.

2 February 1827   Park Theater, New York. C-Conway; V-Stickney; M-?; A-Simpson.

21 May 1827   Theatre Royal, Manchester. C-Vandenhoff; V-Kelly; M-Andrews; A-Bass.

14 June 1827   Theatre Royal, Glasgow. C-Waldron; V-Richardson; M-Livingstone; A-Hooper.

12 July 1827   Theatre Royal, Liverpool. C-Vandenhoff; V-Kelly; M-Andrews; A-Raymond.

8 October 1827   Park Theater, New York. C-Cooper; V-Duff; M-Foot; A-Simpson.

30 November 1827   Theatre Royal, Liverpool. C-Vandenhoff; V-Kelly; M-Andrews; A-Raymond.

7 December 1827   Charleston (Alabama) Theater. C-Hamblin; V-Hughes; M-?; A-Ansell.

18 February 1828   Theatre Royal, Edinburgh. C-Vandenhoff; V-Renaud; M-Mason; A-Pritchard.

12 May 1828	Theatre Royal, Liverpool. C-Vandenhoff; V–Vaughan; M-Andrews; A-Raymond.
23 June 1828	Theatre Royal, Manchester. C-Waldron; V-M'Gibbon; M-Munro; A-Haines. Repeated 5 July.
2 December 1828	Theatre Royal, Liverpool. C-Vandenhoff; V-Vaughan; M-Andrews; A-Raymond.
8 December 1828	Theatre Royal, Bristol. C-Macready; V-Gordon; M-?; A-Gray.
11 December 1828	Theatre Royal, Manchester. C-Waldron; V-M'Gibbon; M-Robson; A-Melville.
9 February 1829	Theatre Royal, Manchester. C-Vandenhoff; V-M'Gibbon; M-Robson; A-Melville.
6 April 1829	Theatre Royal, Birmingham. C-Vandenhoff; V-Barry; M-Hammond; A-Raymond.
12 October 1829	Surrey Theatre. C-Osbaldiston; V-Egerton; M-Pitt; A-Warwick. Repeated 8 January 1830.
23 October 1829	Theatre Royal, Birmingham. C-Macready; V-Clifford; M-Bellamy; A-Montague.
4 November 1829	Chestnut Street Theater, Philadelphia. C-Cooper; V-Wood; M-Stone; A-Maywood.
9 November 1829	Theatre Royal, Liverpool. C-Vandenhoff; V-Pelham; M-Hammond; A-Raymond.
7 December 1829	Theatre Royal, Manchester. C-Waldron; V-M'Gibbon; M-Jones; A-Brindal. Repeated 29 December.
8 February 1830	Theatre Royal, Edinburgh. C-Vandenhoff; V-Stanley; M-Denham; A-Pritchard.
22 May 1830	Theatre Royal, Manchester. C-Waldron; V-M'Gibbon; M-Jones; A-Brindal.
13 November 1830	Theatre Royal, Liverpool. C-Vandenhoff; V-Huddart; M-Smith; A-King.
1 January 1831	Bowery Theater, New York. C-Hamblin; V-Pelby; M-?; A-?. Repeated 5 January.

3 January 1831	Theatre Royal, Hull. C-Butler; V-Penley; M-Strickland; A-Hunt.
5 January 1831	Theatre Royal, Dublin. C-Vandenhoff; V-West; M-Gattie; A-Cooke. Repeated 21 January.
29 January 1831	Theatre Royal, Manchester. C-Anderton; V-Angel; M-Jones; A-Phelps.
27 May 1831	Drury Lane. C-Macready; V-Huddart; M-Dowton; A-Cooper. Repeated 1 June.
21 July 1831	Theatre Royal, Liverpool. C-Vandenhoff; V-West; M-Andrews; A-Cooke.
19 September 1831	Arch Street Theater, Philadelphia. C-Cooper; V-Drake; M-Jones; A-Archer.
6 October 1831	Theatre Royal, Liverpool. C-Vandenhoff; V-West; M-Chippendale; A-Cooke. Repeated 23 November.
14 December 1831	Bowery Theater, New York. C-Butler; V-Waring; M-?; A-Stevenson. Repeated 19 December.
29 December 1831	Theatre Royal, Manchester. C-Vandenhoff; V-West; M-Chippendale; A-Cooke.
14 May 1832	Theatre Royal, Birmingham. C-Vandenhoff; V-Huddart; M-Chippendale; A-Cooke.
17 September 1833	Theatre Royal, Liverpool. C-Vandenhoff; V-Huddart; M-Andrews; A-Cooke. Repeated 9 November [V-Brooks].
16 December 1833	Drury Lane. C-Macready; V-Sloman; M-Blanchard; A-Cooper. Repeated 20 December.
18 January 1834	Theatre Royal, Bath. C-J.W. Wallack; V-Gordon; M-Keene; A-Harrington.
22 March 1834	Theatre Royal, Manchester. C-Macready; V-Brooks; M-Andrews; A-Cooke.
16 June 1834	Theatre Royal, Haymarket. C-Vandenhoff; V-Glover; M-Strickland; A-Rumball. Repeated 18, 20, 23 June; 10 July.

2 October 1834	Covent Garden. C-Vandenhoff; V-Sloman; M-Bartley; A-Cooper. Repeated 6 October [A-King].
14 January 1835	Theatre Royal, Newcastle. C-Anderson; V-Penley; M-Younge; A-Penley.
17 February 1835	Victoria Theatre. C-Osbaldiston; V-West; M-Keene; A-Bender.
27 April 1835	Theatre Royal, Bristol. C-Mude; V-M'Cready; M-Carroll; A-Barry.
20 July 1835	Theatre Royal, Cheltenham. C-Anderson; V-Penley; M-Skerrett; A-Curling.
17 August 1835	Theatre Royal, Glasgow. C-Butler; V-Clifton; M-Stoddart; A-Alexander.
22 February 1836	Theatre, Gloucester. C-Anderson; V-Penley; M-Osborne; A-Willis.
7 July 1836	Theatre Royal, Cheltenham. C-Anderson; V-Crisp; M-Osborne; A-Hill.
10 January 1837	Theatre Royal, Bristol. C-Butler; V-Walton; M-Johnson; A-Griffiths.
23 February 1837	Covent Garden. C-Hamblin; V-West; M-Tilbury; A-Pritchard. Repeated 27 February; 4, 7 March.
6 July 1837	Theatre Royal, Liverpool. C-Vandenhoff; V-Stanley; M-Granby; A-Gray.
23 August 1837	Walnut Street Theater, Philadelphia. C-Conner; V-Meer; M-Porter; A-Procter.
11 September 1837	National Theater, New York. C-Vandenhoff; V-Flynn; M-Gann; A-H. Wallack. Repeated 13 September.
9 October 1837	Chestnut Street Theater, Philadelphia. C-Vandenhoff; V-Flynn; M-Faulkner; A-Harrington. Repeated 12 October.
23 November 1837	Drury Lane. C-Butler; V-Lovell; M-Dowton; A-Cooper.
10 January 1838	Park Theater, New York. C-Forrest; V-C. Cushman; M-Clarke; A-Mason. Repeated 11, 12 January.

22 January 1838	Chestnut Street Theater, Philadelphia. C-Forrest; V-Maywood; M-Faulkner; A-Harrington. Repeated 25 January; 5 February.
29 January 1838	Theatre Royal, Newcastle. C-Green; V-Penley; M-Addison; A-Eustin.
29 January 1838	New Charleston (Alabama) Theater. C-Vandenhoff; V-?; M-?; A-?.
8 March 1838	National Theater, New York. C-Hamblin; V-Sefton; M-Matthews; A-H. Wallack. Repeated 15 March.
12 March 1838	Covent Garden. C-Macready; V-Warner; M-Bartley; A-Anderson. Repeated 19, 26, 29 March; 2,5,19, 26 April [V-Mrs. W. Clifford].
29 March 1838	National Theater, New York. C-Vandenhoff; V-Sefton; M-Matthews; A-H. Wallack.
2 May 1838	Chestnut Street Theater, Philadelphia. C-Vandenhoff; V-Sharpe; M-Faulkner; A-Harrington.
24 September 1838	Covent Garden. C-Vandenhoff; V-Warner; M-Bartley; A-Phelps. Repeated 27 September.
6 May 1839	Covent Garden. C-Macready; V-Warner; M-Strickland; A-Anderson.
20 March 1839	Theatre, Chichester. C-Otway; V-Dacre; M-Clifford; A-White.
2 December 1839	Chestnut Street Theater, Philadelphia. C-Vandenhoff; V-Sharpe; M-Johnson; A-Harrington.
11 January 1840	Park Theater, New York. C-Vandenhoff; V-C. Cushman; M-Chippendale; A-Hield.
18 January 1841	Tremont Theater, Boston. C-Vandenhoff; V-Cramer; M-Gilbert; A-Creswick. Repeated [2 acts] 22 January.
26 April 1841	Arch Street Theater, Philadelphia. C-Forrest; V-Jones; M-Davenport; A-Murdoch.
17 December 1841	National Theater, Philadelphia. C-Forrest; V-Jones; M-Conner; A-J. Wallack.

8 December 1843	New Theatre Royal, Marylebone. C-Otway; V-?; M-?; A-?.
9 October 1843	Bowery Theater, New York. C-Hamblin; V-Shaw; M-?; A-DeBar. Repeated 10, 12 October.
7 September 1844	Park Theater, New York. C-Anderson; V-Sloman; M-Chippendale; A-Dyott. Repeated 11 September.
19 February 1845	St. Charles Theater, New Orleans. C-Anderson; V-Farren; M-Farren; A-Neafie. Repeated 21 February.
14 April 1845	Park Theater, New York. C-Anderson; V-Ellis; M-Chippendale; A-Dyott. Repeated 28 May.
29 July 1845	Walnut Street Theater, Philadelphia. C-J. Wallack Jr.; V-Mrs. J. Wallack Jr.; M-Leman; A-Wheatley. Repeated 31 July; 18 August.
18 October 1845	Walnut Street Theater, Philadelphia. C-Fest; V-Mrs. J. Wallack Jr.; M-Leman; A-Wheatley.
5 December 1845	Theatre Royal, Birmingham. C-Creswick; V-Pope; M-Addison; A-Hield. Repeated 9 December.
2 January 1846	Walnut Street Theater, Philadelphia. C-J.W. Wallack; V-Mrs. J. Wallack Jr.; M-Leman; A-Wheatley. Repeated 30 January.
16 January 1846	Theatre Royal, Newcastle. C-Anderson; V-Rignold; M-Salter; A-Benson.
30 January 1846	Theatre Royal, Bristol. C-Anderson; V-?; M-?; A-?.
3 April 1846	Queen's Theatre, Manchester. C-Anderson; V-Coleman Pope; M-Addison; A-Hield.
13 April 1846	New Theatre Royal, Manchester. C-Graham; V-Weston; M-Cooper; A-Pitt. Repeated 14 [Pitt], 16,18 April.
7 December 1846	Arch Street Theater, Philadelphia. C-Conner; V-Burke; M-Scott; A-Howard.
13 December 1846	Theatre Royal, Glasgow. C-Alexander; V-?; M-?; A-?.
25 January 1847	Theatre Royal, Carlisle. C-Vandenhoff; V-?; M-?; A-?. Repeated 7 February.

9 February 1847	Theatre Royal, Liverpool. C-Vandenhoff; V-Rogers; M-Couldock; A-Mead.
21 February 1848	Walnut Street Theater, Philadelphia. C-J. Wallack Jr.; V-Mrs. J. Wallack Jr.; M-Leman; A-Wheatley.
24 February 1848	Theatre Royal, Manchester. C-Vandenhoff; V-Weston; M-Cooper; A-Sullivan.
15 September 1848	Park Theater, New York. C-Hamblin; V-Winstanly; M-Andrews; A-Hield.
27 September 1848	Sadler's Wells. C-Phelps; V-Glyn; M-Younge; A-Marston. Repeated 28, 29, 30 September; 2, 3, 4, 5, 6, 7, 9, 10 October; 30 November; 5, 6, 10, 11 January 1849.
2 October 1848	Bowery Theater, New York. C-Hamblin; V-Winstanly; M-Andrews; A-Warwick. Repeated 4, 7 October.
16 September 1850	Sadler's Wells. C-Phelps; V-Glyn; M-Younge; A-Waller. Repeated 17, 18, 19, 25, 26 September.
9 December 1850	Surrey Theatre. C-Creswick; V-Cooper; M-?; A-Mead.
6 January 1851	Drury Lane. C-Anderson; V-Weston; M-Emery; A-Cooper. Repeated 13 January.
15 February 1851	Charleston (Alabama) Theater. C-Graham; V-?; M-?; A-?.
7 June 1852	Bowery Theater, New York. C-Hamblin; V-Yeomans; M-Glenn; A-Eddy. Repeated 9 June.
9 May 1853	Great National Standard Theater. C-Anderson; V-?; M-?; A-?. Repeated 12 May.
[?12] February 1855	Metropolitan Theater, San Francisco. C-Stark; V-Stark; M-?; A-?.
23 April 1855	Broadway Theater, New York. C-Forrest; V-Ponisi; M-Whiting; A-Hanchett. Repeated 24, 25, 26, 27, 28, 30 April; 2, 5 May.
24 October 1855	Broadway Theater, New York. C-Forrest; V-Ponisi; M-Whiting; A-Fisher.

31 January 1857	Sadler's Wells. C-Phelps; V-Atkinson; M-Marston; A-Robinson. Repeated 2, 3, 7, 9, 10 February.
14 February 1857	Queen's Theatre and Opera-House, Edinburgh. C-Vandenhoff; V-Cleaver; M-Jones; A-Mead.
8 March 1859	Princess's Theatre, Leeds. C-Loraine; V-Dyas; M-Grainger; A-McKenzie.
17 March 1860	Sadler's Wells. C-Phelps; V-Atkinson; M-Marston; A-Robinson.
15 September 1860	Sadler's Wells. C-Phelps; V-Atkinson; M-Barrett; A-Vezin. Repeated 17, 18, 19, 26, 27, 28 September.
30 May 1862	New Bowery, New York. C-Eddy; V-Farren; M-Petrie; A-Boniface. Repeated 2 June.
27 March 1863	Royal Amphitheatre, Liverpool. C-Brooke; V-Smith; M-Holston; A-Cowper.
2 November 1863	Niblo's Garden, New York. C-Forrest; V-Ponisi; M-Burnett; A-Shewell. Repeated 3, 5, 6, 9, 10, 12, 13, 20 November.
1 February 1864	Boston Theater. C-Forrest; V-Ponisi; M-Curtis; A-Whalley. Repeated 2 February.
5 September 1864	Niblo's Garden, New York. C-Forrest; V-Farren; M-Burnett; A-McCullough. Repeated 6, 8, 9, 12, 13, 15, 16 September; 21 October.
28 November 1864	Academy of Music, Philadelphia. C-Forrest; V-Ponisi; M-W. H. Hamblin; A-McCullough. Repeated 29 November; 1, 2 December.
17 January 1866	Stadt-Theater, New York. C-Hoym; V-Becker-Grahn; M-Frank; A-Knorr. Repeated 18 January.
26 February 1872	Theatre Royal, Sheffield. C-Dillon; V-Hathaway; M-Gomersal; A-Moore.
13 May 1872	New Theatre Royal, Bristol. C-Dillon; V-Manners; M-Knowles; A-?.
6 September 1872	Prince of Wales Theatre, Birminghanm. C-Dillon; V-Booth; M-Gomersal; A-Stuart. Repeated 7 September.

30 September 1872	New Queen's Theatre, Manchester. C-Dillon; V-Booth; M-Gomersal; A-Stewart.
7 February 1878	Boston Theater. C-McCullough; V-Barry; M-Allen; A-James. Repeated 16, 20 February.
16 December 1878	Grand Opera House, New York. C-McCullough; V-Rogers; M-Dean; A-Walcot Jr. [2-week run].
3 January 1883	Thalia Theater, New York. C-Barnay; V-Galster; M-Lupschutz; A-Bollmann. Repeated 4, 5 January.
11 November 1885	Metropolitan Opera House, New York. C-T. Salvini; V-Foster; M-Constantine; A-A. Salvini. Repeated 13, 14 (mat.) November.
17 March 1893	Prince's Theatre, Bristol. C-Tearle; V-Lowe; M-Rouse; A-Scarth.
26 April 1893	Opera House, Northampton. C-Tearle; V-Lowe; M-Rouse; A-Scarth.
8 May 1893	Prince of Wales Theatre, Birmingham. C-. Tearle; V-Lowe; M-Rouse; A-Scarth.
17 August 1893	Shakespeare Memorial Theatre. C-Benson; V-Chapin; M-Swete; A-Stuart. Repeated 18, 19 (mat.) August.
19 April 1898	Shakespeare Memorial Theatre. C-Benson; V-Wetherall; M-Swete; A-Rodney.
13 February 1901	Comedy Theatre. C-Benson; V-Ward; M-Swete; A-Brydone. Repeated 14, 16, 18, 20, 21, 23, 25 February.
15 April 1901	Lyceum Theatre. C-Irving; V-Terry; M-Barnes; A-Ashcroft.
20 May 1904	Court Theatre. Reading sponsored by British Empire Shakespeare Society. C-Leigh; V-Ward; M-Swete; A-Casson.
24 April 1907	Shakespeare Memorial Theatre. C-Benson; V-Ward; M-Nicholson; A-Buchanan.
10 June 1907	Lyric Theatre. Reading sponsored by British Empire Shakespeare Society. C-Waller; V-Ward; M-George; A-Bond.

27 February 1908	Coronet Theatre. C-Benson; V-Ward; M-Nicholson; A-Buchanan.
21 April 1909	Shakespeare Memorial Theatre. C-Benson; V-Ward; M-Nicholson; A-Goodsall.
19 April 1910	His Majesty's. C-Benson; V-Ward; M-Nicholson; A-Maxon.
29 April 1912	Shakespeare Memorial Theatre. C-Benson; V-McDowall; M-Ayrton; A-Holloway.
30 April 1915	Shakespeare Memorial Theatre. C-Benson; V-Ward; M-Stuart; A-Rathbone.
23 April 1919	Shakespeare Memorial Theatre. C-Benson; V-Ward; M-Calvert; A-Rogers.
12 April 1920	Old Vic. C-Warburton; V-Ward; M-Paterson; A-Shaw.
24 March 1924	Old Vic. C-Swinley; V-Britton; M-Walter; A-Hayes.
23 April 1926	Shakespeare Memorial Theatre. C-Skillan; V-Carrington; M-Ayrton; A-Worrall-Thompson.
6 February 1928	Maddermarket Theatre, Norwich. C-Miller; V-Diver; M-Cooper; A-Harwood.
3 March 1928	Marlowe Dramatic Society, Cambridge. [Actors anonymous].
20 July 1928	Haymarket Theatre. British Empire Shakespeare Society Reading. C-Oscar; V-Beringer; M-Llewellyn; A-Skillan.
11 May 1931	Elizabethan Stage Circle, Chelsea Palace Theatre. C-Speaight; V-Allgood; M-Yarrow; A-Walsh.
23 April 1933	Shakespeare Memorial Theatre. C-McMaster; V-O'Day; M-Lathbury; A-Browne.
11 November 1935	Manchester Repertory Theatre. C-Citroen; Draycott; M-Jones; A-King.
13 January 1936	Abbey Theatre, Dublin. C-Jarman; V-Carey; M-Fitzgerald; A-Stephenson.

6 July 1936	Pasadena Community Playhouse, California. C-Ankrum; V-Scott; M-Blanchard; A-Engle.
25 September 1937	Federal Theater Project, Theater of the Four Seasons, Roslyn, Long Island. C-Gage; V-Sorsby; M-Burby; A-Velie.
1 February 1938	Federal Theater Project, Maxine Elliott Theater, New York. C-Gage; V-Sorsby; M-Burby; A-Velie.
19 April 1938	Old Vic. C-Olivier; V-Thorndike; M-Trouncer; A-Devlin.
9 May 1939	Shakespeare Memorial Theatre. C-Clunes; V-Green; M-Leigh; A-Dale.
31 March 1948	Old Vic, New Theatre. C-Clements; V-Atkinson; M-Guinness; A-Andrews.
17 April 1950	Norwich Players, Maddermarket Theatre. [Actors anonymous].
5 March 1951	Marlowe Society and A.D.C., Arts Theatre, Cambridge. [Actors anonymous].
13 March 1952	Shakespeare Memorial Theatre. C-Quayle; V-Ellis; M-Hordern; A-Harvey. [Ellis replaced in latter part of season by Rosalind Atkinson].
26 May 1952	Bath Assembly, Roman Baths, Bath. C-Rideout; V-Stafford; M-Ensor; A-West.
14 January 1954	Phoenix Theater, New York. C-Ryan; V-Natwick; M-Napier; A-Emery.
23 February 1954	Old Vic. C-Burton; V-Compton; M-Squire; A-Daneman.
23 October 1956	Birmingham Repertory Theatre. C-Taylor; V-Jackson; M-Bayldon; A-Finney.
7 July 1959	Shakespeare Memorial Theatre. C-Olivier; V-Evans; M-Andrews; A-Nicholls.
2 March 1960	Oxford University Dramatic Society, Oxford Playhouse. C-Garland; V-Engels; M-Tetlow; A-Croucher.

19 June 1961	Stratford (Ontario) Festival. C-Scofield; V-Stuart; M-Campbell; A-Colicos.
11 December 1963	Nottingham Playhouse. C-Neville; V-Reynolds; M-McKern; A-McKellen.
18 August 1964	National Youth Theatre, Queen's Theatre. C-Nightingale; V-Grimes; M-Stockton; A-Davies.
19 June 1965	American Shakespeare Festival, Stratford, Conn. C-Bosco; V-MacMahon; M-Hines; A-Cunningham.
13 July 1965	New York Shakespeare Festival, Delacorte Theater, Central Park, New York. C-Burr; V-White; M-Cotsworth; A-Ryan.
10 August 1965	Berliner Ensemble, International Theatre Season at Old Vic. C-Schall; V-Weigel; M-Kaiser; A-Thate.
12 April 1967	Royal Shakespeare Theatre. C-Richardson; V-Lacey; M-Mason; A-Cicciarelli.
30 September 1969	Victoria Theatre, Stoke-on-Trent. C-Bond; V-Raitt; M-David; A-Callaghan.
3 March 1970	Liverpool Playhouse. C-Gambon; V-Hamilton; M-Henry; A-Wilson.
6 May 1971	National Theatre. C-Hopkins; V-Cummings; M-Moffatt; A-Quilley.
11 April 1972	Royal Shakespeare Theatre. C-Hogg; V-Tyzack; M-Dignam; A-Stewart.
26 July 1972	Bristol Youth Theatre. C-Bunting; V-Cordery; M-Kosta; A-Reed.
22 November 1973	RSC at Aldwych. C-Williamson; V-Tyzack; M-Dignam; A-James.
15 September 1974	Citizens' Theatre, Glasgow. C-Murphy; V-Bertish; M-Butler; A-Hyde.
17 April 1975	Brecht's *Coriolan,* Everyman Theatre, Liverpool. C-Postlethwaite; V-Amsden; M-LeProvost; A-Washington.

8 September 1976   National Youth Theatre, Shaw Theatre. C-Buffery; V-Buffery; M-Taggart; A-Hope.

20 October 1977   Royal Shakespeare Theatre. C-Howard; V-Audley; M-Crowden; A-Glover.

14 March 1978   RSC at Theatre Royal, Newcastle. C-Howard; V-Audley; M-Crowden; A-Glover.

2 June 1978   RSC at Aldwych. C-Howard; V-Audley; M-Crowden; A-Glover.

14 March 1979   New York Shakespeare Festival, Anspacher/Public Theater, New York. C-Freeman; V-Foster; M-Woods; A-Christian.

28 June 1979   New York Shakespeare Festival, Delacorte Theater, Central Park, New York. C-Freeman; V-Foster; M-Woods; A-Christian.

16 June 1981   Stratford (Ontario) Festival. C-Cariou; V-Chilcott; M-Gordon; A-Hylands.

9 November 1983   Nottingham Playhouse. C-Floy; V-Karlin; M-Barnes; A-Lowrie.

15 December 1984   National Theatre. C-McKellen; V-Worth; M-Treeves; A-Hicks.

17 September 1986   Kick Theatre Company, Almeida Theater, Islington. C-Hodge; V-Townley; M-Kelly; A-Jeune.

6 November 1987   McCarter Theater, Princeton, N.J. C-James; V-Reid; M-Weiss; A-Cumpsty.

28 July 1988   Old Globe, San Diego. A-Jennings; V-Shepherd; M-Matthews; A-Cooper.

22 November 1988   New York Shakespeare Festival, Public Theater, New York. C-Walken; V-Worth; M-Hecht; A-David.

3 May 1989   Young Vic. C-Redgrave; V-Kempson; M-Franklyn-Robbins; A-McFarlane.

30 November 1989   Royal Shakespeare Theatre. C-Dance; V-Jefford; M-O'Conor; A-Storry. Transferred to Barbican Theatre 16 April 1990.

24 September 1990   English Shakespeare Company at Grand Theatre, Swansea. C-Pennington; V-Watson; M-Lloyd; A-Jarvis.

10 April 1991   English Shakespeare Company at the Aldwych. C-Pennington; V-Watson; M-Lloyd; A-Jarvis.

20 May 1992   Renaissance Theatre Company, Chichester Festival Theatre. C-Branagh; V-Dench; M-Briers; A-Glen.

28 May 1993   Théâtre Repère de Québec at Festival de Théâtre des Amériques, Montreal. C-Philip; V-Cadieux; M-Henri-Gagnon; A-Gagnon. Repeated 23 November at Nottingham Playhouse. M-Languirand.

4 May 1994   RSC at the Swan. C-Stephens; V-Blakiston; M-Voss; A-Lynch.

Notes

Chapter 1. Introduction

1. *Coriolanus*'s 3410 lines make it the fourth longest of Shakespeare's plays. While *Hamlet, Richard III,* and *Troilus and Cressida* are considerably longer, *Othello, King Lear, Henry V,* and *Cymbeline* are within a hundred lines of its length.

2. Eric Bentley, *The Dramatic Event* (1954), 186.

3. Ibid., 187.

4. T. S. Eliot, 1919; "Hamlet and His Problems," *Selected Essays: 1917–1932* (1932), 124. Irving is quoted by William Winter, *Shakespeare on the Stage* (3d Series, 1916; reissued Benjamin Blom, 1969), 213.

5. See W. B. Worthen, "Deeper Meanings and Theatrical Technique: The Rhetoric of Performance Criticism," *Shakespeare Quarterly,* 40 (1989): 441–45.

6. *Coriolanus*'s theatrical unpopularity is a persistent myth. The truth is that it has enjoyed about two-thirds as many performances as *Julius Caesar*—a very popular play indeed.

7. John Dennis, Letter to Sir Richard Steele, 26 March 1719. *The Critical Works of John Dennis,* ed. Edward Niles Hooker (Baltimore: 1943), 2:164.

8. Dennis, "Essay on the Genius and Writings of Shakespear," *Critical Works,* 2:9.

9. Ibid., 2:5.

10. Lewis Theobald, Preface to *The Works of Shakespeare* (1733). Cited in *Shakespeare: The Critical Heritage,* ed. Brian Vickers (1974–81), 2:481.

11. Charles Gildon, "Remarks on the Plays of Shakespeare," Rowe's edition, vol. 7, 1710. Cited in *Shakespeare: The Critical Heritage,* 2: 252.

12. Dennis, "Essay on the Genius and Writings of Shakespear," *Critical Works,* 2:7.

13. Thomas Sheridan, Advertisement to *Coriolanus: Or, The Roman Matron* (1755; reprint, Cornmarket Press, 1969), n.p.

14. *Samuel Johnson on Shakespeare,* ed. W. K. Wimsatt, Jr. (1960), 105.

15. Francis Gentleman, Introduction to *Coriolanus,* Bell's edition (1774; reprint, Cornmarket Press, 1969), 5:229.

16. Gildon, "Remarks." Vickers, *Shakespeare: The Critical Heritage,* 2:251.

17. John Upton, *Critical Observations on Shakespeare* (1746), 135–36.

18. Nicholas Rowe, "Some Account of the Life, &c. of Mr. William Shakespeare," Rowe's edition (1709; reprint, Ann Arbor, Mich: Augustan Reprint Society, 1948), xxviii, xxx.

19. Gildon, "Remarks." Vickers, *Shakespeare: The Critical Heritage,* 2:252–53.

20. *Samuel Johnson on Shakespeare,* 105.

21. Sheridan, Advertisement to *Coriolanus: Or, The Roman Matron,* n.p.

22. *Samuel Johnson on Shakespeare,* 28.

23. Gentleman, *Coriolanus,* Bell's edition, 5:231, 292.

24. Ibid., 5:308.

25. Wolstenholme Parr, "On the Tragedy of Coriolanus," extracted in Vickers, *Shakespeare: The Critical Heritage*, 6:615–16.

26. William Hazlitt, *Complete Works*, ed. P. P. Howe (1934), 5:347.

27. Ibid., 5:348.

28. Samuel Taylor Coleridge, *Shakespearean Criticism*, ed. Thomas Middleton Raysor (1960), 1:79.

29. Nathan Drake, *Shakespeare and His Times* (1817; Paris: 1838), 574.

30. Augustus Wilhelm Schlegel, *Dramatic Literature, Lectures*, trans. J. Black (1815), 2:209.

31. Hermann Ulrici, *Uber Shakespeares dramatische Kunst, und sein Verhaltniss zu Calderon und Goethe* (1839); *Shakespeare's Dramatic Art: And His Relation to Calderon and Goethe*, trans. A. J. W. Morrison (1846), 353. After reading Hazlitt and Gervinus, Ulrici moderated his views in later editions of this work. See *Shakespeare's Dramatic Art*, trans. L. Dora Schmitz (1876), 2:192–93.

32. Charles Knight, *Studies of Shakespeare* (1849), 406.

33. Hazlitt, *Complete Works*, 5:348.

34. Ulrici, *Shakespeare's Dramatic Art*, 352, 353.

35. The point was first made by Elizabeth Inchbald a quarter-century earlier in her "Remarks" to her edition of *Coriolanus; or, The Roman Matron*, in *The British Theatre* (1808). "[I]t was [Volumnia]," she observed, "who engrafted that stem of haughtiness which sprouted to his ruin; his manly disposition not temporizing, like hers, to make it pliant by deceit" (5:4).

36. Mrs. [Anna Brownell] Jameson, *Characteristics of Women, Moral, Poetical & Historical* (1832), 2:175, 186.

37. Coleridge, *Shakespearean Criticism*, 1:205.

38. Jameson, *Characteristics of Women*, 2:189–90.

39. Franz Horn, *Shakespeare's Schauspiele erläutert* (Leipzig: 1826), 4:35. Extract translated in *Coriolanus*, New Variorum edition, ed. Horace Howard Furness, Jr. (1928), 669.

40. D. J. Snider, *The Shakespearean Drama: The Histories* (1877–89; 3d edition, St. Louis: 1922), 3:118.

41. G. G. Gervinus, *Shakespeare* (Leipzig: 1849–50); *Shakespeare Commentaries*, trans. F. E. Bunnètt (1863), 2:388, 389.

42. Edward Dowden, *Shakespeare: His Mind and Art* (1875), 328–29.

43. A. C. Swinburne, *A Study of Shakespeare* (1880), 187–88.

44. Gervinus, *Shakespeare Commentaries* (1863), 2:410.

45. Dowden, *Shakespeare: His Mind and Art*, 328.

46. H. N. Hudson, *Shakespeare: His Life, Art, and Characters* (1872), 156. Cited in *Coriolanus*, New Variorum edition, 676.

47. Snider, *The Shakespearean Drama*, 3:107, 111.

48. Wrote Stapfer, "[T]he pride of Coriolanus was essentially a personal pride, and intensely egoistical. . . . his own glory and aggrandizement was, and would remain to the end, his primary consideration." *Shakespeare and Classical Antiquity*, trans. Emily J. Carey (1880), 430–31.

49. Inchbald as early as 1808 associated the character of Martius with that of "a stubborn schoolboy" in her "Remarks" to her edition of *Coriolanus; or, The Roman Matron*, 4.

50. A. C. Bradley, *"Coriolanus," Proceedings of the British Academy*, 5 (1912), 465.

51. Brander Matthews, *Shakespeare as a Playwright* (1913), 270.

52. George Hookham, *Will o'the Wisp* (Oxford: 1922), 114.

53. Wyndham Lewis, *The Lion and the Fox* (1927), 241.

54. John Palmer, *Political Characters of Shakespeare* (1945), 297.

55. Harley Granville-Barker, *Prefaces to Shakespeare* (Princeton, N.J.: 1947), 2:160.

56. Useful studies of the influence of psychoanalysis on Shakespeare criticism include Norman N. Holland, *Psychoanalysis and Shakespeare* (1966), and *The Design Within*, ed. M. D. Faber (1970). Meredith Skura provides a helpful introduction to contemporary challenges to psychoanalytic criticism within the field of literature as a whole in her essay "Psychoanalytic Criticism," *Redrawing the Boundaries: The Transformation of English and American Literary Studies*, eds. Stephen Greenblatt and Giles Gunn (1992), 349–73.

57. Otto Rank, *Das Inzest-Motiv in Dichtung und Sage* (Leipzig and Vienna: 1912); and Jackson E. Towne, "A Psychoanalytic Study of Shakespeare's *Coriolanus*," *Psychoanalytic Review*, 8 (1921): 84–91.

58. Harold C. Goddard, *The Meaning of Shakespeare* (Chicago: 1951), 598.

59. See Charles K. Hofling, "An Interpretation of Shakespeare's *Coriolanus*," *The Design Within*, 287–305. First published in *American Imago*, 14 (1957): 407–37; Gordon Ross Smith, "Authoritarian Patterns in Shakespeare's *Coriolanus*," *Literature and Psychology*, 9 (1959): 45–51; Robert J. Stoller, "Shakespearean Tragedy: *Coriolanus*," *Psychoanalytic Quarterly*, 35 (1966): 263–74; Janet Adelman, "'Anger's My Meat': Feeding, Dependency, and Aggression in *Coriolanus*," *Shakespeare: Pattern of Excelling Nature*, ed. David Bevington and Jay L. Halio (Newark, N.J.: 1978), 108–24; and James Calderwood, *Shakespeare & the Denial of Death* (Amherst, Mass.: 1987), 122–35.

60. Stanley Cavell, "'Who does the wolf love?': Reading *Coriolanus*," *Shakespeare and the Question of Theory*, eds. Patricia Parker and Geoffrey Hartman (1985), 247. First published in *Representations 3* (Summer, 1983).

61. Jameson, *Characteristics of Women*, 2:175.

62. Hudson, *Shakespeare's Life, Art, and Characters* (1872): 2:516.

63. F. J. Furnivall, Introduction to Leopold *Shakspere* (1877), lxxxiii. Cited in *Coriolanus*, New Variorum edition, 660.

64. Grace Latham, "On Volumnia," *New Shakespeare Society Transactions* (1887–92), 90.

65. Gervinus, *Shakespeare Commentaries*, 2:411.

66. Stopford Brooke, *On Ten Plays of Shakespeare* (1905), 246.

67. M. W. MacCallum, *Shakespeare's Roman Plays and Their Background* (1910), 610.

68. Hookham, *Will o' the Wisp*, 114.

69. G. Wilson Knight, *The Imperial Theme* (1931; 1965), 190.

70. MacCallum, *Shakespeare's Roman Plays*, 555.

71. Goddard, *The Meaning of Shakespeare*, 598.

72. Hofling, "An Interpretation of Shakespeare's *Coriolanus*," 292–93.

73. Stoller, "Shakespearean Tragedy: *Coriolanus*," 266.

74. Ralph Berry, "Sexual Imagery in *Coriolanus*," *Studies in English Literature, 1500–1900*, 13 (1973): 302.

75. Janet Adelman, "'Anger's My Meat,'" 109.

76. Phyllis Rackin, "'Coriolanus': Shakespeare's Anatomy of 'Virtus,'" *Modern Language Studies*, 13 (Spring, 1983): 73. For a variety of feminist readings of Volumnia see Coppelia Kahn, *Man's Estate: Masculine Identity in Shakespeare* (1981); Marjorie Garber, *Coming of Age in Shakespeare* (1981); Peter Erickson, *Patriarchal Structures in Shakespeare's Drama* (1985); Lisa Lowe, "'Say I play the man I am': Gender and Politics in *Coriolanus*," *Kenyon Review*, n.s. 8 (1986): 86–95; and Madelon Sprengnether, "Annihilating Intimacy in *Coriolanus*," *Women in the Middle Ages*

and the Renaissance: Literary and Historical Perspectives, ed. Mary Beth Rose (1986), 89–111.

77. Samuel Taylor Coleridge, *Lectures and Notes on Shakespeare* (1849); cited in *Coriolanus,* New Variorum edition, 701.

78. Gervinus, *Shakespeare Commentaries,* 2:392.

79. Hudson, *Shakespeare's Life, Art, and Characters,* 2:504.

80. Dowden, *Shakespeare: His Mind and Art,* 325.

81. Matthews, *Shakespeare as a Playwright,* 272.

82. Bradley, "*Coriolanus,*" 461.

83. Granville-Barker, *Prefaces to Shakespeare,* 2:153.

84. Snider, *The Shakespearian Drama,* 3:115.

85. Palmer, *Political Characters of Shakespeare,* 259.

86. Gervinus, *Shakespeare Commentaries,* 2:415.

87. Snider, *The Shakespearian Drama,* 3:121.

88. E. K. Chambers, *Shakespeare: A Survey,* 1925; reprinted 1958, 264.

89. A. P. Rossiter, *Angel with Horns and Other Shakespeare Lectures,* ed. Graham Storey (1961), 247.

90. *Samuel Johnson on Shakespeare,* 105.

91. Jameson, *Characteristics of Women,* 2:177.

92. Bradley, "*Coriolanus,*" 472.

93. Chambers, *Shakespeare: A Survey,* 264.

94. J. Middleton Murry, *Countries of the Mind* (1922), 35.

95. Una Ellis-Fermor, *Shakespeare the Dramatist and Other Papers,* ed. Kenneth Muir (1961), 74.

96. Goddard, *The Meaning of Shakespeare,* 610.

97. Hofling, "An Interpretation of Shakespeare's *Coriolanus,*" 301.

98. Bradley, "*Coriolanus,*" 470.

99. See Stoller, "Shakespearean Tragedy: *Coriolanus,*" and Berry, "Sexual Imagery in *Coriolanus.*"

100. Stanley D. McKenzie, "'Unshout the noise that banish'd Martius': Structural Paradox and Dissembling in *Coriolanus,*" *Shakespeare Studies,* 18 (1986): 198–99.

101. Gentleman, *Coriolanus,* Bell's edition, 5:311.

102. Augustus Wilhelm Schlegel, *A Course of Lectures on Dramatic Art and Literature,* trans. John Black (1846), 414.

103. Hudson, *Shakespeare: His Life, Art, and Characters,* 2:491.

104. Swinburne, *A Study of Shakespeare,* 188.

105. MacCallum, *Shakespeare's Roman Plays,* 479, 481.

106. For extensive treatment of the influence of modernist criticism on Shakespeare studies see Hugh Grady, *The Modernist Shakespeare* (Oxford: 1991) and Gary Taylor, *Reinventing Shakespeare* (1989), 231–97.

107. Letter to Warburton, 5 February 1719/20. *Illustrations of the Literary History of the Eighteenth Century,* ed. John Nichols (1817; reprint, AMS Press Inc., 1966), 2:477.

108. Horn, *Shakespeare's Schauspiele erlaütert.* Extract translated in *Coriolanus,* New Variorum edition, 669.

109. Bradley, "*Coriolanus,*" 458, 459, 470.

110. Introduction to the Red Letter edition of *Coriolanus* (1907; reprinted in *Shakespeare: A Survey,* 1925), 258.

111. Matthews, *Shakespeare as a Playwright,* 270.

112. Hookham, *Will o'the Wisp,* 114, 115.

113. Bradley, "*Coriolanus,*" 458.

114. Murry, *Countries of the Mind,* 31.

115. Muriel St. Clare Byrne, "Classical Coriolanus," *National Review,* 96 (1931): 427, 429.

116. Mark Van Doren, *Shakespeare* (1939), 243–44.

117. D. J. Enright, "*Coriolanus:* Tragedy or Debate?" *Essays in Criticism,* 4 (1954): 1–19. Van Doren and Enright echo less succinctly and pungently Lytton Strachey's earlier observation that "rhetoric, enormously magnificent and extraordinarily elaborate, is the beginning and the middle and the end of *Coriolanus.* The hero is not a human being at all; he is the statue of a demi-god cast in bronze, which roars its perfect periods . . . through a melodious megaphone." *Books and Characters* (1922), 51–52.

118. George Bernard Shaw, "Epistle Dedicatory to Arthur Bingham Walkley," *Man and Superman* (1903; *Complete Plays with Prefaces,* 1962), 3:509.

119. Oscar J. Campbell, *Shakespeare's Satire* (1943), 198–99.

120. Rossiter, *Angel With Horns,* 245, 251.

121. See Reuben A. Brower, *Hero & Saint: Shakespeare and the Graeco-Roman Heroic Tradition* (1971), 354–81.

122. Richard C. Crowley, "*Coriolanus* and the Epic Genre," *Shakespeare's Late Plays: Essays in Honor of Charles Crow,* eds. Richard C. Tobias and Paul G. Zolbrod (1974), 114–30.

123. See John Holloway, *The Story of the Night* (1961); Kenneth Burke, "*Coriolanus*—and the Delights of Faction," *Language as Symbolic Action: Essays on Life, Literature, and Method* (Berkeley, Calif: 1966), 81–97; and Jay Halio, "*Coriolanus:* Shakespeare's 'Drama of Reconciliation,'" *Shakespeare Studies,* 6 (1972): 289–303.

124. McKenzie, "'Unshout the Noise That Banish'd Martius': Structural Paradox and Dissembling in 'Coriolanus,'" 189.

125. See Arnold Hauser, *Mannerism: The Crisis of the Renaissance and the Origin of Modern Art* (1965), 1:131, 137; and Cyrus Hoy, "Jacobean Tragedy and the Mannerist Style," *Shakespeare Survey,* 26 (1973): 58–62.

126. Cavell, "'Who does the wolf love?'", 262.

127. Jonathan Dollimore, *Radical Tragedy,* 2d ed. (1993), xxvii.

128. Ibid., 218–30.

129. Stephen Greenblatt, *Shakespearean Negotiations* (Berkeley, Calif.: 1988), 1.

130. Useful studies of the evolution and exploitation of Shakespeare as a cultural symbol include Terence Hawkes, *That Shakespeherian Rag: Essays on a Critical Process* (1986); Michael Bristol, *Shakespeare's America / America's Shakespeare* (1989), Gary Taylor, *Reinventing Shakespeare;* and Margreta De Grazia, *Shakespeare Verbatim: The Reproduction of Authenticity and the 1790 Apparatus* (Oxford: 1991).

CHAPTER 2. THE JACOBEAN AND CAROLINE ERA

1. Philip Brockbank, [Introduction to] *Coriolanus,* Arden edition (1976), 24.

2. Geoffrey Bullough, *Narrative and Dramatic Sources of Shakespeare* (1964), 5:559–60.

3. G. B. Harrison, "A Note on *Coriolanus,*" *J. Q. Adams Memorial Studies,* ed. J. G. McManaway *et al* (1948), 239–40.

4. See Bullough, 5:456–58, 553–58, and E. C. Pettet, "*Coriolanus* and the Midlands Insurrection of 1607," *Shakespeare Survey,* 3 (1950): 34–42.

5. *Epicoene or The Silent Woman,* ed. R. V. Holdsworth, Mermaid edition (1979).

6. See E. K. Chambers, *The Elizabethan Stage,* 4.351; and Gerald Eades Bent-

ley, *Shakespeare and His Theatre* (Lincoln, Nebraska: 1964), 72–73. R. B. Parker (*Coriolanus,* The Oxford Shakespeare, ed. R. B. Parker, Oxford, 1994, 86–87) raises the possibility of a private or court performance in the winter of 1608–9.

7. *The Italian Taylor, and his Boy* (1609), A4. Although not a close verbal parallel, Armin's abrupt digression from his tale:

> These busie Subiectes, such they are,
> As be in other lands,
> That carpe at state; and do declare,
> What no man understands:
> They'le seeme to know, and what they thinke,
> Is Chronicle for truth. . . .
>
> (F1-F2)

markedly echoes Martius's arrogant dismissal of the plebeians' right to a say in public affairs at 1.1.190–96.

This text is reprinted by Alexander B. Grosart in *The Works of Robert Armin, Actor 1605–1609* (1880), 135–96.

8. See Oscar James Campbell and Edward G. Quinn, *The Reader's Encyclopaedia of Shakespeare* (1966), 143.

9. See Bentley, *Shakespeare and His Theatre,* 91ff.

10. In a warrant dated c. 12 January 1668/9, allocating the play to Thomas Killigrew for performance at his Theatre Royal, the play is described as "formerly acted at the Blackfryers." See Allardyce Nicoll, *A History of English Drama, 1660–90* (1952), 1:353.

11. "'Gates' on Shakespeare's Stage," *Shakespeare Quarterly,* 7 (1956): 166–67.

12. Johannes Stradanus (?1523–1605), also known as Pieter van der Straet and Giovanni della Strada, a Flemish painter who went south in 1545 to work as an assistant in the studio of Vasari, later became one of the leading popularizers of mannerist art throughout Europe. Some 388 of his paintings and drawings were engraved, mass-produced, and widely distributed. See Bern Dibner, "The 'New Discoveries' of Stradanus," an article which accompanied a reprint of Stradanus's *Nova Reperta,* issued by the Burndy Library, Norwalk, Connecticut, in 1953; E. C. Watson, "*Nova Reperta,*" *The American Physics Teacher,* 6 (February 1938): 25–28; and Welmoet Bok-van Kammen, "Stradanus and the Hunt," (Ph.D. diss., Johns Hopkins University, 1977). For some notion of the vast range of engravings of Roman subjects available in the late sixteenth and early seventeenth centuries see F. W. H. Hollstein, *Dutch and Flemish Etchings, Engravings, and Woodcuts ca. 1450–1700,* 43 vols. (Amsterdam: 1949). Relatively little scholarly attention has been paid to the availability and influence of engravings on the culture of the Elizabethan and Jacobean period.

13. Giulio Romano's archaeologically based paintings of Roman historical subjects had considerable influence on history painters, and perhaps on theatre art as well. See B. P. J. Broos, "Rembrandt and Lastman's *Coriolanus:* the history piece in 17th-century theory and practice," *Simiolus: Netherlands quarterly for the history of art,* 8 (1975/76): 199–228.

14. J. P. Collier (*New Particulars Concerning Shakespeare,* 1836, 27) cites an elegy on Burbage featuring the lines, "Brutus and Marcius henceforth must be dumb / For ne'er thy like upon our stage shall come" (quoted in *Coriolanus,* New Variorum edition, 726). See also Martin Holmes, *Shakespeare and Burbage* (1978), 192–97. So far as I know, the elegy has never come to light.

15. Thomas Whitfield Baldwin, *The Organization and Personnel of the Shakespearean Company* (1961), 249.

16. W. Robertson Davies, *Shakespeare's Boy Actors* (1939), 140–42, 149–50. Mu-

riel Bradbrook shares the same view. See *Shakespeare: The Poet in his World* (1978), 214.

17. See Margaret Lamb, *"Antony and Cleopatra" on the English Stage* (Cranbury, N.J.: 1980), 29ff.

18. "Epitaph on S.[alamon] P.[avy] a child of Q. El. Chappel," *Poems of Ben Jonson*, ed. George Burke Johnston (1954), 63.

19. Parker examines several vexed issues related to Jacobean staging of the play and solutions proposed (Introduction to *Coriolanus*, 90–96).

20. See Clifford Davidson, "*Coriolanus*: A Study in Political Dislocation," *Shakespeare Studies*, 4 (1969): 263–74; F. E. Langman, "Tell Me of Corn: Politics in *Coriolanus*," *Studies in Shakespeare*, ed. Dennis Bartholomeusz, 1 (1990): 1–19; Pettet, "*Coriolanus* and the Midlands Insurrection of 1607," 34–42; Gordon Zeeveld, "*Coriolanus* and Jacobean Politics," *Modern Language Review*, 57 (1962): 321–34.

21. Hauser, *Mannerism*, 1:83. For intensive treatment of the evolution of Renaissance skepticism see William R. Elton, *"King Lear" and the Gods* (San Marino, Calif.: 1966).

22. Annabel Patterson, *Censorship and Interpretation: The Conditions of Writing and Reading in Early Modern England* (Madison: 1984), 18.

23. Paul Yachnin, "The Powerless Theater," *English Literary Renaissance*, 21 (1991): 50.

24. See Hauser, *Mannerism*, 1:131, 137; and Hoy, "Jacobean Tragedy and the Mannerist Style," 61–62.

25. See John Ripley, "*Coriolanus*'s Stage Imagery on Stage, 1754–1901," *Shakespeare Quarterly*, 38 (1987): 338–50.

26. Cavell, "'Who does the wolf love?'" 247.

27. McKenzie, "'Unshout the noise that banish'd Martius,'" 189. I am indebted to this essay for a number of observations which follow.

28. Parker, Introduction to *Coriolanus*, 76.

29. Hand gestures are a particular feature of mannerist art and literature. James V. Mirollo devotes a chapter to this topic—"Hand and Glove: The *Bella Mano* and the *Caro Guanto*"—in his *Mannerism and Renaissance Poetry* (New Haven: 1984), 125–59.

30. McKenzie, "'Unshout the noise that banish'd Martius,'" 192–93.

31. In the Stradanus engraving of the Intercession scene, Virgilia, although she stands closest to Martius ("comes foremost"), seems curiously frail and inconsequential when compared with the significance given the kneeling Volumnia and the gentlewomen on her left.

32. Bradley, "*Coriolanus*," 470.

33. Hauser, *Mannerism*, 1:172.

34. *The Works of Francis Beaumont and John Fletcher*, eds. Arnold Glover and A. R. Waller (1905), 1:177–78.

35. Ibid., 6:7.

CHAPTER 3. FROM TATE TO THOMSON: THE AGE OF PROPAGANDA (1681–1749)

1. Nicoll, *A History of English Drama*, 1:353.

2. "The Epistle Dedicatory" to *The Ingratitude of a Common-wealth: Or, the Fall of Caius Martius Coriolanus* (1682; reprint, Cornmarket Press, 1969), A2-A3.

3. For biographical details see Herbert Francis Scott-Thomas, *The Life and*

Works of Nahum Tate (Baltimore: 1934), and Christopher Spencer, *Nahum Tate* (1972).

4. I am indebted to the following helpful doctoral dissertations dealing with Tate's adaptation: Guy Pierce Allen, "Seven English Versions of the Coriolanus Story" (Ph.D. diss., University of Toronto, 1978); James B. Ayres, "Shakespeare in the Restoration: Nahum Tate's *The History of King Richard the Second, The History of King Lear* and *The Ingratitude of a Common-wealth*" (Ph.D. diss., The Ohio State University, 1964); Sally Marie Gallion, "*Coriolanus* on the Restoration and Eighteenth-Century Stage: Does Virtue 'Lie in th'Interpretation of the Time'?" (Ph.D. diss., University of Missouri-Columbia, 1979); and Ruth Ella McGugan, "Nahum Tate and the Coriolanus Tradition in English Drama, with a Critical Edition of Tate's *The Ingratitude of a Common-wealth*" (Ph.D. diss., University of Illinois, 1965).

5. *The London Stage 1660–1800. Part 1: 1660–1700,* ed. William Van Lennep (Carbondale, Illinois: 1965), 1: 304.

6. Ibid.

7. Some of the Tate material in this chapter appears in my essay "*Coriolanus* as Political Propaganda: Nahum Tate's *Ingratitude of a Common-wealth* (1682)," *Textual and Theatrical Shakespeare: Questions of Evidence,* ed. Edward Pechter (Iowa City: 1996). I am grateful to the University of Iowa Press for permission to reproduce it.

8. See Allardyce Nicoll, "Political Plays of the Restoration," *Modern Language Review,* 16 (1921): 224–42; Virgil L. Jones, "Methods of Satire in the Political Drama of the Restoration," *Journal of English and Germanic Philology,* 21 (1922): 662–69; George W. Whiting, "Political Satire in London Stage Plays, 1680–83," *Modern Philology,* 18 (1930–31): 29–43; and Matthew W. Wikander, "The Spitted Infant: Scenic Emblem and Exclusionist Politics in Restoration Adaptations of Shakespeare," *Shakespeare Quarterly,* 37 (1986): 340–58.

9. See J. Douglas Canfield, "Royalism's Last Dramatic Stand: English Political Tragedy, 1679–89," *Studies in Philology,* 82 (1985): 234–63. Historical treatments of the period include J. R. Jones, *The First Whigs: The Politics of the Exclusion Crisis, 1678–83,* rev. ed. (Oxford: 1970); John Miller, *Popery and Politics in England, 1660–1688* (Cambridge: 1973); Francis S. Ronalds, *The Attempted Whig Revolution of 1678–1681* (Totowa, N.J.: 1974); and Bruce Lenman, *The Jacobite Risings in Britain 1689–1746* (1980).

10. See Whiting, "Political Satire in London Stage Plays, 1680–83," 29–43.

11. See Ronalds, *The Attempted Whig Revolution of 1678–1681,* 81.

12. See H. N. Hudson, *Lectures on Shakespeare* (1848); G. C. D. Odell, *Shakespeare from Betterton to Irving* (1920; reprint, 2 vols., Dover Publications, 1966); and Hazelton Spencer, *Shakespeare Improved: The Restoration Versions in Quarto and on the Stage* (Cambridge, Mass.: 1927).

13. The slaughter of innocents as the outcome of factionalism is a feature of a number of Shakespearian adaptations of this period, and the analogy between family and state is frequently pressed by divine right theorists from James I to Robert Filmer. See Wikander, "The Spitted Infant: Scenic Emblem and Exclusionist Politics in Restoration Adaptations of Shakespeare."

14. Cited by Hauser, *Mannerism,* 1:77.

15. Of Shakespeare's 3409 lines, Tate retains 1274; i.e., he is directly indebted to Shakespeare for 60 percent of the 2164 lines in his adaptation. See McGugen, xxviii.

16. Walter Benjamin, in his analysis of Germany's baroque martyr-drama, with which Tate's *Ingratitude* has affinities, notes that the hero is frequently "a radical stoic, for whom the occasion to prove himself is a struggle . . . ending in torture

and death. A peculiarity is the introduction of a woman as the victim in many of these dramas." See *The Origin of German Tragic Drama*, trans. John Osborne (1977), 73–74.

17. Bradley, "*Coriolanus*," 458.

18. For details of Restoration theatres and their stage practice see Richard Leacroft, *The Development of the English Playhouse* (1973).

19. See *The London Stage*, Part 1: 1660–1700, 1:lvi.

20. On two occasions obvious scene changes are unmarked: the entrance of Brutus and Menenius (43) for a Roman episode after the exit of Aufidius and Nigridius from a sequence set in Corioli, and again in act 5 when, after Volumnia and Virgilia leave Rome, Aufidius and Nigridius must enter on a Corioli setting (54).

21. I am assuming that the Theatre Royal had three grooves, although there may have been more. See Leacroft, *The Development of the English Playhouse*, 110.

22. See Odell, *Shakespeare from Betterton to Irving*, 1: 106.

23. Actresses regularly wore up-to-date fashions in historical plays. As late as 1792, Sarah Siddons was censured for wearing contemporary costume as Volumnia.

24. Judith Hook, *The Baroque Age in England* (1976), 12.

25. For an example of secular transcendence in visual art, Tate need have looked no farther than Rubens's *Apotheosis of James I* on the ceiling of the Banqueting House at Whitehall.

26. John Downes, *Roscius Anglicanus* (1708), 41.

27. The only other contender for the role was Michael Mohun, the company's second leading actor and an outstanding Cassius. He would have had the requisite fire for Martius, but a contemporary description of him as a "little Man of Mettle" (Downes, *Roscius Anglicanus*, 42) suggests that he lacked physical impressiveness.

28. Dennis, *Critical Works*, 2:165.

29. David Erskine Baker, *The Companion to the Play-House* (1764), 1:n.p.

30. Theophilus Cibber, *The Lives of the Poets of Great Britain and Ireland* (1753), 4:221.

31. *The Invader of His Country: or, The Fatal Resentment* (1720; reprint, Cornmarket Press, 1969), 79.

32. See Dennis, *Critical Works*, 2:4.

33. At this period he appears to have withdrawn from active participation in the intellectual milieu. In a letter dated 6 August 1720, he writes, "For these last fifteen Years I have retir'd from the World, and confin'd my Conversation to 3 or 4 of my old Acquaintance" (Ibid., 1:519).

34. Ibid., 2:162.

35. See Richard Hindry Barker, *Mr. Cibber of Drury Lane* (1939), 119–20.

36. Dennis, *Critical Works*, 2:178.

37. Allen, in his dissertation noted above, remarks that "No good Whig would have failed to recognize an instructive parallel between the legitimist position and Coriolanus' autocratic view that the Roman citizens had no rightful place in the political process and no right or qualification to determine their legitimate leaders" (56). Allen finds Dennis's adaptation influenced by the political theory of John Locke.

38. Dennis, "Essay on the Genius and Writings of Shakespear," *Critical Works*, 2:6–7.

39. Dennis, *Critical Works*, 2:168.

40. Gallion calculates that Dennis retains "the essence of only 990 of Shakespeare's 3409 lines and adds 1685 original ones" ("*Coriolanus* on the Restoration and Eighteenth-Century Stage," 156).

41. Dennis, "An Essay Upon the Genius and Writings of Shakespear," *Critical Works*, 2:6.

42. Dennis, "The Advancement and Reformation of Modern Poetry," *Critical Works*, 1: 200.

43. See George C. Branam, *Eighteenth-Century Adaptations of Shakespearian Tragedy* (Berkeley, Calif.: 1956), 114ff.

44. Useful treatments of correspondences between neoclassical art and literature include Walter Friedlaender, *Nicolas Poussin, A New Approach* (1966) and Dean Tolle Mace, "Ut pictura poesis: Dryden, Poussin and the parallel of poetry and painting in the seventeenth century," *Encounters: Essays on Literature and the visual arts,* ed. John Dixon Hunt (1971).

45. Poussin's painting was used as the basis for Kirkall's frontispiece to Rowe's 1709 edition of *Coriolanus* and a number of later editions. See Moelwyn Merchant, *Shakespeare and the Artist* (1959), 178ff. For helpful studies of Poussin's neo-Stoic pieces see Friedlaender, *Nicolas Poussin* and Anthony Blunt, *Nicolas Poussin* (1967).

46. Dennis, "Essay on the Genius and Writings of Shakespear," *Critical Works*, 2:5.

47. Ibid., 2:6.

48. Dennis was particularly incensed by the failure of Shakespeare to ensure the death of Aufidius. "*Aufidius,*" he complains, "the principal Murderer of *Coriolanus, who* in cold blood gets him assassinated by Ruffians, instead of leaving him to the Law of the Country, and the Justice of the *Volscian* Senate . . . thro Jealousy, Envy, and inveterate Malice; this Assassinator not only survives . . . unpunish'd, but seems to be rewarded for so detestable an action" (Ibid., 2:6).

49. Ibid., 2:5.

50. For detailed treatment of language alterations in Shakespearian adaptations of this period, see Branam, *Eighteenth-Century Adaptations of Shakespearean Tragedy.*

51. "Essay on the Genius and Writings of Shakespear," *Critical Works,* 2:9.

52. Ibid., 2:17.

53. Ibid.

54. For a conjectural reconstruction of an eighteenth-century production of *Julius Caesar* based on an extant promptbook, see John Ripley, *"Julius Caesar" on Stage in England and America, 1599–1973* (Cambridge: 1980), 34–41. The change from Coriolanus's house to the Forum for the Banishment scene is not marked, doubtless due to a printer's oversight. Marcius tells his mother just before his exit, however, that he is going to "the *Roman Forum.*" The Voices scene is staged before what is described as "*The Roman Forum.*"

55. Theophilus Cibber, *The Life and Character . . . of Barton Booth, Esq.* (1753), 51.

56. Theophilus Cibber, *The Lives and Characters of the Most Eminent Actors and Actresses of Great Britain and Ireland* (1753), 44.

57. Thomas Davies, *Dramatic Miscellanies* (1783–84), 1:356.

58. Colley Cibber, *Apology for the Life of* (1740), 477, 475.

59. William Cooke, *Memoirs of Charles Macklin* (1804), 25.

60. Dennis, Letter to Sir Richard Steele, 26 March 1719, *Critical Works*, 2:164.

61. Biographical and critical studies of Thomson include Hilbert H. Campbell, *James Thomson* (Boston: 1979); Douglas Grant, *James Thomson: Poet of the Seasons* (1951); G. C. Macaulay, *James Thomson* (1908); James Edward Meeker, *The Life and Poetry of James Thomson* (1917); and James Thomson, *Letters and Documents,* ed. Alan Dugald McKillop (Lawrence, Kansas: 1958).

62. See Lenman, *The Jacobite Risings in Britain 1689–1746,* 235–36.

63. On 12 August 1742, David Mallet, in response to a letter from Aaron Hill noting a current playhouse rumor that Thomson was writing a tragedy on the Black Prince, remarks, "I think I may be positive it never was in his thoughts. He is indeed going upon the subject of Coriolanus." Thomson, *Letters and Documents,* 137.

64. He quotes two lines from 3.3 in a letter to Elizabeth Young, his recalcitrant lover, in a letter dated 4 November 1745. Thomson, *Letters and Documents,* 184.

65. Ibid., 196–97.

66. *Coriolanus, The Works of James Thomson* (1773), 4:286. All citations are from this edition.

67. "Preface to *Troilus and Cressida*" (1679), *Essays of John Dryden,* ed. W. P. Ker (1961), 2:210.

68. Whether Marcius could have eluded his fate by the belated exercise of rational constraint is a moot point: according to Thomson's moral code, he had already doomed himself by "rais[ing] his vengeful arm against his country."

69. See Odell, *Shakespeare from Betterton to Irving,* 1:307–8.

70. See W. M. Merchant, "Classical Costume in Shakespearian Productions," *Shakespeare Survey,* 10 (1957): 71–76.

71. British Library Add. MSS. 12,201. Selected Folios 34–73. This inventory was prepared by John Rich when he was seeking a mortgage from Martha Launder.

72. The curiously-flared base of Quin's costume has often invited comment. It may be explained as simply poor draughtsmanship or, as Merchant suggests (72), "a rococo development of masque or operatic costume."

73. Thomas Davies, *Memoirs of the Life of David Garrick Esq.* (1780): 1:30.

74. Letter from T. Lennard Barrett to Sanderson Miller. *An Eighteenth-Century Correspondence,* ed. Lilian Dickins and Mary Stanton (1910), 136.

Chapter 4. From Sheridan to Kemble: The Making of a Production Tradition (1752–1817)

1. Helpful accounts of the period include Asa Briggs, *The Age of Improvement* (1959); John B. Owen, *The Eighteenth Century 1714–1815* (1974); and Glyn Williams and John Ramsden, *Ruling Britannia: a political history of Britain 1688–1988* (1990).

2. The influence of archaeological investigation on English taste is discussed by Edgar F. Carritt, *A Calendar of British Taste 1600–1800* [1948], 2:231ff; and John Gloag, *Georgian Grace: A Social History of Design from 1660–1830* (1956), 17ff.

3. Johann Joachim Winckelmann, *Reflections on the Imitation of Greek Works in Painting and Sculpture* (1755). German text with English translation by Elfriede Heyer and Roger C. Norton (La Salle, Illinois: 1987), 5.

4. For a detailed account of Sheridan's life and work, see Esther Sheldon, *Thomas Sheridan of Smock-Alley* (Princeton, N.J.: 1967).

5. "Advertisement" to *Coriolanus: or, the Roman Matron* (1755).

6. *CORIOLANUS:/OR, THE/ ROMAN MATRON./ A/ TRAGEDY./ Taken from SHAKESPEAR and THOMSON./ As it is Acted at the/ THEATRE-ROYAL/ IN/ COVENT-GARDEN:/ To which is added,/ The ORDER of the OVATION./ LON-DON:/ Printed for A. MILLAR, in the Strand./ MDCCLV.* In 1757 Sheridan published a second acting edition, featuring his amended text for the 1756 Dublin revival. This script contains more Shakespeare and less Thomson and considerably elaborates the ovation (reprinted by Cornmarket Press, 1969).

7. Sheridan's name does not appear as adaptor, but his authorship was not questioned in his own time or since.

8. Hauser, *The Social History of Art* (1985) 3:130–31.

9. In later productions, to judge by the 1757 acting edition printed in Dublin, Sheridan restored a fair amount of Shakespeare's text in this scene. He was followed in this by Kemble, who seems to have consulted the 1757 version.

10. Robert Hitchcock notes that at Smock Alley "[h]e constantly attended the rehearsals, and settled the business of each scene with precision. Not the most trifling incident of the night's performance was omitted at the next morning's practice. . . . The minutiae of the stage were also diligently attended to. His decorations were truly elegant, and his plays were dressed with characteristic propriety" (*An Historical View of the Irish Stage*, Dublin, 1788, 1:138).

11. "Advertisement" to *Coriolanus; or the Roman Matron* (1755).

12. Ibid.

13. J. Brownsmith, *The Dramatic Time-Piece* (1767), n.p.

14. Unsigned letter, *The Public Advertiser*, 13 December 1754.

15. Ibid.

16. Jonah Barrington, *Personal Sketches of His Own Times* (1827), 2:201.

17. Tate Wilkinson, *Memoirs of His Own Life*, (York: 1790), 4:208.

18. Thomas Wilkes, *A General View of the Stage* (1759), 314.

19. [Paul Hiffernan], *The Tuner, Letter the Third* (1754), 22.

20. *London Chronicle*, 7–9 November 1758.

21. Wilkes, *A General View of the Stage*, 284.

22. *British Chronicle*, 8–13 November 1758.

23. *The Letters of David Garrick*, ed. David M. Little and George M. Kahrl (Cambridge, Mass.:1963), 1:172.

24. Davies, *Memoirs of the Life of David Garrick, Esq.*, 1:96.

25. Wilkinson, *Memoirs of His Own Life*, 4:201.

26. [Hiffernan], *The Tuner, Letter the Third*, 22.

27. Arthur Murphy, *The Life of David Garrick*, (Dublin: 1801), 144.

28. Davies, *Memoirs of the Life of David Garrick, Esq.*, 2:230.

29. Murphy, *The Life of David Garrick*, 144.

30. John O'Keeffe, *Recollections of the Life of* (Philadelphia: 1827), 1:31.

31. Hitchcock, *An Historical View of the Irish Stage*, 1:268.

32. [Hiffernan], *The Tuner, Letter the Third*, 22.

33. *Thraliana: The Diary of Mrs. Hester Lynch Thrale*, ed. Katharine C. Balderston (Oxford: 1951), 2:726.

34. Wilkinson, *Memoirs of His Own Life*, 1:140.

35. Davies, *Memoirs of the Life of David Garrick*, 2:209.

36. The only major actor to challenge Kemble's primacy was George Frederick Cooke who dropped the part after only one performance at Drury Lane in 1804.

37. Inchbald, "Remarks" to *Coriolanus* in *The British Theatre*, 5:5.

38. See Williams and Ramsden, *Ruling Britannia: A political history of Britain 1688–1988*, 152–61.

39. Inchbald, "Remarks" to *Coriolanus*, 5:5.

40. Winckelmann, *Reflections on the Imitation of Greek Works in Painting and Sculpture*, 5.

41. James Boaden, *Memoirs of the Life of John Philip Kemble Esq.* (1825), 1:279. For details of Kemble's life and work see also Herschel Baker, *John Philip Kemble* (1942); Percy Fitzgerald, *The Kembles* (1871); Linda Kelly, *The Kemble Era: John Philip Kemble, Sarah Siddons and the London Stage* (1980); and Charles H. Shattuck's introduction and notes to *John Philip Kemble Promptbooks* (Charlottesville, Virginia: 1974), vols. 1 and 2.

42. Kemble was familiar with the work of Thomas Sheridan, and indeed sought

coaching from him before he played King John in the 1783–84 season. See Baker, *John Philip Kemble,* 93.

43. For detailed treatment of the evolution of neoclassical art theory see Hugh Honour, *Neo-Classicism* (Harmondsworth, Middlesex: 1968); Hauser, *The Social History of Art,* vol. 3; Robert Rosenblum, *Transformations in Late Eighteenth Century Art* (Princeton, N.J.: 1967); and William Vaughan, *Romantic Art* (1988).

44. Sir Joshua Reynolds, "The Third Discourse," *Fifteen Discourses Delivered in the Royal Academy* (Everyman Edition, n.d.), 27, 30.

45. Vaughan, *Romantic Art,* 33.

46. Honour, *Neo-Classicism,* 32.

47. See Marvin Carlson, "David's *Oath of the Horatii* as a Theatrical Document," *Theatre History Studies,* 10 (1990): 15–29.

48. Honour, *Neo-Classicism,* 144.

49. Boaden, *Memoirs of the Life of John Philip Kemble Esq.,* 2:2.

50. James Boaden, *Memoirs of Mrs. Siddons* (1827), 2:250.

51. Reynolds, "The Thirteenth Discourse," 220.

52. William Jaggard, *Shakespeare Bibliography* (Stratford-upon-Avon: 1911).

53. Kemble, perhaps out of modesty, attributes his first acting edition (1789) to Thomas Sheridan, and several reviewers were misled into treating the performance as a revival of the Dublin manager's alteration. Although Kemble's redaction owes a good deal to Sheridan's practice, it is clearly a product of his own artistry.

54. In Shattuck, *John Philip Kemble Promptbooks,* vol. 2.

55. Kemble prints 4.4 in the 1806 acting edition as 4.1, cuts it in the official promptbook, and later marks the scene "In." I can find no reference to it in reviews, and am inclined to think the scene was not played since it would detract from Martius's spectacular discovery in Aufidius's house.

56. Sheridan's acting edition of 1755 employs Thomson's version of the Intercession scene, but his 1757 adaptation relies heavily on Shakespeare.

57. See, for example, Jean-Louis David's *Oath of the Horatii* (1784–85) and *Brutus* (1789), or P.-N. Guerin's *The Return of Marcus Sextus* (1797–99).

58. Kemble mounted *Coriolanus* generously from the first. Sheridan authorized an expenditure of £1000 for the 1789 production, which Kemble managed to exceed by £2000. Archaeological inaccuracies, probably the result of Sheridan's parsimony, plagued early revivals: critics complained in 1792 that "Rome had a Gothic gate, and Hanover-square was the Roman market place" (*Star,* 2 April 1792). Once he obtained a share in the Covent Garden ownership and a freer hand in management, such censure was rare.

59. See Sybil Rosenfeld, *Georgian Scene Painters and Scene Painting* (1981), 146, 174.

60. In the Print Room of the British Museum. West's work is treated in detail by George Speaight in *The History of the English Toy Theatre* (1969). Speaight tells us that settings "were all faithfully copied from actual productions on the London stage" (14). The designs, issued as Toy Theatre sheets in 1815, were no doubt intended to capitalize on Kemble's 1814 revival for which he used the sets prepared in 1811. Although most of the illustrations reproduced here are dated 1824, they are printed from the original 1815 plates.

61. Thomas Goodwin, *Sketches and Impressions,* ed. R. Osgood Mason (1887), 34–35.

62. The imprecise RUE merely indicates an entrance somewhere above the second grooves, according to Shattuck (*The John Philip Kemble Promptbooks,* 1:xix).

63. *London Magazine,* 7 (April 1823), 454–55.

64. The master promptbook lacks details for this entry. Here and elsewhere I

have occasionally supplemented scanty directions in the master-book with fuller directions from the Wister copy when these were available.

65. In the Folger Shakespeare Library (*Cor* 4).

66. For detailed discussion of Kemble's use of music in his *Coriolanus* productions see David Rostron, "John Philip Kemble's *Coriolanus* and *Julius Caesar*," *Theatre Notebook*, 23 (1968): 26–34.

67. See Rosenfeld, *Georgian Scene Painters and Scene Painting*, 146, 174; also her "Scene Designs by Hodgins the Younger," *Theatre Notebook*, 27 (1972/73): 22–25; and "Neo-classical Scenery in England: A Footnote to the Exhibition of the Age of Neo-Classicism," *Theatre Notebook*, 27 (1972/3): 67–71. The accuracy with which West's reproduction follows Hodgins's design further confirms the Juvenile Drama's scenic accuracy.

68. Sheridan lists a "Ram Adorned for the Sacrifice" in the ovation procession in his 1757 acting edition.

69. The ecclesiastical elements in the ovations of Sheridan and Kemble doubtless owe something to the religious procession which opens 3.3 of Thomson's *Coriolanus*.

70. William Robson, *The Old Play-goer* (1846), 35.

71. Mislabeled by West as "Second Scene of the Fourth Act."

72. This direction is crossed out in the Wister book.

73. Mislabeled by West as "1st Scene of 4th. Act.

74. Letter to his sister Eloise, 19 June 1817. Gabriel Harrison, *John Howard Payne* (Philadelphia: 1885), 68.

75. J. M. Williams, *The Dramatic Censor*, 6 (1812): 477.

76. John Ambrose Williams, *Memoirs of John Philip Kemble Esq.*, (1817), 77.

77. Ibid.

78. Robson, *The Old Play-goer*, 35.

79. In the course of one rehearsal Kemble moved so slowly that Schmidt, the trumpeter, "became exhausted and the flourish died out. 'Sir,' said Kemble, with severe dignity, 'did I not tell you to keep on blowing until I stopped?' 'Yes, sir,' meekly answered the breathless trumpeter, 'but mine Gott! who is to find der vind?'" (Goodwin, *Sketches and Impressions*, 36).

80. Williams, *Memoirs of John Philip Kemble Esq.*, 78.

81. Unidentified cutting in Covent Garden Box for 1806, Theatre Museum, London.

82. *Monthly Mirror* 23 (June, 1807): 429.

83. Williams, *Memoirs of John Philip Kemble Esq.*, 79.

84. Ibid., 78.

85. Ibid., 79.

86. John Finlay, *Miscellanies* (Dublin: 1835), 280.

87. J. M. Williams, *The Dramatic Censor*, 6 (1812):477.

88. Williams, *Memoirs of John Philip Kemble, Esq.*, 79.

89. Ibid., 80.

90. Theodore Martin, "An Eye-Witness of John Kemble," *The Nineteenth Century*, 7 (1880):286–87.

91. Williams, *Memoirs of John Philip Kemble, Esq.*, 80.

92. Walter Scott, Review of Boaden's *Kemble*, *The Quarterly Review*, 24 (1826):224.

93. See, for example, Gavin Hamilton's *Andromache Bewailing the Death of Hector* (ca. 1761), Benjamin West's *Agrippina with the Ashes of Germanicus* (1768), and Dance's *Death of Virginia* (1761).

94. Williams, *The Dramatic Censor*, 6 (1812):474.

95. Julian Charles Young, *A Memoir of Charles Mayne Young* (1871), 63.

96. Williams, *The Dramatic Censor,* 6 (1812): 474. Her business at one point in this episode apparently threatened tragic decorum. "In that [scene] where she persuades him to yield to the people, at the market-place," reported the *General Evening Post* critic, "she was not so happy; and there was something in the *thump* she gave him on the shoulder, which, we trust, she will hereafter omit" (17–19 December 1811).

97. Ibid.

98. *London Magazine* 7 (April, 1823): 454.

99. Robson, *The Old Play-goer,* 193.

100. Henry Crabb Robinson, *Diary, Reminiscences, and Correspondence,* ed. Thomas Sadler (1869), 1:229.

CHAPTER 5. The Kemble Tradition Challenged: Elliston-Kean (1820)

1. *New Monthly Magazine,* April 1820, 472.

2. The play was originally advertised to open on 24 January, but the premiere was postponed for a night due to the death of the Duke of Kent.

3. Standard biographies of Edmund Kean include Raymund FitzSimons, *Edmund Kean: Fire from Heaven* (1976); F. W. Hawkins, *The Life of Edmund Kean,* 2 vols. (1869); Harold Newcomb Hillebrand, *Edmund Kean* (1933); J. Fitzgerald Molloy, *The Life and Adventures of Edmund Kean,* 2 vols. (1888); Giles Playfair, *Kean* (1950); and B. W. Procter, *Life of Edmund Kean,* 2 vols. (1835). The only modern biography of Elliston is Christopher Murray's *Robert William Elliston, Manager* (1975). George Raymond's *The Life and Enterprises of Robert William Elliston, Comedian* (1857) is particularly entertaining and useful.

4. William Fleming, *Arts and Ideas,* 6th ed. (1980), 376.

5. Anthony Wood, *Nineteenth Century Britain 1815–1914* (1960), 50.

6. See E. H. Gombrich, *The Story of Art,* 15th ed. (1989), 381–82.

7. See Margreta De Grazia, *Shakespeare Verbatim: The Reproduction of Authenticity and the 1790 Apparatus.* It was, curiously enough, Malone who suggested to Copley the Charles I scene as a subject. See Gombrich, *The Story of Art,* 381.

8. See Murray, *Robert William Elliston, Manager.*

9. *Shakspeare's / CORIOLANUS; / AN / HISTORICAL PLAY. / FROM THE PROMPT COPY OF THE THEATRE ROYAL,/ DRURY LANE./ LONDON; / Printed by J. TABBY, Theatre Royal, Drury Lane. / 1820.* The European Magazine (February 1820, 163) credits George Soane with the alteration; but Elliston took responsibility for it, and was probably at least a close collaborator.

10. Arthur Colby Sprague, "A *Macbeth* of Few Words," . . . *All These To Teach: Essays in Honour of C. A. Robertson,* ed. Robert A. Bryan (Gainesville, Florida: 1965), 86.

11. Hauser, *Mannerism,* 1: 129.

12. For an account of the work of Gaetano Marinari and others see Rosenfeld, *Georgian Scene Painters.*

13. Autopsy report cited by FitzSimons in *Edmund Kean: Fire from Heaven,* 8.

14. James Henry Hackett, *Notes and Comments upon Certain Plays and Actors of Shakespeare* (1864; reprint, Benjamin Blom, 1968), 126–27.

15. Hawkins, *The Life of Edmund Kean,* 2:114.

16. Dr. Doran, *"Their Majesties' Servants": Annals of the English Stage from Thomas Betterton to Edward Kean* (1864), 2:556.

CHAPTER 6. THE KEMBLE TRADITION IN ENGLAND (1819–1915)

1. James E. Murdoch, *The Stage or Recollections of Actors and Acting* (Philadelphia: 1880), 189–90.

2. Macready's promptbook for the 1819 production, a transcription of Kemble's book made in an 1814 edition, survives in the Folger Shakespeare Library (*Cor* 7). It may also have been used for subsequent productions. See David George, "Restoring Shakespeare's *Coriolanus:* Kean versus Macready," *Theatre Notebook,* 44 (1990):101–18.

3. *Macready's Reminiscences, and Selections from His Diaries and Letters,* ed. Sir Frederick Pollock (1875), 1: 290.

4. Useful sources for study of Macready's life and work, in addition to his *Reminiscences* cited above, include *The Diaries of William Charles Macready 1833–1851,* ed. William Toynbee, 2 vols. (1912); and Alan S. Downer, *The Eminent Tragedian: William Charles Macready* (Cambridge, Mass.: 1966).

5. *Macready's Reminiscences, and Selections from His Diaries and Letters,* 424. To be fair to Macready, and perhaps Kemble as well, one should recognize the possibility that their apparent indifference to politics was motivated by Schiller's conviction, shared by many of their contemporaries, that "if we are ever to solve [the] political problem in practice, follow the path of aesthetics, since it is through Beauty that we arrive at Freedom" (Friedrich Schiller, *On the Aesthetic Education of Man,* trans. Reginald Snell [1965], 27).

6. It is a particular irony that the People's Charter was being written even as Macready's *Coriolanus* was played. It was published in May 1838, just after the production closed.

7. Macready's text for the servant sequence was, I suspect, appropriated by Phelps, and may be found in the latter's promptbook. See p. 176.

8. See review in *John Bull,* 1 April 1838.

9. Works on Roman history and archaeology available to Macready included Wilhelm Becker, *Gallus, oder romische Scenen aus der Zeit Augusts* (Leipzig: 1838); Luigi Canina, *Indicazione di Roma Antica* (Rome: 1830); Thomas Swinburne Carr, *Manual of Roman Antiquities* (1836); Antonio De Romanis, *Le Vestigie di Roma Antica* (Rome: 1832); Thomas Hope, *Costume of the Ancients* (1809); and George Ledwell Taylor and Edward Cressy, *Architectural Antiquities of Rome* (1821).

10. Kemble included "Citizens" in his entry directions for this scene, but they were apparently few in numbers and given no significant business.

11. For detailed treatment of this subject see the chapter titled "Transcendent landscapes" in William Vaughan, *Romantic Art,* 132–83.

12. John Coleman, *Players and Playwrights I Have Known* (1888), 1:20. Coleman attributes this account to a review by W. J. Fox, but this material does not appear in either Fox's *Morning Chronicle* notices or his *Collected Works.* It is more likely to be based on Coleman's own recollection.

13. For intensive discussion of Romantic characterization see Joseph W. Donohue, Jr., *Dramatic Character in the English Romantic Age* (Princeton, N.J.: 1970).

14. Charles Reece Pemberton, *The Life and Literary Remains of,* ed. John Fowler (1843), 245.

15. Ibid., 244–45. Pemberton's description of this scene and the Banishment

sequence cited above refers to Macready's 1833 performance when he was playing in Kemble's shadow. Reviews of the 1838 revival, however, indicate that he changed his reading of these episodes very little since it suited a Romantic interpretation quite as well as a neoclassical one.

16. Macready, despite his much admired artistic taste, could not resist including the Kemble business in which the 1st Citizen parodies not so much Martius as the acting style of the star.

17. James R. Anderson, *An Actor's Life* (1902), 73.

18. Ibid.

19. *Macready's Reminiscences,* 428.

20. W. May Phelps and John Forbes-Robertson, *The Life and Life-Work of Samuel Phelps* (1886), 213.

21. He did not stage *Titus Andronicus,* the *Henry VI* plays, *Troilus and Cressida,* or *Richard II.*

22. Henry Morley, *The Journal of a London Playgoer* (1866), 152. For further details of Phelps's production practice see Shirley S. Allen, *Samuel Phelps and Sadler's Wells Theatre,* (Middletown, Conn.: 1971); Dennis Arundell, *The Story of Sadler's Wells 1683–1964,* 2 vols. (1965); John Coleman, *Memoirs of Samuel Phelps* (1886); Sidney Lee, *Shakespeare and the Modern Stage* (1906); Odell, *Shakespeare from Betterton to Irving,* 1:237ff.; and Phelps and Forbes-Robertson, *The Life and Life-Work of Samuel Phelps.*

23. Two transcriptions of the promptbook also survive—*Cor* 13 and *Cor* 15. Occasionally, when a particular direction in *Cor* 13 was more legible, clearer, or fuller than in the original book, I have made a silent substitution. All three books are in the Folger Shakespeare Library.

24. It is worth noting that Macready did not give Phelps any major role when he played Martius himself. Although he employed him as Aufidius to Vandenhoff's Martius, he was companioned by Anderson's Volscian general when he returned to the role in the spring of 1839. See *Chronological Handlist.*

25. *The Complete Works of Shakespeare,* ed. Samuel Phelps (ca.1853), 2:489.

26. The crowd so impressed the audience at one performance that they were summoned for a curtain call. See Clement Scott, *The Drama of Yesterday & To-Day* (1899), 1:287.

27. *The Examiner,* 22 September 1860. Reprinted in Morley, *The Journal of a London Playgoer,* 262.

28. Coleman, *Memoirs of Samuel Phelps,* 27.

29. Accounts of Irving's life and work include Madeleine Bingham, *Henry Irving and the Victorian Theatre* (1978); Austin Brereton, *The Life of Henry Irving,* 2 vols. (1908); Alan Hughes, *Henry Irving, Shakespearean* (1981); Laurence Irving, *Henry Irving: The Actor and His World* (1951); Cary Mazer, *Shakespeare Refashioned: Elizabethan Plays on Edwardian Stages* (Ann Arbor: 1981); and Bram Stoker, *Personal Reminiscences of Henry Irving* (1907).

30. See Michael R. Booth, *Victorian Spectacular Theatre 1850–1910* (1981).

31. In the British Library (Add. Mss. 61996B). The British Library also owns a neat transcription of the promptbook (Add. Mss. 61996C). When promptbook directions were illegible or otherwise unclear, I have silently supplied them from the transcription.

32. Frances Donaldson, *The Actor-Managers* (1970), 84.

33. Kemble acting editions were readily available, and he owned a transcription of Phelps's book (*Cor* 15, now in the Folger Shakespeare Library).

34. For useful studies of Alma-Tadema's life and work, see *Sir Lawrence Alma-Tadema,* [Catalogue of an exhibition at] Mappin Art Gallery, Weston Park, Shef-

field, 3 July-8 August 1976 [and] Laing Art Gallery, Higham Place, Newcastle, 21 August-15 September 1976, [n.d.]; Vern G. Swanson, *Sir Lawrence Alma-Tadema* (1977); and Mario Amaya, "The Roman World of Alma-Tadema," *Apollo,* December 1962, 771–78. The designs were initially prepared when Irving contemplated a production of *Coriolanus* in 1879.

35. R. Phené Spiers, "The Architecture of 'Coriolanus,'" *Architectural Review,* 10 (1901):3–21.

36. "A Talk with Sir Laurence Alma-Tadema," *Daily News,* 16 April 1901. See also Sybil Rosenfeld, "Alma-Tadema's Designs for Henry Irving's *Coriolanus,*" *Deutsche Shakespeare-Gesellschraft West Jahrbuch 1974,* ed. Hermann Heuer, 84–95.

37. Spiers, "The Architecture of 'Coriolanus,'" 5.

38. Rosenfeld, "Alma-Tadema's Designs for Henry Irving's *Coriolanus,*" 87–88.

39. Although the Lyceum theater did not employ the groove and shutter system, the promptbook continues to use the traditional designations for entrances and exits since they were precise and well-understood by actors and stage staff.

40. Rosenfeld, "Alma-Tadema's Designs for Henry Irving's *Coriolanus,*" 88.

41. Frederick Harker, "Irving as Coriolanus," *We Saw Him Act,* ed. H. A. Saintsbury and Cecil Palmer (1939), 382.

42. Ibid.

43. See Ripley, *"Julius Caesar" on Stage in England and America 1599–1973,* 167.

44. Rosenfeld, "Alma-Tadema's Designs for Henry Irving's *Coriolanus,*" 91.

45. Ibid.

46. The *Lady's Pictorial* sketch shows only one chair.

47. Rosenfeld, "Alma-Tadema's Designs for Henry Irving's *Coriolanus,*" 92.

48. As early as 1895 he wrote in a notebook, "The comedy of *Coriolanus* is delicious." See Laurence Irving, *Henry Irving: The Actor and His World,* 585.

49. *Cor* 25. In the Ellen Terry Memorial Museum, Smallhythe.

50. Harker, "Irving as Coriolanus," 383.

51. Ibid.

52. Ibid., 384.

53. Ibid.

54. Ibid.

55. In the Folger Shakespeare Library (*Cor* 24).

56. Harker, "Irving as Coriolanus," 385.

57. Ibid., 383.

58. Gordon Crosse, *Shakespearean Playgoing 1890–1952* (1953), 17.

59. Sir Frank Benson, *My Memoirs* (1930), 184.

60. The *Birmingham Daily Post* (1 May 1915) reports that he played the "Memorial [Theatre] edition" (ed. Charles Flower [1890?]) for the revival of that year. Scene divisions in the program and those for other Benson revivals, to say nothing of comments of critics over the years, fail to support the *Post*'s assertion. The Memorial Theatre editions recorded traditional acting cuts, and I suspect correspondences between the Benson and Flower texts are attributable to the common influence of William Creswick who was advisor to Flower and an early mentor to Benson.

61. Vezin appeared occasionally as a star with the Benson company during its early years.

62. In 1893 the role was played by Alice Chapin; in 1898, a Miss Wetherall attempted it; and in 1912 Ethel McDowall brought her considerable talent to it. None, however, enjoyed much success.

63. Richard Dickins, *Forty Years of Shakespeare on the English Stage* [1907], 99.

64. Harcourt Williams, *Old Vic Saga* (1949), 42.

65. Ibid.

66. Crosse, *Shakespearean Playgoing*, 26.

67. Dickins, *Forty Years of Shakespeare on the English Stage*, 99.

68. Crosse, *Shakespearean Playgoing*, 26.

69. In 1919 he played an abbreviated version as part of a longer program (see Chronological Handlist).

CHAPTER 7. THE KEMBLE TRADITION IN AMERICA (1796–1885)

1. For discussion of the influence of classical learning on postcolonial American culture, see Jean V. Matthews, *Toward a New Society: American Thought and Culture, 1800–1830* (Boston: 1991); and Meyer Reinhold, *Classica Americana: The Greek and Roman Heritage in the United States* (Detroit: 1984).

2. Letter from William Leggett to Edwin Forrest. William Rounseville Alger, *Life of Edwin Forrest* (Philadelphia: 1877), 1:324. Cited by Charles Shattuck, *Shakespeare on the American Stage* (Washington, D.C.: 1976), 66.

3. George Wilkes, *Shakespeare From an American Point of View* (1877), 294.

4. Esther Cloudman Dunn, *Shakespeare in America* (1939), 120.

5. Mrs. Whitlock and her husband were recruited from England by Wignell in 1793.

6. John Bernard, *Retrospections of America 1797–1811*, ed. Mrs. Bayle Bernard (1887), 264.

7. See *Columbian Centinel*, Boston, 1 January 1806.

8. While adhering closely in the main to the Kemble text and business, Ludlow restores the odd Shakespearian line, and removes the Thomsonian interpolations in the scene in which Martius and Tullus meet at the latter's house, although the Kemble business in which Martius is discovered beneath a statue of Mars is retained. Ludlow also restores a number of Shakespeare's lines in the death scene. It is difficult to determine at how early a date Ludlow used this book or precisely when he emended the text. There is no evidence to indicate that the alterations date from Cooper's time, and were probably inspired by Macready's 1838 revival at Covent Garden.

9. The *New York Herald* (24 April 1855) reported that "'Coriolanus' is played at the Broadway from Palmer's Philadelphia edition."

10. The only other American mention of horses I have encountered prior to John McCullough's production in 1878 occurs in an advertisement for an 1811 Philadelphia revival which promised that in the course of the ovation Coriolanus would enter in "A Superb Car drawn by real HORSES" (*Tickler*, Philadelphia, 6 March 1811). In Philadelphia in 1813 Coriolanus appeared in "a superb Car drawn by captives" (*Aurora*, Philadelphia, 15 March 1813).

11. Program for a performance at the Chestnut Theater, Philadelphia, 15 March 1813 in the Billy Rose Theater Collection, New York Public Library at Lincoln Center. The most lavish display of livestock in the play's history occurred during an 1837 performance starring Samuel Butler at Drury Lane when a menagerie on loan from the London zoo for the triumphal procession in *Caractacus* was redeployed in *Coriolanus*. See *Morning Herald*, 24 November 1837.

12. For stock settings used in *Julius Caesar* productions of the period, see Ripley, *"Julius Caesar" on Stage in England and America 1599–1973*, 104.

13. William B. Wood, *Personal Recollections of the Stage* (Philadelphia: 1855), 423.

14. Letter from John Howard Payne to his sister Eloise dated 19 June 1817. Harrison, *John Howard Payne*, 72.

15. Isaac Harby, *A Selection from the Miscellaneous Writings of* (Charleston: 1829), 268.

16. Ibid., 278.

17. N. M. Ludlow, *Dramatic Life as I Found It* (St. Louis: 1880), 235.

18. Harby, *A Selection from the Miscellaneous Writings,* 278.

19. Ibid., 279.

20. His carelessness was frequently scolded by reviewers. In Boston in 1818, "Volumnia had even to remind him in the exclamation—'He turns away'—of his proper action, before the motion was made. This coldness," a critic complained, ". . . does not seem to proceed from a want of the feeling necessary to the character, so much as from a kind of laziness that is generally the result of an overweening confidence" (*Boston Weekly Magazine,* 21 February 1818).

21. The period 1790–1830 Meyer Reinhold calls "the Silver Age of Classical Studies" in America. See his *Classica Americana: The Greek and Roman Heritage in the United States;* also Richard M. Gummere, *The American Colonial Mind and the Classical Tradition* (Cambridge, Mass.: 1963.

22. For a fascinating account of Conway's life see John Tearle, *Mrs. Piozzi's Tall Young Beau* (Cranbury, N.J.: 1991).

23. James Henry Hackett, *Notes and Comments upon Certain Plays and Actors of Shakespeare* (1864; Benjamin Blom, 1968), 125.

24. Biographies of Forrest include William Rounseville Alger, *Life of Edwin Forrest* (1877; reprint, Benjamin Blom, Inc., 1972); Laurence Barrett, *Edwin Forrest* (Boston: 1881); Richard Moody, *Edwin Forrest* (1960); Montrose J. Moses, *The Fabulous Forrest* (Boston: 1929); and James Rees, *The Life of Edwin Forrest* (Philadelphia: 1874).

25. Useful studies of nineteenth-century American theatrical and literary culture include David Grimsted, *Melodrama Unveiled: American Theater and Culture 1800–1850* (Chicago: 1968); Jeffrey D. Mason, *Melodrama and the Myth of America* (Bloomington, Indiana: 1993); Bruce A. McConachie, *Melodramatic Formations: American Theatre & Society, 1820–1870* (Iowa City, Iowa: 1992); and *The Culture of Sentiment: Race, Gender, and Sentimentality in Nineteenth-Century America,* ed. Shirley Samuels (Oxford: 1992).

26. A comparison of reviews of the 1855 production at the Broadway Theater with the 1863 promptbook indicates that the scenographic design was originally Forrest's. Wheatley improved the artistic quality of Forrest's visual effects and provided first-rate stage management.

27. See Paul Boyer, *Urban Masses and Moral Order in America, 1820–1920* (Cambridge, Mass.: 1978), 9; and Bruce A. McConachie, *Melodramatic Formations: American Theatre & Society, 1820–1870,* 29ff.

28. Groove designations in the United States, as in England, no longer invariably imply the use of shutters; as often as not they merely indicate stage positions.

29. Playbill in the Harvard Theater Collection.

30. Thomas Allston Brown claims that there were 154 persons on stage in the Ovation scene in the 1863 revival. See *A History of the New York Stage* (1903; reprint, Benjamin Blom Inc., 1964), 1:196.

31. A number of the Scharf sketches of the 1838 Macready revival are incorporated in Forrest's promptbook, but their influence is obvious only in the Ovation, Senate, and Assassination scenes.

32. Alger, *Life of Edwin Forrest,* 1:251–52.

33. William Winter, *Shadows of the Stage,* 2d ser. (Edinburgh: 1893), 73–75.

34. "Mr. Cooper had been Mr. Forrest's idol; he had looked upon him as the great master of histrionic art, and although not his tutor was the classic model from which he fashioned his own impersonations." Rees, *The Life of Edwin Forrest*, 105.

35. See Moody, *Edwin Forrest*, 172.

36. Grimsted, *Melodrama Unveiled*, 176.

37. Ibid., 207.

38. For treatment of adult ethnic gangs of the mid-nineteenth century, see McConachie, *Melodramatic Formations*, 132ff.

39. Cited by Barrett, *Edwin Forrest*, 138.

40. This direction is most intriguing. Was Forrest familiar with the Quin engraving, and carried a truncheon in emulation of it? Or is this a piece of traditional stage business of eighteenth-century origin not noted in previous promptbooks?

41. McConachie, *Melodramatic Formations*, 100.

42. For details of McCullough's life and art see Susie C. Clark, *John McCullough as Man, Actor, and Spirit* (1905); Joseph I. C. Clarke, *My Life and Memories* (1925); Percy MacKaye, *Epoch: The Life of Steele MacKaye* (1927); Augustus Pitou, *Masters of the Show* (1914); J. R. Towse, *Sixty Years of the Theatre* (1911; 1916); and William Winter, *Other Days* (1908), and *Shakespeare on the Stage*, 3d ser. (1916).

43. See Lewis Mumford, *The Brown Decades: A Study of the Arts in America 1865–1895* (1955).

44. The *Spirit of the Times* writer is here quoting from an unidentified Boston review of McCullough's performances the previous season.

45. Studies of Salvini's life and work include Marvin Carlson, *The Italian Shakespearians* (Cranbury, N.J.: 1985); Charles H. Shattuck, *Shakespeare on the American Stage: From Booth and Barrett to Sothern and Marlowe* (Cranbury, N.J.: 1987), 149–57; and William Winter, *The Wallet of Time* (1913), 1 : 283–90.

46. Tomasso Salvini, *Leaves from the Autobiography of* (1893), 222.

47. *CORIOLANUS. / A TRAGEDY IN FIVE ACTS. / BY WILLIAM SHAKESPEARE.* / As Performed For The First Time On Any Stage By / TOMMASO SALVINI / AT THE METROPOLITAN OPERA HOUSE / UNDER THE MANAGEMENT / AND DIRECTION OF MR. C.A. CHIZZOLA. / NEW YORK: PRESS OF J.J. LITTLE & CO., / 10 To 20 ASTOR PLACE / 1885./ In the Harvard Theater Collection.

48. The rehabilitation of Aufidius may be attributable to the fact that the role was played by Salvini's son Alessandro.

49. Towse, *Sixty Years of the Theater*, 251.

CHAPTER 8. MODERNISM AND ELIZABETHAN METHODISM (1920–1938)

1. Cited by Robert Hughes, *The Shock of the New: Art and the Century of Change* (1980), 9.

2. Clive Bell, *Art* (1913), 117.

3. Cited by Charles Harrison, *English Art and Modernism 1900–1939* (New Haven: 1994), 64.

4. For discussion of the influence of modernism on Shakespeare criticism see Hugh Grady, *The Modernist Shakespeare* (Oxford: 1991).

5. See Bell, *Art*, 11.

6. Ibid., 52.

7. William Poel, *Shakespeare in the Theatre* (1913), 122.

8. Robert Speaight, *William Poel and the Elizabethan Revival*, (1954), 90. In

addition to Speaight's classic account of Poel's work, see also Marion O'Connor, *William Poel and the Elizabethan Stage Society* (Cambridge: 1987), and J. L. Styan, *The Shakespeare Revolution* (Cambridge: 1977), 47–63.

9. Speaight, *William Poel and the Elizabethan Revival,* 113.

10. Letter to *Play Pictorial,* 22(1912), iv. Cited by Styan, *The Shakespeare Revolution,* 82.

11. *New York Times,* 26 July 1914. Cited by Styan, *The Shakespeare Revolution,* 82.

12. For details of Granville Barker's staging, see Dennis Kennedy's *Granville Barker and the Dream of Theatre* (Cambridge: 1985) and *Looking at Shakespeare: A Visual History of Twentieth-Century Performance* (Cambridge: 1993), 72ff.; also Styan, *The Shakespeare Revolution,* 82–104.

13. For details of Gray's productions see Kennedy, *Looking at Shakespeare,* 113–19; Norman Marshall, *The Other Theatre* (1947), 53–71; and Styan, *The Shakespeare Revolution,* 152–53.

14. There had been calls for an end to the convention in the course of Irving's revival. "[W]hen Volumnia comes to intercede for Rome," wrote the *Pall Mall Gazette* reviewer, "she should not be accompanied by so large a train of symmetrically-attired ladies. No doubt these ladies balance the assembled Volscians in the stage picture, but one could very well give them up too" (16 April 1901).

15. Peter Roberts, *The Old Vic Story* (1976), 123.

16. Williams, *Old Vic Saga,* 42.

17. Fenner Brockway, *Socialism Over Sixty Years: the Life of Jowett of Bradford* (1946), 180–83. Cited by Charles Loch Mowat, *Britain Between the Wars 1918–1940* (1955), 153.

18. Accounts of Atkins's tenure as director of production at the Old Vic include *Robert Atkins: An Unfinished Autobiography,* ed. George Rowell (1994); Crosse, *Shakespearean Playgoing (1890–1952),* 50ff; Marshall, *The Other Theatre,* 129–30; Robert Speaight, *Shakespeare on the Stage* (1973), 148–49; and J. C. Trewin, *Shakespeare on the English Stage 1900–1964* (1964), 89–90.

19. Adrian and Nicanor do not appear in the cast-list which suggests that the scene may have been omitted. Atkins's promptbook seems not to have survived.

20. Atkins's arrangement owed much to Granville-Barker's adaptation of the proscenium stage at the Savoy Theatre for his productions there between 1912 and 1914. See Speaight, *Shakespeare on the Stage,* 142.

21. Atkins, *Robert Atkins: An Unfinished Autobiography,* 104.

22. Doris Westwood, *These Players: A Diary of the "Old Vic"* (1926), 209.

23. Herbert Farjeon, *The Shakespearean Scene* (1949), 111.

24. Ibid. The newly-elected Labour cabinet members awaiting the royal swearing-in, if far less sinister than Atkins's tribunes, shared the self-conscious wonderment of Shakespeare's politicians at their unexpected eminence. Wrote J. R. Clynes in his *Memoirs* (1937–39), "As we stood waiting for His Majesty, amid the gold and crimson magnificence of the Palace, I could not help marvelling at the strange turn of Fortune's wheel, which had brought MacDonald, the starveling clerk, Thomas the engine-driver, Henderson the foundry labourer and Clynes the mill-hand, to this pinnacle. . . ." (1:343).

25. Farjeon, *The Shakespearean Scene,* 111.

26. Ibid., 113.

27. Westwood, *These Players,* 217–18.

28. Ibid., 222–23.

29. Ibid., 217.

30. Ibid., 221.

31. Ibid., 207.

32. According to programs in the Theatre Museum, he was replaced at some performances by Robert Glennie.

33. Westwood, *These Players*, 207.

34. Farjeon, *The Shakespearean Scene*, 112.

35. Westwood, *These Players*, 214.

36. See Roberts, *The Old Vic Story*, 122.

37. Lady Benson, *Mainly Players* (1926), 302.

38. "Shakespeare and the Modern Spirit," *Stratford-upon-Avon Herald,* 30 April 1926.

39. Ibid.

40. Kennedy, *Looking at Shakespeare*, 126–27.

41. In Shakespeare Centre Library (*Cor* 29). The same book, with erasures, did duty for both productions. Also in the Shakespeare Centre Library is a more legible copy of this book (*Cor* 30).

42. The *Birmingham Mail* (25 April 1933) reported that "In a week they have gone through six first nights, presented six plays which in the West End would each have six weeks rehearsal. . . . At Stratford the average time for rehearsal of a play is five or six days."

43. Trewin, *Shakespeare on the English Stage 1900–1964,* 166.

44. Accounts of Nugent Monck's life and work include Theodore L. G. Burley, *Playhouses and Players of East Anglia* (Norwich: 1928); Franklin J. Hildy, *Shakespeare at the Maddermarket: Nugent Monck and the Norwich Players* (Ann Arbor: 1986); and Marshall, *The Other Theatre,* 92–97.

45. For architectural details of Monck's theater and analysis of his stagecraft, see Burley, *Playhouses and Players of East Anglia;* and Hildy, *Shakespeare at the Maddermarket.*

46. In the private collection of Jack Hall. I am grateful to Mr. Hall for generously allowing me to consult it.

47. This information comes from an undated *Christian Science Monitor* cutting in a scrapbook (SO 26/236, 505 X 4) in the Norfolk Record Office, Norwich. *The Times* (7 February 1928) also remarks that "The staging of the play was based on a picture by Paul Veronese."

48. *The Times* (7 February 1928), which noticed the production briefly, judged it "one of their best performances."

49. In the archives of the Norfolk Record Office.

50. Marshall, *The Other Theatre,* 95.

51. Monck insisted that Maddermarket actors appear anonymously. The names of the players are recorded, however, in the notebook cited in n. 49.

52. He played Brutus in Bridges-Adams's 1933 production at the Shakespeare Memorial Theatre. His early promise was never fully realized due to the onset of deafness, although he continued to play minor roles.

53. Bradley, '*Coriolanus*', 465.

54. Letter from Sean O Faolain, *The Irish Times,* 15 January 1936.

55. Ibid.

56. Morris Ankrum directed and starred in a production of *Coriolanus* in 1936 at the Padadena Playhouse which was chiefly remarkable for its cinematic lighting effects. A spot, for example, played rapidly over faces in the Banishment scene, darting from speaker to speaker.

57. The production premiered the previous summer at the Theater of the Four Seasons in Roslyn, Long Island.

58. *Coriolanus* Program in Theatre Museum, London.

59. Ibid.

60. Ibid.

61. Robert Speaight, *The Property Basket* (1970), 134.

62. Three typescripts (*Cor* 28) in the Theatre Museum, London. A book in orange covers, designated "A," and another in purple covers, designated "C," were probably Poel's own copies. A third, marked "B," is identified as "Miss Molly Tyson's [the stage manager's] Copy," which I take to be the promptbook or something near it. I have relied primarily on this manuscript, supplemented occasionally with directions from the other two books.

63. Speaight, *William Poel and the Elizabethan Revival,* 262.

64. Ibid., 256.

65. Speaight, *The Property Basket,* 132.

66. "The Principles of Shakespeare Interpretation," *The Shakespeare Review* (September 1928); reprinted in *The Sovereign Flower* (1958), 291.

67. Wilson Knight, *The Wheel of Fire* (1930), 14.

68. Wilson Knight, *Principles of Shakespearian Production,* 1936 (Harmondsworth: 1949), 20.

69. The program for this production is in the Shakespeare Collection of the Birmingham Public Library.

Chapter 9. From Olivier to Olivier: A Romantic Interlude (1938–1959)

1. Studies of the cinema from the thirties to the fifties include Bruce Babington and Peter William Evans, *Biblical Epics: Sacred Narrative in the Hollywood Cinema* (Manchester: 1993); Barbara Deming, *Running Away from Myself: A dream portrait of America drawn from the films of the forties* (1969); Andrew Dowdy, *The Films of the Fifties* (1973); Charles Higham, *The Art of the American Film 1900–1971* (1973); and John Izod, *Hollywood and the Box Office 1895–1986* (1988).

2. For detailed treatment of Olivier's life and work see John Cottrell, *Laurence Olivier* (Englewood Cliffs, N.J.: 1975); Anthony Holden, *Olivier* (1988); Thomas Kiernan, *Sir Larry: The Life of Laurence Olivier* (1981); Laurence Olivier, *Confessions of an Actor* (1982); *Olivier in Celebration,* ed. Garry O'Connor (1987); and Donald Spoto, *Laurence Olivier: A Biography* (1992).

3. Program in the Theatre Museum, London.

4. Peter Hall, "The Job He Liked Best," *Olivier in Celebration,* 120. I have been unable to locate the promptbook for this production.

5. Audrey Williamson, *Old Vic Drama* (1950), 100. The criticism of Bradley, Hookham, and Wyndham Lewis had not been without effect.

6. Ibid.

7. Alan Dent, *Preludes and Studies* (1942), 120.

8. Williamson, *Old Vic Drama,* 101.

9. Cottrell, *Laurence Olivier,* 135.

10. Williamson, *Old Vic Drama,* 101.

11. Thorndike had played the role in a BBC radio version of the play in 1933.

12. Williamson, *Old Vic Drama,* 102.

13. Trewin, *Shakespeare on the English Stage 1900–1964,* 175.

14. Ibid.

15. Williamson, *Old Vic Drama,* 101.

16. Ibid., 102.

17. Crosse, *Shakespearean Playgoing 1890–1952,* 122.

18. The promptbook for this production (*Cor* 32) is in the Shakespeare Centre Library, Stratford-upon-Avon.

19. I have been unable to locate the promptbook. My observations on the acting text are based on the program and contemporary accounts.

20. Crosse, *Shakespearean Playgoing 1890–1952*, 130–31.

21. Ibid., 131.

22. Clifford Leech, "Stratford 1952," *Shakespeare Quarterly*, 3 (1952): 353.

23. In the Shakespeare Centre Library, Stratford-upon-Avon (*Cor* 33).

24. Ellis left the production in July and was replaced in the role by Rosalind Atkinson.

25. John Houseman, *Front and Center* (1979), 436.

26. Ibid.

27. Ibid., 440.

28. Ibid., 441.

29. Shattuck places Houseman's promptbook (*Cor* 34) at the University of California Library, Los Angeles. The Library has to date been unable to locate it.

30. Houseman, *Front and Center*, 436.

31. Ibid., 438.

32. Ibid., 442.

33. Ibid.

34. Arthur Colby Sprague, "Shakespeare on the New York Stage 1953–1954," *Shakespeare Quarterly*, 5 (1954): 314.

35. The promptbook (*Cor* 35) is in the University of Bristol Theatre Collection.

36. For further production details and costume and set photographs see Audrey Williamson, *Old Vic Drama 2* (1957), 155–57; and Roger Wood and Mary Clarke, *Shakespeare at the Old Vic* (1954), 1:32–41, 68–72.

37. Wood and Clarke, *Shakespeare at the Old Vic*, 69.

38. Ibid., 71.

39. There are two major essays on this production: Laurence Kitchin's "Olivier, 1959," *Mid-Century Drama* (1960), 135–41, and Stanley Wells's "Peter Hall's *Coriolanus*," *Royal Shakespeare: Four major productions at Stratford-upon-Avon* (Manchester: 1976), 4–22. I am much indebted to both. My reconstruction is inevitably coloured by my own still-vivid recollections.

40. The promptbook for this production (*Cor* 36) is in the Shakespeare Centre Library, Stratford-upon-Avon.

41. See Peter Hall, "The Job He Liked Best," 120–21.

42. Kitchin, *Mid-Century Drama*, 96.

43. Judith Cook, *Shakespeare's Players* (1983), 94.

44. Ibid.

45. Kitchin, *Mid-Century Drama*, 135.

46. Ibid., 135–36.

47. Ibid., 136.

48. Ibid., 137.

49. Ibid.

50. Kenneth Tynan, *Curtains* (1961), 240.

51. Kitchin, *Mid-Century Drama*, 137.

52. Ibid., 137–38.

53. Trewin, *Shakespeare on the English Stage 1900–1964*, 175.

54. Kitchin, *Mid-Century Drama*, 138.

55. Ibid., 140.

56. Ibid., 136.

57. Tynan, *Curtains*, 241. The Mussolini image was deliberate. Olivier told Ber-

nard Levin at the first-night reception, "We got the idea from Mussolini's death" (*Daily Express*, 1 July 1959).

58. In the course of her talk, she is quoted as saying "An actress has to think about the circumstances in which words are spoken, not only about the actual words, and Volumnia when she first talks about battle and bloodshed is sitting sewing. She sews all through her first scene" (*The Times*, 22 August 1959).

CHAPTER 10. PSYCHOANALYSIS, POLITICS, AND POSTMODERNITY (1961–1994)

1. See H. Stuart Hughes and James Wilkinson, *Contemporary Europe: A History* (Englewood Cliffs, N.J.: 1991), 424 ff., and Paul Johnson, *Modern Times: The World from the Twenties to the Eighties* (1983), 641–46.

2. In a gesture indicative of postwar enthusiasm for Shakespeare as a curriculum subject, the education ministers of all ten Canadian provinces attended the premiere of *Coriolanus* at the Stratford Festival in 1961. See the *Kitchener-Waterloo Record*, 20 June 1961.

3. See François Ricard, *The Lyric Generation: The Life and Times of the Baby Boomers*, trans. Donald Winkler (Toronto: 1994).

4. Christopher Lasch, *The Culture of Narcissism* (1979).

5. Kennedy, *Looking at Shakespeare*, 267.

6. The promptbook for this production (*Cor* 37) is in the archives of the Festival Theatre, Stratford, Ontario.

7. Peter D. Smith, "Sharp Wit and Noble Scenes: A Review of the 1961 Season of the Stratford, Ontario Festival," *Shakespeare Quarterly*, 13 (1962): 75.

8. The innovation might have owed something to Robert Speaight, Poel's Martius, who suggested in a review of the Hall-Olivier revival that "There is a case for bringing *Coriolanus* reasonably up to date. . . . Why not the Directoire? This is a period rich in military and political analogies" (*Tablet*, 8 August 1959).

9. Joan Ganong, *Backstage at Stratford* (Toronto: 1962), 122.

10. Smith, "Sharp Wit and Noble Scenes," 73–74.

11. Ibid., 74.

12. Ganong, *Backstage at Stratford*, 157.

13. Smith, "Sharp Wit and Noble Scenes," 74.

14. Ganong, *Backstage at Stratford*, 116.

15. Ganong recreates the rehearsal of this sequence in *Backstage at Stratford*, 115–16.

16. Robertson Davies, *The Well-Tempered Critic*, ed. Judith Skelton Grant (Toronto: 1981), 88.

17. See Morris Dickstein, *Gates of Eden: American Culture in the Sixties* (1977); Jim Hougan, *Decadence: Radical Nostalgia, Narcissism, and Decline in the Seventies* (1975); and David Riesman, *The Lonely Crowd: A Study of the Changing American Character* (1958).

18. The promptbook for this production is in the Nottingham County Library.

19. Program, Nottingham County Archives. Guthrie discusses the play at greater length in *In Various Directions: A View of Theatre* (1963), 82–92.

20. Program. It is worth noting that in his analysis of the play in *In Various Directions* Guthrie never uses the word homosexual. The nearest he comes is the assertion "In a relationship somewhere between a son and a lover [Coriolanus] throws himself on the mercy of Aufidius" (92). This essay was first published in 1962 as a preface to the Laurel edition of *Coriolanus* (ed. Charles Jasper Sisson).

21. Aufidius's responses during the Intercession scene are carefully marked in the promptbook. In the course of the episode, an intricate physical score is played by the two men, each gesture indicative of unspoken feeling. At various times Aufidius "turns sharply"; another time he is "close behind Cor. watching closely." As Martius capitulates on "Oh, my mother, mother," "Auf moves turns sharply. Cor looks to Auf D. L." In a telling moment, as Martius addresses Aufidius with "Now good Aufidius," he "X to Auf (DL)" while the "women close round Vol." Clearly Martius is here attempting to soften the impact of what Aufidius perceives as a betrayal, and the two forces fighting for mastery are visually highlighted for a final time. When Martius returns to Volumnia, he asks from a distance for Aufidius to "Stand to me in this cause," and as he does so, he directs a "long look" at Aufidius who, in a significant gesture, "changes spear to downst[age] hand." His mind is made up. As Martius leaves the stage, he "turns to look at Auf" once more, and "Auf exit fast R."

22. In Guthrie's Old Vic *Othello* (1938) Olivier had briefly contemplated, and rejected, a simulated orgasm by Iago when Othello had been goaded into paroxysm by the lieutenant's taunts. See Olivier, *Confessions of an Actor*, 105–6.

23. "Study of the First Scene of Shakespeare's 'Coriolanus,'" *Brecht on Theatre*, ed. and trans. John Willett (1964), 255, 258.

24. All references are to Bertolt Brecht, *Collected Plays*, ed. Ralph Manheim and John Willett (1973), vol. 9.

25. See Ruby Cohn, *Modern Shakespeare Offshoots* (Princeton, N.J.: 1976), 21; also *Stage*, 13 December 1962.

26. The Wekworth-Tenschert adaptation was published under the title "Shakespeares *Coriolan* in der Bearbeitung von Bertolt Brecht" in *Spectaculum* 8 (Frankfurt: 1965).

27. Wekworth-Tenschert, "Shakespeares *Coriolan* . . . ," 335, 336. Translation by Cohn, *Shakespeare Offshoots*, 19.

28. See Tenschert's notes to the Berliner Ensemble text in *Spectaculum*, 332–34. I am grateful for the assistance of Gisela Nolting in the translation and analysis of documents in German.

29. Tenschert's notes, p. 333, translated by Gisela Nolting.

30. Kenneth Tynan, "Brecht on Shakespeare," *Observer*, 4 October 1965.

31. Robert Brustein, "Live Blossoms in Dead Soil," *New Republic*, 7 August 1965, 35.

32. Ibid.

33. Ibid., 36.

34. Ibid.

35. According to Benedict Nightingale ("Manly Hopkins," *New Statesman*, 14 May 1971), "[Plummer] withdrew during rehearsals rather than pervert his performance in the manner the directors demanded." See also John Elsom and Nicholas Tomalin, *The History of the National Theatre* (1978), 229–30.

36. The promptbook is in the archives of the Royal National Theatre. I am grateful for the management's kind permission to consult it.

37. Nightingale, "Manly Hopkins."

38. Ibid.

39. Brecht's adaptation was directly or indirectly responsible for two further dramas on the Coriolanus theme. Gunter Grass's *The Plebeians Rehearse the Uprising* (1966) takes Brecht to task for using the workers' 1953 uprising in East Berlin as a research source for a production of *Coriolanus* while refusing to declare unequivocal solidarity with the protesters. John Osborne's *A Place Calling Itself Rome*

(1973), a condensed and politically weighted paraphrase of Shakespeare's script with one new scene added, may be seen as a reactionary response to Brecht's polemic.

40. The promptbook is in the archives of the Festival Theatre, Stratford, Ontario.

41. Ralph Berry, "Stratford Festival Canada," *Shakespeare Quarterly,* 33 (1982): 202.

42. For an extended discussion of Barton's productions see Michael L. Greenwald, *Directions by Indirections: John Barton of the Royal Shakespeare Company* (Newark, N.J.: 1985).

43. The two-volume promptbook is in the Shakespeare Centre Library, Stratford-upon-Avon.

44. For background to this production see Sally Beauman, *The Royal Shakespeare Company: A History of Ten Decades* (1982), 314–17.

45. Promptbooks for both the Stratford-upon-Avon and Aldwych productions are in the Shakespeare Centre Library, Stratford-upon-Avon.

46. *Drama,* Winter 1973, 35.

47. For an account of the tour and a detailed reconstruction of the production, see David Daniell, *"Coriolanus" in Europe* (1980); also J. R. Mulryne, *"Coriolanus* at Stratford-upon-Avon: Three Actors' Remarks," *Shakespeare Quarterly,* 29 (1978): 323–32.

48. The promptbook is in the Shakespeare Centre Library, Stratford-upon-Avon.

49. "A production that does more for Shakespeare than for actors," *Times Higher Educational Supplement,* 23 June 1978, 24.

50. Daniell (167) notes Howard's conviction "that Coriolanus dies in a kind of exhilaration, as a creature from a different sphere. . . . His trip has ended, and he has to return . . . leaving the mayhem behind that the others have created. No father is ever mentioned—it is as if his mother bore him alone, almost like the virgin birth of a god: and Coriolanus is attended by three women everywhere, making a sort of *pietà*."

51. Ibid., 40.

52. My reactions to productions have been conditioned, in ways I cannot always explicitly identify and acknowledge, by the following treatments of postmodernism: Arnold Aronson, *American Set Design* (1985) and "Postmodern Design," *Theatre Journal,* 43 (1991):1–13; Johannes Birringer, *Theatre, Theory, Postmodernism* (Bloomington, Indiana: 1991); David Harvey, *The Condition of Postmodernity* (1989); Grady, *The Modernist Shakespeare,* 190ff.; Fredric Jameson, *Postmodernism* (Durham, N.C.: 1991); and Kennedy, *Looking at Shakespeare,* 266–311.

53. Steve Lawson, "Shakespeare Is Still the Challenge," *New York Times,* 12 August 1979.

54. Michael Goldman, "Papp and Pacino In New York City," *Shakespeare Quarterly,* 31 (1980):192.

55. See Kristina Bedford's detailed record of the rehearsal process in her *"Coriolanus" at the National* (Selinsgrove: 1992) from which much of my information is drawn.

56. The promptbook for this production is in the archives of the Royal National Theatre. I am grateful for the management's kind permission to consult it.

57. Bedford, *"Coriolanus" at the National,* 86.

58. Ibid., 93.

59. Ibid., 129.

60. Ibid., 138.

61. Ibid., 112.

62. Ibid., 129.

63. Ibid., 132.

64. Ibid., 151.

65. Ibid., 63–64.

66. Ibid., 138.

67. Kennedy, *Looking at Shakespeare*, 300.

68. In 1991 Berkoff was invited to direct *Coriolanus* in Munich, a production which differed little in essentials from his New York venture. In 1992 he published his rehearsal diary, which offers helpful insights into his artistic method. See Steven Berkoff, *"Coriolanus" in Deutschland* (Oxford: 1992).

69. Introduction to *Coriolanus*, ed. R. B. Parker, 134.

70. Peter Holland, "Shakespeare Performances in England, 1989–90," *Shakespeare Survey*, 44 (1991):164.

71. Peter Holland, "Shakespeare Performances in England 1990–91," *Shakespeare Survey*, 45 (1992):133.

72. Deborah Warner staged her 1985 *King Lear* around three ladders.

73. Kennedy, *Looking at Shakespeare*, 266.

74. Review by Jean-Marie Maguin, *Cahiers Elisabéthains* (October 1994), 94.

Afterword

1. See Madeleine Doran, "'All's in Anger': The Language of Contention in *Coriolanus*," *Shakespeare's Dramatic Language* (Madison: 1976), 182–217; and R. B. Parker, Introduction to *Coriolanus*, 27.

2. Cook, *Shakespeare's Players*, 94.

3. Granville-Barker, *Prefaces to Shakespeare*, 2:155.

4. See W. S. E. Coleman, "The Peculiar Artistic Quality of Shakespeare's *Coriolanus*," *On-Stage Studies*, 7 (1983):73–84; Parker, [Introduction to] *Coriolanus*, 29ff; Ann Pasternak Slater, *Shakespeare the Director* (Totawa, N.J.: 1982); and Ripley, "*Coriolanus*'s Stage Imagery on Stage, 1754–1901," 339.

Bibliography

BOOKS

Place of publication is noted only when it is other than London or New York.

Alger, William Rounseville. *Life of Edwin Forrest.* 2 vols. Philadelphia: 1877. Reprint, Benjamin Blom, Inc., 1972.

Allen, Guy Pierce. "Seven English Versions of the Coriolanus Story." Ph.D. diss., University of Toronto, 1978.

Allen, Shirley S. *Samuel Phelps and Sadler's Wells Theatre.* Middletown, Conn.: 1971.

Sir Lawrence Alma-Tadema. [Catalogue of an exhibition at] Mappin Art Gallery, Weston Park, Sheffield, 3 July-8 August 1976 [and] Laing Art Gallery, Higham Place, Newcastle, 21 August-15 September 1976. [n.d.].

Anderson, James R. *An Actor's Life.* 1902.

Armin, Robert. *The Italian Taylor, and his Boy.* 1609. Reprint, *The Works of Robert Armin, Actor (1605–1609).* Edited by Alexander B. Grosart. 1880.

Aronson, Arnold. *American Set Design.* 1985.

Arundell, Dennis. *The Story of Sadler's Wells 1683–1964.* 2 vols. 1965.

Atkins, Robert. *Robert Atkins: An Unfinished Autobiography.* Edited by George Rowell. 1994.

Ayres, James B. "Shakespeare in the Restoration: Nahum Tate's *The History of King Richard the Second, The History of King Lear* and *The Ingratitude of a Common-wealth.*" Ph.D. diss., The Ohio State University, 1964.

Babington, Bruce and Peter William Evans. *Biblical Epics: Sacred Narrative in the Hollywood Cinema.* Manchester: 1993.

Baker, David Erskine. *The Companion to the Play-House.* 2 vols. 1764.

Baker, Herschel. *John Philip Kemble.* Cambridge, Mass.: 1942.

Baldwin, Thomas Whitfield. *The Organization and Personnel of the Shakespearean Company.* 1961.

Barker, Richard Hindry. *Mr. Cibber of Drury Lane.* 1939.

Barrett, Lawrence. *Edwin Forrest.* Boston: 1881.

Barrington, Jonah. *Personal Sketches of His Own Times.* 2 vols. 1827.

Beauman, Sally. *The Royal Shakespeare Company: A History of Ten Decades.* 1982.

Beaumont, Francis and John Fletcher. *The Works of Francis Beaumont and John Fletcher.* Edited by Arnold Glover and A. R. Waller. 10 vols. 1905.

Becker, Wilhelm. *Gallus, oder romische Scenen aus der Zeit Augusts.* Leipzig: 1838.

Bedford, Kristina. *"Coriolanus" at the National.* Selinsgrove: 1992.

Bell, Clive. *Art.* 1913.

Bellamy, George Anne. *An Apology for the Life of.* 5 vols. 1786.

Benjamin, Walter. *The Origin of German Tragic Drama.* Translated by John Osborne. 1977.

Benson, Sir Frank. *My Memoirs.* 1930.

Benson, Lady. *Mainly Players.* 1926.

Bentley, Eric. *The Dramatic Event.* 1954.

Bentley, Gerald Eades. *Shakespeare and His Theatre.* Lincoln, Nebraska: 1964.

Berkoff, Steven. "Coriolanus" in *Deutschland.* Oxford: 1992.

Bernard, John. *Retrospections of America 1797–1811.* Edited by Mrs. Bayle Bernard, with an introduction, notes and index by Laurence Hutton and Brander Matthews. 1887.

Bevington, David and Jay L. Halio. eds. *Shakespeare: Pattern of Excelling Nature.* Newark, N.J.: 1978.

Bingham, Madeleine. *Henry Irving and the Victorian Theatre.* 1978.

Birringer, Johannes. *Theatre, Theory, Postmodernism.* Bloomington, Indiana: 1991.

Blunt, Anthony. *Nicolas Poussin.* 1967.

Boaden, James. *Memoirs of the Life of John Philip Kemble Esq.* 2 vols. 1825.

———. *Memoirs of Mrs. Siddons.* 2 vols. 1827.

Booth, Michael R. *Victorian Spectacular Theatre 1850–1910.* 1981.

Boyer, Paul. *Urban Masses and Moral Order in America, 1820–1920.* Cambridge, Mass.: 1978.

Bradbrook, Muriel. *Shakespeare: The Poet in his World.* 1978.

Bradley, A. C. *Shakespearean Tragedy.* 1905.

Branam, George C. *Eighteenth-Century Adaptations of Shakespearian Tragedy.* Berkeley, Calif: 1956.

Brecht, Bertolt. *Brecht on Theatre.* Edited and translated by John Willett. 1964.

———. *Collected Plays.* Edited by Ralph Manheim and John Willett. Vol. 9. 1973.

Brereton, Austin. *The Life of Henry Irving.* 2 vols. 1908.

Briggs, Asa. *The Age of Improvement.* 1959.

Bristol, Michael. *Shakespeare's America / America's Shakespeare.* 1989.

Brockway, Fenner. *Socialism Over Sixty Years: The Life of Jowett of Bradford.* 1946.

Brooke, Stopford. *On Ten Plays of Shakespeare.* 1905.

Brower, Reuben A. *Hero and Saint: Shakespeare and the Graeco-Roman Heroic Tradition.* 1971.

Brown, Thomas Allston. *A History of the New York Stage.* 3 vols. 1903. Reprint, Benjamin Blom Inc., 1964.

Brownsmith, J. *The Dramatic Time-Piece.* 1767.

Bullough, Geoffrey. *Narrative and Dramatic Sources of Shakespeare.* 8 vols. 1964.

Burke, Kenneth. *Language as Symbolic Action: Essays on Life, Literature, and Method.* Berkeley, Calif.: 1966.

Burley, Theodore L. G. *Playhouses and Players of East Anglia.* Norwich: 1928.

Calderwood, James. *Shakespeare & the Denial of Death.* Amherst, Mass.: 1987.

Campbell, Hilbert H. *James Thomson.* Boston: 1979.

Campbell, Oscar James. *Shakespeare's Satire.* 1943.

———, and Edward G. Quinn. *The Reader's Encyclopaedia of Shakespeare.* 1966.

Canina, Luigi. *Indicazione di Roma Antica.* Rome: 1830.

Carlson, Marvin. *The Italian Shakespearians.* Cranbury, N.J.: 1985.

Carr, Thomas Swinburne. *Manual of Roman Antiquities.* 1836.

Carritt, E. F. *A Calendar of British Taste 1600–1800.* [1948].

Chambers, E. K. *The Elizabethan Stage.* 4 vols. Oxford: 1923.

———. *Shakespeare: A Survey.* 1925. Reprint, 1958.

Cibber, Colley. *Apology for the Life of.* 1740.

Cibber, Theophilus. *The Life and Character . . . of Barton Booth, Esq.* 1753.

———. *The Lives and Characters of the Most Eminent Actors and Actresses of Great Britain and Ireland.* 1753.

———. *The Lives of the Poets of Great Britain and Ireland.* 5 vols. 1753.

Clark, Susie C. *John McCullough as Man, Actor, and Spirit.* 1905.

Clarke, Joseph I. C. *My Life and Memories.* 1925.

Clarke, Mary. *See* Wood, Roger.

Clynes, J. R. *Memoirs.* 2 vols. 1937–39.

Cohn, Ruby. *Modern Shakespeare Offshoots.* Princeton, N. J.: 1976.

Coleman, John. *Memoirs of Samuel Phelps.* 1886.

———. *Players and Playwrights I Have Known.* 2 vols. 1888.

Coleridge, Samuel Taylor. *Lectures and Notes on Shakespeare and other English poets.* 2 vols. 1849.

———. *Shakespearean Criticism.* Edited by Thomas Middleton Raysor. Vol. 1. 1960.

Collier, J. P. *New Particulars Concerning Shakespeare.* 1836.

Cook, Judith. *Shakespeare's Players.* 1983.

Cooke, William. *Memoirs of Charles Macklin.* 1804.

Cottrell, John. *Laurence Olivier.* Englewood Cliffs, N.J.: 1975.

Crosse, Gordon. *Shakespearean Playgoing, (1890–1952).* 1953.

Daniell, David. *"Coriolanus" in Europe.* 1980.

Davies, Thomas. *Dramatic Miscellanies.* 3 vols. 1783–84.

———. *Memoirs of the Life of David Garrick Esq.* 2 vols. 1780, 1784.

Davies, W. Robertson. *Shakespeare's Boy Actors.* 1939.

———. *The Well-Tempered Critic.* Edited by Judith Skelton Grant. Toronto. 1981.

De Grazia, Margreta. *Shakespeare Verbatim: The Reproduction of Authenticity and the 1790 Apparatus.* Oxford: 1991.

Deming, Barbara. *Running Away from Myself: A dream portrait of America drawn from the films of the forties.* 1969.

Dennis, John. *The Critical Works.* Edited by Edward Niles Hooker. 2 vols. Baltimore: 1943.

Dent, Alan. *Preludes and Studies.* 1942.

De Romanis, Antonio. *Le Vestigie di Roma Antica.* Rome: 1832.

Dickins, Lilian and Mary Stanton, eds. *An Eighteenth-Century Correspondence.* 1910.

Dickins, Richard. *Forty Years of Shakespeare on the English Stage.* [1907].

Dickstein, Morris. *Gates of Eden: American Culture in the Sixties.* 1977.

Dollimore, Jonathan. *Radical Tragedy.* 2d ed. 1993.

Donaldson, Frances. *The Actor-Managers.* 1970.

Donohue, Joseph, Jr. *Dramatic Character in the English Romantic Age.* Princeton, N.J.: 1970.

Doran, Dr. [John]. *"Their Majesties' Servants": Annals of the English Stage from Thomas Betterton to Edmund Kean.* 3 vols. 1864.

Doran, Madeleine. *Shakespeare's Dramatic Language.* Madison: 1976.

Dowden, Edward. *Shakespeare: His Mind and Art.* 1875.

Dowdy, Andrew. *The Films of the Fifties.* 1973.

Downer, Alan S. *The Eminent Tragedian: William Charles Macready.* Cambridge, Mass.: 1966.

Downes, John. *Roscius Anglicanus.* 1708.

Drake, Nathan. *Shakespeare and His Times.* 1817; Paris: 1838.

Dunn, Esther Cloudman. *Shakespeare in America.* 1939.

Ellis-Fermor, Una. *Shakespeare the Dramatist and Other Papers.* Edited by Kenneth Muir. 1961.

Elsom, John and Nicholas Tomalin. *The History of the National Theatre.* 1978.

Elton, William R. *"King Lear" and the Gods.* San Marino, California: 1966.

Erickson, Peter. *Patriarchal Structures in Shakespeare's Drama.* 1985.

Evans, Peter William. *See* Babington, Bruce.

Faber, M. D., ed. *The Design Within: Psychoanalytic Approaches to Shakespeare.* 1970.

Farjeon, Herbert. *The Shakespearean Scene.* 1949.

Finlay, John. *Miscellanies.* Dublin: 1835.

Fitzgerald, Percy. *The Kembles.* 1871.

FitzSimons, Raymund. *Edmund Kean: Fire from Heaven.* 1976.

Fleming, William. *Arts and Ideas.* 6th ed. 1980.

Fletcher, John. *See* Beaumont, Francis.

Forbes-Robertson, John. *See* Phelps, W. May.

Friedlaender, Walter. *Nicolas Poussin, A New Approach.* 1966.

Gallion, Sally Marie. *"Coriolanus* on the Restoration and Eighteenth-Century Stage: Does Virtue 'Lie in th'Interpretation of the Time'?" Ph.D. diss., University of Missouri-Columbia, 1979.

Ganong, Joan. *Backstage at Stratford.* Toronto: 1962.

Garber, Marjorie. *Coming of Age in Shakespeare.* 1981.

Garrick, David. *The Letters of David Garrick.* Edited by David M. Little and George M. Kahrl. 3 vols. Cambridge, Mass.: 1963.

Gervinus, G. G. *Shakespeare.* 2 vols. Leipzig, 1849–50. Translated by F. E. Bunnètt as *Shakespeare Commentaries.* 2 vols. 1863; 1877.

Gildon, Charles. "Remarks on the Plays of Shakespeare." *The Works of Mr. William Shakespeare.* Edited by Nicholas Rowe. Vol. 7. 1710.

Gloag, John. *Georgian Grace: A Social History of Design from 1660–1830.* 1956.

Goddard, Harold C. *The Meaning of Shakespeare.* Chicago: 1951.

Gombrich, E. H. *The Story of Art.* 15th ed. 1989.

Goodwin, Thomas. *Sketches and Impressions.* Edited by R. Osgood Mason. 1887.

Grady, Hugh. *The Modernist Shakespeare.* Oxford: 1991.

Grant, Douglas. *James Thomson: Poet of the Seasons.* 1951.

Granville-Barker, Harley. *Prefaces to Shakespeare.* Vol. 2. Princeton, N.J.: 1947.

Grass, Gunter. *The Plebeians Rehearse the Uprising.* 1966.

Greenblatt, Stephen. *Shakespearean Negotiations.* Berkeley, Calif.: 1988.

Greenblatt, Stephen and Giles Gunn, eds. *Redrawing the Boundaries: The Transformation of English and American Literary Studies.* 1992.

Greenwald, Michael L. *Directions by Indirections: John Barton of the Royal Shakespeare Company.* Newark, N.J.: 1985.

Grimsted, David. *Melodrama Unveiled: American Theater and Culture 1800–1850.* Chicago: 1968.

Grosart, Alexander B., ed. *The Works of Robert Armin, Actor (1605–1609).* 1880.

Gummere, Richard M. *The American Colonial Mind and the Classical Tradition.* Cambridge, Mass.: 1963.

Gunn, Giles. *See* Greenblatt, Stephen.

Guthrie, Tyrone. *In Various Directions: A View of Theatre.* 1963.

Hackett, James Henry. *Notes and Comments upon Certain Plays and Actors of Shakespeare.* 1864. Reprint, Benjamin Blom, 1968.

Halio, Jay L. *See* Bevington, David.

Harby, Isaac. *A Selection from the Miscellaneous Writings of.* Charleston: 1829.

Harrison, Charles. *English Art and Modernism 1900–1939.* New Haven: 1994.

Harrison, Gabriel. *John Howard Payne.* Philadelphia: 1885.

Hartman, Geoffrey. *See* Parker, Patricia.

Harvey, David. *The Condition of Postmodernity.* 1989.

Hauser, Arnold. *Mannerism: The Crisis of the Renaissance and the Origin of Modern Art.* 2 vols. 1965.

———. *The Social History of Art.* Vol. 3. 1985.

Hawkes, Terence. *That Shakespeherian Rag: Essays on a Critical Process.* 1986.

Hawkins, F. W. *The Life of Edmund Kean.* 2 vols. 1869.

Hazlitt, William. *The Complete Works.* Edited by P. P. Howe. 21 vols. 1930–34.

Hiffernan, Paul. *The Tuner, Letter the Third.* 1754.

Higham, Charles. *The Art of the American Film 1900–1971.* 1973.

Hildy, Franklin J. *Shakespeare at the Maddermarket: Nugent Monck and the Norwich Players.* Ann Arbor: 1986.

Hillebrand, Harold Newcomb. *Edmund Kean.* 1933.

Hitchcock, Robert. *An Historical View of the Irish Stage.* Vol. 1. Dublin: 1788.

Holden, Anthony. *Olivier.* 1988.

Holland, Norman N. *Psychoanalysis and Shakespeare.* 1966.

Holloway, John. *The Story of the Night.* 1961.

Hollstein, F. W. H. *Dutch and Flemish Etchings, Engravings, and Woodcuts ca. 1450–1700.* 43 vols. Amsterdam: 1949.

Holmes, Martin. *Shakespeare and Burbage.* 1978.

Honour, Hugh. *Neo-Classicism.* Harmondsworth, Middlesex: 1968.

Hook, Judith. *The Baroque Age in England.* 1976.

Hookham, George. *Will o'the Wisp.* Oxford: 1922.

Hope, Thomas. *Costume of the Ancients.* 1809.

Horn, Franz. *Shakespeare's Schauspiele erläutert.* 5 vols. Leipzig: 1823–31.

Hougan, Jim. *Decadence: Radical Nostalgia, Narcissism, and Decline in the Seventies.* 1975.

Houseman, John. *Front and Center*. 1979.

Hudson, H. N. *Lectures on Shakespeare*. 1848.

———. *Shakespeare: His Life, Art, and Characters*. 2 vols. 1872.

Hughes, Alan. *Henry Irving, Shakespearean*. 1981.

Hughes, H. Stuart and James Wilkinson. *Contemporary Europe: A History*. Englewood Cliffs, N.J.: 1991.

Hughes, Robert. *The Shock of the New: Art and the Century of Change*. 1980.

Hunt, John Dixon. *Encounters: Essays on Literature and the visual arts*. 1971.

Irving, Laurence. *Henry Irving: The Actor and His World*. 1951.

Izod, John. *Hollywood and the Box Office, 1895–1986*. 1988.

Jaggard, William. *Shakespeare Bibliography*. Stratford-upon-Avon: 1911.

Jameson, Anna Brownell. *Characteristics of Women, Moral, Poetical & Historical*. 2 vols. 1832.

Jameson, Fredric. *Postmodernism*. Durham, N. C.: 1991.

Johnson, Paul. *Modern Times: The World from the Twenties to the Eighties*. 1983.

Johnson, Samuel. *Samuel Johnson on Shakespeare*. Edited by W.K. Wimsatt, Jr. 1960.

Jones, J. R. *The First Whigs: The Politics of the Exclusion Crisis, 1678–83*. Rev. ed. Oxford: 1970.

Jones, Stephen. *The Eighteenth Century*. 1985.

Jonson, Ben. *Epicoene or The Silent Woman*. Edited by R. V. Holdsworth. Mermaid edition. 1979.

———. *Poems of Ben Jonson*. Edited by George Burke Johnston. 1954.

Kahn, Coppelia. *Man's Estate: Masculine Identity in Shakespeare*. 1981.

Kammen, Welmoet Bok-van. "Stradanus and the Hunt." Ph.D. diss., Johns Hopkins University, 1977.

Kelly, Linda. *The Kemble Era: John Philip Kemble, Sarah Siddons and the London Stage*. 1980.

Kennedy, Dennis. *Granville Barker and the Dream of Theatre*. Cambridge: 1985.

———. *Looking at Shakespeare: A Visual History of Twentieth-Century Performance*. Cambridge: 1993.

Kiernan, Thomas. *Sir Larry: The Life of Laurence Olivier*. 1981.

Kitchin, Laurence. *Mid-Century Drama*. 1960.

Knight, Charles. *Studies in Shakespeare*. 1849.

Knight, G. Wilson. *The Imperial Theme*. 1931; 1965.

———. *Principles of Shakespearian Production*. 1936; Harmondsworth, 1949.

———. *The Sovereign Flower*. 1958.

———. *The Wheel of Fire*. 1930.

Lamb, Margaret. *"Antony and Cleopatra" on the English Stage*. Cranbury, N.J.: 1980.

Lasch, Christopher. *The Culture of Narcissism*. 1979.

Leacroft, Richard. *The Development of the English Playhouse*. 1973.

Lee, Sidney. *Shakespeare and the Modern Stage*. 1906.

Lenman, Bruce. *The Jacobite Risings in Britain 1689–1746*. 1980.

Lewis, Wyndham. *The Lion and the Fox*. 1927.

Ludlow, N. M. *Dramatic Life as I Found It.* St. Louis: 1880.

Macaulay, G. C. *James Thomson.* 1908.

MacCallum, M. W. *Shakespeare's Roman Plays and Their Background.* 1910.

MacKaye, Percy. *Epoch: The Life of Steele MacKaye.* 1927.

Macready, William Charles. *The Diaries of William Charles Macready 1833–1851.* Edited by William Toynbee. 2 vols. 1912.

———. *Macready's Reminiscences, and Selections from His Diaries and Letters.* Edited by Sir Frederick Pollock. 2 vols. 1875.

Marshall, Norman. *The Other Theatre.* 1947.

Mason, Jeffrey D. *Melodrama and the Myth of America.* Bloomington, Indiana: 1993.

Matthews, Brander. *Shakespeare as a Playwright.* 1913.

Matthews, Jean V. *Toward a New Society: American Thought and Culture, 1800–1830.* Boston: 1991.

Mazer, Cary. *Shakespeare Refashioned: Elizabethan Plays on Edwardian Stages.* Ann Arbor: 1981.

McConachie, Bruce A. *Melodramatic Formations: American Theatre & Society, 1820–1870.* Iowa City, Iowa: 1992.

McGugan, Ruth Ella. "Nahum Tate and the Coriolanus Tradition in English Drama with a Critical Edition of Tate's *The Ingratitude of a Common-wealth.*" Ph.D. diss., University of Illinois, 1965.

McManaway, J. G. *et al.*, eds. *J. Q. Adams Memorial Studies.* 1948.

Meeker, James Edward. *The Life and Poetry of James Thomson.* 1917.

Merchant, Moelwyn. *Shakespeare and the Artist.* 1959.

Miller, John. *Popery and Politics in England, 1660–1688.* Cambridge: 1973.

Mirollo, James V. *Mannerism and Renaissance Poetry.* New Haven: 1984.

Molloy, J. Fitzgerald. *The Life and Adventures of Edmund Kean.* 2 vols. 1888.

Moody, Richard. *Edwin Forrest.* 1960.

Morley, Henry. *The Journal of a London Playgoer.* 1866.

Moses, Montrose J. *The Fabulous Forrest.* Boston: 1929.

Mowat, Charles Loch. *Britain Between the Wars 1918–1940.* 1955.

Mumford, Lewis. *The Brown Decades: A Study of the Arts in America 1865–1895.* 1955.

Murdoch, James E. *The Stage or Recollections of Actors and Acting.* Philadelphia: 1880.

Murphy, Arthur. *The Life of David Garrick.* Dublin: 1801.

Murray, Christopher. *Robert William Elliston, Manager.* 1975.

Murry, J. Middleton. *Countries of the Mind.* 1922.

Nicoll, Allardyce. *A History of English Drama, 1660–90.* 5 vols. Cambridge: 1952.

Nichols, John, ed. *Illustrations of the Literary History of the Eighteenth Century.* Vol. 2. 1817. Reprint, AMS Press, Inc. 1966.

O'Connor, Garry, ed. *Olivier in Celebration.* 1987.

O'Connor, Marion. *William Poel and the Elizabethan Stage Society.* Cambridge: 1987.

Odell, George C. D. *Shakespeare from Betterton to Irving.* 2 vols. 1920. Reprint, Dover Publications. 1966.

O'Keeffe, John. *Recollections of the Life of.* 2 vols. Philadelphia: 1827.

Olivier, Laurence. *Confessions of an Actor.* 1982.

Osborne, John. *A Place Calling Itself Rome.* 1973.

Owen, John B. *The Eighteenth Century 1714–1815.* 1974.

Palmer, John. *Political Characters of Shakespeare.* 1945.

Parker, Patricia and Geoffrey Hartman, eds. *Shakespeare and the Question of Theory.* 1985.

Patterson, Annabel. *Censorship and Interpretation.* Madison: 1984.

Pechter, Edward, ed. *Textual and Theatrical Shakespeare: Questions of Evidence.* Iowa City: 1996.

Pemberton, Charles Reece. *The Life and Literary Remains of.* Edited by John Fowler. 1843.

Phelps, W. May and John Forbes-Robertson. *The Life and Life-Work of Samuel Phelps.* 1886.

Pitou, Augustus. *Masters of the Show.* 1914.

Playfair, Giles. *Kean.* 1950.

Poel, William. *Shakespeare in the Theatre.* 1913.

Procter, B. W. *Life of Edmund Kean.* 2 vols. 1835.

Quinn, Edward G. *See* Campbell, Oscar James.

Ramsden, John. *See* Williams, Glyn.

Rank, Otto. *Das Inzest—Motiv in Dichtung und Sage.* Liepzig and Vienna: 1912.

Raymond, George. *The Life and Enterprises of Robert William Elliston, Comedian.* 1857.

Rees, James. *The Life of Edwin Forrest.* Philadelphia: 1874.

Reich, Wilhelm. *Charakteranalyse.* Vienna: 1933. Translated by Theodore P. Wolfe as *Character-Analysis.* 1945.

Reinhold, Meyer. *Classica Americana: The Greek and Roman Heritage in the United States.* Detroit: 1984.

Reynolds, Sir Joshua. *Fifteen Discourses Delivered in the Royal Academy.* Everyman Edition. [n.d.]

Ricard, François. *The Lyric Generation: The Life and Times of the Baby Boomers.* Translated by Donald Winkler. Toronto: 1994.

Rich, John. "Covent Garden Inventory of 1744." British Library Add. Mss. 12,201. Selected Folios 34–73.

Riesman, David. *The Lonely Crowd: A Study of the Changing American Character.* 1958.

Ripley, John. *"Julius Caesar" on Stage in England and America, 1599–1973.* Cambridge: 1980.

Roberts, Peter. *The Old Vic Story.* 1976.

Robinson, Henry Crabb. *Diary, Reminiscences, and Correspondence.* Edited by Thomas Sadler. 3 vols. 1869.

Robson, William. *The Old Play-goer.* 1846.

Ronalds, Francis S. *The Attempted Whig Revolution of 1678–1681.* Totowa, N.J.: 1974.

Rose, Mary Beth, ed. *Women in the Middle Ages and the Renaissance: Literary and Historical Perspectives.* 1986.

Rosenblum, Robert. *Transformations in Late Eighteenth Century Art.* Princeton, N.J.: 1967.

Rosenfeld, Sybil. *Georgian Scene Painters and Scene Painting.* 1981.

Rossiter, A. P. *Angel with Horns and Other Shakespeare Lectures.* Edited by Graham Storey. 1961.

Salvini, Tomasso. *Leaves from the Autobiography of.* 1893.

Samuels, Shirley. ed. *The Culture of Sentiment: Race, Gender, and Sentimentality in Nineteenth-Century America.* Oxford: 1992.

Schiller, J. C. F. *On The Aesthetic Education of Man In a Series of Letters.* Translated by Reginald Snell. 1965.

Schlegel, Augustus Wilhelm. *A Course of Lectures on Dramatic Art and Literature.* Translated by John Black. 1846.

————. *Dramatic Literature, Lectures.* Translated by John Black. 2 vols. 1815.

Scott, Clement. *The Drama of Yesterday & To-Day.* 2 vols. 1899.

Scott-Thomas, Herbert Francis. *The Life and Works of Nahum Tate.* Baltimore: 1934.

Shakespeare, William. *The Complete Works of Shakespeare.* Edited by Samuel Phelps. ca.1853.

————. *Coriolanus: or, the Roman Matron A Tragedy. Taken from Shakespear and Thomson.* 1755, 1757. Reprints, Cornmarket Press. 1969.

————. *Coriolanus.* Bell's edition. Edited by Francis Gentleman. Vol. 5. 1774. Reprint, Cornmarket Press. 1969.

————. *Coriolanus; or, The Roman Matron. The British Theatre,* Vol. 5. 1808.

————. *Coriolanus; An Historical Play. From the Prompt Copy of the Theatre Royal, Drury Lane, London.* 1820.

————. *Coriolanus.* T. H. Palmer edition. Philadelphia: 1823.

————. *Coriolanus. A TRAGEDY IN FIVE ACTS. As Performed For The First Time on Any Stage by TOMMASO SALVINI AT THE METROPOLITAN OPERA HOUSE UNDER THE MANAGEMENT AND DIRECTION OF MR. C.A CHIZZOLA.* 1885.

————. *Coriolanus.* Memorial [Theatre] edition. Edited by Charles E. Flower. [1890?].

————. *Coriolanus.* Red Letter edition. 1907.

————. *Coriolanus.* New Variorum edition. Edited by H. H. Furness Jr. 1928.

————. *Coriolanus.* Laurel edition. Edited by Charles Jasper Sisson. 1962.

————. *Coriolanus.* Arden edition. Edited by Philip Brockbank. 1976.

————. *Coriolanus.* The Oxford Shakespeare. Edited by R. B. Parker. Oxford: 1994.

————. *The Ingratitude of a Common-wealth: Or, the Fall of Caius Martius Coriolanus.* 1682. Reprint, Cornmarket Press. 1969.

————. *The Invader of His Country: or, The Fatal Resentment.* 1720. Reprint, Cornmarket Press. 1969.

————. *The Leopold Shakespere.* Edited by Nikolaus Delius. Introduction by F. J. Furnivall. 1877.

————. *Works.* Edited by Nicholas Rowe. 1709–10. Reprint, Ann Arbor, Mich. Augustan Reprint Society, 1948.

————. *The Works of Shakespeare.* Edited with preface by Lewis Theobald. 1733.

Shattuck, Charles H. *John Philip Kemble Promptbooks.* 11 vols. Charlottesville, Virginia: 1974.

———. *Shakespeare on the American Stage.* Washington, D.C.: 1976.

———. *Shakespeare on the American Stage: From Booth and Barrett to Sothern and Marlowe.* Cranbury, N.J.: 1987.

———. *The Shakespeare Promptbooks.* Urbana, Illinois: 1965.

Shaw, George Bernard. *Complete Plays with Prefaces.* Vol. 3. 1962.

Sheldon, Esther. *Thomas Sheridan of Smock-Alley.* Princeton, N.J.: 1967.

Siegel, Paul N. *Shakespeare's Roman and History Plays: A Marxist Approach.* Rutherford, N.J.: 1986.

Snider, Denton J. *The Shakespearean Drama, a Commentary: The Histories.* Vol. 3. St. Louis: 1922.

Speaight, George. *The History of the English Toy Theatre.* 1969.

Speaight, Robert. *The Property Basket.* 1970.

———. *Shakespeare on the Stage.* 1973.

———. *William Poel and the Elizabethan Revival.* 1954.

Spencer, Christopher. *Nahum Tate.* 1972.

Spencer, Hazelton. *Shakespeare Improved: The Restoration Versions in Quarto and on the Stage.* Cambridge, Mass.: 1927.

Spoto, Donald. *Laurence Olivier: A Biography.* 1992.

Stanton, Mary. *See* Dickins, Lilian.

Stapfer, Paul. *Shakespeare and Classical Antiquity.* Translated by Emily J. Carey. 1880.

Stoker, Bram. *Personal Reminiscences of Henry Irving.* 1907.

Strachey, Lytton. *Books and Characters.* 1922.

Styan, J. L. *The Shakespeare Revolution.* Cambridge: 1977.

Summers, Montague. *The Restoration Theatre.* 1934.

Swanson, Vern G. *Sir Lawrence Alma-Tadema.* 1977.

Swinburne, Algernon Charles. *A Study of Shakespeare.* 1880.

Taylor, Gary. *Reinventing Shakespeare: A Cultural History 1642–1986.* 1989.

Taylor, George Ledwell, and Edward Cressy. *Architectural Antiquities of Rome.* 1821.

Tearle, John. *Mrs. Piozzi's Tall Young Beau.* Cranbury, N.J.: 1991.

Tenschert, Joachim. *See* Wekworth, Manfred.

Thomson, James. *Coriolanus, The Works of James Thomson.* 4 vols. 1773.

———. *Letters and Documents.* Edited by Alan Dugald McKillop. Lawrence, Kansas: 1958.

Thrale, Hester Lynch. *Thraliana: The Diary of Mrs. Hester Lynch Thrale.* Edited by Katharine C. Balderston. 2 vols. Oxford: 1951.

Tomalin, Nicholas. *See* Elsom, John.

Towse, John Ranken. *Sixty Years of the Theatre.* 1911; 1916.

Trewin, J. C. *Shakespeare on the English Stage 1900–1964.* 1964.

Tynan, Kenneth. *Curtains.* 1961.

Ulrici, Hermann. *Shakespeare's Dramatic Art.* Translated by L. Dora Schmitz. Vol. 2. 1876.

———. *Uber Shakespeares dramatische Kunst, und sein Verhaltniss zu Calderon und Goethe.* 1839. Translated by A. J. W. Morrison as *Shakespeare's Dramatic Art: And His Relation to Calderon and Goethe.* 1846.

Upton, John. *Critical Observations on Shakespeare.* 1746.

Van Doren, Mark. *Shakespeare.* 1939.

Van Lennep, William, ed. *The London Stage 1660–1800. Part 1: 1660–1700.* Carbondale, Illinois: 1965.

Vaughan, William. *Romantic Art.* 1988.

Vickers, Brian, ed. *Shakespeare, The Critical Heritage: 1774–1801.* 6 vols. 1974–81.

Wells, Stanley. *Royal Shakespeare: Four major productions at Stratford-upon-Avon.* Manchester: 1976.

Westwood, Doris. *These Players.* 1926.

Wilkes, George. *Shakespeare From an American Point of View.* 1877.

Wilkes, Thomas. *A General View of the Stage.* 1759.

Wilkinson, James. *See* Hughes, H. Stuart.

Wilkinson, Tate. *Memoirs of His Own Life.* 4 vols. York: 1790.

Williams, Glyn and John Ramsden. *Ruling Britannia: a political history of Britain 1688–1988.* 1990.

Williams, Harcourt. *Old Vic Saga.* 1949.

Williams, J. M. *The Dramatic Censor.* Vol. 6. 1812.

Williams, John Ambrose. *Memoirs of John Philip Kemble Esq.* 1817.

Williamson, Audrey. *Old Vic Drama.* 1950; 1953.

———. *Old Vic Drama 2.* 1957.

Wimsatt, W. K. *Samuel Johnson on Shakespeare.* 1960.

Winckelmann, Johann Joachim. *Reflections on the Imitation of Greek Works in Painting and Sculpture.* German text with English translation by Elfriede Heyer and Roger C. Norton. La Salle, Illinois: 1987.

Winter, William. *Other Days.* 1908.

———. *Shadows of the Stage.* 2d series. Edinburgh: 1893.

———*Shakespeare on the Stage.* 3 vols. 1911; 1915; 1916.

———. *The Wallet of Time.* 2 vols. 1913.

Wood, Anthony. *Nineteenth Century Britain 1815–1914.* 1960.

Wood, Roger and Mary Clarke. *Shakespeare at the Old Vic.* 3 vols. 1956.

Wood, William B. *Personal Recollections of the Stage.* Philadelphia: 1855.

Young, Julian Charles. *A Memoir of Charles Mayne Young.* 1871.

ARTICLES

Adelman, Janet. "'Anger's My Meat': Feeding, Dependency, and Aggression." In *Shakespeare: Pattern of Excelling Nature,* edited by David Bevington and Jay L. Halio. Cranbury, N.J.: 1978.

Amaya, Mario. "The Roman World of Alma-Tadema." *Apollo* (December 1962).

Aronson, Arnold. "Postmodern Design." *Theatre Journal* 43 (1991).

Berry, Ralph. "Sexual Imagery in *Coriolanus.*" *Studies in English Literature, 1500–1900* 13 (1973).

———. "Stratford Festival Canada." *Shakespeare Quarterly* 33 (1982).

Bradley, A. C. *"Coriolanus." Proceedings of the British Academy* 5 (1912).

Broos, B. P. J. "Rembrandt and Lastman's *Coriolanus:* the history piece in 17th-century theory and practice." *Simiolus: Netherlands quarterly for the history of art* 8 (1975/76).

Byrne, Muriel St. Clare. "Classical Coriolanus." *National Review* 96 (1931).

Canfield, J. Douglas. "Royalism's Last Dramatic Stand: English Political Tragedy, 1679–89." *Studies in Philology* 82 (1985).

Carlson, Marvin. "David's *Oath of the Horatii* as a Theatrical Document." *Theatre History Studies* 10 (1990).

Cavell, Stanley. "'Who does the wolf love?' : Reading *Coriolanus*." In *Shakespeare and the Question of Theory,* edited by Patricia Parker and Geoffrey Hartman. 1985.

Coleman, W. S. E. "The Peculiar Artistic Quality of Shakespeare's *Coriolanus*." *On-Stage Studies* 7 (1983).

Crowley, Richard C. "*Coriolanus* and the Epic Genre." In *Shakespeare's Last Plays: Essays in Honor of Charles Crow,* edited by Richard C. Tobias and Paul G. Zolbrod. 1974.

Davidson, Clifford. "*Coriolanus:* A Study in Political Dislocation." *Shakespeare Studies* 4 (1969).

Dibner, Bern. "The 'New Discoveries' of Stradanus." Essay accompanying reprint of Stradanus's *Nova Reperta.* Issued by the Burndy Library, Norwalk, Connecticut, 1953.

Dryden, John. "Preface to *Troilus and Cressida*." In *Essays of John Dryden,* edited by W. P. Ker. 2 vols. 1961.

Eliot, T. S. "Hamlet and His Problems." In *Selected Essays: 1917–1932.* 1932.

Enright, D. J. "*Coriolanus:* Tragedy or Debate?" *Essays in Criticism* 4 (1954).

George, David. "Restoring Shakespeare's *Coriolanus*: Kean versus Macready." *Theatre Notebook* 44 (1990).

Goldman, Michael. "Papp and Pacino In New York City." *Shakespeare Quarterly* 31 (1980).

Granville-Barker, Harley. Letter to *Play Pictorial* 22 (1912).

Halio, Jay. "*Coriolanus:* Shakespeare's 'Drama of Reconciliation,'" *Shakespeare Studies* 6 (1972).

Hall, Peter. "The Job He Liked Best." In *Olivier in Celebration,* edited by Garry O'Connor. 1987.

Harker, Frederick. "Irving as Coriolanus." In *We Saw Him Act,* edited by H. A. Saintsbury and Cecil Palmer. 1939.

Harrison, G. B. "A Note on *Coriolanus*." In *J. Q. Adams Memorial Studies,* edited by J. G. McManaway *et al.* 1948.

Hofling, Charles K. "An Interpretation of Shakespeare's *Coriolanus*." *American Imago* 14 (1957).

Holland, Peter. "Shakespeare Performances in England, 1989–90." *Shakespeare Survey* 44 (1991).

Hoy, Cyrus. "Jacobean Tragedy and the Mannerist Style." *Shakespeare Survey* 26 (1973).

Inchbald, Elizabeth. "Remarks" to *Coriolanus; or, The Roman Matron.* Vol. 5 of *The British Theatre.* 1808.

Jones, Virgil L. "Methods of Satire in the Political Drama of the Restoration." *Journal of English and Germanic Philology* 21 (1922).

Langman, F. E. "Tell Me of Corn: Politics in *Coriolanus*." *Studies in Shakespeare,* edited by Dennis Bartholomeusz. 1 (1990).

Latham, Grace. "On Volumnia." *New Shakespeare Society Transactions* (1887–92).

Leech, Clifford. "Stratford 1952." *Shakespeare Quarterly* 3 (1952).

Lowe, Lisa. "'Say I play the man I am': Gender and Politics in *Coriolanus*." *Kenyon Review,* n.s., 8 (1986).

Mace, Dean Tolle. "Ut pictura poesis: Dryden, Poussin and the parallel of poetry and painting in the seventeenth century." In *Encounters: Essays on Literature and the visual arts,* edited by John Dixon Hunt. 1971.

Maguin, Jean-Marie. Review of RSC *Coriolanus, Cahiers Elisabéthains* (October 1994).

Martin, Theodore. "An Eye-Witness of John Kemble." *The Nineteenth Century* 7 (1880).

McKenzie, Stanley D. "'Unshout the noise that banish'd Martius': Structural Paradox and Dissembling in *Coriolanus*." *Shakespeare Studies* 18 (1986).

Merchant, W. M. "Classical Costume in Shakespearian Productions." *Shakespeare Survey* 10 (1957).

Mulryne, J. R. "*Coriolanus* at Stratford-upon-Avon: Three Actors' Remarks." *Shakespeare Quarterly* 29 (1978).

Nicoll, Allardyce. "Political Plays of the Restoration." *Modern Language Review* 16 (1921).

Pettet, E. C. "*Coriolanus* and the Midlands Insurrection of 1607." *Shakespeare Survey* 3 (1950).

Rackin, Phyllis. "'Coriolanus': Shakespeare's Anatomy of 'Virtus.'" *Modern Language Studies* 13 (1983).

Ripley, John. "*Coriolanus*'s Stage Imagery on Stage, 1754–1901." *Shakespeare Quarterly* 38 (1987).

Rosenfeld, Sybil. "Alma-Tadema's Designs for Henry Irving's *Coriolanus*." *Deutsche Shakespeare-Gesellschraft West Jahrbuch* (1974).

———. "Neo-classical scenery in England." *Theatre Notebook* 27 (1972/1973).

———. "Scene Designs by Hodgins the Younger." *Theatre Notebook* 27 (1972/73).

Rostron, David. "John Philip Kemble's *Coriolanus* and *Julius Caesar*." *Theatre Notebook* 23 (1968).

Rowe, Nicholas. "Some Account of the Life, &c. of Mr. William Shakespeare." In Rowe's Edition. 1709. Reprint, Augustan Reprint Society. Ann Arbor, 1948.

Schanzer, Ernest. "Plot-Echoes in Shakespeare's Plays." *Deutsche Shakespeare-Gesellschaft West Jahrbuch* (1969).

Scott, Walter. Review of Boaden's *Kemble, The Quarterly Review* 24 (1826).

Skura, Meredith. "Psychoanalytic Criticism." In *Redrawing the Boundaries: The Transformation of English and American Literary Studies,* edited by Stephen Greenblatt and Giles Gunn. 1992.

Smith, Gordon Ross. "Authoritarian Patterns in Shakespeare's *Coriolanus*." *Literature and Psychology* 9 (1959).

Smith, Irwin. "'Gates' on Shakespeare's Stage." *Shakespeare Quarterly* 7 (1956).

Smith, Peter D. "Sharp Wit and Noble Scenes: A Review of the 1981 Season of the Stratford, Ontario Festival." *Shakespeare Quarterly* 13 (1962).

Spiers, R. Phené. "The Architecture of 'Coriolanus.'" *Architectural Review* 10 (1901).

Sprague, Arthur Colby. "A *Macbeth* of Few Words." In . . . *All These To Teach: Essays in Honour of C. A. Robertson,* edited by Robert A. Bryan. Gainesville, Florida: 1965.

———. "Shakespeare on the New York Stage 1953–1954." *Shakespeare Quarterly* 5 (1954).

Sprengnether, Madelon. "Annihilating Intimacy in *Coriolanus.*" In *Women in the Middle Ages and the Renaissance: Literary and Historical Perspectives,* edited by Mary Beth Rose. 1986.

Stoller, Robert J. "Shakespearean Tragedy: *Coriolanus.*" *Psychoanalytic Quarterly* 35 (1966).

Towne, Jackson E. "A Psychoanalytic Study of Shakespeare's *Coriolanus.*" *Psychoanalytic Review,* 8 (1921).

Watson, E. C. "*Nova Reperta.*" *The American Physics Teacher* 6 (February 1938).

Wekworth, Manfred and Joachim Tenschert. "Shakespeares *Coriolan* in der Bearbeitung von Bertolt Brecht." *Spectaculum* 8 (Frankfurt: 1965).

Whiting, George W. "Political Satire in London Stage Plays, 1680–83." *Modern Philology* 18 (1930–31).

Wikander, Matthew W. "The Spitted Infant: Scenic Emblem and Exclusionist Politics in Restoration Adaptations of Shakespeare." *Shakespeare Quarterly* 37 (1986).

Worthen, W. B. "Deeper Meanings and Theatrical Technique: The Rhetoric of Performance Criticism." *Shakespeare Quarterly* 40 (1989).

Yachnin, Paul. "The Powerless Theater." *English Literary Renaissance* 21 (1991).

Zeeveld, Gordon. "*Coriolanus* and Jacobean Politics." *Modern Language Review* 57 (1962).

NEWSPAPERS AND MAGAZINES

Place of publication is London unless otherwise indicated.

Advertiser, Boston: 12 February 1878.

Albion, New York: 19 April 1845; 16 September 1848; 5 May 1855.

Albion and the Star: 19 June 1834.

Athenaeum. 20 April 1901.

Atlas: 29 September 1838.

Aurora, Philadelphia: 15 March 1813.

Bell's Weekly Messenger: 29 June 1817.

Birmingham Daily Gazette: 18 August 1893.

Birmingham Daily Mail: 1 May 1915.

Birmingham Daily Post: 1 May 1915.

Birmingham Evening Dispatch: 10 May 1939.

Birmingham Gazette: 3 May 1910; 10 May 1939.

Birmingham Mail: 25 April 1933; 10 May 1939; 14 March 1952.

Birmingham Post: 23 April 1907; 25 April 1933; 22 April 1938; 1 April 1948; 14 March 1952; 24 February 1954; 23 December 1963.

Boston Evening Transcript: 18 November 1885; 4 December 1885.

Boston Gazette: 30 December 1805.

Boston Patriot: 2 March 1824.

Boston Weekly Magazine: 21 February 1818.

Brantford Expositor: 20 June 1961.

British Chronicle: 8–13 November 1758.

British Monitor: 30 January 1820.

British Press: 26 January 1820.

Cambridge Daily News: 6 March 1928.

Champion: 25 May 1817; 29 January 1820.

Christian Science Monitor, Boston: 1 June 1920; 10 February 1936; 24 April 1948; 23 January 1954; 17 December 1963.

Columbian, Boston: 20 April 1811.

Columbian Centinel, Boston: 1 January 1806.

Courier: 26 January 1820; 13 March 1838.

Cue, New York: 30 January 1954.

Daily Advertiser, New York: 3 June 1799.

Daily Chronicle: 16 April 1901; 13 April 1920.

Daily Courant: 13 December 1718; 1 January 1719/20; 26 December 1720.

Daily Dispatch: 12 November 1935.

Daily Express: 16 April 1901; 1 July 1959; 8 July 1959.

Daily Graphic, New York: 17 December 1878; 4 January 1883.

Daily Herald: 24 February 1954.

Daily Mail: 13 April 1920; 8 July 1959; 13 April 1967.

Daily News: 28 September 1848; 16 April 1901; 13 April 1920.

Daily News, New York: 25 March 1924; 3 February 1938.

Daily Telegraph: 14 February 1901; 16 April 1901; 13 April 1920; 24 April 1926; 12 May 1931; 25 April 1933; 10 May 1939; 1 April 1948; 14 March 1952; 24 February 1954; 30 April 1975.

Douglas Jerrold's Weekly Newspaper: 30 September 1848.

Drama: February 1974.

Dublin Journal: 8–11 April 1749; 18–22 February 1751/2.

Eastern Daily Press, Norwich: 7 February 1928.

Eastern Evening News, Norwich: 7 February 1928.

English Chronicle: 25–27 January 1820.

Entertainer: 12 November 1754.

Era: 16 February 1901; 20 April 1901; 23 April 1910; 14 April 1920.

European Magazine: February 1820.

Evening Mirror, New York: 8 June 1852.

Evening News: 20 April 1938; 1 November 1977.

Evening Post: 13 December 1963.

Evening Post, New York: 25 April 1855; 4 January 1883; 12 November 1885.

Evening Signal, New York: 13 January 1840.

Evening Standard: 20 April 1938; 2 April 1948; 8 July 1959.

Everyman: 21 May 1931.

Examiner: 15 December 1816; 31 January 1820; 18 March 1838; 22 September 1860.

Express, New York: 3 November 1863.

Financial Times: 24 February 1954; 21 October 1977; 17 December 1984.

Frank Leslie's Illustrated Newspaper, New York: 14 November 1863.

Gazette of the United States, Philadelphia: 3 June 1796.

General Evening Post: 17–19 December 1811.

Globe: 16 April 1901; 20 April 1910; 13 April 1920.

Globe and Mail, Toronto: 21 June 1961.

Guardian: 13 December 1963; 17 December 1984; 26 May 1994.

Guardian Journal: 13 December 1963.

Guide: 18 March 1838.

Hamilton (Ontario) Spectator: 17 June 1981.

Hampstead & Highgate Express: 12 September 1986.

Illustrated London News: 6 March 1954; 15 August 1959.

Illustrated Sporting and Dramatic News: 23 February 1901.

Imperial Weekly Gazette: 29 January 1820.

International Herald Tribune: 15–16 May 1971.

Irish Independent, Dublin: 14 January 1936.

Irish Times, Dublin: 15 January 1936; 16 January 1936.

Jewish Chronicle: 29 April 1938.

John Bull. 18 March 1838; 1 April 1838; 30 September 1838.

John O'London's Weekly: 29 April 1938; 12 March 1954.

Kitchener-Waterloo (Ontario) Record: 20 June 1961; 17 June 1981.

Lady: 13 August 1959.

Lady's Pictorial: 27 April 1901.

Leamington Spa Courier: 19 August 1893.

Listener: 25 May 1967.

Liverpool Daily Post: 17 April 1901; 24 February 1954.

London Chronicle: 7–9 November 1758.

London (Ontario) Free Press: 17 June 1981.

London (Ontario) Evening Free Press: 20 June 1961.

London Magazine: February 1820; April 1823.

Loyal Protestant: 7 March 1681/2.

Magnet: 19 March 1838.

Manchester Daily Dispatch: 14 March 1952.

Manchester Evening News: 12 November 1935.

Manchester Guardian: 4 October 1921; 12 May 1931; 26 April 1933; 12 November 1935; 20 April 1938; 2 April 1948; 5 March 1952; 25 February 1954.

Manchester Guardian Weekly: 28 April 1933.

Minerva, New York: 4 October 1823; 21 January 1824.

Mirror of the Times: 22–29 January 1820.

Monthly Mirror: June 1807.

Monthly Review: January 1755.

Morning Advertiser: 26 January 1820; 3 October 1834; 13 March 1838.

Morning Chronicle: 29 October 1816; 26 January 1820; 17 June 1834; 13 March 1838; 22 March 1838; 2 October 1848.

Morning Courier and New York Enquirer. 10 October 1843.

Morning Herald: 24 November 1837.

Morning Leader: 16 April 1901.

Morning News and Public Ledger: 17 June 1834.

Morning Post: 16 December 1811; 29 October 1816; 26 January 1820; 13 March 1838; 28 February 1908.

Morning Telegraph, New York: 9 March 1954.

New England Galaxy & Masonic Magazine, Boston: 11 December 1818; 31 December 1819.

New Monthly Magazine: March 1820; April 1820.

New Republic, New York: 7 August 1965.

News: 22 December 1811; 30 January 1820.

News and Sunday Globe: 25 March 1838.

News Chronicle: 1 April 1948; 14 March 1952; 8 July 1959.

News of the World: 21 April 1901.

New Statesman & Nation: 14 May 1938; 10 April 1948; 22 March 1952; 18 July 1959; 14 May 1971.

New-York Daily Times: 24 April 1855.

New-York Daily Tribune. 24 April 1855; 19 December 1878; 4 January 1883.

New-York Dispatch: 29 April 1855; 8 November 1863.

New Yorker: 30 January 1954.

New York Herald: 15 April 1845; 24 April 1855.

New York Herald Tribune: 20 January 1954; 21 June 1961.

New York Journal and American: 4 February 1938.

New-York Mirror: 31 January 1824.

New York Morning Express: 16 April 1845.

New York News: 3 November 1863.

New York Times: 4 January 1883; 12 November 1885; 26 July 1914; 24 January 1954; 12 August 1979.

New York World: 4 January 1883; 12 November 1885.

Observer: 30 September 1838; 1 October 1848; 24 April 1938; 14 May 1939; 16 March 1952; 1 October 1964; 4 October 1964; 15 August 1965; 16 April 1967; 28 October 1973; 23 December 1984.

Pall Mall Gazette: 16 April 1901; 29 February 1908; 20 April 1910.

Plays and Players: September 1959; February 1964; June 1967; December 1973; June 1994.

Port Folio, Philadelphia: 31 January 1807.

Public Advertiser: 13 November 1754; 15 November 1754, 13 December 1754.

Punch: 12 July 1939.

Queen: 2 April 1924.

Satirist: 30 September 1838.

Scotsman: 14 July 1959.

Sketch: 24 April 1901; 18 March 1908.

Spectator: 17 March 1838; 29 September 1838; 30 September 1848; 21 March 1952; 17 July 1959; 21 April 1967.

Spirit of the Times, New York: 14 December 1878; 21 December 1878; 31 December 1878; 6 January 1883.

Stage: 18 April 1901; 21 April 1910; 27 March 1924; 27 April 1933; 14 November 1935; 7 April 1938; 21 April 1938; 11 May 1939; 20 March 1952; 25 February 1954; 13 December 1962; 19 December 1963.

Standard: 16 April 1901.

Star: 11 February 1789; 2 April 1792; 4 October 1796; 14 February 1901; 16 April 1901.

Stratford (Ontario) Beacon-Herald: 20 June 1961.

Stratford-upon-Avon Herald: 25 August 1893; 22 April 1898; 26 April 1907; 23 April 1909; 7 May 1915; 30 April 1926; 27 August 1926; 12 May 1939; 10 July 1959; 21 April 1967.

Sun: 13 March 1838; 25 September 1838.

Sun, New York: 12 November 1885.

Sunday Dispatch, Dublin: 19 January 1936.

Sunday Express: 28 February 1954.

Sunday Mercury, New York: 8 November 1863.

Sunday Mirror, New York: 8 November 1863.

Sunday Telegraph: 9 May 1971; 23 December 1984.

Sunday Times: 19 February 1837; 26 February 1837; 18 March 1838; 17 February 1901; 24 April 1938; 4 April 1948; 28 February 1954; 12 July 1959; 15 December 1963; 15 August 1965; 16 April 1967; 28 October 1973.

Tablet: 8 August 1959.

Telegram, Toronto: 20 June 1961.

Theatre: 1 October 1893.

Theatre World: April 1954.

Theatrical Inquisitor: January 1820.

Theatrical Journal: 5 October 1848.

Theatrical Observer: 13 March 1838.

Tickler, Philadelphia: 6 March 1811.

The Times: 29 October 1816; 25 June 1817; 29 September 1848; 7 February 1928; 8 May 1939; 10 May 1939; 14 March 1952; 8 July 1959; 22 August 1959; 14 December 1963; 13 April 1967; 7 May 1971; 23 October 1973; 22 October 1977; 17 December 1984; 26 November 1993.

Times Higher Education Supplement: 23 June 1978.

Toronto Star: 17 June 1981.

Tribune: 19 March 1954.

Truth: 9 April 1948; 5 March 1954.

Vanity Fair: 18 April 1901.

Western Daily Press, Bristol: 17 March 1952.

Westminister Gazette: 16 April 1901; 15 April 1920.

Wilkes' Spirit of the Times, New York: 14 November 1863.

World: 9 February 1789; 24 April 1901.

Index

acting editions: Bell's, 16, 109–11, Sheridan's (1755), 97–104, 118, 379 n, (1757), 105, 119, 120, 379 n, Kemble's, 117, 379 n, Elliston's, 145–50, 381 n, Oxberry's, 210, 218, Palmer's Philadelphia Theater, 210, 385 n, Spencer's Boston Theatre, 218, Salvini's, 236, adaptations, by Tate, 54–70, Dennis, 70–82, Sheridan, 96–106, Kemble, 114–23, Brecht, 307–8, Wekworth-Tenschert, 308–9, Osborne, 393–94 n
Adelman, Janet, 22, 24
Admonition scene: Volumnia's manipulation removed by Dennis, 77; in texts of Garrick, 109–10, Kemble, 119, Elliston, 147, Poel, 263; staged by Kemble, 132, Elliston, 156, Macready, 171, Phelps, 183, Irving, 191, Benson, 204, Forrest, 227–28, McCullough, 233, Salvini, 237, 238, Atkins, 249, Poel, 263, Casson, 275, Hall (SMT), 293–94, Hall (National), 325, 326; played by Kemble, 139, Siddons, 141, Kean, 156, Vandenhoff, 162, Macready, 171, Irving, 196, Ward, 204, Britton, 248–49, Thorndike, 275, Olivier, (OV), 275, (SMT), 293–94, Evans, 297, McKellen, 325, Worth, 326
Adorno, Theodor, 22
Adrian-Nicanor scene, 336; cut by Garrick, 110, Kemble, 119–20, Elliston, 147, Phelps, 176, Irving, 186, Benson, 200, Atkins, 388 n, Bridges-Adams, 251, Monck, 255, Payne, 277, Browne, 279, Byam Shaw, 281, Houseman, 284, Benthall, 286, Hall (SMT), 291, Guthrie, 304, Nunn (Aldwych), 318, Hall (National), 324; retained by Poel, 263–64, Casson, 271, Langham (1961), 300, Atkins, 388 n; rewritten by Brecht, 307
Aeschylus: *Agamemnon,* 199
Agate, James, 273, 275

Alger, William R., 224
Allen, Woody, 314
Allgood, Sara, 266
Alma-Tadema, Lawrence, 187, 198, 200, 240
Alvarez, A., 298
American Company, 209
Anderson, J., 174, 184, 211, 215, 217
Andrews, Harry, 280, 297
Andrews, Robert C., 151
Ankers, Kathleen, 279
Ankrum, Morris, 389 n
Ansara, Alan, 306
Antium: Martius's arrival in, locale changed to Corioli by Tate, 67; to military camp by Thomson, 89, Sheridan, 105; staging in *Ingratitude of a Commonwealth,* 67, *Invader of His Country,* 79; Thomson's *Coriolanus,* 89; in text of Elliston, 147, Macready, 164, Phelps, 176, Irving, 186, Benson, 200; staged by Garrick, 110, Kemble, 120, Elliston, 147, Macready, 168, Phelps, 179, Irving, 191, 196, Forrest, 219, Salvini, 238, Poel, 264, Byam Shaw, 281, Houseman, 285, Hall (SMT), 293; played by Kemble, 139, Macready, 171, Irving, 196–97, Ryan, R., 285
Appen, Karl von, 311
Appius, 145
Archer, William, 185
Armin, Robert: *The Italian Taylor, and his Boy,* 34
Arnold, Benedict, 231
Arnus, 145
Aronson, Boris, 291, 294
art: baroque, 69, 169, 265; beau idéal, 74, 136, 164, 199, 203, 339–40; Cubism, 242, Futurism, 242, 249; mannerism, 29, 38, 335–36; modernism, 33, 234, 241, 265, 335; neoclassicism, 76, 82, 83, 98, 115, 116, 144, 164, 334; Post-Impressionism, 240, 241, 249; realism,